THE REAL GUIDE

POLAND

D0839582

THE REAL GUIDES

OTHER AVAILABLE REAL GUIDES
CALIFORNIA AND THE WEST COAST • SAN FRANCISCO
NEW YORK • MEXICO • GUATEMALA & BELIZE • BRAZIL
PERU • FRANCE • PARIS • SPAIN • PORTUGAL • AMSTERDAM
IRELAND • ITALY • VENICE • GREECE • SCANDINAVIA
GERMANY • BERLIN • HUNGARY • CZECHOSLOVAKIA
YUGOSLAVIA • TURKEY • HONG KONG • KENYA • MOROCCO
and **WOMEN TRAVEL**

FORTHCOMING
FLORIDA • EUROPE • HOLLAND • BARCELONA • NEPAL

ROUGH GUIDE CREDITS

Series Editor: Mark Ellingham
Editorial: Martin Dunford, John Fisher, Jack Holland, Jonathan Buckley, Greg Ward
US Text Editor: Marc S. Dubin
Production: Susanne Hillen, Kate Berens, Gail Jammy
Typesetting: Andy Hilliard
Series Design: Andrew Oliver

Both authors would like to thank those at the Real Guides who saw this book through: Andy Hilliard for typesetting and coping with the accents; Kate Berens for proofreading and cartographic assistance; Greg Ward for ingenuity on the Mac; Matthew Yeomans for information from the US; and our editor, Jonathan Buckley, for dedication well beyond the call.

Individually, **Mark** would like to thank Mia for her constant support, encouragement and patience, and the many friends and colleagues here and in Poland whose advice, warmth, and hospitality helped make this book possible. In particular: in Gdańsk—Adam Gosziewski and family, Adam and Gosha, Grzegorz, Leszek, Joanna, Mr Andrzej Januszajtis and the staff of the COIT office; in Warsaw—Marek K, Jacek and Magda Czaputowicz, Ryszard, Krysza and Janek Litynski, Emily, Peter, Jacek and Radka S, Michał Cichy for help with the listings section, Christopher Bobiński of the FT, Jerzy Socała, Piotr Treda and colleagues at ORBIS; in Kraków—Jakub, Bogdan, Janina Pizło of COIT, and above all Marek Czersky for answering all the questions.

Thanks are also due to many others: Jarek Putresza in Białystok; Franek Bachleda in Zakopane; Wiesław Szumiński in Suwałki; the Banachs in Sanok; Jan, Julia Doszna, and fellow Łemkowie for memorable times in the Beskid Niski; Aldona, Arvid Kosa, and all the Griygoutis family for Lithuanian hospitality; Rob Humphreys, fellow author; the comrades of END; everyone at Svenska Freds in Stockholm; Maciej Z; Dominic Ziegler for nearly catching a Bieszczady trout; Anna Wolek of the *Economist* for much advice, humor, and vodka; Geoff Patton and John Saville for tireless and inventive rescue work; David Goldblatt for additional emergency work; to Jack Holland and Bob Ordish for additional material; and last but certainly not least, Piotr Cieplak for a decade of friendship . . . and argument.

Gordon would like to thank: local Orbis directors Edward Giecewicz in Kłodzko, Erwin Piesch in Jelenia Góra, and especially Ireneusz Spychalksi in Wrocław; Paweł Domachowski, PTTK director in Poznań; and Melanie Ellis, Jolanta Wieteska, Zdzisław Ciuk, Lucja Ginko, Małgorzata Raczkowska, Barbara Kowalczyk, Piotr Maniurka, and Tadeusz Hanelt.

Grateful acknowledgement is also made for permission to quote from *All Played Out* by Pete Davies (Heinemann).

The publishers and authors have done their best to ensure the accuracy and currency of all the information in **Poland: The Real Guide**; however, they can accept no responsibility for any loss, injury or inconvenience sustained by any traveler as a result of information or advice contained in the guide.

Published in the United States by
Prentice Hall Press
A division of Simon & Schuster Inc.
15 Columbus Circle
New York, NY 10023

Typeset in Linotron Univers and Century Old Style
Printed in the United States by R.R. Donnelley & Sons.

Illustrations in Part One and Part Three by Ed Briant.
Basics illustration by Simon Fell. Contexts illustration by Tommy Yamaha.

© Mark Salter and Gordon McLachlan 1991

No part of this book may be reproduced in any form without permission from the publisher except for the quotation of brief passages in reviews.

400pp. includes index

Cataloguing-in-Publication Data is available from the Library of Congress.

THE REAL GUIDE
POLAND

Written and researched by

MARK SALTER
and
GORDON McLACHLAN

Edited by
Jonathan Buckley
with Mark Ellingham

PRENTICE
HALL
PRESS

NEW YORK LONDON TORONTO SYDNEY TOKYO SINGAPORE

HELP US UPDATE

We've gone to a lot of effort to ensure that this first edition of *Poland: The Real Guide* is up-to-date and accurate. However, things are changing at an extraordinary speed in Poland, with new businesses cropping up daily and prices in a continual state of flux—so any suggestions, comments, or corrections would be much appreciated.

We'll credit all contributions, and send a copy of the next edition (or any other Real Guide if you prefer) for the best letters. Please write to:

Mark Salter and Gordon McLachlan, The Real Guides, Prentice Hall Trade Division, 15 Columbus Circle, New York, NY 10023.

CONTENTS

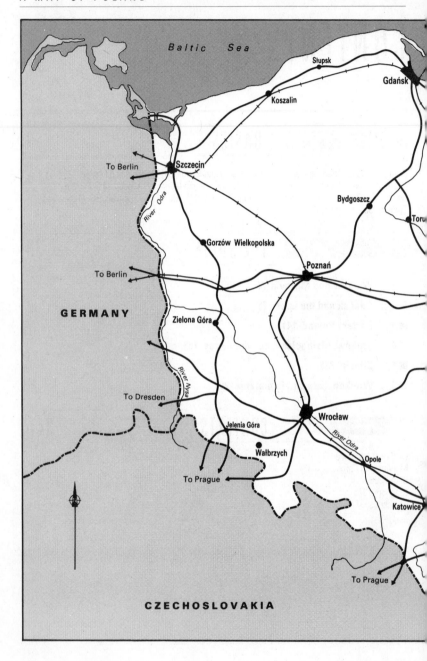

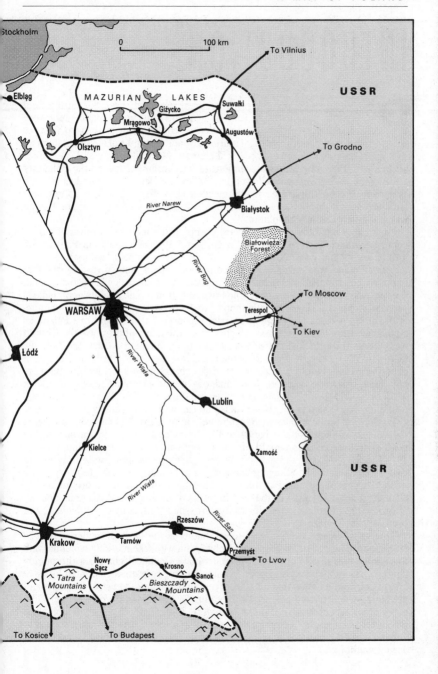

INTRODUCTION

Polish images flooded the world media throughout the 1980s. Strikes and riots at the Lenin shipyards of Gdańsk and other industrial centers were the harbingers of the disintegration of communism in Eastern Europe, and throughout the years of martial law and beyond Poland maintained an exemplary momentum towards political change. At the decade's end, the *annus mirabilis* of 1989 saw the establishment of a government led by the Solidarity trade union, a development followed in 1990 by the victory of union leader Lech Wałęsa in Poland's first presidential election since the 1920s. The pattern was familiar enough through the Eastern Bloc, but the rebirth of democratic Poland was a uniquely Catholic revolution.

For many Poles, the most important events in the movement towards a post-communist society were the visits in 1979 and 1983 of Pope John Paul II, the former archbishop of Kraków. To the outside world this may have been surprising, but Poland was never a typical communist state: Stalin's verdict was that imposing communism on Poland was like trying to saddle a cow. Polish society in the postwar decades remained fundamentally traditional, maintaining beliefs, peasant life, and a sense of nationhood in which the Catholic Church was integral. During periods of foreign oppression—oppression so severe that Poland as a political entity has sometimes vanished from the maps of Europe—the Church was always the principal defender of the nation's identity, so that the Catholic faith and the struggle for independence have become fused in the Polish consciousness. The physical presence of the church is inescapable—in Baroque buildings, roadside shrines, and images of the national icon, the Black Madonna—and the determination to preserve the memories of an often traumatic past finds expression in religious rituals that can both attract and repel onlookers.

World War II and its aftermath profoundly influenced the character of Poland: the country suffered at the hands of the Nazis as no other in Europe, losing nearly one quarter of its population and virtually its entire Jewish community. In 1945 the Soviet-dominated nation was once again given new borders, losing its eastern lands to the USSR and gaining tracts of formerly German territory in the west. The resulting makeup of the population, though far more uniformly "Polish" than at any time in the past in terms of language and religion, incorporates significant ethnic minorities of Byelorussians, Lithuanians, Ukrainians, and even Muslim Tartars.

To a great extent, the sense of social fluidity is the basis of modern Poland's fascination. The government's current obsession with free-market economics and the elimination of all communist legacies makes political change a thoroughly tangible process. Poland is gripped by an austerity program necessitated by a $40 billion debt and inflation that hit 400 percent in one month, yet street markets and privately owned businesses are proliferating in the major towns. Tourism, like every other aspect of the Polish infrastructure, is currently in a state of flux, but it has never been easier to explore the country: foreigners are no longer subject to currency restrictions, and you can travel as you please, if not always as smoothly as you might like.

Encounters with the people are at the core of any experience of the country. On trains and buses, on the streets or in the village bar, you'll never be stuck for opportunities for contact: Polish hospitality is legendary, and there's a natural progression from a chance meeting to an introduction to the extended family. Even the most casual visitor might be served a prodigious meal at any hour of the day—usually with a bottle or two of local vodka brought out from the freezer.

Poles delineate their country's attractions as "the mountains, the sea, and the lakes," their emphasis firmly slanted to the traditional, rural heartlands. To get the most out of your time, it's perhaps best to follow their preferences. The **mountains**—above all the Carpathian range of the Tatras—are a delight, with a well-established network of hiking trails; the **lakes** provide opportunities for canoeing and a host of other outdoor pursuits; and the dozen or so **national parks** retain areas of Europe's last primeval forests, inhabited still by bisons, elks, wolves, bears, and eagles. Yet you will not want to miss the best of the **cities**—Kraków, especially—nor a ramble down rivers like the Wisła for visits to Teutonic **castles**, ancient waterside towns, and grand, Polish **country mansions**, evocative of a vanished aristocratic order. The **ethnic regions** offer insights into cultures quite distinct from the Catholicism of the majority, while the former centers of the **Jewish** community, and the concentration camps in which the Nazis carried out their extermination, are the most moving testimony to the complexity and tragedy of the nation's past.

Where to Go

Unless you're driving to Poland, you're likely to begin your travels with one of the three major cities: Warsaw, Kraków, or Gdańsk. Each provides an immediate immersion in the fast-paced changes of the 1990s, and a backdrop of monuments that reveal the complexities of the nation's history.

Warsaw, the capital, had to be rebuilt from scratch after the war, and much of the city conforms to the stereotype of Eastern European grayness, but the reconstructed Baroque palaces, churches, and public buildings of the historic quarter, the burgeoning street markets, and the bright shopfronts of Poland's new enterprise culture are diverting enough. **Kraków**, however, the ancient royal capital, is the real crowd-puller for Poles and foreign visitors alike, rivaling the Central European elegance of Prague and Vienna. This is the city where history hits you most powerfully: in the royal Wawel complex, in the fabulous open space of the Rynek, in the one-time Jewish quarter of Kazimierz, and in the chilling necropolis of nearby Auschwitz-Birkenau, the bloodiest killing field of the Third Reich. **Gdańsk**, formerly Danzig, the largest of the Baltic ports and home of the legendary shipyards, presents a dynamic brew of politics and commerce against a townscape reminiscent of mercantile towns in the Netherlands.

German and Prussian influences abound in the **north** of the country, most notably in the austere castles and fortified settlements constructed by the Teutonic Knights at **Malbork**, **Chełmno**, and other strategic points along the **Wisła River**—as the Vistula is known in Poland. **Toruń** is one of the most atmospheric and beautiful of the old Hanseatic towns here.

Over in the **east**, numerous minority communities embody the complexities of national boundaries in Central Europe. The one-time Jewish center of **Białystok**, with its Byelorussian minority, is a springboard for the Soviet borderlands, where onion-domed Orthodox churches stand close to Tartar mosques. Farther south, beyond **Lublin**, a famous center of Hassidic Jewry, and **Zamość**, with its magnificent Renaissance core, lie the homelands of Ukrainians, Lemks, and Boyks—and a chance to see some of Poland's extraordinary wooden churches.

In the **west**, ethnic Germans populated regions of the divided province of **Silesia**, where **Wrocław** sustains the dual cultures of the former German city of Breslau and the Ukrainian city of Lwów, whose displaced citizens were moved here at the war's end. The other main city in western Poland is the quintessentially Polish **Poznań**, revered as the cradle of the nation, and today a vibrant and increasingly prosperous university town.

Despite its much-publicized pollution problems, Poland has many regions of unspoiled natural beauty, of which none is more pristine than the **Białowieza forest**, in the extreme southeast; the last virgin forest of the European mainland, it is also the habitat of the largest surviving herd of European bison. A journey westward from here, through the southern uplands, would pass through the wild **Bieszczady** mountains and the alpine **Tatras** before arriving at the bleak **Karkonosze** mountains—all of them excellent walking country, interspersed with less demanding terrain. On the opposite side of the central Polish plain, the wooded lakelands of **Mazury** and **Pomerania** are as tranquil as any lowland region on the continent, while the Baltic coast can boast not just the domesticated pleasures of its beach resorts, but also the extraordinary desert-like dunes of the **Słowinski Park**—one of a dozen national parks.

When to Go

Spring is arguably the ideal season for some serious hiking in Poland's mountainous border regions, as the days tend to be bright—if showery—and the distinctive flowers are at their most profuse. **Summer**, the tourist high season, sees plenty of sun, particularly on the Baltic coast, where the resorts are crowded from June to August and temperatures consistently in the high 70s. The major cities can get pretty stifling at these times, with the effects of the heat compounded by the influx of visitors; accommodation can be tricky in the really busy spots, but a good network of summer hostels provides a low-budget fallback.

Autumn is the best time to come to Poland if you're planning to sample the whole spread of the country's attractions: in the cities the cultural seasons are beginning at this time, and the pressure on hotel rooms is lifting; in the countryside, the golden "Polish October" is especially memorable, the rich colors of the forests heightened by brilliantly crisp sunshine that's often warm enough for T-shirts.

In **winter** the temperatures drop rapidly, as icy Siberian winds blanket many parts of the country with snow for anything from one to three months. Though the central Polish plain is bleak and unappealing at the end of the year, in the south of the country skiers and other winter sports enthusiasts will find themselves in their element. By mid-December the slopes of the Tatras and the other border ranges are thronged with vacationers, straining the few established facilities to the limit.

AVERAGE DAILY TEMPERATURES (°F) AND MONTHLY RAINFALL (mm)

		Kraków	Gdynia	Poznań	Przemśyl	Warsaw
January	Max	32	35	33	32	32
	Min	22	27	24	20	22
	Rain	28	33	24	27	27
February	Max	34	35	34	34	32
	Min	22	25	22	21	21
	Rain	28	31	29	24	32
March	Max	45	40	44	43	42
	Min	30	30	30	29	28
	Rain	35	27	26	25	27
April	Max	55	48	54	55	53
	Min	38	36	37	37	37
	Rain	46	36	41	43	37
May	Max	67	59	67	67	67
	Min	48	45	47	46	48
	Rain	46	42	47	57	46
June	Max	72	66	72	73	73
	Min	54	52	52	53	54
	Rain	94	71	54	88	69
July	Max	76	70	76	75	75
	Min	58	58	57	57	58
	Rain	111	84	82	105	96
August	Max	73	70	73	73	73
	Min	56	57	55	55	56
	Rain	91	75	66	93	65
September	Max	66	64	67	67	66
	Min	49	51	48	48	49
	Rain	62	59	45	58	43
October	Max	56	55	56	57	55
	Min	42	44	41	40	41
	Rain	49	61	38	50	38
November	Max	44	44	43	43	42
	Min	33	36	33	33	33
	Rain	37	29	23	43	31
December	Max	37	38	37	38	35
	Min	28	31	28	28	28
	Rain	36	46	39	43	44

PART ONE

THE
BASICS

GETTING THERE

The easiest way to get to Poland from the US and Canada is to fly direct to Warsaw, though it's also popular and quite economical to fly to a western European city and continue your journey by train. Alternatively, if expense is a main consideration, you may consider flying to London, and then continuing by a combination of bus, train, and ferry. In short, there are options to suit every schedule and sense of adventure.

BY PLANE

LOT (Polish Airlines) flies **direct to Warsaw** from New York's JFK five times a week, once a week from Newark, New Jersey, and twice a week from Chicago's O'Hare airport. As a rule, tickets are not cheap—a low-season, round-trip APEX fare from New York or New Jersey will set you back $870, rising to $1073 in the summer high period (flying from Chicago this increases to $1036 in low season, and $1199 during high season). That said, *LOT* occasionally makes special offers, arranged though the formerly official travel agency *Orbis* (see box on p.7).

Several other carriers, including *PanAm* (☎1-800/221-1212), *JAT* (*Yugoslav Airlines*) (☎1-800/752-6528), *Sabena* (☎1-800/955-2000), and *Lufthansa* (☎1-800/645-3880) offer more reasonable fares to Warsaw **via other European cities**. Flying with *PanAm* for instance, involves a change in Frankfurt: flights to Frankfurt from New York are daily, though onward connections to

Warsaw run only from Sunday to Wednesday. Based on a regular APEX fare with two weeks minimum, three months maximum stay, and mandatory booking at least 21 days in advance, the low season fare is $690, rising to $852 in the high season. Once in Warsaw, *LOT* connects with most of the major Polish cities.

Most **APEX fares** to Poland require a minimum stay of seven days and a maximum of three months, and in the majority of cases must be booked at least 21 days in advance. The cheapest seats available are to be found by booking through *Orbis*, who, though no longer nationalized, retain a special agreement with *LOT* and are able to sell **discounted tickets** on most flights. Other cheap flights can be found by booking through the *Polish American Travel Agency*, which specializes in handling Polish flights and tours, and *American Travel Abroad Inc*, essentially a charter firm but which also sells individual flights on the major airlines (addresses for both these organizations are given below). Specialist agents such as *STA* and *Council Travel* (see overleaf for addresses throughout the US and Canada) sometimes have special arrangements with the airlines and can offer cheap fares, especially if you're under 26. It's also worth checking the travel sections of the major Sunday papers to see what's on offer.

FLIGHTS VIA BERLIN

With cheap flights to Warsaw still something of a rarity, many travel agents suggest flying into Berlin and taking a train to the Polish capital from there—an inexpensive eight-hour journey. *PanAm, TWA* (☎1-800/221-2000), and *Lufthansa* all fly direct to Berlin, *PanAm* offering a round-trip, low-season fare of $500, rising to $580 in high season. Again, it's worth checking with the specialist agents before contacting the airlines.

FLIGHTS FROM CANADA

LOT flies direct to Warsaw from Montreal once a week during the low season and twice a week in high season. The cheapest fares they offer are six-month, round-trip tickets for $1369. All the other major airlines fly to Warsaw as well, but you have to make a change in New York or Western Europe in order to get a cheaper fare.

COUNCIL TRAVEL IN THE US

Head Office: 205 E. 42nd St., New York, NY 10017; ☎212/661-1450

CALIFORNIA
2486 Channing Way, Berkeley, CA 94704; ☎415/848-8604
UCSD Price Center, Q-076, La Jolla, CA 92093; ☎619/452-0630
1818 Palo Verde Ave., Suite E, Long Beach, CA 90815; ☎213/598-3338
1093 Broxton Ave., Suite 220, Los Angeles, CA 90024; ☎213/208-3551
4429 Cass St., San Diego, CA 92109; ☎619/270-6401
312 Sutter St., Suite 407, San Francisco, CA 94108; ☎415/421-3473
919 Irving St., Suite 102, San Francisco, CA 94122; ☎415/566-6222
14515 Ventura Blvd., Suite 250, Sherman Oaks, CA 91403; ☎818/905-5777

COLORADO
1138 13th St., Boulder, CO 80302; ☎818/905-5777

CONNECTICUT
Yale Co-op East, 77 Broadway, New Haven, CT 06520; ☎203/562-5335

DISTRICT OF COLUMBIA
1210 Potomac St., NW Washington, DC 20007; ☎202/337-6464

GEORGIA
12 Park Place South, Atlanta, GA 30303; ☎404/577-1678

ILLINOIS
1153 N. Dearborn St., Chicago, IL 60610; ☎312/951-0585
831 Foster St., Evanston, IL 60201; ☎708/475-5070

LOUISIANA
8141 Maple St., New Orleans, LA 70118; ☎504/866-1767

MASSACHUSETTS
79 South Pleasant St., 2nd Floor, Amherst, MA 01002; ☎413/256-1261
729 Boylston St., Suite 201, Boston, MA 02116; ☎617/266-1926
1384 Massachusetts Ave., Suite 206, Cambridge, MA 02138; ☎617/497-1497
Stratton Student Center MIT, W20-024, 84 Massachusetts Ave., Cambridge, MA 02139; ☎617/497-1497

MINNESOTA
1501 University Ave. SE, Room 300, Minneapolis, MN 55414; ☎612/379-2323

NEW YORK
35 W. 8th St., New York, NY 10011; ☎212/254-2525
Student Center, 356 West 34th St., New York, NY 10001; ☎212/643-1365

NORTH CAROLINA
703 Ninth St., Suite B-2, Durham, NC 27705; ☎919/286-4664

OREGON
715SW Morrison, Suite 600, Portland, OR 97205; ☎503/228-1900

RHODE ISLAND
171 Angell St., Suite 212, Providence, RI 02906; ☎401/331-5810

TEXAS
2000 Guadalupe St., Suite 6, Austin, TX 78705; ☎512/472-4931
Exec. Tower Office Center, 3300 W. Mockingbird, Suite 101, Dallas,TX 75235; ☎214/350-6166

WASHINGTON
1314 Northeast 43rd St., Suite 210, Seattle, WA 98105; ☎206/632-2448

WISCONSIN
2615 North Hackett Avenue, Milwaukee, WI; ☎414/332-4740

STA IN THE US

BOSTON
273 Newbury St., Boston, MA 02116; ☎617/266-6014

HONOLULU
1831 S. King St., Suite 202, Honolulu, HI 96826; ☎808/942-7755

LOS ANGELES
920 Westwood Blvd., Los Angeles, CA 90024; ☎213/824-1574
7204 Melrose Ave., Los Angeles, CA 90046; ☎213/934-8722

2500 Wilshire Blvd., Los Angeles, CA 90057; ☎213/380-2184

NEW YORK
17 E. 45th St., Suite 805, New York, NY 10017; ☎212/986-9470;☎ 800/777-0112

SAN DIEGO
6447 El Cajon Blvd., San Diego, CA 92115; ☎619/286-1322

SAN FRANCISCO
166 Geary St., Suite 702, San Francisco, CA 94108; ☎415/391-8407

TRAVEL CUTS IN CANADA

Head Office: 187 College St., Toronto, Ontario M5T 1P7; ☎416/979-2406

ALBERTA

1708 12th St. NW, Calgary T2M 3M7; ☎403/282-7687. 10424A 118th Ave., Edmonton T6G 0P7; ☎403/471-8054

BRITISH COLUMBIA

Room 326, T.C., Student Rotunda, Simon Fraser University, Burnaby, British Columbia V5A 1S6; ☎604/291-1204. 1516 Duranleau St., Granville Island, Vancouver V6H 3S4; ☎604/689-2887. Student Union Building, University of British Columbia, Vancouver V6T 1W5; ☎604/228-6890 Student Union Building, University of Victoria, Victoria V8W 2Y2; ☎604/721-8352

MANITOBA

University Centre, University of Manitoba, Winnipeg R3T 2N2; ☎204/269-9530

NOVA SCOTIA

Student Union Building, Dalhousie University, Halifax B3H 4J2; ☎902/424-2054. 6139 South St., Halifax B3H 4J2; ☎902/424-7027

ONTARIO

University Centre, University of Guelph, Guelph N1G 2W1; ☎519/763-1660. Fourth Level Unicentre, Carleton University, Ottawa, K1S5B6; ☎613/238-5493. 60 Laurier Ave. E, Ottawa K1N 6N4; ☎613/238-8222. Student Street, Room G27, Laurentian University, Sudbury P3E 2C6; ☎705/673-1401. 96 Gerrard St. E, Toronto M5B 1G7; ☎ (416) 977-0441. University Shops Plaza, 170 University Ave. W, Waterloo N2L 3E9; ☎519/886-0400.

QUÉBEC (known as *Voyages CUTS*)

Université McGill, 3480 rue McTavish, Montréal H3A 1X9; ☎514/398-0647. 1613 rue St. Denis, Montréal H2X 3K3; ☎514/843-8511. Université Concordia, Edifice Hall, Suite 643, S.G.W. Campus, 1455 bd de Maisonneuve Ouest, Montréal H3G 1M8; ☎514/288-1130. 19 rue Ste. Ursule, Québec G1R 4E1; ☎418/692-3971

SASKATCHEWAN

Place Riel Campus Centre, University of Saskatchewan, Saskatoon S7N 0W0; ☎306/343-1601

NOUVELLES FRONTIÈRES

In the United States

NEW YORK 19 W. 44th St., Suite 1702, New York, NY 10036; ☎212/764-6494

LOS ANGELES 6363 Wilshire Blvd., Suite 200, Los Angeles, CA 90048; ☎213/658-8955

SAN FRANCISCO 209 Post St., Suite 1121, San Francisco, CA 94108; ☎415/781-4480

In Canada

MONTREAL 1130 ouest, bd de Maisonneuve, Montréal, P.Q. H3A 1M8; ☎514/842-1450

QUÉBEC 176 Grande Allée Ouest, Québec, P.Q. G1R 2G9; ☎418/525-5255

VIA GREAT BRITAIN

If you're traveling to Poland via Britain as part of a wider European tour, the simplest option is to take one of the daily scheduled flights to Warsaw, taking just 2hr 30min from London's Heathrow airport. If you have the time, however, traveling onward overland can be an excellent way to reach the country, as it allows stopovers en route, and obviously enables you to see much more of Europe along the way.

BY TRAIN

The fastest rail route from London to Warsaw takes you via the Hook of Holland, Hanover, and Berlin, in a journey time of around 33 hours. Trains leave London's Liverpool Street station in the morning from Monday to Saturday, arriving in Warsaw the following evening. Couchettes, if available, cost an extra £9; the pricier sleeping berths are theoretically reserved for people going on to Moscow. Standard tickets, which are valid for two months and allow any number of stop-offs, are not cheap, however; an **ordinary round trip fare** on this route will cost you £212. For this reason most vacationers make use of the variety of **railpasses** available.

Eurail (☎1-800/777-0112), organized through *STA* and *Council Travel*, offers a range of passes that are valid throughout the different European rail networks. Prices vary according to the duration of your trip and the distance you wish to cover. In addition to their all-country youthpass ($425 for one month; $560 for two) which is available only to people under 26, they have a new *East European Flexi Railpass*, which has no age restrictions. Covering Poland, Czechoslovakia, Austria, and Hungary, this allows five days of travel out of a period of fifteen days for $160, or ten days within a month for $259.

BY BUS

Another option, though few but the most budget-oriented traveler would consider it, is to take a cheap flight to London and continue from there by **bus to Warsaw**. An arduous but cheap way to reach Poland, buses are much favored by impoverished, UK-resident Poles during the vacation seasons, and are often packed as a consequence. The most reliable and the costliest services are operated by **Eurolines**, a division of the *National Express* bus company. This runs a regular service **from London to Warsaw** (via Ostend, Brussels, Frankfurt an der Oder, and Poznań) and **to Kraków** (same route to Poznań, then via Wrocław, Opole, and Katowice). Frequency depends on the time of year: weekly in the summer months, but only monthly in January, for example. Journey time for Warsaw is around 36hr, a bit longer for Kraków; cost for both destinations is £125 round trip and £75 one way, with £10–15 reductions for senior citizens and chil-

dren. Tickets can be bought at any *National Express* office in the UK.

In addition, a number of **Polish-emigré run companies** run "buses," which can turn out to mean anything from a double-decker Mercedes to a minibus. The best established of these is *Fregata Travel* (see box next page) which runs vehicles from London to Warsaw via Amsterdam and Poznań, and to Kraków via Amsterdam, Wrocław, and Katowice. Prices are £69 one way, £115 round-trip from London.

HITCHING

Hitching to Poland from the UK, your best bet is to cross the English channel to Ostend (see box next page for ferry companies) and continue via Brussels, Düsseldorf, Hanover, and Berlin. It's worth asking around on the ferry—you may strike lucky and get a truck going through to Düsseldorf or beyond. Alternatively, try the German *Mitfahrzentralen* organization, which links up hitchers and drivers for a smallish fee plus a share of gas costs. They won't get you to Poland, but for $70 you can reach Berlin, a big chunk of your journey. They have an office near London at 50/60 Grant Place, Croydon CRO 6PJ (☎081/654 3210).

BORDER CROSSINGS

Poland shares land borders with Germany, Czechoslovakia, and the Soviet Union. Recent political changes have made the formalities of entering Poland from **Germany or Czechoslovakia** pretty straightforward, though in summer be prepared for long delays at customs points, while Polish officials check their compatriots for smuggled goods. Leaving Poland for Germany or Czechoslovakia can also take time, as Poles still need visas for both countries.

Entering or leaving the **Soviet Union** ought to be less difficult than in the past, with the easing of travel restrictions. However, the mentality of Soviet border guards is lagging well behind the times and the two border posts have proved unable to cope with the flood of visitors between the two countries. In summer, Polish radio broadcasts "border reports" after the weather news, giving details of the length of line (12km on a bad day) and expected waiting time (up to fifty or sixty hours). It's possible that more Polish–Soviet border posts will be opened for international traffic in 1991, but it may be that the number of people leaving the Soviet Union will keep the pressure just as intense.

Current border crossings (all open 24hr) are:

Germany–Poland (north to south)
Ponellen–Kołbaskowo (Berlin–Gdańsk route).
Frankfurt an der Oder–Świecko (Berlin–Warsaw route).
Forst–Olszyna (Berlin–Wrocław/Kraków route).
Görlitz–Zgorzelec (Dresden–Wrocław route).

Soviet Union–Poland (north to south)
Terespol–Brest (Warsaw–Moscow route).
Mędyka (Przemyśl–Lvov/Kiev route).

Czechoslovakia–Poland (west to east)
Jakuszyce (Prague–Wrocław route, via Jelenia Góra).
Kudowa (Prague–Wrocław route, via Kłodzko).
Chałupki (Ostrava– Katowice route).
Cieszyn (Brno/Ostrava–Kraków route).
Chyzne (Ruźomberok–Kraków route).
Łysa Polana (Poprad–Nowy Targ route, via Tatra mountains).
Piwiczna (Poprad–Nowy Sącz route, via Beskids).
Barwinek (Présov–Rzeszów, via Dukla).

ORGANIZED TOURS

With the opening up of Poland, independent travel is gradually becoming easier, but the organized package tour still remains the most popular method of seeing the country. During the communist era, Orbis had unquestioned dominance of this market, and despite a recent growth in the number of small travel operators, most packages from the States will still be booked through them. They have an extensive selection, ranging from 6 to 21 days, including flights, accommodation, and most meals, but they're not especially cheap. A fifteen-day planned excursion called "Panorama of Poland", which takes in the main sights of the country, will cost around $2000, if traveling from New York; from Chicago and Los Angeles you'll need to add on extra for the airfare. "Southern Delight" is a ten-day tour of the country's southern provinces, starting in Warsaw and visiting Kraków, Zakopane, Czestochowa, Wadowice (birthplace of the pope), and Wola, before returning to Warsaw. Between April and October this will cost you $1677 if you fly from New York, or $2092 flying from Los Angeles.

In addition, Orbis arranges tours with a wider scope, taking in other countries. A thirteen-day tour of Poland and the Soviet Union, visiting Warsaw, Kraków, Moscow, and Leningrad between May and September, costs $2649 flying from New York, and $3038 from Los Angeles. Alternatively, a "Highlights of Eastern Europe" tour, visiting Poland, Czechoslovakia, Germany, Hungary, and Austria in sixteen days, costs $2922 flying from New York, $3344 from Los Angeles. This tour runs from June through August.

Orbis also runs a separate tour company for those wishing to roam a bit farther afield, called *Orbis Independent Travel*. This arranges the minimum necessary and leaves exploring up to the individual, while organizing day excursions, for instance to Polish castles and cathedrals, for those that want them. If you're considering this form of travel, bear in mind that rail tickets for journeys within Poland should wherever possible be purchased inside the country, as prices for tickets reserved abroad can be up to fifty percent higher. To bypass this problem, you can take advantage of the internal *Polrail Pass*, also arranged through Orbis, which can cover any period from eight days up to a month. An eight-day pass starts at $35 for second-class, or $50 for first-class travel, rising to a $50 second-class monthly pass, or $75 for the first-class.

AIRLINES AND AGENCIES

LOT, 500 Fifth Ave., New York, NY10110 (☎1-800/223-0593).

Orbis 342 Madison Ave., New York, NY10173; (☎212/867-5011); 338 North Michigan Ave., Chicago, Illinois IL 60601 (☎312/236-9013).

Orbis Independent Travel Address as Orbis.

Polish American Agency Inc.,799 Broadway, New York, NY 10003 (☎212/674-3673).

Polish American Travel Agency, 18 St Mark's Place, New York, NY 10003 (☎212/475-5588)

American Travel Abroad Inc., 250 West 57th St., New York, NY 10107 (☎212/586-5230).

British Rail European Travel Centre Victoria Station, London SW1 (☎071/834 2345).

Eurolines 52 Grosvenor Gdns., London SW1 (☎071/730 3402).

Fregata Travel, 100 Dean St., London W1 (☎071/734 5101).

Scandinavian Seaways, Parkeston Quay, Harwich, Essex CO2 4QG (☎0225/241 234), or 15 Hanover St., London W1 (☎071/493 6696).

P&O, Russell St., Dover, Kent CT16 1QB (☎0304/203 388), or 127 Regent St., London W1R 8LB (☎071/734 4431).

RED TAPE AND VISAS

Although there's a strong probability that the situation will not last for much longer, American and Canadian citizens (and all other westerners) still require visas to enter Poland, the only travel restriction remaining from the communist years.

Visas must be obtained in the applicant's home country before traveling, and although issued for six months don't permit stays of longer

than ninety days at a time. Although you have to stipulate your intended date of arrival, there's no obligation to adhere to this—the visa is valid for any period in the six months following the day of issue.

In order to qualify for a visa, you must have a **full** passport, valid for at least one year beyond the date of your application and with at least one clear page for the authorization stamp. The visa **application form** can be obtained (in person or by mail) either from Polorbis or from a Polish consulate. When completed, the form should be presented along with your passport, two passport-sized photographs, and the appropriate **fee**. The Polish authorities currently charge for each entry you make into the country: $23 for a single entry, $43 for a double, and $63 for a triple within the six-month period. Having made it through the application, the visa will then take around fifteen days to be processed and returned.

Transit visas, valid for 48 hours if you want to stop off in Poland on the way to somewhere else, cost $20 single entry, $30 double; if you want one of these you also have to submit any visa relevant to your ultimate destination.

POLISH EMBASSIES AND CONSULATES

Washington, 2224 Wyoming Ave. NW, DC 20008 (☎202/232-4517).

New York, 233 Madison Ave., NY 10016 (☎212/889-8360).

Toronto, 2603 Lakeshore Blvd. W., Ontario MAV 1GS (☎416/252-5471).

Montreal, 1500 Pine Ave. W., Québec H3G 1B4 (☎514/937-9481).

Ottawa, 443 Daly Ave., Ontario K1N 6H3 (☎613/236-0468).

HEALTH AND INSURANCE

Poland has no reciprocal health agreement with the United States or Canada, so it's essential that you purchase decent health insurance before you travel. An alternative in the bigger cities is provided by the larger western embassies, who run health clinics which nationals can attend for a fee; see the relevant city listings for Warsaw, Kraków, and Gdansk.

Inoculations are not required for a trip to Poland. **Tap water** is officially classified as safe, but in the cities nobody drinks it without boiling it first; mineral water is readily available as an alternative.

PHARMACIES AND HOSPITALS

Simple complaints can normally be dealt with at a regular **pharmacy** (*apteka*), where basic medicines are dispensed by qualified pharmacists, whom Poles consult over most everyday health problems. In the cities many of the staff will speak at least some English or German. In every town there's always one *apteka* open 24 hours a day; addresses are printed in local newspapers.

For more serious problems, or anything the pharmacist can't work out, you'll be directed to a **hospital** (*szpital*), where conditions will probably be pretty horrendous, with too many patients for the beds, a lack of medicines, and often insanitary conditions. Doctors are heavily overworked and scandalously underpaid. Remember to keep any receipts for treatment or medication you receive for your insurance claim when you get back.

INSURANCE

Travel insurance can buy you peace of mind as well as save you money. Before you purchase any insurance, however, check what you have already, whether as part of a family or student policy. You may find yourself covered for medical expenses and loss, and possibly loss of or damage to valuables, while abroad.

For example, **Canadians** are usually covered for medical expenses by their provincial health plans (but may only be reimbursed after the fact). Holders of **ISIC** cards are entitled to $2000 worth of accident coverage and sixty days ($100 per diem) of hospital in-patient benefits for the period during which the card is valid. University **students** will often find that their student health coverage extends for one term beyond the date of last enrollment.

Bank and charge **accounts** (particularly *American Express*) often have certain levels of medical or other insurance included. **Home-owners' or renters'** insurance may cover theft or loss of documents, money, and valuables while overseas, though exact conditions and maximum amounts vary from company to company.

SPECIALIST INSURANCE

Only after exhausting the possibilities above might you want to contact a **specialist travel insurance** company; your travel agent can

usually recommend one—*Travelguard* and *The Travelers* are good policies.

Travel insurance offerings are quite comprehensive, anticipating everything from charter companies going bankrupt to delayed (as well as lost) baggage, by way of sundry illnesses and accidents. **Premiums** vary widely—from the very reasonable ones offered primarily through student/youth agencies (though available to anyone), to those so expensive that the cost for two or three months of coverage will probably equal the cost of the worst possible combination of disasters.

A most important thing to keep in mind——and a source of major disappointment to would be claimants—is that *none* of the currently available policies insures against **theft** of anything while overseas. North American travel policies apply only to items lost from, or damaged in, the custody of an identifiable, responsible third party, i.e. hotel porter, airline, luggage consignment, etc. Even in these cases you will still have to contact the local police to make out a complete report so that your insurer can process the claim.

BRITISH POLICIES

If you are **transiting through Britain**, policies there cost considerably less (under £20/$32 for a month) and include routine cover for theft. You can take out a British policy at almost any travel agency or major bank. ISIS, a "student" policy but open to everyone, is reliable and fairly good value; it is operated by a company called *Endsleigh*, and is available through any student/youth travel agency.

REIMBURSEMENT

All insurance policies—American or Canadian—work by **reimbursing you** once you return home, so be sure to keep all your receipts from doctors and pharmacists. Any thefts should immediately be reported to the nearest police station and a police report obtained; no report, no refund.

If you have had to undergo serious medical treatment, with major hospital bills, contact your consulate. They can normally arrange for an insurance company, or possibly relatives, to cover the fees, pending a claim.

COSTS AND MONEY

Poland is currently one of the great travel bargains. The abolition of all compulsory exchange controls and the effective legalization of the black market mean that most of the essentials of travel, such as food and drink, public transit, and entrance fees are ludicrously cheap for anyone with western (hard) currency. Accommodation is priced on a different scale, but is still inexpensive as a rule. Note that prices are often much higher in Warsaw than in the rest of the country, and are similarly increased in places which see a lot of foreign visitors, such as Kraków and Poznań.

AVERAGE COSTS

Rampant inflation and the lifting of subsidies over the past couple of years have put severe economic pressures on Poles. However, for western visitors, prices for most goods remain very low. You can **eat** and **drink** well for $4 or less even at some of the country's best restaurants, including those in Orbis hotels, which charge western prices for all other services. You should be able to eat in a more basic restaurant for not much more than $2, and substantial hot meals can be had from milk and snack bars for much less than this—40¢ will often buy a main course. Coffee or tea with cakes in a café can be had for a similarly nominal amount.

Prices for **public transit** are little more than pocket money—even traveling across half the length of the country by train or bus only costs around $4. Similarly, you never have to fork out

as much as $2 to visit even the most popular **tourist sights**, with 10¢ the normal asking price.

Faced with such prices, it's almost impossible to get through more than a few dollars a day, unless you go for expensive **accommodation**. Actually, there is plenty of that, with the international hotels in the main cities charging up to $200 per night. On the other hand, if you stick to campgrounds, youth and tourist hostels, or sports hotels, you'll seldom spend much more than $6 on a bed. Budget on about twice as much for a room in a private house or in the cheapest hotels. In the most popular resort areas, full-board terms in pensions and holiday homes can generally be found for $15–20.

CURRENCY

The Polish unit of currency is the **złoty** (abbreviated as zł), which is now fully convertible within the country. The dropping of the artificially high exchange valuation imposed by the communists made its value plummet against hard currencies, though it managed to stabilise during 1990 at around **9000 to the dollar**, with exchange offices offering rates between 8000 and 9500.

The złoty is now almost entirely a paper currency, but **coins** still exist in denominations of 1, 2, 5, 10, and 20 zł. Three different sizes of the 20 zł coin are in circulation: hold on to the medium-sized ones to make phone calls. There are **notes** of 50, 100, 200, 500, 1000, 2000, 5000, 10,000, 20,000, 50,000, 100,000, and 200,000 zł.

TRAVELER'S CHECKS, CREDIT CARDS, AND HARD CURRENCY

Traveler's checks, available from any downtown bank for a one-percent commission, are the easiest and safest way of carrying your money, being fully refundable should they be lost or stolen. The drawback is that in Poland only **main banks**, **Orbis offices**, and **hotels** will accept them, and that the transaction can sometimes be a lengthy process. This is not a particular problem in major cities and tourist areas, but cashiers in provincial towns are often so unfamiliar with the procedure that you can be kept waiting for hours.

Credit cards are more established than you might expect. *Access/Mastercard, American*

Express, Diners Club, Eurocard, JCB, and *Visa* are accepted by Orbis in payment for accommodation, meals, telephone and telex bills, transportation tickets, car rental, and tourist services; you can also arrange a cash advance on most of these cards at their hotels and main offices, though you have to wait for an authorization call to Warsaw. An increasing number of stores, particularly those dealing in hard currency, will also take your plastic.

Poland's desperate need for foreign currency is reflected in the ease with which it's possible to change money. In general, Poles tend to use the **US dollar** as their yardstick and this is the currency they're keenest to acquire; the **Deutschmark** is also in strong demand. It therefore makes sense to take a supply of cash dollars, if only for contingency purposes.

EXCHANGE

As a rule the most competitive **exchange rates** are offered by the **banks** (usually open some-

thing like Mon–Fri 7:30am–5pm, Sat 7:30am–2pm), though you'll almost certainly be kept waiting at the desk. A flat commission of around 20,000zł. per transaction is normally deducted.

Orbis hotels also have exchange desks, which are usually open around the clock; they tend to offer poor rates and charge hefty commissions, though these are not uniformly applied. The main **Orbis office** in each town is supposed to offer a full currency exchange service; this is usually done quickly and efficiently, with a better rate than you'll get in their hotels. However, some offices now seem to be prepared to change cash only.

A whole host of **private banks**, designated by the names *kantor* or *walut*, have sprung up in all the cities, many run in tandem with another retail business. All of these change **cash only**, and may not take anything except US dollars.

The effective legalization of the **black market** rate means that illicit currency transactions are no longer worth the risk.

INFORMATION AND MAPS

There's no direct Polish equivalent to the national tourist boards found in most other European countries; as a result, the provision of information is diffuse, to say the least. Warsaw, for example, has no central tourist office, and tourist information is disseminated by a host of offices, stores, and hotels bearing the sign *Informator*

Turystyczny (IT). What follows is a lowdown on the country's various tourist organizations and the services they provide. As yet, they're still mainly geared to organized group visits, though the importance of independent travel is increasingly being recognized.

ORBIS

By far the largest tourist outfit in Poland is **Orbis**, usually known outside the country as Polorbis. Founded in the 1920s, it was turned by the communists into a vast organization with an unusually wide range of functions. Presumably it will at some time in the future be broken up into several parts, but there's no sign of that happening as yet.

In Poland Orbis at present runs 55 international-type hotels and 160 offices. These offices sell air, rail, bus, and ferry tickets, change money, arrange guided tours, car rental, and special interest activities, make hotel reservations, organize reservations for sports and cultural events, and process visa extensions. Their responsibility for promoting tourism in their own region is rather nebulous, though special offices for foreign visitors do exist in the largest cities, and many other branches are well clued-up on the tourist facilities in their area. Others, however, seem to have brochures on just about anywhere in the world except their own region. The addresses of the most important Orbis offices are listed in the appropriate sections of *The Guide*.

Abroad, the company acts both as the main agent for holidays in Poland and as the nearest equivalent to a state tourist office (see "Getting There" on p.7 for addresses). It's well worth contacting one of their offices to pick up free **promotional material** in English, which can often be difficult to get your hands on in Poland itself. In addition to a series of six glossy brochures covering the whole country, there are also a few booklets on specialist interests (music, architecture, folklore, activity holidays) and an excellent road map ($3).

OTHER TOURIST ORGANIZATIONS

PTTK—which translates literally as "The Polish Country Lovers' Association"—has a rather more direct responsibility for internal Polish tourism than Orbis, administering information offices throughout Poland. In addition, it runs hostels in both city and holiday areas, and rents bungalows for family holidays in the lake regions. Its main foreign service department is at ul. Świętokrzyska 36, Warsaw (☎20-82-41).

Almatur is a student and youth travel bureau—and the obvious contact point for getting to meet young Poles. It arranges international work camps, special study, activity and hobby programs, educational exchanges and, during the summer, accommodation in international student hotels, holiday centers and camps (*Baza Studentowa*). These are open to anyone under 35 on production of Almatur vouchers, which are available from their offices; rates are reduced if you have an ISIC card. Almatur's head office is at ul. Ordynacka 9, Warsaw (☎26-23-56); other addresses can be found in *The Guide* under the appropriate section.

Elsewhere in Poland, a number of individual **city or municipal based tourist offices** dispense information and run tours and excursions for their particular turf. Among the best established of these are *Syrena* in Warsaw and *Wawel Tourist* in Kraków. A host of **local, private tourist agencies** have set up over the past year or two, as well, running a variety of trips and accommodation. See the appropriate parts of *The Guide* for addresses.

MAPS

The maps printed in this book should be sufficient for most purposes. A good detailed **road map** of the country is a useful supplement, however. The Orbis *Poland: Roadmap* (1:750,000) is very useful and widely available in Poland; abroad it is available through Polorbis or in map shops, in slightly modified form, as *Hildebrand: Poland*. PPWK, the state map company, also produces an extremely good, though not easily available, *Atlas Samochodowa* (1:500,000), divided into regions, with supplementary schematic town plans. PPWK also produces the atlas as a series of 16 individual regional maps.

Should you need more detailed **city maps**, try to get hold of the appropriate *plan miasta*, available cheaply at local tourist offices, kiosks, street sellers and bookshops. These index all streets alphabetically, and give exhaustive listings on bus and tram routes, places of entertainment, restaurants, and cafés. Unfortunately, they are prone to go out of print and do not exist at all in the case of several major cities; they're also difficult to buy in advance, though large city bookshops normally keep a reasonable selection.

Even more essential, if you intend doing any serious walking, are the **hiking maps** of the national parks and other tourist areas. Known as *Mapa Turystyczna*, these cost only a nominal amount and are very clear and simple to use: although the texts are usually only in Polish, the keys to the symbols are in several languages, including English. They can be even harder to come by than the city plans: if you see a map you'll need later on in your travels, snap it up rather than take the risk of not being able to get it in the region itself.

Useful **map shops** in the US, which may have some of the PPWK maps in stock, include *Rand McNally*, 150 East 52nd St., New York, NY 10022 (☎212/983 5600), *The Complete Traveller*, 199 Madison Ave., New York, NY (☎212/679 4339), and *Map Link*, 25 East Mason St., Santa Barbara, CA 93101 (☎805/965-4402).

GETTING AROUND

Poland has comprehensive and cheap public transit services, though they can often be overcrowded and excruciatingly slow. As a general rule, trains are the best means of moving across the country, as even the most rural areas are still criss-crossed by passenger lines. Rail buffs, in addition, will find Poland the most fascinating country in Europe: more than two dozen narrow-gauge lines are still in operation (identified in timetables by the word *wąsk*), and steam is used on some of these as well as on a few mainline routes. For information on the major train connections, consult the "Travel Details" section at the end of each chapter. The text of *The Guide* points out those places where it's preferable to take buses—which are usually better for short journeys or in the more remote areas.

Driving is also covered in the section following. You'll find that car-rental prices are similar to the US, but taxis are sufficiently cheap to be worth considering for the occasional inter-town journey, especially if you can split costs three or four ways. Additional and enjoyable means of getting around include coastal and river ferries and, of course, walking in the Tatras and other mountain areas.

TRAINS

Polish State Railroads (*PKP*) is a reasonably efficient organization and runs three main types of train:

● **Express** services (*expresowy*) are the ones to go for if you're traveling long distances, as they stop at the main cities only (although they are still extremely slow by Western European standards). Seat reservations, involving a small supplementary charge, are compulsory; however, leniency is usually shown to dumb foreigners who haven't understood the reservations system. Expresses are marked in red on timetables, with an R in a box alongside.

● So-called **fast** trains (*pośpieszne*), again marked in red, have far more stops, and reservations are optional.

● The **normal** services (*normalne* or *osobowe*) are shown in black and should be avoided whenever possible: in rural areas they stop at every haystack, while even on interurban routes it usually takes about an hour to cover 20km.

Fares won't burn a hole in the pocket of even the most impoverished westerner. Even a long cross-country haul such as Warsaw to Wrocław, Kraków or Gdańsk will set you back little more than $4. With such a price structure, it's well worth paying the fifty percent extra to travel **first-class** or make a **reservation** (*miejscówka*) even when this is not compulsory, as sardine-can-like conditions are fairly common. Reservations can be made up to sixty days in advance, or ninety days for return trips.

Most long intercity journeys are best done overnight; they're often conveniently timed so that you leave around 10 or 11pm and arrive at between 6 and 9am. For these, it's best to reserve either a **sleeper** (*sypialny*) or **couchette**; the total cost will probably be far less than a room in even the cheapest hotel. The second-class sleepers are a particularly good bargain at around $4 per head. They sleep three to a compartment and offer comfortable bunks along with a washbasin, towels, sheets, and blankets; first class has one bed fewer. Although preferable to sitting up, the couchettes (about $2) are rather cramped, with six to a cabin.

TICKETS

Buying tickets is no problem in small places, but in the main train stations of the cities it can be a major hassle, due to the bewildering array of counters, each almost invariably with a long, snaking line. Make sure you start lining up long before your train is due to leave; in the worst cases (eg Warsaw and Poznań), you may have to wait in line for over an hour.

Tickets currently come in all shapes and sizes, but the only time you have to think for yourself is with the recently introduced **undated tickets**, which you validate by sticking in a machine before departure. If you're going for a sleeper or couchette, major stations have special counters. As an alternative to the station lines, you can buy tickets for journeys of over 100km at **Orbis offices**. The main branches of these are also the best places to reserve for **international journeys**, which foreigners still have to pay for in hard currency.

Discounts are available for senior citizens and for kids between four and ten; those under four travel free, though they're not supposed to occupy a seat. **Rail passes** for the whole network are available for periods of eight, fifteen or twenty-one days, or for a whole month, but you'd have to take a lot of trains to justify the outlay.

STATION PRACTICALITIES

In the station, the **departures** are listed on yellow posters marked *odjazdy*, the **arrivals** on white posters headed *przyjazdy*. If you're intending to do a lot of traveling in Poland, it would make sense to invest in the six-monthly network **timetable** (*rozkład*) which can be bought at all main stations—at least while stocks last. Otherwise, you may find yourself having to wait regularly at the information counters, which often have the longest lines of all.

Each **platform** (*peron*) has two tracks, so take care to board the right train; usually only the long-distance services have boards stating their route, so you'll often have to ask. To make matters worse, it's fairly common practice for trains to be re-routed to a different platform at the last minute: if you don't understand Polish, always keep a sharp lookout for the sudden movement of people from one platform to another. Electronic departure boards are increasingly common, though as yet are confined to major cities.

The **main station** in a city is identified by the name *Główny* or *Centralna*. These are open round the clock and usually have such facilities as waiting rooms, toilets, kiosks, restaurants, snack bars, cafés, a luggage consignment counter and a 24 hour post office. Often they're the only place where you'll be able to get something to eat after

about 9pm. The Poles operate an eccentric system for **checking in luggage**. You have to declare its value to the attendant and then pay one-hundredth of this sum as insurance on top of the basic storage charge.

Facilities **on the trains** are much poorer, though some have a buffet car (check on the departure board) and light refreshments are available on all overnight journeys. **Ticket control** is rather haphazard, particularly on crowded services, but it does happen more often than not. If you've boarded a train without the proper ticket, you should seek out the conductor, who will issue one on payment of a small supplement.

BUSES

The extent to which you'll need to make use of the services of *PKS*, the Polish national bus company, depends very much on the nature of your trip. If you're concentrating on cities, then the trains are definitely the better bet: **intercity** buses are often overcrowded and slow, and services less frequent and marginally more expensive (not that this is much of a drawback). There are very few long-haul routes and no overnight journeys. However, in **rural areas**, notably the mountain regions, buses are usually the better means of getting around, scoring in the choice and greater convenience of pick-up points and frequency of service.

TICKETS

In towns and cities, the main **bus station** is usually alongside the train station. **Tickets** can be bought in the terminal building; in larger places there are several counters, each dealing with clearly displayed destinations. Buying this way ensures a seat, as a number will be allocated to you on your ticket. However, the lack of computerized systems means that many stations cannot allocate seats for services starting out from another town. In such cases, you have to wait until the bus arrives and buy a ticket—which may be for standing room only—from the driver.

The same procedure can also be followed, provided the bus isn't already full to overflowing, if you arrive too late to buy a ticket at the counter. With a few exceptions, it isn't possible to buy tickets for return journeys on board.

As with the trains, Orbis offices are the best place to go if you want to reserve on an **international** route.

TIMETABLES

Noticeboards show **departures** and **arrivals** not only in the bus stations, but on all official stopping places along the route. "Fast" buses (which carry a small supplement) are marked in red, slow ones in black. The towns served are listed in alphabetical order, with the relevant times set against each, and mention made of the principal places passed on the way. This can be extremely confusing, as the normal practice is to list only services which terminate in that particular town, and not those which continue onwards. Thus you'll have to check down the "via" (*prez*) column to find additional departure times to your destination.

If in doubt, ask at the information counter, which will be equipped with the multivolume set of timetables listing all *PKS* routes.

PLANES

The domestic network of *LOT*, the Polish national airline, operates **flights from Warsaw** to Gdańsk, Katowice, Koszalin, Kraków, Poznań, Rzeszów, Szczecin, Słupsk, Wrocław, and Zielona Góra—all taking about an hour. Some routes are covered several times a day, but services are sharply reduced on Sunday and during the winter months. Most of the cities mentioned are linked to some of the others, but Warsaw is very much the linchpin of the system. As a general rule, airports are located just outside the cities, and can be reached either by a special *LOT* bus or by a municipal service.

Tickets can be purchased from both *LOT* and Orbis offices, where you can also pick up free **timetables**. Prices are currently in the region of $40–50 one-way (there are no savings on round-trips). Kids up to the age of two travel for ten percent of the adult fare, provided they do not occupy a separate seat; those under twelve go for half price.

BOATS

In summer, ferries and hydrofoils connect towns along the **Baltic coast**, notably around Szczecin, and in the Gdańsk area where they connect the Tri-City of Gdańsk, Sopot and Gdynia with each other and with the Hel Peninsula. The main companies are: *The Szczecin Shipping Company*, Marine Terminal, ul. Jana z Kolna 7, Szczecin (☎225-918), and *The Gdańsk Shipping Company*, ul. Wartka 4, Gdańsk (☎311-975).

PUBLIC TRANSIT IN CITIES

Trams (usually antiquated boneshakers) are the basis of the public transit system in nearly all Polish cities. They usually run from about 5am to midnight, and departure times are clearly posted at the stops. Tickets, which cost around 600zł (about 6¢), must be bought from a *ruch* kiosk; many cities use the same type of ticket, so if you've any left over at the end of your stay you'll probably find you can use them somewhere else. On boarding, you should immediately cancel your ticket in one of the machines; checks by inspectors are rare, but they do happen from time to time. Note that some tickets have to be canceled at both ends (arrows will indicate if this is so): this is for the benefit of children and senior citizens, who travel half-price and thus have to cancel only one end per journey. If you transfer from one tram to another you'll need a second ticket.

The same tickets are valid on the municipal **buses** (which are usually red, in contrast to the yellow favored by *PKS*) and the same system for validating the tickets applies—but note that **night services** require two tickets. The routes of the municipal buses go beyond the city boundaries into the outlying countryside, so many nearby villages have several connections during peak times of the day.

When translated into western money, the price of **taxis** is cheap enough to make them a viable proposition for regular use. In the new free-market economy, plenty of people have turned to taxi-driving, and outside hotels, stations, and major tourist attractions you often have to run the gauntlet of cabbies. Be wary of unmetered taxis (unless you agree the price in advance) and of drivers who demand payment in hard currency, and always ensure that the driver switches on the meter when you begin your journey. Because of the rip-roaring inflation of the past few years, what you actually pay is the meter fare times a multiplier, the current figure for the latter being displayed on a little sign; prices are fifty percent higher after 11pm.

Prices are also raised by fifty percent for journeys outside the city limits. However, costs are always negotiable for longer journeys, between towns, for example, and can work out very reasonable if split among a group.

Inland, excursion boats also run along certain stretches of **canals**—most enjoyably the Augustów near Białystok—and **rivers**, such as the Wisła. Lake cruises are also run on several of the Mazurian lakes. Costs for all are again very modest.

DRIVING AND CAR RENTAL

Access to a car saves a lot of time in exploring rural areas, and driving is relatively easy-going anywhere in the country. Poles are not—as yet—habitual car-owners, and recent inflation has, if anything, cleared the roads still more. The American Automobile Association recommends that anyone planning to drive in Poland should purchase an International Driving Permit, available from all branches of the AAA for $10.

Renting a car is about average for western Europe—crippling by Polish standards—at around $250–400 a week (unlimited mileage). Orbis have rental arrangements with *Avis*, *Hertz*, and *Europcar*, any of whom can make reservations. In Poland, car rental can only be arranged at the main Orbis offices (Gdańsk, Katowice, Kraków, Łódź, Poznań, Szczecin, Warsaw, and Wrocław—see the relevant section for addresses); payment can be made with cash or any major credit card. You can drop the car at a different office from the one where you rented it. The main models on offer are the Fiat 1500, the Polonez, and the Ford Sierra; remember that unless you specify, you'll be driving a stick shift. Note that cars are rented only to people **over 21**, and who have held a full licence for more than a year.

Many **gas stations** in cities and along the main international routes are open 24 hours a day, others from around 6am to 10pm. Diesel is usually available, as is lead-free gas (*benzyna bezołowiowa*) on major routes; always go for the highest octane available—generally 94; 86 is far too low for most western cars. In rural areas it can be a long way from station to station, so always carry a fuel can.

The Polish drivers' organization, *PZMot*, runs a 24-hour **car breakdown** service; for addresses and phone numbers, see the "Listings" section at the end of each main city account. The national headquarters, which can provide some English-language pamphlets on their services, is at ul. Krucza 6/14, Warsaw (☎290-467 or ☎293-541).

The main **rules of the road** are that seatbelts must be worn outside built-up areas, that right of way must be conceded to public transit vehicles, and that you should not drink and drive. **Speed limits** are 60kph in built-up areas (white signs with the place name mark the start of a built-up area, the same sign with a diagonal red line through it marks the end), 90kph on country roads, 110kph on motorways, and 70kph if you're pulling a trailer. In cities, beware of a casual attitude towards traffic lights and road signs by local drivers and pedestrians.

HITCHING

A by-product of the scarcity of private vehicles in Poland is that **hitchhiking** is positively encouraged. PTTK have in fact institutionalized the practice through their *Społeczny Komitet Autostop* (Social Autostop Committee), which sells a package comprising a book of vouchers for 2000km of travel, an ID card, maps, and an insurance policy. The relevant number of vouchers should be given to the driver, qualifying him for various prizes and indemnifying him for any compensation claims. The Autostop packages are valid from May to September (nominal charge), and available to anyone over 17 from larger PTTK offices and some youth hostels; the head Autostop office is ul. Narbutta 27a, Warsaw (☎496-208).

Finally, note that the Polish convention is to stick out your whole arm—not just your thumb.

WALKING

Poland contains some of the best **hiking** country in Europe, specifically in the twelve areas designated as national parks and throughout the mountainous regions on the country's southern and western borders. There's a full network of marked trails, the best of which are detailed in *The Guide*. Many of these take several days, and pass through remote areas served by refuge huts (see "Other Hostels", p.19). However, much of the best scenery can be seen by covering sections of these routes on one-day walks. Few of the trails are particularly strenuous and, although specialist footwear is highly recommended, a well worn-in pair of sturdy shoes is usually sufficient.

ACCOMMODATION

Accommodation will almost certainly account for the majority of your essential expenditure in Poland, though you're by no means confined to the international hotels so heavily touted in most promotional material—almost everywhere, there are now plenty of very cheap alternatives. Listings in the text have been made as wide-ranging as possible to reflect the immense diversity of the available choice: privately run hotels, pensions, hostels, workers' hostels, youth hostels, rooms in private houses, and a good range of campgrounds.

ORBIS HOTELS

Orbis runs some 55 **international hotels** throughout Poland, which can be booked with a minimum of fuss before your departure. A few of these are famous old prewar haunts, but the vast majority date from the last twenty years and are in the anonymous concrete style favored for business purposes the world over. This stock is now being supplemented by some even more luxurious establishments, often as joint ventures with well-known western hotel chains. Needless to say, all such hotels are extremely pricey, but they do have consistently high standards. Minimum

rates, which are based on hard currency and thus an exception to the comments about price fluctuation below, are around $80 for a single, $140 for a double, rising to more than $200 per head in the most exclusive addresses in Warsaw.

Even if this is way beyond your budget, it's still worth knowing about these hotels, as you're more likely to find staff speaking English and other foreign languages here than you are in any tourist office. Non-guests are also able to make use of their very westernized **facilities**. Particularly useful are the 24-hour currency exchange, plus the telex and telephone services—often the easiest means of making an international call. In addition, these hotels have restaurants, cafés, and bars, and may have other facilities such as a swimming pool, tanning studio, sauna, tennis court, hairdresser, hard-currency shop, nightclub, and disco.

Orbis also runs a number of **motels** on the outskirts of major cities; these are usually a bit cheaper than their more central counterparts, but generally only practical if you've got your own transportation.

OTHER HOTELS

Most other hotels have far more rudimentary facilities. They're graded on a **star system**, but these are generously awarded: most four-star Polish hotels would be lucky to be graded as two-star in North America. It's harder to give guidance on prices here than in any other type of accommodation: some highly recommendable hotels charge less than $10 for a double with bath, but you can easily land a tacky room without facilities for three or four times that price somewhere else. If you calculate on paying $20 a day per head as an average, you should end up well in pocket. Generally speaking, savings are

A NOTE ON PRICES

The abolition in July 1990 of specially increased prices for foreigners has led to a state of flux which is likely to last for some time. Some places seem to have raised prices for Poles to the previous level for foreigners, while others have done the reverse, leading to the coexistence of outrageous rip-offs and astonishing bargains. As a result, in many instances it hasn't been possible to give specific prices in the text of *The Guide*. A rough idea of what you can expect to pay for different types of accommodation is given in the sections below, but be prepared for anomalies and fluctuations in price.

made the more people occupy a room, but this seldom amounts to much. Breakfast is sometimes included in the room price, but more often is not. Always ask for prices with and without bath—there may be a substantial difference.

The cheapest of all hotel rooms are provided by **sports hotels** (*Dom Sportowy*), which generally charge around $7 a head. These, however, exist mainly for the use of visiting sporting teams, which means they're likely to be full for at least part of the weekend, and at other times deserted. They're also usually located in a park way out from the center; they don't serve meals; and you may be asked to share a room with a stranger.

PENSIONS AND HOLIDAY HOMES

Some of Poland's best accommodation deals can be found in the **pensions** (*pensjonaty*) situated in the resort towns of major vacation areas such as the Tatras, the Karkanosze, and the Kłodzko Region. These are a particularly attractive option if you're traveling in a group, as triples and quadruples offer substantial savings over doubles; singles are extremely scarce. Half-board terms range from $15 to $30 per head; it's sometimes posssible to get bed and breakfast only, but it would be a pity to miss out on the excellent regional cuisine that's usually provided. For reservations and farther details, contact an Orbis office in the appropriate area.

Another possibility is to rent a **summer cottage**. Available between mid-May and the end of September, these are roughly analogous to the French *gîtes*. Intended for quiet breaks, with opportunities for bicycling, rambling, fishing, and water sports, they are mostly located in secluded rural areas, notably the Mazurian Lakes, the Lubuska region, and Western Pomerania, though there are also some along the Baltic coast. All have a living room with dining area, a bathroom with hot and cold running water, a fully equipped kitchen, a fireplace, and a patio or balcony. They have between one and five bedrooms, sleeping from three to eight people, and are priced accordingly. Obviously they must be booked in advance: for full details, contact Polorbis in New York, or any Orbis office.

A recent addition to the holiday lodging scene are **workers' hostels** (often designated *FWP*), formerly run by unions and factories for their own employees but increasingly privatized and open to general trade.

PRIVATE ROOMS

It's possible to get a **room in a private house** almost anywhere in the country. The disadvantages include sometimes pretty shabby flats, which may well be situated on the outskirts of town, but it's an ideal way to find out how the Poles themselves live.

All major cities have an office providing a room-finding service, usually known as the **Biuro Zakwaterowania**. The charges don't vary much: $12–15, at least half as much again in Warsaw. You should be given a choice of location and category (from 1 down to 3); you register and pay for as many nights as you wish, then are given directions to the house where you'll be staying. You must arrive there before 10pm; there will probably also be a restriction on how early you check in (perhaps 1pm). In case you don't like the place you're sent to, it makes sense not to register for too many nights ahead, as it's easy enough to extend your stay by going back to the *Biuro*, or paying your host directly. Note that there's no scope under this setup for negotiating special rates: the landlady is obliged to inform the *Biuro* if you're staying on, or else is liable to have someone else sent by them to occupy your room.

Some **Orbis offices** also act as agents for householders with rooms available to let. These are often a little more expensive and may be subject to a minimum stay of three nights (or else a hefty surcharge). However, the administration is far less tight than with a *Biuro Zakwaterowania* and you can subsequently extend the length of your stay by negotiation with your host, who'll no doubt be happy to pass on in the form of a price reduction some of the substantial share of your payment that would otherwise go to Orbis.

At the unofficial level, many houses in the main holiday areas hang out **signs** saying *Noclegi* (lodging) or *Pokoje* (rooms). It's up to you to bargain over the price; $5 is the least you can expect to pay. You may get a particularly good deal if you offer hard currency—one reason why you should carry a supply of western cash. In the cities, you won't see any signs advertising rooms, but you may well be approached outside stations and other obvious places. Before accepting, establish the price and check that the location is suitable; the same comments about payment apply.

YOUTH HOSTELS

Scattered throughout Poland are some 200 **official youth hostels** (*Schroniska Młodziezowe*), identified by a green triangle on a white background. However, a large percentage of these are only open for a few weeks at the height of the summer holiday period, usually in converted school buildings, and are liable to be packed solid, while most of the permanent year-round hostels are still very much in line with the hair-shirt ideals of the movement's founders. Children under ten are not allowed in, and preference is supposedly given to those under 26, though there's no upper age restriction. Make sure you bring a sheet sleeping bag.

Two plus points are the **prices** (rarely more than $4 a head, with $2 a likely average) and the **locations**, with many hostels placed close to town centers. Against that, there's the fact that dormitories are closed between 10am and 5pm, that you must check in by 9pm, and that a 10pm curfew is usually enforced.

The most useful hostel **addresses** are given in *The Guide*, but if you need a complete list, either buy the official *IYHF Handbook* or contact the head office of the Polish youth hostel federation (PTSM) at ul. Chocimska 28, Warsaw (Mon–Fri 8am–3:30pm; ☎498-354 or 498-128) for their own comprehensive handbook (*Informator*). It's best to buy an **IYHF** membership card before you go.

OTHER HOSTELS

One reason the youth hostels maintain the accent on youth is that there's a network of adult **tourist hostels**, often run by **PTTK** and called either **Dom Turysty** or **Dom Wycieczkowy**. Found in both cities and rural locations, these are generally cheaper than any hotel, but are often a poor bargain at around $10 for a bed in a small dorm with basic shared facilities.

In July, August, and early September **Almatur** also organizes accommodation in **university hostels** in the main university towns. Rooms have two, three, or four beds; the charges including breakfast are around $8 for students (proof will be required), $12 for others under 35, which

is the age limit. You can eat cheaply at the cafeteria on the premises, and there are often discos in the evenings. The location of these hostels can vary from year to year; contact an Almatur office (relevant addresses are given in the text) or Polorbis before you go.

In mountain areas, a reasonably generous number of **refuges**, which are clearly marked on hiking maps, enable you to make long-distance treks without having to make detours down into the villages for the night. Accommodation is in very basic dormitories, but costs are nominal and you can often get cheap and filling hot meals; in summer the more popular refuges can be very crowded indeed, as they are obliged to accept all comers. As a general rule the refuges are open all year round but it's always worth checking for closures or renovations in progress before setting out.

CAMPING

There are some 400 **campgrounds** throughout the country. The most useful are listed in the text; for a complete list, get hold of the *Campingi w Polsce* **map**, available from bookshops, some travel bureaux or the motoring organization *PZMot*. Apart from a predictably dense concentration in the main holiday areas, they can also be found in most cities; the ones on the outskirts are almost invariably linked by bus to downtown and often have the benefit of a peaceful location and swimming pool. As you'd expect, the major drawback is that most campgrounds are open May to September only, though a few operate all year round. **Charges** usually work out at less than $2 per head, a bit more if you come by car.

One specifically Polish feature is that you don't necessarily have to bring a tent to stay at many camping grounds, as there are often **chalets** for rent, generally complete with toilet and shower. Though decidedly spartan in appearance, these are good value at around $7 per head. In summer, however, they are invariably packed to the gills.

Camping wild, outside of the national parks, is acceptable so long as you're reasonably discreet.

FOOD AND DRINK

Poles take their food pretty seriously, providing snacks of feast-like proportions to the most casual visitors, and maintaining networks of country relatives or local shops for supplies of especially treasured ingredients—smoked meats and sausages, cheeses, fruits and vegetables. The cuisine itself is a complex mix of influences: Russian, Lithuanian, Ukrainian, German, and Jewish traditions have all left their mark. To accompany the dishes, there is excellent beer and a score of wonderful vodkas.

The best meals you'll have in Poland are likely to be at people's homes, if you get the invitation. However, with the move toward a market economy, the country's **restaurants**—most of them specializing in ungarnished slabs of meat during the communist era—have been tidying up. At their best, in fact, they are as good as any in Central Europe, dishing out a spoonful of caviar for starters before moving on through traditional soups and beef, pork, or duck dishes. And, like much else in the country, they are absurdly cheap for western tourists.

Drinking habits are changing. Poles for years drank mainly at home, while visitors stuck to the hotels, with such other **bars** as existed being alcoholic-frequented dives. Over the last couple of years, though, something of a bar culture has been emerging in the cities, supplementing the largely non-alcohol-serving cafés. Elsewhere, drinking is still best done at the local hotel or restaurant.

FOOD

Like their Central and Eastern European neighbors, Poles are insatiable **meat** eaters: throughout the austerities of the past decade, meat consumption here remained among the highest in Europe. Beef and pork in different guises are the mainstays of most meals, while hams and sausages are consumed at all times of the day, as snacks and sandwich-fillers. In the coastal and mountain regions, you can also expect **fish** to feature prominently on the menus, with carp and trout being particularly good.

Although a meal without meat is a contradiction in terms for most Poles, vegetarians will find cheap and dependable refuge in the plentiful **milk bars** (see below), whose dairy-based menus exclude meat almost entirely (continuing Jewish traditions). They have a very mixed reputation, popular on the whole with the young and with students, but often scorned by their elders. At the opposite end of the economic scale, the plusher restaurants normally carry a selection of **vegetarian** dishes (*potrawy jarskie*); if the menu has no such section, the key phrase to use is *bezmiesne* (without meat).

BREAKFAST, SNACKS, AND FAST FOOD

For most Poles, the first meal of the day, eaten at home at around 7am, is little more than a sandwich with a glass of tea or cup of coffee. A more leisurely **breakfast** might include fried eggs with ham, mild frankfurters, a selection of cold meats and cheese, rolls and jam, but for most people this full spread is more likely to be taken as a second breakfast (*drugie śniadanie*) at around midday. This is often taken in the workplace, but a common alternative for younger, city Poles is to stop at a milk bar or self-service snack bar (*samoobsługa*).

Open from early morning till 5 or 6pm (later in the city centers), **snack bars** are soup-kitchen-type places, serving very cheap but generally uninspiring food: small plates of salted herring in oil (*śledź w oleju*), sandwiches, tired-looking meat or cheese, sometimes enlivened by some Russian salad (*sałatka jarzynowa*). **Milk bars** (*bar mleczny*) are even cheaper options, offering a selection of solid, non-meat meals with the emphasis on quantity. Milk bars and snack bars both operate like self-service cafeterias; the menu is displayed over the counter, but if you don't recognize the names of the dishes (the vocabulary section below will help) you can just point.

TAKE-OUT AND FAST FOOD

Traditional Polish **takeout stands** usually sell *zapiekanki*, baguette-like pieces of bread topped with melted cheese; a less common but enjoyable version of the same thing comes with fried mushrooms. You'll also find **hot-dog stalls**, doling out sub-Frankfurter sausages in white rolls, and stalls and shops selling **french fries** (*frytki*); the latter are generally fat and oily, sold by weight, and accompanied by sausage (*kiełbasa*) or chicken (*kurczak*) in the tourist resorts and some city stands, or by fish (*ryby*) in the northern seaside resorts and lakeland areas.

More Western-style **fast food** is starting to take off, too, with hamburger joints opening up in Warsaw and cities such as Gdańsk and Kraków. Like much of the new private enterprise, quality is variable.

DO-IT-YOURSELF SNACKS

If the snacks on offer fail to appeal, you can always stock up on your own provisions.

Most people buy their **bread** in supermarkets (*samoobsługowe*) or from market traders; bakeries (*piekarnia*) are mostly small private shops and still something of a rarity, but when you do find them they tend to be very good, as the lines indicate. The standard loaf (*chleb zakopiański*) is a long piece of dense rye bread, often flavored with caraway seeds. Also common is *razowy*, a solid brown bread sometimes flavored with honey, and *mazowiecki*, a white, sour rye bread. Rolls come in two basic varieties: the more common is the plain, light white roll called a *kajzerka*, the other is the *grahamka*, a round roll of rougher and denser brown bread.

Supermarkets are again a useful source for **fillers**, with basic delicatessen counters for cooked meats and sausages, and cold cases holding a standard array of hard and soft cheeses. Street markets often reveal more choice—certainly for **fruit and vegetables**. Few market stalls supply bags, so bring your own.

COFFEE, TEA, AND SWEETS

Poles are inveterate tea and coffee drinkers, their daily round punctuated by endless cups or glasses, generally with heaps of sugar.

Tea, which is cheaper and so marginally more popular, is drunk Russian-style in the glass, without milk and often with lemon. Cafés and restaurants will give you hot water and a tea bag (Chinese tea as a rule), but in some bars it's more likely to be *naturalna* style—a spoonful of tea leaves with the water poured on top.

Coffee is served black unless you ask otherwise, in which case specify with milk (*z mleckiem*) or with cream (*ze śmietaną*). Most **cafés** (*kawarnia*) offer only *kawa naturalna*, which means a strong brew made by simply dumping the coffee grounds in a cup or glass and pouring water over them. *Expresso*, usually a passable imitation of the Italian original, is confined to the better cafés or restaurants, while *cappuccino* is almost unknown except in the top-notch hotels and trendier new private bars and cafés. In cafés and bars alike a shot or two of vodka or *winiak* (brandy) with the morning cup of coffee is still frequent practice.

CAKES AND ICE CREAM

Cakes, pastries, and other sweets are an integral ingredient of most Poles' daily consumption, and the cake shops (*cukiernia*)—which you'll find even in small villages—are as good as any in Central Europe. *Sernik* (cheesecake) is a national favorite, as are *makowiec* (poppyseed cake), *droźdówka* (a sponge cake, often topped with plums), and *babka piaskowa* (marble cake). In the larger places you can also expect to find *pyszynger*, an Austrian-style *schlagtort* with coffee and chocolate filling, as well as *keks* (fruitcake) and a selection of eclairs, profiteroles, and cupcakes. Wherever you are, go early in the day, as many cake shops sell out quickly, as do the cafés with their more limited selections.

Poles eat **ice cream** (*lody*) at all times of the year, lining up up for cones at street-side kiosks or in *cukiernia*. The standard kiosk cone is watery and pretty tasteless, but elsewhere the selection is better: decent cafés, and in particular the misleadingly named, alcohol-free *cocktail bars*, offer a mouth-watering selection of ices.

RESTAURANT MEALS

The average **restaurant** (*restauracja*, sometimes *jadłojajnia*) is open fom late morning through to mid-evening; all but the smartest close early, though, winding down around 9pm in cities, earlier in the country. Some don't open until 1pm due to the ban on the sale of alcohol before that time. Relatively late-night standbys include Orbis hotel restaurants and, at the other end of the scale, train station snack bars.

Officially restaurants are **graded** from *kat 1* (luxury) down to *kat 4* (cheap), categories which are displayed at the top of the menu; unless your funds are very limited, stick to the top two ratings only—*kat 3* and 4 places can be dirty and dire. Many of the newer private places seem to have eluded this system, however, and categories may well be entirely redefined over the next year or two.

Except in the big hotels and smartest restaurants, **menus** are usually in Polish only; the language section below should provide most of the cues you'll need. While the list of dishes apparently on offer may be long, in reality only things with a price marked next to them will be available, which normally reduces the choice by fifty percent or more. If you arrive near closing time or late lunchtime, the waiter may inform you there's only one thing left.

There are no hard and fast rules about **tipping**, but a common practice is to round the bill up the nearest 1000 złoties, except in upmarket places, where ten percent extra is the established practice.

SOUPS AND APPETIZERS

First on the menu in most places are **soups**, definitely one of Polish cuisine's strongest points, varying from light and delicate dishes to concoctions that are virtually meals in themselves. Best known is *barszcz*, a spicy beet-root broth that's ideally accompanied by a small pastry (*z pasztecikem*). Other soups worth looking out for are *zurek*, a creamy white soup with sausage and potato; *botwinka*, a seasonal soup made from the leaves of baby beet-roots; *krupnik*, a thick barley and potato soup with chunks of meat, carrots, and celery root; and *chłodnik*, a cold Lithuanian beet-root soup with sour milk and vegetable greens, served in summer.

In cheaper places you'll be lucky to have more than a couple of soups and a plate of cold meats, or herring with cream or oil (*śledź w smietanie/oleja*) to choose from as appetizers. In better restaurants, though, the **hors d'oeuvres** selection might include Jewish-style gefillte fish, jellied ham (*szynka w galerecie*), steak tartar (*stek tatarski*), wild rabbit paté (*pasztet zająca*), or hard-boiled eggs in mayonnaise, sometimes stuffed with vegetables (*jajka faszerowane*).

MAIN COURSES

The basis of most main courses is a fried or grilled cut of **meat** in a thick sauce, commonest of which is the *kotlet schwabowy*, a fried pork cutlet. However, Poland's stock of wild animals means that in better restaurants you may find wild boar (*dzik*) and elk (*sarnina*) on the menu. Two national specialties you'll find everywhere are *bigos* (cabbage stewed with meat and spices) and *pierogi*, dumplings stuffed with meat and mushrooms—or with cottage cheese, onion, and spices in the nonmeat variation (*pierogi ruskie*). Another favorite is *flaczki*, tripe cooked in a spiced bouillon stock with vegetables; also worth trying are *gołabki* (cabbage leaves stuffed with meat, rice, and occasionally mushrooms) and *golonka* (pig's leg with horseradish and split peas). Duck (*kaczka*) is usually the most satisfying poultry, particularly with apples, while carp (*karp*), eel (*węgorz*), and trout (*pstrąg*) are generally reliable **fish** dishes, usually grilled or sautéd, occasionally poached. **Pancakes** (*naleśki*) often come as a main course, too, stuffed with cottage cheese (*z serem*).

Main dishes come with some sort of **vegetable**, normally boiled or mashed potatoes and/or cabbage, either boiled or as sauerkraut. Fried potato pancakes (*placki ziemniaczane*) are particularly good, served either in sour cream or in a spicy paprika sauce. Wild forest mushrooms (*boletus*), another Polish favorite, are served in any number of forms, the commonest being fried or sautéd. **Salads** are generally a standard-issue plate of lettuce, cucumber, and tomato in a watery dressing. If available, it's better to go for an individual salad dish like *Mizeria* (cucumber in cream), *buraczki* (grated beet-root) or the rarer *cwikła* (beet-root with horseradish).

DESSERTS

Desserts are usually meager, except in the big hotels and plush restaurants, where a selection of cakes and ice creams will probably be on offer. If it's available try *kompot*, fruit compote in a glass—in season you may chance upon fresh strawberries, raspberries, or blueberries. Pancakes (*naleśki*) are also served as a **dessert**, with jam and sugar or with *powidła*, a delicious plum spread.

FOOD AND DRINK GLOSSARY

BASICS

Śniadanie	Breakfast	*Pieczyste*	Starter	*Jarzyny/*	Vegetables
Obiad	Lunch	*Desery*	Dessert	*warzywa*	
Kolacja	Dinner	*Drób*	Poultry	*Owoce*	Fruit
Nóż	Knife	*Potrawy*	Vegetarian	*Surówka*	Salad
Widelec	Fork	*jarskie*	dishes	*Cukier*	Sugar
Łyzka	Spoon	*Dodatki*	Extras/	*Sól*	Salt
Talerz	Plate		supplements	*Pieprz*	Pepper
Filizanka	Cup	*Ryby*	Fish	*Ocet*	Vinegar
Szklanka	Glass	*Chleb*	Bread	*Olej*	Oil
Przekąska/	Appetizer	*Bułka*	Rolls	*Chrzanem*	Horseradish
zakąska		*Masło*	Butter	*Ris*	Rice
Jadłospis	Menu	*Kanapka*	Sandwich	*Makaron*	Macaroni
Zupa	Soup	*Mleko*	Milk	*Frytki*	French fries
Dania gotowe/	Main	*Jajko*	Egg	*Śmietana*	Cream
głowne danie	Course	*Mięso*	Meat		

SOUPS, FISH, AND POULTRY

Barszcz czerwony—	Beet-root soup	*(zupa) Cebulowa*	Onion soup
z pasztecikem	(borsch)—with pastry	*(zupa) Jarzynowa*	Vegetable soup
Barszcz ukraiński	White borsch	*Kołduny*	Dumplings
Bulion/rosół	Bouillon	*Śledź*	Herring
Zurek	Sour cream soup	*Pstrąg*	Trout
Krupnik	Barley soup	*Łosoś*	Salmon
Chłodnik	Sour milk and vegetable	*Karp*	Carp
	cold soup	*Węgorz*	Eel
Kartoflanka	Potato soup	*Makrela*	Mackerel
Kapuśniak	Cabbage soup	*Sardynka*	Sardine
(zupa) Owocowa	Cold fruit soup	*Kurczak*	Chicken
(zupa) Pomidorowa	Tomato soup	*Kaczka*	Duck
(zupa) Ogórkowa	Cucumber soup	*Indyk*	Turkey
(zupa) Grzybowa	Mushroom soup	*Geś*	Geese
(zupa) Fasolowa	Bean soup	*Bazant*	Pheasant
(zupa) Grochowa	Pea soup		

MEAT

Dzik	Wild Boar	*Kotlet*	Pork	*Bakon,*	Bacon
Sarnina	Elk	*schabowy*	cutlet	*boczek*	
Wątrobka	Liver with onion	*Wołowe*	Beef	*Salami*	Salami
Golonka	Leg of pork	*Befsztyk*	Steak	*Baranina*	Mutton
Wieprzowe	Pork	*Kiełbasa*	Sausage	*Cielęcina*	Veal

VEGETABLES

Marchewka	Carrots	*Pomidor*	Tomato	*Papryka*	Paprika
Kapusta	Cabbage	*Ogórek*	Cucumber	*Kapusta kiszona*	Sauerkraut
Ziemniaki	Potatoes	*Groch*	Peas	*Szpinak*	Spinach
Ciebula	Onion	*Ćwikła/*	Beet-root	*Ogórki*	Gherkins
Czosnek	Garlic	*buraczki*		*Szparagi*	Asparagus
Grzyby/pieczarki	Mushrooms	*Kalafior*	Cauliflower	*Fazola*	Beans

FRUIT, CHEESE, AND NUTS

Banan	Banana	*Maliny*	Raspberries	*Bryndza*	Sheep's cheese
Śliwka	Plum	*Winogrona*	Grapes	*Oscypek*	Smoked goats
Ananas	Pineapple	*Gruszka*	Pears		cheese
Jabłko	Apple	*Czarne jagody*	Blackberries	*Twaróg*	Cottage cheese
Kompot	Stewed	*borówki*		*(ser) Myśliwski*	Smoked cheese
	fruit	*Pomarańcze*	Orange	*(ser) Tylzycki*	Cheddar cheese
Cytryna	Lemon	*Czarne*	Black currant	*Laskowe/orzechy*	Almonds
Morele	Apricots	*poreczki*		*Orzechy włoskie*	Walnuts
Truskawki	Strawberries	*Czereśnie*	Cherries		

CAKES AND DESSERTS

Tort	Tart	*Galaretka*	Jellied fruits	*Pączki*	Doughnuts
Ciastko	Cake	*Mazurek*	Shortcake	*Ciasto*	Yeast cake
Czekolada	Chocolate	*Sernik*	Cheesecake	*drożdżowe*	with fruit
Lody	Ice cream	*Makowiec*	Poppyseed cake		

FOOD TERMS

Mielone	Minced	*Antrykot/wołowy*	Mixed	*Marynowany*	Pickled
Pieczen	Roast meat	*Świerzy*	Fresh	*Surowy*	Raw
Sznycel	Escalope/schnitzel	*Kwaśny*	Sour	*Gotowany*	Boiled
Szaszłyk	Grilled	*Grillowane/z rusztu*	Grilled	*Słodki*	Sweet
Kotlet	Cutlet	*Nadziewany*	Stuffed	*Smacznego!*	Bon appetit!

DRINKS

Herbata	Tea	*Spirytus*	Spirits	*Sok pomarańczowy*	Orange juice
Kawa	Coffee	*Wódka*	Vodka	*Sok pomidorowy*	Tomato juice
Woda	Water	*Piwo*	Beer	*Miód pitny*	Mead
Woda	Mineral water	*Wino*	Wine	*Wino wytrawne*	Dry wine
mineralna		*Koniak*	Cognac/brandy	*Wino słodkie*	Sweet wine
Napój	Bottled fruit drink	*Sok*	Juice	*Na zdrowie!*	Cheers!

DRINKING

Poles' capacity for alcohol has never been in doubt, and drinking is a national pursuit. Much of the drinking goes on in **restaurants**, which in smaller towns or villages are often the only outlets selling alcohol. In the cities and larger towns, you'll come upon **hotel bars** (frequented mainly by westerners or wealthier Poles), a growing number of **privately-run bars** (*bary*), which mimic western models, and the very different and traditional **drink bars**.

The last, basic and functional, are almost exclusively male terrain and generally best avoided; the haunt of hustlers and hardened alcoholics, they reflect the country's serious alcohol problems, caused in part by a preference for spirits rather than beer or wine.

BEER

Poles can't compete with their Czech neighbors in the production and consumption of **beer** (*piwo*), but there are nevertheless a number of highly drinkable, and in a few cases really excellent, Polish brands.

The best and most famous **bottled beers** are all from the south of the country. Zywiec produces two varieties: the strong, tangy *Tatra Pils*, and *Piwo Zywiecki*, a lighter smoother brew, ideal for mealtime drinking. The other nationally available beers are *Okocim* from the Katowice region, and *Lezajsk*, a strongish brew from the town of the same name near Rzeszów. There's also an assortment of regional beers you'll only find locally, *Gdański* and *Wrocława* being two of the most highly rated.

Draft beer (*ciemne*) is a rarity, though wooden barrels of local beer do occasionally crop up in the most unlikely places, particularly villages in the south.

VODKA AND OTHER SPIRITS

It's with **vodka** (*wódka*) that Poles really get into their stride. Such is its place in the national culture that for years the black-market value of the dollar was supposed to be directly pegged to the price of a bottle. If you thought vodka was just a cocktail mixer, you're in for some surprises; reams could be written about the varieties—clear, peppered, honeyed—available. Ideally vodka is served neat, well chilled, in measures of 25 or 50 grammes (a *czysta*—100 grams—is common, too) and bolted "bottoms up", with a mineral water chaser. A couple of these will be enough to put most people well on the way, though the capacities of seasoned Polish drinkers are prodigious—a half-liter bottle between two or three over lunch is nothing unusual.

Best of the **clear vodkas** are *Zytnia* and *Wyborowa*, valuable export earners often more easily available abroad than at home. A perfectly acceptable everyday substitute is *Polonez*, one of the most popular brands and the one you're most likely to encounter in people's houses and in the average restaurant.

Of the **flavored varieties**, first on most people's list is *Zubrówka*, a legendary vodka infused with the taste of bison grass from the eastern Białowieza forest—there's a stem in every bottle. *Pieprzówka*, by contrast, has a sharp, peppery flavor, and is supposedly good for warding off colds. The juniper-flavored *Myśliwska* tastes a bit like gin, while whisky-colored *Jarzębiak* is flavored with rowanberries. Others to look out for are *Wiśniówka*, a sweetish, strong wild-cherry concoction; *Krupnik*, which is akin to whisky liqueur; *Cytrynówka*, a lemon vodka; and *Miodówka*, a rare honey vodka. Last but by no means least on any basic list is *Pajsachówka*, at 75 percent proof by far the strongest vodka on the market and rivaled in strength only by home produced *bimber*, the Polish version of moonshine.

Other popular **digestifs** are *śliwowica*, the powerful plum brandy mostly produced in the south of the country, and *miód pitny*, a heady, mead-like wine. Commonest of all in this category, however, is *winiak*, a fiery Polish brandy you'll find in many cafés and restaurants.

SOFT DRINKS

The commonest **soft drink** is *napój*, a bottled blend of fruit juice and mineral water, the most popular being strawberry (*truskawki*) and apple (*jabkowe*). They are tasty and refreshing, and always preferable to the sickly varieties of *oran-zada* and *lemonada*. There are plenty of sweet, Polish-style Pepsis and Cokes on sale, too, as well as the much higher-priced originals, which are consumed with gusto by Poles keen to identify with the symbols of western consumerism.

Sparkling **mineral water** (*woda mineralna*) from the spas of the south is highly palatable and available throughout the country; the commonest brand name is *Kryniczanka*. Considerably less recommended is *syfon*, the stringent carbonated water you get on train platforms and in some of the cheaper restaurants.

COMMUNICATIONS AND THE MEDIA

POST OFFICES AND MAIL

Post offices in Poland are identified by the name *Urząd Pocztowy* (*Poczta* for short) or by the acronym PTT (*Poczta, Telegraf, Telefon*). Each bears a number, with the head office in each city being no.1. Theoretically, each office has a **poste restante** facility: make sure, therefore, that anyone addressing mail to you includes the "no.1" after the city's name. This service works reasonably well, but don't expect 100 percent reliability. **Mail** to the US currently takes up to three weeks, but seems to move at least twice as fast in the other direction. **Mailboxes** are green, blue, or red; these are respectively for local mail, airmail, and all types of mail.

Opening hours of the head offices are usually Mon–Sat 7/8am–8pm; other branches usually close at 6pm, often earlier in rural areas. A restricted range of services is available 24 hours a day, seven days a week, from post offices in or outside the main train stations of major cities.

TELEPHONES

The antiquated **telephone system** is one of the biggest obstacles to Poland's economic development. Frantic efforts, with a great deal of foreign help, are being made at modernization, but for the present it's a potential cause of frustration every time you need to use it.

At the time of writing, public **pay phones** accepted only 20zł pieces; this coin comes in three sizes, but only the medium-sized ones will work. If you've managed to get your hands on a supply of these, you shouldn't have any problems with local calls, or calling from one city to another (see box below for the main codes). However, you can't dial directly from a city to a small town, even one only a few kilometers away; for that, you have to line up in a post office or an Orbis hotel for an **operator-assisted** call. Thus only local numbers are given in the text of the guide. **Emergency calls** (police ☎997, fire ☎998, ambulance ☎999) are free.

Making **international calls** is a real headache: unless you have a Polish friend equipped with a direct-dial line, there's no alternative to going through an operator. With the single exception of Warsaw, this almost invariably entails a wait, which could be several hours, and even then there's no guarantee of getting through. If you're staying at an Orbis hotel, this problem is minimized; otherwise, try phoning at the least busy times, such as in the middle of the night or early on Sunday morning. To speed up the process, ask for the call to be put through fast (*szybko*), but note that this will double the price. There's no way to call collect.

CODES FOR MAJOR POLISH CITIES

Częstochowa ☎034	Łódź ☎042	Toruń ☎056
Gdańsk/Gdynia/Sopot ☎058	Lublin ☎081	Warsaw ☎022 for six-digit nos.,
Katowice ☎032	Poznań ☎061	☎02 for seven-digit nos.
Kraków ☎012	Szczecin ☎091	Wrocław ☎071

THE MEDIA

With the collapse of communist rule, the Polish media were transformed, leaving the party-line and *samizdat* traditions behind in a sudden rush of legal, free expression. There are today half a dozen variously aligned national papers, numerous regionals, and an ever-increasing roster of specialist magazines. The two state-run TV stations are about to be joined by an independent third channel and the four state radio stations are already in competition with new, independent local broadcasts. The old adage of "Two Poles, Three Opinions" has now found a genuine voice.

NEWSPAPERS AND MAGAZINES

The Polish *samizdat* press of the 1980s was the most sophisticated and widely read in Eastern Europe, forcing a degree of liberalization on the official press through the necessity to compete for readers. The transition from an underground medium has been difficult, and articles are often long on argument and short on reporting; design and style have some way to go to match western equivalents, with poor-quality paper, monotonous slabs of text, and poorly reproduced photographs.

Everything looks set to change, however, as the government has liquidated the *RSW Prasa Ruch* enterprise, former owners of all newspapers and magazine titles, with the intention of selling their assets. Ominously, media barons Rupert Murdoch and Robert Maxwell are both reported to have expressed interest in buying up a number of titles.

Among **Polish-language daily newspapers**, *Życie Warszawy* (Life of Warsaw) is the most popular in the country, having recently eclipsed *Gazeta Wyborcza*, Eastern Europe's first independent daily. The latter, set up in the wake of the 1989 Round Table Agreement, is edited by former Solidarity luminary Adam Michnik, who in recent months has conducted a bitter dispute with Lech Wałęsa and his wing of Solidarity. In autumn 1989 Wałęsa retaliated with a fit of authoritarianism, forcing Michnik to remove the Solidarity logo from the paper's masthead. Other national dailies include the government *Rzeczpospolita*, currently edited by the chairman of the journalists' union, and *Trybuna*, the renamed newspaper of the renamed Communist—now Social Democrat—Party.

Weekly papers also provide a forum for political debate. *Politika* is a theoretical journal, often providing space for critics within Solidarity. *Tygodnik Solidarność*, the union weekly re-legalized in 1989 after an eight-year absence, is widely perceived as a vehicle for Wałęsa, who fired its first new editor and installed his own man. *Tygodnik Powszechny* is a widely respected independent Catholic weekly newspaper. Local weekly papers are, by contrast, pretty unexciting, though useful for details of current events.

Two **English-language papers**, both weekly and both invaluable for political news, are readily available in the big cities, less so out in the sticks. *Gazeta International* is a selection of readable translations from *Gazeta Wyborca*; *Warsaw Voice* is a government-funded publication, with useful listings at the back. **Western newspapers** and magazines are now available the same day in big cities. Most common are the British *Guardian*'s international edition, the *Financial Times*, the *Times* and the *Herald Tribune*, plus magazines like *Newsweek*, *Time*, and *The Economist*. **Ruch kiosks** are the main outlets for papers and magazines. You'll also find foreign newspapers in hotel lobbies, foreign-language bookshops, and foreign press clubs (KMPiK) in major cities.

TV AND RADIO

In addition to the Polish **TV channels**, anyone living in the east of the country can get Soviet stations, anyone in the south Czech or Slovak, and in the west, German. Many Poles consider these a useful supplement to the national network, whose standards (pedestrian news programs, makeshift sets, lots of dubbed imports, shameful soccer coverage) are very slowly becoming more sophisticated. Satellite dishes are making their appearance, too, and in the bigger hotels you can switch on *MTV* (in English) and *Sky* (in German).

The state **radio stations** also present a strange interim picture, broadcasting programs imported from the BBC (in English and Polish) plus German- and French-language programs amid the mix of local bulletins and shows. If you want to pick up the complete **BBC World Service in English**, you'll need a short wave radio tuned to 12.095 MHZ (24.80 meters) or 9.410 MHZ (31.88 meters).

The Polish Radio 1 program broadcasts news and weather reports in English on the hour from 9am–noon in the summer. Wavelengths vary around the country—check the local press for details.

OPENING HOURS AND HOLIDAYS

Most shops are open on weekdays from approximately 10am to 6pm. Exceptions are grocers and food stores, which may open as early as 6am and close by mid-afternoon—something to watch out for in rural areas in particular. Many shops are closed altogether on Saturday, with others opening for just a few hours.

Other idiosyncrasies include *ruch* kiosks, where you can buy newspapers and municipal transit tickets, which generally open from about 6am; some shut up around 5pm, but others remain open for several hours longer. Increasing numbers of **street traders** also do business well into the evening, while you can usually find stores here and there in a major city offering late-night opening throughout the week.

As a rule, **Orbis offices** are open from 9am or 10am until 5pm (later in major cities) during the week; hours are shorter on Saturday, sometimes

with closure on alternate weeks. Other **tourist information offices** are normally open Monday to Friday 9am to 4pm.

PUBLIC HOLIDAYS

The following are national public holidays, on which you can expect most shops and sights to be closed:

January 1
Easter Monday (variable March/April)
May 1 (Labor Day)
May 3 (Constitution Day)
Corpus Christi (variable May/June)
August 15 (Feast of the Assumption)
November 1 (All Saints' Day)
November 11 (National Independence Day)
December 25 & 26

Visiting **churches** seldom presents any problems: the ones you're most likely to want to see are open from early morning until mid-evening without interruption. However, a large number of less famous churches are fenced off beyond the entrance porch by a grille or glass window for much of the day; to see them properly, you'll need to turn up around the times for Mass, ie first thing in the morning and between 6 and 8pm.

The current visiting times for **museums** and **historic monuments** are listed in the text of *The Guide*. They are almost invariably closed on one day per week (usually Monday) and many are closed on another day as well; on the days remaining, many open for only about five hours, often closing at 3pm. Some of the museums in the major cities have managed to extend their opening times recently, but this has often been at the expense of having only a section open to the public at any particular time. Entrance charges seldom amount to more than a few cents.

FESTIVALS

One manifestation of Poland's intense commitment to Roman Catholicism is that all the great feast days of the Church calendar are celebrated with wholehearted devotion, many of the participants donning the colorful traditional costumes for which the country is celebrated. This is most notable in the mountain areas in the south of the country, where the annual festivities play a key role in maintaining a vital sense of community. As a supplement to these, Poland has many more recently established cultural festivals, particularly in the fields of music and drama.

RELIGIOUS AND TRADITIONAL FESTIVALS

The highlight of the Catholic year is **Holy Week**, heralded by a glut of spring fairs, offering the best of the early livestock and agricultural produce. Religious celebrations begin in earnest on **Palm Sunday**, when palms are brought to church and paraded in processions. Often the painted and decorated "palms" are handmade, sometimes with competitions for the largest or most beautiful. The most famous procession takes place at Kalwaria Zebrzydowska near Kraków, inaugurating a spectacular week-long series of mystery plays, reenacting Christ's Passion.

On **Maundy Thursday** many communities take symbolic revenge on Judas Iscariot: his effigy is hanged, dragged outside the village, flogged, burned, or thrown into a river. **Good Friday** sees visits to mock-ups of the Holy Sepulcher—whether permanent structures such as at Kalwaria Zebrzydowska and Wambierzyce in Silesia, or *ad hoc* creations, as is traditional in Warsaw. In some places, notably the Rzeszów region, this is fused with a celebration of King Jan Sobieski's victory in the Siege of Vienna, with "Turks" placed in charge of the tomb. **Holy Saturday** is when baskets of painted eggs, sausages, bread, and salt are taken along to church to be blessed and sprinkled with holy water. The consecrated food is eaten at breakfast on **Easter Day**, when the most solemn Masses of the year are celebrated. On **Easter Monday**, it's the people themselves who are doused, usually by gangs of children armed with buckets and sprays.

Seven weeks later, at **Pentecost**, irises are traditionally laid out on the floors of the house, while in the Kraków region bonfires are held on hilltop sites. Eleven days later comes the most Catholic of festivals, **Corpus Christi**, marked by colorful processions everywhere and elaborate floral displays. Exactly a week later, the story of

ARTS FESTIVALS

January
WROCŁAW Solo Plays
WARSAW Traditional Jazz

February
WROCŁAW Polish Contemporary Music
POZNAŃ Boys' Choirs

March
CZĘSTOCHOWA Violin Music
WROCŁAW Jazz on the Odra

April
KRAKÓW Organ Music
KRAKÓW Student Song

May
WROCŁAW Jazz on the Odra
ŁANCUT Chamber Music
WROCŁAW Contemporary Polish Plays (May/ June)
KRAKÓW "Juvenalia" (student festival)
GDAŃSK "Neptunalia" (student festival)
ŁĄCKO (near Nowy Sącz) Regional Folk Festival

June
PŁOCK Folk Ensembles
KRYNICA Arias and Songs
OPOLE Polish Songs
KRAKÓW Short Feature Films
KAZIMIERZ DOLNY Folk Bands and Singers (June/July)
MRÁGROWO Country and Western Festival

July
JAROCIN Rock Festival
STARY SĄCZ Old Music
GDAŃSK-OLIWA Organ Music
KUDOWA-ZDRÓJ Music of Stanisław Moniuszko
MIĘDZYZDROJE Choral Music

KOSZALIN World Polonia Festival of Polish Songs (every five years—1991, 1996)
RZESZÓW World Festival of Polonia Folklore Groups (every three years—1992, 1995)
SWINOUJSCIE Fama Student Artistic Festival

August
DUSZNIKI-ZDRÓJ Music of Fryderyk Chopin
SOPOT International Songs
KRAKÓW Classical Music
ŻYWIEC Beskid Culture
JELENIA GÓRA Street Theater
GDAŃSK Dominican Fair

September
WARSAW Contemporary Music
ZAKOPANE Highland Folklore
GDAŃSK Polish Feature Films
BYDGOSZCZ Polish Music
SŁUPSK Polish Piano Competition
TORUŃ International Old Music Festival
WROCŁAW "Wratislavia Cantans" (Choral Music)
ZAKOPANE Festival of Highland Folklore
ZIELONA GÓRA International Song and Dance Troupes

October
KRAKÓW Jazz Music
WARSAW Jazz Jamboree
WARSAW Film Week
WARSAW International Chopin Piano Competition (every 5 years, next 1995)

November
POZNAŃ International Violin Competition (every 5 years—1991, 1996)
WARSAW "Theatrical Encounters"

December
WROCŁAW Old Music

the Tartar siege is reenacted as the starting point of one of the country's few notable festivals of secular folklore, the **Days of Kraków**.

St John's Day on June 23 is celebrated with particular gusto in Warsaw, Kraków, and Poznań; at night wreaths with burning candles are cast into the river, and there are also boat parades, dancing, and fireworks. June 26, **St Anne's Day**, is the time of the main annual pilgrimage to Góra Świętej Anny in Silesia.

The first of two major Marian festivals on consecutive weeks comes with the **Feast of the Holy Virgin of Sowing** on August 8 in farming areas, particularly in the southeast of the country. By then, many of the great pilgrimages to the Jasna Góra shrine in Częstochowa have already set out, arriving for the **Feast of the Assumption** on August 15. This is also the occasion for the enactment of a mystery play at Kalwaria Pacławska near Przemyśl.

All Saints' Day, November 1, is the day of national remembrance, with flowers, wreaths, and candles laid on tombstones. In contrast, **St Andrew's Day**, November 30, is a time for fortune-telling, with dancing to accompany superstitious practices such as the pouring of melted wax or lead on paper. **St Barbara's Day**, December 4, is the traditional holiday of the miners, with special Masses held for their safety as a counterweight to the jollity of their galas.

During **Advent**, the nation's handicraft tradition comes to the fore, with the making of cribs to adorn every church. In Kraków, a competition is held on the following Sunday between December 3 and 10, the winning entries being displayed in the city's Historical Museum. On **Christmas Eve** families gather for an evening banquet, traditionally of twelve courses; this is also the time when children receive their gifts. **Christmas Day** begins with the midnight mass; later, small round breads decorated with the silhouettes of domestic animals are consumed. **New Year's Eve** is the time for magnificent formal balls, particularly in Warsaw, while in rural areas of southern Poland it's the day for practical jokes—which must go unpunished.

POLICE AND TROUBLE

Nothing epitomizes recent political change in Poland better than what's happened to the police. Gone now is the secret police structure and the *ZOMO*, the hated riot squads responsible for quelling the big demonstrations during the period of martial law. What's left is the *milicja*—or, as they've been diplomatically renamed now—the **policja**, who are responsible for everyday law enforcement.

Transforming the ethos of a force accustomed to operating outside the bounds of public control is a difficult task, and all in all the *policja* seem to be in a pretty demoralized state, with the entire force supposedly being put through retraining programs. In common with other East European countries Poland has experienced a huge increase in crime over the last year, the police seemingly unable or unwilling to do much about it. Sales of alarms, small firearms, and other security paraphernalia are on the increase, and residents of Warsaw's high-rise towers have resorted to organizing their own night watches to stem the flood of car break-ins.

TROUBLE

For westerners, the biggest potential hassles are **hotel room thefts**, **pickpocketing** in the markets, and **car break-ins**. Sensible precautions should include avoiding leaving cars unattended overnight anywhere in the city centers (larger hotels have guarded parking lots—*parkinge strzezone*); keeping valuables on you at all times; and trying not to look conspicuously affluent. Your best and only protection ultimately is to take out travel insurance, as the chances of getting your gear back are virtually zero.

On a bureaucratic level, Poles are still supposed to carry some form of **ID** with them: you should always keep your passport with you, even though you're unlikely to get stopped unless you're in a car. Western license plates provide the excuse for occasional unprovoked spot checks—particularly late at night, when the police tend to think you'll turn out to be a Pole traveling in a stolen vehicle.

SEXUAL HARASSMENT

Sexual harassment is less obviously present than in the west, but lack of familiarity with the cultural norms means it's easier to misinterpret situations, and rural Poland is still extremely conservative culturally: the more remote the area, the more likely it is that women traveling alone will attract bemused stares.

Polish women tend to claim that men desist as soon as you tell them to leave you alone, but this isn't always the case, particularly with anyone who's had a few drinks. However, if you do encounter problems, you'll invariably find other Poles stepping in to help—the Polish people are renowned for their hospitality to strangers and will do much to make you feel welcome. The only particular places to avoid are the drinking haunts and hotel nightclubs, where plenty of men will assume you're a prostitute.

DIRECTORY

ADDRESSES The street name is always written before the number. The word for street (*ulica*, abbreviated to *ul.*) or avenue (*aleja*, abbreviated *al.*) is often missed out, for example ulica Senatorska is simply known as Senatorska. The other frequent abbreviation is *pl.*, short for *plac* (square). In towns and villages across the country, **street names** commemorating the stars and dates of Polish and international communism are slowly being replaced. Where a prewar name existed, that name is being reinstated, but with new streets there's much controversy over whether to use pre-war names or adopt new heroes (the pope—Jan Paweł II—being a chief contender). Figures on the way out include General Swierczewski, Nowotki, Marchlewski, Dzierzymski, and the once-ubiquitous Lenin.

AIDS Though the exact figures are not known, Poland has the highest incidence of AIDS in Eastern Europe. The Catholic Church's influence is something of a hindrance in combating the disease, but AIDS helplines are becoming established in the major cities.

BOTTLES All nationally produced drinks come in bottles which have a deposit on them. Stores will accept bottles from other outfits providing they stock the type you're trying to fob off on them.

CIGARETTES Most Polish brands are pretty bad. *Extra Moczna* are the cheapest—bonfire-smokey, highly damaging, and popular; *Klubowe*, *Giewont* and *Popularne* are similar; *Carmen* and *Caro* are

more high-class. Among imported brands, *Marlboro* and *Camel* lead the way. Matches are *zapałki*. Smoking is banned in all public buildings and on most public transit within towns.

CINEMA Western movies are released in Poland very soon after their UK or US release, and are usually dubbed, but sometimes subtitled.

CONTRACEPTIVES Polish-produced condoms (*prezerwatywa*) of uncertain quality are available from most kiosks and some pharmacies, though with Catholic mores in operation, many pharmacies are reluctant to stock them. Pewex shops (see below) are a better bet, selling imported rubbers, but it's wiser to bring your own.

DISABLED TRAVELERS At the moment there is very little provision for disabled travelers in Poland, though elevators and escalators are becoming more common in public places.

ELECTRICITY is the standard continental 220 volts supply. Round two-pin plugs are used so you'll need to bring both an adaptor and a transformer.

EMBASSIES AND CONSULATES All foreign embassies are in Warsaw, though a number of countries maintain consulates in Gdańsk and Kraków. See respective listings for addresses.

EMERGENCIES Police ☎997; fire ☎998; ambulance ☎999.

FILM Domestic color films are poor quality (and you may have problems having them developed at home) but imported ones are widely available at Pewex shops.

GAY LIFE The only place there's any developed scene is Warsaw, where a couple of regular newsletters are published.

HARD CURRENCY SHOPS The main hard currency shops are the **Pewex** shops, found in all major towns and in Orbis hotels; their big sellers are alcohol, tobacco, confectionery, and perfumes, though larger Pewex places may also sell electrical goods. Western goods are often cheaper here than back home, and can be exported duty-free, provided all receipts are kept for customs. **Baltona** hard-currency shops are less numerous, and sell western goods only.

JAYWALKING is illegal, and if caught you'll be fined on the spot.

LANGUAGE COURSES Summer Polish language schools are run by the universities of Kraków, Poznań, Lublin (KUL), and Łódź. Courses last from two to six weeks, covering all levels from beginners to advanced; a six-week course with full board and lodging will cost in the region of $700. Information on these courses can be obtained from the Polish Embassy (Cultural Section).

LAUNDRY Laundromats (*pralnia*) exist in the major cities, but are very scarce, and will do attended washes only. Elsewhere you can get things washed for you in the more upscale hotels. Dry cleaners—also *pralnia*—are far more numerous.

SOCCER Franz Beckenbauer described the Polish national squad as "the best team in the world" in 1974, and in that year's World Cup—and the following two tournaments—Polish players such as Lato, Denya, and Boniek became household names. Polish soccer is currently in the doldrums, though—they failed to qualify for the 1990 World Cup, and have no clubs to rank with Europe's best. Nonetheless, the top teams are still worth a look, producing soccer that is up to the standard of middle-order First Division stuff. Top team is Górnik Zabrze (fourteen-times league champions), followed by GKS Katowice, Legia Warszawa, Ruch Chorzow, and the two Łódź sides. The season lasts from August to November, then resumes in March until June.

TAMPONS Sanitary towels (*podpaski higieniczne*) are cheap and available from some pharmacies; tampons (*tampony*) similarly suffer from supply problems and are very poor quality—it's best to bring your own.

TIME Poland is generally nine hours ahead of EST, with the clocks going forward for daylight savings as late as May and back again sometime during September—the exact date changes from year to year.

TOILETS Public toilets (*toalety, ubikacja,* or *WC*) are few and far between (except in the biggest cities) and would win few design awards; restaurants or hotels are a better bet. Once in, you can buy toilet paper (by the sheet) and ask for use of the (yes, *the*) towel from the attendant, whom you also have to tip (signs usually indicate the amount). Only in the top-class hotels does toilet paper come free. Mens is marked ▲, ladies ●.

PART TWO

THE

GUIDE

CHAPTER ONE

WARSAW AND MAZOVIA

Warsaw has two enduring points of definition: the Wisła River, running south to north across the Mazovian plains, and the Moscow–Berlin road, stretching across this terrain—and through the city—east to west. Such a location, and 400 years of capital status, have ensured a history writ large with occupations and uprisings, intrigues and heroism. Warsaw's sufferings, its near-total obliteration in World War II, and subsequent resurrection from the ashes, has lodged the city in the national consciousness, and explains why an often ugly city is held in such affection. In the latest era of political struggle – the fall of communism, the emergence of Solidarity and the current democratic experiment—Warsaw has at times seemed overshadowed by events in Gdańsk and the industrial centers of the south, but its role has been a key one nonetheless, as a focus of popular and intellectual opposition to communism, and the site of past and future power.

Likely to be most visitors' first experience of Poland, Warsaw makes an initial impression which is all too often negative. The years of communist rule have left no great aesthetic glories, and there's sometimes a hollowness to the faithful reconstructions of earlier eras. However, as throughout Poland, the pace of social change is tangible and fascinating, as the openings provided by the post-communist order turn the streets into a continuous marketplace. The formerly gray and tawdry state shopfronts of the city center are giving way to colorful new private initiatives—the Benetton effect, as journalists term it—while the postwar dearth of nightlife and entertainments is gradually becoming a complaint of the past, as a plethora of new bars, restaurants and clubs establish themselves.

Though the villages of **Mazovia**—*Mazowsze* in Polish—are the favored summer abodes of wealthier Varsovians, these surrounding plains are historically one of the poorer regions of Poland, their peasant population eking a precarious existence from the notoriously infertile sandy soil. It is not the most arresting of landscapes, but contains a half-dozen rewarding day trips to ease your passage into the rural Polish experience. The **Kampinoski National Park**—spreading northwest of Warsaw – is the remnant of the primeval forests that once covered this region, with tranquil villages dotted along its southern rim. A little farther west is **Żelazowa Wola**, the much-visited birthplace of Fred Chopin. **Łowicz** is well known as a center of Mazovian folk culture, while the Radziwiłł palace at **Nieborów** is one of the finest and best-preserved aristocratic mansions in the country. Southwest of the capital lies industrial **Łódź**, the country's second city and an important cultural center.

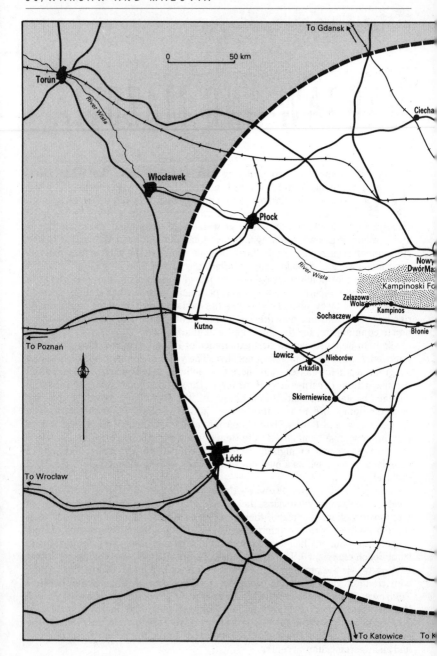

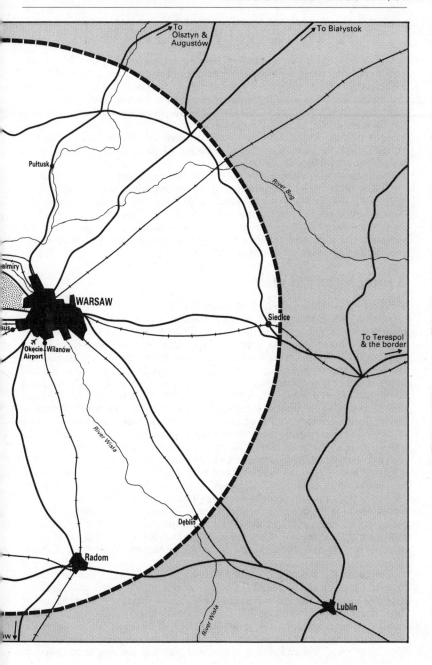

WARSAW (WARSZAWA)

Traveling through the gray, faceless housing estates surrounding **WARSAW**, walking through the grimy Stalinist tracts in the center, you could be forgiven for wishing yourself elsewhere. But a knowledge of Warsaw's rich and often tragic history can transform the city, revealing voices from the past in even the ugliest quarters: a pockmarked wall becomes a precious prewar relic, a housing project the one-time center of Europe's largest ghetto, the whole city a living book of modern history. And among the concrete there are reconstructed traces of Poland's imperial past – a castle, a scattering of palaces and parks, and the restored streets of the historic Old Town.

For those arriving without personal connections or contacts, Warsaw can seem forbidding, with much of the place still shutting down within a few hours of darkness. But Varsovians are generous and highly hospitable people: no social call, even to an office, is complete without a glass of *herbata* and plate of cakes. Postwar austerity has strengthened the tradition of home-based socializing, and if you strike up a friendship here—friendships in Warsaw are quickly formed— you'll find much to enrich your experience of the city.

A Brief History of Warsaw

For a capital city, Warsaw entered history late. Although there are records of a settlement here from the tenth century, the first references to anything resembling a town at this point on the Wisła date from around the mid-fourteenth century. It owes its initial rise to power to the Mazovian ruler **Janusz the Elder**, who made Warsaw his main residence in 1413 and developed it as capital of the Duchy of Mazovia. Following the death of the last Mazovian prince in 1526, Mazovia and its now greatly enlarged capital were incorporated into **Polish** royal territory. The city's fortunes now improved rapidly. Following the Act of Union with Lithuania, the Sejm—the Polish parliament—voted to transfer to Warsaw in 1569. The first election of a Polish king took place here four years later, and then in 1596 came the crowning glory, when **King Zygmunt III** moved his capital 200 miles from Kraków to its current location—a decision chiefly compelled by the shift in Poland's geographical center after the union with Lithuania.

Capital status inevitably brought prosperity, but along with new wealth came new perils. The city was badly damaged by the **Swedes** during the invasion of 1655—the first of several assaults—and was then extensively reconstructed by the **Saxon kings** in the late seventeenth century. The lovely Saxon Gardens (Ogród Saski) for example, right in the center, date from this period. Poles tend to remember the eighteenth century in a nostalgic haze as the golden age of Warsaw, when its concert halls, theaters, and salons were prominent in European cultural life.

The **Partitions** abruptly terminated this era, as Warsaw was absorbed into the Prussian kingdom and occupied. Napoleon's arrival in 1806 gave Varsovians brief hopes of liberation, but the collapse of his Moscow campaign spelled the end of those hopes, and following the 1815 Congress of Vienna, Warsaw was integrated into the Russian-controlled **Congress Kingdom of Poland**. The failure of the **1830 uprising** brought severe reprisals: Warsaw was relegated to the status of "provincial town" and all Polish institutes and places of learning were closed. It was only with the outbreak of **World War I** that Russian control began to crumble, and in 1915 the **Germans** occupied the city, remaining to the end of the war.

Following the return of Polish independence, Warsaw reverted to its position as capital; but then, with the outbreak of **World War II**, came the progressive annihilation of the city. The Nazi assault in September 1939 was followed by round-ups, executions, and deportations—savagery directed above all at the Jewish community, who were crammed into a tiny ghetto area and forced to live on a near-starvation diet. It was the Jews who instigated the first open revolt, the **Ghetto Uprising** of April 1943, which resulted in the wholesale destruction of Warsaw Jewry.

As the war progressed and the wave of German defeats on the eastern front provoked a tightening of the Nazi grip on Warsaw, **resistance** stiffened in the city. In August 1944 virtually the entire civilian population participated in the **Warsaw Uprising**, an attempt both to liberate the city and ensure the emergence of an independent Poland. It failed on both counts. Hitler, infuriated by the resistance, ordered the total elimination of Warsaw and, with the surviving populace driven out of the city, the SS systematically destroyed the remaining buildings. In one of his final speeches to the Reichstag, Hitler was able to claim with satisfaction that Warsaw was now no more than a name on the map of Europe. By the end of the war 850,000 Varsovians—two-thirds of the city's 1939 population—were dead or missing. Photographs taken immediately after the **liberation** in January 1945 show a scene not unlike Hiroshima: General Eisenhower described Warsaw as the most tragic thing he'd ever seen.

The momentous task of **rebuilding** the city took ten years. Aesthetically the results were mixed, with acres of socialist functionalism spread between the Baroque palaces, but it was a tremendous feat of national reconstruction nonetheless. The recovery that has brought the population up to one and a half million, exceeding its prewar level, is, however, marred by a silence—the silence left by the exterminated Jewish community.

Arrival and Transit

The main **points of arrival** are all within easy reach of the city center.

● **Okęcie international airport** is a half-hour journey by bus #175, and there's a *LOT* bus service to their new terminal on al. Jerozolimskie; the **domestic airport** (Lotnisko Krajowe) is ten minutes closer, on bus route #114.

● **Warszawa Centralna**, the main **train station**, is just west of the central shopping area, a ten-minute bus ride from the Old Town. Lines are lengthy at the **luggage consignment** offices, particularly in summer; if you're lucky you might get a locker downstairs. Another option is the luggage consignment counter in the *LOT* building across the road. Most trains run straight through to Centralna but it's possible that you'll stop (or even need to change trains) at **Dworzec Wschodnia** (East) station, out in the Praga suburb, or **Dworzec Zachodni** (West) in the Ochota district. Both stations have regular connections to Centralna.

● **Centralny Dworzec PKS**, the main **bus station**, is across the road from Dworzec Zachodni in Ochota, a ten-minute bus ride into the city center.

● **Arriving by car** isn't too problematic; potholes aside, Warsaw's road system is easy to navigate, with all the major routes—from Gdańsk, Poznań, Kraków, or the Soviet border—leading to the center.

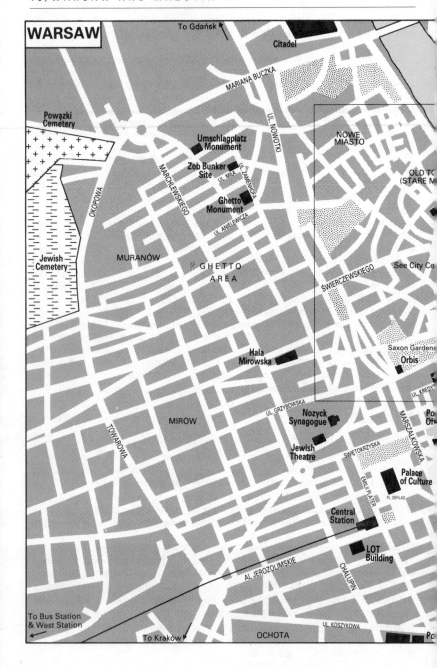

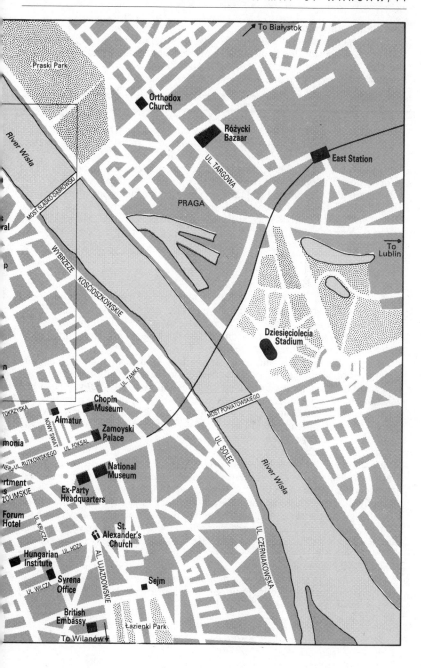

Orientation and Information

The wide open expanse of the Wisła River is the most obvious aid to **orientation**. The heart of Warsaw, the **Śródmieście** district, sits on the left bank; above it is the **Old Town** (Stare Miasto) area, with **plac Zamkowy** a useful central reference, while over on the east bank lies the **Praga** suburb.

Anyone staying for a long period should consider getting hold of a detailed **city map**. Tourist offices hand out town plans of varying quality, but the thing to look out for is the book-format *Warszawa—plan miasta*, which as well as having clear maps is a mine of useful addresses for everything from restaurants to embassies. It's generally available from tourist offices, bookshops, and street sellers, but like all really useful things in Poland could just as easily be impossible to find.

Strangely for a capital city, there's still no reliable source of general practical **information**. The *Informator Turystyczny* (IT) point on plac Zamkowy (8am–6pm) is getting better, though you can't always count on the staff's being multilingual. There are rudimentary information desks in the airport arrivals lounge and the central station. The Orbis office at the corner of Królewska and Marszałkowska has an information desk (that's often crowded), and most of the big hotels have IT points too.

Getting Around

Bus and **tram** are the main forms of city transport, and even after the big price rises of 1990, both are still very cheap for foreigners. They get very crowded at peak hours but services are remarkably punctual. Trams are best for short hops around the center. Regular bus and tram routes close down about midnight; from 11pm to 5am **night buses** leave from behind the Palace of Culture on ul. Emilii Plater at 17 and 47 minutes past the hour.

Tickets for both trams and buses are bought from *ruch* counters (not from drivers), normally in batches of ten or twenty, and are currently 480zl each—but prices will certainly go up. For buses or trams numbered #1–199 you need one ticket, for #400–599 and *pospieszne* (speed) buses marked A–U you need two, and for night buses (#600 and up) four. Punch your tickets in the machines on board—pleas of ignorance don't cut much ice with inspectors, who'll fine you 40,000–50,000zl on the spot if they catch you without a validated ticket.

For Poles, recent price increases have made **taxis** a luxury, though for westerners they're still reasonable—and easy to get. In a bizarre reversal of twenty years' established practice, taxis now line up for customers at the main taxi stops, not vice versa. Make sure the meter is turned on when you set off: the fare is currently the price displayed multiplied by (at last count) 140; there should be a little sign giving the present multiple. At night or from hotels, the airport and the train station, be prepared for drivers charging in hard currency—often at a significant mark-up from the equivalent złoty rate. **Radio taxis** (☎919) are reasonably reliable, though hard to get through to at night; you can order them a day in advance if you have specific needs.

At the time of writing a north–south Warsaw **metro** is under construction. The government's current austerity program, however, means there's little chance of it being finished before the mid-1990s, if at all.

The Warsaw telephone code is ☎022 for six-digit numbers, ☎02 for seven digits.

Accommodation

The listings below give a pretty comprehensive rundown of the accommodation available in the city area: hotels, hostels, private rooms, and even a couple of campgrounds. The lack of cheap, decent-quality hotel accommodation makes renting a private room a particularly attractive option.

As mentioned earlier, finding an office or information point in town to help you make a **reservation** is hard work—the lines, at the airport and train station information desks especially, can be forbidding. The best bets for hotel reservations are the reception of the *Grand Hotel*, ul. Krucza 28 (☎294-051), which can help with Orbis places, and the Syrena office, ul. Krucza 16/22 (☎288-052), which handles Syrena-run hotels. Otherwise it's a case of phoning or calling in person—larger hotels should speak some English or German.

Hotels

The only way to ensure a hotel room in season is to reserve before coming: in summer even the biggest hotels can be packed out solidly for weeks in a row. Rooms in the moderate-to-expensive categories will have a bathroom, and normally include breakfast in the price. Prices have rocketed over the past year.

CHEAPER HOTELS AND PENSIONS

Places at the bottom end of the scale vary a lot in quality and accessibility. At around $19–38 at night, though, these are about the only places, apart from hostels, that most Poles can afford. Consequently, getting a bed can be tricky, especially in summer—and be aware that the three sports-stadium hotels listed at the end of this section are a long way out of town.

ZNP ("Teacher's Hotel"), Wybrzeże Kosciuszki 33 (☎262-600). Near the waterfront, a short walk down from Nowy Świat; takes non-teachers when rooms are free—more likely during school semester than not. A good budget option.

PTTK Dom Turysty, Krakowskie Przedmieście 4/6 (☎263-011). Located just below the university campus. A step down in quality, offering doubles but messy communal bathrooms and toilets.

Druh, ul. Niemcewicza 17 (☎6590-011). West of the main station. A young people's hotel, popular with students—an altogether more attractive option than the *Dom Turysty*; trams #7, #8, #9, and #25.

Pensjonat Stegny, ul. Idzikowskiego 4 (☎422-768). A sports-stadium hotel, on the way to Wilanów.

Skra, ul. Wawelska 5 (☎255-100). Sited next to the Skra stadium in Ochota; bus #167, #187 or #188.

Orzel, ul. Podskarbińska 11/15 (☎105-060). By another stadium in southern Praga; bus #102 or #115.

MODERATE

There's a reasonable selection to consider in the middle price range. All are run by the Syrena tourist office and most are in or close to the city center. Prices run at around $38–75 for a double. Listings are in ascending order of price.

Dom Chłopa, pl. Powstanc ów Warszawy 2 (☎279-251). Used by a wider clientele than its name (Farmers' House) suggests.

Nowa Praga, ul. Brechta 7 (☎195-051). Humdrum place at the cheaper end of the scale—and way out to the east in Praga; any bus going over the Sląsko-Dąbrowski bridge takes you nearby.

Syrena, ul. Syreny 23 (☎328-297). This time well out to the west of town; still, there's generally a good chance of a room here if all else fails.

Saski, pl. Bankowy 1 (☎201-115). The cheapest and nicest of the bunch, well located just off Saski park, with decent rooms and plenty of character.

Warszawa, pl. Powstanców Warszawy 9 (☎269-421). Just off Swiętokrzyska; popular with East European tourist groups.

Polonia, al. Jerozolimskie 45 (☎287-241). Just round the corner from the similar *Metropol* (see below), but noisier. Top end of the scale.

Metropol, Marsałkowska 99a (☎294-001). Sited within easy walking distance of the central station, which means this is often full. Reserve in advance if possible.

MDM, pl. Konstytucji 1 (☎216-211). Rooms here are quieter and pleasanter (though also pricier) than its location and external appearance might suggest.

UPMARKET

Upmarket hotels are quite a growth sector in Warsaw, a by-product of the government's drive to attract western capital. Prices of $190 and up for double rooms are now standard for the top-bracket international hotels (the last four in this list); for the rest (again in ascending order of price), count on around $95–135.

Novotel, ul. 1 Sierpnia 1 (☎464-051). Motel with swimming pool, close to the airport.

Grand, ul. Krucza 28 (☎294-051). One of a string of drab Orbis places—the advantage of this one being its relatively central location.

Solec, ul. Zagórna 1 (☎259-241). Another unexciting Orbis hotel, located south of the center, near the river.

Vera, Wery-Kostrzewy 16 (☎227-4221). Ditto, this time just down from the bus station.

Zajazd Napoleoński, ul.Plowiecka 83 (☎153-068). Small luxury inn reputedly frequented by Napoleon, well out of the center in the Praga district.

Europejski, Krakowskie Przedmiescie 13 (☎265-051). Across from the *Victoria*. The shabbiness of this nineteenth-century building makes it the most appealing upper-bracket hotel.

Victoria, ul. Królewska 11 (☎278-011). Traditional favorite with businessmen, journalists and upmarket tourist groups; overlooking plac Zwycięstwa.

Forum, ul. Nowogrodzka 24/26 (☎210-271). Skyscraper haunt of Orbis package tours, on the corner of busy Marsałkowska and al. Jerozolimskie.

Holiday Inn, ul. Złota 2 (☎220-341). Similar ethos, also within striking distance of the central station.

Marriot, al. Jerozolimskie 65/79 (☎306306). Top of the pile, in terms of price; and a casino for the jet set too.

Hostels and Student Hotels

Warsaw has two **IYHF hostels**. At either, you have to be out of the building from 10am to 5pm, and reception is from 5 to 9pm. The one at **ul. Smolna 30** (☎278-952) is just a five-minute bus ride along al. Jerozolimskie from the main station—any bus heading toward Nowy Świat will drop you at the corner of the street. Predictably, the central location means it gets very crowded in summer. The other one, at **ul. Karolkowa 53a** (☎328-829), is farther out in the western Wola district—take tram #24 north from the main station and get off on al. Świerczewskiego, near the *Wola* department store. It's less likely to be full, but don't bank on it.

During July and August the Almatur-run **international student hotels** are another inexpensive possibility. The Almatur office at ul. Kopernika 15 (☎262-356) has current location details and the required vouchers for those who haven't bought them beforehand (see *Basics*). Reservations for the two- to four-person rooms aren't needed as long as you get there before 2pm.

Private Rooms

The main source of information for **private rooms** is Syrena's often grumpy *biuro kwatery prywatnych* office, ul. Krucza 17 (☎257-201/287-540), a fifteen-minute walk east from the train station, just down from the *Grand* hotel. It's open Monday to Saturday from 8am to 8pm, but get there as early as possible—hoping to find anything after 4pm is pushing your luck. Check locations carefully, as you may well be offered something on the far edge of the city.

Until recently the only alternative to the Syrena office was to trust one of the eager individuals touting rooms at the train station and other tourist haunts. All this is changing under the Solidarity government, and a number of privately run bureaus are now functioning, the most reliable of which is the *Romeo and Juliet*, on the third floor at Emilii Plater 30, across al. Jerozolimskie from the main station (Mon–Sat 9am–7pm; ☎292-993). The English-speaking proprietress guarantees to find you a decent-quality room inside central Warsaw, with a telephone; prices—dollars only—work out similar to those at the Syrena office, at about $19–28 for a double.

Campgrounds

Even in Warsaw camping is extremely cheap and popular, with Poles and foreigners alike. On the whole, site facilities are reasonable too.

Camping Gromada, ul. Zwirki i Wigury 32 (☎254-391). Best and most popular of the Warsaw campgrounds, on the way out to the airport—bus #128, #136, or #175 will get you there. As well as tent space the site has a number of cheap bungalows—though these are often all spoken for.

Wisła, Wery-Kostrzewy 15/17 (☎233-748). Just south of the bus station—take bus #154. Less crowded than the *Gromada* site.

PTTK Camping, ul. Połczyńska 6a. (☎366-716). Out in the Wola district.

Turysta, ul. Grochowska 1. (☎6106-364). Quite a distance out of town on the road to Terespol, useful if you're making an early morning start for the border.

The City

Wending its way north toward Gdańsk and the Baltic Sea, the **Wisła** River divides Warsaw neatly in half: the main sights are located on the western bank, the eastern consisting predominantly of residential and business districts. Somewhat to the north of center, the busy **Old Town (Stare Miasto)** provides the historic focal point. Rebuilt from scratch after the war, like most of Warsaw, the magnificent **Royal Castle**, ancient **St John's Cathedral**, and the **Old Town Square** are the most striking examples of the capital's reconstruction. Baroque churches and the former palaces of the aristocracy line the streets west of the ring of defensive walls and to the north in the quietly atmospheric **New Town (Nowe Miasto)**.

West of the Old Town, in the **Muranów** and **Mirów** districts, is the former **Ghetto** area, where the Nozyck synagogue and the ulica Okopowa cemetery bear poignant testimony to the lost Jewish population. South of the Old Town lies **Sródmiescie**, the city's commercial center, its skyline dominated by the Palace of Culture, Stalin's permanent legacy to the citizens of Warsaw. Linking the Old Town and Sródmiescie, **Krakowskie Przedmieście** is dotted with palaces and Baroque spires, and forms the first leg of the **Royal Way**, a procession of open boulevards stretching all the way from plac Zamkowy to the stately king's residence at **Wilanów** on the southern edge of the city. Along the way is **Łazienki Park**, one of Warsaw's many delightful green spaces and the setting for the charming **Łazienki Palace**, the so-called "palace on the water."

Farther out, the city becomes a welter of high-rise developments, but among them historic suburbs like **Żoliborz** and **Praga**—on the east side of the river— give a flavor of the authentic life of contemporary Warsaw.

The Old Town (Stare Miasto)

The title "Old Town"—Stare Miasto—is in some respects a misnomer for the historic nucleus of Warsaw. Forty-five years ago this compact network of streets and alleyways lay in rubble: even the cobblestones are meticulously assembled replacements. Yet surveying the tiered houses of the main square, for example, it's hard to believe they've been here only decades. Some older residents even claim that the restored version is in some respects an improvement.

Plac Zamkowy (Castle Square), on the south side of the Old Town, is the obvious place to start a tour. Here the first thing to catch your eye is the bronze **statue** of Zygmunt III Waza, the king who made Warsaw the capital. Installed on his column in 1640, Zygmunt suffered a direct hit from a tank in September 1944, but has now been replaced on his lookout; the base, these days, is a popular and convenient rendezvous point.

The Royal Castle

On the east side of the square is the former **Royal Castle** (Zamek Królewski), once home of the royal family and seat of the Polish parliament, now the **Castle Museum** (guided tours Tues–Sun 10am–4pm; last admission 3pm). Dynamited by German troops in the aftermath of the Warsaw Uprising, the seventeenth-century castle was rebuilt as recently as the 1970s. In July 1974 a huge crowd gathered to witness the clock of the domed Zygmunt tower starting up again— the hands set exactly where they were stopped by the first Luftwaffe attack. Attachment to a crucial symbol of independent nationhood explains the resurrected magnificence of the castle: the rebuilding was almost entirely financed by private donations from Poles—from all over the world—and hundreds of volunteers helped with the labor. Though the structure is a replica, many of its furnishings are the originals, spirited away to safety by prescient employees during the first bombing raids.

Entry is through the Senatorial Gate and a vaulted hallway that's always bustling with tourist groups. The obligatory guided tours are often heavily booked up, so get tickets in advance if possible; failing that, get here well before opening time and join the line. The first part of the set tour takes you through the **Jagiellonian Rooms**, overlooking the river from the northeast wing. Originally part of the residence of Zygmunt August, they are adorned with portraits of the Jagiellonian royal families and some outstanding Flemish tapestries, including the ominously titled *Tragedy of the Jewish People*.

Next are the chambers where the Sejm—the parliament—used to meet. Beyond the chancellery, which features more tapestries and portraits of the last dukes of Mazovia, comes the **Chamber of Deputies**, formerly the debating chamber. During parliamentary sessions, the deputies sat on benches on the left side of the chamber, with the Speaker in the center of the room, while members of the public could stand and listen on the right-hand side. Democracy as prac-

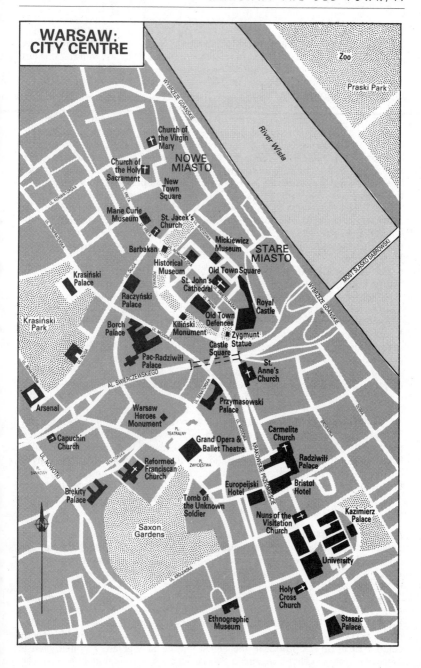

WARSAW: CITY CENTRE

Zoo

Praski Park

River Wisla

WYBRZEŻE GDAŃSKIE

Church of the Virgin Mary

NOWE MIASTO

Church of the Holy Sacrament

New Town Square

Marie Curie Museum

St. Jacek's Church

Mickiewicz Museum

STARE MIASTO

Barbakan

Historical Museum

Old Town Square

Krasiński Palace

St. John's Cathedral

Old Town Defences

Royal Castle

Raczyński Palace

Krasiński Park

Borch Palace

Kiliński Monument

Zygmunt Castle Statue

Pac-Radziwiłł Palace

Castle Square

AL. ŚWIERCZEWSKIEGO

St. Anne's Church

Arsenal

Warsaw Heroes Monument

Przymasowski Palace

Capuchin Church

PL. TEATRALNY

Grand Opera & Ballet Theatre

Carmelite Church

KRAKOWSKIE PRZEDMIEŚCIE

Radziwiłł Palace

PL. ZWYCIĘSTWA

Reformed Franciscan Church

Bristol Hotel

Błękity Palace

Europeijski Hotel

Tomb of the Unknown Soldier

Nuns of the Visitation Church

Kazimierz Palace

Saxon Gardens

University

UL. KRÓLEWSKA

Holy Cross Church

Ethnographic Museum

Staszic Palace

tised here was something of a mixed blessing. On the one hand, the founding decree of the Polish Commonwealth, hammered out here in 1573, demonstrated an exceptionally tolerant attitude to religious differences; on the other, it was also here that the principle of *liberum veto*—unanimity as a prerequisite for the passing of new laws—was established in 1652, often seen as the beginning of the end of effective government in Poland.

The seventeenth-century **Grand Staircase** leads to the most lavish section of the castle, the **Royal Apartments of King Stanisław August**. Through two smaller rooms you come to the magnificent **Canaletto Room**, with its views of Warsaw by Bernardo Bellotto, nephew of the famous Canaletto—whose name he appropriated to make his pictures sell better. Marvelous in their detail, these cityscapes provided important information for the architects rebuilding the city after the war. Next door is the richly decorated **Royal Chapel**, where an urn contains the heart—sacred to many Poles—of Tadeusz Kościuszko, swashbuckling leader of the 1794 insurrection and hero of the American War of Independence. Like many other rooms on this floor, the **Audience Chamber** has a beautiful parquet floor as well as several original furnishings. The four pictures by Bacciarelli, court painter to Stanisław August, symbolize the cardinal virtues of Courage, Wisdom, Piety, and Justice.

The **King's Bedroom**, another lavishly decorated set-up, is followed by the **Study Room**, where Napoleon is supposed to have slept during his short stay—apparently he had Stanisław's bed moved in here, not wishing to sleep in the bedroom occupied so recently by a deposed ruler.

From here you proceed through to the reception rooms, where the **Marble Room** is dominated by portraits of the 22 Polish monarchs, including a much-reproduced portrait of Stanisław August in his coronation robes. Highlight of the parade of royal splendour is the **Ball Room**, the largest room in the castle, with its aptly titled ceiling allegory by Bacciarelli, *The Dissolution of Chaos*. Napoleon met the elite of Warsaw society here in 1806, the occasion on which he made his comments (legendary in Poland) about the beauty of Polish women—his mistress-to-be Countess Marie Walewska included, presumably.

The final leg of the tour—which for the less than obsessionally interested can, by this stage, feel something of an endurance test—is a climb to the upper part of the **north wing**, where paintings by Matejko invest key moments of Polish history with romantic fervour. *Rejtan* shows a deputy blocking the path of a group of other deputies preparing to accept the First Partition, imploring them to kill him rather than Poland, while *The Third of May Constitution* celebrates an enlightened moment—the declaration of one of the first democratic constitutions in Europe—in a similarly intense vein.

North of the Castle

Shops, bars, restaurants, and impromptu sidewalk stalls line **Piwna** and **Swiętojańska**, the two narrow cobbled streets leading northwards from plac Zamkowy. There's a lot of junk about, but occasional nuggets too, especially in the record and book shops.

Each street has a church worth a stop as well. On Piwna there's **St Martin's**, a fourteenth-century structure whose Baroque interior was carefully restored after the war; among those buried here is Adam Jarzębski, king's musician and author of the first guide to Warsaw—written in verse. On Swiętojańska the thirteenth-century **St John's Cathedral**, the oldest church in Warsaw, reconstructed in Mazovian Gothic style, is regaining its old official functions under the Catholic-dominated Solidarity government. The church was scene of some of the bitterest fighting during the Warsaw Uprising, when German tanks entered the building after destroying the southern aisle.

The Old Town Square

The Old Town Square—**Rynek Starego Miasto**—is one of the most remarkable bits of postwar reconstruction anywhere in Europe. Flattened during the Warsaw Uprising, the three-story merchants' houses surrounding the square have been scrupulously rebuilt to their seventeenth- and eighteenth-century designs, multi-colored facades included. By day the Rynek teems with visitors, who are catered to by street musicians, artists, cafés, moneychangers, and *doroski*, the traditional horse-drawn carts that clatter tourists around the Old Town for a sizable fee.

The **Warsaw Historical Museum** (Tues–Sun 10am–4pm) takes up a large part of Strona Dekerta, the north side of the square; entrance is through a house known as the Pod Murzynkiem, where a sculpted black head on the facade symbolizes the first owner's overseas trading concerns. Exhibitions here cover every aspect of Warsaw's life from its beginnings to the present day, with a particularly moving chronicle of everyday resistance to the Nazis—an uplifting complement to the wartime horrors documented in the film shown daily at 10am.

On the square's east side—Strona Barssa—the **Mickiewicz Museum** (same times) is a temple to the Romantic national poet. Among a stack of first editions, contemporary newspapers, and family memorabilia there's actually a shrine room, with portrait and crucifix enveloped in church-like gloom.

If the crowds in the open-air cafés are too much for you, the *Manekin*, in the southeast corner, is a nice little coffee dive with a bar at the back. The south side—Strona Zakrzewskiego—is also mainly about eating and drinking, the exclusive *Bazyliszek* restaurant being the most famous attraction. If you're happy with something a little less grand, the Hortex *Jezuicka* café is an acceptable alternative, and there are a couple of popular café-restaurants and wine cellars on the west side too (see "Eating and drinking")—plus a good poster shop at no. 23.

The Old Town may be liveliest by day, but nighttime is when it's at its most atmospheric. Backstreets like ulica Brzozowa, between the Rynek and the river, are particularly handsome, their slanting tiled roofs, silent courtyards, and tight passageways seemingly untouched by time.

North of the Rynek ... and Across the Water

From the Rynek, ul. Nowomeijska runs north to the edge of the Old Town, passing the city archives (no. 12; entrance by appointment) and an excellent postcard shop (no. 19). The street ends at the sixteenth-century **Barbakan**, which formerly guarded the Nowomeijska Gate, the northern entrance to the city. The fortress is part of the old town defenses, running all the way around from plac Zamkowy to the northeastern edge of the district. In summer the Barbakan attracts street artists and hawkers of kitsch souvenir jewelry.

Walk east along the walls to the Marshal's Tower, and you have a good view over the river to the Praga district. Conversely, some of the best views of the Old Town itself are from the **Praga waterfront**: take any tram over the bridge immediately south of the Old Town (Most Śląsko-Dąbrowski), get off at the first stop and cross into **Praski Park**, then down to the river bank. Walk farther north through the park and you'll find yourself amid the questionable pleasures of the Warsaw Zoo.

The New Town (Nowe Miasto)

Cross the ramparts from the Barbakan and you're into the **New Town** district, which despite its name dates from the early fifteenth century, but was formally joined to Warsaw only at the end of the eighteenth. At that time the wooden buildings of the artisan settlement were replaced by brick houses, and it's in this style that the area has been rebuilt.

Up to the Market Square

The eighteenth-century **Raczyński Palace**, a little way down ul. Długa (the first street to the left over the rampart bridge), was one of several field hospitals in the city center during the Warsaw Uprising; a tablet on the corner with ul. Kilińskiego commemorates over 400 wounded insurrectionists murdered in their beds when the Nazis marched into the Old Town. The Palace is now an archive.

Back up to the bridge, **ul. Freta**—the continuation of Nowomeijska—runs north through the heart of the New Town. On the right, **St Jacek's Church**, a Dominican foundation, is an effective blend of Gothic and early Baroque. The adjoining monastery, the largest in Warsaw, was another field hospital and was heavily bombed as a consequence; hundreds died here when the Nazis regained control in October 1944. The *Pod Samsonen* gallery at ul. Freta 3 holds occasional exhibitions of Asian and Pacific art, shown alongside a small permanent collection (Tues–Sun noon–6pm). For a time the German Romantic writer E.T.A. Hoffman lived at ul. Freta no. 5, and no. 16 was the birthplace of one of Poland's most famous women: **Maria Skłodowska-Curie**, the double Nobel prizewinning discoverer of radium. Inside there's a small **museum** dedicated to her life and work (Tues–Sat 10am–4pm).

Ulica Freta leads to the New Town Market Square—**Rynek Nowego Miasto**—once the commercial hub of the district. Surrounded by elegantly reconstructed eighteenth-century facades, this pleasant square makes a soothing change from the bustle of the Old Town. Tucked into the eastern corner is the **Church of the Holy Sacrament**, commissioned by Queen Maria Sobieska in memory of her husband Jan's victory over the Turks at Vienna in 1683 (see *Contexts*); as you might expect, highlight of the remarkably sober interior is the Sobieski funeral chapel. The architect, Tylman of Gameren, was the most important figure in the rebuilding of Warsaw after the destruction of the Swedish wars in the 1660s. Invited to Poland from Utrecht by Count Jerzy Lubomirski, he went on to redesign what seems like half the city in his distinctive, rather austere Palladian style.

Just off the northern edge of the square, the early fifteenth-century **Church of the Virgin Mary**—once the New Town parish church—has retained something of its Gothic character despite later remodelings; the adjoining belfry is a New Town landmark, easily identifiable from the other side of the river.

The Uprising Monument and Krasiński Palace

The streets northwest of the square lead across ul. Bonifraterska to ul. Marclego Nowotki, a main thoroughfare which marks the boundaries of Muranów (see below). Southwards, ul. Bonifraterska leads to the large plac Krasińskich, recently augmented with the **Warsaw Uprising Monument**, a controversial piece commissioned by the communist authorities and consequently disliked by many Varsovians.

Overlooking the west side is the huge and majestic **Krasiński Palace**, built for regional governor Jan Krasiński by the tireless Tylman of Gameren, its facade bearing fine sculptures by Andreas Schlüter. Most of the palace's collection of documents—40,000 items in all—was destroyed in the war, so today's collection comes from a whole host of sources. Theoretically the building is only open to official visitors but inquiries at the door should get you in to see at least some of the library; the inside of the palace is splendid, the Neoclassical decorations being restored versions of the designs executed by Merlini in the 1780s.

Behind the palace are the **gardens**, now a public park, and beyond that the Ghetto area (see below). If you've got the stomach for it, the **Pawiak Prison Museum**, over to the west at ul. Dzielna 24/26 (Tues–Sat 9am–4pm, Sun 9am–3pm), tells the grim story of Warsaw's most notorious prison from Czarist times to the Nazi occupation.

On and Around ulica Długa

Farther down ul. Bonifraterska, at the corner of ul. Długa and ul. Miodowa, is a small streetside **plaque**, one of the least conspicuous yet most poignant memorials in the city. It commemorates the Warsaw Uprising, and in particular the thousands of half-starved Varsovians who attempted to escape from the besieged Old Town through the sewer network. Many drowned in the filthy passageways, or were killed by grenades lobbed into the tunnels, or were shot upon emerging, but a hundred or so did make it to freedom. The bitter saga was the subject of Andrzej Wajda's film *Kanal*, the second in his brilliant war trilogy.

A number of old patrician residences are to be seen west along ul. Długa, which leads to the **Warsaw Archaeological Museum** (Tues–Fri 9am–4pm, Sat & Sun 10am–5pm), housed in the seventeenth-century arsenal. Starting with Neolithic, Paleolithic, and Bronze Age sites, the museum continues through to early medieval Polish settlements, the highlight being a reconstruction of the early Slav settlements in Wielkopolska.

Palaces on Miodowa

Heading back up to plac Krasińskich and turning south along ul. Miodowa, you find youself in the heart of aristocratic old Warsaw. The palaces lining Miodowa mainly date from the prosperous pre-Partition era, when this section of the city hummed with the life of European high society. Next door to the **Borch Palace**—now the residence of the Catholic Primate, Cardinal Glemp—stands the **Radziwiłł Palace**, designed by Tylman of Gameren and adjoined by the later Pac Palace, with its distinctive frieze-topped entrance.

Close by is the late seventeenth-century **Capuchin Church**, repository of the heart of Jan Sobieski, while off to the left, on ul. Podwale, the **Jan Kiliński monument** commemorates another stirring figure in the country's history. During the 1794 insurrection it was the shoemaker Kiliński who led the citizens of Warsaw in their assault on the Czarist ambassador's residence on this street. His special place in local consciousness was amply demonstrated during World War II after the Nazi governor took down the uncomfortably defiant-looking monument and locked it up in the National Museum. The next day this message was scrawled on the museum wall: "People of Warsaw, here I am! Jan Kiliński."

Muranów and Mirów: Jewish Warsaw

Like Łódź, Białystok, and Kraków, Warsaw was for centuries one of the great Jewish centers of Poland. In 1939 there were an estimated 380,000 Jews living in and around the city—one third of the total population. By May 1945, around 300 were left. Most of Jewish Warsaw was destroyed after the Ghetto Uprising (see box below), to be replaced by the sprawling housing projects and tree-lined thoroughfares of the **Muranów** and **Mirów** districts, a little to the west of the city center. However, a few traces of the Jewish presence in Warsaw do remain, and there's a small but increasingly visible Jewish community here—well supported by its exiled diaspora.

Nożyk Synagogue

First stop on any itinerary of Jewish Warsaw is the **Nożyk Synagogue** on ul. Twarda, the only one of the Ghetto's three synagogues still standing. The majestic Great Synagogue on ul. Tłomackie—which held up to 3000 people—was blown up by the Nazis; in a gesture of crass insensitivity, the Polish authorities decided to build a skyscraper on the site.

The Nożyk, a more modest affair, was built in the early 1900s, gutted during the war, and reopened in 1983 after a complete restoration. The refined interior is theoretically open to tourists only from 10am to 3pm on Thursdays, but in practice it's possible to get in at other times with a little diplomacy. The **Jewish Theater**, rehoused just south of the synagogue on plac Grzybowski, continues the theatrical traditions of the Ghetto.

The Ghetto Heroes Monument and Jewish Cemetery

Marooned in the middle of a drab square to the north of the Ghetto area, the imposing **Ghetto Heroes Monument**—unveiled in 1948 on the fifth anniversary of the Uprising—stresses both the courage of the Jewish resistance and the helplessness of the deportees. It is made from materials ordered by Hitler in 1942 to construct a monument to the Third Reich's anticipated victory.

North along ul. Zamenhofa brings you to ul. Miła and the memorial mound covering the **ZOB bunker** at no. 18 (see box). Continue north, turn left on ul. Stawki, and there on the edge of a housing estate is the *Umschlagplatz*, where, as recorded by the simple stone monument, hundreds of thousands of Jews were loaded onto cattle cars bound for Treblinka and the other death camps.

Walk west along ul. Stawki and down ul. Okopowa for the **Jewish Cemetery** (10am–3pm, closed Fri & Sat), where the tombs range from colossal Gothic follies to simple engraved stones, rather like a Jewish Highgate. Unlike most Jewish cemeteries in Poland, this site was left almost untouched during the war, the reason being that, unlike in smaller Polish towns, the Nazis didn't need the materials for building new roads. Scattered among the plots are the graves of eminent Polish Jews like Ludwig Zamenhof, the inventor of Esperanto, early socialist activist Stanisław Mendelson, and writer D.H. Nomberg. The caretaker at the entrance lodge has detailed guides to the tombstones for anyone wanting to know more.

The Jewish Historical Institute

A final stop should be the **Jewish Historical Institute**, next to the site of the Great Synagogue at ul. Tłomackie 3/5. Itself standing on the site of the prewar Judaic Library, the institute is part museum (Mon–Fri 9am–3pm), part library and research archive (Mon–Fri 8am–4pm). The museum details life in the wartime Ghetto, a fascinating and moving corrective to the familiar images of passive victims.

The international section of the library includes English-language books and journals about Polish Jewry and related issues. To meet increasing demand, the institute has now published an indispensible *Guide to Jewish Warsaw*, also on sale at the cemetery.

THE GHETTO

From the middle of 1940 the Jews of Warsaw were sealed behind the walls of the Nazi-designated Ghetto area, and by the next year nearly one and a half million Jews from all over Poland had been crammed into this insanitary zone, with starvation and epidemics the predictable and intended consequence.

Deportations to the death camps began in summer 1942—300,000 to Treblinka in that summer alone. After further mass round-ups, the Nazis moved in to "clean out" the Ghetto in January 1943, by which time there were only 60,000 people left. Sporadic resistance forced them to retreat, but only until April, when a full-scale Nazi assault provoked the **Ghetto Uprising** under the leadership of the Jewish Combat Organization (ZOB). For nearly a month Jewish partisans battled against overwhelming Nazi firepower, before ZOB's bunker headquarters in ul. Miła were finally taken on May 9, following the suicide of the legendary Mordechai Anieliewicz and his entire staff. A very few combatants survived and escaped to join up with the Polish resistance in the "Aryan" sector of the city. Of those remaining in the Ghetto, 7000 were shot immediately, the rest dispatched to the camps.

Śródmieście

The large area stretching from the Old Town down toward Łazienki Park—Śródmiescie—is the increasingly fast-paced heart of Warsaw, but in keeping with the Polish spirit of reverence for the past, the sector immediately below the Old Town contains an impressive number of reconstructed palaces, parks, churches, and museums, all contributing to a distinctive atmosphere of slightly grubby grandeur. Farther south, below ul. Swiętokrzyska and east of the Palace of Culture, the brash shopfronts, tower blocks and fast-food stands of the main commercial zone epitomise the changing face of Warsaw city life.

From Plac Zamkowy to Aleje Ujazdowskie

Running west from plac Zamkowy is ulica Senatorska, once one of Warsaw's smartest shopping streets, now studded with wall plaques recording the civilian victims of Nazi street executions. As the name suggests, the pseudo-classical giant dominating the nearby plac Teatralny is the **Grand Opera and Ballet Theater**, which stages major theater and opera productions, with an emphasis on classic Polish works (see "Nightlife"). The redoubtable sword-waving figure rising from the stone plinth on the other side of the square is the **Warsaw Heroes Monument**, the state's tribute to the war dead; like most Warsaw monuments, it could do with a cleaner environment.

Continuing west along Senatorska, the Baroque **Reformed Franciscan Church**—a quiet place with restful cloisters—is followed by the **Mniszech Palace** and the **Błękitny Palace**, where Chopin gave one of his earliest concerts at the age of six. Tragically, the palace's destruction in 1944 engulfed the fabulous Zamoyski library of over 250,000 books and manuscripts. Senatorska ends at plac Bankowy, formerly plac Dzierzyńskiego; the giant statue of the unloved Russian Revolutionary who was formerly its namesake has now been removed.

Returning to plac Teatralny, the way from the south side of the theater leads onto an even larger square, **plac Zwycięstwa**, where a huge flower cross lay for some time after martial law was imposed. After the authorities had cleared the cross away, the whole area was closed off for public works for years, presumably to prevent embarrassing demonstrations happening in full view of the tourists staying in the *Victoria* and *Europejski* hotels. These days the military guard in front of the **Tomb of the Unknown Soldier** is the only permanent security presence. Behind it stretch the handsome and well-used promenades of the **Saxon Gardens** (Ogród Saski), laid out by August II for the palace that used to stand here.

Along Krakowskie Przedmieście

Of all the long thoroughfares bisecting central Warsaw from north to south, the most important is the one often known as the Royal Way, which runs almost uninterruptedly from plac Zamkowy to the palace of Wilanów. **Krakowskie Przedmieście**, the first part of the Royal Way, is lined with historic buildings. **St Anne's**, directly below plac Zamkowy, is where Polish princes used to swear homage to the king; founded in 1454, the church was destroyed in 1656 by the besieging Swedes, then rebuilt in Baroque style in the following century. There's a fine view over the Wisła from the courtyard next to the church, though your enjoyment of it is somewhat marred by the traffic thundering through the tunnel below. By the second year of martial law resourceful oppositionists had moved their flower cross to this courtyard after the authorities removed the huge one from plac Zwycięstwa.

South of St Anne's the bus-congested street broadens to incorporate a small green. The **Mickiewicz Statue** stuck in the middle of it is the first of many you'll see if you travel around the country—he's a hero whom everyone seems comfortable with, communist governments included. Just south of the statue stands the seventeenth-century **Carmelite church** whose finely wrought facade is one of the first examples of genuine classicism in Poland. Next door in the **Radziwłł Palace** is where the Warsaw Pact was formally created in 1955, at the height of the Cold War. In front of the palace's large courtyard is a statue of another national favorite, Józef Poniatowski, nephew of the last king of Poland and a die-hard patriot who fought in the 1794 insurrection.

Two grand old hotels face each other a little farther down the street, the *Europejski*, Warsaw's oldest hotel, and the *Bristol*. Begun in the 1850s, the **Europejski**, the only one of the two currently functioning, was badly hit in World War II, but it's been restored well enough to preserve at least a hint of *fin-de-siècle* grandeur. No one's stayed in the *Bristol* for ten years or so—there are rumors that Trust House Forte has bought the franchise. Once owned by musician-president Ignacy Paderewski and a legendary prewar journalists' hang-out, it even used to have its own official guidebook.

Even in a city not lacking in Baroque churches, the **Church of the Nuns of the Visitation** stands out, with its columned, statue-topped facade; it's also one of the very few buildings in central Warsaw to have come through World War II unscathed. Its main claim to fame in Polish eyes is that Chopin used to play the church organ here, mainly during services for school children.

THE UNIVERSITY

Most of the rest of Krakowskie Przedmieście is taken up by **Warsaw University**. Established in 1818, it was closed by the Czar in 1832 as part of the punishment for the 1831 insurrection, and remained closed till 1915. During the Nazi occupation educational activity of any sort was made a capital offense, and thousands of academics and students were murdered, yet clandestine university courses continued throughout the war—a tradition revived in the 1970s with the "Flying University," which involved opposition figures moving around the city giving open lectures on politically controversial issues. Today the university's reputation remains as much political as academic, and even the new political order doesn't seem to have extinguished the traditional radicalism. During semester you'll find groups hustling books and leaflets on the streets outside the main entrance; if they can speak English, a political discussion won't be hard to initiate either—like Poles in general, the students love a good argument. The cafés, restaurants, and milk bars just down the street and around the corner on ul. Oboźna are established student hang-outs.

On the main campus courtyard, the **Library** stands in front of the seventeenth-century **Kazimierz Palace**, once a royal summer residence, while across the street from the gates is the former **Czapski Palace**, now home of the Academy of Fine Arts. Just south is the Baroque **Holy Cross Church** (Kosciól Świętego Krzyza), which was ruined by a two-week battle inside the building during the Warsaw Uprising; photographs of the distinctive figure of Christ left standing among the ruins became poignant emblems of Warsaw's suffering. Another factor increases local affection for this church—on a pillar on the left side of the nave there's an urn containing Chopin's heart.

Biggest among Warsaw's consistently big palaces is the early nineteenth-century **Staszic Palace**, which virtually blocks the end of Krakowskie Przedmieście; once a Russian boys' grammar school, it's now the Polish Academy of Sciences.

The Nowy Świat District

South from the Staszic, the main street becomes **Nowy Świat** (New World), an area first settled in the mid-seventeenth century. Moving down this wide boulevard, the palaces of the aristocracy give way to shops, offices, and cafés: the *Nowy Świat* café, on the corner with Świętokrzyska, is a popular coffee stop, while the *Blikle* farther down still produces the cakes for which it's been famed since 1869. Numerous cultural luminaries have inhabited this street at one time or another, the most famous being Joseph Conrad, who lived at no. 45. A left turn down ul. Ordynacka brings you to the **Chopin Museum** in ul. Okólnik (Mon–Wed, Fri & Sat 10am–2pm, Thurs noon–6pm), also headquarters of the Chopin Society. Memorabilia on display includes the last piano played by him, now used for occasional concerts.

The neo-Renaissance **Zamoyski Palace**, off to the left of Nowy Świat at the end of ul. Foksal, is one of the few Warsaw palaces you can actually see inside. In 1863 an abortive attempt to assassinate the Czarist governor was made here; as a consequence the palace was confiscated and ransacked by Cossacks, who hurled a grand piano used by Chopin out of the window of his sister's flat in the palace. These days it's a suitably elegant setting for an architectural institute, with a restaurant and a nice quiet café open to the public.

Continuing down Nowy Świat, the concrete monster on the southern side of the junction with al. Jerozolimskie was for decades the headquarters of the now-defunct **Polish Communist Party**. It's currently the subject of intense controversy: the university have laid a strong claim to it, but at the moment it looks as though the government may turn it into a banking and finance center.

THE NATIONAL MUSEUM
Immediately west along al. Jerozolimskie is the **National Museum** (Tues 10am–5pm, Wed–Sat 10am–4pm, Sun noon–6pm), an equally ugly and daunting building. Its collections are an impressive compendium of art and archaeology, but be warned that lack of staff means that at least a handful of galleries are always shut. The first floor has the **ancient art** – a large show of Egyptian, Greek, Roman, and Etruscan finds—while the **European galleries** on the upper floors display a wide range of paintings and sculptures—Caravaggio, Bellini, Breughel, and Rodin included.

However, most notable of the museum's collections is the display of **Polish medieval altarpieces and religious sculpture**, featuring some imaginative and exuberant wooden Madonnas, mainly from the Gdańsk region. **Polish art** continues on the upper floors, with a comprehensive collection of canvases by nineteenth-century and modern artists, many of them relatively unknown; an important section is the group of works from the turn-of-the-century *Młoda Polska* school (see "Kraków"). Stanisław Wyspianski's intense self-portraits stand out, as do Jacek Malczewski's haunting images of Death disguised as an angel, and some typically epic Matejko efforts, including the huge *Battle of Grunwald*.

The **Army Museum** next door (same times) stirs pride in many Poles, but few foreigners get farther than the World War II heavy armor outside.

THE PARLIAMENT AND SENATE
South of the museum, plac Trzech Krzyzy (Three Crosses), with the Pantheon-style **St Alexander's** church in the center, leads to the tree-lined sidewalks and magisterial embassy buildings of al. Ujazdowskie. Past the unattractive US embassy and off to the left down ul. Jana Matejki is the squat 1920s **Parliament** (Sejm) and **Senate** building. Hardly worth a mention a few years ago, these days it's where veteran Solidarity oppositionists rub shoulders with, and occasionally dismiss, their former jailers.

Downtown Warsaw

The area below the Saxon Gardens and west of Krakowskie Przedmieście is the busiest commercial zone. **Marszałkowska**, the main road running south from the western tip of the park, is lined with department stores and privately run boutiques and workshops selling everything from jewelry to car spares. South of ul. Swiętokrzyska, in the long narrow streets surrounding Rutkowskiego and Hibnera, it's worth scouting around for good-quality items like heavy winter coats and hand-crafted leather goods.

North of ul. Swiętokrzyska, on ul. Kreditowa, the eighteenth-century **Lutheran Church** stands opposite the **Ethnographic Museum** (Tues, Thurs & Fri 9am–4pm, Wed 11am–6pm, Sat & Sun 10am–5pm), whose collection of over 30,000 items was virtually destroyed in the war. They've done pretty well to revive the place since then, restocking with African tribal artifacts, Latin American outfits, and local folk items. Polish objects take up much of the second floor, a highlight being an absorbing collection of traditional costumes from all over the country. Folklore enthusiasts will enjoy the section devoted to straw men, winter processions, and a host of other arcane rural customs.

Towering over everything in this part of the city is the **Palace of Culture**, a gift from Stalin to the Polish people, and not one that could be refused. Popularly known as "the Russian cake," this neo-Byzantine leviathan provokes both intense revulsion and admiration for its sheer audacity. These days slogans about "capitalizm" and "biznes" have replaced Marx and Lenin on the banners over the giant entrance up the steps from the expansive plac Defilad—currently the subject of a nationwide design competition. Apart from a vast conference hall, the cavernous interior contains offices, movie theaters, swimming pools, some good foreign-language bookshops, and—the ultimate capitalistic revenge—a casino. The locals say that the best view of Warsaw is from the top floor—the only view point from which one can't see the palace. An elevator whisks visitors up to the thirtieth-floor platform from where, on a good day, you can see out into the plains of Mazovia.

Al. Jerozolimskie, the major highway south of the palace, is dominated by the gleaming chrome and marble of the new *LOT* building and Warsaw's latest Western marvel, the luxury **Marriot Hotel**. (The completion of the *Holiday Inn* just north of the station has confirmed this region as Warsaw's top-bracket tourist quarter.) The department stores continue southwards down tram-lined Marsałkowska toward plac Konstytucji, interspersed with tourist offices and cultural institutes of other one-time communist countries. Cross-streets such as Hoźa and Wilcza comprise a residental area whose discreetly well-heeled inhabitants are served by increasing numbers of chic little stores.

West of plac Konstitytucji, on Nowowiejska, is the **Warsaw Polytechnic**, where the local Solidarity Citizens' Committee hold their main meetings. If you happen to be there at the right time, there's nothing to stop you sitting in on these impassioned mini-parliaments, which are sometimes attended by government ministers, and occasionally by the prime minister.

Łazienki Park and Palace

Parks are one of Warsaw's distinctive and most attractive features. South of the commercial district, on the east side of al. Ujazdowskie, is one of the best, the **Łazienki Park**. Once a hunting ground on the periphery of town, the area was bought by King Stanisław August in the 1760s and turned into an English-style park with formal gardens. A few years later the slender Neoclassical **Łazienki Palace** was built across the park lake; designed for the king by the Italian architect Domenico Merlini, in collaboration with teams of sculptors and other architects, it's the best memorial to the country's last and most cultured monarch. Before this summer residence was commissioned, a bathhouse built by Tylman of Gameren for Prince Stanisław Lubomirski stood here—hence the name "Łazienki," meaning simply "baths."

The oak-lined promenades and pathways leading from the park entrance to the palace are a favorite with both Varsovians and tourists. On summer Sunday lunchtimes, concerts and other events take place under the watchful eye of the ponderous **Chopin Monument**, just beyond the entrance; they are an enjoyable introduction to Polish culture in populist form—stirring performances of Chopin études or mazurkas, declamatory readings from Mickiewicz and other Romantics, and so on. On the way down to the lake you'll pass a couple of the many buildings designed for King Stanisław by Merlini. The **New Guardhouse**, just before the palace, is now a pleasant terrace café.

The Palace

The only way to see the **palace interior** (Tues–Sun 10am–4pm; last entrance 3:20pm) is on a group tour, and these fill up early in the day—so get there by

9:30am in summer or be prepared for a long wait. Nazi damage to the rooms themselves was not irreparable, and most of the lavish furnishings, paintings, and sculptures survived the war intact, having been hidden during the occupation.

First on the ground floor are rooms incorporated from the earlier bathhouse; the baths themselves are long gone, but the bas reliefs decorating the walls serve as a reminder of the original waterbound function. Moving into the main section of the palace, the stuccoed **ballroom**, the biggest ground-floor room, is a fine example of Stanisław's classicist predilections, lined with a tasteful collection of busts and classical sculptures. As the adjoining **picture galleries** demonstrate, Stanisław was a discerning art collector. The Nazis got hold of some of the best pieces—three Rembrandts included—but a large collection drawn from all over Europe remains, with an accent on Dutch and Flemish artists.

Upstairs are the **king's private apartments**, most of them entirely reconstructed since the war. Again, period art and furniture dominates these handsome chambers: a stately and uncomfortable-looking four-poster bed fills the royal bedroom, while in the study a Bellotto canvas accurately depicts the original Łazienki bathhouse. An exhibition devoted to the history of Łazienki completes the tour.

The Park

The buildings scattered around the park are all in some way connected with King Stanisław. Just across the lake is the **Myślewicki Palace**, a present from the king to his son Prince Jozef Poniatowski, which imitates the studied decorum of the main palace. In summer the Greek-inspired **Amphitheater**, constructed for the king on an islet just along from the palace, still stages the occasional open-air performance; rustling trees and the background duck chorus are a bit of an intrusion. Back up toward the park entrance, the main **Orangery** houses a well-preserved wooden theater, with room for over 200 people, royal boxes not included; to complete the classical pose, pieces from King Stanisław's extensive sculpture collection fill the long galleries behind the auditorium.

Back out on al. Ujazdowskie, south from the Chopin monument, stands the **Belvedere Palace**, another eighteenth-century royal residence redesigned in the 1820s for the governor of Warsaw, the Czar's brother Konstantine. Official residence of Polish heads of state since the end of World War I (with a brief interlude as home of the Nazi governor Hans Frank), for the last ten years it's been used by General Jaruzelski, soon to be replaced by the country's first freely elected president in over fifty years.

The Royal Way from here slopes gently down toward the Mokotów district, passing the huge **Soviet embassy** building—its security looking a lot more relaxed these days—and the *Universus*, Warsaw's largest bookshop, at the bottom of the hill. The Royal Way then continues a few kilometers south to Wilanów, its ultimate destination.

Wilanów

The grandest of Warsaw's palaces, **Wilanów** is tucked away in almost rural surroundings on the outskirts of Warsaw, and makes an easy excursion from the city center: buses #B, #130, #180, #193, and #422 run to the station just across the road from the palace entrance. Sometimes called the Polish Versailles, it was originally the brainchild of King Jan Sobieski, who purchased the existing manor house and estate in 1677; he spent nearly twenty years turning it into his ideal country residence, which was later extended by a succession of monarchs and aristocratic families. Predictably, it suffered badly during World War II, when the Nazis stole the cream of the Wilanów art collection and tore up the park and surrounding buildings. In 1945 the palace became state property, and for eleven years was extensively renovated and its art collection refurbished. It's now a tourist favorite, and at the height of summer the welter of coach parties can make it almost impossible to get in individually. Your best bets for ensuring entry are either to get there early (as always), to go on a Sunday (theoretically the non-group visitors' day), or to swallow your pride and sign up for an Orbis tour.

The approach to the palace takes you past former outbuildings, including the smithy, the butcher's, and an **inn**, now an exclusive restaurant (see "Eating and drinking"). Also close at hand are some decent **cafés**, welcome refuges after the palace tour. The domed eighteenth-century **St Anne's Church** and ornate Potocki mausoleum across the road lead to the gates, where you buy your tickets—if the crowds are big you'll be given a wooden token telling you what time your designated group is going to be let in.

The Palace

Among the sixty-odd rooms of Wilanów's **interior** (9:30am–2:30pm; closed Tues) you'll find styles ranging from the lavish early Baroque of the apartments of Jan Sobieski and John III to the classical grace of the nineteenth-century Potocki museum rooms. Some might find the cumulative effect of all this pomp and glory rather deadening—even the official guides seem to recognize this, easing off with the facts and figures in the last part of the guided tour.

The first rooms after the entrance, among the oldest in the palace, contain a number of casket images, intended to be interred with the subject but sometimes removed from the coffin before burial. They are part of a total collection of over 250 portraits, most of which are hung in long corridor galleries—an intriguing introduction to the development of Polish fashion, with its peculiar synthesis of Western *haute couture* and Eastern influences such as shaved heads and wide sashes. If you've already visited other museums, the portrait of Jan Sobieski in the **Sobieski Family Room** will probably look familiar—the portly military hero most often crops up charging Lone Ranger-like toward a smoldering Vienna, trampling a few Turks on the way.

After Sobieski's **Library**, with its beautiful marble-tiled floor and allegorical ceiling paintings, you come to the plushest rooms of the bunch—the **Queen's Apartments**, where velvet-covered walls surround a rich collection of seventeenth-century cabinets. In frigid contrast, the **Faience Room** is clad in blue-and-white tiles and topped by a high cupola. Restoration work in the next door **Quiet Room** has uncovered seventeenth-century frescoes of preening Greek goddesses. Of the eighteenth-century rooms the most impressive is King August III's **Great Dining Hall**, complete with galleries for the royal music ensemble. The north wing of the palace mostly consists of nineteenth-century apartments, of which the grandest are the **Crimson Room**, the **Great Crimson Room**, and sections of the **Potocki Art Museum**—dominated by statuary.

The Grounds

If your interest hasn't flagged after the palace tour, there are a couple of other places of note within the grounds. The gate on the left side beyond the main entrance opens onto the stately **palace gardens** (10am till sunset). The ornate statue-topped facade overlooking the gardens contains a golden sundial that tells not just the time but also—thanks to an innovation from the Gdańsk astronomer Hevelius—the astrological sign.

The gardens reach down to the waterside, continuing rather less tidily along the lakeside to the north and south; in autumn this is a fine place for a Sunday afternoon scuffle through the falling oak leaves. Beyond the Orangery is the so-called **English Park**, whose main feature is a Chinese pavilion. Just down from the main gates is the **Poster Museum** (10am–4pm), a mish-mash of the inspired and the bizarre from an art form which has long had major currency in Poland.

The Suburbs

For most visitors anything outside the central town and Royal Way remains an unknown quantity. Visually engaging they may not be, yet some of the Warsaw **suburbs** are worth visiting both for their atmosphere and for their historic resonance, while at its remotest limits the city merges into the villages of the Mazovian countryside, with head-scarved peasants and horse-drawn carriages replacing the bustle of city life.

Zoliborz

Until the last century the **Zoliborz** district, due north of downtown, was an extension of the Kampinoski forest (the Bielany reserve in the northern reaches is a remnant), but then evolved into a blue-collar stronghold. The district's heart is the large square at the top of **ul. Mickiewicza**—the northward extension of Marsałkowska and Nowotki. Officially restored to its prewar name, **plac Wilsona** has a gritty, down-to-earth feeling that contrasts strongly with the gentrified airs of the city center. Politics are gritty here too: the tough campaign fought by local resident and veteran oppositionist Jacek Kuroń in the 1989 elections led to a sizzling confrontation with his Christian Democrat opponent before a packed audience at the old *Wisła* moviehouse on the square.

St Stanisław Kostka's Church, off to the west side of plac Wilsona, was Solidarity priest Jerzy Popiełuszko's parish church until he was murdered by security police in 1985—whereupon his church became a Solidarity sanctuary and a focus for popular opposition. Although western politicians no longer troop here, the custom of newlyweds dropping by to pay their respects at Father Jerzy's shrine continues. In the grounds there's a Via Dolorosa—a path marking the Stations of the Cross—taking you through the major landmarks of modern Polish history.

South of plac Wilsona, bordering on the New Town, is an altogether more sinister place, the **Citadel** (Cytadela). These decaying fortifications are the remains of the massive fortress built here by Czar Nicholas I in the wake of the 1831 uprising. Houses were demolished to make way for it, and Varsovians even had to pay the costs of the intended instrument of their punishment. For the next eighty years or so suspected activists were brought here for interrogation and eventual imprisonment, execution, or exile.

The large steps up the hill lead to the grim **Gate of Executions**, where partisans were shot and hanged, with particular regularity after the 1863 uprising. Uneasy with so obvious a symbol of Russian oppression and Polish nationalist aspirations, the postwar communist party attempted to present the Citadel as a "mausoleum of the Polish revolutionary, socialist and workers' movement". Thus alongside the plaque commemorating the leaders of 1863, there are memorials to the Czarist-era Socialist Party, the Polish Communist Party and "the proletariat." Part of the prison is now a **historical museum** (Tues–Sun 9am–4pm), with a few preserved cells and some harrowing pictures by former inmates depicting the agonies of Siberia. The wagon in the courtyard is a reconstruction of the vehicles used to transport the condemned to that bleak exile.

West of the Citadel across pl. Inwalidów is the grim **Museum of Struggle and Martyrdom**, al. Wojska Polskiego 25 (Wed–Sun 9am–4pm); housed in the former Gestapo headquarters, it focuses on the World War II bloodshed.

Praga

Across the river from the Old Town, the large **Praga** suburb was the main residential area for the legions of Czarist bureaucrats throughout the nineteenth century—particularly the Saska Kempa district, south of al. Waszyngtona. The **Russian Orthodox Church** just beyond Praski Park is one remaining sign of their presence. But Praga's most notorious connection with Russians stems from a later date. At the beginning of September 1944, Soviet forces reached the outer reaches of Praga. Insurrectionists from the besieged town center were dispatched to plead with them to intervene against the Nazis—to no avail. All through the Warsaw Uprising, Soviet tanks sat and waited on the edges, moving in to flush out the Nazis only when the city had been virtually eradicated. For the next forty years, the official account gave "insufficient Soviet forces" as the reason for the non-intervention; as with the Katyn massacre, every Pole knew otherwise.

On a lighter note, Warsaw's best-known and shadiest **flea market**—the Bazar Różyckiego—is five minutes' walk south from the Orthodox church on ul. Zabkowska. The claim that you can buy almost anything here for a price still holds, though with perhaps less drama than in the mid-1980s, when you could reputedly pick up the occasional contraband Kalashnikov from Afghanistan. If you do go, keep all valuables well in hand—pickpockets are numerous and skillful.

For motorists, the other main attraction of Praga may turn out to be the garages and spare-parts shops scattered round its eastern stretches: the high incidence of break-ins on unattended cars nowadays makes a hunt for passenger windows a common exercise for foreigners and Varsovians alike.

Eating and Drinking

As even the proudest Varsovians will admit, the Polish capital is still a long way short of being the gastronome's ideal habitat. Too many **restaurants** are still marred by dingy surroundings, unimaginative menus, and a lack of interest in the concept of service. That said, there are quite a few perfectly good places to eat, and the emergence of an increasing number of small, well-run private restaurants is one of the more encouraging spin-offs from the drive toward a market economy.

Cafés, by contrast, have long been favored for get-togethers, clandestine political exchanges, screaming fights, or just passing the time—though it's a café culture born of sociability rather than affluence: the never-ending economic straits mean that in most places there's not a wide range of choice when it comes to cakes and pastries.

Bars remain a largely underdeveloped phenomenon—though perhaps not for long. Alongside the old-established "drink bars," selling beer, vodka, and other hard spirits to hard-drinking locals, more sophisticated western-influenced places are starting to appear in town, aimed partly at the tourists, partly at the city's young and upwardly mobile.

Meals and Snacks

As throughout Poland, **restaurants** tend to close early. Except in the major tourist hotels you'll be lucky to get served after 9pm—and you're liable to be booted out at 10pm. Foreign-language menus are available in the hotels and pricier restaurants, but don't count on it; if you're stuck, refer to the food section in *Basics* for help with the vocabulary. Remember the basic rule that only things with prices next to them are likely to be available—even then, *niema* (there is none) is a word you'll soon get used to. Unless you're really putting on the dog, nowhere in Warsaw apart from the really top-category places is going to make a serious dent in your finances; our two categories take in "Moderate" (around $9–13 a head) and "First-class" ($13–22). For basic, cheap snacks, **milk bars** (*bar mleczny*) are a useful standby, providing a good feed for under $2.

Moderate Restaurants

Bong Sen, ul. Poznanska 12. Goodish Vietnamese restaurant on a quiet central backstreet. Open 11am–10pm. Reservations recommended (☎212-713).

Habana, ul. Piękna 28. Supposedly Cuban restaurant with very little identifiably Hispanic about it. Passable pork dishes are the mainstay, but beware the occasional evening cabaret/strip shows. Open noon–11pm.

Kamienne Schodki, Rynek Starego Miasta 25. Duck with apples is the house specialty in this simple but popular Old Town hang-out.

Kuźnia, Wiertnicza 2. Wilanów's second-string restaurant. Pork dishes are a good bet, as are the peach and pear desserts. Open 10am–11pm.

Le Petit Trianot. ul. Piwna. Traditional Polish cuisine in a small Old Town tourist trap that's beginning to nudge up into the expensive bracket.

Mekong, ul. Wspólna 35. Excellent small restaurant, owned by a Vietnamese student who stayed on. The fish dishes are definitely worth the extra twenty-minute wait. Open 10am–10pm. Reservations recommended (☎211-881).

Pod Krokodylem, Rynek Starego Miasta 19. Low ceilings and decent Polish cuisine in an Old Town venue that's a favorite with provincial Poles binging it for a weekend in the capital. Open 1pm–3am.

Phenian, ul. Senatorska 27. A passable if characterless Chinese restaurant, a short walk west from the Old Town. It gets full quickly, so turn up early, or better yet reserve (☎279-707).

Pod Retmanem, ul. Bednarska 9. Gdańsk is the theme of the decor in this popular fish-oriented restaurant. Try the house drink, *napój rajeów Gdański*, for a pleasant surprise. Open Mon–Sat 11am–10pm.

Rycerska, ul. Szeroki Dunaj 9/11. Popular Old Town venue swamped in boar's heads and suits of armor. If they're available, the lamb dishes are worth a try. Reservations are a good idea (☎313-688). Open 10am–10pm.

Sinfonia, ul. Jasna 5. The concert hall restaurant. Advantages of this relatively unknown hang-out are the grand decor, the occasional supplies of excellent Russian champagne, and opening hours till midnight.

Sofia, pl. Powstanców Warszawy. Bulgarian joint in the town center. The food is reasonable, the wines excellent. Open 11am–3pm.

Staropolska, ul. Krakowskie Przedmieście 8. Rather gloomy decor and erratic service here is offset by a good, inevitably pork-based menu. A handy place if you're in the university area. Open 5–11pm.

Szanghaj, ul. Marsałkowska 55/57. An ugly building houses Warsaw's best-known but hardly its best Chinese restaurant. The humdrum menu is backed by dubious music most evenings. Open 11am–11pm.

Złota Rybka, Nowy Świat 5/7. Cheapish, uncomplicated fish restaurant in the center of town. Open 11am–10pm.

First-Class Restaurants

Ambassador, ul. Matejki 4 (☎259-961). Luxurious establishment across the road from the US embassy. Good *zurek*, pork dishes, and Georgian mineral water—reputedly Stalin's favorite. Open 11am–11pm.

Bazyliszek, Rynek Starego Miasta (☎311-841). Traditional Polish cuisine, with an emphasis on fish (eels and carp) and game (boar and wild pig) in glamorous old-world surroundings. Open weekdays 10am–midnight, weekends 10am–1am; reservations essential.

Cristal Budapeszt, ul. Marsałkowska 21 (☎253-433). Decent Hungarian nosh and wine with a sprinkling of Polish dishes; has a folk band and dancing in the evenings. Open 11am–11pm.

Europeijski Hotel, ul. Krakowskie Przedmieście 13 (☎265-051). The smaller hotel restaurant is open 11am–9pm, the main restaurant 1pm–midnight, with dancing show and hence obligatory ticket purchase after 7pm. Dependable if unexceptional Orbis fare.

Forum Hotel, ul. Nowogrodzka 24/26 (☎210-271). Has two decent restaurants mainly for tourists, both open 7am–11am & 1pm–midnight—very useful if you arrive in town late and famished, though they like to keep you waiting however empty they are. Reservations are a good idea for larger groups.

Gessler, ul. Senatorska 37 (☎270-633). A newish restaurant that's fast become one of Warsaw's smartest and trendiest. Gourmet European cuisine in demure surroundings. Prices are among the highest in town. Open 10am till late. Reservations definitely advisable.

Lers, Długa 29 (☎635-3888). Within walking distance of the Old Town and much frequented by wealthier tourist groups—which is why a reservation is essential in summer.

Parnas, ul. Krakowskie Przedmieście 4/6 (☎260-071). Posh new Greek restaurant and coffee house.

Szecherezada, ul Zajązkowska 11(☎410-296). New Syrian place, giving Warsaw its first taste of Middle Eastern cuisine.

Victoria Hotel, ul. Królewska (☎278-011). Contains two well-established luxury eateries, the *Canaletto* and the *Hetmańska*, both open 1pm–midnight. The former is one of the best Orbis places in town, with a good line in traditional fowl and game dishes. Reservations essential at weekends.

Wilanów, Wiertnicza 27 (☎421-363). Right outside Wilanów palace. Exclusive and expensive joint frequented by diplomats—many of whom live nearby—and visiting dignitaries. The "old Polish" spread is good, the waiters among the most obsequious you'll ever encounter. Reservations essential.

Zajazd Napoleoński, ul. Płowiecka 83 (☎153-068). Small exclusive Praga restaurant, housed in an inn where Napoleon is supposed to have stayed en route for Moscow. Popular with the smart set. Reservations essential. Open late.

Milk Bars, Snack Bars and Other Cheap Eateries

Ariosto, ul. Poznańska 4. Small and cheap with good, fast lunchtime service.

Bambola, ul. Wspólna 27. Nice pizzeria, with seventeen kinds of pizza to eat in or take away.

Café Pinguin, al. Jerozolimskie 42. Quick-service restaurant offering regular meat-and-potatoes-type lunches.

Expres, ul. Bracka 20. A tiny private operation offering efficient lunch service, but it gets very full around midday.

Victor, ul. Kostancińska 3. New privately run milk bar.

Economistów, Nowy Świat 49. Basic student cafeteria that's as economical as its name suggests. The *barszcz* and chicken dishes are both recommended.

Max, ul. Poznańska 38. Small private bar serving good Arab grub, particularly kebabs and shashlik; close to the central station.

Murżynem, ul. Nowomeijska 13. A good basic spaghetti and pizza house just north of the Old Town square.

Pod Barbakanem, ul. Mostowa 29. Deservedly popular New Town milk bar near the Barbakan, where you can sit outside and watch the crowds.

Pod Gołebami, ul. Piwna. Slightly upmarket Old Town bistro, popular with tourists.

Uniwersytecki, Krakowskie Przedmieście 20. Milk bar much frequented by students; just up from the university gates.

Wygodna, ul. Rutkowskiego 23. Another unpretentious lunchtime restaurant in a useful central shopping location.

Zodiak, ul. Widok 26. Basic town center cafeteria to fill yourself up at lunchtime. Just across from the *Forum* hotel.

Cafés and Bars

Cafés are usually enjoyable in Warsaw, though, as stressed earlier, interest is as much social as gastronomic. In the better-stocked places, the things to ask for are *ciastka* (cakes) and *cukiernia* (sweets); when available, they tend to be excellent. The Hortex cocktail bars (nothing to do with alcohol) are known for some of the best ice creams in town—besides the *Jezuicka* (see below), there's also one at ul. Swiętokrzyska 35 and on plac Konstytucji.

Most of the **bars** are of the archetypal Polish "drink bar" variety. If you don't fancy their atmosphere, hotel bars are always an option; for a good general choice try the places along Krakowskie Przedmieście, the main street south from the Old Town. And if seedy drink bars really do appeal, you'll find a number of them at the top end of ul. Freta, in the New Town.

Cafés

Bowta, ul. Freta. A really nice café at which to sit outside and write postcards while enjoying the New Town square.

Café Columbia, al. Jerozolimskie 42. A center-town joint serving respectable coffee and *ciastka* in rather funereal surroundings.

Danusia, al. Jerozolimskie 57. A cosy little morning coffee shop, next door to the British Institute, close to the main station.

Eljat, al. Ujazdowskie, near pl. Trzech Krzyzy. Small, friendly café owned by the Polish-Israeli friendship society

Harenda, ul. Oboźna 4. Student hang-out.

Jezuicka, Rynek Starego Miasto 15, below the *Bazyliszek* restaurant. A busy Old Town rendezvous. The creamy *ciastka* desserts and ice creams are good, the service unpredictable.

Manekin, Rynek Starego Miasto 27. An enjoyable basement coffee dive on the Old Town square, with a bar at the back.

Nowy Świat, Nowy Świat 17. Venerable prewar café with a mixed clientele of students, tourists, and old folk.

Pod Krokodyl, Rynek Starego Miasto 19. Popular Old Town café-restaurant.

Polonia, al. Jerozolimskie 45. The hotel's *cukiernia* is a nice central stop-off with a good selection of cakes, ice creams and desserts.

U Pana Michała, ul. Freta. Small, rather sedate coffee shop in the New Town.

Bars

Europeijski, Krakowskie Przedmieście 13. In summer the hotel's terrace café is one of the nicest places in town to sit out and enjoy an early evening drink.

Pod Herbami, ul. Piwna 21/23. An archetypal "drink bar"—but one that hip young Varsovians now like to be seen in.

Hacienda, ul. Freta 18. Near the Barbakan. Student pizza joint doubling as a bar.

Studio M, Krakowskie Przedmieście 27. Trendy, expensive designer bar frequented by arty types—there's even a small gallery. Open till 1am.

Na Trakcie, Krakowskie Przedmieście 47. Popular bar with ritzy background muzak, open late. Serves food, too.

U Hopfera, Krakowskie Przedmieście 55. Wine-bar-restaurant that's a favorite with students, but closes at 10pm.

U Fukiera, Rynek Starego Miasta 27. Smoky traditional wine bar on the square, complete with gypsy band.

Nightlife

If Chopin concerts and intense avant-garde dramas are your idea of a good night on the town, you're unlikely to be disappointed by Warsaw **nightlife**; in summer especially, high-quality theater productions, operas and recitals abound, many of them as popular with tourists as with Varsovians themselves. At the other end of the scale there's the schmaltzy nightclub/cabaret scene centered on the big hotels, a bigger pull for businessmen and prostitutes than for your average customer. There's still very little in between—in other words, the sort of places that would appeal to the average fun-loving visitor's idea of a genuine club. Best places for a good bop are the student clubs downtown.

For up-to-date **information** on what's happening, check the back pages of the weekly English-language newspaper *The Warsaw Voice* and the listings in *Wik* magazine, the equivalent of, say, the *LA Reader*. You can buy both at most *ruch*.

Regular Warsaw **festivals** include the excellent annual **Jazz Jamboree** in October (Miles Davis featuring among recent artists), the biennial **Warsaw Film Festival**, the **Festival of Contemporary Music** held every September, and the five-yearly **Chopin Piano Competition**—always a launch-pad for a major international career. The **October Film Week**, organized by the *Hybrydy* club, is a vaguely alternative arts event.

Clubs and Gigs

Warsaw's few decent clubs have been feeling the economic pinch in recent years, and the same goes for the night scene generally—appearances by major western bands are still a rarity. When artists with the pulling power of Stevie Wonder do turn up, they generally play outdoors at the large **Dziesięciolecia** stadium in Praga, near the river.

Except for the big names, the touring circuit for **Polish bands** is confined to student clubs and the occasional one-shot festival. **Jazz clubs** are scarce, a pity in view of the number of excellent local jazz musicians, some of them international figures—such as Zbigniew Namysłowski (tenor sax) and Tomas Stanko (trumpet). As a rule, **discos** are tacky, Europop affairs, frequented by a combination of young reticents and inveterate drunkards. Most of the clubs listed below are known as student venues, though students aren't the only customers.

Akwarium, ul. Emilii Plater 49 (☎205-072). Just behind the Palace of Culture. The only genuine jazz club in town, it has at least one good Polish or foreign act a week. The MTV screen in the café downstairs attracts the Warsaw trendies. Unfortunately it's still plagued by early closing restrictions.

Centrum, Marszałkowska. Upstairs in the shopping center immediately north of the *Forum* hotel. A taste of the archetypal Polish-style disco—if you can get past the bouncer.

Hybrydy, ul. Kniewskiego 7/9. Behind the *Centrum* department store on Marsałkowska. Weekend discos with a decent beat, a "Rap-Club" and occasional live gigs.

Park, al. Niepodległosci 196. In the Piłsudski park, southwest of the town center. Regular late-night dancing; some live bands, too.

Remont, ul. Warynskiego 12. Best of the student clubs, with regular rock, folk and jazz concerts, discos—and weekly Hare Krishna meditation sessions.

Stodola, ul. Batorego 10. Ten minutes' walk from the *Park*. Lively spot at weekends, with a late disco.

Opera and Concerts

Opera is a big favorite in Warsaw, and classical concerts—especially anything with a piano in it (preferably Chopin)—tend to attract big audiences, so it's always advisable to book. Tickets for many concerts are available from the theater ticket office (Kasa Teatralny) at al. Jerozolimskie 25, a little along from the *Forum* hotel (Mon–Thurs 9:30am–5:30pm, Fri closes 5pm; ☎219-454/383).

Filharmonia, ul. Jasna 5. Regular performances by the excellent National Philharmonic Orchestra and visiting ensembles. Tickets from the box office at ul. Sienkiewicza 12.

Academia Muszyczna, ul. Okólnik 2. Regular concerts by talented students.

Chopin Museum, ul. Okólnik 1. Piano recitals and other occasional performances.

Evangelical Church, pl. Małachowskiego. Focus on organ and choral music, often with visiting choirs.

Łazienki Park, al. Ujazdowskie. Varied summer program of orchestral, choral and chamber concerts, often held in the Orangery.

Opera Kameralna, Swierczewskiego 76b (☎312-240). Chamber opera performances in a magnificent white and gold stucco auditorium. Watch out for the Mozart bicentennial season in 1991.

Teatr Wielki, pl. Teatralny (☎263-288). The big opera performances—everything from Mozart to works by contemporary Polish composers such as Moniuszko and Penderecki, in suitably grandiose surroundings. Tickets bookable by phone.

Theater and Movies

Theater is one of the most popular and artistically strong forms of entertainment in Warsaw. Not speaking Polish is of course an obstacle, but for the acting style alone it's worth considering a performance at one of the major theaters such as the *Atenaeum*, ul. Jaracza 2, the *Kameralny*, ul. Folksal 15, or the *Powszechny*, ul. Zamoyskiego 20. There is usually quite a range of productions on offer— translations of Shakespeare, adaptations of classical European drama, and some remarkable home-grown avant-garde.

The traditional mixture in Warsaw's **movie theaters** of "safe" western pictures, Eastern European art movies, and home-grown hits is gradually broadening toward a more varied western selection, including soft porn—much to the church's horror. As on television, subtitling rather than dubbing is the rule. Places with regular showings of **foreign films** include the *Atlantic* and *Non-Stop*, both at ul. Rutkowskiego 33, the *Relax*, ul. Kniewskego 8, and the *Polonia* at Marsałkowska 56.

Gay Warsaw

Gay nightlife has a difficult time in today's Catholic-dominated political climate. Nonetheless, **Warsaw Gay News** has recently been founded, and now publishes an English edition and organizes gay events on a regular basis. It is distributed by an agency called **Pink Service** (9am–5pm; ☎213-227), whose activities include distributing condoms and gay magazines, running a Gay Pride Day, organizing discos in the *Café Fiolka*, and providing a "full tourist service for lesbian and gay visitors"—including arranging accommodation and guides.

The gay **student group**, *Słowazyszenie Grup Lambda*, also welcomes contact and runs a semi-underground club; their address is Uniwersytet Warszawski, ul. Krakowskie Przedmieście 24, 00325 Warszawa.

Shopping

Shopping in Warsaw is a strange experience these days. While shops are being sold off to the highest bidders, political change has brought a significant part of the city's economic life onto the streets themselves, with the throng of vendors making the whole city center seem like one extended market. Not only is trading more energetic than it used to be—generating a sometimes uneasy hustle—but there's also been a widening in the range of goods on offer. Bananas and other exotic fruits, for instance, were virtually unobtainable a short time ago, but can now be picked up for western prices on any central street corner. General goods, too—whether books, records, clothes, or electrical items—are also available in unprecedented plenty—at a price.

Clothes, Crafts, and Hard-Currency Shops

The boutiques at the northern end of Marsałkowska and the streets east of the Palace of Culture are the places to hunt for **clothes**, shoes, and general finery. It's also worth looking in at the big department stores of Marsałkowska for clothes, and women might turn up something at the *Moda Polska* department store on ul. Swiętokrzyska—particularly items like winter coats and hats. Another bargain are handmade shoes, made to high quality by cobblers like the one just below pl. Trzech Krzyzy on al. Ujazdowskie.

Quality and taste is variable at the *Cepelia* **handicraft shops** scattered around town. The biggest is at Marsałkowska 99/101, where you can find wooden boxes and the occasional bit of attractive jewelry. *Polski Len* shops, like the one on ul. Targowa, are worth checking for linen (always 100 percent pure).

Hard-currency *Baltona* and *Pewex* shops aren't quite as important as they used to be, given the increased availability of western goods, but they're still useful for alcohol, tobacco, confectionery, and luxury goods as well as basic items like toothpaste and toothbrushes. You'll find them in the big hotels and at other locations all over town, such as in the *LOT*/Marriot building on al. Jerozolimskie (Mon–Fri 8am–8pm, Sat 8am–4pm).

Books, Cards, and Records

For **books**, the *antiquariats* scattered around the Old Town and central shopping area sometimes produce gems, especially in the art field. Several contemporary bookshops, like the huge *Universus* store at ul. Belwederska 20/22 or the ones in the Palace of Culture, are also worth checking out. The best selection of art **post-cards**, old and new, is in the shop at ul. Nowomeijska 17, near the Barbakan.

Records and **cassettes** are more unpredictable. Really good buys like Chopin boxed sets on the state labels are incredibly hard to get hold of, precisely because they are so good. Selections in the bigger stores, like those on Nowy Świat, are still pretty limited, though for rock music they're now rivaled by the ranks of street entrepreneurs trading in the latest Western sounds, particularly pirated cassettes of varying quality.

Galleries

The commercial galleries scattered around the city center range from the arty to the downright tacky, with the biggest concentrations on Marsałkowska and Krakowskie Przedmieście. *Piotr Nowicki's*, on Nowy Świat, has a good range of modern jewelry, but ignore the paintings. *Desa*, the state-run art and antique outlet, has places all over town: the art at their gallery across the street from *Nowicki's* is worth looking over, as is *Zapiecek* in the Old Town on ul. Zapiecek. The *Dziekanka* and *Kordegarda* galleries on Krakowskie Przedmieście often have interesting exhibitions, as does the *Folksal* gallery in the regal-looking building on the corner of ul. Folksal and Nowy Świat. Another particularly well-known gallery is the *Zachęta* at pl. Malachowskiego 3, just below the Saxon Gardens.

Markets and Bazaars

At weekends, traditional market areas like the **Hala Mirowska** are now packed with stalls and worth visiting for the atmosphere alone. There are also a few established specialist **markets** worth exploring:

Różycki market, Praga (see the "Praga" section). The ranks of Polish and gypsy traders here are swelled these days by increasing numbers of Romanians and Russians—a Warsaw experience not to be missed. All day, every day.

Koło bazaar, ul. Obozowa, in the Wola district (near the end of tram lines #1, #13 and #24). The main antiques and bric-a-brac market, with everything from sofas and old Russian samovars to a genuine Iron Cross available. Sunday.

Ciuchy bazaar, Rembertów, in the south of the Praga district. Look for clothes bargains.

Food market, ul. Polna. If you want avocados or papayas and still can't find them on street stalls, this where the affluent stock up, diplomats included.

Night Shopping

For anyone caught short of a bottle of vodka for an impromptu party, or just desperate for a late-night snack, the following shops will be useful.

Michel Badre, Puławska 53, in Mokotów. A newly opened French establishment open round the clock, selling *baguettes*, beer, champagne, western newspapers, and so on at French prices.

German shop, corner of al. Niepodlegosci and Wawelska. Similar style to the above—substituting Deutsch for Français.

Sklepy Noczne (Night Shops) are at: Grójecka 86 (8am–1pm); ul. Puławska at the corner of ul. Dolna (*Max*; 8pm–2am); al. Swierczewskiego 72 and ul. Targowa 26/30 (*Hala Czluchowska*; 8pm–2am); Przy Agorze 22 (8pm–3am); ul. Targowa (*Kijowanka;* 8pm–6am).

Listings

Airlines The *LOT* building at al. Jerozolimskie 65/79 (☎305-192) makes reservations for domestic and foreign flights, as do all the major Orbis offices. All the big international airlines have offices in the city, mainly on ul. Krucza, ul. Szpitalna and ul. Marsałkowska, as well as reservations desks at Okęcie airport.

Airport Information Domestic airport ☎469-750/70; Okęcie international airport ☎461-731/70.

Autoclub The main office of *PZmot*, the Polish automobile association, is at al. Jerozolimskie 63. Twenty-four-hour breakdown service, run by *PZmot*, is at ul. Kaszubska 2b (☎981 or ☎416-621/410-423). The *Polmozbyt* breakdown service at ul. Omulewska 27 in southern Praga is open 6am–10pm (☎954). Both should be able to track down mechanics for most western makes of car. For spare parts, the *Baltona* shop at ul. Radzymińska 78 in Praga is a good starting point (Mon–Sat 10am–6pm; ☎195-554).

British Institute Al. Jerozolimskie 59 (Mon–Fri 8:30am–5:30pm; ☎287-401); the library has English-language newspapers.

Bus Departures and Tickets The main bus station, Dworzec Centralny Warszawa Zachodnia, out west on al. Jerozolimskie, is for all international departures and for major national destinations south and west. Dworzec Stadion, next to the Praga train station on the line from Dw. Sródmiescie, is for northern and eastern destinations. International bus tickets are available from the main station, from the Orbis office at ul. Puławska 43 (Mon–Fri 9am–4pm) and from the PMKS bureau at ul. Żurawia 26. National bus tickets are available at the appropriate station or from the Syrena office at ul. Krucza 16/22.

Car Rental Orbis rental service, ul. Nowogrodzka 27 (Mon–Sat 8am–8pm; ☎293-875).

Embassies *Australia*, ul. Estońska 3/5 (☎176-081); *Austria*, ul. Gagarina 34, (☎410-081); *Belgium*, ul. Senatorska 34 (☎270-233); *Bulgaria*, al. Ujazdowskie 33/35 (☎294-071); *Canada*, ul. Piękna 2/8 (☎298-051); *Czechoslovakia*, ul. Koszykowa 18 (☎287-221); *Denmark*, ul. Starościńska 5 (☎490-056); *Finland*, ul. Chopina 4/8 (☎294-091); *France*, ul. Piękna 1 (☎288-401); *Germany*, ul. Dąbrowiecka 30 (☎173-011); *Israel*, ul. Krzywickiego 24 (☎250-023); *Italy*, pl. Dąbrowskiego 6 (☎263-471); *Netherlands*, ul. Rakowiecka 19 (☎492-351); *Norway*, ul. Chopina 2a (☎214-231); *Romania*, ul. Chopina 10 (☎283-156); *Sweden*, ul. Bagatela 3 (☎493-351); *UK*, al. Róz 1 (☎281-001/5); *USA*, al. Ujazdowskie 29 (☎283-041/9); *USSR*, ul. Belwederska 49 (☎213-453).

Emergencies Police ☎997; fire ☎998; ambulance ☎999 or ☎282-424.

Hitchhiking The *Biuro Autostop*, ul. Narbutta 27a (Mon–Fri 9am–4pm), has English-language information about the ins and outs of hitching in Poland, and sells maps and auto-stop coupons.

Laundromat Ul. Mordechai Anieliwicza, on corner of the Ghetto monument square; bus #180 passes right by (Mon–Fri 9am–7pm, Sat 9am–4pm).

Lost and Found On city transport, ul. Słowackiego 45. Otherwise the offices at ul. Floriańska 10 and ul. Wery Kostrzewy 11.

Maps The IT on plac Zamkowy and the *Atlas* bookshop at ul. Marchlewskiego 26 have the best selection of Polish maps.

Medical Attention *Central Medical Center*, ul. Hoża 56.

Money Any of the *kantors*, tourist offices, or hotels can change money. Orbis accepts traveler's checks, but they may try to extract a ten-percent commission, so a hotel can be a better bet. The *National Bank* at ul. Świętokrzyska 11/21 can help with transferring money from abroad, though this (like all other transactions) can take a long time.

Newspapers You can now find yesterday's and occasionally the same day's editions of western newspapers like *The Herald Tribune, Le Monde, The Times*, and *The European*, as well as mainstream magazines like *Time* and *Newsweek*, in major hotel lobbies, plus the *Kodak* "Fast Film" photo shops in the *Centrum Shopping Center* on Marszałkowska and in the Old Town, and the *Fuji* shops on ul. Bagatela and in the Old Town. For Polish news, two English-language weeklies are indispensable: the Solidarity-sponsored *Gazeta International* and *The Warsaw Voice*.

Parking Hotel parking lots aside, the multistory parking lot on the appropriately named ul. Parkingowa, behind the *Forum* hotel, is the safest place in the center (hard currency only).

Pharmacies All-night *apteka* at ul. Zielna 45, ul. Freta 13, ul. Leszno 38, ul. Zeromskiego 13 and ul. Puławska 39. For homeopathic treatments try ul. Miła 33 and Marsałkowska 11a.

Post Offices Main offices are at ul. Świętokrzyska 31/33 and in the main train station; both open 24hr for telephones, 8am–8pm for post. Both provide *poste restante*: Warsaw 1 is the code number for the former, Warsaw 120 for the latter.

Train Stations and Tickets The central station serves all international routes and the major national ones—Poznań, Kraków, Gdańsk, Lublin, etc. Northbound trains also stop at Warszawa Gdańska (ul. Buczka 4), west- and southbound at Warszawa Zachodnia (ul. Towarowa 1), eastbound at Warszawa Wschodnia (ul. Lubelska 1). Śródmiescie station, just east of the central station, handles local traffic—Łowicz, Pruszkow, Skierniewice, etc.

For **international tickets**, booking at least 24hr in advance is essential, and in summer 2–3 days advance reservation is the minimum requirement on popular lines—which means pretty much all of them. An alternative to long lines at the station's *kasa międznarodowa* (international counters) is to reserve at Orbis offices, and the same goes for domestic tickets; the offices at ul. Bracka 16, pl. Konstytucji 4, ul. Swiętojańska 23/25 and upstairs in the *Metropol* hotel on Marsałkowska all sell international and domestic tickets. The *Wagon Lits Tourisme* office, Nowy Świat, sells tickets for Western European destinations.

Swimming Pools In summer a number of crowded and over-chlorinated open-air pools are functioning at: ul. Gorczewska 69/73, Namysłowska 8, ul. Puławska 101, ul. Racłaicka 132, ul. Wawelska 5, and at the Gwardia stadium. Indoor pools at the *Victoria, Holiday Inn, Novotel* and *Solec* hotels charge a fee to non-guests, but you might be able to bluff your way in.

Youth Hostels The central office of *PTSM*, the Polish youth hostel federation, is at ul. Chocimska 28, fourth floor, room 423 (Mon–Fri 8am–3pm); they produce a book listing hostels all over Poland.

MAZOVIA

The attractions of **Mazovia**—the plain surrounding Warsaw—are outlined briefly in the introduction to this chapter. If time is limited, then at least take a break outside the city in the beautiful forest of the **Kampinoski National Park**, or to Chopin's birthplace at **Zelazowa Wola**. Southwest of the capital, the great manufacturing city of **Łódź** offers a major dose of culture. Other towns south of Warsaw are less inviting, and industrial centers such as **Skierniewice** and **Radom** are likely to be low on most people's priorities.

Just about everywhere covered in the following section can be reached from Warsaw on **local buses and trains**, though prospective day-trippers to the forest will need to watch out for erratic evening bus services back to the city. Łódź is particularly well served by regular express trains, making a day's outing from Warsaw an easy option.

The Kampinoski National Park

With its boundaries touching the edge of Warsaw's Zoliborz suburb, the Puszcza Kampinoska—or **Kampinoski National Park**—stretches some thirty kilometers west of the capital. An ideal retreat, this open forest harbors the summer houses of numerous Varsovians, and in autumn is a favored weekend haunt for legions of mushroom-pickers. As with all national parks, the forest's nature reserves are carefully controlled to help preserve the rich plant and animal life— elks and wild boars are sighted from time to time—but access for walkers is pretty much unrestricted. Beware that it's all too easy to get lost in the woods, so unless your navigation skills are Scout standard, stick to marked routes: signposts at the edge of the forest show clearly the main paths.

Truskaw and Palmiry

Bus #708 from the Marymont bus station in northern Zoliborz takes you out to **TRUSKAW**, a small village about 10km from town on the eastern edge of the forest. From here it's a pleasant five-kilometer walk to the hamlet of **PALMIRY**, along sandy paths that seem a world removed from the bustle of the city—as do the villages, where children stare at passers-by as much as in the remoter parts of the country. People in the scattered older houses will give you well-water if you ask, and may even part with a jar of the excellent local honey for a price.

The forest's proximity to town made it a center of resistance activity—notably during the 1863 uprising and World War II—and also made it an obvious killing ground for the Nazis. The war cemetery that you pass on this walk contains the bodies of about 2000 prisoners and civilians, herded out to the forest, shot, and hurled into pits. To get back into Warsaw, walk the one-kilometer track north from Palmiry to the main road bus stop and take any bus to Marymont station.

Zaborów, Leszno, and Kampinos

If you're feeling more adventurous, you can head farther into the forest from the villages of **ZABORÓW**, **LESZNO**, or **KAMPINOS**, all of which are sited along the main road that skirts the southern edge of the forest on its way to Zelazowa Wola (see below). To get to them, take a blue regional bus from the Dworzec Zachodnia bus station.

A number of walking options suggest themselves. An obvious one is to get off at Leszno and take the marked forest path to Kampinos, a good twelve-kilometer walk in all (17km from Zaborów), or do the same route in the opposite direction. An advantage of the latter course is that the PTTK hostel and the *GS* hotel in Kampinos both have basic **restaurants** in which to fortify yourself before heading off. Walk north through the village on the marked path and you're soon in the swampy edges of the forest; in summer you'll need to watch out for the particularly bloodthirsty mosquitoes, but the forest itself is a treat, with acres of undisturbed woodland and only very occasional human company. Unless you plan to stay overnight in Kampinos, start out early from Warsaw, as return buses stop at about 6pm, after which the only option is taxi, charging double rates for journeys outside the city.

Zelazowa Wola

Fifty kilometers west of Warsaw, just beyond the western edge of the Kampinoski Forest, is the little village of **ZELAZOWA WOLA**, the birthplace of composer and national hero **Fraderyk Chopin**. The journey through the rolling Mazovian countryside makes an enjoyable day trip from the city: unless you've got a car, you should either sign up with an Orbis excursion, or make the hour-long bus journey from the main bus station (direction Sochaczew).

The house where Chopin was born is now a **museum** (May–Sept Tues–Fri & Sun 10am–5:30pm, Sat 10am–2:30pm; Oct–April Tues–Fri & Sun 10am–4pm, Sat 10am–2:30pm) surrounded by a large garden. The Chopin family lived here for only a year after their son's birth in 1810, but young Fraderyk returned frequently until his departure from the country at the age of twenty, after the suppression of the 1831 uprising. In permanent exile, he transformed the folk forms of the mazurka and the polonaise into high art, writing dozens of piano pieces which have acquired the emotional resonance of anthems in his native country. Lyrical, melancholic, and passionate, his music was described by Schumann as being like "guns hidden in flowerbeds"—an observation that many would find applicable to the national character.

The house itself is a typical *dwór*, the traditional country residence of the *szlacter* (gentleman) class, numerous examples of which can be found all over rural Poland—Mazovia and Małopolska in particular. All the rooms have been restored to period perfection, and contain a collection of family portraits and other Chopin memorabilia, including musical manuscripts and a cast of his left hand. The Sunday **piano recitals** held in the music room in summer are a popular tourist attraction: concerts are held from June to September at 11am and 3pm (check *Wik* magazine for details), and are included in the Orbis tour. Nearby there's a tourist-orientated restaurant for a quick bite before the return journey.

Łowicz and Around

At first sight **ŁOWICZ**, thirty-odd kilometers southwest of Zelazowa Wola, looks like just any other small, concrete-ridden central Polish town, but this apparently drab place is in fact a well-established center of folk art and craft. The ideal time to come here is at **Corpus Christi** (late May/early June)—or, failing that, one of the other major church festivals—when many of the women turn out in beautiful handmade traditional costumes for the procession to the collegiate church. Wearing full skirts, embroidered cotton blouses, and colorful headscarves, they are followed by neat lines of young girls preparing for their first Communion. The crowds gathered in the main square might well contain a sizable contingent of camera-clicking foreigners, but they are never numerous enough to ruin the event's character and sense of tradition.

Łowicz is a ninety-minute train journey from Warsaw; there's a regular local service from Śródmiescie station. The old **Rynek**, ten minutes from the station, is the pivot of the town, along with the vast **Collegiate Church**, a brick fifteenth-century construction, remodeled to its present form in the mid-seventeenth century. Size apart, its most striking features are the richly decorated tombstones of the archbishops of Gniezno, and the ornate series of Baroque chapels. The other attraction is the **local museum** across the square (Tues–Sun 10am–3:30pm), housed in a missionary college designed by Tylman of Gameren. It contains an extensive and carefully presented collection of regional folk artifacts, including furniture, pottery, tools, and costumes whose basic styles are the same as those still worn on feast days. Many houses contain examples of the distinctive colored cut-out decorations on display in the museum too. The back of the museum is a kind of mini-*skansen*, containing two old cottages complete with their original furnishings.

For an overnight stay, the only real options are the basic *Turystyczny* **hotel** at ul. Sienkiewicza 1, south of the main square, and the **youth hostel** at ul. Poznańska 30 (June–July). The hotel has a passable restaurant, otherwise try the *Polonia* in the main square—but don't expect too much.

Arkadia and Nieborów

A short distance east of Łowicz are a couple of sights—a park and a palace—redolent of the bygone Polish aristocracy. They combine for an easy and enjoyable day trip, or, for those into a village stay, a night's stopover.

Arkadia Park

The eighteenth-century **Arkadia Park** is as wistfully romantic a spot as you could wish for an afternoon stroll. Conceived by Princess Helen Radziwiłł as an "ancient monument to beautiful Greece," the classical park is dotted with lakes and walkways, a jumble of reproduction classical temples and pavilions, a sphinx and a mock-Gothic house that wouldn't look out of place in a Roger Corman production. Its air of decay adds to the evocation of an age, only fifty years past, consigned firmly to history.

The park lies about 4km from Łowicz down the Skierniewice road—reached by local bus from the station in the north of town.

Nieborów

The Arkadia bus continues on for 6km to the village of **NIEBORÓW**, whose country **palace** was designed by the ever-present Tylman of Gameren and owned for most of its history, like the park, by the powerful Radziwiłł clan—just one of dozens this family possessed right up until World War II. Now part of the National Museum, the Nieborów palace is one of the handsomest and best-maintained in the country, surrounded by outbuildings and a manicured **park and gardens**.

The palace **interior** (Tues–Sun 10am–3:30pm), restored after the war, is furnished on the basis of the original eighteenth- and nineteenth-century contents of the main rooms—a lavish restoration that makes you wonder whether Polish communists suffered from a kind of ideological schizophrenia. Roman tombstones and sculptural fragments fill a lot of space downstairs, gathered about the palace's prize exhibit, the **Nieborów Apollo**; the grandest apartments (including a library with a fine collection of globes) are on the first floor, reached by a staircase clad in nicely decorated Delft tiles. It all has an air, these days, of studied aristocratic respectability, somewhat belying Radziwiłł history. Karol Radziwiłł, for example, head of the dynasty in the late eighteenth century, used to hold vast banquets in the course of which he'd drink himself into a stupor, and, as often as not, kill someone in a brawl. He would then, as Adam Zamoyski puts it, "stumble into his private chapel and bawl himself back to sobriety by singing hymns"—a far cry from today's genteel environment, which in the spring is host to a much publicized series of **classical concerts** by international artists.

For overnighters Nieborów village offers a small regional-style *Jagusia* **restaurant**, a seasonal **youth hostel** (May–Sept) and a PTTK **campground**. There are springwaters, too, and a sanitarium for those who come to imbibe.

Łódź

Mention **ŁÓDŹ** (pronounced "Woudj") to many Poles and all you'll get is a grimace. Poland's second city is certainly no beauty, but it does have an important place in the country's development—and a unique atmosphere that grows on you the longer you stay. First mentioned in the fourteenth century, at the end of the 1700s it was still an obscure little town of fewer than 200 inhabitants. All this changed rapidly with the industrial revolution, however, and in 1820 Łódź was officially designated a new industrial center of the Congress Kingdom of Poland. Development was rapid, particularly in the textile sector, and by the end of the century the urban proletariat had swelled to over 300,000. Industrialization also brought politicization: by the end of the nineteenth century Łódź, like other new cities such as Białystok, had become a center of working-class and anti-Czarist agitation.

Known popularly as the "Polish Manchester," Łódź is still an important manufacturing center, and much of the city remains unchanged—the tall chimneys and slum buildings, the grand homes of the industrialists, the philanthropic societies, the theaters and art galleries. It was the ready-made location for Andrzej Wajda's *The Promised Land*, a brilliant depiction of life in industrial nineteenth-century Poland, based on the novel by Nobel prize-winning author Władysław Reymont.

In one important respect, though, Łódź, like Warsaw, is a specter of its former self. By the 1930s, **Jews** made up around one-third of the city's 600,000 population, their number including several mill-owning families—the best-known being the Poznańskis, whose luxurious homes now house many of the city's institutions. The Jewish contribution to the cultural life of the city was immense, two of the Ghetto's most famous sons being the great pianist Artur Rubinstein and the poet Julian Tłumin. The Ghetto was liquidated in 1943, when its remaining inhabitants were deported to the death camps.

International business and trade fairs account for most of Łódź's visitors, but its cultural scene is pretty lively as well. The orchestra is one of the best in the country, and there's an impressive array of theaters, art galleries, and opera houses here. The Łódź film school is also internationally renowned, attracting aspiring movie-makers aiming to follow in the footsteps of alumni such as Wajda, Polanski, Kieslowski, and Zanussi.

Arriving and Finding a Place to Stay

The main **train station** (Łódź Fabryczna) and bus station are next to each other in the town center. When taking a train to Łódź, check that it's going to Fabryczna rather than the Chojny or Kaliska stations, both of which are well out of the city center. The **IT office** across from the main station at ul. Narutowicza 27/29 has a good supply of maps and information, and is generally helpful.

The top-bracket **hotels** are the Orbis-run *Grand*, ul. Piotrowska 72 (☎339-920); the nearby *Savoy*, ul. Traugutta 6 (☎329-360); the plush *Centrum*, ul. Kilinskiego 59/63 (☎328-640); and the *Polonia*, ul. Natutowicza 38 (☎328-773). Cheaper possibilities are the *Mazowiecki*, southwest of the center at ul. Hutora 53/57 (☎328-325); and the *Zajazd na Rogach*, ul. Łupkowa 10/16—again well out of town (☎574-616). Another low-cost alternative is the tourist lodge at ul. Skrzydlata 75, a spartan set of log cabins in the middle of the woods north of town (bus #56). The **youth hostel** at ul. Zamenhofa 13 is open all year. If the IT office can't help with **private rooms**, try the office at pl. Wolności 10/11. The **campground** is at ul. Rzgowska 247 near the Chojny station (tram #2, #4 or #5).

The City

The first sight for visitors arriving at Łódź Fabryczna—the central train station—is the **Orthodox Church** across the road; once used by the city's Russian rulers, it's a good example of late nineteenth-century Orthodox architecture, and something of a rarity in central Poland. A couple of blocks to the west from here you'll find yourself on ul. Piotrowska, which bisects the city from north to south. Most of Łódź's sights are located on or around this avenue.

Plac Koscielny, the old market square at the north end of Piotrowska, is dominated by the twin brick towers of the neo-Gothic **Church of the Ascension**.

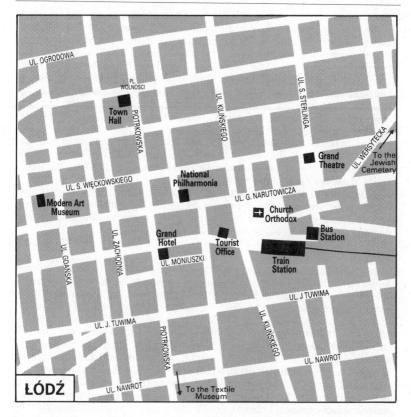

Continue south and you're soon on plac Wolności, with its Neoclassical town hall, regulation Kościuszko statue, and **Ethnographic Museum** (Tues–Sun 10am–4pm), which has a wide-ranging collection of local artifacts, costumes, and archaeological finds.

A few blocks farther on and off to the right is the **Modern Art Gallery** at ul. Więckowskiego 36 (Tues–Sun 10am–4pm), installed in a mock-Renaissance palace—complete with stained glass windows—which once belonged to the Poznański textile clan. Founded in 1925, when it was one of the world's first museums devoted to the avant-garde, it is the finest modern art collection in the country (though it also contains some earlier pieces). Major artists represented include Chagall, Picasso, Paul Klee, Max Ernst, and Fernand Léger, but there's also an excellent selection of work by Polish modern painters such as Strzeminski (quite a revelation if you've not come upon his work before), Wojchekowski, Witkowski, Witkiewicz, and the Jewish artist Jakiel Adler. From a memorable collection of Stalinist-era socialist realism, the lower-floor displays move on to the 1960s and 70s, where for some reason British artists are strongly represented. The ground floor includes an assortment of "events" by contemporary artists—color effects, bricks, rotating boxes and other everyday objects—guaranteed to provoke mirth and infuriate purists.

Łódź is a city dominated by its manufacturing origins, its main architectural features being industrial buildings constructed during the main period of economic expansion. The style is eclectic: huge factories with Gothic facades like the still operational *Poznański* plant at ul. Ogrodowa 17, or the later *Olimpia* factory farther south at Piotrowska 242/250, contrast with streets like ul. Moniuszki, an uninterrupted rank of plush neo-Renaissance family houses. The *Poznański* plant includes weaving and spinning mills, warehouses, tenement houses and the industrialist's palace, which now houses the **City History Museum** (Tues–Sun 10am–4pm).

Further down ul. Piotrowska, beyond the *Olimpia* factory and past St Stanisław Kostka's Church, is the early nineteenth-century **White Factory**, at ul. Piotrowska 282, the oldest mechanically operated mill in the city. It's now a **Textile Museum** (Tues–Sun 9am–4pm).

Of the relics of Jewish life in the city, the most important traces—factories aside—are the **synagogue** at ul. Południowa 28, and the main **Jewish cemetery** on ul. Chryzantem. One of the largest and most poignant in the country, it is located in the north of town, on the edge of the Ghetto area.

Eating and Entertainment

Restaurants aren't Łódź's most exciting feature. Besides those in the hotels—the *Grand* has the best (and most expensive)—a sparse list of recommendations could include the *Europa*, al. Kościuski 116/18, the *Halka*, ul. Moniuszki 1, and a decent Chinese restaurant, the *Złota Kaczka* on ul. Piotrowska, a little south of the *Grand* hotel. There's a string of cheaper places along ul. Piotrowska as well.

As for the **cultural scene**, the *Teatr Wielki* on pl. Dąbrowskiego and the *Teatr Nowy* at ul. Więckowskiego 15 are the major **theaters**; foreign companies regularly perform at both. The concert program of the **National Filharmonia**, ul. Narutowicza 20, features soloists of world renown, while the *Teatr Muzyczny*, ul. Pólnocna 47/51, is the main **opera** venue. Among regular special events are an **opera festival** (March), a **ballet festival** (May–June every other year), and a **student theater festival** (March). Check at the box office at ul. Moniuszki 5 for current details of what's happening in town.

travel details

Trains from Warsaw

Domestic Services: to Białystok (14 daily; 3–4hr); Bydgoszcz (6 daily; 3hr 30min–5hr); Częstochowa (13 daily; 3–5hr); Gdańsk/Gdynia (19 daily; 3hr 30min–5hr; expresses at 6am & 5pm); Jelenia Góra (4 daily; 10hr; couchettes); Katowice (17 daily; 3–5hr); Kielce (12 daily; 3–4hr); Kraków (18 daily; 3–6hr; expresses at 6am, 9am, 4:25pm & 5:45pm); Krynica (2 daily; 10–13hr; couchettes); Lublin (11 daily; 2hr 30min–3hr); Łódź (7 daily; 2–2hr 30min); Olsztyn (8 daily; 3–5hr); Poznań (19 daily; 4hr); Przemyśl (4 daily; 6–8hr); Rzeszów (4 daily; 5–6hr); Suwałki (6 daily; 4–6hr); Świnoujście (3 daily; 10 hr; couchettes); Szczecin (5 daily; 6–8hr); Toruń (6 daily; 3–4hr); Wrocław (16 daily; 5–6hr; couchettes); Zagórz, for Sanok (2 daily; 11hr); Zakopane (6 daily; 6–10hr; expresses at 6:15 & 6:35am; couchettes).

International Services: to Aachen (3 daily); Beograd (1 daily); Berlin (12 daily); Brest (13 daily); Bucharest (1 daily); Budapest (3 daily); Frankfurt (1 daily); Grodno (5 daily); Hook of Holland (3 daily); Istanbul (1 daily); Cologne (4 daily); Kiev (3 daily); Leipzig (2 daily); Leningrad (2 daily); Moscow (7 daily); Munich (1 daily); Odessa (1 daily); Ostend (2 daily); Paris (3 daily); Prague (1 daily); Riga (1 daily); Rome (1 daily); Sofia (1 daily); Vilnius (4 daily); Vienna (2 daily).

Trains from Łódź

Domestic Services: to Bydgoszcz (10 daily; 3–4hr); Częstochowa (9 daily; 2hr 30min–3hr 30min); Gdańsk (6 daily; 6hr); Katowice (7 daily; 4hr); Kraków (6 daily; 5–6hr); Lublin (5 daily; 5–6hr); Poznań (7 daily; 4–5hr); Warsaw (20 daily; 2–3hr); Wrocław (15 daily; 4–5hr).

Buses from Warsaw

Domestic Services: from Dworzec Zachodni to Koszalin (1 daily), Krosno (1 daily), Mikołajki (1 daily), Olsztyn (3 daily), Rzeszów (1 daily), Toruń (1 daily), Zakopane (1 daily); from Dworzec Stadio to Lublin (2 daily), Przemyśl (1 daily), Zamość (3 daily).

International Services. Plenty of new private bus companies are now advertising, particularly in the *Zycie Warszawy* newspaper, but they're not as reliable as the following state-run services.
Orbis: to Hamburg (2 per month); Nuremberg–Munich–Stuttgart (1 weekly); Brunswick–Hanover–Dortmund–Cologne (2 per month); Hanover–London (3 per month).
Pekaes: to Oslo (1 per month); Venice–Bologna–Florence–Rome (2 per month); Hamburg–London–Nottingham–Manchester (1–2 per month); Cologne–Liège–Brussels–Ostend–London (3–4 per month); Frankfurt–Paris (4–5 per month).

Flights from Warsaw

Domestic Flights: to Gdańsk (2–6 daily); Katowice (1 daily, May–Oct only); Koszalin (1–3 daily); Kraków (2–6 daily); Szczecin (1–2 daily); Wrocław (2–6 daily).

International Flights: to Amsterdam (7 weekly); Athens (4 weekly); Barcelona (1 weekly); Belgrade (4 weekly); Berlin (12 weekly); Bratislava (2 weekly); Brussels (5 weekly); Bucharest (3 weekly); Budapest (15 weekly); Copenhagen (10 weekly); Düsseldorf (1 weekly); Frankfurt (13 weekly); Geneva (2–3 weekly); Hamburg (2–3 weekly); Helsinki (3–5 weekly); Istanbul (2 weekly); Cologne (3 weekly); Kiev (2 weekly); Leningrad (5–6 weekly); London (12–14 weekly); Los Angles (2 weekly); Lvov (1 weekly); Lyon (1–3 weekly); Madrid (2–3 weekly); Miami (2 weekly); Milan (3 weekly); Minsk (2 weekly); Montreal (2 weekly); Moscow (14–17 weekly); New York (4–6 weekly); Paris (7–11 weekly); Perth (2 weekly); Prague (12–13 weekly); Rio (1 weekly); Rome (6 weekly); San Francisco (2 weekly); Seattle (3–4 weekly); Singapore (1 weekly); Sofia (10–14 weekly); Stockholm (2–3 weekly); Tel Aviv (1–2 weekly); Tokyo (1 weekly); Vienna (12 weekly); Washington (2 weekly); Zurich (9 weekly).

CHAPTER TWO

GDAŃSK AND THE LAKES

E ven in a country accustomed to shifts in its borders, northeastern Poland presents an unusually tortuous historical puzzle. Successively the domain of a Germanic crusading order, of the Hansa merchants, and of the Prussians, it's only in the last forty years that the region has really become Polish. Right up to the end of World War II large parts of the area belonged to the territories of East Prussia, and although you won't see the old place names displayed any more, even the most patriotic Pole would have to acknowledge that Gdańsk, Olsztyn, and Toruń have made their mark on history under the German names of Danzig, Allenstein, and Thorn. Twentieth-century Germany has left terrible scars: it was here that the first shots of World War II were fired, and the bitter fighting during the Nazi retreat in 1945 left many historic towns as sad shadows of their former selves.

Gdańsk, Sopot, and **Gdynia**—the **Tri-City** as they are collectively known—dominate the area from their coastal vantage point. Like Warsaw, historic Gdańsk was obliterated in World War II but now offers some reconstructed quarters, in addition to its contemporary political interest as the birthplace of Solidarity. It makes an enjoyable base for exploring neighboring **Kashubia**, to the west, with its rolling hills, lakeside forests, and distinctive communities of Prussianized Slavs. While waters around the Tri-City are a dubious proposition, the **Hel Peninsula** and the coast farther west make a pleasant seaside option. On the other side of the Tri-City, **Frombork**, chief of many towns in the region associated with the astronomer Nicolaus Copernicus, is an attractive and historic lagoon-side town.

South of Gdańsk, a collection of **Teutonic castles** and Hanseatic centers dot the banks of the Wisła and its tributaries. Highlights include the huge medieval fortress at **Malbork**, long the headquarters of the Teutonic Knights, and **Toruń**, with its spectacular medieval ensemble. Eastward stretches **Mazury**, Poland's biggest lakeland district, long popular with Polish vacationers and, increasingly, with the Germans. Canoe and yacht rental are the main attractions of its resorts, but for anyone wanting to get away from the crowds there are much less frequented patches of water and nature to explore, both in Mazury and, above all, in the neighboring **Suwalszczyzna** and **Augustów** region.

Southward again, lakes give way to the forests, open plains, and Orthodox villages of **Podlasie**, the border region with the Soviet Union, centered on the city of **Białystok**. Both city and region maintain one of Poland's most fascinating ethnic mixes, with a significant **Byelorussian** population and smaller communities of **Tartars**. The Nazis wiped out the **Jewish** population, but their history is important in these parts too, with one of Poland's finest synagogues well restored at **Tykocin**.

GDAŃSK AND AROUND

With a population of around 750,000, the conurbation comprising **Gdańsk**, **Gdynia**, and **Sopot**—the so-called **Tri-City** (Trojmiasto)—ranks third in size after Warsaw and Łódź. It's an enjoyable area to move about, with ferries shuttling between the three centers and up to the **Hel Peninsula**, and you get a good mix of Poland's northern attractions: politics and monuments in Gdańsk, seaside chic in Sopot, gritty port life in Gdynia, and sandy beaches with clean water up at the Hel Peninsula. The lakes and forests of **Kashubia** are just an hour or two from Gdańsk by bus and **Frombork**, too, makes an easy day trip. As you'd expect, Gdańsk also has excellent **transportation connections** with the rest of Poland, with a host of buses, trains, and flights.

About the only place you won't find detailed in this section—though it falls within the area—is **Elbląg**, an undiluted industrial center, rebuilt after comprehensive damage in the war, and with little to draw the casual visitor.

Gdańsk

For outsiders, **GDAŃSK** is perhaps the most familiar city in Poland. The home of Lech Wałęsa, Solidarity, and the former Lenin Shipyards, its images have flashed across a decade of news bulletins. Expectations formed from the newsreels are fulfilled by the industrial landscape, and suggestions of latent discontent, radicalism, and future strikes are all tangible. What is more surprising, at least for those with no great knowledge of Polish history, is the cultural complexity of the place. Prewar Gdańsk—or **Danzig** as it then was—was forged by years of Prussian and Hanseatic domination, and the reconstructed city center looks not unlike Amsterdam, making an elegant and bourgeois backdrop. What has changed entirely, however, is the city's demography. At the outbreak of the last war nearly all of the 400,000 citizens were German-speaking, with fewer than 16,000 Poles. The postwar years marked a radical shift from all that went before, as the ethnic Germans were expelled and Gdańsk became Polish for the first time since 1308.

Some History

The city's position at the meeting point of the Wisła and the Baltic has long made Danzig/Gdańsk an immense strategic asset: in the words of Frederick the Great, whoever controlled it could be considered "more master of Poland than any king ruling there." First settled in the tenth century, the city assumed prominence when the **Teutonic Knights** arrived in 1308, at the invitation of a population constantly threatened from the west by the margraves of Brandenburg. The Knights established themselves in their accustomed style, massacring the locals and installing a colony of German settlers in their place.

The city's economy flourished, however, and with the ending of the Knights' rule in 1454, Danzig became to all intents and purposes an independent city-state, with its own legislature, judiciary, and monopolies on the Wisła trade routes, restricted only by the necessity of paying homage and an annual tax to the Polish monarch. The key elements of Danzig/Gdańsk history were thus emerging: autonomy, economic power, cultural cosmopolitanism, and German-Polish rivalry for control of the city.

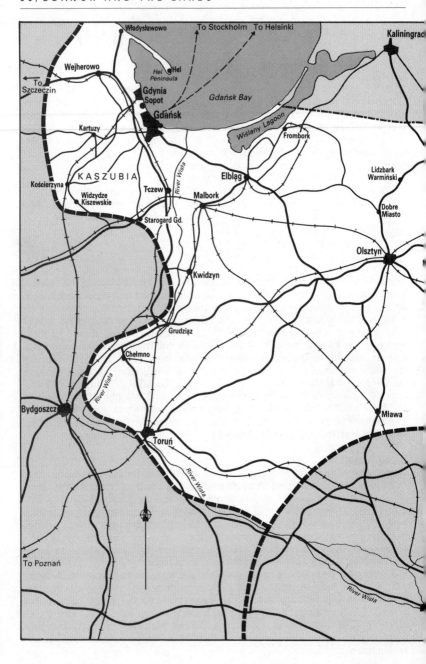

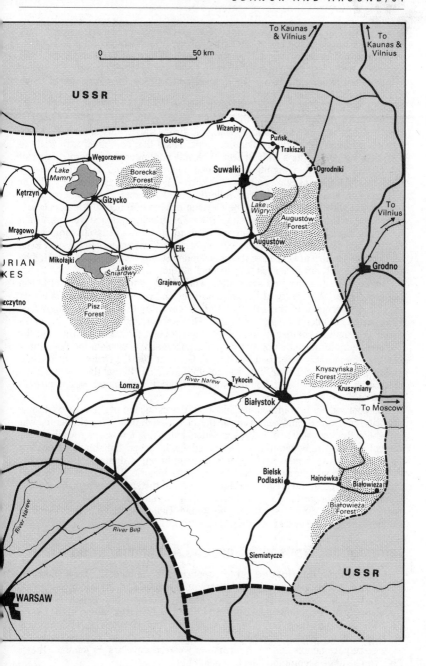

The city's main period of development occurred between the sixteenth century and the Partitions of the late eighteenth century. An indication of the scale of the city's **trading empire** is given by statistics showing that the Danzig Eastland Company had a bigger turnover than even London's mighty East India Company. (One of their major exports was wood, specifically spruce, the very name of which derives from the Polish *Z Prus*, meaning "from Prussia.") Most of the important building took place at this time, as the burghers brought in Dutch and Flemish architects to design buildings that would express the city's self-confidence—hence the strikingly Hanseatic appearance. From the Renaissance period also dates a tradition of religious toleration, a pluralism that combined with trade to forge strong connections with Britain. A sizable contingent of foreign Protestant merchants included a significant Scottish population, who lived in the city districts still known as Stare and Nowe Szkoty—Old and New Scotland.

Prussian annexation of the city, following the Partitions, abruptly severed the connection with Poland. Despite the German origins of much of the population, resistance to Prussianization and support for Polish independence were as strong in Danzig as elsewhere in Prussian-ruled Poland. In 1807, a Prussian campaign to recruit soldiers to fight Napoleon yielded precisely 47 volunteers in the city. Even as German a native of Danzig as the philosopher Schopenhauer was castigated by the Prussian authorities for his "unpatriotic" attitudes.

Territorial status changed again after World War I and the recovery of Polish independence. The Treaty of Versailles created the semi-autonomous **Free City of Danzig**, terminal of the so-called **Polish corridor** that sliced through East Prussia and connected Poland to the sea. This strip of land gave Hitler one of his major propaganda themes in the 1930s and a pretext for attacking the city: the German assault unleashed on the Polish garrison at Westerplatte on September 1, 1939—memorably described by Günther Grass in *The Tin Drum*—was the first engagement of **World War II**. It was not until March 1945 that the city was liberated, after massive Soviet bombardment; what little remained was almost as ruined as Warsaw.

The postwar era brought communist rule, the expulsion of the ethnic German majority, and the formal renaming of the city as **Gdańsk**. The old center was meticulously reconstructed and the traditional shipping industries revitalised. As the communist era began to crack at the edges, however, the shipyards became the harbingers of a new reality. Riots in neighboring Gdynia in 1970 and the strikes of 1976 were important precursors to the historic 1980 **Lenin Shipyards** strike, which led to the creation of **Solidarity**. And the shipyards remained at the center of resistance to General Jaruzelski's government, the last major strike wave in January 1989 precipitating the Round Table negotiations that heralded the beginning of the end of communist rule.

Information, Transportation, and Accommodation

The main **tourist information center**, opposite the station at ul. Heweliusza 8, is one of the best in the country, with extremely helpful and knowledgeable staff. Although their resources get stretched in the summer, they generally have a good supply of maps, timetables, and local tips. The **Almatur office**, in the center of town at Długi Targ 11/13, is also friendly, and employs several English-speakers; unlike most offices they've adapted their style to accommodate the strange requirements—in Polish terms—of western travelers. In summer they'll help you arrange accommodation in student hotels.

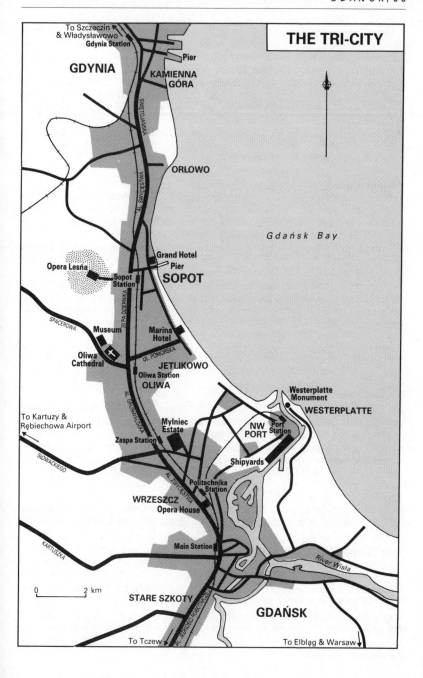

THE TRI-CITY

To Szczecin
& Władysławowo
Gdynia Station

Pier

GDYNIA

KAMIENNA
GÓRA

ŚWIĘTOJAŃSKA

ORŁOWO

Gdańsk Bay

Grand Hotel
Pier

Opera Leśna

Sopot
Station

SOPOT

20 PA DZIERNIKA

SPACEROWA

Museum

Marina
Hotel

UL. POMORSKA

Oliwa
Cathedral

JETLIKOWO

Oliwa Station

OLIWA

Westerplatte
Monument

WESTERPLATTE

To Kartuzy &
Rębiechowa Airport

AL. GRUNWALDZKA

Mylniec
Estate

NW
PORT

Port
Station

Zaspa Station

SŁOWACKIEGO

Shipyards

Politechnika
Station

AL. ŻYWECKIEGO

WRZESZCZ
Opera House

KARTUSZKA

Main Station

River Wisła

0   2 km

STARE SZKOTY

AL. ZWYCIĘSTWA POWSTAŃCÓW

GDAŃSK

To Tczew

To Elbląg & Warsaw

Orientation is fairly straightforward, the main sites of interest being located in three historic districts: Główne Miasto, Stare Miasto, and Stare Przedmieście. **Główne Miasto** (Main Town), the central area, is in easy walking distance of the main station—if you value your life don't be tempted to try jaywalking across Podwale Grodzkie but take the underground passageway like everyone else. The main pedestrianized avenues, ulica Długa and its continuation Długi Targ, form the heart of the district, which backs east onto the attractive waterfront of the Motława Canal and the island of Spichlerze. To the north is the **Stare Miasto** (Old Town), bounded by the towering cranes of the shipyards, beyond which the suburbs of Wrzeszcz, Zaspa, and Oliwa sprawl towards Sopot. South of the center stands the quieter **Stare Przedmieście** (Old Suburb).

Getting Around

Traveling within the urban area is pretty straightforward. A regular **train** service between the main station, Sopot, and Gdynia, with plenty of stops in between, continues well into the evening; tickets can be bought in the passage beneath the main station or at any local station (some have ticket machines).

Trams run within each part of the Tri-City, but not between them. **Buses**, however, operate right across the conurbation. The large-scale **map** of Gdańsk available from kiosks and some bookshops gives all bus and tram routes. Tickets for both trams and buses can be bought from any kiosk (locals generally buy them in multiples of ten). One ticket punched both ends is enough for short hops; you'll need two for night buses and *pospieszne* (speed bus) routes, more for longer journeys.

> The telephone code for the Tri-City is ☎058.

Finding a Place to Stay

As in the other big tourist cities, accommodation in Gdańsk ranges from the ultra-plush to the ultra-basic—and rooms downtown are at a premium in summer. At the top end of the scale, Orbis runs a string of **hotels** aimed very firmly at western tourists and businesspeople. Lower down the price scale, hotels are sparse but **private rooms** are a good option, while **youth hostels** provide the usual not very central fallbacks.

HOTELS
As before, the following hotels are listed in ascending order of price; the last four are all Orbis-run, with doubles priced from $55 to 490; the first four are in the $28–46 range.

Dom Nauczyciela, ul. Hanki Sawickiej 28 (☎419-916). Located out in Wrzeszcz—five minutes' walk north of Gdańsk-Politechnika station—in a quiet side street. Single to four-person rooms, some with toilet and shower.

Motlawa, ul. Wartkiej (☎317-151). An old boat moored to the north along the main waterfront; only ten single rooms, so you'll be lucky to get one in season.

Jantar, Długi Targ 19 (☎316-241). Excellent location in the heart of the Old Town makes it very difficult to get into this one. The view from the top-floor rooms is magnificent.

Mesa, ul. Wały Jagiellońskie 36 (☎318-052). Another decent-quality, reasonable, and hard-to-get-into central option.

Poseidon, ul. Kapliczna 30 (☎530-227). Sited halfway between Gdańsk and Sopot, this is arguably the nicest Orbis hotel in town. Balconied rooms, some with a sea view, others looking onto the woods. Has a popular nightclub.

Marina, ul. Jetlikowska 30 (☎532-079). A "luxury" Orbis hotel on the seafront, complete with a tennis court. No balconies and lots of concrete.

Novotel, ul. Pszenna (☎315-611). A typical and quite friendly motel.

Hewelius, ul. Heweliusza 22 (☎315-631). The big Orbis showpiece—pretentious and a bit too overt a contrast with regular Gdańsk life.

PRIVATE ROOMS

Private rooms can be arranged either with the efficient **Biuro Zakwaterowań** at ul. Elzbietańska 10 (daily 7am–7pm in summer; closes 5pm in winter; ☎319-444/338-840), or with the locals who hang about outside here and at the main train station.

HOSTELS

There are four **youth hostels** open year-round, all of them often full in season:

Ul. Wałowa 21 (☎312-313). The most central hostel—a sizable red brick building ten minutes' walk from the main station.

Ul. Grunwaldzka 238/40 (☎411-660). Near Oliwa in the northern Wrzeszcz suburb. A decent-quality hostel inside a sports center; to get there take a local train to Gdańsk-Zaspa or tram #8, #12, or #15.

Ul. Smoluchowskiego 11 (☎323-820). Also in Wrzeszcz; take tram # 2, #6, #8, #12, #13, or #14.

Ul. Dzierzyńskiego 11 (☎414-108). A lower quality hostel, once again in Wrzeszcz. Take trams # 2, #4, #7, #8, or #14 or walk from the Gdańsk-Wrzeszcz station.

Ul. Karpia 1 (☎318-219). By the canal on the north edge of the Old Town. Open July & Aug only.

CAMPSITES

All the campgrounds below are open from June to September.

Ul. Jetlikowska 23 (☎ 532-731). Near the beach at Jetlikowo. Regular camping facilities plus bungalows—at around $9 a bed, a bargain if you can get one. It's a short walk from the terminal of trams #2, #4, and #15.

Al. Marksa 234 (☎566-531). In the suburb of Brzeźno, due north of the town center; trams #7, #13, and #15, and buses #124 and #148 pass nearby.

Ul. Lazurowa 5 (☎380-739). Even farther out in Orle, east of the city along the Martwa Wisła; bus #112 passes it.

The City

The **Główne Miasto**, the largest of the historic quarters, is the obvious starting point for an exploration of the city; the **Stare Miasto**, across the thin ribbon of the Raduna Canal, is the natural progression. The third, southern quarter, **Stare Przedmieście**, cut off by the al. Leningrafdzka, has its main focus for visitors in the National Museum. Moving north, out toward Sopot, is the **Oliwa** suburb with its cathedral—one of the city's most distinctive landmarks—and park.

North along the canal, **Westerplatte**—with its monument commemorating the outbreak of World War II—can be reached by **boat** from the central waterfront (as can Gdynia, Sopot, and the Hel Peninsula), a trip that allows good views of the famous **shipyards**.

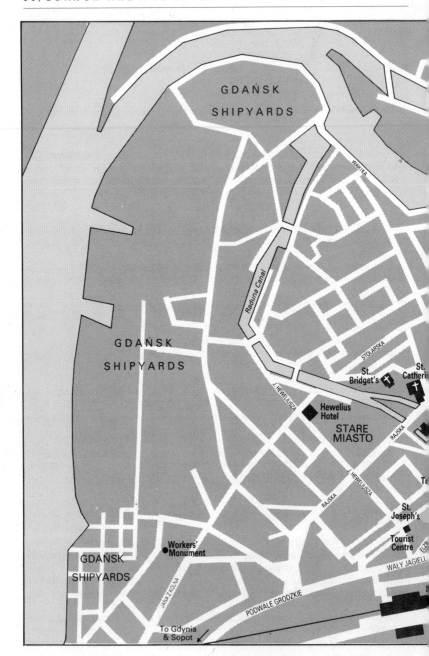

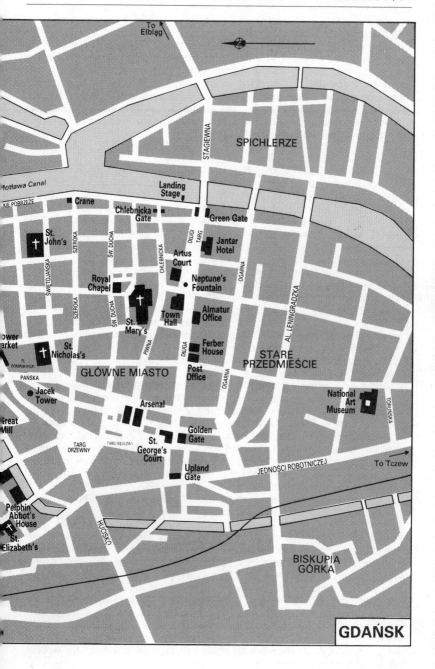

To Elbląg

SPICHLERZE

STAGIEWNA

Mottawa Canal

KIE POBRZEŻE

Crane

Landing Stage

Chlebnicka Gate

Green Gate

St. John's

SZEROKA

ŚW. DUCHA

DŁUGI TARG

Jantar Hotel

Artus Court

CHLEBNICKA

ŚWIĘTOJAŃSKA

SZEROKA

Royal Chapel

ŚW. DUCHA

St. Mary's

Neptune's Fountain

Town Hall

Almatur Office

PIWNA

OGARNA

AL. LENINGRADZKA

ower arket

St. Nicholas's

PL. DOMINIKAŃSK

PAŃSKA

GŁÓWNE MIASTO

Ferber House

DŁUGA

Post Office

OGARNA

STARE PRZEDMIEŚCIE

Jacek Tower

Great Mill

TARG DRZEWNY

TARG WĘGLOWY

Arsenal

St. George's Court

Golden Gate

Upland Gate

National Art Museum

TORUŃSKA

JEDNOŚCI ROBOTNICZEJ

To Tczew

Pelphin Abbot's House

HUCISKO

St. Elizabeth's

BISKUPIA GÓRKA

GDAŃSK

The Main Town (Główne Miasto)

Entering the **Main Town** is like walking straight into a Hansa merchants' settlement. The layout, typical of a medieval port, comprises a tight network of streets, bounded on four sides by water and main roads—the Raduna and Motława canals to the north and east, al. Leningradzka and Wały Jagiellońskie to the south and west. The ancient appearance of this quarter's buildings is deceptive: by May 1945 the fighting between German and Russian forces had reduced the core of Gdańsk to smoldering ruins. A glance at the photos in the town hall brings home the scale of the destruction and of its reversal.

ULICA DŁUGA, THE TOWN HALL, AND DŁUGI TARG

Ulica Długa, the main thoroughfare, and **Długi Targ**, the wide open square on the eastern part of it, form the natural focus of attention. As with all the main streets, huge stone gateways guard both entrances. Before the western entrance to Długa, take a look around the outer **Upland Gate** (Brama Wyżynna) and the Gothic **Prison Tower** which contains a gruesome museum of prison exhibits, some of them displayed in the torture chambers. The gate itself, built in the late sixteenth century as part of the town's outer fortifications, used to be the main entrance to Gdańsk. The three coats of arms emblazoned across the archway— Poland, Prussia, and the free town of Danzig—encapsulate the city's history.

This gate was also the starting point of the "royal route" used by Polish monarchs on their annual state visits. After the Upland Gate they had to pass through the richly decorated **Golden Gate** (Brama Złota), alongside **St George's Court** (Dwór św. Jerzego), a fine Gothic mansion appropriately housing the architects' society. From here, ul. Długa leads down to the town hall, with several gabled facades worth studying in detail—such as the sixteenth-century **Ferber mansion** (no. 28) or the imposing **Lion's Castle** (no. 35), where King Władysław IV entertained local dignitaries.

Topped by a golden statue of King Zygmunt August which dominates the central skyline, the huge and well-proportioned tower of the **Town Hall** makes a powerful impact. Originally constructed in the late fourteenth century, with the tower and spire added later, the building was totally ruined during the last war, but the restoration was so skillful you'd hardly believe it. "In all Poland there is no other, so Polish a town hall" observed one local writer, though the foreign influences on the interior rooms might lead you to disagree. They now house the **Historical Museum** (Tues–Thurs, Sat & Sun 10am–4pm), their lavish decorations almost upstaging the exhibits on display.

From the entrance hall an ornate staircase leads to the upper floor and the main council chamber, the **Red Room** (Sala Czerwona). Interior decoration was obviously one thing that seventeenth-century Gdańsk councillors could agree on—the color red completely dominates the room. The chamber's sumptuous decor, mostly from the late sixteenth century, is the work of various craftsmen: its furniture was designed by a Dutch fugitive who became municipal architect of Gdańsk in the 1590s; Willem Bart of Ghent carved the ornate fireplace—note the Polish-looking Neptunes in the supports; while most of the ceiling and wall paintings were produced by another Dutchman, Johan Verberman de Vries. The central oval ceiling painting, by another Dutchman, Isaac van den Block, is titled *The Glorification of the Unity of Gdańsk with Poland*, a period panorama of the city, stressing its Polish ties. The council used this chamber only in summer; in winter they moved into the adjoining smaller room, entered through the wooden door to the right of the fireplace.

As well as another reconstructed seventeenth-century fireplace, the next room, the **court room**, contains a haunting photomontage of the ruins of Gdańsk in 1945. One floor up, the **archive rooms** now house permanent exhibitions including a display of prewar Gdańsk photographs, plus temporary shows like a recent one of engravings by the city's best-known writer, Günther Grass. The old municipal finance office contains a pair of paintings by van den Block, one a forbidding representation of the Flood, and a statue of King Jagiełło taken from the neighboring Artus Court.

Past the town hall the street opens onto the wide expanses of **Długi Targ**, where the **Artus Court** (Dwór Artusa) stands out in a square filled with many fine mansions. Unfortunately it's closed for reconstruction at the moment, so you'll have to content yourself with admiring the Renaissance frontages of this and the nearby **Golden House** (no. 41). The square itself has many moods: in summer, with tourists and pigeons gathered around the fountain statue of Neptune, the light, open atmosphere recalls an Italian piazza; but on a misty autumn evening, as the streets resound with the chimes of the town hall clock, you could almost imagine yourself in an old Norman cathedral city.

THE WATERFRONT AND ST MARY'S

The archways of the **Green Gate** (Most Zielona), a former royal residence for the annual visit, open directly onto the **waterfront**. From the bridge over the Motława Canal you get a good view of the old granaries on **Spichlerze** island to the right (there used to be over 300 of them), and to the left of the old harbor quay, now a tourist hang-out and local promenade. Halfway down is the massive and largely original fifteenth-century **Gdańsk Crane**, the biggest in medieval Europe; it now houses the **Maritime Museum** (Tues 10am–6pm, Wed–Sun 10am–4pm), which features a model of every ship produced in the nearby shipyards since 1945.

All the streets back into the town from the waterfront are worth exploring. Next up from the Green Gate is **ul. Chlebnicka**, reached through the fifteenth-century **Chlebnicka Gate**. The **English House** (Dom Angielski) at no. 16, built in 1569 and the largest house in the city at the time, is a reminder of the strong Reformation-era trading connections with Britain. Several of the best bars are on Chlebnicka, as is the HQ of the local police—they're the boys sitting around in the carelessly parked cars.

Both this street and neighboring ul. Mariacka, with its gabled terraced houses and expensive boutiques, end at the gigantic **St Mary's Church** (Kosciół Mariacka), reputedly the biggest brick church in the world. Estimates that it could fit 20,000 people were substantiated during the early days of martial law, when huge crowds crammed the cold whitewashed interior. The **high altar**, totally reconstructed after the war, is a powerful sixteenth-century triptych featuring a *Coronation of the Virgin*. Of the chapels scattered round the church, two of the most striking are the **Chapel of 11,000 Virgins**, which has a tortured Gothic crucifix for which the artist apparently nailed his son-in-law to a cross as a model, and the **St Anne's Chapel**, containing the wooden *Beautiful Madonna of Gdańsk* from around 1415. A curiosity is the fifteenth-century **astronomical clock**, which tells not only the day, month, and year, but the whole saints' calendar and the phases of the moon; when completed in 1470 it was the world's tallest clock.

If you're feeling fit, make sure you climb up St Mary's **tower**—on a good day the view over Gdańsk and the plains is excellent; for a few złotys the old man who sits up there all day will let you look around with his binoculars. After the bareness of the church, the Baroque exuberance of the **Royal Chapel**, directly opposite on ul. św. Ducha, makes a refreshing change.

FROM THE ARSENAL TO THE FLOWER MARKET
Ulica Piwna, another street of high terraced houses west of the church entrance, ends at the monumental **Great Arsenal** (Wielka Zbrojowna), an early seventeenth-century armory facing the **Coal Market** (Targ Węglowy). Now a busy shopping center, the coal market leads north to the **Wood Market** (Targ Drzewny), and on to the Old Town over the other side of the canal. Ulica Szeroka, first off to the right, is another charming old street with a nice view of St Mary's from the corner with ul. Furty Groba.

The Dominican-run **St Nicholas' Church** (św. Mikołaja) on ul. Swietojańska is another fourteenth-century brick structure with relatively tasteful Baroque additions, while **St John's** (św. Jana), farther down the same street, is a reputedly beautiful church currently closed for restoration.

The terraced houses and shops tail off as you approach the outer limits of the main town, marked by several towers and other remnants of the **town wall**. **Baszta Jacek**, the tower nearest the canal, stands guard over the Pod Myślinksa, the main route over the canal into the Old Town. The **flower market** opposite is a fine example of the Polish attachment to the finer things of life—even when there was nothing in the food shops, you still found roses or carnations in one of the stalls here. Ceremonious trimming and wrapping make you feel special in a way nothing else quite can.

The Old Town (Stare Miasto) and the Shipyards
Crossing the canal bridge brings you into the **Old Town** (Stare Miasto). Dominating the waterside is the seven-story **Great Mill** (Wielki Mlyn), built in the mid-fourteenth century by the Teutonic Knights and another Gdańsk "largest"—in this case the biggest mill in medieval Europe. Its eighteen races milled corn for 600 years; even in the 1930s it was still grinding out 200 tons of flour a day, and local enthusiasts see no reason why it couldn't be doing the same again. At present it's used as an office building, with a large murky Pewex in the basement to give it that sensitive historical touch.

St Catherine's Church (Katarżynka), the former parish church of the Old Town, to the right of the crossway, is one of the nicest in the city. Fourteenth-century—and built in brick like almost all churches in the region—it has a well-preserved and luminous interior. If you're keen to catch a glimpse of **Lech Wałęsa**, there's a good chance of seeing him at his local church, **St Bridget's** (św. Brigida), next to St Catherine's, on Sundays. Under the charismatic guidance of Father Jankowski, a close confidant of Wałęsa, the church has become a local Solidarity stronghold. The oil painting of the Black Madonna in a tee-shirt sporting the *Solidarność* logo says it all. Although the political importance of the church is diminishing now that Solidarity holds the reins of power, it's still worth visiting places like this—ideally on a Sunday—to experience the specifically Polish mixture of religion and politics that is personified in the man whose statue watches over the church, Karol Wojtyła, aka Pope John Paul II.

Moving farther into the Old Town, the merchants' mansions give way to postwar housing, the tattier sections looking like something off the set of *1984*. The most interesting part of the district is just west along the canal from the mill, centered on the **Old Town Hall** (Ratusz Staromiejski), on the corner of ul. Bielanska and Korzenna. Built by the architect of the main town hall, this delicate Renaissance construction is still occupied by local government offices, but you can wander in to look at the Baroque paintings and sculptures in the main hall. The bronze figure in the entrance hall is of Jan Hevelius, the Polish astronomer after whom Orbis have named their nearby skyscraper hotel. Like the better-known Mr Fahrenheit, he was a Gdańsk boy.

Continuing west from the town hall, Gothic **St Joseph's** (św. Jożefa) and **St Elizabeth's** (św. Elzbiety)—facing each other across ul. Elzbietańska—and the Renaissance **House of the Abbots of Pelplin** (Dom Opatów Pelplińskich) make a fine historic entourage. From here you're only a short walk through the tunnels under the main road (Podwale Grodzkie) from the station.

THE (EX-) LENIN SHIPYARDS

Looming large in the distance are the cranes of the famous **Gdańsk Shipyards** (Stocznia Gdańska)—Lenin's name has now been officially dropped. With the Nowa Huta steelworks outside Kraków, this was the crucible of the political struggles of the 1980s.

Ten minutes' walk or one tram stop north along the main road brings you to the shipyard gates on plac Solidarnośći Robotnicznej. In front of them stands an ugly set of steel crosses, a **monument** to workers killed during the **1970 ship-yard riots**; it was inaugurated in 1980 in the presence of Communist Party, church and opposition leaders. A precursor to the organized strikes of the 1980s, the 1970 riots erupted when workers took to the streets in protest at price rises, setting fire to the Party headquarters after police opened fire. Riots erupted again in 1976, once more in protest at price rises on basic foodstuffs, and then in **August 1980** Gdańsk came to the forefront of world attention when a protest at the firing of workers rapidly developed into a national strike.

The formation of **Solidarity**, the first independent trade union in the Soviet bloc, was a direct result of the Gdańsk strike, instigated by the Lenin Shipyards workers and their charismatic leader **Lech Wałęsa**. Throughout the 1980s the Gdańsk workers remained in the vanguard of political protest. Strikes here in 1988 and 1989 led to the **Round Table Talks** which forced the Communist Party into power-sharing and, ultimately, democratic elections.

Standing at the gates today, you may find it hard to experience this as the place where, in a sense, contemporary Poland began to take shape. Yet ironically the shipyards remain at the leading edge of political developments: the government is attempting (unsuccessfully so far) to sell them off to western investors.

The Old Suburb (Stare Przedmieście)

Stare Przedmieście—the lower part of old Gdańsk—was the limit of the original town, as testified by the ring of seventeenth-century bastions running east from plac Wałowy over the Motława.

The main attraction today is the **National Art Museum** (Tues–Thurs, Sat & Sun 10am–3pm), housed in a former Franciscan monastery at Toruńska 1. There's enough local Gothic art and sculpture here to keep enthusiasts going all day, as well as a varied collection of fabrics, chests, gold, and silverware—all redolent of the town's former wealth. The range of Dutch and Flemish art in the "foreign galleries"—Memling, the younger Breughel, Cuyp, and van Dyck are the best-known names—attests to the city's strong links with the Netherlands.

The museum's most famous work is Hans Memling's colossal *Last Judgement* (1473), the painter's earliest known work—though he was already in his thirties and a mature artist. The painting has had a more than usually checkered past, having been commissioned by the Medici in Florence, then diverted to Gdańsk, looted by Napoleon, moved to Berlin, returned to Gdańsk, stolen by the Nazis and finally, after being discovered by the Red Army, hidden in the Thuringian hills, to be returned to Gdańsk by the Russians in 1956.

Westerplatte

It was at **Westerplatte**, the promontory guarding the harbor entrance, that the German battleship *Schleswig-Holstein* fired the first salvo of World War II. For a full week the garrison of 170 badly equipped Poles held off the combined assault of aircraft, heavy guns, and over 3000 German troops, setting the tone for the Poles' response to the subsequent Nazi-Russian invasion. The ruined army guardhouse and barracks are still there, a more stirring memorial than the 1960s monument raised on the site.

You can get to Westerplatte by the #106 bus from the center, but a much better way is to take one of the tourist **boats** from the main city waterfront, just north of the Brama Zielona. (There are boats to several destinations—Gdynia, Sopot, and Hel included—so make sure you're on the right one.) Taking about thirty minutes, the trip provides an excellent view of the **shipyards**, along with the array of international vessels anchored there.

Oliwa

Back on land, the modern Oliwa suburb, the northernmost area of Gdańsk, has one of the best-known buildings in the city, **Oliwa Cathedral**. To get there, take the local train to Gdańsk-Oliwa station, and walk across the park west of the main Sopot road.

Originally the church of the neighboring Cistercian monastery, the cathedral has been rebuilt several times, its facade combining Gothic brick towers, Renaissance spires, and white Rococo plasterwork to unusually good effect. Centerpiece of a harmonious and predominantly Rococo interior is an exuberantly decorated eighteenth-century organ, the finest such instrument in the country. The **organ recitals** held here, most frequent in the summer months, are definitely worth attending—check the local papers or the tourist office for details.

In the area around the cathedral, the **Oliwa Museum** (Tues–Thurs, Sat & Sun 10am–3pm), housed in the abbots' palace, has a large contemporary art gallery, as well as an interesting display of local ethnography. The **park**, formerly part of the monastery grounds, is a relaxing place for an afternoon stroll. And if you happen to be here on **All Souls' Day** (Nov 1), the large **cemetery** across the road is an amazing sight, illuminated by thousands of candles placed on the gravestones. Whole families come to visit the individual graves and communal memorials to the unknown dead, in a powerful display of remembrance which says much about the intertwining of Catholicism and the collective memory of national sufferings.

Another national monument lives just down the road. **Lech Wałęsa**, having vacated the workers' paradise of the Młyniec housing project, is now in residence in the wealthier zone west of the railroad track.

Like several Polish cities, Gdańsk has a small, low-profile **Tartar** community (see also "Białystok," later in this chapter). They're currently putting the finishing touches to a new **mosque** not far from Wałęsa's house; already in use by local Muslims, including the Arab student population, the mosque is at the south end of ul. Polanki, on the corner with ul. Abrahama (nearest station Gdańsk-Zaspa; trams #6, #12 and #15 also run nearby).

Eating and Drinking

In a city accustomed to tourism, finding a place to eat is relatively straightforward: there's a good range of cafés and snack bars, and even one or two genuinely recommendable restaurants. On the down side, heavy demand in summer makes waiting a frequent ordeal, and with the best places it's quite common to turn up only to find them reserved for tourist groups. As for local specialties, fish dishes are generally worth sampling, as long as you're unworried by a dose of Baltic pollution.

Drinking downtown is essentially confined to a number of bars and cafés on ul. Długa and parallel streets to the north. In summer the attractive terrace cafés of ul. Chlebnicka and Mariacka make the ideal place to sit out and enjoy the sun—and more often than not a decent *espresso*.

Restaurants, Milk Bars, and Fast Food

As throughout Poland, keep in mind that it's difficult to find a restaurant open after 9pm, except in Orbis hotels, which are more adapted to tourist habits.

Neptuny, ul. Długa. One of the city's classic milk bars—look out for daily specials.

Itaka, ul. Długa 25. One of the first genuine Polish fast-food joints, with hamburgers, fries, and all the rest. Poles love it, as much for the novelty of fast (ie normal) service as anything else.

Pod Wzesa, ul. Chlebnicka 50. Quiet pizzeria in the town center.

Pod Żurawiem, ul. Warzywnicza 10. On the waterfront, one of the few places where you can eat outside.

Kubicki, ul. Wartka 5. Good local food in slightly murky maritime-influenced surroundings. Popular with foreign sailors, hence the multilingual menus.

Żółty Kur, Długi Targ 4. A decent cheap eatery in a central location, with Delft tiles for decoration. Chicken specialties.

Karczma Michał, ul. Jana Z. Kolna 8. Cosy little place close to the shipyards, where the world's media used to hang out during the strikes. Good solid local food from the owner's farm outside town.

Tawerna, ul. Powroznicza 19–20. Decent nosh, especially the steak and duck—but only till 8:30pm; drinks till about 10pm.

Athena, ul. Długa. New Greek restaurant. Good value.

Retman, ul. Stągiewna 1. Situated by the waterfront, serving good fish dishes. Increasingly orientated towards German tourists, with prices to match. Open late.

Pod Wieża, ul. Piwna 51. A favorite stopoff with tourists trekking round the Old Town.

Pod Łososiem, ul. Szeroka 54 (☎317-652). The most luxurious and expensive in town. Specializes in seafood; also known locally as originator of *Goldwasser* liqueur, a thick yellow concoction with flakes of real gold that's as Prussian as its name suggests.

Marina, ul. Jetlikowska 30. Good Orbis hotel restaurant; try the duck and poultry.

Hewelius, ul. Heweliusza 22 (☎315-631). If you don't mind paying for it, this Orbis hotel restaurant offers dishes you won't find in many other places. However, the contrast between the champagne and smooth-talking waiters on the inside and the lines outside feels almost colonial.

Cafés, Bars, and Clubs

LOT, Wały Jagiellońskie 2/4. Airline café that serves a decent cup of coffee in upscale surroundings, adorned with paintings by art students.

Palowa, underneath the town hall in Main Town. An ideal rendezvous point, and often has a good selection of cakes, too. Service is what Poles would call "relaxed."

U Szkota, ul. Chlebnicka. Popular, enjoyable bar, small and often difficult to get a table in—but you can normally sit at the bar downstairs.

GTPS Artists' Bar, ul. Piwna. Open till late; helps if you look the part.

Flisak, ul. Chlebnicka 10/11. Smoky dive for serious drinkers only. Open till 2am.

Architects' Club, just off Targ Węglowy. A great spot. Talk your way in with a Polish friend and have a great time with the architecture students.

Vinifera, ul. Brygidzki. A nice canalside bar-café in a tiny little house, with seats outside. A good place to relax in the city.

Zak, ul. Wały Jagiellońskie. Best of a lively bunch of student clubs, just down from the main station.

The **unnamed club** on Wały Piastowskie, open every evening, has some live bands (rock, jazz) and a rousing disco on weekends.

Listings

Airport At **Rębiechowa**, half an hour's bus journey from Targ Węglowy, downtown. International departures to Moscow, Leningrad, Hamburg, and London Heathrow with *LOT* or *Aeroflot*. Domestic connections to Warsaw, Kraków, Katowice, Rzeszów, Wrocław and Zielona Góra. Information ☎415-110/415-162/415-131.

Air tickets From Orbis, plac Gorkiego 1, or the *LOT* building, ul. Wały Jagiellońskie 2/4 (☎311-164/314-026), or the airport (reservations ☎415-251/412-335).

Car Trouble Repairs: ul. Dąbrowszczaków 14 (☎531-652), al. Grunwaldzka 339 (☎522-812). Breakdown service: in Gdańsk, Kartuska 187 (☎323-555) & al. Marksa 132 (☎411-693); in Sopot, ul. Dzierzyńskiego 61 (☎518-030); in Gdynia, ul. Olsztyńska 35 (☎202-541) & ul. 3 Maja 20 (☎210-522).

Consulates *Sweden, Norway & Denmark*, ul. Jana z Kolna 25; *Belgium*, ul. Swietojańska 32; *Holland*, ul. 10—go Lutego 21; *Italy*, ul. Swietojańska 32; *Finland*, ul. Zeromskiego 12 (in Sopot). There are no US or Canadian consulates—the embassies in Warsaw are the nearest.

Festivals The Dominican Fair (*Jarmark*) in August is an important local event, with artists and craftsmen setting up shop in the center of town, often accompanied by street theater and other assorted events.

Gas Stations The following are open 24hr: in Gdańsk, ul. Dąbrowskiego & ul. Elbląska; in Oliwa, ul. Grunwaldzka & ul. Dąbrowszczaków; in Sopot, ul. Dzierzyńskiego; in Gdynia, ul. Kolibki & ul. Chylonksa.

Hospital Ul. Swierczewskiego 1/7, al. XXX–lecia PRL (☎411-000/323-614/323-924).

International Ferries From Nowy Port, opposite Westerplatte. Take a train to Nowy Port station, or the much slower tram #10. Ferries depart for Travemunde (Germany), Nynäshaem (Sweden) and Helsinki. *PolFerries* tickets can be booked through Orbis, or the ferry office at ul. Swiętojańska 132 (☎208-761).

Music and Theater The *National Opera and Philharmonia House*, al. Zwycięstwa 15, features world-class opera and orchestral concerts. The *Gdańsk City Theater*, in the center of town at ul. św. Ducha 2, is well worth checking out, particularly for it's classical Polish theater pieces.

Newspapers Dailies *Głos Wybrzeze* and the new *Gazeta Gdańska* both give detailed listings for local events and a host of other local information, as does the Friday edition of *Dziennik Bałtycki*.

Pharmacies In Main Town: Długa 54/56, Chmielna 47/52, Grobla III 1/6. There are always a few all-night pharmacies on duty on a rotating basis; check the local papers for current details.

Post Office Main office (for *poste restante*, etc) is at ul. Długa 22; open 24hr for telephones, 8am–8pm for postal business.

Shopping The **Hala Targowa** on ul. Pańska has vegetables and fresh chickens outside, loads of small stalls inside, selling anything from caviar to condoms—price often negotiable. There's a good **bookshop** in the shopping arcade on ul. Heveliusa opposite the *Hewelius*. The **Pewex** in the Old Mill by the canal stocks the usual range of luxury western goods. Ul. **Mariacka**, east from Saint Mary's, is a lovely shopping street that somehow retains its peaceful atmosphere even at the height of the summer tourist onslaught. The street-level boutiques sell jewelry, amber products and quality leather at western prices.

Soccer The aptly named Lechia Gdańsk team plays at the BKS Lechia stadium on ul. Traugutta; nearest station is Gdańsk-Politechnika.

Sports Equipment (Sailing, canoeing etc). To rent from *MOSiR*, Ogarna 29.

Swimming Pools Indoor pools at the *Marina* and *Poseidon* hotels.

Train Tickets International train tickets from Orbis, plac Gorkiego 1, and from main stations in Gdańsk and Gdynia.

Sopot

One-time stomping ground for the rich and famous who came from all over the world to sample the casinos and the high life in the 1920s and 1930s, **SOPOT** is still a popular beach resort with landlocked Poles, and is increasingly attractive to westerners—Germans and Swedes in particular. It has an altogether different atmosphere from its neighbor: the fashionable boutiques and bars scattered round ul. Bohaterow Monte Cassino—the main avenue down to the pier—seem light years away from both historic central Gdańsk and the industrial grimness of the shipyards. If you're tired of tramping the streets of Gdańsk, Sopot's an excellent place for a seaside change of air.

The **pier**, constructed in 1928 but later rebuilt, is the longest in the whole Baltic area. Long sandy beaches stretch away on both sides; on the northern section you'll find ranks of bathing huts, some with marvelous 1920s wicker beach chairs for rent. Be warned, though, that the untreated filth pouring from the Wisła means that the whole Gdańsk bay is heavily **polluted**: some locals even consider lying on the sand a bit risky. Farther north from the pier there's a beach restaurant, a sauna and, right at the end, some very cheap tennis courts.

Upper Sopot, as the western part of town is known, is a wealthy suburb of entrepreneurs, architects, and artists—a sort of Polish Cape Cod or Malibu. Here and in other residential areas of Sopot, many of the houses have a touch of Art Nouveau style to them—look out for the turrets built for sunrise viewing. The **park** in upper Sopot offers lovely walks in the wooded hills around Łysa Góra, where there's a ski track in winter.

Accommodation

Sopot's vacation popularity means that rooms can be scarce. As well as the places given below, there are several seasonal hostels and hotels, details of which are given out by the PTTK office on the square opposite the train station. If the hotels are all full, the *biuro zakwaterowań* just down from the station at ul. Dworcowa 4 (daily 8am–6pm; ☎512-617) arranges **private rooms**. If they can't help, you're more than likely to be offered something if you stand around outside long enough.

Best of the **hotels** is the *Grand Hotel*, near the sea on ul. Powstańców Warszawy (☎511-896), which for once more than lives up to its name. Built in the 1920s in regal period style, the *Grand* was a favorite with President de Gaulle, Giscard d'Estaing, and the Shah of Iran, and after a long interval it has recently reopened its casino. Though shabbier than it used to be, it retains some of its former magnificence; huge old rooms at $55–95 a night for doubles, $45–70 for singles, make this an enjoyable indulgence for the westerner, if prohibitive for Poles. Of the other options, the *PTTK Dom Turysty*, al. Sepia 51 (☎510-014), is cheaper, but full in summer; and unfortunately the same goes for the nearby *Pensjonat Maryla*, al. Sepia 22 (☎510-034), and the better-quality *Baltyk* hotel, ul. Bieruta 81 (☎515-751).

There's also a **youth hostel** at al. Niepodlegosci 751 (July & Aug), and, finally, **campers** have two options, both reasonable: the PTTK grounds at Kamienica Potok (train to Kamienny Potok); and *Sopot Camping*, close to the beach at Bitwy Pod Plowcami 79, about a kilometer south from the pier (June–Aug).

Restaurants, Bars, and Cafés

The *Grand Hotel* **restaurant** is a treat, with excellent salmon, trout, and smoked eel; the hotel café is great for afternoon coffee—and men shouldn't miss the luxurious old *pissoirs*. The *Ermitage*, ul. Bohaterów Monte Cassino 23, and *Pod Strecha*, farther up the promenade at no. 17, are both trendy eating places, while the *Dworcowa*, opposite the station at pl. Konstytutcji 3 Maja 2, is more down-to-earth. If you're up in the hills of west Sopot, the old *Parkowy* motel restaurant (the motel part has now disappeared) is a quiet, relaxing spot.

In summer especially, the **pier area** is full of bars, coffee shops, and pleasant old milk bars. The *Zloty Ul* near the pier entrance is the **café** to watch the promenaders from. On ul. Bieruta, just off the promenade, the *Miramar* has lousy service but great cakes, which you may be forced to buy in absurdly large portions. *Spatif*, the artists' club upstairs at no. 54 on the promenade, has an eccentrically decadent cabaret tradition—look artistic to get in.

The lower part of the promenade is the place to be seen in Sopot: the *Marago* and *Alga* **clubs**, near the pier, are popular evening hang-outs, especially with Arab students and Syrians from Berlin.

Entertainments

The open-air **Opera Leśna**, in the peaceful hilly park in the west of Sopot, hosts big-scale productions including an **International Song Festival** in July. It's hoped to include big names from the western rock scene alongside the usual homegrown performers at future festivals. The "Friends of Sopot" hold **chamber music** concerts every Thursday at ul. Czyzewskiego 12 (off al. Bohaterow), in a room where Chopin is said to have played.

The *Baltyk* hotel has a **swimming pool** and good **tennis courts**—Davis Cup matches are sometimes played here. In upper Sopot there's a racecourse that puts on show-jumping and horse races every June.

Gdynia

Half an hour's train journey from central Gdańsk (trains every 5–10min), **GDYNIA** is the northernmost section of the Tri-City. Originally a small Kashubian village, from the fourteenth to the eighteenth century it was the property of the Cistercian monks of Oliwa. Boom time came after World War I, when Gdynia, unlike Gdańsk, returned to Polish jurisdiction. The limited coastline ceded to the new Poland—a twenty-mile strip of land stretching northward from Gdynia—left the country strapped for coastal outlets, so the Polish authorities embarked on a massive port-building program, which by the mid-1930s had transformed Gdynia from a small village into a bustling harbor. Following its capture in 1939, the Germans deported most of the Polish population, established a naval base, and to add insult to injury renamed the town Gotenhafen. Their retreat in 1945 was accompanied by wholesale destruction of the harbor installations, which were subsequently rebuilt by the communist authorities. The endearingly run-down, almost seedy atmosphere of today's port makes an interesting contrast to the more cultured Gdańsk.

Unless you like faceless 1950s city centers, the place to head for is the **port area**, directly east across town from the main station. From the station walk down ul. Starowiejska past the *Bristol* hotel, and after the bizarre concrete "Monument of Thankfulness" to the Soviets you'll find yourself at the foot of the large southernmost **pier**. Moored on its northern side is the *Błyskawica*, a World War II destroyer now housing a miniature **maritime museum** (May–Sept Tues–Sun 10am–4pm). Often anchored in the yacht basin beyond the ferry embarkation point is another proudly Polish vessel, the three-masted frigate *Dar Pomorza*, now a training ship; guided tours are given when it's in dock (Tues–Sun 10am–4pm). At the very end of the pier, a ham-fisted monument to Polish seafarer and novelist Joseph Conrad stands near the **aquarium**, where the fish are presumably healthier than the ones being caught by the fishermen ranged along the pier head. If you want more local maritime history, the **Naval Museum** on Bulwar Nadmorski, south of the pier (Tues–Sun 10am–4pm), fills in the details of Polish seafaring from early Slavic times to World War II. To complete the tour there's a nice view over the harbor from the hilltop of Kamienna Góra, a shortish walk south of the town center.

Accommodation

The *Gdynia*, ul. 22 Lipca 22 (☎206-661), is a flashy modern Orbis joint for the rich sailing contingent who hang out here in the summer; the rooms are nothing much to talk about, and prices are the same as Orbis hotels in Gdańsk. The *Bristol*, on ul. Starowiejska in the town center, is a sensibly priced alternative. Other options, in declining order of quality, are the *Nadmorski*, ul. Ejsmonda 2, the *Garnizonowy*, ul. Jana Z Kolna 25, and the *Dworcowy*, ul. Dworcowa 11a.

Private rooms are organized by the *biuro zakwaterowań* at ul. Dworcowa 7 (daily 8am–5pm; ☎210-531). The main **youth hostel**, open all year, is at ul. Czerwonych Kosynierów 108C (☎2044-23); take the local train to Gdynia-Grabowek, or bus #109, #125, #141, or tram #22, #25, #26, or #30. There's also a summer **hostel** at ul. Wiczlinska 93. There are two **campgrounds** in south Gdynia: at ul. Swiętopelka 19/23 right by the sea, and at Spacerowa 7; for both, take the train to Gdynia-Orłowo station.

Restaurants, Bars, and Cafés

The *Gdynia* has a restaurant which is considered by some to be one of the best in the region—fine if you like an expensive westernized menu and can put up with the jet set. The *George* at ul. 3 Maja 21, *Ermitage* at Świętojańska 39, and *Mysliwśka* at ul. Abrahama 18, are all better priced and more Polish alternatives.

Likewise, the *Bristol* has a restaurant and adjoining beer bar that's popular with the locals. There's also a host of assorted milk bars and greasy spoons dotted around the town center. For a coffee break, the *Ambrozja*, at ul. Starowiejska 14, usually has a good selection of *sernik* and other cakes.

Entertainments

The **Musical Theater** (*Teatr Muszyczny*), plac Grunwaldzki 1, near the Gdynia hotel, is a favorite haunt with Poles and tourists alike, featuring quality Polish musicals, as well as all-too-frequent productions of the Andrew Lloyd Webber oeuvre. Tickets from the box office or the Orbis bureau in the *Gdynia*.

The Hel Peninsula

For the bucket-and-spade brigade, relief from the pollution of the Gdańsk bay is at hand in the shape of the **Hel Peninsula**, a long thin strip of land sticking out into the Baltic sea twenty kilometers above Gdańsk. The sandy beaches dotted along the north side of the peninsula are well away from the poisonous Wisła outlet, making the water around here as clean as you'll get on the Baltic coast; what's more, they are easily accessible and almost never overcrowded.

Hel...

HEL, the small fishing port at the tip of the peninsula, is the main destination. It's an enjoyable two-and-a-half-hour trip from Gdańsk in an open boat from the Motława waterfront (first departure 9am in summer), giving you the chance to see the shipyard complex on the way out to sea.

Despite heavy wartime fighting—a German army of 100,000 men was rounded up on the peninsula in 1945—the main street retains some nineteenth-century wooden fishermen's cottages. For the locals the main attraction seems to be the bar/restaurant on this main drag, which unlike virtually any known bar in Gdańsk serves strong "Gdańsk Export" draft beer in apparently limitless quantities.

Hel's **Maritime Museum** (Tues–Sun 10am–4pm), housed in the village's Gothic former church, has plenty of model ships and fishing tackle as well as some local folk art. As on the adjoining mainland, the people of the peninsula are predominantly Kashubian (see "Kashubia," below), as evidenced in the local dialect and the distinctive embroidery styles on show in the museum.

... and beyond

If you're not in a hurry to get back to town, you could take one of the regular trains along the wooded, sandy shoreline for an afternoon swim; the really energetic could do the thirty-odd kilometers of the peninsula in a solid day's walking, beach stops included. Whichever way you do it, two worthwhile stopping-off places are the small harbor at **JASTARNIA**, a few kilometers west of Hel, and **KUŹNICA**, a little beyond. Jastarnia has a **PTTK hostel** at ul. Baltycka 5, a campground, and one or two basic eating places; Kuznica, like nearby CHALUPY, is basically a good beach with camping space nearby.

You touch down on the mainland at **WŁADYSŁAWOWO**, a small but busy fishing port. The old fish hall, the **Dom Rybacka**, has a restaurant on the second floor—the local fish dishes are excellent, but some customers might be deterred by the pollution hazards. For an overnight stay in town ask at the **biuro zakwate-rowań** at ul. 22–go Lipca 4, just up from the hall; there's a summer campground on ul. Helska too. Regular local trains run from here to Gdynia and Gdańsk, taking between an hour and ninety minutes.

A five-kilometer bus journey farther up the coast is **JASTRZĘBIA GÓRA**, a popular seaside resort with a 1930s atmosphere and some good beaches nearby. The handful of *pensjonats* are likely to have space, as the town is shifting identities from a subsidized workers' resort to a privatized one. If cash is short, try the *Pod Zagłem* hostel on ul. Zeromskiego (often full though), or the campground at LISI JAR just east of the main resort.

Kashubia

The large area of lakes and hills to the west of Gdańsk—**Kashubia**—is the home-land of one of Poland's lesser-known ethnic minorities, the **Kashubians**. "Not German enough for the Germans, nor Polish enough for the Poles"—Grandma Koljiaczek's wry observation in *The Tin Drum*—sums up the historic predica-ment of this group. Originally a western Slav people linked ethnically to Poles, they were subjected to a German cultural onslaught during the Partition period, when the area was incorporated into Prussia. The process was resisted fiercely: in the 1910 regional census, only 6 out of the 455 inhabitants of one typical village gave their nationality as German.

But the Kashubians' treatment by the Poles has not always been better, and it's often argued that Gdańsk's domination of the region has kept the development of a Kashubian national identity in check. Certainly the local museums are some-times guilty of consigning the Kashubians to the realm of quaint historical phenomena, denying the reality of what is still a living culture. You can hear the distinctive Kashubian language spoken all over the region, particularly by older people, and many villages still produce such Kashubian handicrafts as embroi-dered cloths and tapestries.

Zukowo and Kartuzy

The old capital of the region, Kartuzy, is tucked away among the lakes and woods 30km west of Gdańsk. From the main Gdańsk station a bus winds its way through the hills, passing en route through **ZUKOWO**, the first really Kashubian village. The fourteenth-century **Norbertine church and convent** here has a rich Baroque interior and organ, resembling a country version of St Nicholas in Gdańsk. The arrangement of buildings – church, convent, vicarage, and adjoining barns—has a distinctly feudal feel. Leaving Zukowo, on the Kartuzy road, gour-mets should keep an eye out for a Swiss restaurant signposted off to the right—it's among the best in the region.

Though reached in just an hour, the dusty, rather run-down market town of **KARTUZY** feels a long way from Gdańsk. The **Kashubian Regional Museum** at ul. Ludowa Polskiego 1 (March–Oct Tues–Sat 9am–4pm, Sun 9am–3pm; Nov–April closed Sun) introduces you to the intricacies of Kashubian domestic, cultural, and religious traditions. Highlight of the curator's guided tour is his performance of a Kashubian folk song complete with dramatic accompaniment—introducing the musical and theatrical delights of such instruments as the *bazuna, burchybas,* and *skrzypce diabelskie.* The Gothic **church**, part of a group of buildings erected in 1380 on the northern edge of town by Carthusian monks from Bohemia, is a somber sort of place—the fact that the building is coffin-shaped may have something to do with it. Otherwise nothing much remains of the original monastery. More appealing are the paths through the beech groves surrounding nearby **Lake Klasztorne**, a nice place to cool off on a summer's day.

If you decide to make a night of it, you can try either the *Rugan* **hostel**, ul. 1 Maja 34 (☎15-83), or ask about **private rooms** at the **tourist office** at ul. Dworcowa 4/8 (☎20-86). There's also a summer **youth hostel** at ul. Ks Sciegiennego 3. A few *kawiarnia* aside, the only actual restaurant in Kartuzy is the *Kashubska* at ul. Szymbaka 6; don't expect too much.

The Strawberry Festival

In the postwar years, Kashubia has gathered some wealth through the development of strawberry production: if you want to sample the crop, the June **strawberry festival** held on a hill 2km out of Kartuzy (anyone will direct you) provides an ideal opportunity. The occasion is part market, part fair—a little like a German *Jahrmarkt*—with the local farmers bringing baskets of strawberries to the church at nearby WYGODA, which is situated in the middle of a field.

Around Kashubia

Behind Kartuzy the heartland of Kashubia opens out into a high plateau of **lakes**, low hills, and tranquil woodland dotted with villages and the occasional small town. Running around the whole area is the **Ostrzydkie Circle**, an Ice-Age hill formation that has a winter ski slope at **Wiezyca**, some 10km south of Kartuzy on the road to Kościerzyna. Being an intensely religious region, Kashubia is especially worth visiting during any of the major **Catholic festivals**—Corpus Christi for example, or Marian festivals such as the Dormition of the Virgin on August 15.

Buses and a couple of local **train lines** service the region, but a car is a definite bonus. In the past, tourist excursions have also been offered from Gdańsk to Wdzydze Kiszewski and elsewhere; it could be worth asking at Orbis or the tourist offices.

Chmielno and Sierakowice

Set among the lakes west of Kartuzy, **CHMIELNO** is a center of Kashubian ceramics and pottery as well as a busy Polish holiday target. A youth hostel and private rooms (ask at the tourist office) are available in the village, and there's a campground nearby on the edge of Lake Klodno.

The much larger **Lake Radunia**, a couple of kilometers to the south, is a popular sailing area: **canoes** and **yachts** are both available for rent in an informal kind of way if you ask at the lakeside workers' hostels—which may also be able to provide accommodation.

Moving west, **SIERAKOWICE** (20km from Kartuzy on the Lembork railroad line) is a typically charming Kashubian haunt, with classic wooden church, in the midst of some lovely countryside. It has a few private rooms.

Wdzydze Kiszewskie

At the village of **WDZYDZE KISZEWSKIE**, 25km southwest of Kartuzy (and 5km south of Kościerzyna), there's an open-air museum, or *skansen* (Tues–Sun 10am–4pm), devoted to Kashubian architecture and folk culture, its exhibits including windmills and old barns reassembled from the region. A weekend summer combination **festival-market** is held here every July, an event for which many of the locals deck themselves out in traditional Kashubian costume.

The village has some accommodation: the *Pod Niedźwiadkiem* tourist **hostel** and a couple of summer **campgrounds** (June–Sept). Like so many Kashubian villages, it too is on the edge of a lake, with negotiable boats and the like.

Frombork

A little seaside town 90km east along the Baltic coast from Gdańsk, **FROMBORK** was the home of Nicolaus Copernicus, the Renaissance astronomer whose ideas overturned church-approved scientific notions, specifically the earth-centred model of the universe. Most of the research for his famous *De Revolutionibus* (see box overleaf) was carried out around this town, and it was here that he died and was buried in 1543. Just over a century later, Frombork was badly mauled by marauding Swedes, who carted off most of Copernicus' belongings, including his library. The town was wrecked in World War II, after which virtually none of the old quarter was left standing. Today it's an out-of-the-way place, as peaceful as it probably was in Copernicus' time.

The only part of Frombork to escape unscathed from the last war was the **Cathedral Hill**, up from the old market square in the middle of town. A compact unit surrounded by high defensive walls, its main element is the dramatic fourteenth-century Gothic **Cathedral**, with its huge red-tiled and turreted roof. Inside, the lofty expanses of brick rise above a series of lavish Baroque altars— the High Altar is a copy of the Wawel altarpiece in Kraków. The seventeenth-century **organ** towering over the nave is one of the best in the country, and the Sunday afternoon recitals in summer are an established feature: check the concert program at the tourist office in Gdańsk. If you like organ music but can't make it to a concert, Frombork organ records are available from the unofficial guide who hangs around outside the cathedral; he also happens to be an authority on the intricacies of local ethnic history.

To the west of the cathedral, the **Copernicus Tower** is supposed to have been the great man's workshop and observatory. Doubting that the local authorities would have let him make use of a part of the town defenses, some maintain that he's more likely to have studied at his home, just north of the cathedral complex. The **Radziejowski Tower**, in the southwest corner of the walls, houses an assortment of Copernicus-related astronomical instruments and has an excellent view of the Wislany lagoon stretching seventy kilometers north towards the Soviet naval base of Kaliningrad (formerly Königsberg). More equipment and memorabilia of the astronomer are to be found in the **Copernicus Museum** in the Warmia Bishops' Palace, across the tree-lined cathedral courtyard (Tues–Sun 9am–3pm). Among the exhibits are early editions of Copernicus' astronomical treatises, along with a number of his lesser-known works on medical, political, and economic questions, a collection of astrolabes, sextants, and other instruments, plus pictures and portraits.

NICOLAUS COPERNICUS

Nicolaus Copernicus—Mikołaj Kopernik as he's known to Poles — was born in Toruń in 1473. The son of a wealthy merchant family with strong church connections, he entered Kraków's Jagiellonian University and subsequently joined the priesthood. Like most educated Poles of his era, he traveled abroad to continue his studies, spending time at the famous Renaissance universities of Bologna and Padua.

On his return home in 1497 he became administrator for the northern bishopric of Warmia, developing a wide field of interests, working as a doctor, lawyer, architect, and soldier (he supervised the defense of nearby Olsztyn against the Teutonic Knights)—the archetypal Renaissance man. He lived for some fifteen years as canon of the Frombork chapter house and here constructed an observatory, where he undertook the research that provided the empirical substance for the *De Revolutionibus Orbium Caelestium,* whose revolutionary contention was that the sun, not the earth, was at the center of the planetary system. The work was published by the church authorities in Nuremberg in the year of Copernicus' death in 1543; it was later banned by the papacy.

Practicalities

For an overnight stay the best of a limited choice of rooms is a decent-quality **PTTK hostel** at ul. Krasickiego 3. The other options are the *Słoneczny*, a basic hotel near the cathedral at ul. Koscielna 2, or the summer youth hostel at ul. Elblągska 1. The **PTTK campground** on ul. Braniewska (May 15–Sept 15) is some way from the center. Apart from some summer takeout bars, the only places to eat are the *Pod Wzgorzem* on ul. Rynek and the restaurant in the PTTK hostel.

Frombork's **bus and train stations** are next to each other near the seafront; you're likely to use the PKP only if you're heading for Elbląg. The bus journey from Gdańsk central station takes between two and three hours—for a day trip take the earlier of the two morning buses, returning late afternoon: if there's no direct bus back, take one to Elbląg and change there.

ALONG THE WISŁA

Following the course of the **Wisła** south from Gdańsk takes you into the heart of the territory once ruled by the **Teutonic Knights**. From a string of fortresses overlooking the river this religio-militaristic order controlled the lucrative medieval grain trade, and it was under their protection that merchant colonists from the northern Hanseatic League cities established themselves down the Wisła as far south as Toruń. The Knights' architectural legacies are distinctive red brick constructions: tower-churches, sturdy granaries, solid burghers' mansions surrounded by rings of defensive walls and protected by castles. **Malbork**, the Knights' headquarters, is the prime example—a town settled within and below one of the largest fortresses of medieval Europe. Continuing downriver, a string of lesser fortified towns – **Kwidzyn**, **Grudziąz** and **Chełmno**—lead to the ancient city of **Toruń**.

During the Partitions era—from the late eighteenth century up until World War I—this upper stretch of the Wisła was **Prussian** territory, an ownership that has left its own mark on the neat towns and cities. After 1918, part of the territory returned to Poland, part remained in East Prussia; in World War II, as throughout this region, much was destroyed during the German retreat.

Physically, the **river delta** is a flat plain of isolated villages, narrow roads, and drained farmland, with the towns an occasional and imposing presence. The river itself is wide, slow-moving, and dirty, the landscape all open vistas under frequently sullen skies. **Travel connections** aren't too bad, with buses and trains between the main towns, all of which are within reasonable striking distance of Gdańsk.

Malbork

For Poles brought up on the novels of Henryk Sienkiewicz, the massive riverside fortress of **MALBORK** conjures up the epic medieval struggles between Poles and Germans that he so vividly described in *The Teutonic Knights*. Approached from any angle, the intimidating stronghold dominates the town, imparting the threatening atmosphere of an ancient military headquarters to an otherwise quiet, undistinguished, and—following war damage—predominantly modern town.

The history of the town and castle is intimately connected with that of the **Teutonic Knights** (see box overleaf), who established themselves here in the late thirteenth century and proceeded to turn a modest fortress into the labyrinthine monster whose remains you can see today. After two centuries of Teutonic domination, the town returned to Polish control in 1457, and for the next 300 years the castle was a royal residence, used by Polish monarchs as a stopover en route between Warsaw and Gdańsk. Following the Partitions, the **Prussians** turned the castle into a barracks and set about dismantling large sections of the masonry—a process halted only by public outcry in Berlin. Except for the eastern wings, the castle came through World War II unharmed.

The Castle

You approach the main fortress (May–Sept Tues–Sun 9am–4:30pm; Oct–April 9am–3pm) through the old outer castle, a zone of utility buildings which was never rebuilt after the war. The fortress itself was restored from 1817, work seen as a glorious reminder of Prussia's medieval past, and which has been continued by the Poles—with rather less of an eye to ideology—since the 1950s.

Passing over the moat and through the daunting main gate, you come to the **Middle Castle**, built following the Knights' decision to move their headquarters to Malbork in 1309. Spread out around an open courtyard, this part of the complex contains the Grand Master's palace, of which the **Main Refectory** is the highlight. Begun in 1330, this huge vaulted chamber is one of the few rooms still preserved in pretty much its original condition; the elegant palm vaulting, supported on slender granite pillars, shows the growing influence of the Gothic cathedral architecture developed elsewhere in Europe. Displays of weaponry are arranged around the refectory, but more interesting is the painting that fills one of the walls: *The Battle of Grunwald* is archetypal Matejko romanticism, a heroic, action-packed interpretation of a key moment in Polish history.

Leading off from the **courtyard** are a host of dark, cavernous chambers. The largest ones contain collections of ceramics, glass, sculpture, paintings, and—most importantly—a large display of Baltic **amber**, the trade in which formed the backbone of the order's fabulous wealth. Innumerable amber pieces of all shapes

THE TEUTONIC KNIGHTS

The Templars, the Hospitallers and the **Teutonic Knights** were the three major military-religious orders to emerge from the Crusades. Founded in 1190 as a fraternity serving the sick, the order combined the ascetic ideals of monasticism with the military training of a knight. Eclipsed by their rivals in the Holy Land, the Knights—the Teutonic Order of the Hospital of Saint Mary, to give them their full title—established their first base in Poland at Chełmno in 1225, following an appeal from Duke Konrad of Mazovia for protection against the pagan Pomeranians and Prussians. The Knights proceeded to annihilate the Prussian population, establishing German colonies in their place. It's ironic that the people known as Prussians in modern European history are not descendants of these original Slavic populations, but the Germanic settlers who annihilated them.

With the loss of their last base in Palestine in 1271, the Teutonic Knights started looking around for a European site for their headquarters. Three years later they began the construction of Malbork Castle—**Marienburg**, "the fortress of Mary," as they named it—and in 1309 the Grand Master transferred here from Venice.

Economically the Knights' chief targets were control of the **Hanseatic cities** and the trade in Baltic amber, over which they gained a virtual monopoly. Politically their main aim was territorial conquest, especially to the east—which, with their religious zealotry established in Palestine, they saw as a crusade to set up a theocratic political order. Although the Polish kings soon began to realise their mistake in inviting the Knights in, until the start of the fifteenth century most European monarchs were still convinced by the order's religious ideology; their cause was aided by the fact that the Lithuanians, Europe's last pagan population, remained unconverted until well into the fourteenth century.

The showdown with Poland came in 1410 at the **Battle of Grunwald**, one of the most momentous clashes of medieval Europe. Recognizing a common enemy, an allied force of Poles and Lithuanians inflicted the first really decisive defeat on the Knights, yet failed to follow up the victory, and allowed them to retreat to Malbork unchallenged. It wasn't until 1457 that they were driven out of their Malbork stronghold by King Kazimierz Jagiełło. The Grand Master of the Order fled to Prussian-ruled Königsberg.

The Knights' political power, however, was soon to revive. In 1525, the Grand Master, Albrecht von Hohenzollern, having converted to Lutheranism, decided to dissolve the order and transform its holdings into a secular duchy, with himself as head. Initially, political considerations meant he had to accept the Polish king as his overlord, and thus he paid homage before King Zygmunt in the marketplace at Kraków in 1525. But the duchy had full jurisdiction over its internal affairs, which allowed for the adoption of Protestantism as its religion. This turned out to be a crucial step in the history of Europe, as it gave the ambitious Hohenzollern family a power base outside the structures of the Holy Roman Empire, an autonomy that was to be of vital importance to them in their ultimately successful drive to weld the German nation into a united state.

and sizes are on show here—everything from beautiful miniature altars and exotic jewelry pieces to an assembly of plants and million-year-old-flies encased in the precious resin. If you're visiting in summer, the main courtyard provides the spectacular backdrop for the castle's sound-and-light shows.

From the Middle Castle a passage rises to the smaller courtyard of the **High Castle**, the oldest section of the fortress, dating from the late thirteenth century. Climbing up from the courtyard you enter a maze of passages leading to turrets whose slit windows scan the approaches to Malbork. The religious focus of the Knights' austere monasticism was the vast **Castle Church**, complete with seven-pillared refectory and cloisters; features from the church's delicately sculptured **Golden Gate** are mirrored in the portals of the **Chapel of St Anne**, a later extension of the main structure. The Knights' spartan sleeping quarters are nearby, down the passageway running to the Gdanisko Tower—the castle toilet.

When you've finished looking around inside, head **over the bridge** to the other side of the river (technically the Nogat—a tributary of the Wisła), where the view of the castle allows you to appreciate what a Babylonian project it must have seemed to medieval visitors and the people of the surrounding country. The hot-dog stall stationed on hand might help fuel the imagination.

Practicalities

The castle aside, there is little to say about Malbork, whose old town was virtually razed in World War II. Evidence of the intense fighting in these parts is to be seen in the Allied war cemetery on the edge of the town.

The **train and bus stations** are sited next to each other about ten minutes' walk south of the castle; Malbork is on the main Warsaw line, so there are plenty of trains from Gdańsk (1hr) as well as a regular bus service. Tourist **information** is available from the **PTTK office** inside the castle area at ul. Hibnera 4, or from the *Hotel Zbyszko*, between the stations and castle.

There are three **hotels**. The *Zbyszko*, ul. Kościuski 43 (☎3394), is preferable to the dingy *Sportowy* (☎2413) east of the castle at ul. Portowa 3, or the *Dom Wycieckowy* (☎3311) at ul. Mickiewicza 26. If you'd rather stay in someone's home, **private rooms** should be available through the reception at the *Zbyszko*. The youth **hostel** is at ul. Zeromskiego 45 (July & Aug), about 2km south of the station along al. W. Polskiego. There's a decent **campground** at ul. Portowa 1 (June–Sept). For a **meal** try either the *Zbyszko* restaurant or *Nad Nogatem* on pl. Słowianski, just west of the castle complex; neither is anything out of the ordinary.

Kwidzyn

Set in the loop of a tributary a few kilometers east of the Wisła, **KWIDZYN** is a smallish fortified town amid a sprawling, dirty industrial belt. The first stronghold established by the Teutonic Knights—in the 1230s, some forty years before the move to Malbork—its original fortress was rapidly joined by a bishop's residence and cathedral. Three hundred years later, the castle was demolished and rebuilt, but the cathedral and bishop's chapter house were left untouched; unlike the rest of the Old Town area, the entire complex survived the fierce fighting in 1945 unscathed.

The Castle Complex

Most of the **Castle** is poised on a hilltop over the Liwa River, but the most immediately striking feature is the tower stranded out in the river bed; connected to the main building by means of a precarious roofed walkway, it looks more like the remains of a bridge-builder's folly than a solid defensive structure. Ranged around a large open courtyard, the castle houses a rather run-down local **museum** (Tues–Sun 9am–4pm), charting the early development of human settlements along the Wisła basin, with additional sections on folklore, natural history, and the tangled ethnography of the region. Despite later reconstructions the large, moody **Cathedral**, adjoining the castle, retains several original Gothic features, the most noteworthy being a beautiful late fourteenth-century mosaic in the southern vestibule.

Practicalities

There's no particularly good reason to stop over in what—cathedral and castle apart—is a pretty undistinguished sort of place. However, **accommodation** is provided by the **hotels** *Saga*, ul. Chopina 42 (☎3433), the *Miejski*, ul. Braterstwa Narodów 42 (☎3732), the *Pensjonat Miłosna* on ul. Miłosna (☎3249), and the **youth hostel** (June & July) on ul. Braterstwa Narodów 58 (☎3876). There's also a **campground** on ul. Sportowa, on the edge of town. For **eating**, the *Piastowska* and the *Kaskada* on ul. Chopina are the main options. Tourist information is handled by the *Saga*.

The town has regular **bus** services to Tczew, Malbork, and Grudziąz. Trains run to Gdańsk twice daily (1hr 30min).

Grudziąz

GRUDZIĄZ, 35km downriver from Kwidzyn, was another early Teutonic stronghold and is again flanked by unprepossessing industrial development. Bus and train terminals are right in the center—a shortish walk west toward the river and you're soon inside the more attractive confines of the atmospheric **Old Town**, overlooking the river.

The Old Town

Grudziąz has changed hands several times. The Knights took over control of an early Polish settlement, then were obliged to hand it back in 1454. Included in the territory annexed by Prussia during the Partition period, it became part of the inter-war Polish corridor, was nabbed by the Germans in 1939 and finally returned to Poland in 1945. Those years of Prussian control explain the distinctively Germanic feel of the town, which despite the usual war damage retains several of its old buildings. For all the faded shopfronts and crumbling houses, the orderly arrangement of the charming **Rynek** bespeaks Prussian orderliness and sense of proportion. As the cars and buses parked below the old quarter indicate, slowly but surely Germans are coming back to old haunts like these, to visit the homes of their ancestors or even the scenes of their own childhoods.

Most of the sights are a short walk from the Rynek. The Gothic **Parish Church** to the north is a typically Teutonic high-brick construction with an equally typical Baroque overlay to the interior. To the south, the **Benedictine Monastery** houses a museum (Tues–Sun 10am–4pm, Wed 10am–3pm), as interesting for the exhibitions by local artists as for the established displays recounting the town's history.

Above the river, the **granaries** built into the hillside fortifications are a reminder of the importance once attached to the grain trade. Together with the **mansions** topping the walls, they form the centerpoint of the famous view of the town from the other side of the river; one of the best vantage points is from the train to or from Bydgoszcz and Gdańsk. The hill north of the Rynek—**Góra**

Zamkowa—is the former castle site, now scattered with just a few foundations and an obelisk modeled on an ancient pagan statue of Światowid, a Slav deity.

Practicalities

For an overnight stay in the town, the *Nadwiślanin*, a short walk south of the Old Town at ul. 1 Maja 28 (☎260-30), is definitely the **hotel** to go for; as well as an IT point selling local maps, it's got the best **restaurant** in town. Other options are the *Pomorzanin*, ul. Kwiatowa 28 (☎261-41), the *Garnizonowy*, ul. Świerczewskiego 53 (☎264-46), and the all-year **youth hostel** at ul. Obr. Stalingradu 102 (☎231-18), a bus ride south from the center.

Trains run frequently to Bydgoszcz and Toruń (both 1hr) and twice daily to Gdańsk (2hr). There are **bus** connections with Kwidzyn, Chełmno, and Toruń.

Chełmno

The hilltop town of **CHEŁMNO**, another important old Prussian center, escaped from World War II undamaged, and has remained untouched by postwar industrial development. Perhaps the most memorable thing about the place is its atmosphere—the archetypal quiet rural town, steeped in the powerful mixture of the Polish and Prussian that characterizes the region as a whole.

Although a Polish stronghold is known to have existed here as early as the eleventh century, Chełmno really came to life in 1228 with the arrival of the Teutonic Knights. They made the town their first political and administrative center, which led to rapid and impressive development. An academy was founded in 1386 on the model of the famed University of Bologna, and despite the damage inflicted by the Swedes in the 1650s, the town continued to thrive right up to the time of the Partitions, when it lapsed into provincial Prussian obscurity.

The Old Town

To enter the Old Town area, cars and people alike pass through the **Grudziąż Gate**, a well-proportioned, fourteenth-century Gothic construction topped by fine Renaissance gables. Continue along ul. Grudziązka and you're soon amid the Prussian ensemble of the **Rynek**, a grand open space at the heart of the grid-like network of streets. Gracing the center of the square is the brilliant white **Town Hall**, its facade exuding a real hat-in-the-air exuberance. Rebuilt in the 1560s on the basis of an earlier Gothic hall, its elegant facade, decorated attic, and soaring tower are one of the great examples of Polish Renaissance architecture. It houses a rather inconsequential **museum** (Tues–Sun 10am–4pm), whose main attraction is the chance to look around the building.

Most of Chełmno's seven churches are Gothic, their red brick towers and facades punctuating the streets of the Old Town at regular intervals. Best of the bunch is the **Parish Church** standing just off the Rynek to the west, an imposing thirteenth-century building with a fine carved doorway. The interior retains sculpted pillars, a Romanesque stone font, and fragmentary frescoes. Further west, past St James' church, is an early fourteenth-century **monastery**, former home to a succession of Cistercian and Benedictine orders. Its church features some original Gothic painting and a curious twin-level nave. The church backs onto the western corner of the town walls, crumbling but complete and walkable for excellent views over the Wisła and low-lying plains.

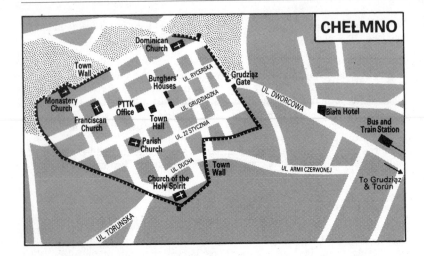

Practicalities

For a town with some potential commercial pull, there are precious few tourist facilities here. The **train and bus stations** (buses are easiest, coming from Grudziądz) are next to each other on ul. Dworcowa, a fifteen-minute walk to the west of the Old Town.

There's no real information office to speak of, but it might be worth trying the PTTK on the main square at no. 12. The *Biala*, ul. Dworcowa 23(☎86/0212), just up from the station, is the only decent **hotel** and the only **restaurant** worthy of the name. Enter the *Pod Kogutem* at Rynek 5 at your peril—it's a serious dive. A **youth hostel** (June & July) operates at ul. Klasztorna 12 (☎86/2470), on the western edge of the Old Town.

Toruń

Poles are apt to wax lyrical on the glories of their ancient cities, and in the case of **TORUŃ**—the biggest and most important of the Hanseatic trading centers along the Wisła—it is more than justified. Miraculously surviving the recurrent wars afflicting the region, the historic core is one of the country's most evocative, bringing together a rich assembly of architectural styles. The city's main claim to fame is as the birthplace of Nicolaus Copernicus, whose house still stands. Today, it is a university city: large, reasonably prosperous, and—once you're through the standard postwar suburbs—with a definitely cultured air.

Some History

The pattern of Toruń's early history is similar to that of other towns along the northern Wisła. Starting out as a Polish settlement, it was overrun by Prussian tribes from the east towards the end of the twelfth century, and soon afterward the Teutonic Knights moved in. The Knights rapidly developed the town, thanks to its access to the burgeoning river-borne grain trade, a position further consolidated with its entry to the Hanseatic League. As in rival Gdańsk, economic prosperity was expressed in a mass of building projects through the following century; together these make up the majority of the historic sites in the city.

Growing disenchantment with the Teutonic Knights' rule and heavy taxation, especially among the merchants, led to the formation of the Prussian Union in 1440, with Toruń as its base. In 1454, as war broke out between the Knights and Poland, the townspeople destroyed the castle in Toruń and chased the Order out of town. The 1466 Treaty of Toruń conclusively terminated the Knights' control of the area.

The next two centuries brought even greater wealth as the town thrived on extensive royal privileges and increased access to goods from all over Poland. The Swedish invasion of the 1650s was the first significant setback, but the really decisive blow to the city's fortunes came a century later with the Partitions, when Toruń was annexed to Prussia and thus severed from its hinterlands, which by now were Russian. Like much of the region, Toruń was subjected to systematic Germanization, but as in many other cities a strongly Polish identity remained, clearly manifested in the cultural associations that flourished in the latter part of the nineteenth century. Toruń returned to Poland under the terms of the 1919 Versailles treaty as part of the "Polish corridor" that was to enrage Hitler; it was liberated from the Nazis in 1945.

> The Toruń area telephone code is ☎056.

Arriving and Finding a Place to Stay

The principal **stations** are on opposite sides of the Old Town. Toruń Główny, the main **train station**, is south of the river; buses #12 and #22 run over the bridge to pl. Rapackiego, on the western edge of the Old Town. From the **bus station** on ul. Dąbrowskiego it is a short walk north to the center. The **PTTK**, pl. Rapackiego 2 (Mon–Fri 8am–4:30pm, Sat & Sun 10am–1pm), is the most useful general **information** point. **Orbis**, on the corner of the Rynek at ul. Zeglarska 31, issues travel tickets, while **Almatur**, in the university area at ul. Gagarina 21, can arrange beds in student hotels.

There's a reasonable choice of **accommodation** on offer. Orbis has two hotels aimed at foreign tourist groups: the *Kosmos*, ul. Portowa 2 (☎289-00), west near the river, and the inferior *Helios*, ul. Kraszewskiego 1/3 (☎250-33), northwest of downtown. Slightly cheaper and a lot more attractive is the *Zajazd Staropolski*, ul. Zeglarska 12/14 (☎260-61/260-63), well situated just down from the Rynek; it's very popular in summer though, so you'll be lucky to get a room on a walk-in basis. A step down in quality are the *Polonia*, pl. Armii Czerwonej 5 (☎230-28), and the *Pod Orłem*, ul. Mostowa 15 (☎250-24), though both are in easy walking distance of the Rynek. The *Pod Trzema Koronami*, ul. Stary Rynek 21 (☎260-31), is a further step down—tatty rooms and dubious shared bathrooms—but it makes up for everything with its location on the edge of the Rynek, overlooking the town hall. Consider the PTTK hostel, well north of the center at ul. Zjednoczenia 24, only as a last resort.

Of the two all-year **youth hostels**, the one at ul. Podmurna 4 (☎235-53) is excellently located in a Gothic tower overlooking the river. If you can't get in—a distinct possibility in summer—you'll have to settle for the one across the river some way to the east of the train station at ul. Rudacka 15 (☎272-42); bus #13 runs nearby. The *Tramp* **campground** at ul. Kujawska 14, a short walk west of the train station, has some bungalows as well as tent space—and it's not a bad setting. Finally, in summer the university runs **international student hotels**—details from the Almatur office (see above).

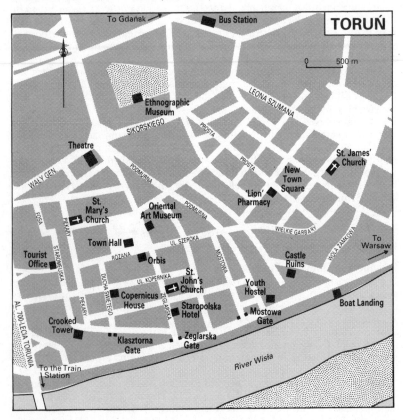

The City

The historic core of Toruń is divided into "Old Town" and "New Town" areas, both established in the early years of Teutonic rule. Traditional economic divisions are apparent here, the Old Town quarter being home for the merchants, the other for the artisans; each had its own square, market area and town hall.

Overlooking the river from a gentle rise, the medieval nucleus constitutes a relatively small section of the modern city and is clearly separated from it by a ring of main roads. Approached from along the river, the ramparts, the Gothic spires, and towers are unmissable, their shapely forms dominating the surroundings. Arriving from other directions can pose more problems, since there's a lack of signs pointing to the center; ask for the way to the Stare Miasto.

The Old Town (Stare Miasto)

The westerly Old Town area is the obvious place to start looking around—and as usual it's the **Rynek**, in particular the **Town Hall**, that provides the focal point. Town halls don't come much bigger or more striking than this: raised in the late fourteenth century on the site of earlier cloth halls and trading stalls, this immensely elegant work is one of the finest Gothic buildings in northern Europe. A three-story brick structure topped by a sturdy tower, its outer walls are punctuated by indented windows, framed by a rhythmic succession of high arches peaking just beneath the roof, and complemented by graceful Renaissance turrets and high gables.

The south side entrance leads to an inner courtyard surrounded by fine brick doorways, the main one leading to the **Town Museum** (Tues–Sat 10am–4pm), which now occupies much of the building. Over the centuries Toruń's wealth attracted artists and craftsmen of every type, and it's their work that features strongest here. Most of the ground floor—once the wine cellar—is devoted to medieval artifacts, with a gorgeous collection of the **stained glass** for which the city was famed and some fine **sculptures**—especially the celebrated "Beautiful Madonnas." Also housed on this floor is an extensive archaeological section, bringing together highlights of a vast array of neolithic and early Bronze-Age relics uncovered in this region. On the upper floor, painting takes over, with rooms covered in portraits of Polish kings and wealthy Toruń citizens. A small portrait of the most famous city burgher, Copernicus, basks in the limelight of a Baroque gallery. Before leaving the town hall it's also worth climbing the **tower** for the view of the city and the winding course of the Wisła, stretching into the plain on the southern horizon.

Lining the square itself are the stately mansions of the Hansa merchants, many of whose high parapets and decorated facades are preserved intact. The finest houses flank the east side of the square. Number 35, next to one of the Copernicus family houses, is the fifteenth-century **Pod Gwiazdą**, with a finely modeled late Baroque facade; inside, a superbly carved wooden staircase ends with a statue of Minerva, spear in hand. The house is now a small **Oriental Museum** (Tues–Sun 10am–4pm), based on a private collection of art from China, India, and other Far Eastern countries.

Off to the west of the square stands **St Mary's Church**, a large fourteenth-century building with elements of its early decoration retained in the somber interior. There's no tower to the building, supposedly because the church's Franciscan founders didn't permit such things; monastic modesty may also help to explain the high wall separating the church from the street. Back across the square, on the other side of the town hall, a blackened but noble **statue of Copernicus** watches over the crowds scurrying round the building.

South of the square, on the dusty, narrow, and charmingly atmospheric ul. Zeglarska, is **St John's Church**, another large and magnificent Gothic structure, whose clockface served as a reference point for loggers piloting their way downstream. The presbytery, the oldest part of the building, dates from the 1260s, but the main nave and aisles were not completed till the mid-fifteenth century. Entering the building from the heat of the summer sun, you're immediately enveloped in an ancient calm, an aura heightened by the damp, chilly air rising from the flagstones, and by the imposing rose window. The tower, completed late in the church's life, houses a magnificent fifteenth-century bell, the *Tuba Dei*, which can be heard all over town.

West of St John's runs ul. Kopernika, halfway down which you'll find the **Copernicus Museum** (Tues–Sat 10am–4pm), installed in the high brick house where the great man was born. Restored in recent decades to something resembling its original layout, this Gothic mansion contains a studiously assembled collection of Copernicus artifacts: priceless first editions of the momentous *De Revolutionibus*, models of gyroscopes and other astronomical instruments, original household furniture, early portraits. Authenticity is abandoned on the upper floors, which are taken up by products of the modern Copernicus industry: Copernicus coins, badges, stamps, even honey pots and tea labels.

Ulica Kopernika and its dingy side streets, lined with crumbling Gothic mansions and granaries, evoke a blend of past glory and shabbier contemporary reality. Farther down towards the river, the high, narrow streets meet the old defensive **walls**, now separating the Old Town from the main road. These fortifications survived virtually intact right up to the late nineteenth century, but then some enterprising Prussian town planners decided to knock them down, sparing only a small section near the river's edge which didn't obstruct their plans. This short fragment remains today, the walls interspersed by the old gates and towers at the ends of the streets.

To the west, at the bottom of ul. Pod Krzywa Wieza, stands the mid-fourteenth-century **Crooked Tower** (Krzyza Wieza), followed in quick succession by the **Monastery Gate** (Brama Klasztorna) and **Sailors' Gate** (Brama Zeglarska), all from the same period, the last originally leading to the main harbor.

Heading east, past the large **Bridge Gate** (Brama Mostowa), brings you to the ruins of the **Teutonic Knights' Castle**, sandwiched between the two halves of the medieval city. While not in the same league as the later Malbork fortress, the scale of the ruins here is enough to leave you impressed by the Toruń citizenry's efforts in laying it waste. In the vaults, a small **museum** (summer Tues–Sun 10am–4pm) recounts the history of this redoubtable building.

A little farther east along the river bank is a **landing stage**, from which in summer you can take a ninety-minute **boat trip** downriver and back. One glance at the state of the water will be enough to wipe out any thoughts of a quick dip.

The New Town (Nowe Maisto)

Following ul. Przedzamcze north from the castle brings you onto ul. Szeroka, the main thoroughfare linking the Old and New Town districts. Less grand than its mercantile neighbor, the **New Town** still boasts a number of illustrious commercial residences, most of them grouped around the **Rynek Nowomiejski**. On the west side of this square, the fifteenth-century **Pod Modrym Faruchem** inn (no. 8) and the Gothic **pharmacy** at no. 13 are particularly striking, while the old **Murarska** inn at no. 17, on the east side, currently houses an art gallery displaying children's work from all over the country.

The fourteenth-century **St James' Church**, south of the market area of the Rynek, completes the city's collection of Gothic churches. Unusual features of this brick basilica are its flying buttresses—a common enough sight in western Europe but extremely rare in Poland. Inside, mainly Baroque decoration is relieved by occasional Gothic frescoes, panel paintings and sculpture—most notably a large fourteenth-century crucifix.

North of the square, ul. Prosta leads onto Wały Sikorskego, a beltway which more or less marks the line of the old fortifications. Across it there's a small park, in the middle of which stands the former arsenal, now an **Ethnographic**

Museum (Tues–Sat 10am–4pm) dealing with the customs and crafts of northern Poland. The displays covering historical traditions are enhanced by imaginative attention to contemporary folk artists, musicians, and writers, whose work is actively collected and promoted by the museum.

The Park

If you're feeling the need for a bit of tranquillity, there's a pleasant park along the water's edge west of downtown, reached by tram #3 or #4 from pl. Rapackiego. On weekends you'll be joined at the waterside by picknickers and the occasional group of horseback-riders.

Eating, Drinking, and Entertainment

The hotels provide most of the decent places to **eat**. Gothic brickwork, stone floors, and high wooden ceilings are the decor in *Zajazd Staropolski* restaurant, which offers a considerably better-than-average menu. The *Helios* and *Kosmos* have the usual uninspiring Orbis decor but decent, if predictable, Orbis food. The noisier *Polonia* is okay, as is the *Staromeijska* at ul. Szcztyna 2/4, but avoid the *Pod Trzema Koronami*'s restaurant: food poisoning and drunken brawlers are not unknown. Additional, if undistinguished, eateries and milk bars include the *Pomorzanka*, ul. Szeroka 22, *Hungaria*, ul. Prosta 19, and *Pod Arkadami*, ul. Rózana 1—there's really not much difference between them.

Cafés are in good supply, with terrace places on streets such as ul. Szeroka providing an opportunity to enjoy the atmosphere of the Old Town. The regal *Pod Atlantem* in ul. św. Ducha stays open late, while at the nearby *Flisaka*, an old loggers' haunt, you can sit outside and enjoy the view over the river. And don't leave town without trying some **gingerbread**, a local delicacy already popular here by the fourteenth century—as attested by the molds in the town museum. It comes in ornate shapes: stagecoaches, eighteenth-century figures, and Copernicus are among the most popular. Numerous shops around the Old Town sell the stuff; eat it on the spot, as it goes rock-hard pretty quickly.

Finally, if you're up for a bit of local culture, see what's playing at the grand old **Toruń Theater** on pl. Armii Czerwonej, home of one of the country's most highly regarded repertory companies—and check the listings in the local newspaper for occasional classical **concerts** in the town hall. During school semester, the university area can be worth a look around, too, for the occasional **gig** or **disco**.

THE LAKES

The woodlands that open up to the east of Malbork signal the advent of **Mazury**, the "land of a thousand lakes" that occupies the northeast corner of the country, stretching for some 300km towards the Lithuanian border. A sparsely populated area of thick forests and innumerable lakes and rivers, Mazury is one of the country's main vacation districts—and rightfully so. It's a wonderful haunt for walkers, campers, watersports enthusiasts, or just for taking it easy.

Coming from Gdańsk, **Olsztyn** is the first major town and provides a good base for exploring the lesser-known western parts of Mazury, a landscape of rolling woodland interspersed with farming villages. Enjoyable as this area is, though, most vacationers head east to the area around lakes **Mamry** and

Śniardwy—the two largest of the region—and to more developed tourist towns like Giżycko, Mrągowo, and Mikołajki. Still farther east, up beyond Ełk, is the Suwalszczyzna, tucked away by the border, in many ways the most enchanting part of the region. As with other border areas there is a minority population, in this case Lithuanians.

Transportation links within the region are reasonably well-developed if slow. Local trains and/or buses run between all the main destinations; farther afield, notably in the Suwalszczyzna, the bus service becomes more unpredictable, so you may have to rely on hitching—not too much of a problem in the holiday season. Approaching Mazury from the south can be tricky, however, as the lakelands were in a different country until 45 years ago. Olsztyn and Augustów are on main rail lines from Warsaw; anything in between may involve a couple of

---

EAST PRUSSIA

Present-day Warmia and Mazury make up the heartlands of what until forty years ago was called **East Prussia** (Ostpreussen). Essentially the domains ruled by the Teutonic Knights at the height of their power, the main part of the territory—Royal Prussia—passed into Polish control following the Peace of Toruń in 1466, after which Polish settlers began moving into the area in numbers. The eastern part of the territory—Ducal Prussia as it became known from 1525 onward—became a state paying homage to the Polish king.

This was not the end of the original **"German question,"** however, for in 1657, under the pressure of the Swedish wars, King Jan Kazimierz released the branch of the powerful Hohenzollern family ruling Ducal Prussia from any form of Polish jurisdiction, allowing them to merge the province with their own German territories. By 1704 King Frederick was able to proclaim himself king of an independent Ducal Prussia, and impose limits on Polish settlement in the region: the way was now cleared for—from the Polish point of view – the disastrous slide to Frederick the Great and Partition-era Prussia. After World War II East Prussia was sliced across the middle, the northern half, including the capital Königsberg, designated a new province of the Russian Federation (though separated from it by Lithuania), the southern half becoming part of Poland.

Prusso-German culture had a strong impact on the character of the area, as evidenced by the many Protestant churches and German-looking towns dotted around—Olsztyn was once known as Allenstein, Elbląg as Elbling, Ełk as Lyck. Today the most obvious sign of Prussian influence is the influx of Germans who flock to the major lakeside holiday resorts in the summer. The Mercedes and BMW bikes look out of place in tatty Polish tourist towns, but many of the older visitors had family roots here until 1945, when—as in other areas of newly liberated Poland—everybody of German origin was ordered to leave. Most fled to West Germany, joining the millions of other displaced or uprooted peoples moving across Europe in the immediate postwar period.

A particularly sad example of the Polish government's rigid displacement policy occurred with the **Autochtones**, a peasant minority from the villages around Olsztyn. Like the other historic peoples of Warmia, the Autochtones were of Slavic origin, but unlike the original Slavic Prussians they survived the onslaughts of the Teutonic Knights, only to be strongly Germanized, then Polonized during the Polish rule of Ducal Prussia. Yet after centuries of tending the forests, they were pressured into leaving the Olsztyn area for good on account of the German taint in their history—and they're probably not the ones now coming back in the BMWs either.

changes, so the bus from Warsaw to Mikołajki may be a better idea if you're heading direct to the central lakes.

For **trekking** or **canoeing**, a tent, a sleeping roll, food supplies, and the right clothing are essential—don't count on being able to buy equipment in Poland. Canoe rental can usually be organized by Almatur or PTTK, and sometimes by Orbis, though all three should be contacted well in advance (see *Basics* for addresses). As tourism develops, however, there's a fair chance that you may find facilities available from new local operators, or established workers' holiday homes which are now having to make their own way.

Olsztyn

Of several possible jump-off points for the lakes, **OLSZTYN** is the biggest and the easiest to reach, and owing to the summertime tourist influx it's well equipped to deal with visitors. The town itself is located in pleasant woodland, but owing to wartime destruction much of the old center is the usual residential post-war grayness. Nestled among the concrete blocks and dusty main thoroughfares, though, quiet streets of the neat brick houses built by the city's former German inhabitants remain, their durability and calm orderliness forming a strong contrast with the often shabby modern constructions.

Olsztyn was something of a latecomer, gaining municipal status in 1353, twenty years after its castle was begun. Following the 1466 Toruń treaty, the town was reintegrated into Polish territory, finally escaping the clutches of the Teutonic Knights. Half a century later Nicolaus Copernicus took up residence as an administrator of the province of Warmia, and in 1521 helped organize the defense of the town against the Knights.

Coming under Prussian control after the First Partition, it remained part of East Prussia until 1945. Resistance to Germanization during this period was symbolized by the establishment here, in 1921, of the Association of Poles in Germany, an organization dedicated to keeping Polish culture alive within the Reich. With Hitler's accession, the Association became a target for Nazi terror, and most of its members perished in the concentration camps. The town also suffered, roughly forty percent being demolished by 1945.

Nonetheless, postwar development has established Olsztyn as the region's major industrial center, with a population of nearly 100,000. Ethnically they are quite a mixed bunch: the majority of the German-speaking population, expelled from the town after World War II, were replaced by settlers from all over Poland, particularly the eastern provinces annexed by the Soviet Union, and from even farther afield—hence a small community of Latvians.

The Town

The main places to see are concentrated in the **Old Town**, fifteen minutes' walk to the west of the **bus and train stations**. As an alternative to walking, just about any bus heading down al. Partyzantów will drop you at **plac Wolności**, the town's main square, with the Gothic **High Gate** (Brama Wysoka)—the entrance to the Old Town—a short stroll away at the end of ul. 22 Lipca.

Once through the gate, ul. Staromiejska brings you to the **Rynek**, which retains a few of its old buildings, most notably the Prussian-looking town hall, appearing rather stranded in the middle.

Over to the west stands the **Castle**, fourteenth-century but extensively rebuilt, surveying the steep little valley of the Lyna River. Its **museum** (Tues–Sun 10am–4pm) is an institution with a mission: to set the historical record of Mazury straight and to promote the cause of Warmian culture. The ethnography section contains a good selection of folk costumes, art, and furniture, while the historical section stresses the Warmians' general resistance to all things German. There's also a large archaeological collection, including objects from ancient burial grounds—look out for the mysterious granite figure in the castle courtyard, a relic of the original Slavic Prussians. **Copernicus' living quarters**, on the first floor of the southwest wing, are the castle's other main feature; along with a wistful portrait by Matejko and several of the astronomer's instruments, the rooms contain a sundial supposed to have been designed by Copernicus himself.

Just up from the castle entrance there's a stern neo-Gothic **Protestant church**, formerly used by the predominantly non-Catholic German population. To get to the early fifteenth-century—and Catholic—**Cathedral**, walk back across the Rynek. Originally a grand parish church, this retains some of its original Gothic features, and despite extensive renovations is still a moody, atmospheric place.

Practicalities

The well-organized **COIT office**, part of a tourist office complex just down from the High Gate at ul. Warszawska 13, will give you all the information you need, probably in English. A good **place to stay** right in the center is the **PTTK hostel** (☎236-75); housed in the gate itself, it makes a nice, unpretentious overnight, if you can get a room. **Hotels** include the classy *Kormoran*, near the station at ul. Kościuszki 6 (☎335-864), the *Relax*, ul. Zolnierza 13a (☎335-864), and the *Garnizonowy*, Gietkowska 1. Renovation of the upscale *Warminski*, ul. Głowackiego 8 (☎246-64), should be complete soon, too, with one of the best restaurants in town included. The Orbis *Novotel* motel is out on the western edge of town, at ul. Sielska 3a (☎240-81).

For **private rooms**, ask at reception at the *Nad Lyna*, al. Wojska Polskiego 14 (☎266-401). There are also two **youth hostels**: the main one at ul. Kopernika 45 (☎274-062; open all year), the other at ul. Kętrzynskiego 6 (☎335-045; July & Aug). In summer, cheap beds are also available in the **student hotels** at the Agricultural College in the southern suburb of Kortowo; ask at the COIT office or go straight to the **Almatur** office on the site (☎278-653). Finally, there's a good, large PTTK **campground** by Lake Krzywe, near the *Novotel* (May–Sept).

Restaurants in Olsztyn seem to be improving. Aside from the *Warmiński*, there is a new French place, the *Francuska* at ul. Mickiewicza 9a, and a Syrian restaurant, the *Arabska* at ul. Marchlewskiego 3–4 in the Old Town. Cheaper if unexciting standbys include the *Pod Zaglami*, ul. Pieniężego 22, the *Frykas*, ul. Kolobrzesko 13, and the *Kolorowa*, al. Wojska Polskiego 74, all fairly central.

North of Olsztyn

If you're not eager to press straight on to the lakes, it's worth considering a day trip—feasible by bus—through the attractive countryside north of Olsztyn to the town of **Lidzbark Warmiński**.

The forty-kilometer journey takes you through the open woodlands and undulating farmland characteristic of western Mazury, and if you've caught an early bus there's enough time for a stop off en route at **DOBRE MIASTO**, a small town with a vast Gothic church, rising majestically from the edge of the main road. Baroque ornamentation overlays much of the interior, and there's a florid late Gothic replica of Kraków's Mariacki altar; the collegiate buildings around the back house a minor local museum.

Lidzbark Warmiński

Set amid open pastureland watered by the Lyna River, **LIDZBARK WARMIŃSKI** started out as one of the numerous outposts of the Teutonic Knights. When they'd finished conquering the region, they handed the town over to the bishops of Warmia, who used it as their main residence from 1350 until the late eighteenth century. Following the Toruń treaty, Lidzbark came under Polish rule, becoming an important center of culture and learning—Copernicus lived here (of course), just one member of a community of artists and scientists. A later luminary of the intellectual scene in Lidzbark was **Ignacy Krasicki** (1735–1801), a staunch defender of all things Polish; after Prussian rule had deprived him of his job as archbishop, he turned his attention to writing, producing a string of translations, social satires, and one of the first Polish novels.

The Castle

Sadly, much of the old town was wiped out in 1945, with only the parish church, town gate, and a few sections of the fortifications managing to survive the fighting. Lidzbark's impressive Teutonic **Castle**, however, came through unscathed, a stylish, well-preserved, riverside fortress which ranks as one of the architectural gems of the region. Used as a fortified residence for the Warmian bishops, it has the familiar regional period look to it: the square brick structure echoes Frombork cathedral in its tiled roof, Malbork in the turreted towers rising from the corners.

Through the main gate you find yourself in a courtyard, with arcaded galleries rising dreamily above, while at ground level there are Gothic cellars with delicate ribbed vaulting. Inside the main structure, fragments of fifteenth-century frescoes are visible in places, and the **chapel** retains its sumptuous Rococo decorations. But the chief interest comes from the exhibits in the **regional museum** (Tues–Sun 10am–4pm) that now occupies much of the building. The displays begin with excellent Gothic sculpture in the **Great Refectory**, featuring the tombstones of several Warmian bishops, whose heraldic devices still cover the walls. On the second floor are a collection of modern Polish art, not very riveting, and an exquisite exhibition of **icons**. These come from the convent at Wojnowo (see below), where the nuns are members of the strongly traditionalist Starowiercy (Old Believers) sect, which broke away from official Orthodoxy in protest at the religious reforms instigated by Peter the Great.

The east wing of the castle was torn down in the mid-eighteenth century to make way for a bishop's palace and gardens. The **winter garden** opposite the approach to the castle is the most attractive bit left, with a Neoclassical orangery that wouldn't be out of place in a royal residence. Into the town center the tall **Parish Church** is another Gothic brick hall structure, similar in style to Dobre Miasto; the aisles off the vaulted nave reveal some fine Renaissance side altars and old tombstones. The old **Protestant Church** in town is now an Orthodox *cerkiew* used by the Eastern settlers who moved here following the postwar border shifts.

Practicalities

The High Gate, now the local **PTTK hostel** (☎521), is a good place for an over-night stay. Virtually the only other options are the **youth hostel** at ul. Ziednoczenia Partii 3 (July & Aug; ☎31-47), not far from the station, and the summer **campground** at ul. Olsztyńska 4. Close to the campground is *Pod Klobukiem*, one of the better **restaurants**.

The Mazurian Lakes

East of Olsztyn, the central Mazury lakeland opens out amid thickening forests. In summer the biggest lakes—**Mamry** and **Śniardwy**—are big attractions, with all the advantages and disadvantages that brings. On the plus side, tourist facili-ties are well-developed in many places, and you can rent sailing and canoeing equipment in all the major resorts. On the other hand, the crush can be intolera-ble, and the primitive sewage facilities of the bigger towns has led to severe pollu-tion. If solitude and clean water are what you're after, the best advice is to get a detailed map and head for the smaller lakes; as a general rule, tranquillity increases as you travel east.

Among highlights, **Mrągowo**, the most westerly of the major holiday resorts, is now at least as well known for its Country-and-Western festival. Perched on the southern edge of Lake Mamry, **Giżycko** attracts yachters and canoeists and would be a useful base for exploring the lakes. And in a region of summer cottages and wooded lakes it's quite a shock to come upon Hitler's wartime base at **Gierloz**—one of the strangest and most chilling of all World War II relics.

On the whole, **transportation** around the lakes isn't too problematic. While a car is a definite advantage for venturing into the remoter reaches, bus and train connections between the main centers are more than adequate.

Mrągowo and Around

MRĄGOWO, situated on the main Olsztyn–Augustów road, is one of the princi-pal hubs of the district, and if you're anywhere near in July it would be folly to miss its acclaimed **Country Picnic Festival**, held in an amphitheater adjoining the Orbis *Hotel Mrągowia*. In Poland, as elsewhere in Eastern Europe, C&W is big news, and the festival is an opportunity for aspiring Slavic Hank Williams and Dolly Partons to croon their hearts out in front of large, appreciative audiences; American stars add a bit of muscle.

The rest of the year, Mrągowo is rather less compelling. Yet thanks to brochure hyping that attracts plenty of foreigners, the wealthier of whom stay at the *Mrągowia*, a plush **hotel** at ul. PPR 6 with a fine lakeside site (☎32-22). Other than this, there is only a drab hotel at ul. Warszawska 10, a **youth hostel** at ul. Zwyciezców 1a, and a **campground** by the lake on the eastern side of the town.

Sorkwity and the Krutynia Route

SORKWITY, 12km west of Mrągowo, is the starting point for a beautiful and popular canoeing run which ends 90km downstream at Lake Bełdany, adjoining the western edge of Lake Sniardwy. The Orbis hotel in Mrągowo can help arrange canoe rental for the trip, but in summer advance notice is virtually essen-tial (see also the Almatur entry in *Basics*).

Canoeists generally start from the PTTK waterside hostel (*stanica wodna*; May–Sept) at the edge of Sorkwity village. Known as the **Krutynia route**, after the narrow, winding river that makes up the last part of the journey, the route takes you through a succession of eighteen lakes, connected by narrow stretches of river, the banks often covered with dense forest. The journey takes a minimum of five days, with Mikołajki the final destination. Overnight stops are usually in the following places (in *stanica wodna* unless specified; open June–Sept): **day one** at BIENKI or BABIĘTA, 20km and 25km downstream respectively (there's also a July & Aug youth hostel in the latter); **day two** in KRUTYN (at the PTTK hostel; June–Sept); **day three** at UKTA on the Krutynia; **day four** at Kamień on Lake Bełdany.

Between Krutyn and Ukta the Krutynia flows by the village of WOJNOWO, where a small convent and *cerkiew* hidden back from the river are home to the only surviving settlement of Starowiercy nuns in Poland (see "Lidzbark Warmiński," p.117).

Mikołajki

MIKOŁAJKI, on the northern shores of Lake Bełdany, is one of the smaller and most atmospheric of the lakeside resorts. The town—really more a glorified village—has cobbled streets and half-timbered houses, and an affluent feel as the main base for yachting on Lake Śniardwy. An unusual attraction is the **nature reserve** around Lake Łukajno, 4km east of town, the home of one of Europe's largest remaining colonies of wild swans. The *Pensjonat Wodnik*, ul. Kajki 130 (☎161-41), is the main **place to stay** in town, alternatives being the **youth hostel** (July & Aug), in a school near the station, or the **campground** at ul. Leśna 2.

South from Mikołajki, several well-signposted **hiking trails** lead south through the lakeside forests for 22km to **RUCIANE NIDA**, another popular holiday resort in the heart of the huge **Pisz forest**. Alternatively, day-long boat excursions do the same journey along the narrow lakes between the two centers.

Kętrzyn and the Wolf's Lair

Known as Rastenburg until its return to Polish rule in 1945, **KĘTRZYN** is a quiet, unexceptional town, whose main interest lies in its proximity to Gierłoz—Hitler's "Wolf's Lair" (see below).

With time to spare, the Teutonic **castle** is an easy walk from the bus or train stations, though it was almost totally burned out in World War II; it contains a local museum. Down the road, the **Gothic church** survived the war rather better, while the chapel nearby, a fourteenth-century construction rebuilt in the late seventeenth, is now a Protestant church, much to the official guidebook's annoyance. On the other side of town at ul. Mickiewicza there's also an early nineteenth-century freemasons' lodge, now a Dom Kultury.

Gierłoz

GIERŁOZ lies 8km east of Kętrzyn and can be reached by local bus or the Węgorzewo train (be careful to check return times). Here, deep in the Mazurian forests, Hitler established his military headquarters in the so-called **Wolf's Lair** (Wilczy Szaniec; Tues–Sun 8am–6pm), a huge underground complex from which the Germans' eastward advance was conducted. Encased in several meters of concrete were private bunkers for Göring, Bormann, Himmler, and Hitler

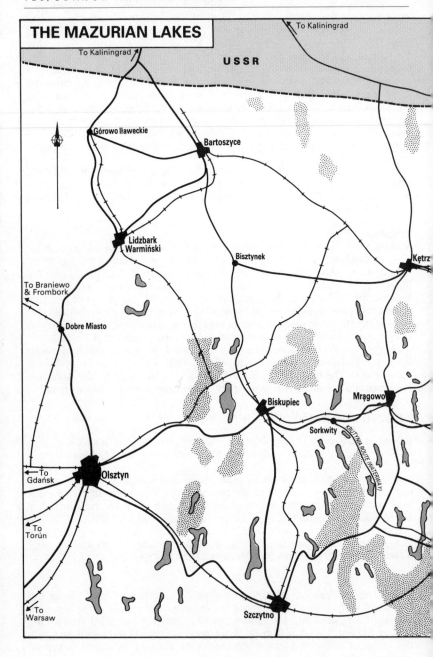

THE MAZURIAN LAKES

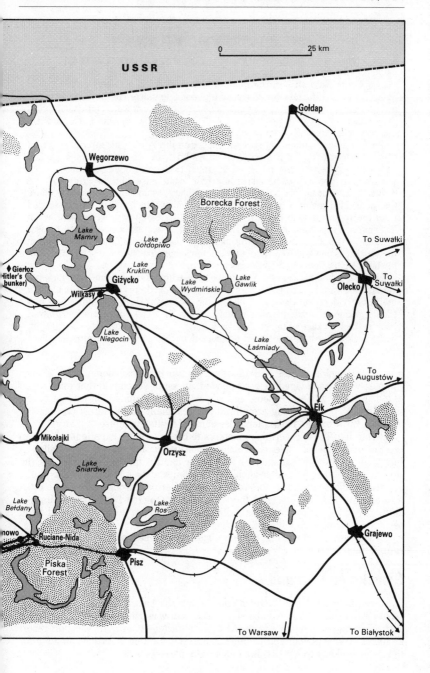

THE JULY BOMB PLOT

In the summer of 1944, the Wolf's Lair was the scene of the assassination attempt on Adolf Hitler that came closest to success—the **July Bomb Plot**. Its leader, **Count Claus Schenk von Stauffenberg**, an aristocratic member of the General Staff, had gained the support of several high-ranking officers of the German army, who, like him, were sickened by atrocities on the Eastern front and convinced of the certainty of defeat. It was decided to kill the Führer, seize control of army headquarters in Berlin, and sue for peace with the Allies.

On July 20th, Stauffenberg was summoned to the Wolf's Lair to brief Hitler on troop movements on the Eastern front. In his briefcase was a small bomb, packed with high explosive; once triggered, it would explode in under ten minutes. As Stauffenberg approached the specially built conference hut, he triggered the device, then took his place a few feet from Hitler, positioning the briefcase under the table. Five minutes before the bomb exploded, Stauffenberg quietly slipped from the room, unnoticed by the generals and advisors, who were absorbed in listening to a report on the central Russian front. One of the officers moved closer to the table to get a better look at the campaign maps; he found the briefcase was in the way of his feet and so picked it up and moved it. Now, the very solid support of the table leg lay between the briefcase and Hitler.

At 12:42 the bomb went off. Stauffenberg, watching the hut from a few hundred yards away, was shocked by the force of the explosion: there could be no doubt that the Führer, along with everyone else in the room, was dead. He hurried off to a waiting plane and made his way to Berlin to join the other conspirators. However, back at the wreckage of the conference hut, Hitler staggered out into the daylight, badly shaken but having suffered no more than a perforated eardrum and minor

himself, alongside offices, SS quarters, and operations rooms. The 27-acre complex was camouflaged by a suspended screen of vegetation that was altered to match the changing seasons, and was permanently mined "in case of necessity." In 1945 the retreating army fired the detonator, but it merely cracked the bunkers, throwing out flailing tentacles of metal reinforcements.

Peering into these cavernous monsters today is an eerie experience. You can see the place, for example, where the assassination attempt on Hitler failed in July 1944 (see box above) and look around the airstrip, the SS living quarters, the staff movie theater, and other ancillaries of domestic Nazi life. Gruesome photographs and films remind visitors of the scale of German atrocities, but as so often with official anti-fascist material, there's a tendency to resort to horrifying images at the expense of information and critical understanding. It will be interesting to see if the Solidarity-led government changes this at all.

For anybody up to staying, there's a basic **hostel**, **campground**, and **restaurant** at the bunker site.

Giżycko and Around

Squeezed between Lake Niegocin and the marshy backwaters of Lake Mamry, **GIŻYCKO** is one of the main lakeland centers. It was flattened in 1945, however, and the rebuilding didn't create a lot of character—if grayish vacation resort architecture lowers your spirits, don't plan to stay for long before heading out for the lakes. Wilkasy (see p.124) is a much more pleasant base.

injuries. After being attended to, he prepared himself for a meeting with Mussolini later that afternoon, and dispatched Himmler to Berlin to quell the rebellion.

When word that the Führer was still alive reached the Supreme Command building in Berlin, headquarters of the plot, the conspirators tried to persuade high-ranking officials to join them. But the Bendlerstrasse HQ was already being surrounded by SS troops. The coup was over. The conspirators were gathered together, given paper to write farewell messages to their wives, taken to the courtyard of the HQ and shot by firing squad. Stauffenberg's last words were "Long live our sacred Germany!"

Hitler's ruthless revenge on the conspirators was without parallel even in the bloody annals of the Third Reich. All the colleagues, friends, and immediate relations of Stauffenberg and the other conspirators were rounded up, tortured and taken before a "People's Court," where they were humiliated and given more-or-less automatic death sentences. Anyone whose name was blurted under torture was also quickly arrested, the most notable being Field Marshal Rommel, who, because of his popularity, was given the choice of a trial in the People's Court or suicide and a state funeral. Most of those others found guilty were executed at Plötzensee prison in Berlin. Under the Führer's instructions, they were hanged from meat hooks by piano wire, their death agonies prolonged by slow strangulation. A film of the executions was made for Hitler's private delectation.

All in all, the July Bomb Plot caused the deaths of perhaps 5000 people, including many of those who would have been best qualified to run the postwar German government. Within six months the country lay in ruins as the Allies advanced; had events at Rastenburg been only a little different, the course of the war—and European history—would have been altered incalculably.

Incongruously, the **Orbis** office at ul. Dąbrowskiego has glossy brochures and ticket-booking facilities for anywhere on the other side of the globe, but absolutely nothing about Giżycko or its surroundings. As indicated by the ranks of German vehicles parked outside, the central *Wodnik* **hotel**, ul. 3 Maja 2 (☎38-72), is the hub of foreign tourist activity; it's expensive and difficult to get into. More likely to have space is the *Zamek*, a large motel in the ruins of the Teutonic castle at ul. Moniuszki 1 (☎24-19), with a **campground** close by (☎34-10). Within walking distance of the train station there are also two **youth hostels**, at ul. Mickiewicza 27 (☎29-87) and ul. Wiejska 50 (☎21-35); both are open July to September only.

Lakes near Giżycko

East of Giżycko, the tourists thin out and the lakes get quieter and cleaner. There's little accommodation, though, so you'll need to come equipped with a tent or a car, allowing you to venture out for day trips along the picturesque country roads.

Ten kilometers northeast from Giżycko are the adjoining **Gołdopiwo** and **Kruklin lakes**, a couple of kilometers from the edge of the **Borecka forest**. A bus from Giżycko will take you to the village of KRUKLANKI on the southern edge of Lake Gołdopiwo, and from there you're pretty much on your own. Twenty kilometers to the southeast of Giżycko there's another enchanting string of lakes—**Wydmińskie**, **Jedzelewo**, and **Lasmiady**—linked by the Gawlik River: they're all easily reached, being close to stations on the Giżycko–Ełk rail line.

Wilkasy

WILKASY is a five-kilometer bus ride southwest of Giżycko; the train from Kętrzyn stops here too, at the Niegocin station. If you want to see how Poles take their Mazurian vacation, this is the place to head for, with its assortment of lakeside rest homes, summer cabins, and hostels. Apart from some nice enclosed swimming areas by the lake, the other attraction of Wilkasy is that it's much easier to **rent canoes or kayaks** here. Before they are allowed to set oar to water, Poles have to produce an official card proving they can swim, but you should be able to persuade the attendants to let you aboard. It makes for a pleasant day, paddling round the lake, peeling off into reed beds or canals as the fancy takes you—even though the pollution becomes more obvious the nearer you get to Giżycko.

A good place to stay is the **PTTK hostel** (May–Sept; ☎30-78) near the bus stop just up from the water; they or one of the neighboring houses will also allow camping in the garden for a small fee. The **restaurant** across the road is mainly used by holiday groups eating set meals in timed seatings; it isn't exactly a gastronomic paradise but is certainly very Polish, and as in all major tourist resorts you won't have any trouble getting a beer or ten—if you want to follow local male vacationing habits.

Ełk

EŁK, the easternmost main town of Mazury, is the area's major bus and train interchange. Established by the Teutonic Knights as a base from which to "protect" the locals and keep an eye on the heathen Lithuanian hordes, the town was colonized by Poles in the sixteenth century, before becoming an East Prussian border post during the Partitions. It remained Prussian until 1945, and suffered comprehensive damage during the war; the ruins of the Teutonic castle apart, it's got little to show for its past now.

Most visitors don't get much farther than the shabby square below the train station; there really isn't much to detain you in the sprawling, tatty town center. If you're forced to spend the night here, head for the **hotel** *Mazurski*, at ul. Słowackiego 26 (☎32-15), or failing that the *Dom Turystyczny* at ul. Armii Czerwonej 23 (☎24-19), where there's also a basic **restaurant**. For local information, the **Orbis office** at ul. Mickiewicza 15 is not far from the train and bus stations, both of which are close to downtown.

Augustów and the Suwalszczyna

The region around the towns of **Augustów** and **Suwałki** is one of the least visited areas of Poland; even for Poles, anything beyond Mazury is still pretty much terra incognita. As with most parts of eastern Poland, the region north of Suwałki—the **Suwalszczyna**—is little developed economically, a region of peasant farmers and tortuous ethnic and religious loyalties. And like the Bieszczady mountains (see Chapter Three), its counterpart in obscurity, the Suwalszczyna is one of the most beautiful, unspoiled territories in Europe.

Much of the southern stretch of this region is covered by the **Puszcza Augustówska**, the remains of the vast forest that once extended well into Lithuania. In the north, by contrast, wonderfully open countryside is interspersed with villages and lakes, some reasonably well known—like **Lake Hańcza** (the deepest in Poland); others, often the most beautiful, rarely visited. Wandering through the fields and woodland thickets you'll find storks, swallows, brilliantly colored butterflies, and wild flowers in abundance, while in the villages the twentieth century often seems to have made only modest incursions, leaving plenty of time to sit on the porch and talk.

Getting around isn't exactly straightforward: buses operate in most of the region, but frequency declines the closer you get to the Lithuanian border. Suwałki and Augustów both have main line train connections to Warsaw.

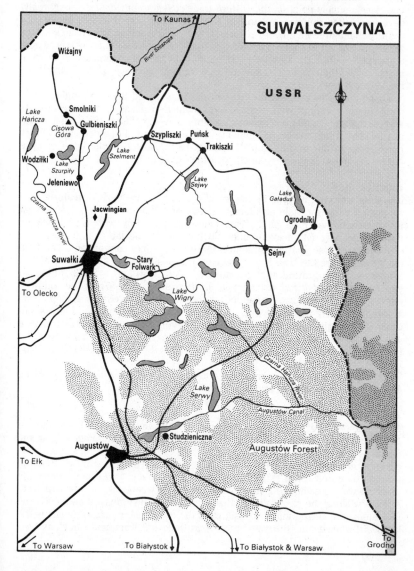

Augustów and Around

The region around AUGUSTÓW was settled at some indistinct time in the early Middle Ages by Jacwingians, a pagan Baltic Slav tribe. By the end of the thirteenth century, however, they had been wiped out, leaving as testimony only a few sites such as the burial mound near Suwałki (see p.128) and a scattering of place names. The area remained almost deserted for the next two centuries or so, until the town's establishment in 1557 by King Zygmunt August (hence the name) as a supply point on the eastern trade routes from Gdańsk. It only really developed after the construction of the **Augustów canal** in the nineteenth century. A hundred-kilometer network of rivers, lakes, and artificial channels, this waterway was cut to connect the town to the Niemen River in the east, providing a transport route for the region's most important natural commodity, wood. Still in use today, the canal offers the most convenient approach to the heart of the forest (see below).

Thanks to its location on the edge of the *puszcza* and the surrounding abundance of water, Augustów has carved out a niche for itself as a vacation center. As a town, though, it's no great shakes. Caught on the frontline of the Soviet assault in late 1944, it has few prewar buildings, except a handful of nineteenth-century tenements, an old sawmill, and the 1920s PTTK hostel on the edge of Lake Necko. Its appeal is as a base for countryside exploration.

Practicalities

The **bus station** is right in the middle of town, the nearest **train** stop—Augustów Port—a couple of kilometers' bus ride from the center. The **tourist information center** on pl. J. Krasickiego is reasonably with it and helpful, though they may not be able to offer much on **accommodation** in high season. Considering it's such a tourist center, there aren't that many options. The first-choice places are the *Dom Nauczyciela* at ul. 29 Listopada 9 (☎20-21), the **PTTK hostel** and **campground** at ul. Sportowa 1 in Augustów Port (☎20-42), or—most expensively—the *Polmozbytu* motel at ul. Mazurska 4 (☎35-67) on the southern edge of town. From July to September there's a **youth hostel** at ul. Konopnickiej 4; if there are any **private rooms** going, the information office will know about them. It's just possible that you'll arrive to find everything full up, in which case, if you have a sleeping bag, make for the Almatur *baza studentowa* (student base) by the lakeside at STUDZIENICZNA, a six-kilometer bus journey east; there's no food, so bring your own.

In town, the only **restaurants** worth mentioning are the *Albatros* at ul. Armii Czerwonej 5, in the center, and the motel.

The Forest

The combination of wild forest, lakes, and narrow winding rivers has made the *puszcza* a favorite with canoeists, walkers, and naturalists alike. Following in the footsteps of their partisan ancestors, whose anti-Czarist forces found shelter here, adventurous Poles spend days and sometimes weeks paddling or trekking through the forest. Such expeditions require preparation, so for most people the practical way to sample the mysteries of the forest is to take a **day trip** from Augustów along the canal system. Boats leave from the embarkation point at ul. 29 Listopada 7, fifteen minutes' walk from the town center—*zéglug* (boat) is the key word when asking the way. First departure is at 8:30am, and you should get there early to line for tickets. It's also a good idea to take some food: most boats don't have any, and restaurant stops on the way are unpredictable.

The shortest trips—a couple of hours—go east through the **Necko**, **Białe**, and **Studzieniczne** lakes to SWOBODA or SUCHA RZECZKA, giving at least a taste of the beauty of the forest. Other boats go onward to PLASKA and the lock at PERKUC, returning in the evening; beyond this point, the canal is for canoeists only, and even they can only go another twenty-odd kilometers to the Soviet border.

The **forest** is mainly coniferous, but with impressive sections of elm, larch, hornbeam, and ancient oak creating a slightly somber atmosphere, particularly along the alley-like section of the canal between Swoboda and Sucha Rzeczka— the tallest trees blot out the sun, billowing reeds brush the boat, and the silence is suddenly broken by echoing bird calls. Amongst the varied wildlife of the forest, cranes, gray herons, and even the occasional beaver can be spotted on the banks of the canal, while deeper into the *puszcza* you might glimpse wild boars or elks.

Suwałki and Around

Founded as late as the 1720s, **SUWAŁKI** is another slow-paced provincial town with a decidedly eastern ambience. Perhaps feeling the need to keep the intellectuals in touch with life out in the sticks (or vice versa), Solidarity nominated the medieval historian Bronisław Geremek and the film director Andrzej Wajda as candidates for the Suwałki region in the 1989 elections. Accounts of their campaign encounters with local farmers suggest it wasn't all plain sailing, skepticism about the men from Warsaw's capacity to represent regional concerns being a key issue.

A rambling, unfocused sort of place, Suwałki presents a mix of fine Neoclassical architecture and Russian-looking nineteenth-century buildings, with the usual postwar blocks around the outskirts. Religion is a mixed business here as well: the majority Catholic population uses the stately Neoclassical parish church of Saint Alexandra on pl. Wolnosci, but there's also an Evangelical church, farther down on the main ul. Kosciuszki, and the **Molenna**, a small wooden *cerkiew* serving one of the few surviving Starowiercy congregations and retaining some fine original icons. It is tucked away on a side street off al. Armii Czerwonej close to the station; the only reliable time to gain entry is during the Sunday morning service.

PRACTICALITIES

The **train station**, terminal of the line from Warsaw, lies east of the center—take bus #1, #8, or #12 into town. The **bus station**, on ul Brzostowskiego, is more central. Information is available from the **tourist office** at ul. Kościuszki 37.

Suwałki doesn't go overboard on **hotels**. The *Hancza* at ul. Wojska Polskiego 2 (☎32-81), near the river in the south of town, is reasonably comfortable, reasonably priced, and also has a restaurant. That's it, apart from **private rooms**, available from the *Wigry* office in the *Hańcza* building, and a summer **youth hostel** at ul. Klonowa 51 (☎51-40). The only real **restaurants**, apart from the *Hancza*, are the *Jacwieska*, 1 Maja 14, and the *Wigry* at ul. Lenina 32, both in the central area and both distinctly ordinary.

The Jacwingian Burial Site

The ancient Jacwingian burial ground, 4km north of Suwałki, is one of the few definite signs of the presence of these ancient people, and a must for lovers of mystic sites. To reach it take a #7 bus to SZWACJARIA, or the Jeleniewo road by car—in both cases you'll see a sign at the roadside pointing you to the **Cementarzysko Jacwingów**. A short walk through the fields and over an overgrown ridge brings you to the burial mounds, discernible through a tangled mass of trees and undergrowth. Little is known of this pagan people but stay long enough in this beautiful and peaceful spot and you begin to conjure up your own images of how they might once have lived.

Lake Wigry

Lake Wigry, the largest lake in this district, and one of the most beautiful, is just 11km southeast of Suwałki. To get there, take a local bus to the holiday center of STARY FOLWARK, where there's a **PTTK hostel** (☎12-23) and **campground** near the water. You may be able to **rent canoes** or other boats here.

If you do manage to get hold of a boat, head straight across the lake from Stary Folwark and you come to **Wigry church**, part of a monastery founded here by King Władysław IV Waza in the 1660s. A typical piece of Polish Baroque, it has exuberant frescoes in the main church and monks' skeletons in the catacombs. The **monastery** itself has been turned into a combo conference center-hotel (☎12-28), with a decent restaurant; it's worth considering for a comfortable stop in peaceful surroundings. Other good trips are to be had out to the western shores, where there are a couple of beaver colonies and the landlocked expanse of **Lake Biale**.

The Suwalszczyzna

North of Suwałki the forests give way to the lush, rolling hills of the **Suwalszczyzna**. Two roads take you through the heart of the region, towards the Lithuanian border: the first heads due north then veers westward through sporadic villages to **Wiźajny**; the other—along with a highly recommended steam railroad—runs some way to the east, covering the 30km to **Puńsk**.

Suwałki to Wiźajny

The great appeal of this route lies in getting right off the beaten track—and tracks don't get much less beaten than that to **WODZIŁKI**, tucked away in a quiet wooded valley around 10km north of Suwałki. The hamlet is home to a small community of Starowiercy, whose original wooden *cerkiew* is still in use, along with a nearby *bania* (sauna). Life in this rural settlement seems to have changed little since the first settlers moved here in the 1750s: the houses are simple, earth-floored buildings with few concessions to modernity, the old men grow long white beards, the women don't appear to cut their hair, the children run barefoot. If you're lucky enough to get invited into one of their homes, you'll see amazing collections of icons, rosaries, Bibles, and other precious relics.

The easiest way to get to the hamlet is to take the bus through JELENIEWO. If possible take one that's turning off to TURTUL RUTKA, from where it's thirty minutes' walk north to Wodziłki; otherwise get off at Sidorówka, the next stop after Jeleniewo, which leaves five kilometers' walk west, skirting **Lake Szurpiły**. The lake itself is great for swimming, and an ideal camping spot, provided the mosquitoes aren't out in force.

CISOWA GÓRA

The next bus stop after Sidorówka is **GULBIENISKI**, the point of access for the hill called **Cisowa Góra**. Though known as "The Polish Fujiyama," at 258m it looks more like an Indian burial mound in the Midwest than a mountain, a comparison which in fact goes beyond superficial resemblance—it was the site of pre-Christian religious rituals, and it's rumored that rites connected with Perkun, the Lithuanian fire-god, are still observed here. Bear in mind that the Lithuanians, who still make up a small percentage of the population of this region, were the last Europeans to be converted to Christianity, in the late fourteenth century. Czesław Miłosz's semi-autobiographical novel *The Issa Valley*, set in neighboring Lithuania, bears witness to the durability of pre-Christian beliefs right into the present century. Whatever the historical reality of the hill, it's a powerful place.

LAKE HANCZA

North of Gulbieniski the road divides: Wiżajny to the left, Rutka Tarta to the right. Continuing along the Wiżajny route the next village is **SMOLNIKI**, just before which there's a wonderful panorama of the surrounding lakes; if you're on the bus ask the driver to let you off at the *punkt wyściowy* (viewpoint).

A couple of kilometers west of Smolniki, along a bumpy track through the woods, is **Lake Hancza**, the deepest in Poland at 108m, and quiet, clean, and unspoiled. There's a **youth hostel** on the southeast edge at BŁASKOWIZNA; camping isn't allowed within the Suwałki National Park, of which this area is part. To get to the hostel take the Wiżajny bus from Suwałki and get off at BACHANOWO, a kilometer beyond Turtul Rutka; it's a short walk from here.

From Suwałki to Puńsk and Sejny

Lithuanians are one of Poland's minorities, most of the 15,000-strong community living in a little enclave of towns and villages north and east of Suwałki. The farther you go into the countryside, the more common it becomes to catch the lilt of their strange-sounding tongue in bars and at bus stops.

The village of **Puńsk**, right up by the border, has the highest proportion of Lithuanians in the area and is surrounded by some of the loveliest countryside. There are two ways of covering the 30km from Suwałki. The first is to take the twice-daily **train** to TRAKISZKI and then walk the last two kilometers. The attraction of this is that the line is still run almost exclusively by old **steam trains**, which enhances the time-warp quality of a journey that takes you through ancient meadows—their hedgerows a brilliant mass of flora—and fields tilled by horse-drawn ploughs. Keep your passport handy as the border police are sometimes on hand in Trakiszki to check what you're up to. If you're in the mood for a swim first, **Lake Sejwy**, 3km down the road, is an excellent spot.

The other option is to make the journey by **bus**, changing at SZYPLISZKI. The bar opposite Szypliszki's bus stop serves a decent local beer, or if you prefer a more wholesome pastime you could walk the couple of kilometers west through the fields to **Lake Szelment**, another untouched corner of the region.

PUŃSK

Tucked away a few kilometers from the Lithuanian border, **PUŃSK** used to be sunk in complete obscurity, but since 1989 has been the object of unprecedented attention. The reason is the village's **Lithuanians**—some seventy percent of the population—who, despite their small numbers, maintain a Lithuanian cultural center, choir, and weekly newspaper, giving the place a decidedly un-Polish feel.

In the summer of 1989 Lithuanian flags and the symbol of Sajudis (the Lithuanian Popular Front) were becoming common sights here, and when the Soviet blockade of Lithuania began in March 1990, the response in Puńsk was immediate: it became the collection point for supplies to Lithuania from all over Poland, and demonstrations in support of Lithuanian independence were held after Mass every Sunday.

The neo-Gothic **parish church** might look nothing special as a building, but turn up on a Sunday at 11am and you'll find the place packed for Mass in Lithuanian. If it's a major feast day, you may also see a procession afterward, for which the women, especially, don the curiously Inca-looking national costume. Inquiries in the bar or shops should track down the old man who set up the local **Lithuanian museum**, on the edge of the village; it's not yet officially open but if you've got a car, offers of transportation will help persuade him to show you around. Inside there's an interesting collection of local ethnography, including some wonderful decorative fabrics and crafts, bizarre-looking farm implements, and prewar Lithuanian books and magazines, as well as maps that illuminate the tangled question of the Polish-Lithuanian border. There's also recent Sajudis material, a section that will doubtless grow over the next few years.

Although there is no regular **accommodation** in the village, Lithuanians are immensely hospitable people, so it's worthwhile asking at the *Rutka* restaurant/ bar about the possibility of a bed for the night. The *Rutka* isn't the best you'll ever visit, but a couple of beers into a chat with locals and you'll probably get some insights into local Polish-Lithuanian relations. Despite their support for Lithuanian independence and general lack of enthusiasm for things Polish, most seem content to stay in Poland, at least for the moment. As with other Polish minorities, however, there's a strong desire for more cultural rights, including more provision for Lithuanian language-teaching in local schools. It remains to be seen how far the overwhelmingly Polish Solidarity-led government is prepared to go on this issue.

As well as Lithuanians, the Puńsk area was for centuries home to another minority—Jews. Almost every Jew from this region was either slaughtered or uprooted, but a few signs of the past—predictably ignored in the official Polish guides and maps—are still left. The *Dom Handlowy* on the main street in Puńsk used to be the rabbi's house, and the older locals can point you in the direction of the abandoned **Jewish cemetery**, on the northern edge of the village, where a few Hebrew-inscribed headstones are still visible among the grass and trees. A visit is a reminder of the power of forgetting.

SEJNY

Instead of returning directly to Suwałki, you might consider making the return bus trip via the market town of **SEJNY**, 25km south of Puńsk, a cross-country journey that's a treat in itself. Sejny is dominated by a Dominican **monastery complex** at the top of the town, which contains a grandiose late Renaissance church refurbished in Rococo style in the mid-eighteenth century. The surrounding monastic buildings are currently under restoration, and likely to remain so for some time. At the other end of town is the former **synagogue**, its size suggesting the Jewish population here used to be quite large. Carefully restored, it's now a **museum** and cultural center. If your Polish is up to it, the curator can fill you in on local history, particularly the Lithuanian, Jewish, and Old Believer minorities.

Despite signs in the town center, the information office does not exist any more, while the only chance of a room is at the very basic **restaurant** *Na Skarpie* at ul. Armii Czerwonej 15 (☎65), the main street, or at the summer **youth hostel** on the outskirts at ul. Łąkowa.

THE BORDER
Don't be surprised to see Soviet registration cars and trucks rumbling through Sejny. OGRODNIKI, the only border crossing into Lithuania, is just 20km to the east. Even if you've got a Soviet visa, though, the political tensions produced by Lithuania's de facto declaration of independence mean that westerners are very unlikely to get through here; reports from recent travelers indicate that the Polish border guards may let you pass but the Soviet guards on the other side will almost certainly turn you back.

BIAŁYSTOK AND THE BYELORUSSIAN BORDERLANDS

Heading south from the lakes or east from Warsaw, you find yourself in a region of complex ethnicity, up against the borders of Soviet Byelorussia. The Poles call the area the **Podlasie**—literally "Under the Trees"—which gives little hint of its landscape of wide, open plains, tracts of primeval forest, and dark skies. Even without the increasing presence of onion-domed Orthodox churches, it would feel intrinsically eastern, more like Russia than Poland. It also feels extremely poor, and is one of the most neglected regions of the country, with an overwhelmingly peasant population. On the long potholed country roads you see as many horsecarts as cars, in the fields as many horse-drawn plows as tractors. In the **Białowieża forest** the isolation has ensured the survival of continental Europe's last belt of virgin forest—the haunt of bison, elk, and hundreds of varieties of flora and fauna, and home, too, of the wondrous *Zybrówka* "bison grass" vodka.

Byelorussians constitute the principal ethnic minority, numbering some 200,000 in all. Before the war, Polish territory stretched far to the east, across the current Soviet border, and today communities on either side are scarcely distinguishable, save that the Soviets are, if anything, poorer still. Another historic, but declining, minority are the **Tartars**, who settled here centuries ago, and whose wooden mosques at **Bohoniki** and **Kruszyniamy** are one of the sights of the Polish east. (There are many more across the border.) Also distinctive is the **Jewish** legacy: the restored synagogue complex at **Tykocin** is one of the most evocative monuments in the country, though the community itself was eradicated by the Nazis.

Once again, local **transportation** consists mainly of buses, with services diminishing the nearer the border you get.

Białystok

Even the habitually enthusiastic official Polish guidebooks are mute on the glories of **BIAŁYSTOK**, the industrial center of northeast Poland; it's not a beautiful place, its main development occurring during the industrialization of the nineteenth century. Unique among major Polish cities today, however, it has retained the healthy ethnic and religious mix—Poles, Byelorussians and Ukrainians, Catholic and Orthodox—characteristic of the country before the war, though the Jews, of course, are absent. And despite all the industry, it's one of the country's least polluted cities.

Some History

According to legend, Białystok was founded in 1320 by Gedymin, the Grand Duke of Lithuania, but its emergence really began in the 1740s when local aristocrat Jan Branicki built a palace in the town center. Partitioned off to Prussia and then to Russia, Białystok rapidly developed as a textile city, in competition with Prussian-controlled Łódz. In both cities industrialization fostered the growth of a sizable urban proletariat and a large and influential Jewish community. Factory strikes in the 1880s demonstrated the potency of working-class protest, as did the anti-Czarist demonstrations which broke out here in 1905. Echoing protests in other parts of the Russian empire, they elicited a similar response—an officially instigated pogrom, during which many Białystok Jews lost their lives. Fifteen years later, anticipating a victory that never came against Piłsudski's apparently demoralized forces, Lenin's troops installed a provisional government in Białystok led by Felix Dzierzyński, the notorious Polish commander of the Cheka or Soviet secret police.

World War II brought destruction and slaughter to Białystok. Hitler seized it in 1939, then handed it over to Stalin before reoccupying it in 1941—which is when the Jewish population was herded into a ghetto area before deportation to the death camps. The heroic Białystok **ghetto uprising** of August 1943—the first within the Reich—presaged the extinction of the city's Jewry. Nor was the killing confined to Jews. By 1945, over half the city's population were dead, with three-quarters of the town center destroyed.

Following the end of the war, the authorities set about rebuilding the town and its industrial base. From a strictly utilitarian point of view they succeeded: Białystok is a developed economic center for textiles, metals, and timber, with a population of over 250,000. The aesthetic cost has been high, though—the usual billowing smokestacks, ugly high-rises and faceless open streets of postwar development. But Białystok has its share of historic sights—mostly associated with its Orthodox Byelorussian community—and it makes an ideal base for exploring the border region to the east.

The Town

Białystok's historic centerpoint is the **Rynek**, an unusual triangular-shaped space with a large Baroque town hall in the middle. The main sights are situated on and around ul. Lipowa, the main thoroughfare cutting from east to west across the city center. The church of **St Nicholas** here was built in the 1840s to serve the swelling ranks of Russian settlers. A typically dark, icon-filled place of Orthodox devotion, its ornate frescoes are careful copies of those in the Orthodox cathedral in Kiev. It is filled to capacity for the Sunday services—worth coinciding with to hear the choir. Further down ul. Lipowa the **Orthodox cemetery** contains another enchanting *cerkiew*—though your only chance of getting in to look around is during the Sunday morning service.

Catholic competition comes from the huge **parish church** nearby and the imposing 1920s **St Roch**, at the western end of the street. The parish church is

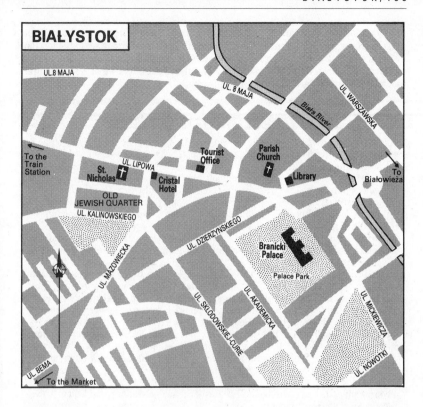

something of a historical curiosity: next to it is a small seventeenth-century parish church built by the Branicki family, while the main structure is a vast 1900-vintage neo-Gothic building, almost twenty times the size and only permitted by the Czarist authorities because its official request billed it as an "addition." The streets south of ul. Lipowa comprise the old **ghetto area**; a tablet on an apartment house near the court house commemorates the 3000 Jews burned to death in June 1941, when the Nazis set fire to the **Great Synagogue** which used to stand on this site.

The most striking building downtown is the **Branicki Palace**, destroyed by the Nazis in 1944 but rebuilt on the lines of the eighteenth-century building commissioned by Jan Branicki—itself a reconstruction of an earlier palace. It's difficult to get inside, as the main building is now a medical academy, but you can stroll unhindered through the park and admire its classical grandeur from a distance. Look out, too, for the main front balcony, the so-called **Dzierżyński Balcony**, from which Felix Dzierżyński and associates proclaimed the creation of the Polish Soviet Socialist Republic in 1920.

Białystok's proximity to the Soviet border ensures it a key place among the growing number of Polish towns heavily involved in "trade tourism." On Sunday mornings the open-air **market**—strategically located by the police station on ul. Bem—is thronged with Soviet citizens plying a strange assortment of consumer goods: gold, clothes, hi-fi, antiques, cosmetics, anything that Poles are prepared to buy. If you want **caviar**, this is the place to buy it, as the nearer the border you get, the lower the price: Gdańsk is fifty percent higher, Warsaw seventy-five. Pay in dollars only if you have to, be prepared to bargain, buy glass containers (not metal), and bear in mind that taking caviar out of Poland is illegal. Keep in mind, too, that the crowds are a haven for pickpockets.

POLES AND BYELORUSSIANS

Poles and Byelorussians have a long history of living together but also one of long-suppressed cultural and political antagonisms, which have recently begun to surface. In the communist era, minorities were actively recruited into the party and state security apparatus, and their religion given active state backing—so long as the community kept its separatist or nationalist impulses in check. Use of the Byelorussian language was forbidden in public, and there were no concessions to the culture in schools or cultural institutions. Despite this, a handful of Byelorussian *samizdat* publications circulated during the communist years.

The result of these years of active state co-option, inevitably, was to reinforce Catholic Polish suspicion of their neighbors, which, with the state controls off, is surfacing in openly expressed hostility. Meanwhile, for Byelorussians, the new Polish political climate and freedoms, the disintegration of the Soviet empire, and ever-burgeoning Polish nationalism, have reawakened their own search for a meaningful national identity. In Białystok, nationalist Byelorussian candidates ran against Solidarity in the 1989 elections and the community is taking steps to re-establish its language and culture. In 1989 a Byelorussian association was set up with the agreement of the local authorities—although to date it has been extremely cautious, using, for instance, the Polish language for its meetings. A current controversy is whether to replace the Slav church services with Byelorussian services, an innovation resisted by their own conservative church authorities.

As in other borderlands, the underlying issue here is whether the Solidarity-led government policy on minorities will go further than declarations, and lead to active support for their development.

Practicalities

The main **train station**, a dingy pink building that wouldn't look out of place in Moscow, is a five-minute bus ride (#4) west of the city center—supposedly it was built outside the center as a punishment for anti-Czarist protests in the city. Close by, on ul. Manifestu Lipcowego, is the **bus station**. The **tourist information office**, in the center of town at ul. Rynek Kościuszki 26, has a plentiful supply of maps and brochures, and can make useful suggestions about places to stay. **Almatur**, at ul. Zwierzyniecka 14, runs a lot of youth and student camps in the area, as well as arranging boat and canoe rental. They may also be able to tell you the current whereabouts of **student hotels** (open June–Aug), whose locations change year by year.

Among **hotels**, the best are the *Cristal*, ul. Lipowa 3 (☎250-61), smack in the middle of town, and the *Leśny*, ul. Zwycięstwa 77 (☎511-641). The *Turkus* at ul. Zwycięstwa 54 (☎513-278) is cheaper and reasonable quality; the *Cristal Nowy*, ul. Malmeda 1 (☎260-41), and the less inviting *Zwierzyniec*, ul. Swierczewskiego 28 (☎226-29), are two lower-quality alternatives. The **youth hostel** (☎231-38) is at ul. Stołeczna 6, and there's a makeshift **campground** next to the *Leśny* hotel.

All the main hotels have **restaurants**, of which the *Cristal* and *Turkus* are the more enticing. The *Grodno* at ul. Sienkiewicza 28 offers its version of Byelorussian cuisine, while the *Kaunas*, ul. Wesola 18, has Lithuanian specialties like *chłodnik*. Other options are the *Karczma Słupska* on ul. Manifestu Lipcowego, and *Hubertówka* at Ul. Broniewskiego 4.

Tykocin

Forty kilometers west of Białystok, north of the main Warsaw road (E18), is the quaint, sleepy little town of **TYKOCIN**, set in the open vistas of the Podlasie countryside. Tykocin's size belies its historical significance. As well as the former site of the national Arsenal, it also has one of the best-restored **synagogues** in Poland today, a reminder that this was once home to an important Jewish community. It's a one-hour journey from the main bus station in Białystok; buses leave regularly throughout the day.

The Town

The bus deposits you in the enchanting **town square**, surrounded on several sides by well-preserved, nineteenth-century wooden houses. The **statue** of Stefan Czarnecki in the center was put up by his grandson Jan Branicki in 1770, while Branicki was busy rebuilding this town and his adopted home of Białystok. The Baroque **parish church**, commissioned by the energetic Branicki in 1741 and recently restored, has a beautiful polychrome ceiling, a finely ornamented side chapel of the Virgin, and a functioning Baroque organ. Also founded by Branicki was the nearby **Bernardine Convent**, now a Catholic seminary. Next to the church looking on to the river bridge is the **Alumnat**, a hospice for war veterans founded in 1633—a world first. Continue out of town over the Narew River and you'll come to the ruins of the sixteenth-century **Radziwiłł Palace**, where the national Arsenal was once kept; it was destroyed by the Swedes in 1657.

Jews first came to Tykocin in 1522, and by the early nineteenth century seventy percent of the population was Jewish, the figure declining to around fifty percent by 1900. The original wooden **synagogue** downtown was replaced in 1642 by the Baroque building still standing today. Carefully restored in the 1970s, it now houses an excellent **Jewish museum** (Tues–Sun 10am–5pm), where background recordings of Jewish music and prayers adds to a mournfully evocative atmosphere. Information sheets in English and German give detailed background on both the building and the history of Tykocin Jewry. Beautifully illustrated Hebrew inscriptions adorn parts of the interior walls, but most striking of all is the Baroque *bima*, the four-pillared central podium from which the cantor led the services. Valuable religious artifacts are on display, as well as historical documents relating to the now-lost community. Over the square in the old **Talmud house** there's a well-kept **local history museum**, featuring an intact apothecary's shop.

Practicalities

The only **restaurant** in town, the *Narnianka*, just off the square on ul. Bernardynska, is pretty squalid—wait to get back to Białystok before eating unless you're starving. The **PTTK hostel** is closed at the moment, so the only official accommodation is a **youth hostel** on ul. Kochanowskiego (June & July; ☎136-85).

Kruszyniamy and Bohoniki

Hard up near the Byelorussian frontier, the old Tartar villages of **Kruszyniamy** and **Bohoniki** are an intriguing ethnic component of Poland's eastern borderlands, with their wooden mosques and Muslim graveyards. The story of how these people came to be here is fascinating in itself (see box below), and a visit to the villages is an instructive and impressive experience.

Getting to them is no mean feat. Direct **buses to Kruszyniamy** from Białystok are scarce; the alternative is to take the bus to KRYNKI (about 40km) and wait for a connection to Kruszyniamy. If there aren't any of these, the only thing left to do is hitch. The only **buses to Bohoniki** are from SOKOŁKA, an hour's train journey north of Białystok. If you're trying to visit both villages in the same day, the best advice is to go to Kruszyniamy first, return to Krynki (probably by hitching), then take a bus towards Sokołka. Ask the driver to let you off at STARA KAMIONKA, and walk the remaining 4km eastwards along the final stretch of the "Tartar Way" (Szlak Tartarski Duzy), which runs between the two villages. To get back to Białystok, take the late afternoon bus to Sokołka, then a train back to the city.

THE TARTARS

Early in the thirteenth century, the nomadic Mongol people of central Asia were welded into a confederation of tribes under the rule of Genghis Khan. In 1241 the most ferocious of these tribes, the **Tartars**, came charging out of the steppes and divided into two armies, one of which swept towards Poland, the other through Hungary. Lightly armored, these natural horsemen moved with a speed that no European soldiery could match, and fought in a fashion as savage as the diet that sustained them—raw meat and horse's milk mixed with blood. On Easter Day they destroyed Kraków, and in April came up against the forces of the Silesian ruler Duke Henryk the Pious at Legnica. The Silesians were annihilated, and a contemporary journal records that "terror and doubt took hold of every mind" throughout the Christian west. Before the eventual withdrawal of the Tartar hordes, all of southern Poland was ravaged repeatedly—Kraków, for example, was devastated in 1259 and again in 1287.

By the fourteenth century, however, the greatest threat to Poland was presented by the Teutonic Knights (see "Malbork," p.103), and the participation of a contingent of Tartars in the Polish defeat of the Knights at Grunwald in 1410 signalled a new kind of connection. Communities of Tartars were now living close to the borders of the country (the Cossacks, for instance, were an offshoot of a Tartar tribe) and were steadily encroaching westward. It was in the late seventeenth century that Poland received its first peaceable Tartar settlers, when King Jan Sobieski granted land in eastern Poland to those who had taken part in his military campaigns.

Today some 6000 descendants of these first Muslim citizens of Poland are spread all over the country, particularly the Szczecin, Gdańsk, and Białystok areas. Though thoroughly integrated into Polish society, they are distinctive both for their Asiatic appearance and their faith—the Tartars of Gdańsk, for example, have just completed a mosque. Apart from the mosques and graveyards at Bohoniki and Kruszyniamy, little is left of the old settlements in the region east of Białystok, but there are a number of mosques still standing across the border in Byelorussia.

The Villages

Walking through **KRUSZYNIAMY** is like moving back a century or two: the painted wooden houses, cobbled road, and wizened old peasants staring at you from their front porches are like something out of Tolstoy. Surrounded by trees and set back from the road is the eighteenth-century **mosque**, recognizable by the Islamic crescent hanging over the entrance gate. Despite initial protests and general grumpiness, the imam will let you in if you're properly dressed, which means no bare legs or revealing tops. Though the Tartar population is dwindling, the mosque's predominantly wooden interior is well maintained—a glance at the list of Arab diplomats in the visitor's book explains where the money comes from, and the imam won't refuse a donation from you either.

The mosque in remoter **BOHONIKI** is a similar building, looked after by a woman who is a direct descendant of the settlers who established themselves here in 1697. She lives at number 26 (there's only one road), and she or one of her family will open up the mosque, and the village *ruch* if you want postcards. In the **Tartar cemetery**, hidden in a copse half a kilometer south of the village, gravestones are inscribed in both Polish and Arabic with characteristic Tartar names like Ibrahimowicz and Bohdanowicz—in other words, Muslim names with a Polish ending tacked on. Search the undergrowth at the back of the cemetery and you'll find older, tumbled-down gravestones inscribed in Russian, from the days when Bohoniki was an outpost of the Czarist empire. Tartars from all over Poland are still buried here, as they have been since Sobieski's time.

The Białowieża Forest

For a country with a reputation as an environmental disaster zone, Poland has an amazing number of beauty spots. One hundred kilometers southeast of Białystok is one of the best-known of these, the **Białowieża Forest** (Puszcza Białowieska). Covering 312,000 acres and spreading way over the border into the Soviet Union, Białowieża is the last primeval forest in Europe, but its fame and popularity rest as much on the forest's large population of **European bison** as on its antiquity and beauty.

For centuries Białowieża was a private hunting ground for a succession of Lithuanian and Byelorussian princes, Polish kings, Russian Czars, and other potentates—patronage which ensured the forest survived largely intact. Recognizing its environmental importance, the Polish government turned large sections of the *puszcza* into a national park in the 1920s, not least to protect its bison herds, which had been hunted almost to extinction by famished soldiers during World War I. Like most *puszcza*, Białowieża has hidden its fair share of partisan armies, most notably during the 1863 uprising and World War II; monuments scatter the area, as no doubt do the bones of countless unknown dead.

A large section of forest on the Polish side of the border is now a strictly controlled reserve, but the rest is open for **guided visits**. The unique atmosphere of the place makes even a day trip an experience not to be missed.

Getting There

Białowieża is a bus journey of a couple of hours from Białystok; for a day trip there and back, take the 6:30am bus—and get there early in summer, as tickets sell out quickly. (There are trains too, but they involve changes at BIELSK PODLASKI and HAJNÓWKA, and take much longer.) On the way through the flat, wooded greenery of the Podlasie countryside you'll probably see more Orthodox onion domes than Catholic spires; the recently renovated *cerkiew* in Hajnówka, the last town before the forest area, is a spiritual center of the Byelorussian revival.

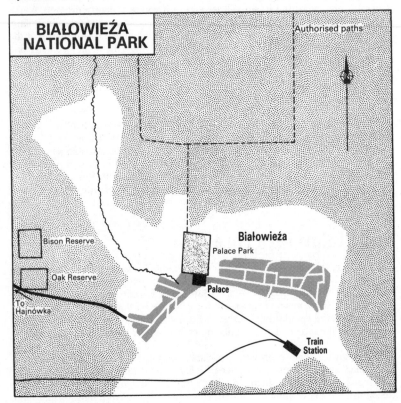

Białowieża Village and the Forest

From Hajnówka the road runs straight for 20km through the forest to the village of **BIAŁOWIEŻA**, a mere 2km from the border. The bus stops at the gates of the **Palace Park**, opposite a typical late nineteenth-century *cerkiew*, with a unique tiled iconostasis. Inside the park, the Białowieża **museum** (Tues–Sun 8am–4pm) provides a detailed introduction to the natural history of the forest, including examples of the amazingly diverse flora and fauna.

Access to the forest itself is controlled: unless you want to negotiate for a private guide to take you into the reserve, the only way in is to charter a horse-drawn cart from the nearby tourist office. Prices are reasonable, but you may have to wait some time if there are a lot of people around—a good argument for getting there early. The two-to-three-hour cart tour takes you along the forest paths to the **bison reserve** (open all year), a few kilometers from the village, where some of the forest's 250 specimens can be seen lounging around—the rest are out in the wilds. The horses also kept in the reserve area are wild **tarpans**, relations of the original steppe horses which are gradually being bred back to their original genetic stock after centuries of interbreeding.

Interesting though these animals are, the main impressions of the forest stem from the ancient *puszcza* itself. At times the serenity of the forest's seemingly endless depths is exhilarating, then suddenly the trunks of oak, spruce, and hornbeam swell threateningly to a dense canopy, momentarily pierced by shafts of sunlight that sparkle briefly before subsiding into gloom. One memorable cluster, which the guide will take you to, consists of a group of forty-meter-high oaks, each named after a Polish monarch.

Apart from the rarer animals such as elk and beaver, the forest supports an astounding profusion of **flora and fauna**: over 20 species of tree, 20 of rodents, 13 varieties of bat, 228 of birds—all told over 3000 species, not counting around 8000 different insect species.

Staying

The *Iwa* **hotel** in the park grounds (☎122-60/123-84) is geared to western tourist requirements, and priced accordingly. The nearby **PTTK hostel** (☎125-05) is a perfectly comfortable, cheaper alternative. In season both places get very busy, so reserving in advance is a good idea—they'll probably understand English or German at reception. The decent-sized **youth hostel** in the village at ul. Waszkiewicza 4 (☎125-60) is open all year. For meals, head for the *Iwa* hotel **restaurant**, especially if you need a good breakfast after the early-morning bus journey.

travel details

Trains

Gdańsk to Białystok (2 daily; 8–9hr); Bydgoszcz (hourly; 2–3hr); Częstochowa (5 daily; 7–8hr); Elbląg (11 daily; 1–2hr); Hel (6–9 daily; 2hr–2hr 30min); Katowice (8 daily; 7–8hr; couchettes); Kołobrzeg (4 daily; 4–5hr); Koszalin (13 daily; 3–4hr); Kraków (6 daily; 6–10hr); Lublin (2 daily; 7hr 30min); Łódź (6 daily; 5hr 30min–7hr); Olsztyn (6 daily; 3hr 30min); Poznań (7 daily; 4hr); Przemyśl (1 daily; 13hr); Rzeszów (1–2 daily; 11–14hr; couchettes); Szczecin (8 daily; 4hr 30min–6hr); Toruń (5 daily; 3–4hr); Warsaw (19 daily; 3hr 30min–5hr); Wrocław (7 daily; 7–8hr; couchettes); Zakopane (1 daily; 13hr; couchettes).

Toruń to Bydgoszcz (30min–1hr); Gdańsk (5 daily; 3–4hr); Kraków (3 daily; 7–8hr); Łódź (11–14 daily; 2–4hr); Olsztyn (7–9 daily; 2–3hr); Poznań (5 daily; 2–3hr); Rzeszów & Przemyśl (1 daily June–Sept; 10hr 30min; couchettes); Warsaw (6 daily; 3–5hr); Wrocław (2 daily; 5–6hr).

Olsztyn to Białystok (4 daily; 5–7 hr); Elbląg (10 daily; 1hr 30min–2hr); Gdańsk (6 daily; 3–4hr); Kraków (2 daily; 7–12hr); Poznań (4 daily; 5–7hr); Suwałki (2 daily; 5–6hr); Szczecin (5 daily; 8–10hr); Toruń (8 daily; 3–4hr); Warsaw (8 daily; 3hr 30min–6hr); Wrocław (2 daily; 7–8hr); Zakopane (1 daily; 16hr).

Suwałki to Białystok (4 daily; 2hr 30min–3hr 30min); Kraków (1 daily June–Sept; 12hr); Olsztyn (2 daily; 6–8hr); Warsaw (4–6 daily; 4–8hr; couchettes June–Sept).

Białystok to Gdańsk (2 daily; 9hr; couchettes); Kraków (1 daily; 9hr; couchettes); Lublin (1 daily; 9hr); Olsztyn (5–6 daily; 6hr); Poznań (1 daily;

10hr; couchettes); Suwałki via Augustów (4–5 daily; 2hr 30min–3hr).

Useful bus routes

Gdańsk to Kartuzy, Kwidzyn, Grudziądz, Chełmno, Toruń.

Toruń to Bydgoszcz, Gdańsk, Olsztyn, Warsaw.

Chełmno to Toruń, Bydgoszcz, Grudziąz.

Olsztyn to Lidzbark Warmiński, Mrągowo, Białystok, Ełk, Augustów.

Augustów to Olsztyn, Suwałki, Warsaw, Białystok, Ełk, Giżycko, Sejny.

Białystok to Lublin, Olsztyn, Augustów.

Suwałki to Gdańsk, Warsaw, Grudziąz, Bydgoszcz, Olsztyn, Kwidzyn.

CHAPTER THREE

EASTERN POLAND

T he **East** is the least populated and least known part of Poland: a great swath of border country, its agricultural plains punctuated by remote backwoods villages and a few market towns. It is peasant land, the remnants of the great European *latifundia*—the feudal grain estates— whose legacy was massive emigration from the late 1800s until World War II to France, Germany, and, above all, the USA.

Borders have played an equally disruptive role in recent history. Today's **Polish–Soviet frontier**, established after the last war, sliced through the middle of what was long the heartland of the Polish **Ukraine**, leaving towns like Lublin (and Lwów, inside the Soviet Union) deprived of their historic links. As border restrictions ease, the prewar links are reasserting themselves in the flood of Soviet "trade tourists"—essentially car-trunk salesmen—who give an international touch to the street markets of towns like Przemyśl and Rzeszów. On the Polish side, potatoes are now a major peasant crop of the southeast, for private sale to Soviet Ukrainians. In the genuine wilderness of the **highland areas** you come upon a more extreme political repercussion of the war, with the minority **Lemks** and **Boyks** just beginning to re-establish themselves, having been expelled in the wake of the civil war that raged here from 1945 to 1947. And this area's ethnic diversity is further complicated by the religious divisions between Catholic, Uniate, and Orthodox communities.

None of this may inspire a visit, yet aspects of the east can be among the highlights of any Polish trip. The **mountains**, though not as high nor as dramatic as the Tatras to the west, are totally unexploited. A week or so hiking in the **Bieszczady** is time well spent, the pleasures of the landscapes reinforced by easy contact with the locals—a welcoming bunch, and drinkers to match any in the country. The **Beskid Niski**, to the west, has some great rewards too—in particular its amazing **wooden churches** or *cerkwi* (*cerkiew* in the singular), whose pagoda-like domes and canopies are among the most spectacular folk architecture of Central-Eastern Europe.

Lublin, the region's major city and for centuries the home of a famous Jewish community, is hard to find appealing, due in large part to the somber sight of the Majdanek death camp on its outskirts. However, the smaller towns, like the old trading centers of **Kazimierz Dolny** and **Sandomierz** along the Wisła River, are among the country's most beautiful, long favored by artists and retaining majestic historic cores—though again the absence of the Jews casts a pall. Over to the east, **Zamość** has a superb Renaissance quarter, miraculously preserved from the war and well worth the detour needed to get there, while in the south there is the stately **Łancut Castle**, an extraordinary reminder of prewar, aristocratic Poland. Each summer the castle hosts a chamber music festival, one of the most prestigious Polish music events. The most intriguing of the region's festivals, however, takes place at nearby **Rzeszów** in June and July every third year, when folklore groups from *emigracja* communities get together for a riot of singing, dancing, and nostalgia.

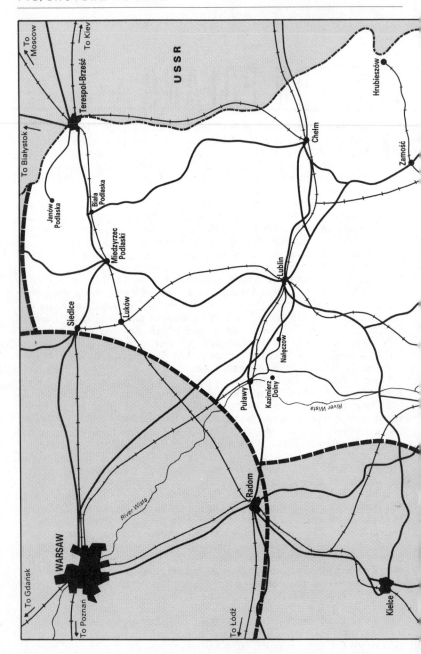

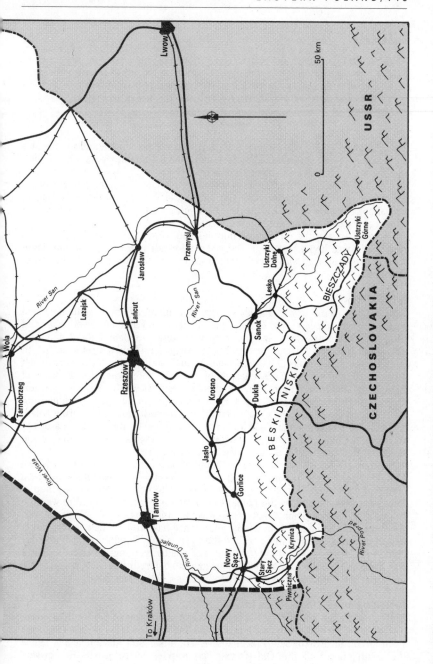

Lublin

In the shops, oil lamps and candles were lit. Bearded Jews dressed in long cloaks and wearing wide boots moved through the streets on the way to evening prayers. The world beyond was in turmoil. Jews everywhere were being driven from their villages. But here in Lublin one felt only the stability of a long established community.

Isaac Bashevis Singer, *The Magician of Lublin.*

The city of **LUBLIN**, the largest in Eastern Poland, presents an all too familiar ambivalence, with sprawling high-rises and Stalinist smokestacks surrounding the historic center. Once you're in the heart of the place, however, it's all cobbled streets and dilapidated mansions—a wistful reminder of the city's past glories. The fabric of this old quarter came through World War II relatively undamaged, and although years of postwar neglect have left it in a pretty disheveled state, a slow reconstruction program is now under way.

Tucked between the numerous churches you'll find reminders that for centuries Lublin was home to a large and vibrant **Jewish community**, a population exterminated in the Nazi concentration camp at **Majdanek**, just 3km from downtown.

Some History

Like many eastern towns, Lublin started as a medieval trade settlement and guard post, in this case on the trade route linking the Baltic ports with Kiev and the Black Sea. Somehow managing to survive numerous depredations and invasions—the fearsome Tartar onslaughts in particular—Lublin by the sixteenth century was well established as a commercial and cultural center. As every Polish schoolchild knows, the city's finest hour came in 1569 when the Polish and Lithuanian kings met here to unite the two countries—the so-called **Lublin Union**—thereby creating the largest mainland empire in Europe, stretching from the Baltic to the Black Sea. Over a century of prosperity followed, during which the arts flourished and many fine buildings were added to the city. The Partitions rudely interrupted this process, leaving Lublin to languish on the edge of the Russian-ruled Duchy of Warsaw for the next hundred years or so.

Following World War I and the regaining of national independence in 1918, a Catholic university—the only one in Eastern Europe—was established, now a cradle of the Polish Catholic intelligentsia. It was to Lublin, too, that a group of Polish socialists known as the Lublin Committee returned in 1944 from wartime refuge in the Soviet Union to set up a new communist government. Since the war, the town's industrial and commercial importance has grown considerably, with a belt of factories mushrooming around the town center. Lublin may also one day come to be seen as one of the birthplaces of Solidarity. Some Poles claim that it was a strike in Lublin in May 1980—four months before the Gdańsk shipyard sit-ins—that first demonstrated the power of workers' self-organization.

Arriving and Finding a Place to Stay

You're most likely to arrive at the **train station**, some way to the south of downtown; from here it's best to take a taxi (if the line isn't too long) or bus #50 to the main street, ul. Krakowskie Przedmieście. The main **bus station** is just below the castle, north of the Old Town. The **tourist office** at ul. Krakowskie

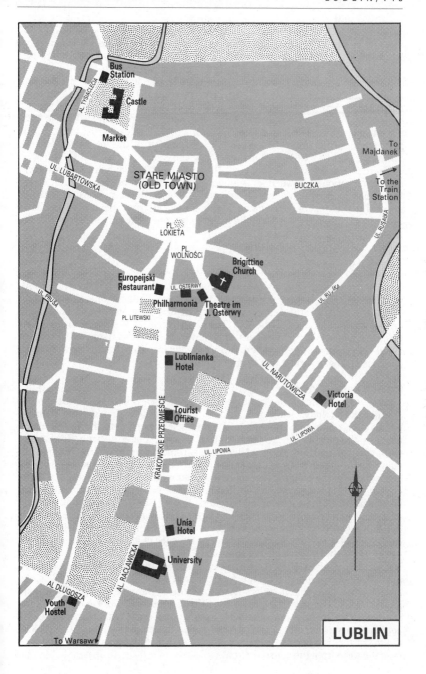

Przedmieście 78 (☎244-12) has a reasonable amount of maps and other information, but rarely has English-speaking staff. The **Almatur office**, ul. Langiewicza 10 (☎332-37), is more likely to have an English-speaker; they can also tell you about student hotels on the university campus (available July 15–Sept 15).

There are few **hotels**, but they are generally adequate. *Dom Noclegowy*, ul. Academicka 4 (☎382-35), is a cheap, basic place near the university. The *Hotel Lublinianka*, Krakowskie Przedmieście 56 (☎242-61), a Stalin-era extravaganza, has reasonable rooms, a separate coffee shop and restaurant, and is in easy walking distance of the Old Town. The *Victoria*, ul. Narutowicza 56/58 (☎290-26), is pricier and farther from the center. Most expensive of the lot is the *Unia*, al. Raclawickie 12 (☎320-61), part of the Orbis chain.

There is also a **youth hostel**, at ul. Długosza 4a (☎306-28; bus #50 or #54 from the train station), crowded in summer, and a **PTTK hostel** at Krakowskie Przedmieście 29, which offers cheap beds in four-berth dormitories. The **campground** in the west of the city at ul. Sławinkowska 46 (June–Sept) has bungalows as well as tent places, but you'll be lucky to get one; take bus #18 from the city center, #20 from the station.

The City

The busy plac Łokieta forms the main approach to the Stare Miasto (Old Town), with an imposing nineteenth-century **New Town Hall** on one side. Straight across the square is the fourteenth-century **Brama Krakowska** (Kraków Gate), one of three gateways to the Old Town. Originally a key point in the city's defenses against Tartar invaders, this now houses the **Historical Museum** (Wed–Sun 9am–4pm); the contents aren't greatly inspiring, but the view from the top floor makes it worth a visit to orient yourself.

Into the Stare Miasto

A short walk around to the right along ul. Królewska brings you to the **Brama Trinitarska** (Trinity Gate), and opposite it the **Cathedral**, a gloomy Baroque building with little to commend it. The gate itself opens onto the Rynek, dominated by the outsize **Old Town Hall**; built in 1389, it later became the seat of a royal tribunal, and was given a Neoclassical remodeling in 1781 by Merlini, the man who designed Warsaw's Łazienki Palace. Getting around the square is tortuous, as a lot of the buildings are under reconstruction; a fair number of the laborers are Vietnamese *gastarbeiter*, invited here a few years ago in a spirit of socialist brotherhood. Of the surrounding burghers' houses, the **Sobieski Mansion** (no. 12)—where Charles XII of Sweden and Peter the Great were both once guests—has Renaissance sculptures decorating its exterior, while the Lubomelski house (no. 8) hides some racy fourteenth-century frescoes in its wine cellars, which the workmen might be persuaded to show you.

East of the square, down the narrow ul. Złota, lies the fine **Dominican Church and Monastery**, founded in the fourteenth century and reconstructed in the seventeenth. The church suffers from the familiar Baroque additions, but don't let that deflect you from the Renaissance **Firlej Family Chapel** at the end of the southern aisle, built for one of Lublin's leading aristocratic families, nor the eighteenth-century panorama of the city just inside the entrance. Round the back of the monastery is a popular playhouse, the **Teatr im. Andersen**, with a good view over the town from the square in front.

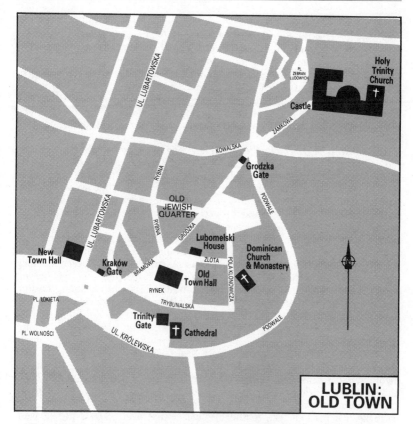

LUBLIN: OLD TOWN

The Old Town's other theater, **Studio Teatralne**, near the center at ul. Grodzka 32, has a gallery featuring local artists. Grodzka was part of the **Jewish quarter** and several of the buildings on the street bear memorials in Polish and Yiddish to the former inhabitants. Lublin was one of the main centers of Hassidic Jewry and its **Yeshiva**—now a medical academy—was the world's largest Talmudic school right up to the war.

The Castle Complex

On a hill just east of the Old Town is the **Castle**, an offbeat 1820s neo-Gothic edifice built on the site of Kazimierz the Great's fourteenth-century fortress, and linked by a raised pathway from the Brama Zamkowa (Castle Gate) at the end of ul. Grodzka.

The castle houses a sizable **museum** (summer daily 9am–3pm; winter Wed–Sun only), the high points of which are the **ethnography** section, including a good selection of local costumes, religious art, and woodcarving, and the **art gallery**, where moody nineteenth-century landscapes and scenes of peasant life mingle with portraits and historical pieces. Among the latter, look out for two famous and characteristically operatic works by Matejko: the massive *Lublin*

Union portrays Polish and Lithuanian noblemen debating the union of the two countries in 1569; the equally huge *Admission of the Jews to Poland* depicts the Jews' arrival in Poland in the early Middle Ages, the two sides eyeing each other suspiciously. Another upstairs room contains an excellent collection of eighteenth- and nineteenth-century **Orthodox icons** from the Brest (formerly Brzesc) area, now just over the other side of the Soviet border. The section of the museum devoted to World War II recalls the castle's use by the Nazis as a prison and interrogation center. Polish civilian prisoners were shot in the courtyard and over 400,000 Jews were detained here before being sent to Majdanek or other concentration camps.

The **Church of the Holy Trinity**, behind one of the two remaining towers in the corner of the courtyard, is closed for restoration, but a request to the main castle office should get you in. Behind rickety scaffolding are a glorious set of Byzantine-looking frescoes, unlike anything you'll find in your average Roman Catholic church. Uncovered in the last century, they were painted by a group of Ruthenian artists from the Ukraine—exceptionally for the time, the main artist, Master Andrew, signed his name and the date, 1418.

On the way back to the Old Town, check out the **market** just below the castle; you may find something interesting among the mixture of junk and contraband. As in many eastern towns, the squat peasants with stand-out accents selling caviar, gold, and radios for dollars are Russians from just over the border. They're what are euphemistically known as "trade tourists," an enduring Eastern European practice whereby itinerant traders buy and sell products unobtainable in neighboring countries.

Majdanek

The proximity of **Majdanek**, the largest Nazi death camp after Auschwitz, is a shock in itself. This was no semi-hidden location that local people could claim to be or strive to remain in ignorance of—a plea that is more debatable at Auschwitz and Treblinka. Inside the camp, the shock intensifies. Wandering among the barbed wire and watchtowers, staring at crematoria and rows of shabby wooden barracks, it's hard to take in the brutal fact that over 360,000 people were murdered here, the huge majority of them Jews. The **camp museum** (summer Tues–Sun 8am–6pm; closes 3pm in winter) in a former barracks tells the terrible story in detail.

Buses #14, #23, #28, and #153 run to Majdanek from pl. Wolności. For further details on the camps and Polish-Jewish relations, see the Auschwitz section in Chapter Four.

Eating, Drinking, and Entertainment

For a city of its size, Lublin offers remarkably little in the way of diversion. Decent **restaurants** in particular are thin on the ground, with the trend toward private ownership taking its time to penetrate east. The *Unia* hotel, an old party dignitaries' haunt, has the best and most expensive food in town—fine if you're prepared for obsequious waiters and the inevitable "dancing" band blasting away in the corner. The restaurant of the *Lublinianka* hotel stays open later than most, does a good *zurek* soup, and attracts a contingent of hardened local boozers. The *Europeijski* at Krakowskie Przedmieście 29 is gloomy, while the *Karczma Lubelska* at pl. Litewski 2 is okay but nothing more.

Milk bars, as reliable as ever, include the *Staromeijski*, just inside the Old Town at ul. Trybunalska 1, and a string of places along Krakowskie Przedmieście: the *Turstyczny* (no. 29), *Centralny* (no. 56), and *Ogrodowy* (no. 57). For breakfast, the *kawiarnia* in the *Lublinianka* does scrambled eggs and coffee till quite late. Of the few Old Town **cafés,** the *Czarcia Lapa* on ul. Bramowa has a good cheesecake.

Despite its student population, the city doesn't exactly bristle with **nightlife,** either. During semester the *Chata Zaka* club, behind the Catholic University (KUL) on ul. Nowotki, is a popular student dive. There are a number of other **student clubs** dotted around the university campuses and residence halls. The best bet is to wander into either KUL or the nearby state university area and ask what's going on; many students speak English, and there's an even chance of getting invited to some event or other, usually of a heavy drinking nature.

On a more cultural front, the *Philharmonia,* ul. Osterwy 7, has a regular program of high-quality classical **concerts,** and the *Teatr im. J Osterwy,* ul. Narutowicza 17, offers mainly classical Polish **drama**—worth seeing even if you don't speak the language.

West to Kazimierz

The Lublin–Warsaw route has a major attraction in the town of **Kazimierz,** an ancient and highly picturesque grain town set above the Wisła. To reach it on public transit, the easiest approach from Warsaw is to go by train to **Puławy** and catch a connecting bus from there; from Lublin there are direct buses, via the old spa town of **Nałęczów.**

Nałęczów

Twenty-five kilometers west of Lublin (regular buses: destination Puławy and/or Kazimierz Dolny), **NAŁĘCZÓW** saw its heyday at the end of the last century, when Polish writers and artists, including the popular novelists Bolesław Prus and Stefan Zeromski, and pianist-prime minister Ignacy Paderewski, hung out here.

Today the spa is still renowned for its therapeutic waters, heart specialists, and generally medicinal climate, and the town retains much of its old-time appearance and atmosphere. A leisurely stroll through the town park brings you to the Neoclassical **Małachowski Palace,** part health center and part **museum** (Tues–Sun 10am–3pm), devoted to Prus and the "positivist" literary movement he promoted in reaction to traditional insurrectionary romanticism. Nearby is the **sanatarium,** fronted by a monument to **Zeromski,** and, across the road, up ul. Zeromskiego, the writer's Podhale-style cottage—now a small museum. For an instant iron-deficiency remedy, you can taste the local **waters** in the park.

There is just one **hotel** in town, the *Dom Wycieczkowy* at ul. 1 Maja 6, which provides the bare essentials, restaurant included; it might also be able to arrange **private rooms.**

Puławy

PUŁAWY is a grubby, medium-sized industrial town, whose only real attraction is the seventeenth-century **Czartoryski Palace** and its landscaped gardens. A mock-Gothic Temple of the Sibyl and an orangery, both built in the second half of the eighteenth century by Adam Czartoryski and his wife Izabella, give the park a slightly decadent air, reminiscent of the royal residence at Wilanów. During the

Partition period the palace—now an agricultural research institute—became an important intellectual center, amassing a huge library and art collection in the process. The Russians confiscated the whole estate following the failure of the 1831 insurrection, in which the Czartoryskis were deeply implicated. The main palace collection was moved to Kraków, where it makes up the core of the Czartoryski Museum (see Chapter Four).

If you're stranded, there are various accommodation options: the *Hotel Izabella*, ul. Dzierzinskiego 1 (☎3041), aimed at foreign tourists and with a decent if expensive restaurant; a **PTTK hostel** at ul. Rybacka 7 (☎30-48), cheaper and more basic; and an all-year **youth hostel** at ul. Włostowicka 27 (☎33-67). The main **tourist information point** is in the *Izabella* hotel. The town is on a major train line from Warsaw (3hr) and has regular bus connections with Lublin (1hr).

Kazimierz Dolny

Don't be surprised if your first impression of **KAZIMIERZ DOLNY** is one of *déjà vu*; recognizing celluloid potential when they see it, numerous film directors—and not just Polish ones—have used the scenic backdrop of this well-preserved town for historical thrillers and tragic romances. Artists, too, have long been drawn to Kazimierz's effervescent light and ancient buildings.

Historically, the place is closely associated with its royal namesake, Kazimierz the Great (1333–70), who rescued Poland from dynastic and economic chaos, and transformed the country's landscape in the process. It is said of him that he "found a wooden Poland and left a Poland of stone," and Kazimierz Dolny (Lower Kazimierz) is perhaps the best remaining example of his ambitious town-building program. Thanks to the king's promotion of the Wisła grain trade, a minor village was transformed into a prosperous mercantile town by the end of the fourteenth century, and much of the money that poured in was used to build the ornate burghers' houses that are today's prime tourist attraction.

It was during this period, too, that Jews began to settle in Kazimierz and other neighboring towns, grateful for the legal protection proclaimed for them throughout Poland by King Kazimierz. Dynamic Jewish communities of traders and shopkeepers were integral to the character of towns like Kazimierz for over 500 years: at one time eighty percent of the inhabitants of Kazimierz were Jewish. The soul of the town, you feel, died in the concentration camps.

Arriving and Finding a Place to Stay

Unless you have access to a car, the only way to get to Kazimierz Dolny is by **bus** from Puławy, 15km to the north. From Puławy's bus and train stations there are frequent buses to Kazimierz, but note that not all the return buses go to the Puławy train station. The Kazimierz bus station—really just a drop-off point—is on ul. Podzamcze, within spitting distance of the Rynek.

There's a helpful **PTTK office** at no. 27 on the Rynek; for **accommodation**, the best bet is a **private room**, available at reasonable prices (even in summer) from the *Biuro Zakwaterowania* at ul. Lubelska 7 (Mon–Sat 9am–3pm; ☎101). The *Dom Architectowy* at no. 20 on the Rynek offers beds, decent food, and an excellent setting, though it's not a regular tourist place and you may need to be persuasive. Otherwise, you'll be forced farther out to the **PTTK hostel**, a converted fourteenth-century granary south of the town center on ul. Krakowska 59 (☎36). There's a **campground** here, too, and a noisier one at ul. Senatorska 24.

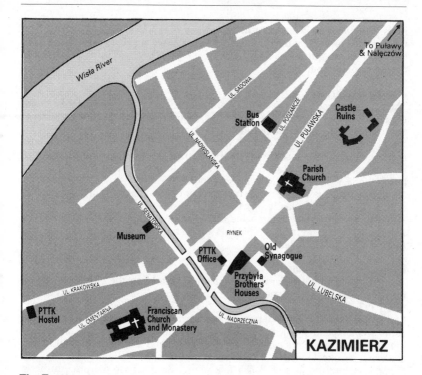

KAZIMIERZ

The Town

The **Rynek**, with its solid-looking wooden well at the center, is a classic Orbis poster image. Most striking of the merchants' residences around the square—all restored after the war—are the **Przybyła Brothers' Houses** on the southern edge. Built in 1615, they bear some striking Renaissance sculpture; the guidebooks say that the largest one shows Saint Christopher, but his tree trunk of a staff and zodiacal entourage suggest something more like a Polish Jolly Green Giant.

Other houses still carrying their Renaissance decorations can be seen on ul. Senatorska, which runs alongside the stream south of the square. One of these, no. 17, houses the **Town Museum** (Tues–Sun 10am–3pm); along with paintings of Kazimierz and its surroundings, the museum documents—albeit sketchily—the history of the town's Jewish community. The nineteenth-century paintings focus largely on the Jews—a kind of Orientalist fascination seems to have gripped the largely gentile Polish artists—and evoke an almost palpable atmosphere. On the streets it's not hard to conjure up this atmosphere, either, though specifically Jewish buildings are scarce. The old **synagogue** is off ul. Lubelska, to the east of the Rynek; it was once a fine building, constructed in King Kazimierz's reign, but war damage and conversion to a movie theater have left little evidence of this.

Crossing the stream and following ul. Cmentarna up the hill brings you to the late sixteenth-century **Franciscan church and monastery**, from where there's a nice view back down over the winding streets and tiled rooftops. Up the hill on the other side of the square is the **Parish Church**, remodeled impressively in the early seventeenth century. Farther up, there's an excellent view from the ruins of the fourteenth-century **Castle**, built by King Kazimierz and destroyed by the Russians in 1792, in the prelude to the Second Partition. The panorama from the top of the **watchtower** above the castle is even better, taking in the Wisła and the sweep of the countryside.

Into the Countryside

There's some good **walking** territory around Kazimierz. If you really want to get the feel of the town's gentle surroundings, follow one of the marked paths from the town center—either the five-kilometer green path southwest past the PTTK hostel and along the **river cliff** to MECMIERZ, or the four-kilometer red path northeast to the ruined **castle** of BOCHOTNICA. One of King Kazimierz's favorite mistresses, a Jewess called Esterka, is said to have lived at Bochotnica in a house connected to the castle by a secret tunnel.

Another option is to take the **ferry** (summer only) to the ruins of the sixteenth-century **Firlej family castle** at JANOWIEC, also situated in attractive countryside. There's an equally improbable tunnel story connected with this castle as well, namely that the well doubled as the entrance to a passage joining this fortress to that of Kazimierz.

Eating and Entertainment

There's little in town as far as **food** is concerned. Apart from the *Dom Architectowy*, the only restaurant on the square is the *Esterka* at no. 13, a dubious greasy spoon. The PTTK hostel has a restaurant too, though it's hardly worth a special trek. Rumor has it that a number of **private restaurants** may be opening soon—check at the accommodation office on ul. Lubelska for the latest. Otherwise, the *kawiarnia* on the square offer snacks, and you can get chips and (sporadically) fish or chicken at a makeshift take-out joint just off the south end of the square.

For sampling the joys of Polish folk music, Kazimierz is the place to be in summer: a week-long **Folk Groups and Singers Festival** takes place here in late June or early July. Unless you have a tent, expect to rough it if you're in town then, as the meager accommodation is snapped up instantly.

Sandomierz

SANDOMIERZ, 80km south of Kazimierz along the Wisła, is another of those small towns described as "quaint" or "picturesque" in the brochures. Its hilltop location certainly fits the bill, though the charm is dented by the evil stench rising from the polluted Wisła. However, a visit is definitely worthwhile, and access is straightforward, with regular train services from Warsaw and buses from Lublin. The one problem is accommodation: the town gets a lot of summer tourists and rooms in season can be very tricky to find; if you're energetic, it's a conceivable day trip from Lublin.

Like other towns in the southeast, Sandomierz rose to prominence through its position on the **medieval trade route** running from the Middle East, through southern Russia and the Ukraine, into central Europe. The town was sacked by the Tartars (twice) and the Lithuanians, in the thirteenth and fourteenth centuries respectively, then completely rebuilt by **Kazimierz the Great**, who gave it a castle, defensive walls, cathedral, and street plan—still visible in the Old Town. Subsequently Sandomierz flourished on the timber and corn trade, with its links along the Wisła to the Baltic ports. It was also the scene of one of the key religious events in Poland. In 1570, while Catholics and Protestants were slitting each others' throats in the rest of Europe, members of Poland's non-Catholic churches met here to formulate the so-called **Sandomierz Agreement**, basis for the legally enshrined freedom of conscience later established throughout the country.

Physically, Sandomierz suffered badly at the hands of the Swedes, who blew up the town castle in 1656, and it was only thanks to a minor miracle that it survived World War II intact. In August 1944, as the **Red Army** pushed the Germans back across Poland, the front line moved closer and closer to Sandomierz. The story goes that one Colonel Skopenko, an admirer of Sandomierz, managed to steer the fighting away from the town. He was later killed farther west; his last wish, duly honored, was to be buried in the cemetery at Sandomierz.

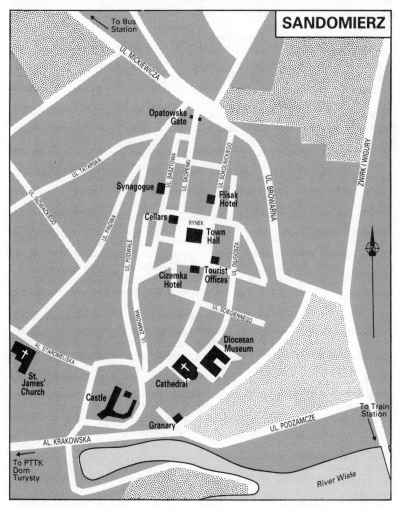

The Town

The **train and bus stations** are on opposite sides of town, a bus ride from the center. Coming in through the nondescript slabs of modern Sandomierz, get off at the fourteenth-century **Brama Opatowska**, part of King Kazimierz's fortifications and the entrance to the Old Town.

From here on it's alleyways and cobblestones, as ul. Skopenki leads to the delightful **Rynek**, an atmospheric square with plenty of places for a leisurely coffee. At its heart is the fourteenth-century **Town Hall**, a Gothic building which had its decorative attic, hexagonal tower, and belfry added in the seventeenth and eighteenth centuries. Many of the well-preserved **burghers' houses** around positively shout their prosperity: nos. 5 and 10 are particularly fine Renaissance examples. There's a Tuesday market on the square, which on the first Tuesday of the month becomes a major rural event, with livestock and produce driven in from the countryside.

A hidden aspect of old Sandomierz is revealed by a PTTK guided tour (Tues–Sun 10am–5pm) of the wine and grain **cellars** under the Rynek; entered from ul. Olesnickich, just off the square, the cellars extend under the town hall, reaching a depth of twelve meters at one point. The registrar's office on nearby ul. Basztowa was an eighteenth-century **synagogue**, though there is—as so often—little to indicate its origins.

A stroll down either of the streets leading off the southern edge of the square brings you to the murky **Cathedral**, constructed around 1360 on the site of a Romanesque church, now with substantial Baroque additions. It is worth a look within for the Byzantine-looking **murals** in the presbytery, and a gruesome series of paintings in the nave, showing the Tartars enjoying a massacre of the populace in 1259 and the Swedes blowing up the castle four centuries later.

Set back from the cathedral, the **Diocesan Museum** (summer Tues–Sun 10am–5pm; winter closes 3pm) was the home of Jan Długosz (1415–80), author of one of the first histories of Poland. The building is filled to bursting with religious art, ceramics, glass, and other curios, including a collection of Renaissance locks and keys, and a wonderful old pipe supposed to have belonged to Mickiewicz. Among the best works are a twelfth-century stone *Madonna and Child*, a *John the Baptist* by Caravaggio, and a fifteenth-century *Three Saints* triptych from Kraków.

Downhill from the cathedral is the **castle**, currently being restored; it is used occasionally for concerts and plays but otherwise has little going for it. Toward the river stands a medieval **granary**; others are to be found north along the river. Aleja Staromeijska runs from in front of the castle to the **Church of St James** (Kościół św. Jakuba), a linden-shaded late Romanesque building that's thought to be the first brick basilica in Poland; its restored entrance portal is particularly striking. The area around the church was the site of the original town, destroyed by the Tartars; recent archaeological digs in the area uncovered a twelfth-century chess set, the oldest in Europe. This whole southern district has had to be shored up, owing to subsidence caused by the network of tunnels and cellars dug for grain storage and running for hundreds of meters through the soft subsoil.

Head back down the path in front of St James and you re-enter the town walls through the **Ucho Igielne**, a small entrance shaped like the eye of a needle.

Practicalities

The town has two **tourist offices**, next door to each other in a corner of the Rynek: Orbis (at no. 24) deals with ticket reservations, PTTK (no. 25/26) with maps and other local information, including accommodation.

Accommodation is in extremely short supply. The *Hotel Cizenka*, Rynek 27 (☎36-38), is ideally situated but has just fifteen rooms. The *Flisak*, off the square at ul. Gen. Sokolnickiego 3 (☎24-25), is also small and thus generally full. The only other options are the very basic PTTK *Dom Wycieczkowy* at ul. Stefana Zeromskiego 10 (☎30-88), on the way into town from the bus station; the more pleasant *Dom Turysty PTTK*, ul. Krakowska 34 (☎22-84), which has a restaurant but is farther out of town; and the **youth hostel**, ul. Flisaków 26 (☎25-63). There is also a **campground** on ul. Podzamcze, right by the river.

The best **restaurants** are in the hotels. The *Cizenka* does an excellent *krupnik* soup but otherwise predictable food; its basement bar is popular with tourists and the local drinking crowd. The only serious alternative downtown, the *Ludowa* at ul. Mariacka 5, is drab; while the restaurant in the *Dom Turysty*, though better, is only worth visiting if you're staying there. The *Flisak* doesn't serve meals, but has a friendly **bar**. As Sandomierz is a day-trippers' favorite, ice cream and coffee bars are open all over the town center in summer.

Zamość

The old towns and palaces of southeast Poland often have a Latin feel to them, and none more so than **ZAMOŚĆ**, 96km from Lublin. The brainchild of the dynamic sixteenth-century chancellor Jan Zamoyski (he of the vodka), the town is a remarkable demonstration of the way the Polish intelligentsia and ruling class looked towards Italy for ideas, despite the proximity of Russia. Zamoyski, in many ways the archetypal Polish Renaissance man, built this model town close to his childhood village to his own ideological specifications, commissioning the design from Bernardo Morando of Padua—the city where he had earlier studied. Morando produced a beautiful Italianate period piece, with a wide piazza, grid-plan streets, an academy, and defensive bastions. These fortifications were obviously well thought out, as Zamość was one of the few places to withstand the seventeenth-century "Swedish Deluge" that flattened so many other Polish towns.

War returned to Zamość early this century, when the area was the scene of an important battle during the Polish-Russian war of 1919–20. The Red Army, which only weeks before had looked set to take Warsaw, was beaten decisively near the town, forcing Lenin to sue for peace with his newly independent neighbors. Somehow, Zamość managed also to get through World War II unscathed, so what you see today is one of Europe's best-preserved Renaissance town centers, classified by UNESCO as an outstanding historical monument.

The Old Town

Standard-issue urban development surrounds Zamość's historic core, and both **bus** and **train stations** are located some way from the center. It's worth taking a bus or taxi to the edge of **plac Wolności**, bordering the Rynek. Once there, you should have no problem finding your way around the Renaissance grid.

The **Rynek**, also known as plac Mickiewicza, is a couple of blocks in from plac Wolności and the partly preserved circuit of walls. Ringed by a low arcade and the decorative former homes of the Zamość mercantile bourgeoisie, the square is dominated by the **Town Hall**, with its sweeping double stairway. Inside there's a room commemorating the socialist theorist **Rosa Luxemburg**, though staff don't rush to open it; she was born east of the square at ul. Staszica 37. Behind the

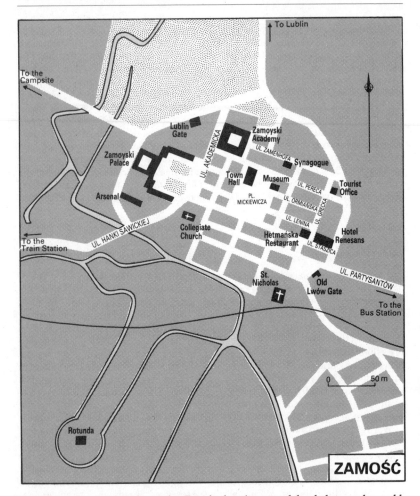

ZAMOŚĆ

arcade on the south side of the Rynek there's a good bookshop and an old-fashioned pharmacy. More evocative is the **Town Museum** to the right of the town hall (Tues–Sun 10am–3pm), with its well-preserved facade, wooden ceilings, and original interior decorations. Unsurprisingly, the museum boasts plenty of portraits of the town's patron, and other assorted Zamoyskiana.

West of the Rynek stands the **Collegiate Church**, a fine Mannerist basilica by Morando; the interior, refreshingly devoid of the usual Baroque additions, features paintings of the life of Saint Thomas attributed to Domenico Tintoretto, and an inevitable Zamoyski family chapel, including the tomb of Chancellor Jan. Just west of the church is the old **Arsenal**, now a military museum, and the former **Zamoyski Palace**. Due north along ul. Academicka are the **Lublin Gate**, oldest of the town entrances and, close by, the old **Zamoyski Academy**, a center of Renaissance learning in Poland. To the east, the former **synagogue** on ul.

Zamenhofa (built as part of Zamoyski's scheme) is now a public library; some of the religious decorations still peer out from above the bookshelves.

In the southern section of the Old Town, around plac Wolności, are a couple more churches: the simple, former Greek Orthodox church of **St Nicholas**, at the bottom of ul. Bazylianka, in which original stucco work was recently uncovered, and a former **Franciscan church**, now the town cinema. Across the road is the **Old Lwów Gate**, built by Morando. Stroll around the remains of the town's **fortifications** from here and you'll appreciate why those marauding Swedes drew a blank at Zamość.

The Nazis spared the buildings of Zamość, but not its people. In the **Rotunda**, a nineteenth-century arsenal south of the Old Town on ul. Wyspiańskiego, over 8000 local people were executed by the Germans; a simple museum there tells the story of the town's wartime trauma. In fact, Zamość (preposterously renamed "Himmlerstadt") and the surrounding area was the target of a brutal "relocation" scheme of the kind already carried out by the Nazis in Western Prussia. From 1942 to 1943 nearly 300 villages were cleared of their Polish inhabitants and their houses taken by German settlers—all part of Hitler's plan to create an Aryan eastern bulwark of the Third Reich. The remaining villages were apparently left alone only because the SS didn't have enough forces to clear them out.

Practicalities

Zamość is easiest approached by bus from Lublin; trains take a very roundabout route. The main **bus station** is over to the east of the town center; for details of departures, check at the **tourist office** on ul. Łukasińskiego, two blocks north of plac Wolności (Mon–Fri 7am–4pm, Sat 9am–noon). The nearby Orbis office at ul. Grecka 10 deals with advance bus and train tickets.

The best **hotel** option is the ugly *Renesans*, behind the tourist office on ul. Grecka 6 (☎20-01); it's moderately priced and conveniently close to the historic district, but very full in summer. A cheap, central alternative is the basic *Dom PTTK*, ul. Zamenhofa (☎26-39), though it is again extremely busy in season. The *Hotel Jubilat* in al. Lenina is noisy, more expensive and a long walk from the Old Town. The **youth hostel**, ul. Partyzantów 14 (June–Aug), is better placed, between the bus station and the Old Town. And, as ever, it's always worth asking at the tourist office about **private rooms**, especially in summer; taxi drivers or people hanging around at the stations are other sources of information. The PTTK **campground** on ul. Krolowej Jadwigi is some way to the west of the town center.

The only **restaurant** worth mentioning is the *Hetmańska*, ul. Staszica 1 (off the Rynek), though it's still pretty dingy and offers little more than soup plus the inevitable pork chop. The **bar** upstairs in the house to the right of the town hall is the place for a night of serious drinking—and perhaps best left when the glasses start flying. With a little cajoling, the **café** at the *Renesans* will serve up a standard breakfast of eggs, cheese, and coffee.

Rzeszów

RZESZÓW was essentially a postwar attempt to revive the southeast, providing industry and an administrative center for an area that had seen the previous half-dozen decades' heaviest emigration. The city's population of over 100,000 is evidence of some sort of success, even if this rapid expansion has produced a soulless urban sprawl. Yet the hinterland still consists of the small villages characteristic of this corner of Poland for centuries, which explains why in 1980 Rzeszów became a nucleus of Rural Solidarity, the independent farmers' and peasants' union formed in the wake of its better-known urban counterpart. If the above suggests you might not want to spend Christmas in Rzeszów, there's little that a visit will do to persuade you otherwise—this is a city to see in transit.

Coming in, the **bus and train stations** are adjacent to each other, a short walk north of downtown. The city also has an **airport** (11km out), which could provide a useful route into the region from Warsaw, Gdańsk, or Szczecin; there is a LOT office at pl. Zwycięstwa 6 (☎332-34 or ☎335-50). **Tourist information** is available at ul. Asynka 10, near the stations, or from the main tourist office at ul. Zeromskiego 2, between the stations and the Old Town (all Mon–Fri 9am–4pm).

As for sights, the **Rynek**, as ever, is the focus of interest, with its **Town Hall** plumped in the middle. From the west side of the square, ul. 3 Maja runs south to a Piarist monastery, now the **Regional Museum** of crafts and folk art (Tues, Fri & Sat 10am–6pm, Wed, Thurs & Sun 10am–3pm). From here the same street continues to the seventeenth-century **castle**, formerly owned by the powerful Lubomirskis, one of Poland's main aristocratic clans. The castle was converted into a prison by the Austrian rulers of Galicia—of which Rzeszów was a part—at the turn of the century and is now the law courts. Heading back up into the center, on ul. Boznicza, northeast of the square, are two old **synagogues**, both rebuilt after the war: the **Old Town Synagogue**, a fine late sixteenth-century building, and the **New Town Synagogue** from a hundred years later, now an arts center.

Practicalities

All the **hotels** are reasonably close to the stations. The *Rzeszów*, al. 22 Lipca 2 (☎374-41), is reasonable in the drab, unexciting way of modern Polish hotels. The *Polonia*, ul. Grottgera 16 (☎320-61), is cheaper and dirtier, but very close to the stations. The *Sportowy*, ul. Turkienizca 23a (☎340-77), is low-grade and slightly farther out. Right by the station at plac Kilińskiego 6 is the *Dom Wycieczkowy* (☎356-76), a typical PTTK place—cheap, basic, but all right. The all-year **youth hostel** (☎344-30) is in the town center at Rynek 25.

Among **restaurants**, the *Rzeszów* hotel is the businessmen's hang-out, offering local specialties including duck, goose, and wonderful *Lezajsk* beer from the nearby town of the same name. Alternatives are the *Relax* at ul. Moniuszki 4, the *Rarytas* at ul. Marszałkowska 15, and the *Rzeszówska* at ul. Kościuszki 9, all within walking distance of the center. If you prefer **milk bars**, there's the *Centralny* at ul. 3 Maja 8, or the downstairs bar of the PTTK hostel.

Appropriately enough for a town with such a long history of emigration, the **Festival of Polonia Music and Dance Ensembles** takes place in Rzeszów in June and July every third year (next one is in 1992). It's a riotous assembly of groups from *emigracja* communities all over the world—Britain, France, USA, Argentina, and Australia.

Łańcut

First impressions of the **fortress** that dominates the center of ŁAŃCUT (pronounced "Winesoot"), 17km east of Rzeszów, suggest that it must have seen rather more high-society engagements than military ones. There has been some serious action around here, though. The first building on the site, constructed by the Pilecki family in the second half of the fourteenth century, was burned down in 1608 when royal troops ambushed its robber-baron owner Stanisław Stadnicki, known by his contemporaries as "The Devil of Łańcut." The estate was then bought by Stanisław Lubomirski, who set about building the sturdier construction that forms the basis of today's castle. Following contemporary military theory, the four-sided castle was surrounded by a pentagonal outer defense of moat and ramparts, the outlines of which remain.

The fortifications were dismantled in 1760 by Izabella Czartoryska (see "Puławy" on p.149), wife of the last Lubomirski owner, who turned Łańcut into one of her artistic salons, laid out the surrounding park, and built a theater in the castle. Louis XIII of France was among those entertained at Łańcut during this period, and the next owners, the Potocki family, carried on in much the same style, Kaiser Franz Josef being one of their guests. Count Alfred Potocki, the last private owner, abandoned the place in the summer of 1944 as Soviet troops advanced across Poland. Having dispatched 600 crates of the castle's most precious objects to liberated Vienna, Potocki himself then departed, ordering a Russian sign reading "Polish National Museum" to be posted on the gates. The Soviets left the castle untouched, and it was opened as a museum later the same year.

The Castle

Forty or so of the castle's hundreds of rooms are open to the public (Tues–Sat 9am–4pm, Sun 9am–3:30pm, opens Sun 10am in winter; closed Mon & Dec 15–Jan 15; last entry 1hr before closing), and in summer they are crammed with organized tour groups. Ask at the ticket office if one of the two English-speaking guides can take you around—they're worth it for the anecdotes. If you're really lucky your guide might be the highly knowledgeable museum curator.

Most of the interesting rooms are on the **first floor**, reached by a staircase close to the entrance hall, which is large enough to allow horse-drawn carriages to drop off their passengers. The **corridors** are an art show in themselves: family portraits and busts, paintings by seventeenth-century Italian, Dutch, and Flemish artists, and eighteenth-century classical copies commissioned by Izabella. Some of the nearby bedrooms have beautiful inlaid wooden floors, while the bathrooms have giant old-fashioned bathtubs and enormous taps.

Moving through the **Chinese apartments** (remodeled by Izabella at the height of the vogue for chinoiserie), the **ballroom** and **dining room**, you reach the **old study**, decorated in frilliest Rococo style—all mirrors and gilding—and with a fine set of eighteenth-century French furniture. In the west corner of this floor, the domed ceiling of the **Zodiac Room** still has its Italian seventeenth-century stucco decorations. Beyond is the old **library**, where among the leather tomes you'll find bound sets of English magazines like *Country Life* and *Punch* from the 1870s—which only goes to show how the old European aristocracy stuck together.

On the **ground floor**, the **Turkish apartments** contain a turbaned portrait of Izabella and a suite of English eighteenth-century furniture. Don't miss the extraordinary eighty-seater **Łańcut theater** commissioned by Izabella; as well as the ornate gallery and stalls, the romantic scenic backdrops are still there, as is the stage machinery to crank them up and down.

The **Carriage Museum** (same hours) in the old coach house is a treat, including horse-drawn vehicles for every conceivable purpose, from state ceremonies to delivering the mail. Next door, the **old stables** house a beautiful collection of Ruthenian **icons**, so numerous that they are hung from the walls in huge racks.

The Town

Łańcut town has one other main point of interest, the old **synagogue**, just off the main square on ul. Zamkowa. It's currently closed for renovation and reconstruction of its museum, but if you ask at the castle office you should be able to find someone to let you in. Built in 1751 on the site of an old wooden synagogue, it has somehow retained some of its original ceiling decorations.

The **Jewish cemetery**, ten minutes' walk south of the town center, off ul. Bohaterow Westerplatte, contains the Ohel, grave of the famous nineteenth-century Hassidic rabbi Hurwitz.

Practicalities

Łańcut's **train station** is a taxi ride north from the center; the **bus station**, however, is only five minutes' walk from the castle. If you're planning to stay overnight, first choice is the wonderful *Zamkowy* **hotel** (☎2671 or ☎2672), a period piece occupying the south wing of the castle, with a good **restaurant** just opposite. This small hotel is predictably popular, and in the summer you won't get in unless you've reserved three months in advance (sic). The only other option is the **PTTK hostel** at ul. Dominikańska 1 (☎2512), just north of the Rynek; it too has a restaurant, as well as housing a PTTK tourist office. As an alternative, the *Zamkowy* hotel staff can sometimes help with fixing **private rooms** in town.

Every May, Łańcut castle hosts a series of **international chamber music** concerts, and in the summer there are international master classes for aspiring young instrumentalists.

Przemyśl

Overlooking the San River, just 10km from the Soviet border, with the foothills of the Carpathians peering out of the distance, the grubby but haunting border town of **PRZEMYŚL** has plenty of potential. Climbing the winding streets of the old quarter is like walking backwards through history to some far-flung corner of the Habsburg empire. As yet, though, it's very little visited and even by normal Polish standards has a serious dearth of accommodation, restaurants, or entertainment. Access is straightforward, however, with both trains and buses from Rzeszów and Łańcut.

Founded in the eighth century, Przemyśl is the oldest town in southern Poland after Kraków, and for its first few centuries its location on the borders between Poland and Ruthenia made it a constant bone of contention. Only under Kazimierz the Great did Poles establish final control of the town, developing it as a link in the trade routes across the Ukraine. Przemyśl maintained a commercial preeminence for several centuries, despite frequent invasions (notably by the Tartars), but as with many Polish towns economic decline came in the seventeenth century, particularly after Swedish assaults in the 1650s.

Much of the town's character derives from the period after the First Partition, when Przemyśl was annexed to the Austrian empire. In 1873 the Austrians added a huge castle to the town's defenses, creating the most important fortress in the eastern Austro-Hungarian Empire. During World War I this region was the scene of some of the fiercest fighting between the Austrians and Russians: throughout the winter of 1914 Russian forces besieged the town, finally bringing its surrender in March 1915, then losing it again only two months later. The devastation of both town and surrounding region was even more intense then than during the Nazi onslaught 25 years later, with only small sections of the sturdy fortifications surviving the siege.

The Town

The main **train station** (Przemyśl Główny) is within walking distance of the center. Don't be surprised if you find Russians on the platform—a glance at the timetables shows that post-glasnost Przemyśl gets a lot of cross-border traffic, with daily trains to Kiev and the once Polish city of Lwów, for example. The **bus station** is just behind, on ul. Czarnieckiego.

Fragments of the **Austrian fortifications** can be seen on the approach to the Old Town, opposite the Reformed Franciscan church on the corner of ul. Mickiewicza. Ulica Franciszkańska brings you to the **Rynek**, where the **Franciscan Church** offers a demonstration of unbridled Baroque. The same goes for the **Cathedral**, farther along the cobbled streets leading up to the castle—its 71-meter bell tower points the way. Remnants of the first twelfth-century rotunda can be seen in the crypt, and there's a fine Renaissance alabaster

Pietà on the main altar, but Baroque dominates the interior, most notably in the Fredro family chapel.

The fourteenth-century **castle**, home to the town theater and currently under restoration, isn't much to look at, but the view from the ramparts makes the climb worthwhile. Of the other churches dotted around the old town, the seventeenth-century **Jesuit Church** contains an extraordinary pulpit shaped like a ship, complete with rigging. Partisans of Catholic religious paraphernalia can take a look at the **Diocesan Museum** in the adjacent Jesuit college (Tues–Sun 10am–4pm), which nuns take you around. The seventeenth-century **Carmelite Church** functioned as the Uniate (Greek Catholic) cathedral until 1945, when it was handed over to the Roman Catholics; the old wooden iconostasis is on display in the **local museum** just across the road (Tues–Sun 10am–2pm). As well as a good selection of local ethnography, including some gorgeous folk costumes, the museum contains one of several excellent collections of Uniate icons you can find in the region (see "Sanok").

Fifty years ago Przemyśl had much greater ethnic diversity than today: old guidebooks indicate that the area around the Carmelite church was the **Ruthenian district**. There are two **Orthodox churches** still functioning in the east of the town, both of them nineteenth-century constructions. The **Jewish quarter** was more to the north of the old center. Numbers 33 and 45 on ul. Jagiellońska were both synagogues before World War II, and there was another across the river – off to the left from ul. 3 Maja.

Out of Town

For an excellent view, especially towards the Carpathians, the **Kopiec Tartarski** (Tartar Monument) on the southern outskirts of town is worth a trip: buses #28 and #28A deposit you at the bottom of the hill. According to legend, the monument at the top marks the burial place of a sixteenth-century Tartar Khan who is reputed to have died nearby.

For a slightly longer excursion from Przemyśl, the obvious destination is **Krasiczyn Castle**, a ten-kilometer ride by bus #5. Built in the late sixteenth century for the Krasicki family by Italian architect Gallazzo Appiani, the castle is a fine example of Polish Renaissance architecture. Extensive restoration is in progress, but you can still see most of the building, including the courtyard. The wooded **park** that shelters the castle makes a cool, relaxing spot for a stroll. When the Austrian-funded restoration is completed (1993 by current projections), Krasiczyn castle will become a conference center and hotel; till then the hotel and restaurant in the castle will probably remain out of action.

Practicalities

The well-organized **tourist center** opposite the station is both an information center and Orbis ticket office (information ☎5615; Orbis ☎3366).

The best **place to stay** in town—which isn't saying much—is the privately run *Pod Białym Orłem* at ul. Galińskiego 13 (☎61-07); it's twenty minutes' walk west along the river from the station, or take bus #10 or #10A. Cheap and peacefully located on the edge of a wood, the hotel has a restaurant serving home-cooked specialties. The *Przemysław* (☎40-32), next to the tourist center at ul. Dworskiego 4, is a basic bed-and-breakfast place, generally full in season, though the reception here can help with **private rooms** too. The *Sportowy* at ul. Adama

Mickiewicza 30 (☎38-49), ten minutes' walk east from the station, is of similar quality but less likely to be full. The teachers' union hostel (*Dom Nauczycielstwa NZP*), near the castle at ul. Chopina 1 (☎27-68), is cheap, as is the nearby *Podzamcze PTTK* at ul. Waygarta 5. The **youth hostel** at ul. Lelewela 6 (☎57-14) stays open all year, while the *Zamek* **campground** at ul. Manifestu Lipcowego 8a, about half a mile west of the old town, has bungalows as well as tent space. If you're in a car, consider the *U Medarda pensionat* (☎18-94) in DYBAWKA, about 6km west of Przemyśl on the Krasiczyn road.

The *Białym Orłem* also comes first in the **restaurant** recommendations. If you want to eat late, there's the *Karpacka* at ul. Kościuszki 5, though you may be subjected to a local "dancing band"; the same holds true for the *Adria*, opposite the station entrance road at ul. Mickiewicza 6. In the town center the *Polonia* at ul. Franciszańska 35, the *Bałtycka* in ul. Dąbrowskiego, and the *Kmiecianka* at ul. Wieniawskiego 2 will at least fill you up, while for **milk bar** fans the *Expres*, opposite the station, does the honors. If you have a car you could try the Hungarian *Eger* at ul. Grunwaldzka 134, some way out on the Rzeszów road, or the *Troika*, ul. Lwowska 18, on the border road—both are bar-restaurants.

The Sanok Region

There are two good routes south from Przemyśl towards the **Bieszczady Mountains**, one direct, the other more circuitous. The first involves a two-hour train journey into and out of the **Soviet Union**, ending up in **Ustrzyki Dolne** (see below), in the foothills of the Bieszczady. If nothing else, it's a unique chance to travel into Soviet territory without a visa. Trains leave once a day—currently 2:30pm—passing through several Ukrainian towns and villages without stopping. Polish and Soviet soldiers ride on board to ensure no-one tries any funny business. Controls used to be rigorous: in the early 1980s some Solidarity activists flushed leaflets in Russian down the toilets on the Soviet side; the train stopped, and didn't move until the soldiers had recovered every single one. Nowadays the reduced troop contingent keeps a pretty low profile, but taking photos on the Soviet side is a bad idea, however innocuous you may find snapshots of passing fields and trees.

The alternative option is to go by bus through **Sanok**, sixty-odd kilometers and a two-hour ride southwest from Przemyśl. The advantage of this route is the journey through the foothills: in spring and autumn the mountains are at their most alluring, the sun intensifying the green, brown and golden hues of the beech forests. If you've the time to spare, consider stopping off at picturesque little towns such as **Bircza** or **Tyrawa Wołoska** to soak up the atmosphere; a number of villages with wooden *cerkwi* are tucked away in easy walking distance of Tyrawa.

Sanok

Perched up on a hilltop above the San valley, **SANOK** looks a sleepy sort of place. It's best known within Poland for its rubber and bus factories, whose *AutoSan* vehicles can be seen all over the country. For the southbound traveler, though, the important thing about Sanok is that it's the last real town before the Bieszczady mountains, which loom through the mists on the horizon.

A number of things in and around the town make it a place worth visiting in its own right, too. The reconstructed fourteenth-century **parish church** on the edge of the Rynek hosted the wedding of King Władysław Jagiełło in 1417. Nearby, the remnants of the sixteenth-century **castle** are largely devoted to a **town museum**, containing an interesting collection of modern art from the region.

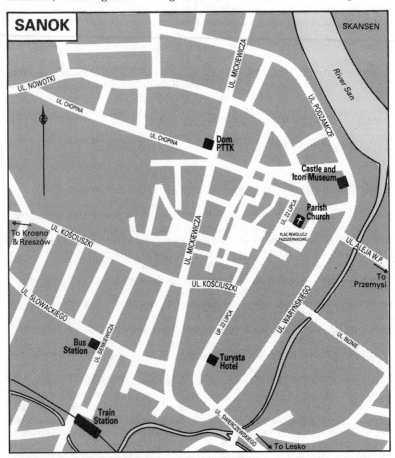

But the building to head for is the one overlooking the valley, looking like the ancestral manor of some Scottish laird. Two rooms house the fabulous Sanok **Icon Museum** (April 15–Oct 15 Tues–Sun 9am–3pm), the largest collection of Ruthenian icons in the world after the one in Moscow. Though most of the pieces date from the sixteenth and seventeenth centuries, the oldest comes from the mid-1300s, so the collection gives a clear impression of the development of the **Ukrainian school** of painting, which evolved in tandem with an autonomous and assertive local church. Unlike Russian and Greek Orthodox iconography, however, much of the work on display here is still pretty unknown to anyone but art historians and specialists, despite its quality. The best of the early icons have both the serenity and severity of Andrei Rublev's greatest works. In contrast, later icons manifest the increasing influence of western Catholicism—which culminated in the formation of the Uniate Church in 1595 (see box on p.168)—both in their style and subject matter, with an encroaching Renaissance approach to the portraiture. In a few cases, the figures show strong Tartar influences too. Look out too for a large *Icon of Hell*, an icon of a type traditionally housed in the women's section of Orthodox churches; such lurid depictions of the torments of the underworld must have kept a few people in check.

As with all such collections, the presence of these icons is related to postwar "resettlements." With many local villages deserted in the aftermath of "Operation Vistula" (again, see box), their wooden *cerkwi* neglected and falling apart, the oldest and most important icons were removed to museums. Genuine artistic concern prompted their removal, but now that local people are returning to the villages and using the churches again, it's high time for the authorities to consider handing the icons back.

Also worth a visit is the **skansen** in the Biała Góra district, 2km north of the center (Tues–Sun 8am–5pm); if you don't want to walk, take a bus north along ul. Mickiewicza to the bridge over the river—the *skansen* is on the other side, spread along the river bank. This open-air museum, one of the best in the country, brings together examples of the different styles of all the region's main ethnic groups—Boyks, Lemks, Dolinianie ("Inhabitants of the Valley"), and Pogorzanie. (If you want detailed ethnography, an English guidebook is available at the entrance.) Specimens of every kind of country building have been carefully moved here: smithies, inns, granaries, windmills, pigsties, and churches. Up on the hillside, a couple of graceful eighteenth-century *cerkwi* nestle in the shade of the trees. In the nineteenth-century school building, you'll find some amazing old textbooks: note too the carefully preserved maps of pre-1914 Poland, showing this area as a region of the Austro-Hungarian province of Galicia—hence the portrait of Kaiser Franz Josef behind the teacher's desk.

Practicalities

The **bus station** is close to the train station, about fifteen minutes walk from the middle of town, on the corner of ul. Sienkiewicza and Słowackiego; most buses from here will take you up to the main square. Of the **tourist offices**, the most helpful are the *Turysta* bureau in the hotel of the same name at ul. Swierczewskiego 13, and the PTTK office a little farther up the road at ul. 22 Lipca 18; if any office has maps and general information, including for the Bieszczady mountains, the latter will. Orbis, at ul. Grzegorza 2, deals with tickets.

For an **overnight stay**, the best place in town is the *Turysta* (address above; ☎306-64); it is modern, soulless, and quite expensive but worth the prices if you can get a top-floor view over the San valley, and the downstairs bar is a weekend hangout for the Sanok smart set. Other options are considerably more modest: the *Bieszczady* **hostel** just down the road at ul. Świerczewskiego 16 (☎321-02), which also theoretically organizes **private rooms**; or the *Dom PTTK* at ul. Mickiewicza 29 (☎314-39), some way west from the main square, which has its own modest restaurant. The **youth hostel** is at ul. Lipińskiego 34 (☎319-80), the easterly continuation of the Lesko road. You can **camp** either in Biała Góra, near the *skansen*, or at the *AutoCamping* on al. Wojska Polskiego, to the east on the town side of the river.

The privately run *Bartlek* on ul. Padlewskiego, a side-street on the way to the *skansen* (ask locals for directions), is a reasonable **restaurant**, but open erratically. Out of town there's the *Adria*, ul. Lipińskiego 58, and the *Dąbrowianka* on ul. Krakowska, the Krosno road. Unless beer rather than food is your main interest, avoid eating at the *Karpacka*, ul. Świerczewskiego 24, at all costs.

The Foothills

En route for the mountains most buses stop in the Rynek at **LESKO**, another hill town, 13km south of Sanok. If you break the journey, take a look at the nearby *Dom Kultury* on ul. Moniuszki, reconstructed after the war from a fortified seventeenth-century **synagogue**—plans are afoot to turn it into a Jewish museum. The nearby Jewish cemetery contains some impressive tombstones, the oldest dating back to the fifteenth century.

South from here the bus continues through **UHERCE**, where many Polish tourists veer off towards the **Jezioro Soliński**, an artificial lake created in the 1970s for hydroelectric power and water sports purposes. The custom-built lakeside villages of SOLINA, POLAŃCZYK and MYCZKÓW have more restaurants than anywhere else in the area, but there's little else to recommend them apart from their access to the water. In all three your best bets for accommodation now are the numerous workers' holiday houses. Yacht and kayak rental can be arranged with the *Bieszczady* tourist office in Solina.

Ustrzyki Dolne

Back on the main road, **USTRZYKI DOLNE**, 25km east of Lesko, is the main base for the mountains, swarming in summer with backpacking students and youth groups, many of them fresh off the afternoon "Soviet Express" from Przemyśl (see above). Otherwise this is a small agricultural town with just a scattering of minor monuments: a synagogue (now a library) and a *cerkiew*—both nineteenth-century—and several memorials connected with the Ukrainian resistance (see box again). **Accommodation** can be very hard to find in the hiking season. Best bets are the *Laworta* at ul. Zielona 1 (☎365), the biggest hotel in town and so most likely to have a room, the smaller *Strwiąz* on ul. Radziecka (☎303), and the *Pensjonat Otryt* at ul. Rzeczna 20 (☎320). The **PTTK bureau** on the main ul. 1 Maja doubles up as a hostel in season (ask about **private rooms** here also), as does the *Bieszczady* office on the same street. There's plenty of **camping** space, both at the official site on ul. PCK and in the fields around the edge of town.

Lines for **buses into the mountains** form early at the stops ranged along the road down from the train station, and everyone has to shove their way on board. Before leaving, stock up in the shops around the station area; supplies of anything edible are unpredictable beyond here.

Krościenko

Nine kilometers north of Ustrzyki Dolne is the village of **KROŚCIENKO**, last train stop before the Soviet border (local buses run there too). The Bieszczady region is full of surprises, and this is one of them. Following the outbreak of civil war in Greece, a small community of Greek partisans and their families escaped to Poland in 1946 and settled in this area. The monument in the village center is to **Nikos Baloyannis**, a Greek resistance hero executed by the generals in Athens soon after his return in 1949. There's a fine eighteenth-century **cerkiew** in the village too, and another older one a little farther north in the Wolica district.

The Bieszczady Mountains

The valleys and mountain slopes of the **Bieszczady Mountains** were cleared of their populations—a mix of Boyks, Lemks, and Ukrainians—in "Operation Vistula," following the last war (see box again). Today, these original inhabitants and their descendants are coming back, but the region remains sparsely populated and is largely protected as national park or nature reserves. All of the reserves are carefully controlled to protect the wildlife, but are open to the public—quite a change from a decade ago, when the Communist Party elite still maintained various sections for its own high-security hunting lodges.

Ecologically, the area is of great importance, with its high grasslands and ancient forests of oak, fir and, less frequently, beech. Among the rarer species of fauna inhabiting the area you may be lucky enough to sight **eagles**, **bears**, **wolves**, **lynx**, and even **bison**, introduced to the Bieszczady in the 1960s.

Even the highest peaks in the region, at around 1300 meters, won't present too many **hiking** problems, as long as you're properly equipped. Like all mountain regions, however, the **climate** is highly changeable throughout the year; on the passes over the *połoninas* (meadows) for example, the wind and rain can get very strong. The best time to visit is late autumn—here, as in the Tatras, Poles savor the delights of the "Golden October." Mountain temperatures drop sharply in winter, creating excellent skiing conditions.

BOYKS, LEMKS, AND UNIATES

Up until World War II, a large part of the population of southeast Poland was classified officially as **Ukrainian**. For the provinces of Lwów, Tarnopol, and Volhynia, in
the eastern part of the region (all in the Soviet Union today), this was accurate.
However, for the western part, now Polish border country, it was seriously misrep-
resentative, as this region was in fact inhabited by **Boyks** (Boykowie)and **Lemks**
(Lemkowie). These people, often collectively called "Rusini," are historically close
to the Ukrainians but have their own distinct identities, both groups being descendants of the nomadic shepherds who settled in the **Bieszczady** and **Beskid Niski**
regions between the thirteenth and fifteenth centuries.

For centuries these farming people lived as peacefully as successive wars and
border changes allowed. Their real troubles began at the end of World War II,
when groups of every political complexion were roaming around the ruins of
Poland, all determined to influence the shape of the postwar order. One such movement was the **Ukrainian Resistance Army (UPA)**, a group fighting against all
odds for the independence of their perennially subjugated country. Initially
attracted by Hitler's promises of an autonomous state in the eastern territories of
the Third Reich, by 1945 the UPA were fighting under the slogan "Neither Hitler or
Stalin," and had been encircled by the Polish, Czech and Soviet armies in this
corner of Poland. For almost two years small bands of partisans, using carefully
concealed mountain hideouts, held out against the Polish army, even killing the
regional commander of the Polish army, General Karol Swierczewski, at Jabłonki in
March 1947.

This is where the story gets complicated. According to the official account, UPA
forces were fed by a local population more than happy to help the "Ukrainian
fascists." The locals give a different account, claiming they weren't involved with
the UPA, except when forced to provide them with supplies at gunpoint. The Polish
authorities were in no mood for fine distinctions. In April 1947 they evacuated the
entire population of the Bieszczady and Beskid Niski regions in a notorious opera-

Ustrzyki Dolne to Ustrzyki Górne

The main road out of **Ustrzyki Dolne** winds south through the mountain valleys
towards **Ustrzyki Górne**, a ninety-minute journey by bus. If you've developed an
enthusiasm for the wooden churches of this area, and you've time to spare, you
could consider a diversion a few kilometers east off the road to the border
villages of JAŁOWE, BANDARÓW NARODOWY, and MOCZARY (the first two
are reachable by bus) to see the fine examples there. Back on the main road,
you'll also find wooden churches at HOSZÓW, CZARNA GÓRNA, SMOLNIK,
and—on a road off to the east—at BYSTRE and MICHNIOWIEC (bus from
Czarna Górna).

Coming over the hill into **LUTOWISKA** you'll see makeshift barracks and
drilling rigs, signs of the oil industry that has developed here sporadically since
the last century. Locals insist that the Soviets for years blocked full development
of the region's resources, fearing Polish economic independence. The grubby
roadside restaurant in the village caters mainly for the oil workers.

Ustrzyki Górne
USTRZYKI GÓRNE has a wild, end-of-the-world feel, spread out along the
bottom of a peaceful river valley and surrounded by the peaks of the Bieszczady.

tion codenamed **"Operation Vistula"** (Akcja Wisła). Inhabitants were given two hours to pack and leave with whatever they could carry, then were "resettled" either to the former German territories of the north and west, or to the Soviet Union.

From the Gorlice region of the Beskids, a traditional Lemk stronghold, an estimated 120,000–150,000 were deported to the Soviet Union and another 80,000 were scattered around Poland, of whom about 20,000 have now returned. The first arrived in 1957, in the wake of Prime Minister Gomulka's liberalization of previously hard-line policy. (Rumor has it that this was Gomulka's way of thanking the Lemks who had helped him personally during the war.) The trickle of returnees in the 1960s and 1970s has, since the demise of communist rule, become a flow, with Lemks and Boyks reclaiming the farms that belonged to their parents and grandparents. This return to the homeland is bringing a new level of political and cultural self-assertion. In the June 1989 elections, Stanisław Mokry, a Solidarity candidate from near Gorlice, openly declared himself a Lemk representative. Like other minorities in Poland, Lemks and Boyks want their own schools, language teaching, and the right to develop their own culture.

But the question of self-identity is entangled by the religious divisions within the community. Like their Ukrainian neighbors, in the seventeenth century many previously Orthodox Boyks and Lemks joined the **Uniate Church**, which was created in 1595 following the Act of Union between local Orthodox metropolitans and Catholic bishops. The new church came under papal jurisdiction, but retained Orthodox rites and traditions—including, for example, the right of priests to marry. Today the majority of Lemks in the Bieszczady and Beskid Niski classify themselves as Uniate (or "Greek Catholic," as Poles know them). Encouraged both by the pope's appointment of a Polish Uniate bishop and political changes in the Ukraine, where Uniates are finally coming into the open after years of persecution, Lemk Uniates are tentatively beginning to adopt a higher religious profile, rebuilding and reclaiming churches.

The vacation development at the north end of the village may change things in time, but for the moment Ustrzyki is little more than a few houses, a shop, and a clutch of take-out stands.

The main accommodation is provided by a **PTTK hostel** at the southern end of the village; like most others in the region, it is pretty basic but it guarantees to find you at least some floor space, however crowded it gets. For **campers** there's no problem in putting up your tent next to the hostel, or even elsewhere in the valley, as long as you don't make a mess. Nearby, a *baza studentowa* (student camp) operates in the summer months: you can probably get a mattress in a tent on short notice here, though as always this is easier if you've got some Almatur vouchers. A costlier but more comfortable alternative is to ask around for **private rooms** in the houses up the hill on the other side of the road from the PTTK.

Beside the smoky dive of a restaurant across from the PTTK hostel, the only **food** options in Ustrzyki are a couple of stand-up places by the main road. The wooden hut just up from the PTTK, on the same side of the road, has very rudimentary food but plentiful supplies of *Lezajsk*, from the brewery near Rzeszów; a small but devoted band of locals seem to spend most of their time camped around the bar, joined in the early evening by hard cases off the Ustrzyki Dolne bus, which pulls up here. Anglers might note that the stream running through Ustrzyki is prime trout-fishing territory—not that it appears on local menus; signs on the river banks warn that fishing rights are controlled by the fishing club, but permission should be easy to get.

Hiking in the Bieszczady

Walking and winter skiing are the main reasons for coming to the Bieszczady region. From Ustrzyki there are a number of **hiking options**, all of them attractive and accessible for anyone reasonably fit; times given below are reckoned for an average walker's speed, including regular stops and landscape gazing. **Skiers** will need to bring along all equipment and be prepared for minimum facilities—there are lifts at just three villages: Ustrzyki Górne, Cisna and Polańczyk. The best **map** is the *Bieszczady Mapa Turystczyna* (1:75,000).

East to Tarnica and the Soviet Border

There are two initial routes east from Ustrzyki, both leading to the high Tarnica valley (1275m). The easier is to follow the road to the hamlet of WOŁOSATE (there's a **campground** just beyond at BESKID, right on the border) then walk up via the peak of Hudow Wierszek (973m)—about four hours in all. Shorter but more strenuous is to go cross-country via the peak of Szeroki Wierch (1268m), a three-hour hike. **Tarnica peak** (1346m) is another half-hour hike south of the valley.

From Tarnica valley you can continue east, with a stiff up-and-down hike via **Krzemien** (1335m), **Kopa Bukowska** (1312m), and **Halicz** (1333m; 3hr) to **Rozsypaniec** (1273m), the last stretch taking you over the highest pass in the range. This would be a feasible day's hike from the Beskid campground; the really fit could do an outing from Ustrzyki to Krzemien and back in a day.

Adventurous walkers could consider trekking into the region to the north of Tarnica valley in search of the **abandoned Ukrainian villages** and tumbled-down *cerkwi* scattered along the border (delineated by the San River). Some, like BUKOWIEC and TARNAWA WYZNIA, are marked on the map, but others aren't, so you have to keep your eyes peeled. Many villages were razed to the ground, the only sign of their presence being their orchards. The Polish **border police** who shuttle around the area in jeeps are nothing to worry about as long as you're carrying your passport with valid visa, and have a plausible explanation of what you're up to. The Russians who watch this area are a different proposition, though, so don't on any account wander into Soviet territory—police detention of hikers in Lwów has been known to occur.

West Toward the Czech Border

There are some easy walks west to the peak of **Wielka Rawka** (1307m), flanked by woods on the Czech border. One option is to go along the Cisna road and then left up the marked path to the summit (3hr). Another is to head south to the bridge over the Wołosate River, turn right along a track, then follow signs to the peak of Mała Szemenowa (1071m), from where you turn right along the border to the peaks of Wielka Szemenowa (1091m) and Wielka Rawka (4hr).

Northwest of Ustrzyki

The best-known walking areas of the Bieszczady are the **połoninas** or mountain meadows. These desolate places are notoriously subject to sudden changes of weather—one moment you can be basking in autumn sunshine, the next the wind is howling to the accompaniment of a downpour. The landscape, too, is full of contrasts: there's something of the Scottish highlands in the wildness of the passes, but wading through the tall rustling grasses of the hillsides in summer you might imagine yourself in the African savannah. Walking the heights of the passes you can also begin to understand how Ukrainian partisans managed to hold out for so long up here (see box on previous page); even for the most battle-hardened Polish and Soviet troops, flushing partisan bands out from this remote and inhospitable landscape must have been an onerous task.

Note that you can save walking time in this region by taking a **bus** from Ustrzyki Górne though Wetlina, Dołzyca, and Cisna. If you've only got a very short time, you could take just a brief detour off the road north from Ustrzyki Górne to Ustrzyki Dolne. Take the bus a couple of kilometers west to the **Przelec Wyzniańska** pass, the first stop, from where a marked path leads up through the woods on the right-hand side of the road to the **Połonina Caryńska** (1107m)—a steep climb of roughly 45 minutes. You'll have time to walk along the pass a bit to get a feel for the landscape, and then get back down to catch the next onward bus.

For a more extended trip from Ustrzyki Górne, take the steep trail marked in red and green north through the woods up to the eastern edge of the **Połonina Caryńska**, and walk over the top to the western edge (1297m; 2hr 30min). Continue down the hill to the village of BRZEGI GÓRNE where there's a **campground** near the road. From here either take a bus to Ustrzyki Górne (or on to Sanok), or take the red-marked path up the wooded hill to the right to the all-year PTTK **hostel** on the eastern edge of the **Połonina Wetlińska** (1228m; 1hr 30min from Brzegi)—views from this windswept corner are spectacular. Sleeping arrangements involve mattresses in ten-person rooms; theoretically you should bring your own food, but the young couple who run the place will probably be happy to feed you from the communal pot.

Beyond the hostel there's an excellent walk over the Połonina Wetlińska to **Przelec Orłowicza** (1075m), where the path divides in three. A sharp left takes you down the hill to WETLINA (2hr 30min from the hostel), where there's a larger **PTTK hostel** and **campground** (open all year), a restaurant and a bus stop for journeys north to Sanok or south to Ustrzyki Górne. The middle path goes to **Smerek** (1222m) and down through the woods to the bus stop in SMEREK village (2hr). The right-hand path is for the long-distance hike via Wysokie Berdo (940m), Krysowa, Jaworzec, Kiczera, Przerenina, and Fałówa to DOŁZYCA (7hr; PTTK hostel), or even on to the villages of Jabłonki and Baligród (see overleaf).

Continuing west from Dołzyca brings you to **CISNA**, a small village where you might be able to get a room and could certainly camp. A kilometer to the south-west is **MAJDAN**, little more than a couple of houses but also the site of an **open-air rail museum** and a station for the **narrow-gauge railroad** which runs once a day through the forests along the Czech border to Nowy Łupków (2hr 30min), continuing occasionally to Rzepedz (see overleaf). This is a great journey, with the driver reputedly happy to stop along the way if anyone wants to have a longer look at the scenery. The train leaves Majdan at 6:30am.

NOWY ŁUPKÓW itself is a tiny place whose name is familiar to Poles for the nearby internment camp, to which Lech Wałęsa was consigned during martial law. If you have transportation, there is an interesting Uniate *cerkiew* at the village of SMOLNIK, just to the east.

Out of the Mountains

There is a choice of routes out of the western Bieszczady back to Sanok. The main one runs **from Nowy Łupków through Komańcza** and a series of tiny Uniate villages such as Rzepedz. The other is a more obscure, winding road north from **Cisna**, via **Jabłonki** and **Baligród**. Buses run along both roads, while trains serve only the main route.

Komańcza and Rzepedz

Once or twice a week the narrow-gauge railroad from Nowy Łupków makes its way to Rzepedz, but more regular transport is provided by buses and PKP trains north to the village of **KOMAŃCZA**, whose two churches illustrate graphically the religious tensions of the region. Near the main road is a modern building recently constructed by the majority **Uniate** population, while hidden away in the woods on the edge of the hill is a nineteenth-century *cerkiew*, used by the small **Orthodox** community. In 1980 the Uniates petitioned the local authorities for their own place of worship but the *cerkiew* was given instead to the Orthodox worshippers—a good example of the divide-and-rule tactics used to manipulate the smaller religious groupings. At the other end of the village, uphill to the left, the **Nazarene Sisters Convent** is something of a shrine for Polish tourists; it was here that Cardinal Wyszyński, the redoubtable former Primate of Poland, was kept under house arrest in the early 1950s during the Stalinist campaign to destroy the independence of the Catholic Church. The **PTTK hostel** just down the hill will put you up for the night, as might the convent.

You could have a fascinating time searching the Komańcza area for *cerkwi*: modern maps of the region mark them clearly. (Uniate buildings are identified in the key as "churches in ancient orthodox churches.") A particularly fine one is at **RZEPEDZ**, a few kilometers off the main road and rail line north from Komańcza. Nestled away on a hillside surrounded by tranquil clusters of trees, the church merges into the landscape—a common quality in *cerkwi* that may explain how they escaped the destruction of Bieszczady villages in the wake of "Operation Vistula." Unless it's Sunday, you'll have to ask for the key (*klucza*) from the nearby house. The interior gives a sense of the twin strands of Uniate worship: on the one hand western Madonnas and insipid oil paintings; on the other the Eastern iconostasis, the absence of an organ (in the Orthodox tradition the choir provides all the music), the pale blue Ukrainian saints, and Ukrainian-script wall inscriptions.

From Rzepedz, buses and trains take you the twenty-odd kilometers onward to Zagórz and Sanok.

North of Cisna

From **Cisna** (see previous page) buses head to Lesko and Sanok, through a region which was the scene of some of the heaviest fighting between the Polish Army and the Ukrainian resistance. At **JABŁONKI** there's a monument to **General Karol Swierczewski**, the veteran Spanish Civil War commander killed here in March 1947, while farther north at the village of **BALIGRÓD** a monument commemorates the Polish soldiers—but not, as yet, the Ukrainians. This was the headquarters of the Polish Army during the conflict, and if you root around in the hills you'll see fortifications and the sites of various villages cleared in 1947.

The Beskid Niski

West from Sanok the main road, closely paralleled by the slow rail line, heads toward Gorlice through the Wisłok valley—a pleasant pastoral route, with a succession of wooden villages set back in the hills of the **Beskid Niski** to the south. There's not a great deal to detain you, though, until you get west of Krosno, to the medieval town of **Biecz** and on to Gorlice, the center for Beskid Niski hikes.

Also covered in this section is **Dukla**, an isolated old town that has long controlled the Przelec Dukielska pass into Czechoslovakia—the most important crossing point in the east of the country.

Krosno

Sited at the heart of the country's richest oil reserves, **KROSNO** is the petroleum capital of Poland, but for the moment the resource is under-exploited, and the town seems more rooted in the past than expectant of future riches. A statue on plac Zwyiecęstwa commemorates **Ignacy Łukasiewicz** (1822–82), who sunk what's claimed to be the world's first oil well in 1854 at the village of BÓBRKA, 10km south. The pioneering Pole's drilling derrick and oil shaft are preserved in an **open-air museum** set up there, which can be reached by local bus. Back in town, at ul. Nowotki 16, there's also a **district museum** (Tues–Sat 10am–4:30pm, Sun 10am–2:30pm) devoted to the mining trade, with collections of old kerosene lamps, of which Ignacy was also the inventor.

The main **bus and train stations** are next to each other, ten minutes' walk to the west of the Old Town, with its scattering of arcaded Renaissance houses. For **tourist information** in Krosno there's a *Bieszczady* office at ul. Staszica 20, a PTSM (youth hosteling) office at ul. Waryńskiego 43, and an Orbis bureau at ul. Blich 1. **Accommodation** includes two modest hotels: the *Polonia*, near the center at ul. M. Nowotki 18 (☎220-34), and the seasonal *Dom Wycieckowy*, ul. Czajkowskiego 43. There's also the expensive, three-star *Krosno-Nafta*, ul. Lwowska 21 (☎220-11), and, for anyone with a car, the *Motel Moderówka* (☎17-96) at Moderówka, 8km west on the Gorlice road. Krosno also has a **youth hostel**, well north of the center at ul. Konopnickiej 5 (July & Aug; ☎210-09), and the *Bieszczady* tourist office may also be able to help fix up **private rooms**.

Best of an indifferent bunch of **restaurants** is the *Stylowa*, in the *Krosno-Nafta* hotel. On the main square, the *Wojtowska* at Rynek 29 will at least dish up the basic mashed potatoes and *kotlet schwabowy*. Genuine greasy spoons are located on ul. Sienkiewicza and Franciszkańska, just off the main square.

Around Krosno

If you feel like venturing around the Krosno area, the ruins of the fourteenth-century **Castle Kamieniec**, one of the oldest fortresses in the Carpathian mountains, can be seen at **ODRZYKOŃ**, 8km north (occasional buses).

At **HACZÓW**, 12km east (again occasional buses), there's a beautiful mid-fifteenth-century **cerkiew**, as well as some fine timber houses.

Dukla

DUKLA, 24km south of Krosno, was for centuries the main mountain crossing-point on the trade route from the Baltic to Hungary and central Europe. The loca-

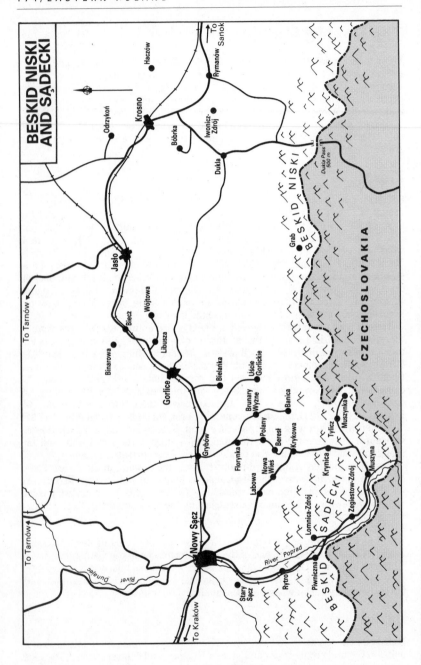

BESKID NISKI
AND SĄDECKI

tion has also ensured an often bloody history, the worst episode occurring in the last war, when over 60,000 Soviet soldiers and 6500 Czechoslovaks died trying to capture the valley from the Germans.

Today, rebuilt after comprehensive damage in the fighting, Dukla is a windy, quiet, and rather bleak place—every bit the frontier town with its eerie, stage-set main square. There are no real sights, save for a Rococo parish church and a local **museum** (Tues–Sun 10am–4pm), which gives chilling details of the wartime fighting in the "Valley of Death" to the south.

For an overnight **stay** it's a choice between the PTTK **hostel** on the main square (☎46), the **youth hostel** at Trakt Wegierski 14 (☎8; summer only), or **private rooms** (ask at the PTTK hostel). For food and drink, check out the *Basztowa*, opposite the squat town hall in the main square, or the slightly better *Granicze* around the corner on ul. Kościuszki.

West of Dukla, one or two buses a day cover the backwoods route **to Gorlice**, taking you along the edge of the hills. If you have a vehicle, or time to hike, the tiny roads leading south into the Beskid Niski are well worth exploring.

Biecz

BIECZ, one of the oldest towns in Poland, was the conduit for nearly all the wine exported north from Hungary in medieval times. This thriving trade in the early equivalents of *Bull's Blood* continued until the mid-seventeenth century, when the "Swedish Deluge" flattened the economy—but fortunately not the town.

Trains and buses both stop near the center, with the Old Town a short walk up on the top of the hill. The **Rynek** here is dominated by the fifty-meter tower of the late Renaissance **Town Hall**. Nearby, the large **parish church**, complete with fortified bell tower, contains Renaissance and Gothic pews, as well as a fine seventeenth-century pulpit decorated with musicians. Across the road on ul. Kromera, the local **museum** (May–Sept Tues–Sun 9am–4pm; Oct–April closes 3pm), housed in a burgher's home that used to be part of the fortifications, has an intriguing collection of artifacts, featuring Baroque musical instruments, carpenters' tools, and the entire contents of the old pharmacy—sixteenth-century medical books, herbs, and prescriptions included. For the record, guides inform you that Biecz once had a school of public executioners. They were kept busy: in 1614, for example, 120 public executions took place in the square.

For an overnight stay there are two options, the *Adrianka* **hotel**, ul. Świerczewskiego 35 (☎157), and the **youth hostel** at ul. Parkowa 1 (☎14). About the only places to eat are the *Smakosz* restaurant and a *kawiarnia*, both on the edge of the main square.

Churches Around Biecz

Several villages near Biecz have beautiful wooden churches. In the woods at **LIBUSZA**, 9km south, off the Gorlice road, the sixteenth-century chapel still retains some of its Renaissance polychromy. Two kilometers east, the church at **WÓJTOWA**, another sixteenth-century specimen, is similarly splendid.

If you've got time for only one sortie, go to **BINAROWA**, 5km north of Biecz (local bus or taxi). Constructed around 1500, the timber **church** here has an exquisitely painted interior, rivaling the better-known one at Debno in the Podhale (see Chapter Four); the polychromy is part original, part eighteenth-century additions, and all meriting close attention. If he's around, and you can speak Polish, try to get a tour with the local priest, an entertaining commentator who declares that King Kazimierz the Great, who was very fond of visiting Biecz, often stopped off at the Binarowa church on his way home.

Gorlice

GORLICE is a curious base for the **Beskid Niski**, the westerly extension of the Bieszczady; you'll know when you're approaching the town by the suddenly foul air. Like Krosno, the town has for a century been associated with the oil industry, Ignacy Łukasiewicz having set up the world's first refinery here in 1853. If you want farther doses of petroleum history, the **local museum** on ul. Wąska (Tues–Sun 10am–4pm) is devoted to Łukasiewicz and the oil industry generally. That aside, there's not a lot to be said—Gorlice is not the most beautiful of towns.

The **bus and train stations** are both close to the center on the northern side of town. The train station is the terminal of the Krosno line—trains to Tarnów and on to Kraków leave from Gorlice Zagorzany, 2km up the line (frequent train and bus connections). **Tourist information** is available at the PTTK office, ul. Tysiaclecia 3, and the IT bureau in the rudimentary *Wiktoria* hostel at ul. 1 Maja 10 (☎206-44). Other **accommodation** options are the *Parkowa* hotel (☎214-60) in the Park Meijskipark, the *Dom Nauczyciela* teachers' hostel at ul. Wróblewskiego 10, and the summer-only **youth hostel** at ul. Michałusa 16 (☎211-83; July & Aug). For **food** your best bets are the *Magura*, ul. Waryńskiego 16, or the *Gorlicka*, ul. Słoneczna 6, both designated as "category 1" restaurants. For a simple snack try the *kawiarnia* in the basement of the town hall.

South of Gorlice: Walks in the Beskids

The **Beskid Niski** are a hilly rather than mountainous range, less dramatic than the Bieszczady, but nevertheless excellent walking country. The people—predominantly **Lemks** (see box above)—provide a warm welcome to the few hikers who do get to this area, and many of their settlements have fine examples of the region's characteristic **wooden churches**. As a rule you'll find these deliberately tucked away amid the trees, their rounded forms and rustic exteriors seeming almost organic to the landscape. The earliest date from the fifteenth century, most from the eighteenth and beyond. In the Gorlice area, a noticeable feature of most church **cemeteries** are the international names on the tombstones, a legacy of an Austro-Hungarian battle against the Russians in 1915, which left 20,000 dead.

Details of all the hill walks are given in the **PTSM youth hostel handbook** (see *Basics*), and should be provided by the tourist offices in towns such as Krosno and Gorlice. A good local map will greatly increase your enjoyment of this region, though the best one, *Beskid Niski i Pogorze*, is currently out of print; you might track one down in a shop or tourist office.

The most ambitious **route**, marked in blue on the *Beskid Niski i Pogorze* map, runs some 80km from GRYBOW, 12km west of Gorlice, along the Czech border to KOMAŃCZA (see "The Bieszczady Mountains," p.167). **Youth hostels** (July & Aug) are strategically placed at twenty- or thirty-kilometer intervals at USCIE GORLICKIE and HAŃCZOWA (day 1), GRAB (day 2), BARWINEK (day 3) and RZEPEDZ (day 4), all with bus stops nearby.

Bielanka

The physical return of the Lemk and Boyk minorities to their roots has been accompanied by a revival of interest in their cultural and linguistic traditions. **BIELANKA**, 10km southwest of Gorlice, is the base of the *Lemkyownya* **music and dance ensemble**, which has already toured the Ukraine, Canada, and the USA. Turn up in Bielanka on a Thursday evening and you may catch them rehearsing in the village hall.

The Beskid Sądecki

West from Gorlice the hills continue through a range known as the **Beskid Sądecki**, another low-lying stretch of border slopes sheltering a sizable and expanding Lemk population. **Nowy Sącz**, the regional capital, is the obvious base for the area, which otherwise comprises very small market towns, scattered villages, and traditional peasant farms.

Nowy Sącz

NOWY SĄCZ, the main market town of the Beskid Sądecki, nestles on the banks of the Dunajec River, an out-of-the-way place these days and ideal as a base for exploring the hills. It was once better known, having been a royal residence from the fourteenth to the seventeenth centuries, and in the fifteenth century having seen the birth of the **Kraków-Sącz School** of painters, the first recognized Polish "school."

The Town

There are two **train stations**: the Miasto station, near the old town, handles Kraków trains; the Dworzec Główny station, 2km south of town, all other destinations. Local buses shuttle between the Dworzec Główny and downtown, via the **bus station** on ul. Staszica.

The center of the spacious **Rynek**, in the old town, is occupied by the incongruous neo-Gothic **Town Hall**, which hosts occasional chamber music concerts as well as council meetings. The Gothic parish church of **St Margaret** (św. Małgorzata), off the east side of the square, has the familiar Baroque overlay, two Renaissance altars excepted.

Over the road on ul. Lwowska, the sixteenth-century Canonical House contains the **town museum** (Tues–Thurs, Sat & Sun 10am–2:30pm, Fri 10am–6pm), which displays those few pieces from the Kraków-Sącz school that haven't been taken off to the national museums in Kraków and Warsaw. Other rooms hold a collection of icons gathered from *cerkwi* in the surrounding region—not as extensive as that in Sanok but amply demonstrating the distinctive regional style of icon painting. There's plenty of folk art on show too, including some typically Polish *Christus Frasobliwy* sculptures, showing a seated Christ propping his mournful face on one hand. Finally there's an interesting collection of works by the Lemk artist Nikifors (1895–1968), known locally as the "Matejko of Krynica." Bearing inscriptions in spidery, childlike handwriting (Nikifors didn't learn to write until late in life), some of the pictures are reminiscent of Lowry's scenes of industrial northern England.

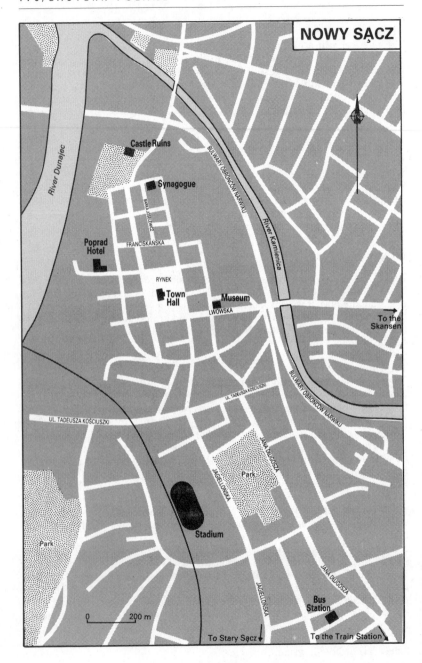

NOWY SĄCZ

River Dunajec

Castle Ruins

Synagogue

BANKA KAZELNICZ

Poprad Hotel

FRANCISKAŃSKA

RYNEK

Town Hall

Museum

LWOWSKA

River Kamienica

BULWARY OBROŃCÓW NARWIKU

To the Skansen

BULWARY OBROŃCÓW NARWIKU

UL. TADEUSZA KOŚCIUSZKI

UL. TADEUSZA KOŚCIUSZKI

JANA DŁUGOSZA

Park

JAGIELLOŃSKA

Stadium

Park

JAGIELLONSKA

JANA DŁUGOSZA

Bus Station

0   200 m

To Stary Sącz

To the Train Station

The seventeenth-century **synagogue** on ul. Berka Joselewicza, in the ghetto area north of the Rynek, houses a contemporary art gallery (Wed–Sun 10am–2:30pm); the building has been so well modernized that there's nothing visibly Jewish left. Farther up on the northern edge of the old town, the ruins of the **castle**, built during Kazimierz the Great's reign, give a good view over the valley below. After being used for mass executions of local civilians, the castle was blown up by the Germans in 1945.

A few kilometers east of town by bus #14 or #15 from the train or bus station, the **skansen** (May–Sept Tues–Fri 9:30am–4pm, Sat & Sun 9:30am–5pm) has an extensive and still growing collection of regional peasant architecture. If you've already visited the *skansen* at Sanok, the buildings in the Lemk and Pogorzanie sections here will be familiar. What you won't have seen before, however, are buildings like the fragments of a Carpathian Gypsy (*Cyganie*) hamlet—realistically situated some distance from the main village—and the assortment of manor houses, including a graceful seventeenth-century specimen from Małopolska, complete with its original interior wall paintings.

Practicalities

Of the various **tourist offices** in town, the most helpful are the *Poprad* bureau in the *Hotel Panorama* on ul. Romanowskiego, just off the main square, the PTTK office at Rynek 6, and the *WOIT* bureau at ul. J. Długosza 21.

Choice of **accommodation** is not over-inspiring. The *Panorama* at ul. Romanowskiego 4a (☎218-78) is the preferable hotel, central and cheaper and more congenial than the Orbis *Beskid Hotel* near the main station at ul. Limanowskiego 1 (☎207-70). Other options are the small *Zajazd Sądecki* hostel, ul. Król. Jadwigi 67 (☎267-17), a standard PTTK hostel at ul. Jamnicka 2 (☎250-12), and the **youth hostel** on ul. Batorego 72 (☎215-12; July & Aug; buses #14 and #15 stop outside). For **camping** there's tent space near the PTTK hostel in summer. Ask at the PTTK office for **private rooms**: when demand is high the *Poprad* bureau (see above) also doles out sleeping places around the town.

Restaurants by contrast are pretty good. The cookery-school-assisted *Staropolska*, on the east edge of the main square in ul. Kościelna, serves an appetizing selection of local specialties such as *płacek* (potato pancakes). Other places to consider are the *Panorama* and *Beskid* hotel restaurants, both reasonable, and the shabbier *Imperial* and *Stylowa*, both south of the main square on ul. Jagiellońska. Milk bars, *kawiarnia*, and assorted drinking dives can be found all over town, especially in the bustling shopping area around the Rynek.

A Loop Around the Beskid Sądecki

The **Poprad River**—which feeds the Dunajec just south of Nowy Sącz—creates the broadest and most beautiful of the **Beskid Sądecki valleys**. A minor road follows its length to the Slovak border, which it then proceeds to trail for the best part of 25km. Meandering along this route is as good an experience of rural Poland as you could hope for, winding through fields where farmers still scythe the grass, with forests covering the hills above. Tracks lead off to tiny, remote hamlets, ripe for a couple of hours' church-hunting, while along the main body of the valley you can boost your constitution at Habsburg-looking spa towns like **Krynica**. North of Krynica, the road loops back up another valley to Nowy Sącz, making a satisfying circuit.

Stary Sącz

Nowy Sącz's smaller sister town of **STARY SĄCZ**, 10km south (bus #8, #9, #10, #21, or #24; or train on the Krynica line), was first recorded in 1163, and is the oldest urban center of the region. It's situated on a hill between the Dunajec and Poprad rivers, whose confluence you pass soon after leaving Nowy Sącz.

Like its modernized neighbor, the town's cobbled **Rynek** has an expansive feeling to it, the main difference being in the height of the buildings—none of the eighteenth-century houses around the Stary Sącz square has more than two storys. Even in a town this small, though, you still find two thirteenth-century churches: a fortified Gothic **parish church** south of the square, and the convent **Church of the Poor Clares**, to the east, relieved by some sixteenth-century wall paintings. The **town museum** on the square (Tues–Sun 10am–1pm) will kill half an hour.

Accommodation is limited to basic rooms at the *Szalas* (☎600-77), the **youth hostel** (July & Aug) at ul. Kazimierza Wielkiego 14, and the *Poprad* **campground** on ul. Bylych Wiezniow Politycznych. The *Poprad* tourist office in Nowy Sącz may also be able to find **private rooms** in or around town. The only real **restaurant** is the *Staromeijska* on the Rynek (closes 9pm), while the tallest of the Rynek's houses has a good *kawiarnia* upstairs, the *Maryszenka*. **Tourist information** is available from the *Kinga* bureau on the Rynek.

The Poprad Valley

By local train or bus it's a scenic two-hour ride along the deep, winding Poprad valley from Stary Sącz to Krynica, and if you're not in too much of a hurry, a few places are worth hopping off at before the terminal.

At **RYTRO**, 16km down the line, there are ruins of a thirteenth-century castle, and lots of hiking trails up through the woods into the mountains; there's a hotel here too. Radziejowa summit (1262m), reached along a ridge path to the southwest, is a popular destination, about two hours' walk from the village. The stretch of the river after nearby **PIWNICZNA** forms the border between Poland and Czechoslovakia, and is one of the most attractive parts of the valley, with trout-filled water of crystalline clarity. If you're not hoping to catch the fish yourself, call in at the *Poprad* restaurant in **ZEGESTIÓW-ZDRÓJ**, a lovely spa town farther down the valley, for excellent poached trout. The old village, farther uphill from the station, makes for an enjoyable, leisurely post-lunch stroll.

MUSZYNA, next along the valley, has sixteen mineral springs, spa buildings, and the ruins of a thirteenth-century castle, just north of the train station. The town museum (Wed–Sun 9:30am–3pm), installed in a seventeenth-century tavern, focuses on local woodwork, agricultural implements in particular. From Muszyna the Poprad runs south and the railroad north to Krynica via the village of POWROZNIK, with its fine seventeenth-century *cerkiew*.

Krynica

If you only ever make it to one spa town in Poland, **KRYNICA** should be it. Evocative of *fin-de-siècle* Central Europe, its combination of woodland setting, rich mineral springs and moderate altitude (600m) have made it a popular resort for over two centuries. In winter the hills (and a large skating rink) keep the vacation trade coming in.

At the northern end of the promenade, past a statue of Mickiewicz, a **funicular train** (summer daily 9am–midnight) ascends a 741-meter hill for an overview of town. Ranged below you are a fine array of **sanatariums**, including an old-fashioned pump room, assorted "therapeutic centers," and mud-bath houses. The **pump room** is the place to try the local waters. Rent or buy a tankard from the desk here before heading for the taps, where the regulars will urge you to try the purply-brown *Zuber*. Named after the professor who discovered it in 1914, it is reckoned to be the most concentrated mineral water in Europe—certainly it's the worst-smelling. *Zdroj Główny*, a mixture of three or four different waters, is one of the more palatable brews.

Krynica hasn't yet worked out how to deal with foreigners. **Accommodation** is difficult to track down, and the singularly unhelpful PTTK tourist office at ul. Kraszewskiego 14, off the southern end of the promenade, seems to have little interest in revealing what is available. In fact, PTTK not only offers **private rooms**, but also runs the *Rzymianka* **hostel** at ul. Dąbrowskiego 17 (☎22-27). Otherwise there's the *Belweder* **hotel** at ul. Kraszewskiego 17 (☎540); it's run by the *Jaworzyna* tourist bureau on ul. Pułaskiego, who also deal with private rooms. There's a seasonal **youth hostel** at ul. Kraszewskiego 158 (☎442), and a **campground** some way out from the center on ul. Czarny Potok.

Restaurants are less of a struggle to find. The *Havana* on ul. Bieruta (the Nowy Sącz road) and the *Roma* at ul. Puławskiego 93 are both reasonable—though bedeviled by the usual "dancing bands." More basic are the *Dworcowa* on ul. Waryńskiego, the *Hokejowa* on ul. Sportowa, the *Cichy Kacik* at ul. Nowasadecka 100, and the *Krynicka* milk bar, ul. Dietla 15.

East of Krynica

The region **east from Krynica** is particularly rich in attractive villages and *cerkwi*, including some of the oldest in the country. Villages such as WOJKOWA, TYLICZ, and MUSZYNKA, up in the hills by the Slovak border, have fine seventeenth-century examples. Local buses run occasionally from Krynica, or you could take a taxi—it won't break the bank.

North of Krynica

North of Krynica buses run to Nowy Sącz and Grybów, to the west of Gorlice. For the first 6km both routes follow the main road to KRZYKOWA, where the road divides. For Nowy Sącz you continue through the wooded groves of the Sącz Beskids, via villages such as NOWA WIES and ŁABOWA.

The **Grybów road** is an even more attractive backroads route, due north through open countryside. The village of **BEREST**, 5km north of the main Nowy Sącz road, is a real treat. Set back from the road in pastoral surroundings, it has an eighteenth-century *cerkiew*, an archetype of the harmonious beauty of this region's wooden churches. The doors, opened by a huge metal key that's kept by an ancient peasant caretaker, creak open to release a damp draft from inside; muted scufflings from the priest's small herd of goats will probably be the only sounds to break the silence. Just a couple of kilometers up the road is **POLANY**, where a contemporary icon painter named Eugeniusz Forycki has a workshop in an old Lemk house; in summer you can visit his workshop—a sort of private *skansen*. From here to Grybów the valley is a gorgeous riverside route; if you have a car, a brief detour south to BRUNARY-WYZNE, then on to the border villages of BANICA and IZBY, is worthwhile, since all three have magnificent wooden *cerkwi*. From **GRYBÓW**, you have the choice of frequent buses and trains west to Nowy Sącz or east to Gorlice, or trains north to Tuchow and Tarnów.

travel details

Trains

Lublin to Białystok (1 daily; 9hr); Gdańsk (2 daily; 8hr); Katowice (4 daily; 6–7 hr); Kielce (8 daily; 3–4hr); Kraków (4 daily; 6–8hr); Przemyśl (1 daily; 6hr); Warsaw (11 daily; 2–3hr); Zamość (4 daily; 3–4hr).

Zamość to Kraków (3 daily; 6–10 hr); Lublin (4 daily; 2–4hr); Rzeszów (1 daily; 6hr); Tarnów (3 daily; 4–8 hr); Warsaw (2 daily; 5–7hr).

Rzeszów to Gdańsk (2 daily; 11hr); Kraków (20 daily; 2–4hr); Krosno (2 daily; 3hr); Przemyśl (hourly; 1–2hr); Tarnów (20 daily; 1–2hr); Warsaw (4 daily; 5–7hr).

Łańcut to Przemyśl (15 daily; 1–2hr), via Jarosław (1hr).

Przemyśl to Kraków (15 daily; 3–6hr); Lublin (1 daily; 4hr 30min); Opole (5 daily; 7–9 hr); Rzeszów (20 daily; 1–2 hr); Tarnów (15 daily; 4–6 hr); Warsaw (4 daily; 7–8 hr); Zamość (frequent local train to Jarosław then bus; 3–4hr). Also overnight couchettes to Wrocław and Szczecin and international trains to Lwów, Bucharest, and Sofia.

Sanok to Kraków (2 daily; 7 hours); Krosno (hourly; 2hr); Lublin (1 daily; 8hr); Przemyśl (2 daily; 3–4hr); Rzeszów (2 daily; 3–5hr); Tarnów (2 daily; 3–5hr); Warsaw (2 daily, including one sleeper; 10hr).

Nowy Sącz to Krynica (hourly; 2hr).

Buses

Lublin to Nałęczów, Kazimierz Dolny, Zamość, Sandomierz and Kraków.

Łańcut to Rzeszów.

Krynica to Gorlice and Nowy Sącz.

Nowy Sącz to Kraków, Rzeszów, Tarnow, Zakopane and Warsaw.

Sanok to Ustrzyki Dolne and into the Bieszczady mountains.

Gorlice to Nowy Sącz and Kraków.

Zamość to Przemyśl, Lublin, Sandomierz and Kraków.

CHAPTER FOUR

KRAKÓW, MAŁOPOLSKA, AND THE TATRAS

T he Kraków region attracts more visitors—Polish and foreign—than any other in the country, and its attractions are clear enough from just a glance at the map. The **Tatra Mountains**, for centuries the political border with Czechoslovakia, are Poland's grandest and most beautiful, snowcapped for much of the year and markedly alpine in feel. Along with their foothills, the **Podhale**, and the neighboring, more modest peaks of the **Pieniny**, they have been an established center for hikers for the better part of a century. And with much justice, for there are few ranges in northern Europe where you can get so authentic a mountain experience without having to be a committed climber. The region as a whole is perfect for low-key rambling, mixing with vacationing Poles, and getting an insight into the culture of the indigenous *górale*, as the highlanders are known. Other outdoor activities are well provided for, too, with raft rides down the Dunajec gorge in summer and some fine winter skiing on the higher Tatra slopes.

Kraków itself is equally popular and impressive: a city that ranks with Prague and Vienna as one of the architectural gems of Central Europe, with an old town which retains an atmosphere of *fin-de-siècle* stateliness. A long-time university center, its streets are a cavalcade of churches and aristocratic palaces, while at its heart is one of the grandest of European squares, the Rynek Główny. The city's significance for Poles goes well beyond the aesthetic, though, for this was the country's ancient royal capital, and has been home to many of the nation's greatest writers, artists, and thinkers, a tradition retained in the thriving cultural life. The Catholic church in Poland has often looked to Kraków for guidance, and its influence in this sphere has never been greater—Pope John Paul II was Archbishop of Kraków until his election in 1978. Equally important are the city's **Jewish roots**: until the last war, this was one of the great Jewish centers in Europe, a past whose fabric remains clear in the old ghetto area of Kazimierz, and whose culmination is starkly enshrined at the death camps of **Auschwitz-Birkenau**, west of Kraków.

For the rest, this chapter takes in an area which loosely corresponds to **Małopolska**—a region with no precise boundaries, but which by any definition includes some of the historic heartlands of the Polish state. Highlights here—in countryside characterized by rolling, open landscape, market towns, and farming villages—include **Kielce**, springboard for hikes into the **Świętokrzyskie Mountains**, and the pilgrim center of **Częstochowa**, home of the Black Madonna, the country's principal religious symbol.

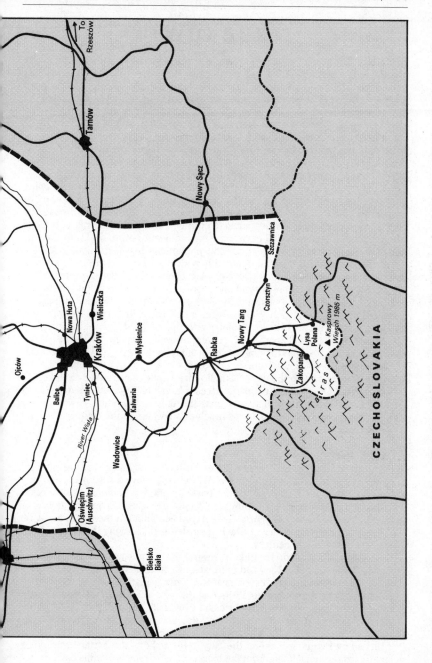

KRAKÓW

KRAKÓW, the ancient capital of Poland and residence for centuries of its kings, was the only major city in the country to come through World War II essentially undamaged. Its assembly of monuments, without rival in Poland, has now been listed by UNESCO as one of the world's twelve most significant historic sites. All the more ironic, then, that the government has had to add another tag: that of official "ecological disaster area"—for Kraków's industrial suburbs represent the communist experiment at its saddest extreme.

Up until the war, the city revolved about its **Jagiellonian University**, founded back in the fourteenth century, and its civic power was centered on the university's Catholic, conservative intelligentsia. The communist regime, wishing to break their hold, decided to graft a new working class onto the city by developing on the outskirts one of the largest steelworks in Europe, **Nowa Huta**. It was like dropping Pittsburgh onto the periphery of Oxford, and within a few decades its effects were apparent as the city began to crumble. Consequently Kraków is faced with intractable economic and environmental problems: how to deal with the acid rain of the steelworks, how to renovate the monuments, how to maintain jobs.

Yet the city remains a visual treat, with **Wawel Hill** one of the most striking royal residences in Europe and the old inner town a mass of flamboyant monuments. For Poles, these are a symbolic representation of the nation's historical continuity, and for visitors brought up on gray Cold War images of Eastern Europe they are a revelation. Kraków's recent **political history** is also of major importance. It was at Nowa Huta—along with the Lenin Shipyards in Gdańsk—that things started to fall apart for the communist government. By the 1970s the steelworkers had become the epitome of hostility to the state, and with the birth of Solidarity in 1980 Nowa Huta emerged as a center of trade union agitation. Working-class unity with the city's Catholic elite was demonstrated by Solidarity's call to increase the officially restricted circulation of *Tygodnik Powszechny*, a Kraków Catholic weekly which was then the only independent newspaper in Eastern Europe. It was in Kraków, as much as anywhere in the country, that the new order was created.

A Brief History

The origins of Kraków are obscure. An enduring legend has it that the city was founded by the mythical ruler **Krak** on Wawel Hill, above a cave occupied by a ravenous dragon. Krak disposed of the beast by offering it animal skins stuffed with tar and sulphur, which it duly and fatally devoured. In reality, traces of human habitation from prehistoric times have been found in the city area, while the first historical records are of **Slavic peoples** settling along the banks of the Wisła here in the eighth century.

Kraków's position at the junction of several important east–west trade routes, including the long haul to Kiev and the Black Sea, facilitated commercial development. By the end of the tenth century it was a major market town and had been incorporated into the emerging **Polish state**, whose early **Piast** rulers made Wawel Hill the seat of a new bishopric and eventually, in 1038, the capital of the country. Subsequent development, however, was rudely halted in the mid-thirteenth century, when the Tartars left the city in ruins. But the urban layout established by **Prince Bolesław the Shy** in the wake of the Tartar invasions, a geometric pattern emanating from the market square, remains to this day.

Kraków's importance was greatly enhanced during the reign of **King Kazimierz**. As well as founding a **university** here in 1364—the oldest in Central Europe after Prague—Kazimierz rebuilt extensive areas of the city and, by giving Jews right of abode in Poland, paved the way for a thriving **Jewish community** here. The advent of the Renaissance heralded Kraków's emergence as an important European center of learning, its most famous student (at least, according to local claims) being young **Nicolaus Copernicus**. Part and parcel of this was a reputation for religious tolerance at odds with the sectarian fanaticism stalking sixteenth-century Europe. It was from Kraków, for example, that King Zygmunt August assured his subjects that he was not king of their consciences—bold words in an age of despotism and bloody wars of religion.

King Zygmunt III Waza's decision to **move the capital to Warsaw** in 1596, following the union of Poland and Lithuania, was a major blow. The fact that royal coronations (and burials) continued on Wawel for some time was little compensation for a major loss of status. Kraków began to decline, a process accelerated by the pillaging of the city during the Swedish invasion of 1655–57.

Following the **Partitions**, after a brief period as capital of a tiny, notionally autonomous republic (1815–46), the city was incorporated into the **Austro-Hungarian** province of Galicia. The least repressive of the occupying powers, the emperor granted Galicia autonomy within the empire in 1868, the prelude to a major revival. The relatively liberal political climate allowed Kraków to become the focus of all kinds of underground political groupings: **Józef Piłsudski** began recruiting his legendary Polish legions here prior to World War I, and from 1912 to 1914 Kraków was **Lenin**'s base for directing the international communist movement and the production of *Pravda*. **Artists and writers** attracted by the new liberalism gathered here too. Painter Jan Matejko produced many of his stirring paeans to Polishness during his residency as art professor at the Jagiellonian University, and the city was the source of Wyspiański and Malczewski's **Młoda Polska** (Young Poland) movement.

The brief interlude of independence following World War I ended for Kraków in September 1939 when the **Nazis** entered the city. Kraków was soon designated capital of the Central Government, incorporating all Polish territories not directly annexed to the Reich. Hans Frank, the notorious Nazi governor, moved into the royal castle on Wawel Hill, from where he exercised a reign of unbridled terror, presaged by the arrest and deportation to concentration camps of many professors from the Jagiellonian University in November 1939. The elimination of the **Kraków ghetto**, most of whose inhabitants were sent to nearby Auschwitz (Oswięcim), was virtually complete by 1943.

The main event of the immediate postwar years was the construction of the vast **Nowa Huta steelworks** a few miles east of the city, a daunting symbol of the communist government's determination to replace Kraków's Catholic, intellectually oriented past with a bright new industrial future. The plan did not work: the peasant population recruited to construct and then work in the steel mills never became the loyal, anti-religious proletariat the Party hoped for. Kraków's reputation as a center of conservative Catholicism was enhanced by the election of **Pope John Paul II** in 1978, who until then had been Archbishop of Kraków.

An unforeseen consequence of the postwar industrial development is one of the highest **pollution** levels in Europe; dangerously high toxic levels are wreaking havoc with the health of the local population as well as causing incalculable damage to the ancient city center. If you find yourself feeling exhausted or dizzy after a few days here—a common experience—then blame it on Nowa Huta, and the fumes blown in from the Katowice region. After years of prevarication, cleaning up the city is now a major local political issue, and in 1989 Kraków actually elected a Green mayor.

Orientation, Arrival, and Transit

Kraków is bisected by the **Wisła River**, though virtually everything of interest is concentrated on the north bank. At the heart of things, enclosed by the **Planty**— a green belt following the course of the old ramparts—is the **Stare Miasto**, the Old Town, with its great central square, the **Rynek Główny**. Just south of the Stare Miasto, looming above the river bank, is **Wawel**, the royal castle hill, beyond which lies the old Jewish quarter of **Kazimierz**.

Thanks to the lack of wartime damage, the **inner suburbs** have more character than usual, the modern high-rises being interspersed with the occasional villa and nineteenth-century residential area. The more recent outer suburbs are no more characterful than the norm. If you come in from the east, you'll see and smell the steelworks at **Nowa Huta**, their chimneys working overtime on acid rain production.

The main points of arrival are all fairly convenient.

● **Kraków Główny**, the central **train station**, is within walking distance of the Stare Miasto. All principal lines run to here. The luggage consignment is open 24 hours a day.

● **Dworzec PKS**, the main **bus station**, is opposite the train station.

● **Arriving by car**, major roads from all directions are well-signposted, though once downtown, you'll have to cope with trams, narrow streets, and heavy daytime traffic. There are official parking lots on pl. św. Ducha and pl. Szczepański; and, although they are technically for hotel guests only, you could also try the *Cracovia*, *Holiday Inn*, and *Wanda* hotels.

● **Balice airport** handles both domestic and international flights. It is half an hour west of the city, connected with the main bus station by bus #208; taxis are always available, too, and pretty reasonable at around $9–15.

Getting Around

The central area of Kraków is compact enough to get around on foot; indeed parts of the **Stare Miasto**—including the Rynek—are pedestrian zones.

For exploring farther afield, **trams** are plentiful, start early and run till late at night. Tram routes radiate out from the Planty to the suburbs; useful services are detailed as relevant in the text. **Buses** can also be useful, complementing the trams and keeping similarly long hours, with night buses taking over from around 11pm to 5am; they provide the main links with outer suburbs such as Tyniec and Nowa Huta, and local towns such as Wieliczka. **Local train** services can be handy for trips out of the city center, such as to Płaszów.

Taxis are still affordable for westerners, though as elsewhere in the country they are highly priced for the local economy. There are ranks around downtown at pl. św. Ducha, Mały Rynek, pl. Dominikański, pl. Szczepański, pl. Wiosny Ludów, and at the main train station.

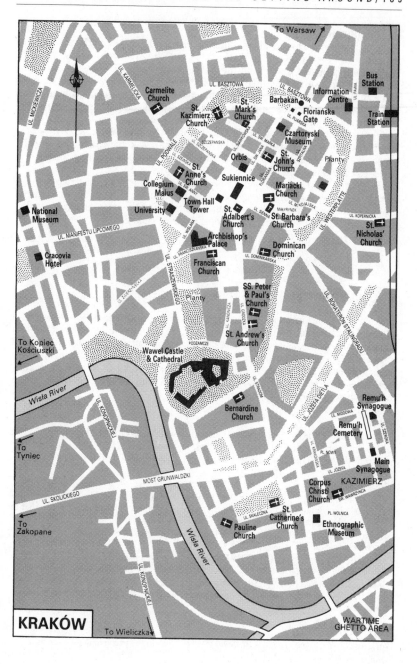

KRAKÓW

Information and Maps

Possibly in response to the sheer volume of visitors, Kraków's city tourist office is far and away the best-organized of any Polish city. The **main office**, run by *Wawel Tourist*, is just down from the station at ul. Pawia 8 (Mon–Fri 8am–4pm, Sat 8am–noon), with all the maps and brochures you could want. The **Almatur** office at Rynek Główny 7/8 is also worth a call; it handles student accommodation and is good for advice on nightlife and alternative events. As usual, **Orbis** also has information points in their hotels as well as a central office at Rynek Główny 41. They organize city tours and day excursions to Tyniec, Wieliczka, Ojców park and Pieskowa Skała castle, Oświęcim (Auschwitz), Zakopane, and the Dunajec gorge; details from the main office or the information points in the *Cracovia* or *Holiday Inn* hotels.

The **maps** we've printed should be functional enough for most purposes. If you plan a longer stay, or are staying out in the suburbs, it might be worth investing in the fold-out **plan miasta**—available (if stocks have been printed recently) at the tourist offices, the *ruch*, bookshops, or street vendors.

> The Kraków telephone code is ☎012.

Accommodation

Kraków is turning into one of Europe's prime city destinations—so you should contact hotels ahead in summer. If you don't, be prepared to try your luck with a private room, which, as ever, may well be some way out of the center. **Prices** for hotels are higher than in most Polish cities but nevertheless marginally lower than Warsaw's. The cheapest places come out at around $19–28 for a double; moderate ones at around $36–72; Orbis hotels from around $95–130. Private rooms run at around $19–22 for a double.

Hotels

A bureau inside the *Warszawski* hotel at ul. Pawia 6, a couple of doors down from the main tourist office, deals with **hotel reservations** (☎221-509 for advance booking; ☎229-370 for same day). Listings are in ascending order of price.

CHEAPER HOTELS

PTTK Dom Turysty, ul. Westerplatte 15/16, near the station (☎229-566). Few singles, lots of doubles plus eight-person dormitories. Popular student venue, nearly always crowded in season; double rooms are small but decent. Self-service restaurant.

Juventur Hotel, ul. Sławkowska 3 (☎214-222). Useful central location and again popular with students—Polish and foreign.

Korona, ul. Pstrowskiego 9/15 (☎666-511). Located out in the southern Podgorze district, on the edge of the wartime ghetto area, this is a cheap, lesser-known sports hotel.

Wisła, ul. Reymonta 22 (☎334-922). Another sports hotel, set in a pleasant park in the western Czarna Wieś district, next to the main soccer stadium. Bus #144 (from the main bus station) passes close by.

MODERATE HOTELS

Warszawski, ul. Pawia 6 (☎220-622). Good location close to the train station—but noisy.
Polonia, ul. Basztowa 25 (☎221-661). Ditto.

Europeijski, ul. Lubicz 5 (☎220-911). Ditto.

Polera, ul. Szpitalna 30 (☎221-044). New name and (private) management; calm, central location.

Krakowianka, ul. Zywiecka (☎664-191). A last resort—well south of downtown.

Monopol, ul. Warynskiego 6 (☎227-666). A bit more expensive than most in this category, but worth it for better-quality rooms.

Polski, ul. Pijarska 17 (☎221-144). Higher end of the price scale, again a very central and quiet location.

Pod Kopcem, al. Waszyngtona (☎230-355). Housed in an old fortress on a hill west of the center, this is a delightfully peaceful hotel—well worth the higher-than-average prices. Increasingly popular.

Motel Krak, ul. Radzikowskiego 99 (☎372-122). Well outside the city—see "Campgrounds," below, for transportation details. Its advantage is a swimming pool.

Pod Róża, ul. Floriańska 14 (☎229-399). Venerable place, now taken over by the crowd using its much-advertised casino.

EXPENSIVE HOTELS

The fancy hotels remain dominated by Orbis, who own four of the five listed below. However, their ranks are shortly to be joined by the old and elegant *Franczuski*, coming to the end of a major refurbishment.

Cracovia, al. Puszkina 1 (☎228-666). Oldest and best-located of the Orbis hotels, a tram ride (#15 or #18) west of the center.

Forum, ul. Konopnickiej 28 (☎669-50). Fading but still plush 1970s block south of Wawel near the river—much used by tour groups.

Holiday Inn, ul. Koniewa 7 (☎375-044). Luxury international hotel favored by the tourist jet set, well out of the city center on the main Balice–Katowice road.

Wanda, ul. Koniewa 9 (☎371-677). Not quite up to the mark of its neighbor, the *Holiday Inn*.

Grand, ul. Sławkowska 19. The newest luxury hotel in town, due to open imminently.

Private Rooms

The office next door to the main tourist information, at ul. Pawia 6 (Mon–Fri 7am–9pm, Sat 1–6pm; ☎221-921) organizes **private rooms**, which can be a good bet during the summer. Ask carefully about addresses, which tend to be a long way out.

Student Hotels and Youth Hostels

Student hotels operate throughout the summer months (June–Sept). Details of locations (which change each year) are available from the **Almatur** office on the main square at Rynek Główny 7/8 (☎226-352).

There are three regular **youth hostels**.

Ul. Oleandry 4 (☎338-920). The main hostel is a huge concrete construction behind the *Cracovia* hotel—but still manages to fill up in summer. Open all year.

Ul. Kościuszki 88 (☎221-951). A smaller place, housed in a former convent overlooking the river (trams #1, #2, #6, #21). Open all year.

Ul. Złotej Kielni 1 (☎372-441). Open July & Aug only.

Campgrounds

Krak Camping, ul. Radzikowskiego 99, near the motel of the same name (see "Moderate Hotels," above), in the northwest of the city. The most popular camping site. Buses #118, #173, #208, # 218, and #223 pass the motel.

The City

The area covered in this section is basically the city center; with the Rynek Główny as a starting point, almost everything is within half an hour's walk. The heart of the district is the **Stare Miasto**, the Old Town, bordered by the greenery of the **Planty**. Within this area, a broad network of streets stretch southward to the edge of **Wawel Hill**, with its royal residence, and beyond to the Jewish quarter of **Kazimierz**. Across the river, on the edge of the **Podgórze** suburb, is the old wartime ghetto. And finally, a little farther out to the west, **Kościuszko's Mound** offers an attractive stretch of woods and countryside, just a ten-minute bus ride from the center.

Rynek Główny

The **Rynek Główny** was the largest square of medieval Europe: a huge expanse of flagstones, ringed by magnificent houses and towering spires. Long the marketplace and commercial hub of the city, it's an immediate introduction to Kraków's grandeur and stateliness. By day things can get obscured by the crowds, but venture into the square late at night and you can immerse yourself in the aura of the city in its *fin-de-siècle* heyday and of the great events played out here, like the rallying call to national independence made by revolutionary leader Tadeusz Kościuszko in 1794. In this atmosphere the sound of the *hejnał*—the trumpet call played each hour from the Mariacki church (see below)—becomes an achingly mournful sound.

The square is more open today than it used to be. Until the last century much of it was occupied by market stalls, a tradition maintained by the flower sellers and ice cream vendors, and by the booths in the **Sukiennice**, the medieval cloth hall (see below) at the heart of the square, which divides it into west and east sections, the latter dominated by the **Mariacki**.

Around the Square

In the east section, the focus is a statue of the romantic poet **Mickiewicz**, a facsimile of an earlier work destroyed by the Nazis, and a favorite meeting point. To its south is the copper-domed **St Adalbert's** (św. Wojchecha), the oldest building in the square and the first church to be founded in Kraków. The saint was a Slav bishop, reputed to have preached here in around 995 before heading north to convert (and get martyred by) the Prussians. Go down into the basement—reconstructed in the eighteenth century—and you can see the foundations of the original tenth-century Romanesque building. Traces of an even earlier wooden building, possibly a pre-Christian temple, and an assortment of archaeological finds are also on display.

Many of the **mansions** ranged around the square are associated with artists, writers, and wealthy local families, though these days most of them are in use as shops, offices or museums. The eastern side of the square has some of the oldest in the city. The **Grey House** (no. 7), for example, despite its later appearance, has many of its Gothic rooms intact; its ex-residents include Poland's first elected king, Henri de Valois, and Tadeusz Kościuszko, who used the house as his headquarters during the 1794 uprising. The Gothic **Boner House** (no. 9) was for some time the home of the Kraków writer and painter Stanisław Wyspiański.

Moving anticlockwise, around to the west section of the square, the **Potocki Palace** (no. 20) is a good example of a classical Kraków mansion, while the **Pod Baranami** (no. 27) is another aristocratic home, constructed from four adjacent burghers' houses in the sixteenth century. The nucleus of nineteenth-century social life, it's nowadays a cultural center (see "Entertainment and Nightlife"). Farther around the square, an orderly collection of shopfronts and restaurants added on to the old burghers' houses ends at the **Krzysztofory Palace** (no. 39), another well-preserved mansion created by fusing burghers' houses into a single building; it now houses a few sections of the history museum on the first floor.

The tall **tower**—facing the Pod Baranami—is all that remains of the original, fourteenth-century **town hall**, demolished during the 1820s by the authorities as part of a misguided improvement plan. It's worth the climb for an excellent overview of the city. The top floor features occasionally illuminating local exhibitions (Wed–Sun 9am–3pm); the Gothic vaults below are currently occupied by the *Teatr Satyry*, a popular satirical cabaret outfit (see "Entertainment and Nightlife").

The Sukiennice

The **Sukiennice** is one of the most distinctive sights in the country: a colonnaded medieval cloth hall, topped by a sixteenth-century attic dripping with gargoyles. Its commercial traditions are perpetuated by a **covered market**, which bustles with tourists and street sellers at almost any time of year. Inside, the stalls of the darkened central arcade display a hotch-potch collection of junk and genuine craft items from the Podhale region. Popular buys include painted boxes in every shape and size and thick woollen sweaters from the mountains; prices are inevitably inflated, so if you're traveling on to the south, it's better to wait until you get to the market at Nowy Targ (see "South to Zakopane," p.227). The **terrace cafés** on either side of the hall are classic Kraków haunts, where locals idle away the afternoon over tea and *sernik*.

The **Art Gallery** on the upper floor of the Sukiennice (Thurs noon–6pm, Fri–Mon 10am–4pm) is worth a visit for its collection of works by nineteenth-century Polish artists, among them Matejko, Malczewski, Gierymski, and Chełmonski. The Matejkos here include two political heavyweights, the *Homage of Prussia* and the stirring *Kościuszko at Racławice*. As usual with Matejko, the impact is heightened if you appreciate the historical reference points, in this case the homage of the Teutonic Knights in 1525 (see "Malbork," in Chapter Two) and the Polish peasant army's victory over the Russians in 1794.

Mariacki Church and Square

Mariacki Church (St Mary's) was founded in 1222 and destroyed during the mid-century Tartar invasions. The current building, begun in 1355 and completed fifty years later, is one of the finest Gothic structures in the country—the taller of its towers topped by an amazing ensemble of spires, elaborated with a crown and helmet.

Legend has it that during one of the early Tartar raids the watchman positioned at the top of this tower saw the invaders approaching and took up his trumpet to raise the alarm; his warning was cut short by a Tartar arrow through the throat. The legend lives on, and every hour on the hour a lone **trumpeter** plays the sombre *hajnał* melody, halting abruptly at the precise point the watchman was supposed to have been hit. The national radio station broadcasts the *hajnał* live at noon every day and Polish writers are still apt to wax lyrical on the symbolism of the trumpet's warning.

First impressions of the **church** are of a cavernous, somewhat gloomy expanse. What little light there is comes from the high windows at each end, the ancient altar window facing the stained glass of the west end, an Art-Nouveau extravaganza by Kraków artist Stanisław Wyspiański. Walking down the nave, you'll have to pick your way past devotees kneeling in front of the fifteenth-century **Chapel of Our Lady of Częstochowa**, with its copy of the venerated image of the Black Madonna, which locals claim has actually been here longer than the original has existed.

Continuing down the high Gothic nave, under arched stone vaulting enhanced in blue and gold, the walls—like those surrounding the high altar—are decorated with **Matejko friezes**. Separating the nave from the aisles are a succession of buttressed pillars fronted by Baroque marble altars. The aisles themselves lead off to a number of lavishly ornamented chapels, fifteenth-century additions to the main body of the building. Focal point of the nave is the huge stone **crucifix** attributed to Veit Stoss (see below), hanging in the archway to the presbytery.

The biggest crowds are drawn by the majestic **high altar** at the far east end. Carved by the Nuremberg master craftsman Veit Stoss (Wit Stwosz, as he's known in Poland) between 1477 and 1489, the huge linden-wood triptych is one of the finest examples of late Gothic art. The outer sides of the folded triptych feature illustrations from the life of the Holy Family executed in gilded polychromy. At noon (Sundays and saints' days excluded) the altar is opened to reveal the inner panels, with their reliefs of the Annunciation, Nativity, Adoration of the Magi, Resurrection, Ascension, and Pentecost; for a good view, arrive at least a quarter of an hour before the opening. These six superb scenes are a fitting backdrop to the central panel—an exquisite **Dormition of the Virgin** in which the graceful figure of Mary is shown reclining into her final sleep in the arms of the watchful Apostles. Like most of the figures, the Apostles—several of them well over life-size—are thought to be based on Stoss's contemporaries in Kraków. Certainly there's an uncanny mastery of human detail that leaves you feeling you'd recognize their human counterparts if you met them in the street.

ST BARBARA'S CHURCH AND MARIACKI SQUARE

The side door on the south side of the chancel brings you in to **Mariacki Square**, a small courtyard replacing the old church cemetery closed down by the Austrians in the last century. On the far side of the courtyard stands the fifteenth-century **St Barbara's** church; during the Partitions the ruling Austrians took over the Mariacki, so the locals were forced to use this tiny place for services in Polish. The back of the church looks onto the tranquil **Mały Rynek** whose terrace cafés make an enjoyable venue for postcard sessions or a quiet beer.

From Mały Rynek, the narrow **ul. Sienna** offers an alternative route back to the main square. On the street outside no. 5 there's normally a bunch of students touting political books and badges, alternately amusing, informative, or impenetrable to the foreigner. The first floor of the building houses the local branch of the **Catholic Intellectuals Club** (KIK), an organization that's more approachable than it sounds. Founded in the wake of the post-Stalinist political thaw of the 1950s, the KIK was for over thirty years one of the few officially sanctioned independent structures in the country, and its national network played an important part in the last decade's political events. It was to the KIK offices in Kraków, for example, that local steelworkers and farmers came for help when setting up the first Solidarity organizations in 1980. Today, a number of KIK people are now prominent Solidarity politicians, ex-Prime Minister Mazowiecki included.

Around the Stare Miasto

Like the Rynek, the streets around the Stare Miasto still follow the medieval plan, while their **architecture** presents a rich Central European ensemble of Gothic, Renaissance, and Baroque. They are a hive of commercial activity, too, with privately owned shops sprouting up in place of the old state enterprise outlets, and a mass of **street traders**, ranging from young Poles touting western cassettes to Russian peasants holding up gold trinkets. West of the Rynek, the atmosphere is generated by the academic buildings and student haunts of the **university district**.

Ulica Floriańska

Of the three streets leading north off the Rynek, **ul. Floriańska** is the busiest and most striking. Tucked between the myriad shops, cafés and restaurants are some attractive fragments of medieval and Renaissance architecture. At no. 5, for example, a beautiful early Renaissance stone figure of the *Madonna and Child* sits in a niche on the facade. At no. 14, **Pod Róża**, the oldest hotel in Kraków, has a Renaissance doorway inscribed in Latin "May this house stand until an ant drinks the oceans and a tortoise circles the world"—it doesn't seem to get much attention from the moneyed revelers who flock to the hotel's casino, recently re-opened amid much hype. Famous hotel guests of the past include Franz Liszt, Balzac, and the occasional czar. Farther up the street at no. 41 is the sixteenth-century **Matejko House**, home of painter Jan Matejko. A small museum (Wed, Thurs, Sat & Sun 10am–4pm, Fri noon–6pm) comprises mementoes of the industrious artist's life and work, with two rooms preserved as they were during his lifetime.

Floriańska Gate, at the end of the street, marks the edge of the Old Town proper. A square, robust fourteenth-century structure, it's part of a small section of fortifications saved when the old defensive walls were torn down in the early nineteenth century. The walls lead east to the fifteenth-century Haberdashers' (Pasamoników) Tower and west to the Joiners' (Stolarska) Gate, which is separated from the even older Carpenters' (Cieśli) Gate by the arsenal. The original fortifications must have been an impressive sight—three kilometers of wall ten meters high and nearly three meters thick, interspersed with no fewer than forty-seven towers and bastions. The strongest-looking defensive remnant is the **Barbakan**, just beyond Floriańska Gate. A bulbous, spiky fort, added in 1498, it's unusual in being based on the Arab as opposed to European defensive architecture of the time. The covered passage linking the fort to the walls has disappeared, as has the original moat—all of which leaves the bastion looking a little stranded.

The Czartoryski and History Museums

Back through Floriańska Gate and past the reproduction Pop Art collections displayed on the old walls, a right turn down the narrow **ul. Pijarska** brings you to the corner of ul. św. Jana and back down to the main square. On the way, on your right, is the Baroque monastery and church of the **Holy Transfiguration**; on your left, linked to the church by an overhead passage, is the Czartoryski Palace.

THE CZARTORYSKI PALACE

A branch of the National Museum, the **Czartoryski Palace** houses Kraków's finest art collection (Mon, Tues & Fri–Sun 10am–4pm). Its core was established by Izabella Czartoryska at the family palace in Puławy (see Chapter Three) and was then moved to Kraków following the confiscation of the Puławy estate after the 1831 insurrection, in which the family were deeply implicated. The family were legendary collectors, particularly from the Paris salons of the seventeenth and eighteenth centuries, and it shows, despite the Nazis' removal—and subsequent loss—of many precious items.

The **ancient art** collection alone contains over a thousand exhibits, from sites in Mesopotamia, Etruria, Greece, and Egypt. Another intriguing highlight is the collection of **trophies from the Battle of Vienna** (1683), which includes sumptuous Turkish carpets, scimitars, and other Oriental finery.

The **picture galleries** contain a rich display of art and sculpture ranging from thirteenth- to eighteenth-century works, the most famous being Rembrandt's brooding *Landscape Before a Storm* and Leonardo da Vinci's *Lady with an Ermine*. A double pun identifies the rodent-handler as Cecilia Gallerani, the mistress of Leonardo's patron, Lodovico il Moro: the Greek word for this animal is *galé*—a play on the woman's name—and Lodovico's nickname was "Ermelino," meaning ermine. There is also a large collection of Dutch canvases and an outstanding array of fourteenth-century Sienese primitives. As in all Polish museums you may find several galleries closed off (often the best ones), ostensibly for lack of staff; passing yourself off as an art student or amateur enthusiast may gain you admission.

THE KRAKÓW HISTORY MUSEUM

On down ul. św. Jana towards the Rynek, there are more wealthy Old Town residences, like the Neoclassical Lubomirski palace at no. 15 and the eighteenth-century Kołłątaj House at no. 20, once a meeting place for the cultured elite. The Gothic palace at ul. św. Jana 12 houses a section of the **Kraków History Museum** (Wed–Sun 9am–3pm, closed first Sat & Sun of the month). The museum is not very inspired, focusing on the development of the city's defenses, with an offbeat display of military objects, including armor, cannon, and swords; the top floor houses a large, jumbled collection of clocks and other timepieces.

The University District

Head west from the Rynek on any of the three main thoroughfares—ul. Szczepańska, ul. Szewska or ul. św. Anny—and you're into the **university area**. The main body of buildings is south of ul. św. Anny, the principal Jewish area of the city until the early 1400s, when the university bought up many of the properties and the Jews moved out to the Kazimierz district.

THE COLLEGIUM MAIUS

The Gothic **Collegium Maius** building, at the intersection of ul. św. Anny with ul. Jagiellońska, is the historic heart of the university complex. The university got off to something of a false start after its foundation by King Kazimierz in 1364, floundering badly after his death six years later until it was revived by King Władysław Jagiełło in the early fifteenth century, when the university authorities began transforming these buildings into a new academic center.

Through the passageway from the street, you find yourself in a quiet, arcaded **courtyard** with a marble fountain playing in the center—an ensemble that, during the early 1960s, was stripped of neo-Gothic accretions and restored to something approaching its original form. The cloistered atmosphere of ancient academia makes a enjoyable break from the city in itself, though actually getting into the building is not so easy. Now the **University Museum**, the Collegium is open to guided tours only (Mon–Sat noon–2pm), for which you need to reserve places at least a day in advance (☎220-549). If you just turn up, you might be able to talk your way onto a tour, but in summer they're full more often than not. You could assess your chances at the shop in the courtyard arcade, which seems to have caught onto the logo craze, selling mugs, pens, sweatshirts, and anything else you can think of sporting the Jagiellonian University crest.

Inside, **tours** proceed through the **ground-floor** rooms, which retain the mathematical and geographical murals once used for teaching; the **Alchemy Room**, with its skulls and other wizard's accoutrements, was used according to legend by the fabled magician Doctor Faustus. Stairs up from the courtyard bring you to an elaborately decorated set of **reception rooms**. The principal assembly hall has a Renaissance ceiling adorned with carved rosettes and portraits of Polish royalty, benefactors, and professors; its Renaissance portal carries the Latin inscription *Plus Ratio Quam Vis*—"Wisdom rather than Strength." The professors' common room, which also served as their dining hall, boasts an ornate Baroque spiral staircase and a Gothic bay window with a replica statuette of King Kazimierz. In the **Treasury** the most valued possession is the copper Jagiellonian globe, constructed around 1510 as the centerpiece of a clock mechanism, and featuring the earliest known illustration of America—labeled "a newly discovered land." If you find old scientific instruments interesting, ask the guide if you can see the other old laboratories and globe rooms.

THE REST OF THE DISTRICT
Several other old buildings are dotted around this area. The Baroque university church of **St Anne**, on the street of the same name, was designed by the ubiquitous Tylman of Gameren (see "Warsaw"). The **Collegium Minus**, just around the corner on ul. Gołębia, is the fifteenth-century arts faculty, rebuilt two centuries later; Jan Matejko studied and later taught here. On the corner of the same street stands the enormous **Collegium Novum**, the neo-Gothic university administrative headquarters, with an interior modeled on the Collegium Maius. The **Copernicus statue**, in front of the Collegium Novum, on the edge of the Planty, commemorates the university's most famous supposed student—though some local historians doubt that he really did study here.

In term time the university district's **cafés** and **restaurants** are usually lively (see "Food, Drink, and Entertainment"), while the graffiti-sprayed southern section of **ul. Jagiellońska** and adjoining **ul. Gołębia** are invariably lined with students hawking books, posters and, of course, Solidarity badges—though that's mainly for the tourists these days. Student artwork, however, remains a fount of political comment: for example, a poster of a grinning mohawk-coiffed Lenin saying "I ♥ Perestroika."

The Route to Wawel Hill
The traditional route used by Polish monarchs when entering the city took them through the Floriańska Gate, down ul. Floriańska to the Rynek, then southward

along ul. Grodzka—part of the old trade route up through Kraków from Hungary—to the foot of **Wawel Hill**. Ulica Grodzka's first intersection is with the tram lines circling the city center at plac Dominikańska, across which stands the large brickwork basilica of the thirteenth-century **Dominican church and monastery**. It was badly damaged by fire in the 1850s, but the rather somber cloisters retain sections of the Romanesque walls; **exhibitions** by local artists and students are often held here, featuring the kind of works that only a few years ago were still considered politically sensitive.

On the opposite side of the square is the equally ancient **Franciscan church**, whose monks arrived in Kraków from Prague in 1237. Also victim of fires in the last century, its darkened interior was redone in suffocating neo-Gothic, an effect enhanced by a set of paintings by Wyspiański, who was also the creator of the stained glass windows in the choir and chancel. On down ul. Grodzka, past the self-explanatory **Lions House** and **Elephants House** (nos. 32 and 38), turn into ul. Poselska to find the house (no. 12) where novelist **Joseph Conrad** spent his childhood.

Back down Grodzka there's a last string of churches before you reach the hill. The first, **Saints Peter and Paul's**, a little way back from the street, is fronted by imposing statues of the two Apostles, actually copies of the pollution-scarred originals, now kept elsewhere for preservation's sake. Modeled on the Gesù church in Rome, it's the earliest Baroque building in the city, commissioned by the Jesuits when they came to Kraków in the 1580s to quell Protestant agitation. Next comes the Romanesque **St Andrew's**, remodeled in familiar Polish Baroque style, where the local people are reputed to have holed themselves up and successfully fought off marauding Tartars during the invasion of 1241; it looks just about strong enough for the purpose. A little farther on, **St Martin's**, built in the seventeenth century on the site of a Romanesque foundation, now belongs to Kraków's small Lutheran community. For the final haul to Wawel, the most atmospheric route is to cross the small plac Wita Stwosza opposite the church, and turn south down ul. Kanonicza, a largely unrestored Gothic street. At the end of the street, you emerge opposite the main path up to the castle.

Wawel Hill: the Cathedral and Castle

For over 500 years the country's rulers lived and governed on **Wawel Hill**, whose main buildings stand pretty much as they have done for centuries. Even after the capital moved to Warsaw, Polish monarchs continued to be buried in the cathedral, and it's at Wawel that many of the nation's venerated poets and heroes lie in state. As such, Wawel represents a potent source of Polish national and spiritual pride: unusually in Kraków, there are always far greater crowds of Poles than foreigners looking around.

The cobbled path up Wawel negotiates lines of souvenir touts, silhouette artists, and horoscope sellers. At the top, a typically dramatic statue of Tadeusz Kościuszko—a copy of the one destroyed by the Nazis—stands before the sixteenth-century Waza Gate. As you emerge, the cathedral rears up to the left, with the castle and its outbuildings and courtyards beyond. Directly ahead is a huge, open square, once the site of a Wawel township, but cleared by the Austrians in the early nineteenth century to create a parade ground.

Official **opening hours** are 10am to 3pm (Tues–Sun) for the cathedral, and 10am to 3pm (Tues, Thurs, Sat & Sun) or noon to 6pm (Wed & Fri) for the castle.

However, times do vary so it's a good idea to check beforehand at one of the tourist offices or in the listings in *Krak* magazine. Keep in mind, too, that Wawel is extremely popular at all times of year—and from May to September, you need to turn up at least an hour and a half before opening for any chance of a ticket. Be sure to specify that you want **tickets** for the castle *and* royal chamber, and the cathedral *and* its museum. Guides for small groups are available for rent from the PTTK counter opposite the ticket office; Orbis also arranges tours of the Stare Miasto and castle, complete with tickets, if you're not keen on lining up.

The Cathedral

"The sanctuary of the nation . . . cannot be entered without an inner trembling, without an awe, for here—as in few cathedrals of the world—is contained a vast greatness which speaks to us of the history of Poland, of all our past." So was Wawel Cathedral evoked by former Archbishop Karol Wojtyła of Kraków. As with Westminster Abbey or St Peter's, the moment you enter Wawel, you know you're in a place overloaded with history.

The first cathedral was built here around the time King Bolesław the Brave established the Kraków bishopric in 1020. Fragments of this building can still be seen in the west wing of the castle and the courtyard between the castle and the cathedral, while the St Leonard's crypt survives from a second Romanesque structure. The present brick and sandstone basilica is essentially Gothic, dating from the reigns of Władysław the Short (1306–33) and Kazimierz the Great (1333–70), and adorned with a mass of side chapels, endowed by just about every subsequent Polish monarch and a fair number of the aristocratic families too.

The view down the nave of the cathedral, with its arched Gothic vaulting, is blocked by the **shrine of Saint Stanisław**, an overwrought seventeenth-century silver sarcophagus commemorating the bishop who was murdered by the king in 1079 for his opposition to royal ambitions. Beyond it stands the Baroque **high altar** and choir stalls. However, most people are drawn immediately to the outstanding array of side chapels which punctuate the entire length of the building.

THE CHAPELS

All except four of Poland's forty-five monarchs are buried in the cathedral, and their tombs and side chapels are like a directory of the Central European architecture, art, and sculpture of the last six centuries.

Beginning from the right of the entrance, the Gothic **Holy Cross Chapel** (Kaplica Świętokrzyskia) is the burial chamber of King Kazimierz IV Jagiełło (1447–92). The boldly colored, Byzantine-looking paintings on the walls and ceiling were completed by artists from Russian Novgorod, while the king's marble tomb is the characteristically expressive work of Veit Stoss, of Mariacki fame. Two carved Gothic altars and a beautiful triptych of the Holy Trinity in the side panels round off a sumptuously elegant masterpiece.

Moving down the aisle, the next two chapels celebrate aristocratic families rather than kings: the **Potocki** (a Neoclassical creation) and **Szafraniec** (a Baroque ensemble at the foot of the Silver Bells tower). They are followed by the majestic **Waza** chapel, a Baroque mausoleum to the seventeenth-century royal dynasty, and the **Zygmuntowska** chapel, whose shining gilded cupola—its exterior regularly replated owing to the corrosive effects of pollution—dominates the courtyard outside. Designed for King Zygmunt the Old by the Italian architect

Bartolomeo Berrecci, it's an astonishing piece of Renaissance design and ornamentation, with intricate sandstone and marble carvings, and superb sculpted
figures above the sarcophagi of the king, his son Zygmunt August, and his wife
Queen Anna. The two altarpieces are spectacular, too; the silver *Altar of the
Virgin* was designed by craftsmen from Nuremberg and includes Passion paintings by George Pencz, a pupil of Dürer.

Venerable fourteenth-century bishops occupy several subsequent chapels,
while the Gothic, red Hungarian marble **Tomb of King Kazimierz the Great**,
immediately to the right of the high altar, is a dignified tribute to the revered
monarch. The fourteenth-century **St Mary's** chapel, directly behind the altar and
connected to the castle by a passage, was remodeled in the 1590s to accommodate the austere black marble and sandstone tomb of King Stefan Batory (1576–
86). The **Tomb of King Władysław the Short** (1306–1333), on the left-hand
side of the altar, is the oldest in the cathedral, completed soon after his death; the
reclining, coronation-robed figure lies on a white sandstone tomb edged with
expressive mourning figures.

THE TREASURY, TOWER, AND CRYPTS
The highlights of the cathedral **Treasury** (in the northeast corner, behind the
sacristy) include a collection of illuminated texts and some odd items of Polish
royal and ecclesiastical history—Saint Maurice's spear (a present to King
Bolesław the Brave from Emperor Otto), an eighth-century miniature of the four
Evangelists, and King Kazimierz the Great's crown.

An ascent of the **Zygmuntowska Tower** (access again from the sacristy) gives
a far-reaching panorama over the city and close-up views of the five medieval
bells. The largest, known as Zygmunt, is two and a half meters in diameter, eight
in circumference, and famed for its deep, sonorous tone, which local legends
claim scatters rain clouds and brings out the sun. These days it doesn't get too
many chances to perform, as it's only rung on Easter Sunday, Christmas Eve, and
New Year's Eve.

Back in the cathedral, the **crypt** (in the left aisle) houses the remains of the
poets **Adam Mickiewicz** and **Juliusz Słowacki**, while **St Leonard's Crypt**, part
of a long network of vaults reached from near the main entrance, contains the
tombs of national heroes Prince Józef Poniatowski and Tadeusz Kościuszko. The
equally sanctified prewar independence leader Jozef Piłsudski lies in a separate
vault nearby. Standing with the crowds filing past this pantheon, you catch the
passionate intensity of Polish attachment to everything connected with past resistance and independent nationhood.

Finally, as you leave the cathedral, look out for the bizarre collection of **prehistoric animal bones**—a mammoth's shinbone, a whale's rib, and the skull of a
hairy rhinoceros—in a passage near the main entrance. As long as they remain,
so legend maintains, the cathedral will too.

The Castle
Entering the tiered courtyard of **Wawel Castle**, you might imagine that you'd
stumbled on an opulent Italian palazzo. That's just the effect Zygmunt the Old
intended when he entrusted the conversion of King Kazimierz's Gothic castle to a
Florentine architect in the early 1500s. The major difference from its Italian
models lies in the response to climate: the window openings are enlarged to maxi-
mise the available light, while to withstand snow the roofing has a distinctly

northern functionalism. A spate of fires, and more recently the corrosive effects of Kraków's atmosphere, have taken their toll on the building, but it still exudes a palatial bravura.

Essentially the palace remained a grand residence for as long as the kings stuck around. The rot set in after the capital moved to Warsaw, and the castle was already in a dilapidated state when the Austrians pillaged it and turned it into a barracks. Reconstruction began in earnest in 1880, following Emperor Franz Josef's removal of the troops, continuing throughout the interwar years. Wawel's nadir came during World War II, when governor Hans Frank transformed the castle into his private quarters, adding insult to injury by turning the royal apartments over to his Nazi henchmen. Luckily many of the most valuable castle contents were spirited out of the country at the outbreak of war, eventually being returned to Wawel from Canada in 1961, after years of wrangling. Alongside many pieces from individual Poles at home and abroad—some of these, incidentally, items plundered by the Nazis but subsequently spotted at the big art auctions—they make up the core of today's amply stocked and well-restored collection.

The **castle** is divided into three main sections: the state rooms, crown treasury, and a separate exhibition of oriental art. The state rooms are the section to focus on if time is limited, with their art collections accumulated by the Jagiellonian and Waza dynasties.

THE STATE ROOMS AND ART COLLECTIONS
The centerpiece of the art collections is King Zygmunt August's splendid assembly of **Flanders tapestries**, scattered throughout the first and second floors. The 136 pieces—about a third of the original collection—are what remain from the depredations of Czarist, Austrian, and Nazi armies. Outstanding are three series from the Brussels workshops of the "Flemish Raphael," Michel Coxien, the first and most impressive of which is a group of eighteen huge Old Testament scenes, featuring a lyrical evocation of Paradise and a wonderfully detailed tapestry of Noah and family in the aftermath of the Flood. The oldest tapestry in the castle is the mid-fifteenth-century French *Story of the Swan Knight* displayed in Zygmunt the Old's upstairs bedroom.

In the northwest corner of the same floor is a remnant of the original Gothic castle, a tiny two-roomed watchtower named the **Hen's Foot Tower**. In contrast to other parts of the castle, the rooms of the north wing are in early Baroque style, the result of remodeling following a major fire in 1595. Of the luxurious apartments in this section, the **Silver Hall**, redesigned in 1786 by Domenico Merlini (of Warsaw's Łazienki park fame), achieves a particularly harmonious blending of the old architecture with period classicism.

The **state rooms** on the top floor are among the finest in the building, particularly those in the **east wing** where the original wooden ceilings and wall paintings are still visible. A glance upward at the carved ceiling of the **Audience Hall** at the southern end of the wing will tell you why it's nicknamed the "Heads Room." Executed for King Zygmunt in the 1530s by Sebastian Tauerbach of Wrocław and Jan Snycerz, only thirty of its original array of nearly 200 heads remain, but it's enough to give you a feeling for the contemporary characters they were based on—from all strata of society. The frieze by Hans Dürer illustrates *The Life of Man*, a sixteenth-century retelling of an ancient Greek legend, while the magnificent tapestries of Garden of Eden scenes are again from the Coxien workshop.

Back down the corridor is the **Zodiac Room**, ornamented by an astrological frieze—an ingenious 1920s reconstruction of a sixteenth-century fresco—as well as another series of Biblical tapestries. The northeast corner towers contain the private royal apartments. The **Chapel**, rebuilt in 1602, looks onto the king's bedchamber, while the walls of the **Study**, with its fine floor and stucco decorations, are a mini-art gallery in themselves, crammed with works by Dutch and Flemish artists, among them a Rubens sketch and a painting by the younger Breughel. The seventeenth-century **Bird Room**, named after the wooden birds that used to hang from the ceiling, leads on to the **Eagle Room**, the old court of justice, with a Rubens portrait of Prince Władysław Waza. Last comes the large **Senators' Hall** with a collection of tapestries illustrating the story of Noah and the Ark, another impressive coffered ceiling, and a sixteenth-century minstrel's gallery still used for the occasional concert.

THE TREASURY AND ARMORY

If you've got the stamina, the next thing to head for is the **Royal Treasury and Armory** in the northeast corner of the castle (entrance on the ground floor). The paucity of crown jewels on display, however, is testimony to the ravages of the past. Much of the treasury's contents had been sold off by the time of the Partitions to pay marriage dowries and debts of state. The Prussians did most of the rest of the damage, purloining the coronation insignia in 1795, then melting down the crown and selling off its jewels. The vaulted Gothic **Kazimierz Room** contains the finest items from a haphazard display of lesser royal possessions including rings, crosses, the coronation shoes of Zygmunt August, and the burial crown of Zygmunt August. The oldest exhibit is a fifth-century ring inscribed with the name MARTINVS, found near Kraków.

The prize exhibit in the next-door **Jadwiga and Jagiełło Room** is the solemnly displayed *Szczerbiec*, the thirteenth-century weapon used for centuries in the coronation of Polish monarchs. The other two exhibits here are an early sixteenth-century sword belonging to Zygmunt the Old and the oldest surviving royal banner, made in 1533 for the coronation of Zygmunt August's third wife, Catherine von Habsburg. In the following room are displayed a variety of items connected to **Jan Sobieski**, most notably the regalia of the Knights of the Order of the Holy Ghost sent to him by the pope as thanks for defeating the Turks at Vienna. Things get more military from here on. The next barrel-vaulted room contains a host of finely crafted display weapons, shields and helmets, while the final **Armory Room** is about serious warfare, with weapons captured over five centuries from Poland's host of foreign invaders, including copies of the banners seized during the epic Battle of Grunwald.

THE ORIENT OF THE WAWEL, LOST WAWEL, AND THE CAVE

The **Orient of The Wawel** exhibition, housed in the older west wing of the castle, focuses on Oriental influences in Polish culture. The first floor has an interesting section on early contacts with Armenia, Iran, Turkey, China, and Japan, but the main "influences" displayed here seem to be war loot from the seventeenth-century campaigns against the Turks. The centerpiece is a collection of **Turkish tents and armor** captured after the Battle of Vienna. Other second-floor rooms display an equally sumptuous assortment of Turkish and Iranian carpets, banners, and weaponry seized during the fighting—the sixteenth-century **Paradise Carpet** must have gone very nicely in the royal front room.

The **Lost Wawel** exhibition, beneath the old kitchens south of the cathedral, takes you past the excavated remains of the hill's most ancient buildings, including the foundations of the tenth-century **Rotunda of Saints Felix and Adauctus**, the oldest known church in Poland. A diverse collection of medieval archaeological finds is displayed in the old coach house.

Before leaving Wawel, take in the view over the river from the terrace at the western edge of the hill. And if you're feeling energetic, you could, instead of returning directly to town, clamber down the steps to the **Dragon's Cave** at the foot of the hill—the legendary haunt of Krak (see "A Brief History") and the medieval site of a fishermen's tavern.

Kazimierz, the Ghettoes, and Płaszów

South from Wawel Hill lies the **Kazimierz** district, originally a distinct town and named after King Kazimierz, who granted the founding charter in 1335. Thanks to the acquisition of royal privileges the settlement developed rapidly, trade centering around a market square almost equal in size to Kraków's. The decisive influence on the character of Kazimierz, however, was King Jan Olbracht's electing to move Kraków's already significant **Jewish population** into the area from the ul. św. Anny district in 1495.

In tandem with Warsaw, where a **ghetto** was created at around the same time, Kazimierz grew to become one of the main cultural centers of Polish Jewry. Jews were initially limited to an area around modern-day ul. Szeroka and Miodowa, and it was only in the nineteenth century that they began to spread into other parts of Kazimierz. By this time there were ghettoes all over the country, of course, but descriptions of Kazimierz in Polish art and literature make it clear that there was something special about the Oriental atmosphere of this place.

The life of the area was to perish in the gas chambers of nearby Auschwitz, but many of the buildings, synagogues included, have survived. Walking around the streets today, you feel the weight of an absent culture. Yiddish inscriptions fronting the doorways, an old pharmacy, a ruined theater: the details make it easier to picture what has gone than do the drab housing projects covering the former Warsaw ghetto.

Around the Ghetto

If you're coming from the center of town take a tram (#3, #9, #11, or #13) down ul. Bohaterów Stalingradu and get off at the corner of ul. Miodowa. A left off ul. Miodowa into ul. Szeroka and you're into the heart of the ghetto.

The tiny **Remu'h synagogue** at ul. Szeroka 40 is one of two still functioning in the quarter. Built in 1557 on the site of an earlier wooden synagogue, it was ransacked by the Nazis and restored after the war. It's named after Moses Isserles, also known as Rabbi Remu'h, an eminent Polish writer and philosopher and the son of the synagogue's founder. On Fridays and Saturdays the small local congregation is swelled by some of the increasing number of Jews visiting Poland these days. Behind the synagogue is the **Remu'h cemetery**, established twenty or so years earlier, and in use till the end of the eighteenth century. Many of the gravestones were unearthed in the 1950s; one of the finest is that of the still venerated Rabbi Remu'h, its stele luxuriously ornamented with plant motifs. Tombstones torn up by the Nazis have been collaged together to form a high, powerful Wailing Wall just inside the entrance.

Continuing down ul. Szeroka, no. 16 is the **Poper's Synagogue**, built in 1620 by a merchant of the same name. Restored since the war, it's now a cultural center. Other synagogues no longer used for worship are the late sixteenth-century **Wysoka** (High Synagogue) at ul. Józefa 38, the **Ajzyk** (Isaac) synagogue nearby at ul. Jakuba 25, built in the 1630s, and the 1590 **Kupa** synagogue, a little farther north at ul. Warszauera 8. The nineteenth-century **Postępowa-Tempel** synagogue at the corner of ul. Miodowa and Podbrzezie alternates with the Remu'h for regular services.

The grandest of all the Kazimierz synagogues was the **Old Synagogue** on ul. Szeroka, the earliest surviving Jewish religious building in Poland. Modeled on the great European synagogues of Worms, Prague, and Regensburg, the present Renaissance building was completed in 1557 after a fire destroyed much of the area. The synagogue's story is entwined with the country's history: it was here, for example, that Kościuszko came to rally the Jews in 1794, a precedent followed by the Kazimierz rabbi Ber Meissels during the uprisings of 1831 and 1863. Since the war it's been carefully restored and turned into a **museum** of the history and culture of Kraków Jewry (Mon & Tues 9am–3pm, Wed, Thurs, Sat & Sun 9am–3pm, Fri 11am–6pm; closed first Sat & Sun of the month). Nazi destruction was thorough, so the museum's collection of art, books, manuscripts, and religious objects has a slightly cobbled-together feel to it. The wrought-iron *bima* in the center of the main prayer hall is original though, the masterful product of a sixteenth-century Kraków workshop.

Western Kazimierz

As the presence of several churches indicates, the western part of Kazimierz was where non-Jews tended to live. Despite its Baroque overlay, the interior of the Gothic church of the **Holy Sacrament**, on the corner of ul. Bożego Ciała, retains early features including stained glass windows installed around 1420. The Swedish king Charles Gustaf is supposed to have used the building as his operational base during the mid-seventeenth-century siege of the city. The high church looks onto **plac Wolnica**, the old market square of Kazimierz, now much smaller than it used to be, thanks to the houses built along the old trade route through it in the nineteenth century. The fourteenth-century **Town Hall**, later rebuilt, stands in what used to be the middle of the square, its southern extension an overambitious nineteenth-century addition. It now houses the largest **Ethnographic Museum** in the country (Mon 10am–6pm, Wed–Sun 10am–3pm). The collection focuses on Polish folk traditions, although there's also a selection of artifacts from Siberia, Africa, Latin America, and various Slavic countries. A detailed survey of life in rural Poland includes an intriguing section devoted to ancient folk customs and an impressive collection of costumes, painting, wood-carving, fabrics, and pottery—an excellent introduction to the fascinating and often bizarre world of Polish folk culture.

Two more churches west of the square are worth looking in on. On ul. Skałeczna stands fourteenth-century **St Catherine's**, founded by King Kazimierz for Augustine monks imported from Prague. The large basilican structure is a typical example of Kraków Gothic, though the interior has suffered everything from earthquakes to the installation of an Austrian arsenal. Farther down the road is the **Pauline church and monastery**, perched on a small hill known as Skałka (the Rock). Tradition connects the church with Saint Stanisław, the bishop of Kraków, whose martyrdom by King Bolesław the Generous in 1079 is supposed to have happened here. An altar to him stands in the left aisle of the remodeled Baroque church, and nearby you can see the block on which he's supposed to have been beheaded. Underneath the church is a **crypt** cut into the rock of the hill, which was turned into a mausoleum for famous Poles in the late nineteeth century. Eminent artists, writers and composers buried here include Kraków's own Stanisław Wyspiański, composer Karol Szymanowski, and the medieval historian Jan Długosz.

The Wartime Ghetto

Following an edict from Hans Frank, in March 1941 the entire Jewish population of the city was crammed into a tiny **ghetto** across the river, south of Kazimierz, in the area around modern-day plac Bohaterów Getta. It was sealed off by high walls and anyone caught entering or leaving unofficially was summarily executed. After waves of deportations to the concentration camps, the ghetto was finally liquidated in March 1943, thus ending seven centuries of Jewish life in Kraków. The area is the setting of Thomas Keneally's novel *Schindler's Ark*, which recreates life in the ghetto from the stories of survivors saved by the German industrialist Oskar Schindler.

If you know what you're looking for, it's still possible to detect signs of past Jewish presence in what is now a quiet, rather run-down suburban district. The most obvious is the **Apteka Pod Orłem** on the southeast corner of plac Bohaterów: the old ghetto pharmacy, this is now a museum (10am–4pm, closed Sat). Its wartime proprietor Dr Pankiewicz was the only non-Jewish Pole permitted to live in the ghetto and the exhibition touches on the sensitive question of Polish wartime aid to Jews, as well as life in the ghetto area.

At the bottom of ul. Lwówska, which runs southeast of the square, there's a fragment of the **ghetto wall**. West of the square on ul. Węgierska is the burnt-out shell of what looks like an old Jewish theater, while around the corner on ul. Jozefinska, the state mint turns out to be the former **Jewish bank**. Careful hunting round the area may produce other traces; if you want a break first, however, the coffee shop on the corner of ul. św. Benedykta and Limanowskiego is a restful place, with a gallery next door that often features Jewish artists (Mon–Fri 10am–5pm).

Płaszów Concentration Camp

As well as imprisoning people in the ghetto, the Nazis also relocated many Jews to the **concentration camp at Płaszów**, built near an old Austrian hill fort a couple of kilometres south of Kazimierz. Leveled after the war, the camp's desolate hilltop site is now enclosed by fields and concrete residential high-rises. Although none of the local guidebooks mention the site, it is marked on the large *Kraków: plan miasta* city map by two "Pomnik Martyrologii" symbols, just above the junction of ul. Kamienskiego and ul. Wielicka.

To **get there**, take a local train (Tarnów direction) to Płaszów station, walk down to ul. Wieliczka and cross over. From here it's about ten minutes' walk west to the site; the large hilltop monument is clearly visible from the main road below. Like all concentration camps the site has an eerie, wilderness atmosphere, all the more so for the lack of buildings. Scratch beneath the surface of the grass-covered mounds and you'll find shards of pottery, scraps of metal, and cutlery—telltale evidence of its wartime use.

The Kościuszko Mound and Beyond

This 300-meter-high hill stands a short distance west of the city center, capped by a memorial mound erected in the 1820s in honor of Poland's greatest revolutionary hero, **Tadeusz Kościuszko**. A veteran of the American War of Independence, Kościuszko returned to Poland to lead the 1794 insurrection against the Partitions. With the failure of this uprising, he was imprisoned for two years in St Petersburg, then—after returning for a while to America to promote Polish independence—lived the rest of his life in exile in France and Switzerland. For Poles he is the personification of the popular insurrectionary tradition that involved peasants rather than just intellectuals.

The mound is quite an oddity, having been added onto the hill by the citizenry of Kraków, using earth from Kościuszko's battle sites—both from Poland and (reputedly) from the United States. Access to this section of the hill is only possible via an effusive **museum** of Kościuszko memorabilia (Tues–Sat 10am–4pm). It's worth the few złotys' admission for the view alone. Lower down the hill, the deer roaming about the hillside are a surprising sight so close to a city center, but the polluted grass can't do them much good. There is also a nineteenth-century Austrian **fort** and an upmarket **hotel and restaurant**, the *Pod Kopcem*.

From the city center (plac Matejki) bus #100 runs to the hotel, but if you feel like a walk out of town you can cross the **Błonia**—a green belt west of the Stare Miasto—and then, crossing a couple of roads, follow one of the overgrown pathways up the slopes.

Las Wolski

For a more extended bout of countryside, you could take an hour's walk west from the mound to the wonderful stretch of woodland known as **Las Wolski**. At its center there's a restaurant, a zoo, and another mound—this one erected, in emulation of Kościuszko's, to the 1920s ruler Jozef Piłsudski. Bus #134 runs from the city center to the mound.

The Outskirts

If Wawel Hill and the main square are quintessential old Kraków, the steel mills, smokestacks, and grimy housing projects of **Nowa Huta**, 10km east of the city, are the embodiment of the postwar communist dream, and any Cracovian will want to show them to you. South of the city, a fifteen-kilometer bus ride offers a glimpse at an earlier industrial past in the medieval **Wieliczka salt mine**, a beautiful, UNESCO-listed site that demands a visit. **Tyniec**, 15km southwest of the city, along the river, is a fine Benedictine abbey, with summer organ recitals.

Nowa Huta

Built from scratch in the late 1940s on the site of an old village, the vast industrial complex of **NOWA HUTA** now has a population of over 200,000, making it by far the biggest suburb, while the vast steelworks accounts for more than fifty percent of the country's production. It's worth visiting for the insights it offers into the working-class culture of postwar Poland and the immense ecological problems facing the country.

From downtown Kraków it's a forty-minute tram journey (#4, #9, #15, or #22) to **plac Centralny**, the main square, now bereft of its statue of Lenin, which was replaced in 1990 by a small replica of the Gdańsk Crosses. From here, endless streets of residential blocks stretch out in all directions. East along the main road are the mills known until recently as the **Lenin Steelworks**, now renamed but still belching out the thick smoke that covers the whole area with layers of filth.

In keeping with the anti-religious policies of the postwar government, churches were not included in the original construction plans for Nowa Huta. After years of intensive lobbying, however, the ardently Catholic population eventually got permission to build one in the 1970s. The **Church of the Ark**, in the northern Bieńczyce district, is the result—an amazing ark-like concrete structure encrusted with mountain pebbles. Go there any Sunday and you'll find it packed with steel workers and their families decked out in their best, a powerful testament to the seemingly unbreakable Catholicism of the Polish working class. The other local church, the large **Maximilian Kolbe** church in the Mistrzejowice district, was consecrated by Pope John Paul II in 1983, a sign of the importance the Catholic hierarchy attaches to the loyalty of Nowa Huta. Kolbe, canonized in 1982, was a priest sent to Auschwitz for giving refuge to Jews; in the camp, he took the place of a Jewish inmate in the gas chambers. Trams #1, #16, and #20 from plac Centralny all pass by the building.

Tyniec

Within easy striking distance of the city center, 15km along the river, is the village of **TYNIEC**. City bus #112 takes you there, as do excursion boats in summer, a nice trip provided you don't inspect the water too carefully.

The main attraction here is **Tyniec Abbey**, an eleventh-century foundation that was the Benedictines' first base in Poland. Perched on a white limestone cliff on the edge of the village, the abbey makes an impressive sight from the riverbank paths. The farm plots and traditional wooden cottages dotted around the village lend the place a rural feel at odds with its location so close to the city center; it's a popular place for a Sunday afternoon stroll.

The original Romanesque abbey was rebuilt after the Tartars destroyed it during the 1240 invasion, and then completely remodeled in Gothic style in the fifteenth century, when the defensive walls were also added. The interior of the church subsequently endured the familiar Baroque treatment, but portions of the Gothic structure are left near the altar and in the adjoining (but usually off-limits) cloisters. From June to August the church holds a series of high-quality **organ concerts** during which the cloisters are opened.

In the village, the *Srerbna Góra* on ul. Benedyktyńska is a famed fish **restaurant** that Cracovians drive out to for the evening in droves.

Wieliczka

Fifteen kilometers south of Kraków is the salt mine at **WIELICZKA**, described by one eighteenth-century visitor as being "as remarkable as the Pyramids and more useful." Salt deposits were discovered here as far back as the eleventh century, and from King Kazimierz's time onward local mining rights and hence income were strictly controled by the crown. As mining intensified over the centuries a huge network of pit-faces, rooms, and tunnels proliferated—nine levels in all, extending to a depth of 327m. Scaled-down mining continues today, and there's a sanatarium 200m down, to exploit the supposedly healthy saline atmosphere.

To **get to Wieliczka** take a local train—there are plenty of them—or bus #D from the main Kraków station. Both drop you a little way from the mine, but it isn't hard to locate the pit's solitary chimney and squeaky conveyor belt.

Down the Mine

Entrance to the mine (Tues–Sun 8am–6pm) is by guided tour only, in groups of thirty or so; in summer there are some French-, German- and English-speaking guides around; if you turn up you might strike lucky, otherwise book in advance with Orbis. Be prepared for a bit of a walk—the tour takes two hours, through nearly two miles of tunnels.

A clanking lift takes you down in complete darkness to the first of the three levels included in the **tour**, at a depth of 135m. The rooms and passageways here were hewn between the seventeenth and nineteenth centuries, and while the lower sections are mechanised, horses are still used to lug things around on the top three levels. Many of the first-level chambers are pure green salt, including one dedicated to Copernicus, which he is supposed to have visited.

The deeper you descend, the more spectacular and weirder the chambers get. As well as underground lakes, carved chapels, and rooms full of eerie crystalline shapes, the second level features a chamber full of jolly salt gnomes carved in the 1960s by the mineworkers. The star attraction, **Blessed Kinga's Chapel**, comes on the bottom level: everything in the ornate fifty-meter-long chapel is carved from salt, including the stairs, bannisters, altar, and chandeliers. The chapel's acoustic properties—every word uttered near the altar is audible from the gallery—has led to its use as a concert hall. A **museum**, also down at the lowest level, documents the history of the mine, local geological formations, and famous visitors such as Goethe, Balzac, and the Emperor Franz Josef.

Food, Drink, and Entertainment

Kraków's tourist status has given rise to a decent selection of **restaurants**, with new places springing up every week. For the moment, however, keep in mind that demand is also high and for the better places reservations are essential. You need to turn up early, too—this is not a late-night city, its life instead revolving around a Central European café culture of afternoon and early evening socializing. There is, however, a good deal happening on the **cultural front**, with one of the best **theater** groups in Europe, a long-established **cabaret** tradition, and numerous **student events**. The compact size of Kraków's city center and the presence of the university gives a general buzz that's largely absent, say, in Warsaw.

For local **listings** and general information, the weekly magazine *Krak* is invaluable, as is the newspaper *Gazeta Krakowska*.

Restaurants and Snack Bars

Kraków's Jewish past seems to have rubbed off on some of the better restaurants, with dishes like jellied carp and various versions of *gefillte fisch* appearing on menus. Otherwise it's pretty much a case of traditional Polish fare tempered by splashes of European cuisine—Western and Eastern—plus the new (for Poland) phenomenon of fast food and snacks. Recommendations within the restaurant section are in roughly ascending order of price.

Restaurants

Pani Stasia's, ul. Mikołajska. Small, privately-owned fast-food joint, east of the Rynek. Popular with students and the like, with home cooking including great *pierogi* (cabbage pancakes). It's hidden from the street but lines are conspicuous. Lunchtime only.

Cechowa, ul. Jagiellońska 11. Handy if you're in the university area, with excellent pancakes and a fast lunchtime service.

Hawełka, Rynek Główny 34. Popular, noisy haunt serving *kasha i zrasy* (buckwheat with rolled meat) and traditional fortified *miody pitne* wines.

Myśliwska, pl. Szczepański 7. Good straightforward Polish food.

Kurza Stopka, pl. Wiosny Ludów. Cheap, clean, and has a good reputation among locals.

Balaton, ul. Grodzka 37. Good but cramped Hungarian restaurant; be prepared for a wait, especially in summer.

Polski, ul. Pijarska 17. Cheap and basic hotel restaurant (pork with sauerkraut, etc), close to the city center. Live music in the evenings.

Grodzka, pl. Dominikański 6. Frequented by tourist groups but still worth a visit for dishes like *sztuka mięsa chrzanowy* (beef with horseradish sauce). Live music in the evenings; speedy lunchtime service.

Ermitage, ul. Karmelicka 3. Regular Polish cuisine and dinner-dancing till late.

Dniepr, ul. 18 Stycznia 55. Big modern place near Pewex. Ukrainian specialties—and dancing.

Cyganeria, ul. Szpitalna 38. Art Deco interior, gypsy music and old-style Polish cuisine pull in the city's nouveaux riches.

Staropolska, ul. Sienna 4. Deservedly popular Old Town venue with an emphasis on traditional pork and poultry dishes. Reservations essential in the evening (☎225-821).

Pod Kopcem, al. Waszyngtona. Restaurant of the elegant hotel below the Kościuszko Mound, specializing in fish from the Tatras. Reservations essential in season (☎220-311/ 355).

Cracovia, al. Puszkina 1. A pricey but good hotel restaurant in striking distance of the center, with a resident dance band. Reservations advisable, especially at weekends (☎228-666). Open until midnight.

Pod Róża, ul. Floriańska 14. Another excellent hotel restaurant.

Wierzynek, Rynek Głowny 1. This stately place is Kraków's most famous restaurant. On a good night it's one of the best in the country with specialties like mountain trout and the house *wierzynek* dish. For westerners prices remain very reasonable at around $27 a head; to have any chance of a table reserving is essential (☎221-035). Open till 11pm.

Grand, ul. Sławkowska 19. The city's newest luxury hotel has an excellent, if also rather pricey, restaurant.

Milk Bars and Snacks

Żywiec, ul. Floriańska 19; **Pod Basztą**, ul. Floriańska 55. Two reliable snack bars in a street (just north of the Rynek) that offers plenty of cheap places to eat. **Florian** at no. 7 is distinctly rougher—frequented by hustlers and prostitutes in the early morning for revitalizing vodka and herrings.

Akademicki, ul. Podwale 5. Cheap student milk bar in the university district.

Piccolo Pizza, ul. Szewsk 14a. Useful pizza parlor, again in the university district.

Pod Zegarem, ul. Basztowa 12. Regular lunchtime milk bar on the north edge of the Planty.

PTTK Hostel, ul. Westerplatte 15–16. Self-service restaurant offering large portions of solid, no-nonsense meat and veg. Near the train station.

Grodzki, ul. Grodzka 47. Another self-service place, just south of the Rynek.
Giermek, ul. Karmelicka 57. Similar to the above on a street to the west of the Planty.

Cafés and Bars

The *cukiernia* dotted around the city center provide delicious cakes to most Kraków **cafés**. However, the best of these cake shops—like *Michałek's* on ul. Krupnicza—sell out quickly, so go early in the day. **Bars** are increasingly numerous—and increasingly trendy—but still a bit on the sporadic side; as a last resort, you can always get a drink at one of the larger hotels until around midnight, while the Orbis hotel nightclubs keep going through to around 3 or 4am.

Cafés

Austropol, Rynek Główny (opposite the State Bank). Mouth-watering cakes at this café on the main square, once the center for black-market moneychangers.
Antyczna, Rynek Główny (near the corner with ul. Sławkowska). A cosy haunt with a splendid Art-Nouveau interior; the coffee's better than average too.
Rio, ul. Jana. Stand-up café-bar with excellent coffee, frequented by actors and literary types.
Jama Michalika, ul. Floriańska 45. A pleasant café by day before the evening cabaret (see "Theater and Cabaret," below).
Staromiejska, Mały Rynek. Nice place to sit out and enjoy the atmosphere of this attractive square. The **Pasieka** next door is somewhat grander.
U Zalipianek, ul. Szewska 24. Traditionally decorated, serving a range of herbal teas to a trendy crowd.
Literacka, ul. Pijarska 7. A lovely Art-Deco café with marble tables and fine brews.
Zigi, ul. Grodzka. One of the more stylish stand-up coffee bars that are increasingly coming into fashion in the city. **Pod Pawiem**, on the same street, is a good second if the *Zigi* is full.

Bars

ZPAF Photographers' Club, ul. św. Anny 3. The gallery has a basement dive across the courtyard at the back that's a trendy student hang-out.
Pod Strzelnicą, ul. Królowej Jadwigii 184. Small, private *kneiper*, serving snacks, beer, and vodka.
Feniks, ul. Jama 2. Traditional drinking bar, open till late.
Maxime, ul. Floriańska 32. Old established bar, again open late.

Entertainment and Nightlife

Even if you don't speak the language, some of Kraków's **theatrical events** are worth catching. In addition to consulting *Krak* magazine, look in at the **Pod Baranami** at Rynek Główny 27, which serves as the city's main cultural center and a clearing house for information and tickets (room 37). In summer everything sells out fast. For **rock** or vaguely alternative events, check posters in the university district or consult the *Almatur* office on the Rynek.

Theater and Cabaret

Ever since Stanisław Wyspiański and friends made Kraków the center of the **Młoda Polska** movement at the beginning of this century, many of Poland's greatest actors and directors have been closely identified with the city. Until his death in December 1990 the most influential figure on the scene was avant-garde director **Tadeusz Kantor**, who used the **Cricot 2** theater (ul. Kanonicza 5) as the base for his visionary productions; the company's future is uncertain.

The **Stary Theater** perform at three different sites: a main stage at ul. Jagiellońska 1 (☎228-566), and studio stages in a basement at ul. Sławkowska 14 and Bohaterów Stalingradu 21. They place a strong emphasis on visuals, making the productions (mostly reinterpretations of Polish and foreign classics) unusually accessible; they have built up an international following from appearances at the Edinburgh Festival and other such jamborees.

Of the city's other fifteen or so theaters, the **Teatry im. J. Słowackiego** on plac św. Ducha is the biggest and one of the best known, with a regular diet of classical Polish drama and ballet, plus occasional opera. Check too, for the latest productions at places like the **Miniatura** (pl. św. Ducha), the **STU** (al. Krasińskiego 18) and the **Bagatela** (ul. Karmelicka 6). **Ewa Demarczyk**, "the Polish Edith Piaf," has her own theater at ul. Floriańska 55.

Cabaret is also an established feature of Kraków. Two of the best-known venues are the **Jama Michalika** café on ul. Floriańska (an old Młoda Polska haunt), and the **Teatr Satyry**, beneath the town hall tower on the Rynek. The **Pod Baranami** (see above) also has a cabaret venue—considered the best in Poland—in its cellar.

Classical Music

For classical concerts, the **Filharmonia Szymanowskiego**, ul. Zwierzyniecka 1, is home of the Kraków Philharmonic, one of Poland's most highly regarded orchestras (box office 9am–noon & 5–7pm).

Jazz and Student Clubs

Pod Jaszczurami, Rynek Główny 7/8, is a **jazz** club with occasional **discos**, which in the summer months are usually completely packed out with a combination of locals and foreign students. Other lively **student clubs** include the *Karlik*, ul. Reymonta 17, and the *Forum*, ul. Mikołajska 2, and the *Rotunda* out at Błonia.

FESTIVALS

June is the busiest month for festivities, with three major events: the **Kraków Days** (a showcase for a range of concerts, plays, and other performances), the **Folk Art Fair**, and the **Lajkonik Pageant**. The last, based on a story about a raftsman who defeated the Tartars and made off with the khan's clothes, features a brightly dressed Tartar figure leading a procession from the Salwator church in the western district of Zwierzyniec to the Rynek. Over the **Christmas** period, a Kraków specialty is the *szopki* Nativity scene; examples are displayed in the Rynek with a prize for the best new design. The tradition goes back a long way, and you can see some fourteenth-century *szopki* year-round in St Andrew's church.

On the cultural front, there are **organ concerts** at Tyniec (see "The Outskirts") from June to August, and at various of the city's churches in April. The **Graphic Art Festival**, held from May to September in even-numbered years, is a crowd-puller, too. And finally, on a somewhat smaller scale, there's an annual **International Short Film Festival** (May–June).

Listings

Airlines *LOT*, Ul. Basztowa 15 (☎225-076/227-078); *Pan Am*, ul. Szpitalna 36 (☎226-105).

Airport information ☎116-700.

Bus tickets are available in advance from Orbis at ul. św. Marka 25. Buying international tickets in summer can involve hours or even days of waiting.

Car rental Try the agency at ul. Koniewa 9 (☎371-120).

Car repairs *Polmozbyt* offices are at al. Pokoju 61 (Mon–Fri 6am–10pm, Sat & Sun 10am–6pm; ☎480-034), on ul. Kawiory (daily 7am–10pm; ☎375-575) and al. 29 Listopada 90 (daily 6am–10pm; ☎116-044). There are now plenty of private places too—ask at the tourist offices, hotels, cafés, or the big garages themselves.

Consulates *France*, ul. Stolarska 15 (☎223-390); *USSR*, ul. Westerplatte 11 (☎222-647); *USA*, ul. Stolarska 9 (☎221-400).

Galleries Among the numerous Stare Miasto galleries, you might check out: *Sztuka Polska*, ul. Floriańska 34; *Krzysztofory*, ul. Szczepańska 2; *Desa*, ul. Św. Jana 3; and the exhibitions in the Pod Baranami on the Rynek.

Gas stations 24-hr stations are to be found on ul. Wielicka; ul. Podgórska; ul. Gagarina; ul. Kamienna; ul. Powst. Wielkopolskich os. Strusia; and ul. Zakopiańska.

Post office Main office is at ul. Wielopole 2, including poste restante and 24-hr phone services.

Soccer Wisła Kraków is one of the oldest clubs in the country, six times league champions, but these days in and out of the first division. It plays out at the Wisła stadium, ul. Reymonta, in the western Czarna Wieś district (bus #144 passes close by).

Swimming pool The most central one is at the *Hotel Cracovia*, al. 3 Maja; non-residents can get in for a small fee.

Train tickets are available from the Orbis office at Rynek Główny 41 and in the train station (from the ticket hall over the track from the main hall). International tickets can take a very long time to obtain.

MAŁOPOLSKA

The name **Małopolska**—literally "Little Poland"—in fact applies to a large swathe of the country, for the most part a rolling landscape of traditionally cultivated fields and quiet villages. It is an ancient region, forming with Wielkopolska the early medieval Polish state, though its geographical divisions, particularly from neighboring Silesia, are a bit nebulous. The bulk of Małopolska proper sits north of Kraków, bounded by the Świętokrzskie mountains to the north and the broad range of hills stretching down from Częstochowa to Kraków—the so-called Eagles' Nests trail—to the west.

    Kielce, a large industrial center and the regional capital, provides a good stepping-off point for forays into the **Świętokrzyskie Mountains**, really no more than high hills but enjoyable walking territory. **Częstochowa**, the only other city of the region, is famous as the home of the Black Madonna, which draws huge crowds for the major religious festivals and annual summer pilgrimages from all over the country. Pope John Paul II is a native of the region, too, and his birthplace at **Wadowice** has become something of a national shrine, while the Catholic trail continues to the west at **Kalwaria Zebrzydowska**, another pilgrimage site.

    West of Kraków at **Oświęcim** is the **Auschwitz-Birkenau** concentration camp, preserved more or less as the Nazis left it.

Oświęcim: Auschwitz-Birkenau

When you go in there's a sign in five languages that says, 'There were four million'.

I broke down about halfway round Auschwitz, walking away from the wall against which 20,000 people were shot. There's a shrine there now; schoolgirls were laying flowers and lighting candles.

But it wasn't that particular detail that got to me. And it wasn't the stark physical evidence in earlier blocks of the conditions in which people had lived, sleeping seven or nine together on straw in three-high tiers the size of double beds.

It wasn't the enormous glass-fronted displays in which, on angled boards sometimes dozens of feet long, lay great piles of wretchedly battered old boots, or children's shoes. It wasn't the bank of suitcases, their owners' names clumsily written on them in faded paint, or the heaps of broken spectacles, of shaving brushes and hairbrushes.

It wasn't the case the length of a barrack room in the block whose subject was the 'Exploitation of Corpses', the case filled with a bank of human hair, or the small case to one side of that, showing the tailor's lining that was made from it.

It wasn't the relentless documentary evidence, the methodical, systematic, compulsive bureaucracy of mass murder.

And it wasn't the block beside the yard in which the shrine now stands, in whose basement are the 'standing cells' used to punish prisoners, measuring ninety by ninety centimeters. People were wedged together into these bare brick cubicles, and left to starve or suffocate pinned helplessly upright. In other cells in the same basement, the first experiments with Zyklon B as a means of mass extermination were conducted.

It was all these things cumulatively crushing you, a seeping of evil from every wall and corner of the place, from every brick of every block, until you reach your limit and it overwhelms you. For a short while I found myself crying, leaning against the wire. Like they tell you—the birds don't sing.

In paintings and drawings by Auschwitz inmates, the guards are shown leering and jeering at the suffering of their victims—enjoying themselves.

On the morning of the October day that England qualified for Italia '90 [the World Cup soccer tournament], a small group of Englishmen were seen by some of the sports press at Auschwitz, laughing and posing as they took pictures of each other—doing the Nazi salute.

From Pete Davies's *All Played Out* (Heinemann, 1990).

Seventy kilometers west of Kraków, **OŚWIĘCIM** would in normal circumstances be a nondescript industrial town—a place to send visitors on their way through without a moment's thought. The circumstances, however, are anything but normal here. In 1940 Oświęcim, then an insignificant rural town, well away from prying eyes in the border region between Silesia and Małopolska, became the site of the Oświęcim-Brzezinka concentration camp, better known by its German name of **Auschwitz-Birkenau**. Of the many concentration camps built by the Nazis in Poland and the other occupied countries during World War II, this was the largest and most horrific: between the camp's construction and its liberation in 1945 something approaching four million people—two and a half million of them Jews—were imprisoned and systematically murdered.

The physical scale of the Auschwitz-Birkenau camp is a shock in itself. Most visitors see only the Auschwitz section, but this was just one component in a vast complex designed for slave labor and extermination, complete with its own rail-road network and factories. It is only by visiting Birkenau, 2km down the road from Auschwitz, that you begin to grasp the enormity of the Nazi death machine.

Practicalities

To get to Auschwitz-Birkenau from Kraków, you can take either of the regular bus or train services to Oświęcim station, an hour and a half's journey. From there it's a short bus ride to the gates of Auschwitz; there's no bus service to Birkenau, but taxis are available. Rather grotesquely, there's a hotel and a large cafeteria inside the Auschwitz camp.

Auschwitz-Birkenau is unfathomably shocking. If you want all the specifics on the camp, you can pick up a detailed guidebook (in English and other languages) with maps, photos, and an horrendous array of statistics. Alternatively, you can join a guided group, often led by former inmates. It's perhaps best to go with friends rather than alone—mutual support and emotional back-up is extremely helpful. Children under thirteen are not admitted to Auschwitz.

POLES, JEWS, AND THE CONCENTRATION CAMPS

The general issue of Polish-Jewish relations, both historical and current, is an emotive and sensitive area, and what follows can be no more than a brief sketch of its contours.

The immediate context for the glaring omission of the Jewish perspective in the official Polish guidebooks and tours of the concentration camps is straightforwardly political. For Poland's postwar communist regime, like those in other East European countries, the horrors of World War II were a constant and central reference point. Following the official Soviet line, the emphasis was on the war as an anti-fascist struggle, in which good (Communism and the Soviet Union) had finally triumphed over evil (Fascism and Nazi Germany).

This interpretation provided an important legitimizing prop for the new regimes: the Soviet Union, aided by loyal national communists, were the people who had liberated Europe from Hitler, and as inheritors of their anti-fascist mantle the newly installed communist governments were heirs to all that was noble and good. In this schematic view of the war there was no room for the racial aspects of Nazi ideology. People were massacred in the camps because fascists were butchers, not because the victims were Jews or Poles or Gypsies. Hence the camps were opened up first and foremost as political monuments to the victims of fascism rather than to the Holocaust.

The broader issue is that of anti-Semitism, a prejudice that many commentators suggest is as current now as it ever has been. The debate was given a recent focus by Claude Lanzemann's film documentary *Shoah* (1985), a relentless and shocking exploration of the Holocaust; shown only in edited form on Polish television, it was denounced by press and politicians—including President Jaruzelski—as "anti-Polish." It is not hard to see why the film caused a stir. Lanzemann's interviews with Polish peasants in the Auschwitz region, for example, revealed deep levels of ignorance and hostility—displaying a medieval Catholic primitivism, they were heard to decry the Jews as Christ-killers who deserved their annihilation. The charge that hurt most was the implication that the Polish nation actively aided and abetted in the Nazi's destruction of the Jews and that the location of the death camps inside Poland was no mere geographical coincidence.

Auschwitz

Most of the Auschwitz camp buildings, the barbed-wire fences, watch towers, and the entrance gate inscribed "Arbeit Macht Frei" (Work Makes Free) have been preserved as the **Museum of Martyrdom** (daily Jan, Feb & late Dec 8am–3pm; March & Nov–Dec 15 8am–4pm; April & Oct 8am–5pm; May–Sept 8am–6pm).

The **movie theater** is a sobering starting point. The film was taken by the Soviet troops who liberated the camp in May 1945—harrowing images of the survivors and the dead confirming what really happened. A board outside lists timings for showings in different languages. The bulk of the **camp** consists of the prison cell blocks, the first section being given over to "exhibits" found in the camp after liberation. Despite last-minute destruction of many of the **store-houses** (there were 35 of them in all) used for the possessions of murdered inmates there are rooms full of clothes and suitcases, toothbrushes, dentures, glasses, a huge collection of shoes, and a mound of women's hair—154,322 pounds of it. It's difficult to relate to the scale of what's shown.

Poles react strongly to such charges. How, they argue, were Poles supposed to help Jews when such assistance was made a capital offence? And how were farmers supposed to have resisted the acquisition of land for the camps? They point out that for several centuries Poland was home to—and in some senses a refuge for—Europe's largest Jewish community. While other European nations were persecuting and expelling their Jewish populations, the Polish-Lithuanian Commonwealth allowed its Jews unrivaled rights and political status. In everything from architecture and language to humor and cooking, Polish and Jewish cultures are deeply intertwined.

The problem is that there are two victim nations demanding recognition: Poles and Jews. Polish indignation over charges of wartime anti-Semitism is certainly guilt-tinged—for every Pole who assisted Jews during the war there were plenty who made a living out of spotting and denouncing them—but it is also the overreaction of the fellow-sufferer. And in this context, as historian Norman Davies put it, debating who suffered most is the meanest of controversies.

However, anti-Semitism has been a recurrent postwar issue. Many Jews who had survived the war left for Israel in 1968, following a communist government campaign against Jewish student leaders. And the early years of Solidarity-led rule have been equally blemished. Both the 1989 parliamentary election campaign and the 1990 presidential campaign were marked by startlingly chauvinistic outbursts, most notably Lech Wałęsa's populist insistence that he's a "true Pole" and his remarks that some politicians should stop "hiding behind Polish names"—a presumed reference to the Jewish origins of certain of his Solidarity rivals, such as Adam Michnik and Bronesław Geremek. In the summer of 1989, too, a furious dispute arose over a convent set up by Catholic nuns inside the Auschwitz camp perimeter. The nuns claimed they simply wanted to establish a place of prayer for the dead but many Jews were incensed by what they saw as a misguided attempt to "baptise" the Holocaust. Cardinal Glemp in turn suggested that a world Jewish media conspiracy was being directed against the Church, a remark which provoked several noted Catholic intellectuals to publicly censure him. Wałęsa was also much criticized within Poland over his "Polish names" comments. But taken together, the incidents hint at a nasty undercurrent to Polish politics, and it's unnerving that anti-Semitism should remain a useful political tool in a country where virtually no Jews remain.

Block 11, farther on, is where the first experiments with Zyklon B gas were carried out on Soviet POWs and other inmates in 1941. And between two of the blocks stands the flower-strewn **Death Wall**, where thousands of prisoners were summarily executed with a bullet in the back of the head. As at the other concentration camps, the Auschwitz victims included people from all over Europe—over twenty nationalities in all. Many of the camp barracks are given over to **national memorials**, moving testimonies to the sufferings of inmates of the different countries—Poles, Russians, Czechs, Slovaks, Norwegians, Turks, French, Italians . . ..

Another barrack is labeled simply **"Jews."** Normally ignored by the official guided tours, its atmosphere is of quiet reverence, in which the evils of Auschwitz are felt and remembered rather than detailed or observed. On the second floor there's a section devoted to Jewish resistance both inside and outside the camp, some of which was organized in tandem with the Polish AK (*Armia Krajowa*; Home Army), some entirely autonomously. Despite the strength and power of this memorial, it's disconcerting to find it lumped with the others, as if Jews were just another "nationality" among many to suffer at the hands of the Nazis. This relates to a wider issue, the tendency in Auschwitz, as in the other death camps, to downplay the centrality of Jews in the murderous Nazi ideology. Thus the official Auschwitz guidebook hardly uses the words "Jew" or "Holocaust"—nor "Romany" or "Homosexual," to name two other persecuted groups—opting instead for the Soviet "anti-fascist" interpretation of the camps (see box on previous page).

The prison blocks terminate by the **gas chambers** and the ovens where the bodies were incinerated. "No more poetry after Auschwitz," in the words of the German philosopher Theodor Adorno.

Birkenau

The **Birkenau camp** (same hours) is much less visited than Auschwitz, though it was here that the majority of captives lived and died. Endless rows of symmetrical barracks stretch into the distance, where hundreds of thousands of people lived in appalling conditions. Not that most prisoners lived long. Killing was the main goal of Birkenau, most of it carried out in the huge **gas chambers** at the back of the camp, damaged but not destroyed by the fleeing Nazis in 1945. At the height of the killing, this clinically conceived machinery of destruction gassed and cremated 60,000 people a day.

Most of the victims arrived in closed **trains**—cattle cars mostly—to be driven directly from the railroad ramp into the gas chambers. Railroad line, ramp, sidings—they are all still there, just as the Nazis abandoned them. In the dark, creaking huts the pitiful bare bunks would have had six or more shivering bodies crammed into each level: wander around the barracks and you soon begin to imagine the terror and degradation of the place. A monument to the dead, inscribed in ten languages, stares out over the camp from between the chambers.

Kalwaria Zebrzydowska and Wadowice

Southwest of Kraków are two places of great religious significance to Poles: **Kalwaria Zebrzydowska**, a center of pilgrimage second only to Częstochowa, and **Wadowice**, birthplace of a certain Karol Wojtyła. From Kraków, buses are straightforward to either destination; local trains are slower.

Kalwaria Zebrzydowska

The object of pilgrims' devotions is perched on the hill overlooking **KALWARIA ZEBRZYDOWSKA**: a Bernardine church and Via Dolorosa built by the Zebrzydowski family in the early seventeenth century, following a vision of three crosses here on the family estate. Miracles followed.

The Zebrzydowskis sent an envoy to Jerusalem for drawings and models of the holy places and, on his return, began building a sequence of **chapels** across the nearby hills, many of them modeled on buildings in the city. The main **church** is a familiar Baroque effusion, with a silver-plated Italian figure of the Virgin standing over the high altar.

The site always has its crowds, but they are at their most intense during August, the traditional time of pilgrimage throughout the country, and at Easter, when the Passion Plays are performed here. The heady atmosphere of collective catharsis accompanying these events offers an insight into the inner workings of Polish Catholicism; to anyone from more sober northern climes the realism (figures are tied on crosses, while spectators are dressed as Romans) can all be very perplexing, even frightening. As the *Misteria* photo album available in many bookshops throughout the country reminds you, however, gruesome enactments of the Crucifixion are a feature of peasant Catholic festivals throughout Europe.

Wadowice

Fourteen kilometers farther down the road is the little town of **WADOWICE**, whose rural obscurity was shattered by the election of local boy Karol Wojtyła to the papacy in October 1978. Almost instantly the town became a place of pilgrimage, with the souvenir industry quick to seize the opportunities.

The **pope's birthplace** at ul. Kościelna 7, off the market square, has been turned into a shrine-like museum, while the nearby **parish church** displays the record of its most famous baptism, in 1920. For the truly devout, the local **soccer field**—where young Karol kept goal with some success—could be an additional point of pilgrimage.

The Ojców Valley and the Eagles' Nests

To the northwest of Kraków, the **Ojców Valley** offers an easy respite from the pollution of the city. This deep limestone gorge of the Prądnik River has a unique microclimate and astonishingly rich variety of plants and wildlife, virtually all of it now protected by the **Ojców National Park**. It's a beautiful area for a day's trekking, particularly in September and October, when the rich colors of the Polish autumn are at their finest.

The valley also gives access to the most southerly of the **castles** built by King Kazimierz to defend the southwestern reaches of the country from the Bohemian rulers of Silesia. Known as the **Eagles' Nest Trail**, these fortresses are strung along the hilly ridge extending westwards from Ojców towards Częstochowa.

Ojców: the Castle and Łokieta's Cave

To get to the gorge, take a bus (direction Olkusz) to **OJCÓW**, poised above the valley 25km from Kraków. Unremarkable in itself, the village is capped by a fine, ruined **castle**, the southern extremity of the **Eagles' Nest Trail**; it's an evocative place in the twilight hours, circled by squadrons of bats. There's not much of the castle left, though a Gothic tower houses a small **museum** devoted to the valley's flora and fauna (April 15–Oct 31 Tues–Sun 10am–5pm). Basic accommodation is provided by the *Hotel Zosia* (☎8).

From the village, you can walk down to the valley along marked trails from the bus stop. A notable feature of the gorge is its strange assortment of **caves** and other geological formations, in several of which traces of prehistoric human habitation have been discovered. The best-known is **Łokieta's Cave** (daily 8am–5pm), the largest of a sequence of chambers burrowing into the cliffs outside Ojców. According to legend it was here that King Władysław the Short was hidden and protected by loyal local peasants following King Wenceslas of Bohemia's invasion in the early fourteenth century.

Halfway down the valley is the curious spectacle of a **wooden church** straddling the river on brick piles. This odd site neatly circumvented a nineteenth-century czarist edict forbidding religious structures to be built "on solid ground," part of a strategy to subdue the intransigently nationalist Catholic Church.

Pieskowa Skała

At **PIESKOWA SKAŁA**, 9km north of Ojców (45min by bus from Kraków), there's a **castle** in rather better shape, the fourteenth-century original having been rebuilt in the 1580s as an elegant Renaissance residence. As in Wawel castle, the most impressive period feature is the delicately arcaded castle courtyard, a photogenic construction that's a regular feature in the travel brochures. The castle **museum** (Tues–Sun 10am–3:30pm) is divided into two main exhibitions: one covering the history of the building, the other illustrating the development of European art from the Middle Ages to the nineteenth century, drawing extensively on the Wawel National Museum's collection, period furniture included. To finish off a visit, head for the excellent **restaurant** at the top of one of the fortified towers. In summer they put tables out on the roof terrace, where you can enjoy a fine view over the valley, and—if they've got it—some mouth-watering local trout.

The End of the Trail

The remaining castles of the Eagles' Nest Trail are very ruined, but they're as dramatic and photogenic as their Spanish counterparts, seeming to spring straight out of the Jurassic rock formations. You really need your own vehicle to follow most of the route from here; although all castles are accessible by bus, this entails long waits and frequent detours, and it's unlikely you'd be able to find anywhere to stay. However, the most impressive of these castles are also the easiest to get to. **OGRODZIENIEC**, some 35km north of Pieskowa Skała on the main road between OLKUSZ (served by bus from Kraków) and ZAWIERCIE, preserves the substantial shell of a frontier fortress which was partly remodeled as a palace during the Renaissance.

Even more accessible is **OLSZTYN**, just a few kilometers outside the city boundaries of Częstochowa, to which it's linked by several buses an hour. The castle here is the one generally used to promote the route on tourist brochures and posters. Unusually, it's laid out in two parts, with a round watchtower crowning one outcrop of rock, and a keep on top of another; from each there's a superb view over the whole upland region.

Note that if you're traveling between Ogrodzieniec and Olsztyn by car or bike, there are other castles to see at MIRÓW, BOBOLICE, and OSTRĘŻNIK.

Częstochowa

Seen from a distance, **CZĘSTOCHOWA** shows the country at its absolute worst. Its steelworks and textile factories unleash a noxious cocktail of multicolored fumes, while the city center is ringed by jerry-built concrete projects thrown up to accommodate a fast-growing population, currently numbering over 250,000. Yet all this is overshadowed by the city's status, courtesy of the **monastery of Jasna Góra** (Bright Mountain), as one of the world's greatest places of pilgrimage. Its famous **icon of The Black Madonna**, which has drawn the faithful here over the past six centuries, is an inescapable image: reproductions of it can be seen everywhere in Poland, with at least one adorning almost every church in the country.

The special position that Jasna Góra and its icon hold in the hearts and minds of the majority of Poles is due to a rich web of history and myth. It's not a place you can react to dispassionately, but even if you find its heart-on-sleeve fervor overbearing, an awareness of the background to it will at least make it comprehensible. Central to this is the tenuous position Poland has held on the map of Europe; at various times the Swedes, the Russians, and the Germans have sought to annihilate it as a nation. Each of these traditional and non-Catholic enemies has laid siege to Jasna Góra, yet failed to destroy it, so adding to the icon's reputation as a miracle-worker—and the guarantor of Poland's very existence.

A Brief History

The hill known as Jasna Góra was probably used as part of the same defensive system as the castles along the Eagles' Nest Trail, but in the fourteenth century it came under the control of **Ladislaus II**, whose main possession was the independent duchy of Opole on the other side of the Silesian frontier. In 1382 he founded the monastery here, donating the miraculous icon a couple of years later. Ladislaus spent his final years imprisoned in his own castle, having fallen into disgrace for trying to prevent the union with Lithuania. Nevertheless, the monastery quickly attracted pilgrims from a host of nations and was granted the special protection of the Jagiellonian and Waza dynasties, though it was not until the fifteenth century that a shrine of stone and brick was built.

In the first half of the seventeenth century the monastery was enclosed by a modern **fortification system** as a bulwark of Poland's frontiers—and its Catholic faith—at a time of Europe-wide political and religious conflicts. Its worth was proved in the six-week-long **siege of 1655** by the Swedes, who failed to capture it in spite of having superior weapons and almost 4000 troops ranged against just 250 defenders. This sparked off an amazing national fightback against the enemy, who had occupied the rest of the country against little resistance, and ushered in Poland's short period as a European power of the first rank.

In 1717 the Black Madonna was crowned **Queen of Poland** in an attempt by the clergy to whip up patriotism and fill the political void created by the Russian-sponsored "Silent Sejm," which had reduced the nation to a puppet state. Jasna Góra was the scene of another heroic defense in 1770, when it was held by the Confederates of Bar against greater Russian forces, and retained by them until after the formal partitioning of Poland two years later. Częstochowa was initially annexed by Prussia, but after a few years as part of Napoleon's Duchy of Warsaw, it served as a frontier fortress of the Russian empire for more than a century. It was incorporated into the new Polish state after World War I, when the icon's royal title was reaffirmed.

In 1945, Soviet troops defused bombs left by the retreating Nazis which might finally have destroyed the monastery. They later had cause to regret their actions: while Częstochowa itself developed into a model communist industrialized city, Jasna Góra became a major **focus of opposition** to the communist regime. The Church skillfully promoted the pilgrimage as a display of patriotism and passive resistance, a campaign which received a huge boost in 1978 with the election of **Karol Wojtyła**—Archbishop of Kraków and a central figure in its conception—as Pope John Paul II. His devotion to this shrine ensured worldwide media attention for Poland's plight, and one consequence of the publicity he created is that praying at Jasna Góra has become an essential photo-opportunity for the new breed of democratic politicians.

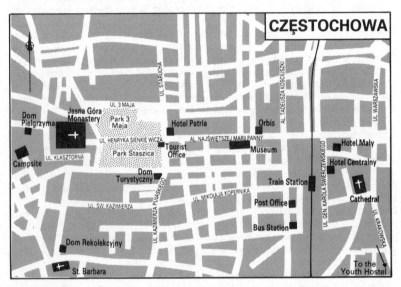

Jasna Góra

A dead-straight, three-kilometer-long boulevard, aleja Najświętszej Marii Panny (abbreviated as al. NMP), cuts through the heart of Częstochowa, terminating at the foot of **Jasna Góra**. On most days, ascending the hill is no different from taking a walk in any other public park, but the huge podium for open-air Masses gives a clue as to the atmosphere on the major **Marian festivals**—May 3, August 15, August 26, September 8 and December 8—when up to a million pilgrims converge here, often in colorful traditional dress. Many come on foot: every year, for example, tens of thousands make the nine-day walk from Warsaw to celebrate the Feast of the Assumption.

Although there's little of the souvenir-peddling tackiness characteristic of Europe's other leading Marian shrines, Jasna Góra could hardly be called beautiful: its architecture is generally austere, while the defensive walls give the hill something of a fortress-like feel. Entry is still via four successive **gateways**, each one of which presented a formidable obstacle to any attacker.

The best way to begin an exploration is by ascending the 100-meter-high **tower** (Mon–Sat 8am–4pm, Sun 8am–10:30am & 1–5pm), a pastiche of its eighteenth-century predecessor, which was destroyed in one of the many fires which have plagued the monastery. An earlier victim was the monastic **Church**, which has been transformed from a Gothic hall into a restrained Baroque basilica. Not that it's without its exuberant features, notably the colossal high altar in honor of the Virgin, and the two sumptuous family chapels off the southern aisle, which parody and update their royal counterparts in the Wawel Cathedral in Kraków.

Inevitably, the **Chapel of the Blessed Virgin**, a separate church in its own right, is the centerpiece of the monastery. It's also the only part to retain much of the original Gothic architecture, though its walls are so encrusted with votive offerings that this is no longer obvious. Masses are said here almost constantly and you'll have to come very early or very late if you want much of a view of the **Black Madonna** (see box below). Much of the time, the icon is invisible behind a screen, each raising and lowering of which is accompanied by a solemn fanfare from a brass band hidden from the eyes of the believers. Even when **on view** (normally 6am–noon, 3:30–4:40pm, 7–7:45pm & 9–9:10pm) you don't get to see very much of the picture itself, as the figures of the Madonna and Child are almost always decked out in crowns and robes made of diamonds and rubies. For an idea of the impassioned reverence it inspires, on the other hand, try to coincide your visit with one of the frequent pilgrim groups, who piously hobble around the image on bended knee.

THE BLACK MADONNA

According to tradition, **The Black Madonna** was painted from life by **Saint Luke** on a beam from the Holy Family's house in Nazareth. This explanation is accepted without question by most believers, though the official view is kept deliberately ambiguous. Scientific tests have proved the icon cannot have been executed before the sixth century and it may even have been quite new at the time of its arrival at the monastery. Probably Italian in origin, it's a fine example of the hierarchical **Byzantine** style, which hardly changed or developed down the centuries. Incidentally, the "black" refers to the heavy shading characteristic of this style, subsequently darkened by age and exposure to incense.

What can be seen today may well only be a copy made following the picture's first great "miracle" in 1430, on the occasion of its theft. According to the official line, this was the work of followers of the Czech reformer Jan Hus, but it's more likely that political opponents of the monastery's protector, King Władysław Jagiełło, were responsible. The **legend** maintains that the picture increased in weight so much that the thieves were unable to carry it. In frustration, they slashed the Virgin's face, which immediately started shedding blood. The icon was taken to Kraków to be restored, though its condition may have precluded this. When it reappeared it had a gash (still visible), in confirmation of the truth of the miracle.

Sceptics have pointed out that during the Swedish siege, usually cited as the supreme example of The Black Madonna's miracle-working powers, the icon had been moved to neutral Silesia for safekeeping. Yet such was its hold over the Polish imagination that its future seemed to occasion more anguished discussion at the time of the Partitions than any other topic. In the present day, the **pope's devotion to the image** has also been a mixed blessing. It may have helped to focus the world's attention on Poland, but such emphasis on unreformed and nationalistic Catholicism has also been the main reason why this charismatic religious leader has so clearly failed—in circumstances which have never been so favorable—to make a significant breakthrough towards Christian unity.

To the north of the chapel, a monumental stairway leads to the **Knights' Hall**, the principal reception room, adorned with flags and paintings illustrating the history of the monastery. There are other opulent Baroque interiors, notably the **refectory**, whose vault is a real tour de force, and the **library**. However, you'll have to inquire at the information office by the main gateway for permission to see them, as they are normally closed to the public.

Jasna Góra's treasures are kept in three separate buildings. The most valuable liturgical items can be seen in the **Treasury** above the sacristy, entered from the southeastern corner of the ramparts (summer Mon–Sat 9am–11:30am & 3:30–5:30pm, Sun 8am–1pm & 3–5:30pm; winter Mon–Sat 9am–10:30am & 3:30–4:30pm, Sun 9am–12:30pm & 3:30–5pm). There's usually a long line for entry, so be there well before it opens.

At the southwestern end of the monastery is the **Arsenal** (summer Mon–Sat 9am–noon & 2–6pm, Sun 9am–noon & 2–6pm; closes 5pm in winter), devoted to the military history of the fortress, and containing a superb array of weapons, including Turkish war loot donated by King Jan Sobieski. Alongside is the **600th Anniversary Museum** (daily 11am–4:30pm), which tells the monastery's story from a religious standpoint. Exhibits include the seventeenth-century backing of The Black Madonna, which illustrates the history of the picture, and votive offerings from famous Poles, prominent among which is Lech Wałęsa's 1983 Nobel Peace Prize.

Around Town

Other than Jasna Góra, Częstochowa has very few sights, although the broad tree-lined boulevards at least give the heart of the city an agreeably spacious, almost Parisian feel. On pl. Biegańskiego, just off al. NMP, is the **District Museum** (Tues & Thurs–Sat 9am–3pm, Wed noon–6pm, Sun 10am–3pm), which has a decent archaeology section plus the usual local history displays. If you want to continue with the ecclesiastical theme, visit the small Baroque church of **St Barbara** to the south of Jasna Góra, allegedly the place where The Black Madonna was slashed. At the opposite end of town, close to the train station, is the massive neo-Gothic **Cathedral**, remarkable solely for its size.

Near the suburban station of Raków, reached by any southbound tram, is an important **Archaeology Reserve** (Wed noon–6pm, Thurs & Fri 9am–3pm, Sat 9am–2pm, Sun 10am–3pm), with 21 excavated graves from the Lusatian culture of the sixth and seventh centuries BC; it's seemingly subject to random closures.

The Częstochowa telephone code is ☎034.

Practicalities

The **Orbis** office is at al. NMP 40/42 (☎479-87), while **Almatur** is at ul. Zawadzkiego 29 (☎541-06). There's also a well-stocked **tourist information center** in the underground passageway at the intersection of al. NMP and ul. Pułaskiego (☎413-60).

The regular pilgrim influxes mean that you might have problems finding somewhere to stay: consider reserving in advance, or visiting on a day trip from Kraków or Opole. Normally, the likeliest **hotel** bets are the *Centralny* at ul. Świerczewskiego 9 (☎440-76) and *Mały* at ul. Katedralna 18 (☎433-91); they are both by the train station, but the latter is much the better bargain. Just below Jasna Góra is a luxurious Orbis hotel, *Patria*, ul. Starucha 2 (☎470-01). There are also three **motels** on the outskirts—*Orbis*, al. Wojska Polskiego 287 (☎556-07), *PZMot*, al. Wojska Polskiego 58 (☎522-36), and *Turysta*, ul. Makuszyńskiego 58 (☎522-36).

As you'd expect, there's a fair choice of **hostel** accommodation, including two geared specifically to pilgrims—*Dom Pielgrzyma* beside the parking lot on the west side of the monastery and *Dom Rekolekcyjny* south of the hill at ul. św. Barbary 43. There's also a *Dom Wychieczkowe* conveniently sited at ul. Pułaskiego 4, but the **youth hostel** is very much a last resort, being way to the southeast of the station, at the opposite end of town from Jasna Góra, at ul. Wacławy Marek 12 (☎312-96). However, there's a **campground** (☎326-28), with a few chalets, ideally placed directly opposite the *Dom Pielgrzyna*.

Częstochowa is very poorly off for places to **eat** and **drink**. Top choice is the *Hotel Patria*; otherwise, there's the usual cluster of snack bars and restaurants around the station, best of which is *Polonia*. For a lively **café**, try *Adria*, about twenty minutes' walk north of the center at al. Zawadzkiego 58.

Kielce and Northern Małopolska

Most people see nothing more of the northern reaches of Małopolska than the glimpses snatched from the window of a Warsaw to Kraków express—a pity, because the gentle hills, lush valleys, strip-fields, and tatty villages that characterise the region are quintessential rural Poland. The main town is **Kielce**, roughly halfway between Warsaw and Kraków, but the main attraction for visitors lies in rambling about in the **Świętokrzyskie Mountains**—in reality more of a hillwalkers' range.

Kielce

KIELCE is nothing much to look at, having undergone the standard postwar development, but has a relaxed, down-at-heel, rural atmosphere and a pleasant main square, **plac Partyzantów**, lined by crumbling eighteenth- and nineteenth-century mansions. One of these (no. 3/5) houses a **regional museum** (Tues–Sun 10am–4pm), which has good local ethnography and history sections, but is silent on the 1946 pogrom for which Kielce is notorious: the mob massacre of Jews followed a rumor about the murder of a Christian child.

Just south on another square you'll find the **Cathedral**—Romanesque features lost in later reconstruction—and the early Baroque **palace** built for the bishops of Kraków, the town's owners in the mid-seventeenth century. Now a **Museum of Polish Art** (Tues–Sat 10am–4pm), the building's outstanding features are its period interiors, designed in the 1640s. For major **religious festivals** the square east of the cathedral is packed with smartly dressed locals, many in regional folk costume, for the solemn procession round the square.

The town's **train and bus stations** are close by each other on the west side of town, a ten-minute walk down ul. Sienkiewicza into the town center. The **PTTK** offices, upstairs at ul. Sienkiewicza 34, provide local information—though maps of the town are currently unavailable. For **accommodation**, the dingy *Hotel Centralny* (☎420-41), opposite the train station, is cheap and reasonably clean, though the same can't be said for its restaurant, which seems to be the favored haunt of just about the entire local contingent of drunks and prostitutes. The central *Hotel Bristol*, ul. Sienkiewicza 21(☎469-65), is similarly priced but nicer, with a smaller but better restaurant. The reception at the *Bristol* can also arrange **private rooms**, and there is an all-year **youth hostel** at ul. Szymanowskiego 5 (☎237-35).

The Świętokrzyskie

In this low-lying region, the **Świętokrzyskie Mountains** stand out more than their height—600m maximum—would suggest. Running east from Kielce, their long ridges and valleys, interspersed with isolated villages, are a popular and rugged hiking territory. During World War II the area was a center of armed resistance to the Nazis; a grim, essentially factual account of life in the resistance here appears in Primo Levi's *If Not Now, When?*, in which he refers to the area as the Holy Cross Mountains, a literal translation of their name.

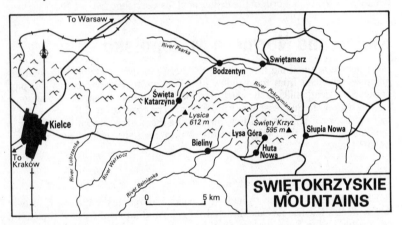

The Łyso Góry

The fifteen-kilometer-long **Łyso Góry** range is the most popular destination in the Świętokrzyskie. The place to head for is SWIĘTY KRZYŻ, one hour by bus from the main Kielce station (five departures daily, from 7am). The journey takes you along the edge of the range and eventually up a lovely mountainside road to the edge of the Świętokrzyskie National Park, stopping at a parking lot near Łysa Gora (Bald Mountain; 595m); across the way is the *Jodłowy Dwór*, an ugly **hotel** (☎107-28) with a good restaurant.

The bus continues through the park—the only vehicle allowed to do so—but you're better off walking from here, through the protected woodland habitat of a range of birds and animals, including a colony of eagles. The path leads to a clearing—from where you can pick up the road again—then past a huge TV tower to the **Święty Krzyż abbey**, established up here by Italian Benedictines in the early twelfth century. The buildings have changed beyond recognition, about the only remnant of the original foundation being the abbey church's Romanesque doorway. The isolated mountain site, however, maintains an ancient feel: the abbey itself replaced an earlier pagan temple, traces of which were discovered nearby some years ago. On a more somber note, the abbey buildings were turned into a prison following the enforced dissolution of the Benedictine order in 1825; it remained one right up to 1945, having been used by the Nazis as a concentration camp for Soviet POWs. Just how appalling conditions were then is indicated by photographs in the old monastery building of camp signs (in Russian and German) forbidding cannibalism.

The abbey **museum** (Tues–Sun 10am–4pm) houses one of the country's best natural history collections, covering every aspect of the area's wildlife, with exhibits ranging from butterflies and snakes to huge deer and elks. There's a good view down into the valley below the edge of the abbey, and you can also see some of the large tracts of broken stones that are a distinctive glaciated feature of the hilltops.

The path due east down the mountain leads to the village of **NOWA SŁUPIA** with its **Museum of Ancient Metallurgy** (Tues–Sun 10am–4pm), located on the site of iron-ore mines and smelting furnaces developed here as early as the second century AD. For nearly a thousand years this was one of Europe's biggest ironworks. From Nowa Słupia you can take a bus back to Kielce, or you can climb back up and catch one from Święty Krzyż. If you want to stay over there's a year-round youth hostel in the village too.

The highest point of the Łyso Góry is a hill known as **Łysica** (611m), a standard hikers' destination at the far end of the range. If you set out for Święty Krzyż early in the morning you could make it there with a good day's walk along the marked path—plenty of people do. Otherwise, catch a bus from Kielce to the village of **ŚWIĘTA KATARZYNA**, at the foot of the hills, and take the woodland path, past memorials to resistance fighters hunted down by the Nazis, to the summit—a legendary witches' meeting place and an excellent viewpoint. In Święta Katarzyna itself, there's a **convent** that's been home to a sequestered order of nuns since the fifteenth century—you can peer in at the church. For accommodation, there is a choice between a PTTK **hotel and restaurant** (☎110-111) and an all-year **youth hostel** (☎110-114).

PODHALE AND THE TATRA MOUNTAINS

Ask Poles to define their country's natural attractions and they often come up with the following simple definition: The Lakes, The Sea and The Mountains. "The Mountains" consist of an almost unbroken chain of ridges extending the whole length of the southern border, of which the highest, most spectacular and most revered are the **Tatras**—or *Tatry* as they're known in Polish. Eighty kilometers long, with peaks rising to over 2500m (8200ft), the Polish Tatras are actually a relatively small part of the range, most of which rises across the border in Czechoslovakia. As the estimated three million annual tourists show, however, the Polish section has enough to keep most people happy: high peaks for the dedicated mountaineers, excellent trails for hikers, cable cars and creature comforts for day-trippers, and ski slopes in winter.

Podhale—the Tatra foothills, beginning to the south of Nowy Targ—is a sparsely populated region of lush meadows, winding valleys and old wooden villages. The inhabitants of Podhale, the **górale**, are fiercely independent moun-

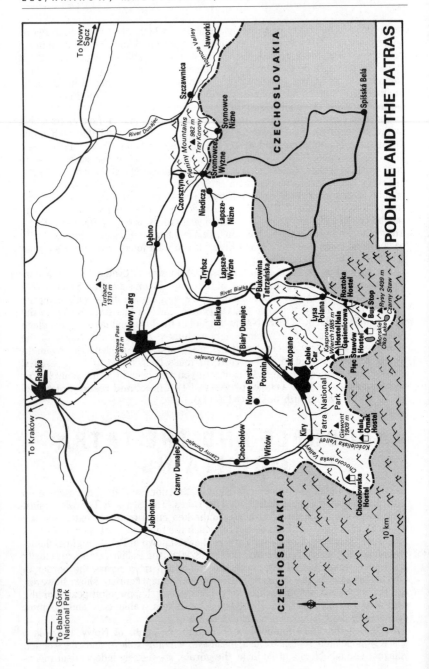

PODHALE AND THE TATRAS

tain farmers, known throughout Poland for their folk traditions. The region was "discovered" by the Polish intelligentsia in the late nineteenth century and the *górale* rapidly emerged as symbols of the struggle for independence, the links forged between intellectuals and local peasants presaging the anticipated national unity of the post-independence era. As in other neglected areas of the country, the poverty of rural life led thousands of *górale* to emigrate to the United States in the 1920s and 1930s. The departures continue today, with at least one member of most households spending a year or two in Chicago, New York, or other US Polish emigré centers, returning with money to support the family and, most importantly, build a house.

Of late the traditional bonds between Podhale and the rest of the country have been shaken by what many locals see as central government's insensitivity to their specific concerns. Tensions surfaced following Solidarity's refusal to adopt a popular *górale* community leader as their main candidate in the elections of summer 1989, choosing instead a union loyalist.

Despite the influx of vacationers, the *górale* retain a straight-talking and highly hospitable attitude to outsiders. If you're willing to venture off the beaten track, away from the regular tourist attractions around Zakopane, there's a chance of real and rewarding contacts in the remoter towns and villages.

South to Zakopane

From Kraków the main road south—parts of it, for once, divided highway—heads through the foothills towards **Zakopane**, the main base for the Tatras. Most buses (and most visitors) run straight through but, with a little time on your hands, it's worth considering a couple of journey breaks.

Rabka and the Gorce

The climb begins as soon as you leave Kraków, following the course of the Raba River from Myślenice to Lubień and then on, with the first glimpses of the Tatras ahead, to **RABKA**. This is a quiet little town, with a beautiful seventeenth-century **church** at the base of the hill, now housing a small **ethnographic museum** (Tues–Sun 9am–4pm).

Surrounding Rabka is a mountainous area known as the **Gorce**, much of it national parkland. It's fine, rugged hiking country, with paths clearly signposted and color-graded according to difficulty. There are trails to several mountain-top hostels: Luboń Wielki (1022m), Maciejowa (815m), Groniki (1027m) and—highest and best of all—Turbacz (1310m), a solid six-hour walk east of town. Before setting out, try to pick up the **map** *Beskid Makowski (Beskid Średni)*.

Nowy Targ

From Rabka the road continues over the **Obidowa Pass** (812m), then down onto a plain crossed by the Czarny Dunajec river and towards Podhale's capital, **NOWY TARG** (New Market). The key attraction of this squat, undistinguished town—the home of many a Polish-American—is, as the name suggests, a **market**, held each Thursday on a square near the center. This is basically a farmer's event, with horse-drawn carts lining the streets from early morning, when serious trading in animals takes place around the edges of the square. The central area is taken up by stalls laden with local produce and solid locally produced domestic appliances—tools, baskets, huge cooking pots, and carved wooden plates. As with all Polish markets, there's also a lively trade in scarce or newly available consumer imports from the west. But for most visitors, the main shopping attractions are the chunky sweaters that are the region's hallmark—prices are lower and the quality generally better here than in either Kraków or Zakopane. Be prepared to bargain for anything you buy (wool and crafts especially) and arrive early if you want to get the real atmosphere. By 10am or so, with business done, most of the farmers retreat to local greasy spoons for a hearty bout of eating and, especially, drinking.

As far as sights go, the town center offers **St Catherine's Church**, which has a Gothic presbytery, and there's an attractive larchwood chapel across the river. The unofficial Podhale **Lenin trail** begins at the town, too; the old prison beyond the southeast corner of the main square is where he was held in 1914 on suspicion of spying—by then he'd been living in the area for nearly two years. A further Soviet connection is revealed in the local cemetery: a fierce battle for the town during the Red Army's advance in early 1945 left over a thousand Soviet soldiers dead.

If you're spending the night in town, the *Janosik*, ul. Hanka Sawickiej 8 (☎2876), is the best **hotel**, and modestly priced. There is also a **youth hostel** at Dzielnica Niwa (☎2522; July & Aug), while **private rooms** can be arranged through the **Podhale Information Office** on pl. Pokoju. For food, there's little to distinguish the *Podhalanka* and the *Dunajec*, both on pl. Pokoju, and the *Tatry*, ul. Kopernika 12.

Zakopane

South of Nowy Targ the road continues another 20km along the course of the Biały Dunajec before reaching the edges of **ZAKOPANE**, a major mountain resort, crowded with visitors throughout its summer hiking and winter skiing seasons. It has been an established attraction for Poles since the 1870s, when the purity of the mountain air began to attract the attention of doctors and their consumptive city patients. Within a few years this inaccessible mountain village of sheep farmers was transformed, as the medics were followed by Kraków artists and intellectuals, who established a fashionable colony in the final decades of Austro-Hungarian rule. These days Zakopane is popular with everyone, but even in July, the peak of the tourist influx, it's still a remarkably relaxed place.

The Town

The **bus** and **train stations** are both a ten-minute walk east of the main street, **ul. Krupówki**. A bustling pedestrianized zone, this is the focus of the town, devoted to a jumbled collection of restaurants, cafés, and souvenir shops. Uphill the street merges into **ul. Zamoyskiego**, which runs on out of town past the fashionable *fin-de-siècle* wooden villas of the outskirts, while in the other direction it follows a rushing stream down towards **Gulbałówka** hill (see below).

The **Tatra Museum** (Tues–Sun 9am–3:30pm), near the center of ul. Krupówki, covers local wildlife, ethnography, and history, including a section on the wartime experiences of the *górale*, who were brutally punished by the Nazis for their involvement with the Polish resistance and cross-mountain contacts with Allied intelligence. The museum is dedicated to T. Chałubinski, the doctor who "discovered" Zakopane in the 1870s.

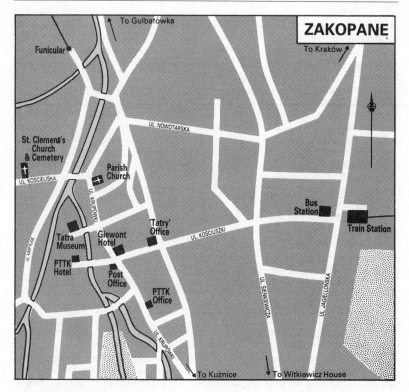

In the cemetery of the **wooden church** on ul. Kościeliska you'll find the graves of many of the town's best-known writers and artists, among them that of Stanisław Witkiewicz (1851–1915) who developed the distinctive "Zakopane" architectural style based on traditional wooden building forms. Alongside the famous are the graves of old *górale* families, including well-known local figures such as the skier Helena Marusarzówna, executed by the Nazis for her part in the resistance. West of the main street is **Willa Atma**, a traditional-style villa and longtime home of composer Karol Szymanowski, now a museum dedicated to its former resident (Tues–Sun 10am–4pm).

Two Witkiewicz buildings can be seen just east of Zakopane: the **Willa Pod Jedlami** at BYSTRE and a wooden **chapel** at CHŁABÓWKA; both are on the Morskie Oko bus route. Ten minutes' walk west along ul. Kościeliska is the **Willa Koliba**, Witkiewicz's first experiment.

The Zakopane area telephone code is ☎0165.

Practicalities

Zakopane has several **tourist offices**, each useful for different purposes: the *Tatry* office at ul. Kościuszki 7 is the main information center for the whole area;

Orbis at ul. Krupowki 22 helps with hotels, train and bus reservations, and local trips; the PTTK office at ul. Krupówki 37 has maps, local guidebooks, and information about mountain huts (which they operate). Opening hours for the tourist offices are generally 8am to 6pm, Monday to Friday, 8am to noon on Saturdays; only the PTTK is open on Sundays.

All the tourist offices have **rooms** available, many in *pensjonat*, whose stock has greatly increased following the privatization of many workers' vacation homes. Orbis runs several *pensjonat*, reservable—along with other accommodation— through the reception desk at the *Hotel Giewont*. *Tatry* operates accommodation services for groups at its main office and for individuals (mainly rooms in houses) at ul. Kościuszki 23a. Although privatizations have relieved the town's perennial accommodation problems, it's still worth reserving rooms well in advance in midsummer or during the skiing season. The following **hotels and hostels** are listed in ascending order of price, which varies considerably according to season.

Youth Hostel, ul. Nowotarska 45 (☎662-03). Open all year.

Juventur, ul. Stołeczna 2a (☎662-53). Student hotel.

Dom Turysty, ul. Zaruskiego 5 (☎3281). Cheap hotel popular with Polish students; laundry and showers on the second floor are handy.

Gazda, Zaruskiego 2 (☎5011); **Morskie Oko**, Krupówki 30 (☎5076); **Warszawianka**, Jagiellońska 7 (☎3261); **Imperial**, ul. Balzera 1 (☎4021). Mid-range, central hotels.

Giewont, Kościuszki 1 (☎2011). The town's smart hotel, right in the center; chances of getting a room if you haven't called ahead are virtually zero.

Kasprowy, Polana Szymoszkowa (☎4011). Luxury hotel west of town, looking onto the mountains.

There is a **campground** at the end of ul. Zeromskiego, on the east side of town.

Eating is never a problem in Zakopane. If you want a fast snack there are plenty of cafés, milk bars, and streetside *zapiekanki* merchants to choose from. Restaurants are plentiful, too, with very good ones in the hotels *Gazda* and *Giewont* (at night there's often a lengthy wait for a table), and a very proper one at the *Kasprowy*. Other reasonable options are the *Jędruś*, ul. Swierczewskiego 5, where the waitresses dress up in folk costume; the *Watra*, ul. Zamoyskiego 2, which has ploddy live music on many nights; and *Obrochtowka*, ul. Kraszewskiego 10a, a small haunt favored by locals. The *Robber's Hut* on ul. Jagiellońska is a recent commercial venture—a mock mountain-smuggler's den.

Around Zakopane

If hiking in the Tatras proper sounds too energetic, there are a number of easy and enjoyable walks in the foothills and valleys surrounding Zakopane. For navigation purposes, the **map** to look out for is *Tatry i Podhale* (1:75,000).

Gubałówka Hill

There's an excellent view of the Tatras from the top of **Gubałówka Hill** (1120m) to the west, but everyone knows this, as you discover when you join the long lines for the **funicular from Zakopane** (follow ul. Krupówki out from the center). From the summit, a good day reveals the high peaks to the south in sharp relief against clear blue mountain skies.

Most people linger a while over the view, browse in the souvenir shops, and head back down again, but the long wooded hill ridge is the starting point of several excellent **hikes**, taking you through a characteristic Podhale landscape.

To the **west** from the top of the funicular the trails begin as a single path, which soon divides. Continue straight along the ridge and you gradually descend to the Czarny Dunajec valley, ending up at the village of WITÓW, around two hours' walking in all; buses back to Zakopane take fifteen minutes. Alternatively, take the north fork and it's a four-hour hike to the village of CHOCHOŁÓW, with its fine wooden houses and church; you can get there by two paths, either following a track (which soon becomes a road) through the village of DZIANISZ, or taking the cross-country route marked *Szlak im. Powstania Chocołówskiego* on the *Tatry i Podhale* map.

East of the funicular, the main path leads to PORONIN, on the Zakopane–Kraków road, a sleepy village distinguished by a statue of Lenin. The great man spent nearly two years here (1913–14), events which used to be commemorated in a small Lenin museum, closed for the new political era. A steep climb up the marked path east of the village takes you to a hilltop area with wonderful views. Continue east from here and you come to BUKOWINA TATRZAŃSKA, a fair-sized village with buses back to Zakopane (15min), a pension (the *Morskie Oko*; ☎7212), private accommodation office (☎7293) and restaurant.

Dolina Białego and Dolina Strążyska

For some easy and accessible valley hiking, Dolina Białego and Dolina Strążyska each provide a relaxed long afternoon's walk from Zakopane, and if you're feeling energetic you could combine the two in one day.

Leaving Zakopane to the south, along the Strążyska road, you reach **Dolina Strążyska** in around an hour. At the end of the valley (3hr) you can climb to the **Hala Strążyska**, a beautiful high mountain pasture (1303m); the **Siklawica waterfall**, a stream coursing down from the direction of Giewont, makes an enjoyable rest point on the way. Walk east along the meadow to the top of **Dolina Białego** and you can descend the deep, stream-crossed valley back to the outskirts of Zakopane (6–7hr in total).

Dolina Chocołowska and Dolina Kościeliska

Two of the loveliest valleys of the area are Dolina Chocołowska and Dolina Kościeliska, both a bus ride west of town.

Dolina Chocołowska, the longest valley in the region, follows the course of a stream deep into the hills. From the parking lot at the head of the valley it's a good hour's walk to the *Chocołowska* hostel, beautifully situated overlooking the meadows, with the high western Tatras and the Czech border behind. The steep paths up the eastern side lead to ridges that separate the valley from Dolina Kościeliska—one from a little way beyond the parking lot connects the two valleys, making a round trip possible.

Dolina Kościeliska is a classic beauty spot, much in evidence on postcards of the region. To get there take the bus to the hamlet of KIRY and set off down the stone valley track ahead. For a stiffish price a horse-drawn cart will run you down the first section of the valley to a point known as Pisana Polana, but from there on it's walkers only; the crowds diminish here, but there are always quite a few more dedicated types who carry on. A distinctive feature of Kościeliska are the **caves** in the limestone cliffs, once the haunts of robbers and bandits, legend has it. Take a detour off to the left—marked *jaskinia* (caves)—and you can visit various examples, including **Jaskinia Mroźna**, where the walls are permanently encased in ice.

Beyond Pisana Polana the narrow upper valley is a beautiful stretch of crags, gushing water, and greenery reminiscent of upper New England, leading to the *Hala Ornak* **hostel**, a popular overnight stop with a restaurant. Two marked paths continue up beyond the hostel: the eastern route takes you the short distance to **Smreczyński Staw** (1226m), a tiny mountain lake surrounded by forest; the western route follows a high ridge over to Dolina Chocołowska—a demanding walk only for the fit.

The Tatras

Poles are serious mountaineers, with an established network of climbing clubs, and it's in the **Tatras** that everyone starts and the big names train. Most of the peaks are in the 2000–2500m range, but the unimpressive statistics belie their status, and their appearance. For these are real mountains, snowbound on their heights for most of the year and supporting a good skiing season in December and January. They are as beautiful as any mountain landscape in northern Europe, the ascents taking you on boulder-strewn paths alongside woods and streams up to the ridges, where grand, windswept peaks rise in the brilliant alpine sunshine. Wildlife thrives here: the whole area was turned into a national park in the 1950s and supports rare species like lynx, golden eagles, and brown bear—which for once you might even glimpse.

Though many of the peak and ridge climbs are for experienced climbers only, much is accessible to regular walkers, with marked paths which give you the top-of-the-world exhilaration of bagging a peak. For skiers, despite the relative paucity of lifts and hi-tech facilities, there are some high-quality pistes, including a dry slope.

Afraid of their citizens catching "the Polish disease" (ie Solidarity), the Czechs virtually closed this part of the border in 1980, and throughout the decade hikers were confronted with the somewhat comical sight of uniformed police sweating it over the mountain passes. Things have eased up these days, with the latest edition of the *Tatry i Podhale* map showing cross-border walks in great detail, though the police are still in evidence and Poles still need visas to cross into Czech territory. Most foreigners can cross with just a passport stamp, however, and the new political climate means that exploration of the whole Tatra region is possible for the first time since the war. (See the *The Real Guide: Czechoslovakia* for details of the Czech High Tatras.)

Practicalities

A decent **map** of the mountains is indispensable. The best is the *Tatrzański Park Narodowy* (1:30,000), which has all the paths accurately marked and color-coded. The *Tatry Polskie* **guidebook** is likewise invaluable, giving all the main walking routes in several languages, English included.

Overnighting in the PTTK-run **huts** dotted across the mountains is an experience in itself. There are seven of them in all, clearly marked on the map (for up-to-date information on openings, check at the PTTK office in Zakopane). In summer the huts are crammed to the gills with student backpackers from all over the country; as they generally can't afford the beds they crash on the floor, and if it's really crowded you'll probably be joining them too. **Food** is basic, but pricey for Poles, most of whom bring their own; the huts are an ideal place to mix in, preferably over a bottle of vodka. Even if you don't want to lug large weights around the mountain tops, a supply of basic rations is a good idea. **Camping** isn't allowed in the National Park area, rock-climbing only with a permit—ask at the PTTK for details. And for anyone attempting more than a quick saunter, the right **footwear and clothing** are, of course, essential.

Walks in the Tatras

The easiest way up to the peaks is by **cable car** from the hamlet of KUŹNICE, a three-kilometer walk or bus journey south from Zakopane along the Dolina Bystrego. In summer the cable car is a sell-out, making advance reservations at the Orbis office a virtual necessity, unless you're prepared to turn up before 8am; the only way around this—and it doesn't always work—is to buy your ticket for ten times the normal price from the touts lurking near the entrance.

Kasprowy Wierch—and Descents to Kuźnice

The cable car ends near the summit of **Kasprowy Wierch** (1985m), where weather-beaten signs indicate the border. From here many day-trippers simply walk back down to Kuźnice through the Hala Gąsienicowa (an equally popular option is to walk up and return by cable car). A somewhat longer alternative is to strike west to the cross-topped summit of **Giewont** (1909m) and head down to Kuźnice through the Dolina Kondratowa past the *Hala Kondratowa* hostel. This is fairly easy going and quite feasible in a day if you start out early.

East: the Eagles' Path and Morskie Oko Lake

East of Kasprowy Wierch the walking gets tougher. From Świnica (2300m), a strenuous ninety-minute walk, experienced hikers continue along the **Orła Perć** (Eagles' Path), a challenging, exposed ridge with spectacular views. The *Pięc Stawów* **hostel**, in the high valley of the same name, provides overnight shelter at the end.

From the hostel you can hike back down Dolina Roztoki to **Łysa Polana**, a border crossing point in the valley, and get a bus back to Zakopane. An alternative is to continue a short distance east to the **Morskie Oko Lake** (1399m). Encircled by spectacular sheer cliff faces and alpine forest, this large glacial lake is one of the Tatras' big attractions, most frequently approached on the winding forest road from Łysa Polana. In summer the paths around the lake are packed with bus-tour parties out for the day from Zakopane. If you want to do it by bus, advance tickets from Orbis are strongly recommended, though you might find regular PKS buses with seats left over on the day.

The lakeside *Morskie Oko* **hostel** provides a base for the ascent of **Rysy** (2499m), the highest peak in the Polish Tatras. Closer to hand on the same red-marked route is **Czarny Staw** (1580m), an even chillier-looking lake half an hour's walk up from Morskie Oko.

East to the Pieniny

East of the Tatras the mountains scale down to a succession of lower ranges— *beskidy* as they're known in Polish—stretching along the Czechoslovak border. The walking here is less dramatic than in the Tatras but excellent nonetheless, and the locals are a good bunch too, including *górale* and a long-established Slovak minority. The highlights of the region are the **Pieniny Mountains**, hard by the Slovak border, and the raft run through the **Dunajec gorge**, far below.

Transportation in this little-known region can be a struggle, away from the immedate vicinity of **Szczawnica**, a spa town that makes the best Pieniny base.

The Spisz Region

The road east from Nowy Targ to Szczawnica is one of the most attractive in the country, following the broad valley of the Dunajec through the **Spisz**, a backwoods region whose villages are renowned for their wooden houses, churches, and folk art. Buses cover the route four or five times a day.

DĘBNO, 14km from Nowy Targ, boasts one of the best-known wooden churches in the country, a shingled, steep-roofed building with a profile vaguely reminiscent of a snail. Inside, the full length of walls and ceiling are covered with exuberant, brilliantly preserved fifteenth-century polychromy and wooden carving. Their subjects are an enchanting mix of folk, national, and religious motifs, including some fine hunting scenes and curiously Islamic-looking geometric patterns. In the center of the building fragments survive of the original roodscreen, supporting a tree-like cross, while the altarpiece triptych features an unusually militant-looking Saint Catherine.

Just to the south of the road, 12km on from Dębno, is **CZORSZTYN**, a small village with a memorable if very ruined castle. From its heights you get a sweeping view over the valley and to the castle of Niedicza (see below) across the mouth of the Dunajec gorge. The valley itself is the subject of a controversial hydroelectric **dam project**, whose initial stages are already disfiguring the land below Czorsztyn. Environmentalists fear that the flooding of the Czorsztyn area will transform the Spisz into mosquito-ridden marshland, but despite strong protests and considerable technical problems the project is inching ahead, supported by the heavy-industry lobby—though the government has recently promised a review of the whole project.

Niedicza—and West Along the Slovak Border

NIEDICZA lies just across the gorge from Czorsztyn, reachable on foot in a half-hour walk to the south and over a pedestrian bridge or, more circuitously, by road to the west of Czorsztyn; some of the Nowy Targ to Szczawnica buses take a detour here en route.

The village occupies a strategic position at a major confluence of the Dunajec, with a substantial tributary plunging down from Slovakia. Control of this valley and the border territory explains the presence of the **castle**, perched above the river. Originally raised in the fourteenth century, it was reconstructed in its current Renaissance style in the early 1600s, and today lies under threat from the hydroelectric scheme, which some experts believe will erode its rock foundations. It today houses a **museum of Spisz folk art** (Tues–Sun 8am–5pm) and an artists' retreat. A Tintin-like folktale associates the castle with the Incas. The wife of the last descendant of the Inca rulers allegedly lived here in the late eighteenth century, and left a hidden document detailing the legendary Inca treasure buried in Titicaca lake in Peru—a document supposedly discovered in 1946.

To the **west of Niedicza**, a little-frequented backroad winds its way toward Nowy Targ and Zakopane through the heart of the Spisz. Most villages here were effectively cut off from the outside world well into the nineteenth century, and serfdom was only abolished here in 1931. It still feels like another world, particularly in villages like TRYBSZ and ŁAPSZE with their Slovak populations. If you get the chance, visit on a Sunday morning, since the local choirs are reputedly wonderful.

Szczawnica and Around

East of the Tatras there's a plethora of spa towns amid the river gorges and steep valleys of the border area. **SZCZAWNICA** is a highly picturesque example, sited on the edge of the sparkling Dunajec River below the peaks of the Pieniny. It is also by far the most visited town in the region, crowded through the summer with all types of mountain vacationers: canoeists setting off down the gorge, hikers heading off to the hills, industrial workers recuperating in the sanatariums.

Buses run here from both Nowy Targ (40km) and, on a slightly roundabout route, from Zakopane (50km), dropping you in the middle of town, by the river. From here it's a short walk up to the bustling square, and the staid health establishments of the **upper town**. Most of Szczawnica's alkaline spring water is consumed by miners and steelworkers; casual visitors are free to wander in and sample the waters. There's little else to see in town, unless you happen to be around during *górale* folk events. The attraction for most foreign visitors lies in getting out to explore the Pieniny and the Dunajec gorge.

There are no real hotels, but accommodation isn't a problem—in season half the town population rent out **rooms** in their homes for next to nothing. You can arrange lodgings through the Podhale tourist office at ul. Szalaya 84, or at Orbis, on the main square at pl. Dietla 7. A more spartan alternative is the *Orlica* **PTTK hostel**, right on the edge of the gorge, a kilometer south along the river.

Krościenko

The small town of **KROŚCIENKO**, a short bus ride north of Szczawnica, is an alternative base for the Pieniny, located right at the edge of the mountains and starting point for hikes to the Trzy Korony (see below). It again has the possibility of **private rooms**, arranged through the **PTTK office** at ul. Jagiellońska 28 (☎3059), and an undistinguished collection of restaurants.

Dolina Homole

A short local excursion worth considering is to the **Dolina Homole**, 8km east of Szczawnica. This is a peaceful valley of wooded glades and streams, and you can walk up to the surrounding hilltops in less than two hours. There's a PTTK **campground** up here too.

Buses run from Szczawnica to the village of **JAWORKI**, starting point for the walk and an interesting example of the ethnic and religious twists characterizing the eastern hill country. At first sight the **church** looks like a regular Catholic building but a glance at the iconostasis behind the altar indicates a different history. Although now Roman Catholic, it was originally a Uniate *cerkiew*, in what was the westernmost point of Lemk settlement in Poland (see Chapter Three). Today only a couple of Lemk families remain. If you find the church closed, ask for the key from the house next door. A basic **bar-restaurant** (closed Mon) in the village serves fine fish dishes and *Okocim* beer.

The Pieniny

A short range of Jurassic limestone peaks, rearing above the spectacular Dunajec gorge, the Pieniny offer some stiff hill-walking and the appeal of requiring no serious climbing to reach its 1000-meter summits. Jagged outcrops are set off by abundant greenery, the often humid mountain microclimate supporting a rich and varied flora. Like the Tatras, the Pieniny are an officially designated national park and have a network of controlled paths. The detailed *Pieniński Park Narodowy* (1:22,500) **map** is useful; it's theoretically available in the Szczawnica tourist offices.

Trzy Korony

The main range, a ten-kilometer stretch between Czorsztyn and Szczawnica, is the most popular hiking territory, with the peaks of **Trzy Korony** (Three Crowns; 982m) the big target.

There are several routes up, the best-known leading from **Krościenko**. From the bus stop here you can follow the signs—and in summer the packs of hikers – southward on the yellow route. The path soon begins to climb through the mountainside woods, with plenty of meadows and lush clearings on the way. Around two hours from Krościenko you'll finally reach **Okrąglica**, the highest peak of the Trzy Korony, via some chain-bannistered steps. On a clear day there's a excellent view over the whole area: the high Tatras off to the west, the slopes of Slovakia to the south, and the Dunajec gorge far below.

Many hikers take the same route back, but two alternatives are worth considering. One is to walk to Szczawnica, a two- or three-hour trip. Head back along the route you came as far as Bajków Groń (679m), about three-quarters of the way down, and from there follow the blue path across the mountains south to Sokolica and down to the river, where you can get a boat across to the *Orlica* hostel. The other, if you want to combine the walk with the Dunajec gorge, is to descend the mountain south to Sromowce Nizne, one of the two starting points for the raft trip upriver (see below).

PIENINY GÓRALE: MUSIC EVENTS

Like the Podhale, the Pieniny region is populated by *górale* highanders who for much of the century have been migrating to the United States in great numbers; it's not uncommon to come across broad Chicago accents in the villages. To the outsider, the main distinction between the Podhale and Pieniny clans are their **costumes**—the reds, browns, and blacks of the western Podhale giving way to the purple-blues of the Pieniny decorated jackets. There are also, however, significant differences in **dialect**, and even if you're a Polish-speaker a Pieninski going full tilt is hard to follow.

Music is the most accessible aspect of their culture. In summer you may well catch vocal ensembles at open-air folk evenings held in Szczawnica or Krościenko—a good excuse for everyone to dress up and sing their hearts out. While the harmonies and vocal style are similar in both *górale* regions, the Pieninski make more use of instruments—violins and a thumping bass in particular—to create a sound that has marked similarities to Slovak and Hungarian country styles. The visiting crowds are overwhelmingly Polish at these traditional old-time romps, and for the atmosphere alone it's well worth joining them.

The Dunajec Gorge

Below the heights of the Pieniny the fast-moving Dunajec twists and turns below great limestone rockfaces and craggy peaks. The river is a magnet for **canoeists**, who shoot fearlessly through the often powerful rapids; for the less intrepid, the two-hour **raft trip** provides an enjoyable version of the experience.

The most popular **starting point** for this trip is KĄTY, a few hundred meters east of SROMOWCE WYZNE; regular buses run to Kąty from Szczawnica and Nowy Targ. There's a second landing stage farther downriver at SROMOWCE NIZNE, easier to reach if you've been hiking in the Pieniny; this village has a largish PTTK hostel, and lies across the river from the Slovak settlement and monastery of ČERVENY KLÁŠTOR, the main Czechoslovakian starting point for raft trips.

Trips currently run from April to late August, starting at 8am and finishing around 4pm. In season, if you turn up on the day you can expect to wait a couple of hours for a place; tickets can be reserved through local Orbis offices, regional hotels (in Kraków and Zakopane for example), and tourist offices, including *Tatry* and *Związek Podhalański* bureaux.

The rafts are sturdy log constructions, carrying up to ten passengers plus two navigators in traditional Pieniny costume. Here, as farther east, the river forms the border with Czechoslovakia and at several points Slovak villages face their Polish counterparts across the banks, with their own rafters and canoeists hugging the southern side of the river. After plenty of sharp twists and spectacular cliffs, the rafts end up at Szczawnica, from where buses return to Kąty until 4pm.

travel details

Trains

From Kraków to Białystok (1 daily; 10hr); Bydgoszcz (3 daily; 7–9hr); Częstochowa (12 daily; 2–4hr); Gdańsk (6 daily; 5–11hr); Katowice (26 daily; 1hr 30min–2hr); Kielce (11 daily; 2–3hr); Krynica (8 daily; 5–6hr); Lublin (3 daily; 5–7hr); Nowy Sącz (11 daily; 3–4hr); Poznań (7 daily; 7–8hr); Przemyśl (15 daily; 3–5hr); Rzeszów (20 daily; 2–3hr); Szczecin (5 daily; 12–14hr); Warsaw (19 daily; 2hr 30min–6hr; expresses from 6–7am and 6:40–8pm); Wrocław (15 daily; 4–6hr); Zakopane (15 daily; 3–5hr). Also **international connections** to Budapest, Prague, and Vienna.

From Częstochowa to Kraków (11 daily; 2–3hr); Kielce (10 daily; 2hr); Katowice (hourly; 1–2hr); Warsaw (14 daily; 3–4hr); Łódź (15 daily; 2–3hr).

From Kielce to Kraków (8 daily; 2–3hr); Częstochowa (10 daily; 2hr); Warsaw (12 daily; 3–4hr); Łódź (1 daily; 4hr).

From Zakopane to Kraków (15 daily; 3–5hr); Częstochowa (3 daily; 7–8hr; sleepers); Gdańsk (1 daily; 12hr; sleeper); Warsaw (6 daily; 5–12hr).

Buses.

From Kraków to Nowy Targ (12 daily; 1–2hr); Sandomierz (2 daily; 4–5hr); Tarnów (15 daily; 1–1hr 30min); Zamość (2 daily; 6–8hr); Zakopane (8–10 daily; 2hr 30min–3hr).

From Zakopane to Nowy Targ (hourly; 30min); Szczawnica (5 daily; 1hr).

Flights

From Kraków Daily flights to Gdańsk (2hr; July & Aug) and Warsaw (50min; May–Oct).

CHAPTER FIVE

SILESIA

I n Poland it's known as *Śląsk*, in Czechoslovakia as *Sleszko*, in Germany as *Schlesien*; all three countries hold part of the frequently disputed province that's called in English **Silesia**. Since 1945, Poland has had the best of the argument, holding all of it except for a few of the westernmost tracts, a dominance gained as compensation for the Eastern Territories, which were incorporated into the USSR in 1939 as a result of the Nazi–Soviet pact, and never returned.

Silesia presents a strange dichotomy. On the one hand there's its notorious heavy industry, especially the huge **Katowice** conurbation, by far the largest unmodernized "Rust Belt" left in Europe. An even worse environmental disaster exists in **Wałbrzych**, one of the most polluted towns in the world. Similar problems, albeit on a smaller scale, also affect the province's chief city, **Wrocław**, holding back its potential to become a rival to Kraków, Prague, and Budapest as one of Central Europe's most enticing cosmopolitan centers.

Silesia's other face, ironically enough, is its role as a national playground, as the Sudeten mountain chain at its western extremity contains two of the most popular recreation areas in the country. Of these, the **Karkanosze National Park** offers the more rugged scenery, while the **Kłodzko Region** has a richer and more surprising range of landscapes, with the lazy ambience of its spa resorts providing a counter-attraction to bracing mountain hikes.

Along with Wielkopolska and Małopolska, Silesia was a key component of the early Polish nation. Following the collapse of the country's monarchical system, the Duke of Silesia, a member of the Piast dynasty, sometimes served as Poland's uncrowned king. However, this system fell by the wayside in the wake of the Tartar invasions in the thirteenth century, and the duchy was divided into **Lower** and **Upper Silesia**. As the succeeding dukes divided their territory among their sons, Silesia became splintered into eighteen principalities: hence what you see today is the legacy of a series of pint-sized former capitals, each with its fair share of castles, palaces, churches, and other monuments.

As each line died out, its land was incorporated into **Bohemia**, which eventually took over the entire province when the Piasts were extinguished in 1675—by which time Bohemia itself had become part of the Austrian-dominated **Habsburg Empire**. In 1740, Frederick the Great, king of the militaristic state of **Prussia**, launched an all-out war on Austria, his pretext being a dubious claim his ancestors had once had to one of the Silesian principalities. After changing hands several times, all but the southern part of the province was taken over by the Prussians in 1763, becoming part of Bismarck's Germany in 1871.

In 1921 a plebiscite resulted in the industrial heartland of the province becoming part of the recently resurrected Polish state. Another 860,000 Silesians opted for Polish rather than German nationality when given the choice in 1945, and displaced Poles from the Eastern Territories were brought in to replace the Germans who were now evacuated from the region. Yet, although postwar Silesia has developed a strongly Polish character, people with strong family roots in the province are often bilingual and, in a situation analogous to the Scots or Welsh, consider their prime loyalty to lie with Silesia rather than Poland. To complicate the picture further, many have German ancestors, and are targeted—not without success—by right-wing political extremists in Germany bent on recreating the prewar Reich. It was only as a result of international pressure that the German government decided not to stake a claim to Silesia as part of the unification talks; notwithstanding the November 1990 treaty confirming the borders, the issue will probably only be buried completely when Poland manages to close the gap in living standards between the two countries.

SILESIAN PLACE-NAMES

When Poland took over parts of Silesia in 1921 and 1945, all German names were replaced with Polish ones, often the towns' original names. Sometimes there is an obvious connection, as with Katowice/Kattowitz or Legnica/Liegnitz; at other times there is not, as with Jelenia Góra/Hirschberg or Legnickie Pole/Wahlstatt. The problem is that the German names still have their adherents, notably among long-established Silesian families. Throughout this chapter, therefore, the German name is given in parenthesis after the initial mention of the Polish name. If communicating in German—not only the *lingua franca* of Eastern European tourism, but also an acceptable substitute for Polish in parts of Silesia—the normal convention is to use German versions.

WROCŁAW AND AROUND

Lower Silesia's historic capital, **WROCŁAW** (BRESLAU), is the fourth largest city in Poland and has an exhilarating big-city feel to it, yet behind this animated appearance lies an extraordinary story of emergence from the verge of ruin. Its special nature comes from the fact that it contains the soul of two great cities. One of these is the city that has long stood on this spot, Slavic in origin but for centuries dominated by Germans and generally known as **Breslau**. The other is **Lwów**, capital of the Polish Ukraine, which was annexed by the Russians in 1939 and retained by them in 1945. After the war, its displaced population was encouraged to take over the severely depopulated Breslau, which had been confiscated from Germany and offered them a ready-made home.

Part re-creation of Lwów, part continuation of the tradition of Breslau, postwar Wrocław has a predominantly industrial character. However, there's ample compensation for this. The multinational influences which shaped the city are graphically reflected in its architecture: the huge Germanic **brick Gothic churches** which dominate the skyline are intermingled with Flemish-style Renaissance mansions, palaces and chapels of Viennese Baroque, and boldly utilitarian public buildings from the early years of this century. The tranquillity of the parks, gardens, and rivers—which are crossed by over eighty **bridges**—offer a ready escape from the urban bustle, while the city has a vibrant cultural scene, its **theater** tradition enjoying worldwide renown.

The city is encircled by rural terrain that is rivaled within Silesia only by the far better-known—and consequently far more touristy—Karkonosze Mountains and Kłodzko Valley. After the account of Wrocław itself you'll find a rundown on the most attractive places within easy reach of the city.

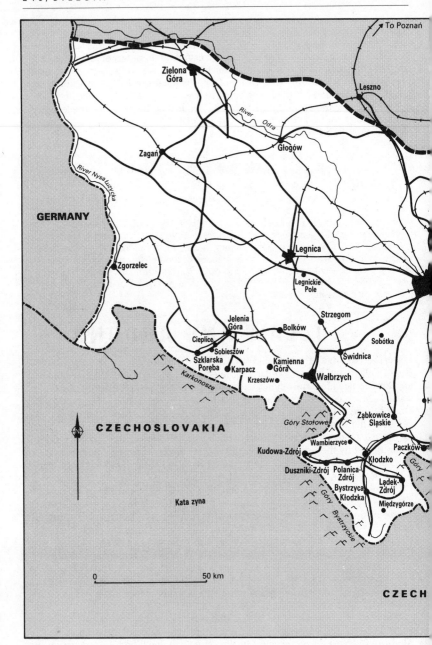

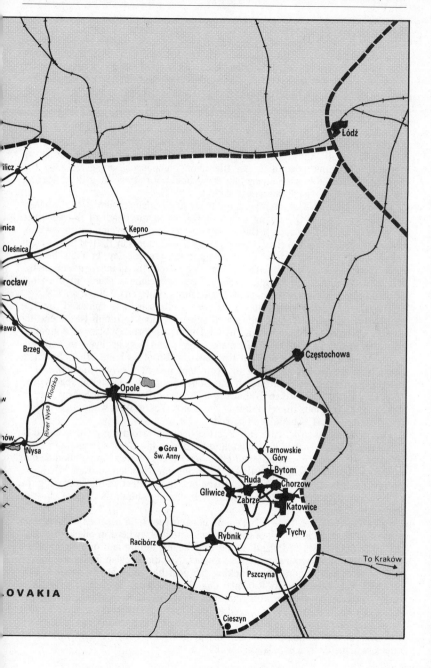

Wrocław's History

The origins of Wrocław are unknown. There may well have been a community here in Roman times, but the earliest documentary evidence is a ninth-century record of a Slav market town called **Wratislavia** situated on a large island at the point where the Odra River receives three tributaries. Subsequently, this became known as **Ostrów Tumski** (Cathedral Island) in honor of the bishopric founded here in 1000 by Bolesław the Brave.

German designs on Wratislavia came to the fore in 1109, when the army of Emperor Henry V was beaten off by Bolesław the Wrymouth. The site of the battlefield became known as **Psie Pole** (Dogs' Field), which today is one of the city's five administrative districts; the name supposedly arose because the Germans retreated in such chaos that they could not retrieve their dead, leaving the carcasses to the local canine population.

This proved to be only a temporary setback to German ambitions. Immediately after the creation of the duchy of Lower Silesia on the death of Bolesław the Wrymouth in 1138, German settlers were encouraged to develop a new town on the southern bank of the river. Destroyed by the Mongols in 1241, this was soon rebuilt on the grid pattern which survives to the present day. In 1259 the city, now commonly known as **Breslau**, became the capital of an independent duchy. It joined the Hanseatic League, and its bishop became a prince of the Holy Roman Empire of Germany, ruling over a territory centered on Nysa.

The duchy lasted only until 1335, when Breslau was annexed by the **Bohemian kings**, a dynasty which had sufficient clout to rebuff Kazimierz the Great's attempts to reunite it with Poland. During the two centuries of Bohemian rule the mixed population of Germans, Poles, and Czechs lived in apparent harmony, and the city carried out the construction of its huge brick churches. Most of these were transferred to Protestant use at the Reformation, which managed to take root even though the Bohemian crown passed in 1526 to the staunchly Catholic **Austrian Habsburgs**. However, Breslau paid heavily for the duality of its religious makeup during the Thirty Years' War, when its economy was devastated and its population halved.

The years of Austrian rule saw Breslau become increasingly Germanized, a process accelerated when it finally fell to Frederick the Great's **Prussia** in 1763. It became Prussia's most important city after Berlin, gaining a reputation as one of the most loyal lynchpins of the state during the Napoleonic wars, when the French twice occupied it, only to be driven out. In the nineteenth century it grew enormously with the industrial revolution, becoming one of the largest cities of the German nation.

After World War I, Breslau's **Polish community** held a series of strikes in protest at their exclusion from the plebiscite held elsewhere in Silesia to determine the boundaries of Poland. Being only 20,000 strong and outnumbered by thirty to one, their actions made little impact. Nor did Breslau figure among the targets of Polish leaders when looking for possible gains at the expense of a defeated Nazi Germany. As it turned out, they gained it by default. The Nazis made the suicidal decision, on retreating from the Eastern front, to turn the entire city into a fortress. It managed to hold out for four months against the Red Army, only capitulating on May 6, the day before the unconditional surrender. However, street fighting had left seventy percent of the city in ruins, with three-quarters of the civilian population having fled west.

The subsequent **return to Poland** of this huge city, rechristened with the modern Polish version of its original name, shocked the Germans more than any other of their many territorial losses. Its second transformation occurred much faster than that of seven centuries earlier: over the next few years, most of the remaining German citizens were shunted westward, while the inhabitants of Lwów were transferred here across Poland, bringing many of their institutions with them.

A relatively modest amount of government aid was made available for the restoration of the city, much of which remained in ruins for decades. Nonetheless, a distinctive and thoroughly Polish city has gradually emerged, one whose revival finally seemed complete in the 1980s when its population level surpassed the prewar figure of 625,000.

> The Wrocław telephone code is ☎071.

Arrival, Information, and Getting Around

The main **train station**, Wrocław Główny—itself one of the city's sights—faces the broad boulevard of ul. Gen. Karola Świerczewskiego, about fifteen minutes' walk south of downtown. All international and most major domestic services stop there, but there are two other stations you may find yourself using. **Wrocław Świebodzki**, close to the inner beltway on pl. Sergiusza Kirowa, is used by most trains between Wrocław and Jelenia Góra, plus some of those to and from Legnica and Głogów. On pl. Staszica, well to the north of Ostrów Tumski and connected to the center by trams #0 and #1, is **Wrocław Nadodrze**, for trains to and from Łódź, Trzebnica, and Oleśnica.

At the time of writing, the main **bus station** was still at pl. Konstytucji, diagonally opposite Wrocław Główny, but was due to be moved to ul. Sucha, at the back of the train station. The small bus stations beside each of the other rail terminals are only for destinations within the Wrocław district.

Bus #106 runs between Wrocław Świebodzki and the **airport**, which lies in the suburb of Strachowice, 10km to the southwest.

Best source for **tourist information** is the **Orbis** office at no. 45 on the Rynek (April–Sept Mon–Sat 8am–5pm; Oct–March Mon–Fri 8am–5pm; ☎44-79-46 or 76-79 or 41-09). The full range of Orbis services, including international train and bus tickets and currency exchange, is provided at no. 29 on the Rynek (Mon–Fri 8am–7pm, Sat 8am–5pm; ☎326-65/347-80) and at ul. Świerczewskiego 62 (same times; ☎387-45 or 44-87-17). There's a small **tourist office** at ul. Kazimierza Wielkiego 39 (Mon–Sat 10am–4pm; ☎44-31-11), but you're unlikely to find anyone there who speaks English. Other sources of information are the **Biuro Usług Turystycznych** at ul. Świerczewskiego 98 (Mon–Fri 9am–5pm, first Sat in month 9am–2pm; ☎44-41-01), and, for students, **Almatur** at ul. Tadeusza Kościuszki 34 (☎44-30-03).

The **trams** cover almost the entire built-up area of the city; the #0, a circular route around the central area, makes an easy introduction to the city. A pair of historic trams, known as *Jaś i Małgosia* (Hänsel and Gretel) run throughout the summer.

Finding a Place to Stay

Wrocław has accommodation to suit every taste and pocket; the entries which follow are more or less exhaustive. Prices within each category are a good bit lower than in Warsaw, a touch lower than in Poznań, and roughly comparable to Kraków's. There is no especially busy time of year.

Cheaper Hotels

A cluster of inexpensive hotels, mostly with a two-star rating, can be found near the main train station. Best of these is the *Grand*, ul. Świerczewskiego 100 (☎360-71). On the same street are *Europejski* at no. 88 (☎310-71) and *Polonia* at no. 66 (☎310-21), plus the less classy *Piast* at no. 98 (☎300-33), while the *Odra* is just around the corner at ul. Stawowa 13 (☎375-60). Cheaper and closer to downtown is *Domu Kultury*, Kazimierza Wielkiego 45 (☎44-38-66).

Most of the other bargain options entail a certain amount of commuting. *Żeglarz* is near the Nadodrze station and on the tram #14 route at ul. Władysława Reymonta 4 (☎21-29-96); *Oficerski* is in the southwestern suburbs at ul. Adama Próchnika 130 (☎60-33-03), near tram routes #13, #14 and #20; *Śląsk* is in a park farther west near ul. Oporowska (☎61-16-11), served by trams #1, #4, #5, #13, #16, #18 and #20; *Nauczycielski* is at ul. Nauczycielski 2 on Ostrów Tumski (☎22-92-68) and is reached by trams #0, #1, #2, #10, or #12; the sports hotel *DOSiR* is west of the center at ul. Wejherowska 2 (☎55-01-98), the end of the line of the #127 bus route.

Luxury Hotels

The five Orbis hotels all have the standard international facilities and prices to match. Most prestigious and expensive of the three four-star options is the *Wrocław*, ul. Powstańców Śląskich 7 (☎61-46-51), in a far-from-ideal situation southwest of the main train station and on the route of trams #6, #7, #8, #13, #14, and #20. *Novotel*, ul. Wyścigowa 35 (☎370-41), is inconveniently placed at the extreme southern edge of the city near the terminal of tram #17, whereas *Panorama* has a much more central position on the east side of the city center at pl. Feliksa Dzierżyńskiego 8 (☎44-36-81). The three-star *Motel* is way to the northwest of downtown at ul. Lotnicza 151 (☎51-81-53), served by trams #3, #10, #18, #21, #22, and #23. A similar rating is given to the venerable *Monopol*, right in the heart of the city at ul. Modrzejewskiej 2 (☎370-41). Taking into account its character, location and lower prices, this is the best bet for a classy stay.

Hostels and Private Rooms

The PTTK **tourist hostel** has an excellent location at ul. Szajnochy 11 (☎44-30-73). One of the city's two **youth hostels** is close to the main station at ul. Hugona Kołłątaja 20 (☎388-56); the other is 3km northwest at Na Grobli 30 (☎374-02), some distance off any tram routes. Nearby is one of the **campgrounds** (☎344-42), but the better one is on the east side of town near the Olympic Stadium at al. Ignacego Padarewskiego 35 (☎48-46-51)—trams #9, #16, and #17 go close. Chalets can also be rented at both sites. Information on summer **student hostels** is available at Almatur (see above).

Rooms in **private houses** can be booked at the *Biuro Zakwaterowania* at ul. Świerczewskiego 98 (☎44-41-01).

The City

Wrocław's central area, laid out in an approximate chessboard pattern, is delineated by the Odra River to the north and by the bow-shaped ul. Podwale—the latter following the former fortifications, whose ditch, now bordered by a shady park, still largely survives. The main concentration of shops—many housed in grandiose Stalinist buildings—and places of entertainment are found at the southern end of the center and in the streets leading south to the train station; this is also where most of the new market traders have set up. Immediately bordering the Odra at the northern fringe of the center is the university quarter. Beyond are a number of peaceful traffic-free islets, formerly sandbanks, linked to each other and to the mainland by graceful little bridges. The southern part of the much larger island of Ostrów Tumski, farther east, is the city's ecclesiastical heart, with half-a-dozen churches and its own distinctive hubbub. Farther north is an area of solidly nineteenth-century tenements, while the city's main green belt lies off the eastern side of the island.

The Rynek

Center of the chessboard is occupied by the vast space of the **Rynek**. Unlike the central squares in Poland's other main cities, this is still open to traffic, though it may not remain so for much longer. No longer a place of commerce, it now has a tourist and leisure-oriented tone, being devoted mainly to museums, restaurants, cafés, travel agencies, and bookshops. Unfortunately, a lot of scaffolding is usually in evidence: although the historic buildings are well looked after, the pollution from local factories makes it necessary to clean them every few years.

The Town Hall

The magnificent **Town Hall**, symbol of the city for the last seven centuries, was originally a modest one-story structure erected after the Tartar invasion, and was progressively expanded over the years. Its present appearance dates largely to the fifteenth-century high point of local prosperity, when the south aisle was added and the whole decorated in an elaborate late Gothic style. The international mix of stylistic influences reflects the city's status as a major European trading center at the time.

The **east facade**—the one which figures in all of Wrocław's promotion material—features an astronomical clock from 1580, and an elaborate central gable, decorated with intricate terra-cotta patterns and exquisite pinnacles. In contrast, the west facade (the main entrance) is relatively plain, save for the octagonal Gothic belfry with its tapering Renaissance lantern. It's the **south facade** which is the real show-stopper, with its huge Renaissance windows crowned with spire-like roofs, its filigree friezes of animals and foliage, and its rich statuary—in which the saints and knights are overshadowed by an old crone and a yokel. This pair appear above the doorway leading to the vaulted cellars of the *Piwnica Świdnicka*, a tavern since the thirteenth century, and named after the famous beer of Świdnica.

Relieved of its municipal duties by the adjoining nineteenth-century offices, the town hall now serves as the city's **Historical Museum** (Wed–Fri 10am–4pm, Sat 11am–5pm, Sun 10am–6pm). However, it's the largely unaltered interior itself which constitutes the main attraction.

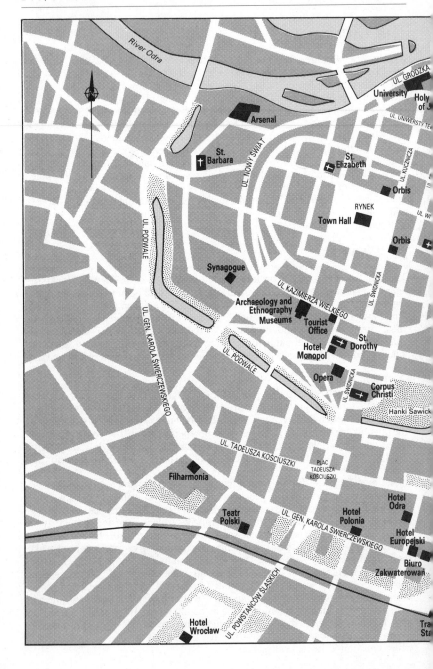

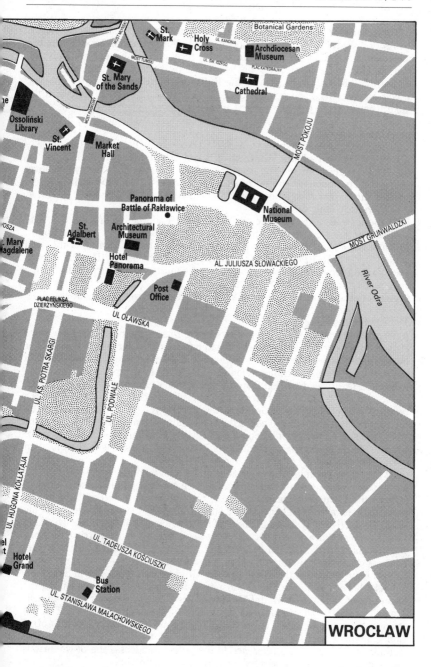

St. Mark

Holy Cross

Botanical Gardens

UL. KANONIA

Archdiocesan Museum

MOST MŁYŃSKI

MOST TUMSKI

St. Mary of the Sands

UL. ŚW. IDZIEGO

PLAC KATEDRALNY

Cathedral

ne

Ossoliński Library

St. Vincent

Market Hall

MOST PIASKOWY

MOST POKOJU

Panorama of Battle of Rakławice

National Museum

MOSTY GRUNWALDZKI

.OSZA

. Mary agdalene

St. Adalbert

Architectural Museum

River Odra

Hotel Panorama

AL. JULIUSZA SŁOWACKIEGO

PLAC FELIKSA DZIERZYNSKIEGO

Post Office

UL. OŁAWSKA

UL. KS. PIOTRA SKARGI

UL. PODWALE

UL. HUGONA KOŁŁĄTAJA

el t

Hotel Grand

UL. TADEUSZA KOŚCIUSZKI

Bus Station

UL. STANISŁAWA MAŁACHOWSKIEGO

WROCŁAW

The kernel of the town hall, dating back to the 1270s, is the twin-aisled **Burghers' Hall** on the ground floor. Not only the setting for important public meetings and receptions, it also did service throughout the week as a covered market, functioning as such for 450 years. The next part to be built, at the very end of the thirteenth century, was the **Bailiff's Room** immediately to the east, which was the office and courtroom of the official who governed the city in the duke's name. Over the centuries, it gained an extravagant stellar vault and a couple of Renaissance doorways, which lead to the chambers which were progressively added as needs arose.

A tasteless nineteenth-century marble staircase goes upstairs to the resplendent, three-aisled **Knights' Hall**, which supplanted the Burghers' Hall as the scene of civic celebrations. The keystones of the hall's vault are highly inventive, some of them character studies of all strata of society. Even more richly decorated is the coffer-ceilinged oriel window, which gives a Renaissance flourish to the otherwise Gothic design.

At the far end of the hall are two stone portals adorned with wild men. The southern of these gives access to the Alderman's Office and the **Strong Room**, which was actually the customs house, the treasury being located in the oriel behind, under whose wacky vault are stored coins of the period. The other portal leads to the **Princes' Room**, a pure example of fourteenth-century Gothic with a vault resting on a single central pillar. It was built as a chapel, but takes its name from its later use as a meeting place for the rulers of Silesia's principalities.

The Rest of the Rynek

Among the cluster of modern buildings to the rear of the adjoining New Town Hall is the celebrated **Laboratory Theater** founded by **Jerzy Grotowski**. For two decades this was one of the most famous centers for experimental drama in the world. Contrary to the impression given in tourist brochures, the company no longer exists; it was dissolved following Grotowski's emigration to Italy in 1982, and its successor, founded by his pupils, has also been broken up. In its place is a research institute devoted to Grotowski's work, and you can see an exhibition on the Laboratory Theater if you ask at the offices down the alley to the left. The tiny studio theater, on the second floor of the building, is still used—on average once a week—for experimental performances by visiting actors; check the billboard outside for details.

Of the mansions lining the main sides of the Rynek, those on the western side are the most distinguished and colorful. Among several built in the self-confident style of the Flemish Renaissance, no. 2, the **Griffin House** (Pod Gryfami), is particularly notable. Number 5, with a superb Mannerist facade, is known as the **Waza Court** (Dwór Wazów), in honor of the tradition that it was the place where King Zygmunt Waza stayed during secret negotiations for his marriage to Anna von Habsburg. The mansion has recently been converted into Wrocław's chief gourmet citadel (see "Eating, Drinking, and Entertainment").

Next door at no. 6 is the **House of the Golden Sun** (Pod Złotym Słońcem), behind whose Baroque frontage is a suite of Renaissance rooms containing the **Museum of the Art of Medal-Making** (Tues–Sun 11am–6pm); its shop sells examples of the craft, which must be the classiest souvenirs in town. The last striking house in the block is no. 8, again Baroque but preserving parts of its Gothic predecessor; it's known as the **House of the Seven Electors** (Pod Siedmioma Elektorami), a reference to the seven grandees—one of whom was the king of Bohemia—who elected the Holy Roman Emperor.

West of the Rynek

At the southwest corner of the Rynek is a second, much smaller square, **plac Solny**. Its traditional function as a market has recently been revived, with flowers the dominant item, just as salt was in centuries past. Most of the buildings date back no earlier than the early nineteenth century, with pride of place taken by the Neoclassical former **Stock Exchange**, which occupies the lion's share of the southern side of the square.

Just off the northwest corner of the Rynek are two curious Baroque houses known as **Jaś i Małgosia**, linked by a gateway giving access to the cul-de-sac of **St Elizabeth**. Proving that brick is not an inherently dull material, this is the most beautiful of Wrocław's churches. Since the end of the fourteenth century its stately ninety-meter **tower**, which was under construction for 150 years, has been the city's most prominent landmark. Sadly, the church was gutted by fire under suspicious circumstances in 1976; restoration work has as yet a long way to go, and the whole area is still sealed off.

Facing the inner ring road just west of here is the only other block of old **burghers' houses** surviving in the city. Across the road and down ul. Antoniego Cieszyńskiego is the **Arsenal**, originally sixteenth-century but considerably altered by the Prussians a couple of hundred years later. Most of it is dilapidated, but a restored section houses a splendidly fusty branch of the **Historical Museum** (Tues, Thurs & Fri 10am–4pm, Sat 11am–5pm, Sun 10am–6pm).

On the next street to the south, ul. Mikołaja, stands the Gothic church of **St Barbara**, which has been given to Russian Orthodox exiles from Lwów. If you come here on Saturday evening or on Sunday between 8am and 1pm you can hear their gravely beautiful sung services, which last for well over two hours. At other times, only the chapel entered from the cemetery on the north side of the church is kept open.

Two streets farther to the south is the plain Baroque church of **St Anthony**, immediately to the east of which is the maze-like former **Jewish quarter**, whose inhabitants fled or were driven from their tenements during the Third Reich and were never to return. It seems that the postwar authorities have always been unsure as to how to react to this embarrassing legacy of the city's German past: a recent Polish guidebook to Wrocław makes no mention of the quarter's existence. The Neoclassical **Synagogue**, tucked away on a tiny square halfway down an alley, must once have been a handsome building, despite its shocking dilapidation.

South of the Rynek

Immediately to the east of the Jewish quarter is a part of the city built in obvious imitation of the chilly classical grandeur of the Prussian capital, Berlin. Indeed it was Carl Gotthard Langhans, designer of the Brandenburg Gate, who built the Neoclassical palace on the northern side of ul. Kazimierza Wielkiego, now the **New University Library**. He also had a hand in the monumental **Royal Palace** on the opposite side of the street. The central block of this now houses the **Archaeology Museum** (Wed & Fri 10am–4pm, Thurs 9am–4pm, Sat & Sun 10am–5pm), a dry survey of the prehistory of the region. Somewhat more fun is the **Ethnographical Museum** (Wed–Sun 10am–4pm) in the southern wing, a good place to visit if you have kids in tow. Its main attraction is a large collection of dolls decked out in what are deemed to be traditional dresses from all around the world—something guaranteed to bring a smile to the face of anyone from Scotland, Canada, or Australia.

The royal flavor of this quarter is continued in a different vein with the lofty Gothic church of **St Dorothy**, otherwise known as the "Church of Reconciliation." This was founded in 1351 by Charles IV, King of Bohemia and the future Holy Roman Emperor, in thanks for the conclusion of his negotiations with Kazimierz the Great, which secured Bohemia's rule over Silesia in return for a renunciation of its claim to Poland. Unlike most of Wrocław's other brick churches, this stayed in Catholic hands after the Reformation, becoming a Franciscan monastery. Its interior was whitewashed and littered with gigantic altars in the Baroque period, giving it a very different appearance from its neighbors, which still bear the hallmarks of four centuries of Protestant sobriety.

Behind St Dorothy's stands the **Opera House**, built by Carl Ferdinand Langhans in a faithful continuation of his father's Neoclassical style. Facing it is another example of fourteenth-century Gothic, **Corpus Christi** (Kościół Bozego Ciała), distinguished by the delicate brickwork of its facade porch and gable, and by the elaborate interior vaulting.

East of the Rynek

Returning to ul. Kazimierza Wielkiego and proceeding eastward, you come to the part-Gothic, part-Renaissance church of **St Christopher**, used by the small minority of German-speaking Protestants who remain here. Behind it stretches the vast esplanade of **plac Feliksa Dzierżyńskiego**. Until 1945 there was a heavily built-up quarter on this spot, but this was so badly damaged in the street fighting that it had to be completely razed. There's some compensation for this loss in the unusually wide **view** of the old city which has been opened up as a result.

The twin-towered **St Mary Magdalene**, just west of the square, is another illustration of the seemingly inexhaustible diversity of Wrocław's brick churches: this one is unusual in having flying buttresses, giving it a French feel. A bevy of funeral plaques and epitaphs line its exterior, though the most striking adornment is the twelfth-century stone **portal** on the south side. This masterpiece of Romanesque carving (whose tympanum has been moved for conservation to the National Museum) came from the demolished abbey of Ołbin in the north of the city. At the opposite side of the church is a separate entrance to a beautifully pure Gothic chapel, now a commercial gallery.

At the northern end of pl. Feliksa Dzierżyńskiego are the buildings of the **Dominican monastery**, centered on the thirteenth-century church of **St Adalbert** (św. Wojciecha), which is embellished with several lavish Gothic and Baroque chapels. A couple of blocks east, the gargantuan former **Bernardine Monastery** stands in splendid isolation; there's a particularly fine view of its barn-like church from the park beyond. The last important example of Gothic brickwork in the city, the monastery was begun in the mid-fifteenth century and finished only a few years before the Reformation, whereupon it was dissolved and the church used as a Protestant parish church. Severely damaged during the war, the church and cloisters have been painstakingly reconstructed to house the somewhat misleadingly named **Museum of Architecture** (Tues, Thurs & Fri 10am–3:30pm, Wed & Sat 10am–4pm, Sun 10am–5pm). In fact, this is a fascinating documentary record, using sculptural fragments and old photos, of the many historic buildings in the city which perished in the war.

Just east of here is the main post office building, with a **Museum of Posts and Telecommunications** (Mon–Sat 10am–3pm, Sun 11am–2:30pm) containing an impressive collection of stamps from the period of the Russian-controlled Kingdom of Poland; a couple of old mail coaches and all kinds of antiquated equipment are also on display.

The Racławice Panorama

Wrocław's best-loved sight, the **Panorama of the Battle of Racławice** (daily 8am–8pm), is housed in a specially designed rotunda in the park by the Bernardine monastery. This gigantic painting, 120m long and 15m high, was commissioned in 1894 to celebrate the centenary of the defeat of the Russian army by the people's militia of Tadeusz Kościuszko near the village of Racławice, between Kraków and Kielce. Ultimately this triumph was in vain: the third and final Partition of Poland, which wiped it off the map altogether, occurred the following year. Nonetheless, it was viewed a century later by patriots of the still-subdued nation as a supreme example of national will and self-sacrifice, which deserved a fitting memorial.

For a few decades, panorama painting created a sensation throughout Europe and North America, only to die abruptly with the advent of cinema. In purely artistic terms, most surviving examples are of poor quality, but this one is an exception, due largely to the participation of **Wojciech Kossak**, one of the most accomplished painters Poland has produced. Amazingly, he and his co-worker, **Jan Styka**, completed the project in just nine months. Seven other painters were hired for the execution of details, but the vast majority of the canvas is the work of these two men.

The subsequent **history of the painting** is a remarkable saga which tells much about the political situation of Poland. Despite an attempt by Polish-Americans to buy it and ship it across the Atlantic, it was placed on public view in Lwów, which was then part of Austria—the only one of the partitioning powers which would have tolerated such nationalist propaganda. It remained there until 1944, when a bomb substantially damaged it. Although allocated to Wrocław, as the cultural heir of Lwów, it was then put into storage—officially because there were no specialists to restore it, and no money to build the special structure the painting would need. The truth was that it was politically unacceptable to allow Poles to glory in their ancestors' slaughter of Russians.

That all changed with the events of 1980. Within five years the painting had been immaculately restored and was on display in a snazzy new building, with much attention being paid to natural foreground of soil, stones, and shrubs, which greatly adds to the uncanny appearance of depth. Not only is it Poland's most hi-tech tourist attraction, it's also one of the most popular, an icon second only in national affection to the Black Madonna of Jasna Góra. Poles flock here in droves, and you may have to reserve several hours in advance for a showing. This lasts for about 45 minutes—make sure you ask to hear the **English-language cassette** which explains all the details of the painting. Be warned that everyone is marched out as soon as the tape stops playing; you can, however, study the scale model of the battlefield downstairs at leisure.

The National Museum

At the opposite end of the park is the ponderously Prussian neo-Renaissance home of the **National Museum** (Wed & Fri–Sun 10am–4pm, Thurs 9am–4pm), which unites the collections of Breslau and Lwów. At the moment you need to come on two consecutive days to see everything—to save money, only half of the museum is open each day. However, one of the most important sections, **medieval stone sculpture**, is housed in the hall around the café and is open daily. Here you can see the delicately linear carving of *The Dormition of the Virgin* which formed the tympanum of the portal of St Mary Magdalene. The other major highlight is the poignant early fourteenth-century *Tomb of Henryk the Righteous*, one of the earliest funerary monuments to incorporate the subsequently popular motif of a group of weeping mourners.

On the first floor, one wing is devoted to an impressive display of Silesian **polychrome wood sculptures**. The most eye-catching exhibits are the colossal, late fourteenth-century statues of saints from St Mary Magdalene, their raw power compensating for a lack of sophistication. More pleasing are the many examples of the "Beautiful Madonnas" which were for long a favorite subject in Central European sculpture; a particularly fine example is the one made in the early fifteenth century for the cathedral.

The **foreign paintings** in the opposite wing include only a few worth specially seeking out. Among these are Cranach's *Eve*, originally part of a scene showing her temptation of Adam which was cut up and repainted as two portraits of a burgher couple in the seventeenth century. *The Baptism of Christ* is a fine example of the art of Bartholomeus Spranger, the leading exponent of the erotic style favored at the imperial court in Prague at the turn of the seventeenth century.

One of the star pieces in the comprehensive collection of **Polish paintings** on the top floor is the amazingly detailed *Entry of Chancellor Jerzy Ossoliński into Rome in 1633* by Bernardo Bellotto, best known for his documentary record of eighteenth-century Warsaw (see Chapter One). The other leading exhibit here is an unfinished blockbuster by Matejko, *Vows of King Jan Kazimierz Waza*. Set in Lwów Cathedral, it illustrates the monarch's pledge to improve the lot of the peasants at the end of the war against his invading Swedish kinsmen. Other works to look out for are Piotr Michałowski's *Napoleon on Horseback*, the *Fatherland Triptych* by Jacek Malczewski, and some mountain landscapes by Wojciech Gerson. A number of galleries are devoted to **contemporary arts and crafts**, much of it surprisingly daring for work executed under communist rule.

The University Quarter

Wrocław's academic quarter can be reached in just a few minutes from the Rynek by ul. Kuznicza, but the most atmospheric approach is to walk there from the National Museum along the south bank of the Odra, for a series of wonderfully peaceful **views** of the ecclesiastical quarter opposite.

Overlooking the Piaskowsky Bridge is the **Market Hall** (Hala Targowa), an early twentieth-century secular update of the idiom of the brick churches. It is piled with irresistible food and other goods, and boasts that it was equally replete even during martial law. From this point, the triangular-shaped university quarter, jam-packed with historic buildings, is clearly defined by two streets, ul. Universytecka to the south and ul. Grodzka, which follows the Odra.

Along the northern side of the former are three religious houses. First is **St Vincent**, founded as a Franciscan monastery by Henryk the Pious not long before his death at the Battle of Legnica (see "Legnica," below). One of the grandest of the city's churches, it was severely damaged in the war and is not yet fully restored. Its Baroque monastic buildings overlooking the Odra are now used by the university. Henryk also founded the **Ursuline Convent** alongside, which served as the mausoleum of the Piasts, who ruled the city during its period as an independent duchy.

Last in the row is the fourteenth-century church of **St Matthew** (św. Macieja), containing the tomb and memorial portrait of the city's most famous literary figure, the seventeenth-century mystic poet Johann Scheffler—better known as **Angelus Silesius** ("the Silesian Angel"), the pseudonym he adopted after his conversion to Catholicism. Many of Scheffler's poems still enjoy worldwide popularity as hymns, though his epigrams (standards of any anthology of German verse) represent his finest achievement. Facing the south side of the church is the Renaissance palace of the Piasts of Opole, while across ul. Szewska is the Baroque residence of their cousins from Brzeg-Legnica; both are now used by the university.

Behind St Matthew's stands one of Wrocław's most distinguished buildings, the domed **Ossoliński Library**. Originally a hospital, it was erected in the last quarter of the eighteenth century to designs by the Burgundian architect Jean Baptiste Mathey. The library collections are another legacy from Lwów, where they were assembled by the family whose name they still bear; among the many precious manuscripts is the original of the Polish national epic, Mickiewicz's *Pan Tadeusz*. Check on the boards outside for details of exhibitions.

The elongated plac Uniwersytecki begins on the southern side with a dignified eighteenth-century palace, **Dom Steffensa**, again owned by the university. Facing it is one of the most obviously Austrian features of the city, the **Church of the Holy Name of Jesus**, built at the end of the seventeenth century in the rash of Counter-Reformation religious building in the Habsburg lands. Its most arresting feature is the huge allegorical ceiling fresco by the most celebrated Austrian decorative painter of the day, Johann Michael Rottmayr.

Adjoining the church is the 171-meter-long facade of the Collegium Maximorum of the **University**, founded in 1702 by Emperor Leopold I. The wide entrance portal bears a balcony adorned with statues symbolizing various academic disciplines and attributes; more can be seen high above on the graceful little tower.

A frescoed staircase leads up to the main assembly hall or **Aula** (daily 9am–3:30pm, but frequently closed). The only historic room left in the huge building, it's one of the greatest secular interiors of the Baroque age, fusing the elements of architecture, painting, sculpture, and ornament into one bravura whole. Lording it from above the dais is a statue of the founder, armed, bejeweled, and crowned with a laurel. The huge illusionistic **ceiling frescoes** by Christoph Handke show the *Apotheosis of Divine and Worldly Wisdom* above the gallery and auditorium, while the scene above the dais depicts the university being entrusted to the care of Christ and the Virgin Mary. On the wall spaces between the windows are richly framed oval portraits of the leading founders of the university, while the jambs are frescoed with *trompe l'oeil* likenesses of the great scholars of Classical antiquity and the Middle Ages.

Wyspa Piasek, Ostrów Tumski and Eastward

From the Market Hall, the Piaskowsky Bridge leads to the sandbank of **Wyspa Piasek**, about half of whose area is green, with a cluster of historic buildings crammed together in the center. The first you come to on the right-hand side is the **University Library**, installed in an Augustinian monastery which was used as the Nazi military headquarters. Beside it is the fourteenth-century hall church of **St Mary of the Sands** (Kościół NMP na Piasku), dull on the outside, majestically vaulted inside. The aisles have an asymmetrical tripartite rib design known as the Piast vault, which is peculiar to this region. In the south aisle is the Romanesque tympanum from the previous church on the site, illustrating the dedication by its donor, Maria Włast. Across the road stands the Baroque church of **St Anne**, now used by a Uniate community from Lwów (see Chapter Three), and other parts of the Augustinian monastic complex, while at the far end of the islet are two old **mills**, known as *Maria i Feliks*.

Ostrów Tumski

The two elegant little painted bridges of Most Młyński and Most Tumski, which look as though they should belong in an ornamental garden, connect Wyspa Piasek with Ostrów Tumski. For those not already sated by medieval churches, there's a concentration of five more here, beginning just beyond Most Tumski with the fifteenth-century **Saints Peter and Paul**, behind which is the squat hexagonal **St Mark** of a couple of centuries earlier.

Far more prepossessing than these is the severe and imperious **Holy Cross and St Bartholomew**, which, with its massive bulk, giant buttresses, and pair of dissimilar towers, looks like some great fortified monastery. In fact, it's really two churches, one on top of the other. The lower, dedicated to St Bartholomew, is more spacious and extensive than an ordinary crypt, but lacks the exhilarating loftiness of its partner upstairs. The complex was founded in 1288 by Duke Henryk the Righteous as his own mausoleum, but his tomb has now been removed to the National Museum. A highly elaborate Baroque **monument to St Jan Nepomuk** stands in the square outside; his life is illustrated in the column bas-reliefs.

Ulica Katedralny leads past several Baroque palaces (among which priests, monks, and nuns are constantly scuttling) to the twin-towered **Cathedral**. Grievously damaged in 1945, this has been fully restored to its thirteenth-century form, but is not one of the more attractive of Wrocław's churches. The one exterior feature of note is the elaborate **porch**, though its sculptures, with the exception of two delicate reliefs, are mostly nineteenth-century pastiches. Three chapels behind the high altar make a visit to the dank and gloomy interior worthwhile. On the southern side is **St Elizabeth's Chapel**, built in the last two decades of the seventeenth century, its integrated architecture, frescoes, and sculptures created by Italian followers of Bernini. Next comes the Gothic **Lady Chapel**, with the masterly Renaissance funerary plaque of Bishop Jan Roth by Peter Vischer of Nuremberg. Last in line is the **Corpus Christi Chapel**, a perfectly proportioned and subtly decorated Baroque gem, begun in 1716 by the Viennese court architect Fischer von Erlach. To see the chapels, you'll probably have to ask at the sacristy, or tag onto one of the organized groups passing through.

Opposite the northern side of the cathedral is the tiny thirteenth-century church of **St Giles** (św. Idziego), the only one in the city to have escaped destruction by the Tartars, and preserving some finely patterned brickwork. Down ul. Kanonia is the **Archdiocesan Museum** (Tues–Sun 10am–3pm), a sizable and ramshackle collection of sacred artifacts. For a bit of relief from cultural indigestion, you can escape from the same street into the **Botanical Gardens** (Mon–Fri 9am–7pm or dusk, Sat & Sun 10am–6pm).

Ulica Szczytnicka leads eastward to the elongated avenue of plac Grunwaldzki, which gained notoriety in 1945 when it was converted into an airstrip to allow the defeated Nazi leaders to escape. At its southern end is the most famous of the city's bridges, **Most Grundwaldzki**, built in 1910.

East of Ostrów Tumski

Wrocław's most enticing stretch of greenery is the **Park Szczytnicki**, east of Ostrów Tumski, on the route of trams #1, #2, #4, #10, and #12. Its focal point is the **Hala Ludowa**, a huge hall built in 1913 to celebrate the centenary of the liberation of the city from Napoleon. Designed by Max Berg, the innovative municipal architect, it combines traditional Prussian solidity with a modernistic dash—the unsupported dome, with a diameter of 130 meters, is an audacious piece of engineering even by present-day standards. The hall is still used for exhibitions, sporting events, and other spectaculars, but even if there's nothing scheduled you can ask at the porter's desk to see inside.

In the same park is a work by a yet more famous architect: the box-like **Kindergarten** with peeling whitewash is Eastern Europe's only building by Le Corbusier. Along with the huge steel needle beside the hall, this is a legacy of the Exhibition of the Regained Territories, held here in 1948. Other delights in the park include a reassembled seventeenth-century wooden church, an amphitheater, a Japanese garden and pagoda, an artificial lake, and hundreds of different trees and shrubs—including oaks that are more than 600 years old. Across the road lie the **Zoological Gardens** (summer 9am–7pm, winter 9am–5pm), with the largest collection of wild animals in Poland.

Eating, Drinking, and Entertainment

Wrocław has a good selection of places to eat and drink, most of which are within a relatively small area—the episcopal and university quarters are noticeably barren. All the Orbis hotels, plus some of those around the main station, have both a restaurant and a café, but although these are all safe bets, Wrocław is one city where you can generally eat better elsewhere. Nightlife isn't exactly a Wrocław strong point, but the city's theater is maintaining its high reputation.

Restaurants

Dwór Wazów, Rynek 5. The "King's Restaurant" of this new complex is the best and most expensive in town, specializing in regal banquets with flambé meat dishes. Reservations recommended (☎44-16-33).

Dwór Wazów, ul. Kiełbaśnicza 6/7. The "Burghers' Restaurant," entered from the first street west of the Rynek, is just as recommendable as its pretentious stablemate, yet its prices are only marginally higher than those of the basic restaurants.

Piwnica Świdnicka, Rynek-Ratusz. This famous old restaurant under the Town Hall is a must, but beware of outrageously marked-up imported drinks which can easily double the price of a meal. Dancing in the evenings.

Ratuszowa, Rynek 9. Another cellar-restaurant, this time under the New Town Hall, serving cheap and solid food.

Zorba, Rynek-Ratusz. Tiny authentic Greek restaurant hidden away in the alley behind the New Town Hall. Open noon–6pm.

KDM, pl. Tadeusza Kościuszki 5/6. By far the best choice for inexpensive but hearty traditional dishes, serving Polish drinks only. Dancing in the evenings.

Czardasz, pl. Tadeusza Kościuszki 20. In theory the local Hungarian restaurant, but standard Polish dishes predominate.

Bieriozka, ul. Marcelego Nowotki 13. Close to the Jewish quarter, the cuisine in supposedly Russian but again there's little evidence of this.

Pod Chmielem, ul. Odrzańska 17. Beer hall serving high-quality food.

Grunwaldzka, pl. Grunwaldzki 6. Pick of the restaurants on Ostrów Tumski.

Snack Bars

Kambuz, ul. Ruska 58. Excellent and reasonably priced little fish restaurant, with changing daily specials.

Pod Złoty Dzbanem, Rynek 23. Slightly upscale snack bar.

Ratuszowy, Rynek 27a. The most conveniently sited of the city's milk bars.

Wojtus, Rynek 37. Very cheap and decent snack bar.

Pizzeria, Rynek 46/47. Specializes in pizzas, but with a range of hot snacks as well.

Miś, Kuźnicza 48. Milk bar close to the university quarter.

Wzorcowy, ul. Świerczewskiego 80. Best of the fast-food joints in the vicinity of the station.

Cafés

Dwór Wazów, Rynek 5. Situated above the restaurant, with a real palm-court atmosphere. There's also the alternative of sitting outside in the courtyard at the back.

Prospera, Rynek 28. Another upper-story café, with a predominantly young clientele.

Zak, Rynek-Ratusz 7. Has a tempting array of high-calorie desserts.

Małgosia, corner of Rynek and ul. Odrzańska. Relaxed basement café in one of Wrocław's most famous houses.

Hortex, pl. Tadeusza Kościuszki 1. Probably the most popular rendezvous point; frequently packed.

Pod Kalamburem, ul. Kuźnicza 29a. Beautiful Jugendstil decor, very low prices.

Saba, ul. św. Jadwigi. Housed in a splendid Baroque palace on Wyspa Piasek; one of the few refreshment spots in the episcopal quarter.

Cocktail Bar, ul. Komandorska 4a. Close to the station, with the best ice creams and milk shakes in town.

Entertainment and Festivals

Outside the big hotels, lively **nightspots** in Wrocław are thin on the ground. The most obvious place to drink and dance the night away is *Winiarnia Bacchus* at no. 16 on the Rynek, which is open from 10pm to 5am. There's live music every evening at the *Rura* jazz club, ul. Łazienna 4, while the main student club, *Pałaczyk*, ul. Tadeusza Kościuszki 34, has discos each Saturday.

Despite the demise of Grotowski's famous studio, Wrocław remains a major **theater** center. Henryk Tomaszewski, a former associate of Grotowski, has built up an international reputation for his pantomime company, which performs in alternation with classic drama at the *Teatr Polski*, ul. Gabrieli Zapolskiej 3 (☎386-53). *Teatr Kameralny*, ul. Świdnicka 28 (☎372-44), is the other main venue for straight plays, while the experimental mantle has been taken up by *Kalambur*, ul. Kuźnicza 29a (☎351-47). *Jedliniok*, a student song-and-dance ensemble decked out in colorful traditional costumes, performs at the *Teatr Gest*, pl. Grunwaldzki 63 (☎21-00-14). *Teatr Lalek*, pl. Teatralny 4 (☎44-12-17), is a celebrated puppet theater—reserve well in advance for its regular weekend shows, which are invariably sold out. The city's annual **drama festivals** include one devoted to monologues in January, and a contemporary Polish play season in May and June.

There's a similarly wide choice in classical **music**. Both the *Opera*, ul. Świdnicka 35 (☎307-27), and the *Operetka Wrocławska*, ul. Gen. Karola Świerczewskiego 67 (☎356-52), maintain high standards; tickets are easy to obtain and absurdly cheap by New York or Los Angeles standards. Orchestral concerts and recitals take place regularly at the *Filharmonia*, ul. Gen. Karola Świerczewskiego 5 (☎44-20-01).

Wrocław hosts two contrasting **international music festivals** each year: the renowned *Jazz on the Odra* in May, and *Wratislavia Cantans*, devoted to oratorios and cantatas, in September. There's also a festival of early music at the beginning of December.

Listings

Airline *LOT*, ul. Świerczewskiego 36 (☎363-76).

Bookshops Main concentration is on the Rynek, including one devoted to Russian and another to imported publications, both with many titles in English; others on ul. Świdnicka.

Car breakdown *PZMot*, ul. Jagiellończyka 18 (daily 6am–10pm; ☎981); *Polmozbyt*, pl. Grunwaldzki 47 (daily 7am–10pm; ☎954).

Car rental Orbis, Rynek 29 (☎347-80/326-65).

Exchange facilities Best rate from the bank at ul. Oławska 2.

Gas station The one at ul. Zmigrodzka is open 24hr and has a lead-free pump.

Post offices Head office is at ul. Zygmunta Krasińskiego 1; there's a branch at Rynek 28 and another, with a restricted 24-hr service, in the square in front of the main train station.

The Wrocław District

The administrative **district of Wrocław**—covering a roughly circular area, with the city itself at the center—is predominantly rural, with the River Odra and its tributaries draining some of the most productive agricultural land in the country. Yet the scenery is very varied, ranging from an isolated massif in the southwest through several forests to a chain of small lakes in the northwest. Due to the extensive **public transit** network, Wrocław itself makes a perfectly adequate touring base, though there's a reasonable amount of basic **accommodation** elsewhere should you prefer to stay in a more tranquil location.

Ślęza and Sobótka

The flatness of the plain south of the Odra is abruptly broken some 30km from Wrocław by an isolated outcrop of rocks with two peaks, the higher of which is known as **Ślęza** (718m). One of the most enigmatic sites in Poland, Ślęza was used for pagan worship in Celtic times, and was later settled by the Slav tribe after whom the mountain—and Silesia itself—are named.

Ślęza is normally approached from **SOBÓTKA** (ZOBTEN), which is on the rail line and some bus routes to Świdnica. Between the bus terminal and the train station is the Gothic parish church, outside which stands the first of several curious ancient **sculptures** to be seen in the area—consisting of one stone placed across another, it's nicknamed "The Mushroom". On the slopes of Ślęza there's a large and voluptuous statue of a woman with a fish, while the summit has a carved lion on it. Exactly what these carvings symbolize is not known; some certainly postdate the Christianization of the area, but that hasn't prevented their association with pagan rites. Even though the site hasn't achieved the cult status of its English counterparts—Glastonbury, Avebury, and Stonehenge—it's not exactly a place to look for quiet mystery, being enormously popular with day-trippers, and often teeming with busloads of schoolchildren.

Five separate **hiking trails** traverse the hillsides, some of them stony, so it's essential to wear shoes with a good grip. More than an hour is needed for the busiest stretch, the direct ascent from Sobótka to the top of Ślęza by the route marked by yellow signs. The summit is spoiled by a number of ugly buildings including the inevitable television tower, while the neo-Gothic chapel is a poor substitute for the castle and Augustinian monastery which once stood here. Recompense comes with the most extensive panoramic view in Silesia.

Should you wish to stay, there are a couple of **tourist hostels** in Sobótka: *Pod Misiem*, ul. Mickiewicza 7 (☎199), and *Pod Wiezycą*, ul. Zymierskiego 13 (☎147). At SULISTROWICE, 2km to the south, there's a **campground** (☎604) with chalets. On Sobótka's main square is a bar which serves very cheap meals; other-wise you'll have to stock up at the grocery store.

Oleśnica

OLEŚNICA (OELS), 30km west of Wrocław, is today a market town of some 35,000 people, yet was once the capital of a tiny principality. Some of the feel of an old ducal capital lingers on, largely owing to the **Castle** which still completely dominates the town. Raised in the fourteenth century, it was transformed in the sixteenth into a magnificent palace in the German Renaissance style for a member of the Bohemian royal family. Most of the building is now used as offices, but there's also a small archaeological museum (Tues–Sun 10am–3pm).

The Gothic **parish church**, once the duke's chapel, is linked to the castle by a covered archway; other reminders of its ducal past are the grandiose tombs in the chancel. Oleśnica was a bastion of the Reformation, with the local Polish-speaking population seemingly as enthusiastic as their German overlords. Although the church has now been returned to the Catholics, its arrangement of wooden galleries is a legacy of the Protestant emphasis on preaching. The only other notable monument in Oleśnica is an extensive section of the **town walls**, including an impressive but unkempt gateway across from the bus station.

There are two **hotels** here: the one-star *Śląsk*, at no. 12 on the Rynek (☎20-54), and the three-star *Perła* at ul. Zawadzkiego 12 (☎35-19). Best choice for a meal is the *Piast* restaurant on the same square.

Trzebnica

TRZEBNICA (TREBNITZ), 24km north of Wrocław, is even smaller and more unassuming than Oleśnica, yet is another place with a long and distinguished history, having been granted a charter in 1202 by Duke Henryk the Bearded. It was his marriage to the German princess Saint Hedwig (known in Poland as Jadwiga) which was largely responsible for shifting Silesia towards a predomi-nantly German culture, setting the trend for the next six centuries.

The couple established a **Cistercian convent** in the town, the sole monument of note. Built in the severe style favored by this order—still Romanesque in shape and feel, but already with the Gothic pointed arch and ribbed vault—it was progressively remodeled and now has a predominantly Baroque appearance. A survival from the original building is the **portal**, which was found during excava-tion work and re-erected, half-hidden, behind the porch. Its sculptures, showing

King David playing the harp to Bathsheba and a maidservant, are among the most refined European works of the thirteenth century. The northern doorway also survives, but is of a far lower standard of workmanship.

Inside the church, the main feature is the large Gothic **St Hedwig's Chapel** to the right of the choir. The princess, who spent her widowhood in the convent, was canonized in 1267, just twenty-four years after her death, whereupon this chapel was immediately built in her memory. In 1680, her simple marble and alabaster sepulchral slab was incorporated into a grandiose tomb, whose sides are lined with mourners. At the same time, a considerably less ostentatious memorial to her husband was placed in the choir, its entrance guarded by statues of Saint Hedwig and her even more celebrated niece, Saint Elizabeth of Hungary.

The only places to stay in Trzebnica are the three-star **motel** on ul. Prusicka (☎12-00-48) and the **campground** (which also has chalets) at ul. Leśna 2 (☎12-12-26). There's a very basic **restaurant** opposite the convent, and a couple of even more basic snack bars in the town center.

The Zmigród and Milicz Lake District

North of Trzebnica lies a lake district with several nature reserves, centered on the small towns of **ZMIGRÓD** (TRACHENBERG) and **MILICZ** (MILITSCH), which both lie in the valley of the Barycza, a tributary of the Odra. The former is on the main rail line to Leszno and Poznań, the latter on a different northbound route.

Although there are also buses connecting these towns with Trzebnica and Wrocław, the most entertaining way to travel in this region is on the **narrow-gauge train** from Trzebnica. One of Poland's best-loved lines with visiting train enthusiasts, it continues to thrive despite being under threat of closure for years. The tiny diesel is in a very dilapidated state, and there are only two passenger services per day. As one of these runs before dawn, effectively the only option is the departure just after 11am. Don't look for a station—there isn't one—but for a painted sign like a bus stop by the tracks at the northeastern edge of town. The line divides at PREDZKOWICE, but if you want to see the whole stretch you should continue to the first terminal at Zmigród; the train then backtracks to the junction before continuing eastward via Milicz to the other terminal of SULMIERZYCE, arriving at 4:40pm. After a pause, it returns to Trzebnica, but if you're staying in Wrocław it's best to alight at Milicz and change to a mainline train.

The journey between Milicz and Sulmierzyce is particularly intriguing, as it takes you through one of Europe's most important **bird reserves**. Over 170 different water and moorland species breed in the area, while an even larger number use it as a stop-off point on their migration. Black and white storks, swans, herons, seagulls, cranes, cormorants, and great crested grebes are among the species most likely to be seen, apart from the inevitable ducks and geese. If you're lucky, you might even be able to spot sea eagles, who spend the winter here. Autumn, as the birds prepare to leave, is the best season for a visit: they are less timid at this time and more likely to be seen in groups in the open countryside.

Although it's usually possible to see some birds from the train, if you're seriously interested you'll need to go on foot. There are marked trails throughout the area, and an observation tower at the Wzgórze Joanny (Joanna Hill) south of Milicz. Other parts of this lake district are **forest reserves**, in some of which wild boar and both red and fallow deer roam freely. Be warned, however, that the marshy soil often means that stretches of this countryside are impassable.

Accommodation is limited: Zmigród has a **tourist hostel**, *Zmigrodzianka*, at ul. Wojska Polskiego 5 (☎37-38), while a **campground** with chalets can be found at ul. Poprzeczna 13 (☎412-15) in KARŁOWO, just south of Milicz.

AROUND SILESIA

Though much of the Silesian countryside is flat farmland, the scenery at the western edge of the province is its strongest selling point. The **Karkonosze National Park** and the valleys around **Kłodzko** have some of Europe's best hiking country, along with a series of resorts offering everything from spa treatments to winter sports. None of the other old ducal capitals, such as **Legnica**, **Świdnica**, **Brzeg, Opole**, and **Cieszyn**, are developed to anything like the same extent as Wrocław, and some still have an attractively small-town air. Many of the province's finest surviving monuments are to be found in these towns; other slightly less central sights are the medieval fortifications of **Paczków** and the Baroque monasteries of **Legnickie Pole** (close to Legnica) and **Krzeszów**. The southern part of the province is dominated by one of Central Europe's largest conurbations, centered on **Katowice**; its heavy industry has been crucial to Poland's economy, but the failure to modernize has led to an environmental disaster which is currently one of the country's most challenging problems.

Traveling by **public transit** should present few problems, but bear in mind that the varied terrain means that journeys often take even longer than usual. There's plentiful **accommodation** in the most popular areas, though choice in many other parts of the province is often restricted.

Legnica

In 1241 the Tartar hordes won a titanic battle 60km west of Wrocław against a combined army of Poles and Silesians, killing its commander, Duke Henryk the Pious. Silesia's subsequent division among Henryk's descendants into three separate duchies began a process of dismemberment which was thereafter to dog its history. One of the new capitals was **LEGNICA** (LIEGNITZ), a fortified town a few kilometers from the battlefield, one of the few in the area to have escaped destruction. It remained a ducal seat until the last of the Piasts died in 1675, but by then its role as their main residence had been taken over by Brzeg.

Although often ravaged by fires, and badly damaged in World War II, Legnica has maintained its role as one of Silesia's most important cities, and is nowadays a busy regional center preserving a wide variety of monuments—admittedly interspersed with a fair amount of shoddy concrete—as evidence of its varied history.

The Town

Arriving at the **train station** to the northeast of the old city, or the **bus station** diagonally opposite, the main sights are best covered by a circular walk. Following either ul. Dworcowa (between the stations) or the parallel ul. Pocztowa (behind the bus station) to the right, you shortly come to the ample plac Zamkowy, site of the early fifteenth-century **Głogów Gate** (one of only two surviving parts of the city wall) and the enormous **Castle**.

The latter is a bit of a mish-mash, and now houses administrative offices, with no interesting interiors to see. Nonetheless, it has some outstanding features, particularly the **gateway** in the form of a triumphal arch, the only surviving part of the Renaissance palace built here. Two towers survive in restored form from the earlier defensive castle, replaced by a Romantic pseudo-fortress designed by the great Berlin architect Karl Friedrich Schinkel.

Continuing down ul. Nowa, which offers the best overall view of the castle, you arrive at ul. Pantyzanow, the axis of a well-preserved Baroque quarter. On the right are the Jesuit buildings, with the church of **St John** and the college next door united in a single, sweeping facade. Protruding from the eastern side of the church, its orientation and brick Gothic architecture looking wholly out of place, is the presbytery of the thirteenth-century Franciscan monastery which formerly occupied the spot. It owes its survival to its function as the Piast mausoleum; inside you can see several sarcophagi, plus Baroque frescoes illustrating the history of Poland and Silesia under the dynasty.

Across the road stands the **Regional Museum** (Wed–Sun 11am–5pm), housed in the former mansion of the Cistercian monastery of Lubiąz. Another fine palace of the same epoch, the **Rycerska Academy**, can be found in the street immediately behind, ul. Chojnowska. Here also is the late fourteenth-century **Chojnow Tower**, plus a small section of the medieval wall.

This same street runs into the elongated **Rynek**. Sadly, this has lost much of its character—the two rows of historic buildings placed back-to-back along the central part of the square are now set off by functional modern dwellings, which have transformed the Rynek from a public meeting place into a residential area. Eight arcaded Renaissance houses, all brightly colored and some decorated with graffiti, have survived. At the end of this block is the **Town Hall**, a restrained Baroque construction, while behind stands the **Theater**, built in the first half of the nineteenth century in a style reminiscent of a Florentine palazzo. There's also a fine but blackened eighteenth-century fountain dedicated to Neptune.

The far end of the square is closed by the large twin-towered brick church of **Saints Peter and Paul**, with its fairytale neo-Gothic exterior, which fits very well with the monumental turn-of-the-century buildings in and around the small plac Chopina on its south side. Two exquisite fourteenth-century portals have survived: the northern one, featuring a tympanum of *The Adoration of the Magi* flanked by statues of the church's two patrons, overshadows the more prominent facade doorway with its *Madonna and Child*. The furnishings of the interior, which largely retains its original form, range from a late thirteenth-century font with bronze bas-reliefs to an elaborate Renaissance pulpit and a theatrical Baroque high altar.

Ulica Piotra i Pawła and ul. Rosenbergów both lead to pl. Mariacki, with the brick Gothic church of **Our Lady**, whose gaunt exterior brings to mind military rather than ecclesiastical architecture. Notwithstanding its dedication, it's still the place of worship of the remnant of the Protestant community, who were in a majority here until 1945.

Legnickie Pole

LEGNICKIE POLE (WAHLSTATT), 9km southeast of the city, occupies the site of the great battleground; it can be reached by any bus going to JAWOR, or by the municipal services #9, #16, #17, and #20. Extensive repair work has been in progress on the village's monuments for several years, with the optimistic aim of having them restored in time for the 750th anniversary of the battle in 1991.

A church was erected on the spot where Henryk the Pious's body was found (according to tradition, his mother was only able to identify the headless corpse from his six-toed feet), and in time this became a Benedictine monastery—popularly but implausibly said to be the rustic Gothic building in the center of the village. A Protestant parish for four centuries, the church has been secularized to house the **Museum of the Battle of Legnica** (Tues–Sun 11am–5pm), which includes diagrams and mock-ups of the conflict and a copy of Henryk's tomb (the original is in Wrocław's National Museum).

The Benedictines, who were evicted during the Reformation, returned to Legnickie Pole in the early eighteenth century and constructed the **Abbey** (Tues–Sun 11am–5pm) directly facing their alleged former premises. It was built by **Kilian Ignaz Dientzenhofer**, the creator of much of Prague's magnificent Baroque architecture. His characteristic use of varied geometric shapes and the interplay of concave and convex surfaces is well illustrated here. The interior of the church, an oval nave plus an elongated apse, is exceptionally bright, an effect achieved by the combination of white walls and very large windows. Forming a perfect complement to the architecture are the bravura **frescoes** covering the vault by the Bavarian **Cosmos Damian Asam**. Look out for the scene over the organ gallery, which shows the Tartars hoisting Henryk's head on a stake and celebrating their victory, while the duke's mother and wife mourn over his body.

Since the second dissolution of the monastery in 1810, the **monastic buildings** (currently a women's hospice) have been put to a variety of uses. For nearly a century they served as a Prussian military academy; its star graduate was Paul von Hindenburg, German commander-in-chief during World War I and President from 1925 until his death in 1934.

Practicalities

In Legnica, the only **hotel** is the four-star *Cuprum* (☎285-44) at no. 7 on ul. Skarbowa, which leads from pl. Mariacki back to the bus station; this also has the best restaurant and café in town. The other accommodation possibility is the **youth hostel** at ul. Jordana 17 (☎254-12). Alternative places to **eat** and **drink**, on the other hand, are reasonably plentiful, and include another restaurant on ul. Skarbowa, *Polonia*. Across from the train station are a restaurant, *Piast*, and a milk bar, *Ekspres*. A similar choice is available on the Rynek with *Stary Zagora* and *Kefirek*, along with a busy café, *Ratuszowa*. The **Orbis** office is due east of pl. Mariacki at ul. Wrocławska 10/18 (☎229-23). Several more travel bureaus can be found around the Rynek; you should be able to pick up leaflets on the town, though most likely only in Polish.

In Legnickie Pole there's an officially designated **restaurant**, *Rycerska*, on the main square; don't expect too much from the food, though there's beer on tap. At the edge of the village is the only **campground** (☎823-97) in the Legnica area; it also has chalets for rent.

Głogów and Zielona Góra

Northwestern Silesia is little visited and contains nothing in the way of obvious tourist attractions. However, it has a couple of old towns which are, for very different reasons, worth a passing look.

Głogów

GŁOGÓW (GLOGAU), 60km north of Legnica, is a name which crops up quite frequently in history books. The capital of one of the myriad Piast duchies, it has produced a remarkable number of influential citizens for a place whose population has never numbered more than a few thousand. These include Jan of Głogów, the teacher of Copernicus; Andreas Gryphius, the greatest German poet and dramatist of the seventeenth century; and Arnold Zweig, the Jewish novelist who became a leading intellectual figure in Israel and then in the German Democratic Republic. The town also provided the setting for one of E.T.A. Hoffmann's chilling fantasies on the theme of schizophrenia, *The Jesuit Chapel at G___*.

In 1945, Głogów was turned into a fortress by the retreating Nazis and completely destroyed. Visiting it today is still a shocking experience. The historic quarter, which lies about ten minutes' walk to the left of the station, has never been rebuilt and stands as an overgrown wasteland, around which has sprung up a modern town with no real heart to it. An abortive attempt was made to patch up the parish church, formerly a handsome piece of brick Gothic architecture, but clearly it was too badly damaged for full restoration. However, the **Jesuit college** described in Hoffmann's story has somehow managed to survive, rising in defiance above the desolation. Inside, a photographic exhibition provides a poignant documentary record of the appearance of the town before its destruction.

Zielona Góra

The wartime experience of **ZIELONA GÓRA** (GRÜNBERG), 60km northwest of Głogów, was very different. Hardly damaged at all, it has grown to become an important center for the machine and textile industries since passing into Polish hands, and now has a population numbering some 100,000. It also has a somewhat esoteric claim to fame as being the only place in Poland where wine is produced.

Although it lacks any outstanding sights, the whole central area of Zielona Góra has a certain novelty value, full of examples of the sorts of buildings which in most other Polish towns tended to fall to the bulldozers if they hadn't already been destroyed in the war. It's a patchwork of the architectural styles practiced in turn-of-the-century Germany, with the solidly orthodox Wilhelmine rubbing shoulders with the experimental forms of Jugendstil. There are also a few older landmarks in the midst of these, including a couple of towers surviving from the fifteenth-century ramparts, the Gothic church of St Hedwig and the much-remodeled Renaissance town hall in the center of the Rynek. Most imposing of all is the large **parish church**, an eighteenth-century example of the Silesian penchant for half-timbered ecclesiastical buildings.

Orbis obviously thinks highly of Zielona Góra, as it has a prestigious international **hotel**, the *Polan*, just a couple of blocks east of the station at ul. Staszica 9a (☎700-91). The company's travel bureau is at ul. Świerczewskiego 28 (☎659-58), while **Almatur** is at ul. Westerplatte 30 (☎728-67). Pick of the many **restaurants** in the town are *Topaz* on ul. Boharetów Westerplatte and *Ostoja* on ul. Poznańska. The best time for a visit here is September, when there are **festivals** devoted to the wine harvest and to international song and dance troupes.

Jelenia Góra and Around

JELENIA GÓRA (HIRSCHBERG), which lies 60km southwest of Legnica and some 110km from Wrocław, is the gateway to one of Poland's most popular holiday and recreation areas, the Karkonosze National Park. Its name means "Deer Mountain," but the rusticity this implies is scarcely reflected in the town itself, a manufacturing center for the past five centuries. Founded as a fortress in 1108 by King Bolesław the Wrymouth, Jelenia Góra came to prominence in the Middle Ages through glass and iron production, with high-quality textiles taking over as the cornerstone of its economy in the seventeenth century. With this solid base, it was hardly surprising that after coming under Prussian control the town was at the forefront of the German industrial revolution.

The Town

Some of Jelenia Góra's present-day factories look stuck in a nineteenth-century time-warp, and pollution is a major problem. Thankfully, however, industry has always been confined to the peripheries, and the traffic-free historic quarter is remarkably well-preserved. Even in a country with plenty of prepossessing central squares, the **plac Ratuszowy** is outstanding. Not the least of its attractions is that it's neither a museum-piece nor the main commercial center: most of the businesses are restaurants and cafés, while the tall mansions are now subdivided into apartments. Although their architecture ranges from the late Renaissance via Baroque to Neoclassical, the houses form an unusually coherent group, all having whitewashed walls and an arcaded front at street level. The latter feature, which provides protection against the harsh winter climate, is unique in Poland. Occupying the familiar central position on the square is the large mid-eighteenth- century **Town Hall**. Its graceful tower is one of the dominant features of the skyline, while the unpainted stonework provides the best possible foil to the houses.

To the northeast of pl. Ratuszowy rises the slender belfry of the Gothic parish church of **Saints Erasmus and Pancras**. Epitaphs to leading local families adorn the outer walls, while the inside is chock-full of Renaissance and Baroque furnishings. Yet another eye-catching tower can be seen just to the east, at the point where the main shopping thoroughfare, ul. Marii Konopnickiej, changes its name to ul. 1 Maja. Originally part of the sixteenth-century fortifications, it was taken over a couple of centuries later to serve as the belfry of **St Anne's Chapel**. The only other survivor of the town wall is the tower off ul. Jasna, the street which forms a westward continuation of pl. Ratuszowy.

Continuing down ul. 1 Maja, you come in a couple of minutes to the Baroque chapel of **Our Lady**; it's normally kept locked, but if you happen to be here on a Sunday morning you can drop in to hear the fervent singing of its Russian Orthodox congregation. At the end of the street, enclosed in a walled, park-like cemetery, is another Baroque church, **Holy Cross**, built during the early eighteenth century by a Swedish architect, Martin Franze, on the model of St Catherine's in Stockholm. Though sober from the outside, the double-galleried interior is richly decorated with *trompe l'oeil* frescoes.

From the bustling al. 15 Grudnia, which skirts the old town to the south, ul. Jana Matejki leads to the **District Museum** (Tues, Thurs & Fri 9am–3:30pm, Wed, Sat & Sun 9am–5pm), set just below the wooded Kościuski Hill. Apart from temporary exhibitions, the display space here is devoted to the history of **glass** from antiquity to the present day, with due emphasis on local examples and a particularly impressive twentieth-century section.

For the best **viewpoint** in town, go west from pl. Ratuszowy along ul. Jasna, then cross ul. Podwale and continue down ul. Obrońców Pokoju into the woods and over the bridge. Several paths lead up the hill, which is crowned with a watchtower that's permanently open. From the top there's a sweeping view of Jelenia Góra and the surrounding countryside.

Jelenia Góra Practicalities

The main **train station** is about fifteen minutes' walk east of the center at the far end of ul. 1 Maja. Local buses plus a few services to nearby towns leave from the bays in front, but the **bus station** for all interurban departures is at the opposite end of town off ul. Obrońców Pokoju.

PTTK have a tourist information bureau at al. Wojska Polskiego 40 (Mon–Sat 8am–4pm; ☎220-00). English is spoken at the **Orbis** office, ul. 1 Maja 1 (Mon–Fri 8am–5pm, Sat 8am–1/2pm; ☎262-11); ask here if you want a room in a **private house** in Jelenia Góra or one of the nearby resorts. Other services available here include the renting of mountain guides, and flights by hang-glider or helicopter (not outrageously expensive if you're in a large enough group).

Another Orbis agency is in the spanking new five-star **hotel,** *Jelenia Góra* (☎240-81), located on ul. Gen. Karola Świerczewskiego at the southeastern edge of town, on the road to Kowary and Karpacz. This is one of the best-equipped hotels in Poland, with prices to match. The considerably less glamorous alternatives are *Europa* at ul. 1 Maja 16 (☎232-21) and *Sportowy* (☎269-42) in the park between *Hotel Jelenia Góra* and the town center; the park also has the only **campground**. Of the two **youth hostels**, *Bartek*, ul. Bartka Zwycięzcy 10 (☎257-46), is handy for the station, whereas *Michałek* is inconveniently sited to the far north of town at ul. Wiejska 86 (☎241-55). There's also a **PTTK hostel** at ul. 1 Maja 88 (☎230-59).

On the western side of pl. Ratuszowy are three **restaurants**, *Pokusa, Retro*, and *Pod Smokiem*, all with outside tables. The last named, specializing in flambé dishes, is the pick of the trio, though its local nickname of "the Chinese restaurant" refers to the decor rather than to the cooking. Fiery Hungarian-style dishes are served at *Tokaj* on ul. Pocztowa, just around the corner from another good choice, *Staropolska Karczma* on ul. 1 Maja. There are plenty of **snack bars** and **cafés** in the center, among which *Hortex* on pl. Ratuszowy is particularly good.

Cultural life centers on the Secessionist-style **Cyprian Norwid Theater** at al. Wojska Polskiego 38 (☎232-74), whose main season is in the autumn. Jelenia Góra hosts concerts of chamber and organ music in July, while early to mid-August sees a **festival** of street theater.

Cieplice Śląskie-Zdrój

The municipal boundaries of Jelenia Góra have recently been extended to incorporate a number of communities to the south, nearest of which is the old spa town of **CIEPLICE ŚLĄSKIE-ZDRÓJ** (BAD WARMBRUNN), 8km away. Local bus #9 passes through the center of Cieplice; #7, #8, and #15 stop on the western side of town, enabling you to connect with buses and trains to Szklarska Poręba (see "The Karkonosze Mountains"), while #4, #13, and #14 stop on the eastern side, with bus connections to the other main resort in the range, Karpacz.

Although it has a number of modern sanatariums, along with concrete apartment houses in the suburbs, Cieplice seems to bask in the aura of an altogether less pressured age. To catch this atmosphere at its densest, attend one of the regular concerts of **Viennese music** in the spa park's delightful Neoclassical **theater**.

The broad main street of Cieplice is oddly designated as a square—plac Piatowski. Its main building is the large eighteenth-century **Schaffgotsch Palace**, named after the German grandees who formerly owned much of the town. There are also a couple of Baroque **parish churches**—the one for the Catholics stands in a cul-de-sac at the western end of the street and is generally open, whereas its Protestant counterpart to the east of the palace is locked except on Sunday mornings. In the Park Norweski, which continues the spa park on the southern side of the Podgórna River, is a small **Ornithological Museum** (Tues–Sun 9am–4pm).

At the western edge of the spa park at ul. Cervi 11 is the **hotel** *Cieplice* (☎510-41); until recently it was the most prestigious in the region though its facilities (only light meals available) hardly justify its four-star rating. There's also a **tourist hostel**, *Pod Rózami*, at pl. Piatowski 26 (☎514-54). The **campground**, *Rataja* (☎525-66), is near the Orłe train station outside town to the southwest, on the routes of buses #7 and #15. In the assembly rooms beside the spa theater is a good **café** with a cold buffet service and dancing in the evenings. The hostel has a **restaurant**, and there's a decent **milk bar** at the western end of pl. Piatowski, but you'll have to go to Jelenia Góra if you want a full meal later than 5pm.

Sobieszów and Jagniątków

Buses #7, #9 and #15 all continue the few kilometers south to **SOBIESZÓW** (HERMSDORF). Once again, there are two Baroque **parish churches**, both located off the main ul. Cieplicka: the one built for the Protestants is appropriately plain, while that for the Catholics is exuberantly decorated. In an isolated location on the southeastern outskirts is the **Regional Museum** (Tues–Sun 9am–4pm), with displays on the local geology, flora, and fauna.

From there, the red and black trails offer a choice of ascents to **Chojnik Castle** (Tues–Sun 9am–4pm), which sits resplendently astride the wooded hill of the same name. It's actually much farther from town than it appears—allow about an hour for the ascent. Founded in the mid-fourteenth century, the castle is celebrated in legend as the home of a beautiful, man-hating princess who insisted that any suitor had to travel through a treacherous ravine in order to win her hand. Many perished in the attempt: when one finally succeeded, the princess chose to jump into the ravine herself in preference to marriage. The castle was badly damaged in 1675, not long after the addition of its drawbridge and the Renaissance ornamentation on top of the walls. Yet, despite its ruined state, enough remains to give a good illustration of the layout of the medieval feudal stronghold it once was, with the added bonus of a magnificent **view** from the round tower.

The castle houses a restaurant and **tourist hostel** (☎535-35), though its isolated position makes the novelty value the sole reason for staying. Sobieszów itself has another hostel, *Nad Wrzosówką* at ul. Cieplicka 213 (☎536-27), along with a **campground**, *Łazienkowska*, at the northern edge of the town center on ul. Łazienkowska. Also on ul. Cieplicka are a **restaurant**, *Ostoja*, and a couple of snack bars.

Jagniątków

At the very edge of the Karkonosze, just south of Sobieszów, is the village of **JAGNIĄTKÓW** (AGNETENDORF), once home of the German novelist and playwright **Gerhart Hauptmann**, winner of the 1912 Nobel Prize for Literature. Having fallen afoul of the Nazis he formerly supported, Hauptmann spent his last years in this isolated corner of his native province, staying on even when it came under Polish rule in 1945. The psychological novels he wrote here have worn less well than his earlier naturalistic works, notably his drama of Silesian industrial life, *The Weavers*. **Hauptmann's house**, a spectacular Jugendstil mansion with a Great Hall lined with giant murals, is now a convalescent home for child victims of industrial pollution from the Katowice conurbation. You're free to look in and see the memorial room, which contains first editions of his major works.

The Karkonosze Mountains

The **Karkonosze** (Riesengebirge, or "Giants' Mountains") are the highest and best-known part of the chain known as the Sudeten mountains, which stretch 300km northwest from the Beskids, forming a natural border between Silesia and Czechoslovakia. Known for its raw, highly volatile climate, the predominantly granite Karkonosze range rises abruptly on the Polish side, and its lower slopes are quite heavily forested with fir, beech, birch, and pine. At around 1100m, these trees give way to dwarf mountain pines and alpine plants, some of them imported. Above 1350m the summits have an unusually stark appearance for this part of Europe.

Primarily renowned as **hiking** terrain, these mountains formerly rivaled the Black Forest as Germany's most popular scenic region. Set beneath dramatically changing skies, its peaks often blanketed by mist, the range strongly stirred the German Romantic imagination, and was hauntingly depicted by the greatest artist of the movement, Caspar David Friedrich. From the amount of German you hear spoken in the resorts, and from the turned-up *lederhosen* and feathered hats worn by so many hikers, you might think that this area still belonged to Germany. Yet the Polish tourist authorities aren't complaining at the Germanic hordes who pour in to take advantage of the low prices and in many cases to cast wistful glances at the former holiday homes of their ancestors. The collapse of communism has depleted the system of trade-union holiday homes and reduced the numbers of other Eastern Europeans, who are now free to travel wherever they please. As a result, even with the steady flow of BMW-drivers, the Karkonosze resorts find themselves facing the prospect of economic ruin. The easiest way to avert this, and the one currently being heavily touted, would be to develop the area's potential as a **winter sports** region; it has some facilities at the moment, but they are still fairly rudimentary.

The upper reaches of the Karkonosze have been designated as a **national park**. Lying just outside its boundaries are two sprawling resorts, Szklarska Poręba and Karpacz, which make the most convenient centers for exploring the mountains, though Jelenia Góra and its satellites are viable alternatives. As the area is relatively compact—the total length of the Karkonosze is no more than 37km—and the public transit system good (if circuitous), there's no need to use more than one base.

HIKING IN THE NATIONAL PARK

The **map** of the national park available from kiosks and travel offices is a must if you intend to do any serious walking: it shows all the best viewpoints, and marks where avalanches may occur. Special care should be taken if visiting in winter, even though the area is patrolled by mountain rescue teams with St Bernard dogs, as many paths are impassable or dangerous for months on end.

No matter what the season, the summits are battered by wind almost every day and have an **average annual temperature of around freezing point**, so make sure you take warm clothing even if it's a sunny summer's day. **Mist** is encountered on about 300 days in the year, so always stick to the marked paths and if necessary take shelter in the refuge huts which are liberally sprinkled throughout the area. Finally, many of the trails pass sections of the **frontier** with Czechoslovakia and often converge with paths coming up from the opposite side of the border. These are generally controlled by guards, but in any event resist the temptation to cross— this is still illegal and the signposts are clear enough to make any protestations of linguistic ignorance untenable as an excuse.

Szklarska Poręba

SZKLARSKA PORĘBA (SCHREIBERHAU) lies 18km southwest of Jelenia Góra and just to the west of a major international road crossing into Czechoslovakia. It can be reached from Jelenia either by train, which deposits you at the station on the northern heights of the town, or by bus, whose terminal is at the eastern entrance to the resort.

Whichever way you choose to arrive, make sure you walk the last few kilometers of the bus route from PIECHOWICE (which also has a train station); although not actually in the national park, this offers some of the most beautiful scenery in the Karkonosze. The road closely follows the course of the **Kamienna**, one of the main streams rising in the mountains, which is joined along this short stretch by several tributaries, in a landscape reminiscent of the less wild parts of the Scottish highlands. Much the best vistas are to be had from the road itself, which has a lane set aside for walkers; the views from the hiking trails are obscured by trees most of the time. However, you do need to make a detour down one of the paths in order to see the **waterfall** formed by the Szklarka just before it joins the Kamienna; the point to turn off is well signposted from the bus stop and parking lot by the main road, and it's usually thronged with souvenir sellers.

The Kamienna slices Szklarska Poręba in two, with the main streets in the valley and the rest of the town rising high into the hills on each side. It's well worth following the stream all the way through the built-up part of the resort, as there follows another extremely picturesque stretch, with some spectacular rock formations (the **Kruce Skalny**) towering above the southern bank. Beyond, at the extreme western edge of town, is the celebrated **Huty Julia** glassworks, whose nineteenth-century core can be visited on a guided tour on weekday mornings. From here, you can ascend by the black or red trails into the mountains.

Taking the **red trail**, you enter the national park at the **waterfall** of the Kamienczyka, which is about a third of the way up the trail to **Szrenica** (1362m). Tumbling down the valley in a single slanting dive and beautifully framed by woodland, it's the most picturesque of the falls in the Karkonosze. Unfortunately, the observation platforms are currently fenced off for safety reasons.

The easiest and quickest way into the mountains is by **chair lift**, which goes in two stages to the summit of Szrenica. Its departure point is at the southern end of town: from the bus station, follow ul. 1 Maja, then turn right into ul. Turystyczna, continuing along all the way to the end. Despite its rickety appearance, the chair lift is quite secure, the only drawback being that it stops running at around 3:30pm.

Practicalities

As you'd expect, Szklarska Poręba has a great variety of accommodation. At the time of writing, the resort's main **hotel** was closed for repairs, leaving *COS*, by the chair lift at ul. Turystyczna 26 (☎30-35), and the motel *Relax* (☎26-95), on the Piechowice road about 1km east of town. The **Biuro Zakwaterowania** across from the bus station at ul. 1 Maja 4 (☎23-93) can arrange stays in private homes, while the **Orbis** office around the corner at ul. Jedności Narodowej 13a (☎23-47) has access to **pensions** offering good-value comprehensive deals. Just north of the center are the **campground**, ul Demokratów 6, and a **tourist hostel**, ul. Sportowy 6 (☎22-37). The **youth hostel** is a less enticing option, being out in the sticks at ul. Piastowska 1 (☎21-41), on the wrong side of town for the best walks. Ulica Jedności Narodowej offers the main concentration of places to **eat** and **drink**; several alternatives can be found on ul. Turystyczna.

Karpacz

KARPACZ (KRUMMHÜBEL), 15km south of Jelenia Góra, is an even more scattered community than Szklarska Poręba, occupying an enormous area for a place with only a few thousand inhabitants. Much of it is built around one street, ul. 1 Maja, which stretches and curves 3km uphill to the *Hotel Biały Jar*. This is the convergence of three hiking trails and also the terminal for some of the buses, though others continue up the road to the adjoining village of BIERUTOWICE.

The stop before Bierutowice is the place to alight for the path leading to the most famous, not to say curious, building in the Karkonosze—the **Wang Chapel**. This twelfth-century Romanesque church, which boasts some wonderfully refined carving on its portals and capitals, stood for nearly 600 years in a village in southern Norway. By 1840, it had fallen into such a state of disrepair that the parishioners sought a buyer for it. Having failed to interest any Norwegians, they sold it to the most powerful architectural conservationist of the day, King Friedrich Wilhelm IV of Prussia. He had the church dismantled and shipped to this isolated spot, where it was punctiliously reassembled over a period of two years; the stone tower, added at the beginning of the present century, is the only feature which is not original. In deference to Friedrich Wilhelm's wishes, it's still used on Sunday mornings for Protestant worship. Otherwise, it's opened only for groups, but as these come here very frequently in season, you shouldn't have any trouble getting in.

Immediately above the Wang Chapel is one of the entry points to the national park, from where the blue hiking trail goes up into the mountains. Faster access is by the **chair lift** midway between here and the *Biały Jar*. This ascends directly to the summit of **Kopa** (1375m); try not to be put off by the machinery, which is even more decrepit-looking than its counterpart in Szklarska Poręba. Again, it operates only until around 3:30pm.

A short distance west of the chair lift is the first of two **waterfalls** on the Łomnica River, which rises high in the mountains and flows all the way through Karpacz, defining much of the northern boundary of the town, as well as the course of ul. 1 Maja, which follows a largely parallel line. The second waterfall, well downstream near the center, stands in complete contrast to the rustic charm of its predecessor, having been altered to form a dam. However, on its northern bank there's the attraction of the pleasantly secluded wooded heights of Karpatka.

The only other sightseeing attraction in Karpacz itself is the small **Museum of Sport and Tourism** (Tues–Sun 9am–4pm), housed in an alpine chalet on ul. Kopernika, close to the second bus stop on ul. 1 Maja. Below the museum is the valley of the Dolna, which offers a superb **view** over the national park.

Hikes from Karpacz

The most obvious goal of any walk is the austere **Śniezka** (Schneekoppe, or "Snow Peak"), at 1602m the highest peak in the range and normally covered with snow for half the year. Lying almost due south of Karpacz, it can be reached by the black trail in about three hours from the *Biały Jar*, or in about fifty minutes if you pick up the trail at the top of the Kopa chair lift. From the chair lift you pass through the **Kocioł Łomniczki**, whose abundant vegetation includes Carpathian birch, gentian, cloves, Alpine roses, and monk's hood; only moss, lycopod, Alpine violets and lichen grow on the slopes of Śniezka itself. Access to the actual summit is by either the steep and stony "Zigzag Way" (the red trail) which ascends by the most direct method, or the easier "Jubilee Way" (the blue route) around the northern and eastern sides of the mountain. At the top is a large modern weather station-snack bar, where you can get cheap hot meals; there are also refreshments available in the refuges on Kopa and at the junction of the two trails.

On a clear day, the **view** from Śniezka stretches for 80km, embracing not only other parts of the Sudeten chain in Poland and Czechoslovakia, but also Wrocław, Śleza, Legnica, and the Lausitz Mountains in Germany. However, good visibility is a rarity; the more usual misty effects at least offer a highly atmospheric consolation.

The **red trail**, which passes close to the frontier in covering all the main summits in the national park, makes the most obvious basis for a walking route. One section particularly worth seeing is that immediately to the west of Śniezka, which runs above two glacial **lakes**, Mały Stam and Wielki Stam. If you don't want to continue onward to Szklarska Poręba, you can then descend by the black trail, then switch to the blue, which brings you out at the Wang Chapel.

Practicalities

In the Dolna valley, at ul. Obrońców 5 is Karpacz's leading **hotel**, the luxurious and ultra-modern Orbis-run *Skalny* (☎721). The alternatives are the aforementioned *Biały Jar*, ul. 1 Maja 79 (☎319), and *Orlinek*, just before the chair lift at ul. Olimpijska 9 (☎548). There's a **tourist hostel** in the town center at ul. Waryńskiego 6 (☎513), and another just across the road from the *Skalny* (☎789). The **youth hostel** is also quite centrally placed at ul. Gimnazjalna 9 (☎290). Near the entrance to Karpacz at ul. 1 Maja 8 are the **campground** (☎316) and the **Biuro Zakwaterowania** (☎453). Information about **pensions** offering full and half board should be available from **Orbis** at no. 50 on the same street (☎547). A wide variety of places to **eat** and **drink** can also be found around here.

From the Karkonosze to the Kłodzko Region

In the stretch of land between the Karkonosze Mountains and Silesia's other main recreation area—the Kłodzko Valley to the southeast—lie several historic towns, most of them connected with the former **Duchy of Świdnica**, which lasted only from 1290 to 1392, but exerted a profound influence on Silesian culture. The places mentioned are best visited in passing from the one holiday district to the other, or on day trips from Wrocław or the resorts themselves. Accommodation is very limited, and there's not likely to be a reason for wanting to spend the night anyway.

Kamienna Góra

Weaving became the staple craft of Silesia in the fourteenth century, and **KAMIENNA GÓRA** (LANDESHUT), which lies 38km southeast of Jelenia Góra, carries on this uninterrupted tradition with its silk, linen, and clothing works. Founded as a fortress to protect Świdnica against the Bohemians, Kamienna Góra's greatest moment came in 1345, after it had fallen to the enemy, in an incident still celebrated in local folklore. Taking a leaf out of the book of the Greeks in their siege of Troy, the counter-attacking troops smuggled themselves back into the town hidden in hay carts, then emerged to rout the garrison. Not surprisingly, wars have featured strongly in the town's history: it was the scene of a rare Austrian victory over the Prussians in 1760, then in 1813 was the rallying point of the allied armies ranged against Napoleon.

The central square, **plac Wolności**, is lined with a number of fine old houses, of which no. 11 houses the **museum** (Tues & Fri–Sun 10am–4pm, Wed & Thurs 10am–3pm), devoted mainly to weaving in the region. Nearby stands the Gothic church of **Saints Peter and Paul**, which seems to have never really recovered from its sacking at the hands of followers of the Czech reformer Jan Hus. Far more imposing is the **Church of Peace** on a hillock at the southern side of town, a Greek-cross design which is one of half a dozen Silesian churches specially built in the early eighteenth century for Protestant worship.

There's a **hotel**, *Karkonosze*, at ul. Świerczewskiego 33 (☎22-30) and a **tourist hostel** at no. 2 on the same street (☎22-21). The usual range of places to eat and drink can be found, but don't expect anything wonderful.

Krzeszów

The village of **KRZESZÓW** (GRÜSSAU), 8km south of Kamienna Góra by regular bus, lies in the shade of a huge **Abbey** complex which ranks, historically and artistically, among the most significant monuments in Silesia. It was first settled in 1242 by Benedictines at the instigation of Anne, widow of Henryk the Pious. However, they stayed for less than half a century; the land was bought back by Anne's grandson, Bolko I of Świdnica, who granted it to the Cistercians and made their church his family's mausoleum. Despite being devastated by the Hussites and again in the Thirty Years' War, the abbey flourished, eventually owning nearly 300 square kilometers of land, including two towns and forty villages. This economic base funded the complete rebuilding in the Baroque period, but not long afterward the community went into irreversible decline as the result of the confiscation of its lands during the Silesian Wars.

For over a century the buildings lay abandoned, but in a nicely symmetrical turn of events they were reoccupied by Benedictine monks from Prague in 1919, with a contingent of nuns joining them after World War II. Even so, this is no more than a token presence, and the unkempt appearance of the courtyard strikes you immediately. Restoration work is well under way, but will clearly continue for some time yet.

The two churches are very different in size and feel. The smaller and plainer of the two, **St Joseph's**, was built in the 1690s for parish use. In replacing the medieval church, its dedication was changed to reflect the Counter-Reformation cult of the Virgin Mary's husband, designed to stress a family image which was overlooked in earlier Catholic theology. The magnificent **fresco cycle**, in which Joseph—previously depicted by artists as a shambling old duffer—appears to be little older than his wife and is similarly transported to heaven from his deathbed, is a prime artistic expression of this short-lived cult. Executed with bold brush-work and warm colors, it is the masterpiece of **Michael Willmann**, an East Prussian who converted to Catholicism and spent the rest of his life carrying out commissions from Silesian religious houses. On the ceiling, Willmann continued the family theme with various Biblical genealogies.

The **Monastic Church**, in the grand Baroque style, was begun in 1728 and finished in just seven years—hence its great unity of design, relying for effect on a combination of monumentality and elaborate decoration. Three altarpieces in the transept are by Willmann, but the most notable painting is a Byzantine icon which has been at Krezesów since the fourteenth century. The nave ceiling fres-coes illustrate the life of the Virgin, and thus form a sort of counterpoint to those in the parish church; that in the south transept shows the Hussites martyring the monks.

From the south transept you pass into the **Piast mausoleum** behind the high altar. This is kept open when tourist groups are around (which is quite frequently in summer); at other times you'll have to persuade a monk or nun to open it up. Focal point of the chapel is the grandiose colored marble monument to Bernard of Świdnica, to each side of which are more modest Gothic sarcophagi of Bolko I and II. The history of the abbey is told in the frescoes on the two domes.

Other buildings in the close include the monastic quarters adjoining the church, the now derelict hostelry beside St Joseph's, a shrine which is part of a series of wayside chapels continued outside the precincts, and the former estate management offices fronting the entrance gateway. The gateway previously housed a restaurant, but this was closed at the time of writing, with the stores left as the only places to buy food.

Bolków and Strzegom

The very name of **BOLKÓW** (BOLKENHAIN), 35km east of Jelenia Góra and 19km north of Kamienna Góra, proclaims its foundation by the first Duke of Świdnica, Bolko I. Although a ruin, his **Castle** (Tues–Fri 9am–4pm, Sat 8am–3pm, Sun 9am–4pm) is still an impressive sight, rising imperiously above the little town. Later converted into a Renaissance palace, it passed into the control of the monks of Krzeszów, and was finally abandoned after their Napoleonic suppression. A section of the buildings has been restored to house a small museum on the history of the town, and you can ascend the tower for a huge panoramic view.

There's little to see in the lower town, though the gaudily painted Gothic parish church and the sloping Rynek have a certain charm. On the square there's a cheap and decent restaurant, *Kosmos*.

STRZEGOM (STRIEGAU), 20km east on the road and train routes to Wrocław, is Silesia's oldest town, and might even be the oldest in Poland. An important center for the extraction of granite and basalt, it has long been predominantly industrial, with few suggestions of its antiquity. The only worthwhile monument is the **parish church**, a lofty Gothic design chiefly notable for its monumental facade illustrating *The Last Judgement* and the southern porch with a tympanum of *The Dormition of the Virgin*.

Wałbrzych and Książ

Visiting **WAŁBRZYCH** (WALDENBURG) is like traveling back to the Britain of Dickens' *Hard Times*. This unsightly industrial town, located between two of the country's main resort areas, is Poland's biggest environmental disaster area and one of the most polluted places in Europe. Unlike Katowice or Łódź, there are no saving graces among the belching factories, putrid air, and heavy grime of Wałbrzych. This bastion of outdated technology is very largely a modern creation. Although its lead and coal mines had been worked for several hundred years, the number of inhabitants numbered only a few hundred in 1800 and it was still a modest town early in this century, before accelerating to its present population of 125,000—the highest in Lower Silesia after Wrocław.

Other than for its shock value, the only reason for coming to Wałbrzych is because of its proximity to **KSIĄŻ** (FÜRSTENSTEIN), which lies just off the few kilometers of road leading to the smaller but only marginally less unpleasant industrial town of ŚWIEBODZICE. Given the surrounding environment, it's miraculous that Książ gives the appearance of being deep in rural countryside. There's even a **stud farm** offering riding holidays here; you're allowed to wander around its stables for a nominal fee.

Książ's tranquillity is disturbed only by the presence of the tourists drawn by the vast **Castle** (May–Sept Mon–Fri 9am–5pm, Sat & Sun 9am–6pm; Oct & April Mon–Fri 9am–4pm, Sat & Sun 9am–5pm; Nov–March Mon–Fri 9am–3pm, Sat & Sun 9am–4pm), which commands a thickly wooded valley and is a magnificent sight from a distance. Close up, it's less impressive, due to the disparate styles in which it's built, taking in practically everything from the thirteenth-century Romanesque of Duke Bolko I's original fortress to nineteenth-century Romanticism. Some of it is even more modern, as work was carried out to transform it into a bomb-proof bunker for Hitler. Nonetheless, a few fine interiors remain, notably the **Maximilian Hall**, a piece of palatial Baroque, complete with carved chimneypieces, gilded chandeliers, a fresco of Mount Parnassus, and multicolored marble paneling. The basement houses a good cheap **restaurant**, while one of the outbuildings has been converted into a **hotel**.

Świdnica

Few adjacent towns could be less similar than Wałbrzych and **ŚWIDNICA** (SCHWEIDNITZ), less than 20km to the northeast and connected by numerous buses and trains. Twentieth-century growth has largely bypassed what was for centuries Silesia's second most important city, and its population today barely tops the 40,000 mark. Yet, aided by the fact that it suffered little damage in World War II, it still preserves much of the grandeur of a former princely capital, and is one of the most attractive Silesian towns.

Although Świdnica's period of independent glory—which came not long after its twelfth-century foundation—was short-lived, the town continued to flourish under Bohemian rule. Not only was it an important center of trade and commerce, it ranked as one of Europe's most renowned brewing centers, with its famous *Schwarze Schöps* forming the staple fare of Wrocław's best-known tavern, and exported as far afield as Italy and Russia.

A few minutes' walk north from the **train and bus stations**, the **Rynek** is predominantly Baroque, though the core of many of the houses is often much older. Two particularly notable facades are at no. 7, known as **The Golden Cross**, and no. 8, **The Gilded Man**. In the central area of the square are two fine fountains and the handsome early eighteenth-century **Town Hall**, which preserves the tower and an elegant star-vaulted chamber from its Gothic predecessor.

Off the southwestern corner of the Rynek, the main street, ul. Staromiejska, curves gently downhill. The view ahead stretches past a number of Baroque mansions to the majestic **belfry**—the second highest in Poland—of the Gothic parish church of **Saints Stanislaw and Wenceslas**. Intended as one of a pair, the tower was so long under construction that its final stages were built after the start of the Reformation. The church also boasts a splendidly monumental **facade**, in front of which are placed a Baroque statue of Saint Jan Nepomuk and a beautiful late Gothic relief of *St Anne, the Virgin, and Child*. Around the early fifteenth-century portals, the two patrons occupy a privileged position in the group of Apostles framing the Madonna. Look also at the Bridal Doorway on the north side of the nave, so called because it was reserved for wedding ceremonies: it features chauvinistic carvings of *Samson and Delilah* and *Aristotle and Phyllis*, as a warning to the bridegroom of woman's potential for corrupting man.

During the Thirty Years' War, the church was returned to Catholic use and shortly afterward given to the Jesuits, who subsequently erected the large college building on the south side. They also carried out a Baroque transformation of the **interior**, respecting the original architecture while embellishing it to give a richer surface effect. A massive high altar with statues of the order's favorite saints dominates the east end; the organ with its carvings of the heavenly choir provides a similar focus to the west, while the lofty walls were embellished with huge Counter-Reformation altarpieces, some of them by Willmann.

The **Church of Peace** (Kościół Pokoju), at the northern edge of the town center, was built after the Thirty Years' War for the displaced Protestant congregation, and survives unaltered. The name derives from the Peace of Westphalia of 1648 which brought this morass of religious and dynastic conflicts to an end, but could equally apply to its tranquil setting in a walled courtyard. At first glance, the rusticity of the surroundings seems to be mirrored in the half-timbered architecture and the irregular chapels. However, it's actually a highly sophisticated piece of design: for all its compact shape, 4000 worshippers can be seated inside, thanks to the double two-tiered galleries.

Świdnica has two **hotels**—*Piast*, just off the Rynek at ul. Marksa 11 (☎230-76), and *Śląsk*, ul. Saperów 16 (☎231-05). There's also a **campground** with chalets at ul. Śląska 37 (☎225-32). The *Piast* has a **restaurant**; other places to eat and drink can be found in and around the Rynek, including a café in the town hall. At no. 31 on the square is an **Orbis** office (☎226-74).

The Kłodzko Region

Due south of Wrocław is a rural area of rocky mountains, wooded hills, gentle valleys, and curative springs that provides the perfect antidote to the heavy industry of so much of Silesia. Known as the **Kłodzko Region** after its largest town, it's surrounded on three sides by Czechoslovakia, with the Sudeten mountains forming a natural frontier. This is one of the most popular holiday areas in Poland, catering to all inclinations from the sedentary to the hyperactive.

On the one hand, there are five **spa resorts** (identified by the suffix *-Zdrój*), the largest concentration in the country, and a reminder of the area's long period under the rule of Germany, a nation addicted to this type of therapy. The slightly run-down appearance of these towns only adds to their appeal, their somnambulent atmosphere providing a tantalizing evocation of prewar Central Europe. For the people who congregate here for rest and rehabilitation, the day's most arduous activity is a meander down to the pump room to fill up their beakers with the local spring water—which is actually mild and refreshing, with not a hint of the sulphuric taste characteristic of that of so many other spas.

High above these resorts are some of Poland's best **hiking routes**, passing through marvelously varied and often bizarre landscapes. A network of marked paths covers the entire region, in which there are several separate ranges. To the northwest are the **Góry Stołowe** (Table Mountains), which give way to the **Wzgórza Lewińskie**. Farther south are the **Góry Orlickie** and **Góry Bystrzyckie**, the former lying predominantly within Czechoslovakia. The southeast of the area is taken up by the massif of the **Masyw Śnieżnika**, beyond which are the **Góry Bialskie**, while much of the eastern boundary is defined by the **Góry Złote** (Golden Mountains).

Many trails follow a complete circuit and take several days, but it's easy enough to make up your own shorter routes if you want to base yourself in one place. Some of the ascents can be quite strenuous, though if you're reasonably fit and wearing sturdy shoes you shouldn't have any problems. The *Ziemia Kłodzka* **map**, variably available from tourist offices and newsagents in the area, is a must if you intend to do any serious walking, but beware of occasional divergences in detail from the actual marking of the paths. **Winter sports** ensure the area attracts activity vacationers all year round, even if the facilities have as yet not been developed to their full potential.

Accommodation throughout the Kłodzko Region is plentiful and, with the winding down of subsidized factory vacations, is currently undersubscribed. It's possible to stay here very cheaply—the custom-built **pensions** offering half-board terms are particularly good value, even though their rates are based on hard currency. For **getting around**, buses take second place to walking; picturesque rail lines hug the valleys, but the stations are usually on the outskirts of the towns.

Kłodzko

Dominated as it is by two large fortresses rising on the heights above the River Nysa Kłodzka, it's immediately obvious that **KŁODZKO** (GLATZ) was once a place of enormous strategic importance. This becomes even clearer from a glance at a map—several rivers converge in the immediate vicinity, giving the town control over access to a number of valleys, including what was the main trade route between Bohemia and Poland. Until the eighteenth-century Prussian takeover, Kłodzko's orientation had been towards the former, and its main Polish connection prior to 1945 was that it once belonged to the father of Adalbert, the Czech saint who was to have a crucial impact on the development of Poland (see "Gniezno," Chapter Six).

The main survivor of the medieval fortifications is the Gothic **bridge** leading into the old town. Its defensive function by then being obsolete, it was embellished in the Baroque period by sacred statuary, among which a *Coronation of the Virgin* stands out. Nowadays, the bridge has been taken over by the market traders, including dealers in paintings and artifacts. Before crossing over, take a look at the restrained Baroque **Franciscan church**, originally part of a Jesuit college.

On the opposite bank, impressively grand nineteenth-century mansions rise high above the river. Passing them, you ascend to the sloping Rynek, which has a number of fine old houses from various periods. Standing in the center is the **Town Hall**, which retains the handsome Renaissance belfry of its predecessor; the rest would look very much at home in Hartford or Charleston, being a good example of the sort of self-confident architecture favored during the last two centuries by newly prosperous cities.

Just to the south, and closer to the river, is a smaller and quieter square dominated by the parish church of **Our Lady**. Like its namesake in Świdnica, this Gothic building was adapted to Baroque without being ruined in the process. Look out for the fourteenth-century tomb of the founder, Bishop Ernst of Pordolice, which somehow managed to survive the desecrations of the Hussites five centuries ago.

From the Rynek, pathways ascend to the huge Prussian-built **Fortress** (Tues–Sun 9am–5pm), the more important of the two commanding the valley, now crudely adorned with the name of the town in huge letters. Its former impregnability—which enabled it to withstand a siege in 1807 by the all-conquering army of Napoleon—is still obvious, with the natural rock providing the first line of defense. To travel along the whole length of its **underground passages** would take hours; some of these are so narrow that you're virtually forced to get down on your hands and knees. As a complete contrast, there are superb **views** over the town and its surroundings.

Practicalities

If you're arriving by rail, get off at the Kłodzko Miasto **train station**, which is beside the **bus station** and only a few minutes' walk from the center; this is also the best place to catch trains heading south, and to the two spa valleys to the east and west. The main station, Kłodzko Główny, is over 2km north and only worth using if you're heading to Wrocław or Jelenia Góra.

The helpful **Orbis** office, located just beside the bridge at ul. Grottgera 1 (Mon–Fri 10am–5pm, alternate Sats 10am–noon; ☎27-75), can help you find a place to stay anywhere in the region. An alternative source of information is the **tourist office** on the corner of the Rynek (Mon–Fri 10am–4pm). Although Kłodzko makes an ideal touring base, Orbis tends not to plug it, as accommodation is far scarcer than in the nearby spas. Of the **hotels**, *Astoria* on pl. Jedności (☎30-35) is worth considering for convenience, being right beside the bus station. The alternatives are *Nad Młynówka* at ul. Daszyńskiego 16 (☎25-63) and an out-of-town motel, *Zosia* (☎37-37). For a cheaper deal, try for a chalet at the **campground**, beyond the fortress on ul. Nowy Świat (☎30-31).

Kłodzko is a bit short on places to **eat** and **drink**, with a couple of cafés being all that the upper town has to offer. Outside the hotels, the only two restaurants are on ul. Grottgera between the bus station and Orbis office. Of these, *Wilcza Jama* is particularly recommended, with decent opening hours and excellent Czech beer; *Czardasz* across the road is acceptable enough.

Polanica-Zdrój

The nearest resort to Kłodzko is **POLANICA-ZDRÓJ** (BAD ALTHEIDE), 15km to the west, which was only really developed this century. Lacking any kind of commercial center, the spa quarter is Polanica's heart, and its gardens—ablaze with rhododendrons and azaleas in the spring—are the town's chief joy.

Lying just out of the mountains, Polanica isn't ideally placed for the best scenery, but there are still some good **walks** in the immediate vicinity. Taking the black trail to the southwest brings you into the Góry Bystrzyckie; about two and a half hours are required to ascend to the first main viewpoint, **Wolarz** (850m). A similar length of time is needed to reach the other summit within easy reach, **Szczytnik** (589m), via the yellow route going northwest; this has a neo-Gothic castle and a view over the glass-making village of SZCZYTNA below.

Where Polanica really scores is in its choice of accommodation. The **PTTK** at ul. Zdrojowa 15 (☎312), just south of the spa quarter, will help you find a room if there isn't space in its own hostel. Both **hotels** are farther south, on the way to the train station: *Polonia* is at ul. Wojska Polskiego 4 (☎500), the more luxurious *Polonica* at ul. Warszawska 14a (☎605). The **youth hostel**, at ul. Wojska Polskiego 25, is only open for a few weeks in midsummer. The **campground** (☎210) and another **tourist hostel** are northeast of the spa park on ul. Sportowa. There are also at least half-a-dozen **pensions** offering bargain all-inclusive rates; ask at PTTK or **Orbis**, ul. Zdrojowa 5 (☎412), for details. Plenty of cafés are scattered throughout the resort, but the only **restaurant** other than those in the hotels is *Globus*, Kłodzka 7.

Duszniki-Zdrój

Ten kilometers west of Polanica lies the far more venerable and attractive spa of **DUSZNIKI-ZDRÓJ** (BAD REINERZ). Despite the short distance between the two, their climates are quite different, Duszniki's being more fluctuating and extreme, with hotter summers and harsher winters. The town is a well-known cultural center, with a beautiful nineteenth-century theater as a centerpiece of the spa quarter. In the first half of August each year, a **Chopin Musical Festival**, which usually manages to feature at least one world-famous pianist, is held here, commemorating the concerts given during a convalescence by the sixteen-year-old composer in 1826.

Duszniki divides into two halves, with the old town lying midway between the spa quarter and the train station. On the **Rynek**, Renaissance and Baroque styles are mingled in the Town Hall and the burghers' houses, one of which bears a plaque recording Chopin's stay. Down ul. Adama Mickiewicza is another fine square, pl. Warszawy, where the former **drapers' guild hall** can be identified by the emblem of a lamb with the tools of the draper's trade.

Ulica Kłodzko, the oldest street in town, is dominated by the parish church of **Saints Peter and Paul**, a bland example of early eighteenth-century Baroque put into the extraordinary class by two fantastically ornate **pulpits**; one of these—a unique and slightly morbid specimen—is shaped like the whale which swallowed Jonah, with the creature's mouth fixed open to form a platform for the preacher.

At the bottom of the same street is the **Museum of the Paper Industry** (Tues–Sun 10am–3pm), which occupies a large paper mill dating from the beginning of the seventeenth century. One of Poland's most precious industrial buildings, its fine half-timbering, sweeping mansard roof, and delicate rosette decoration make it a handsome piece of Baroque. Following ul. Sprzymierzonych south from here, then turning left up ul. Wiejska, brings you to a tiny chapel which now houses the **Museum of the Chopin Festival** (Tues–Fri 10am–3pm, Sat & Sun 1–3pm), with photos and programs of past events.

If you continue uphill, you reach Nawojowa (675m), one of the **viewpoints** within easy reach of the town. The other, just to the south, is Ptasia Góra (736m), which is connected by the brown trail leading back to the spa quarter. Among longer hikes, the **red trail** leads south in about three and a half hours to ZIELENIEC, the highest village in the region and a winter sports center. A short distance to its east is the **Topieliska nature reserve**, a high-altitude peat bog with tundra-like flora, including cotton grass and dwarf birch. Another worthwhile section of the red trail goes west from Duszniki, arriving after a couple of hours at the ruined thirteenth-century Lewin Castle, another fine viewpoint. The **blue trail** leads north from Duszniki into the Góry Stołowe (see below).

Practicalities

The **PTTK** office, at no. 14 on the Rynek (☎540), operates a room-finding service. This organization's own **tourist hostel** is *Pod Muflonem* (☎339), just below Ptasia Góra; the **youth hostel** is far more conveniently sited in a school building at Kłodzka 22 (☎255), but is open only during the summer holidays. Other options include a **hotel**, *Miejski*, just off the Rynek at ul. Karola Świerczewskiego 2 (☎504), a **pension**, *Blachownia*, in the northeastern corner of the spa quarter at ul. Wojska Polskiego 64 (☎100), and the **campground**, close to the station at Dworcowa 6 (☎489). The only **restaurant** is *Slowianka* on the Rynek, but cafés and snack bars are dotted all around town.

Kudowa-Zdrój and the Góry Stołowe

KUDOWA-ZDRÓJ (BAD KUDOWA) lies in a wide basin at the foot of the Góry Stołowe and Wzgórza Lewińskie, 16km west of Duszniki and a couple of kilometers before a major road crossing into Czechoslovakia. More than any of the other resorts in the Kłodzko Region, Kudowa preserves much of the feel of the bygone days when it was patronized by the internationally rich and famous. Spacious nineteenth-century villas set in their own grounds give Kudowa its aristocratic air, yet it has no obvious center other than the **spa park**. This can claim the largest sanatarium and pump room in the region, along with an extensive *jardin anglais* with over 300 different species of tree and shrub. From here, it's a gentle ascent north to the Wzgórze Kapliczne (420m), which takes its name from the Protestant chapel on its summit.

Orbis and **PTTK** both have offices on ul. Zdrojowa—at no. 47 (☎266) and no. 42a (☎222) respectively. The main room-finding agency, however, is in the resort's leading **hotel**, *Kosmos* at ul. Mariana Buczka 8a (☎511). On ul. Łąkowa, just off ul. Gen. Karola Świerczewskiego (the street leading to the border crossing) are the other hotel, *OSiR* (☎627), and the **campground** (☎627), while the **tourist hostel** *Pod Strzechą* is on ul. Słone (☎262), slightly nearer the frontier. **Pensions** include *Gwarek*, ul. Juliusza Słowackiego 10 (☎661), and *Marysieńka*, ul. 1 Maja 3. There's a wide variety of places to **eat** and **drink**, with the restaurants in the *Kosmos* and the tourist hostel probably the best bets.

Each July, Kudowa hosts a **festival** devoted to Stanisław Moniuszko, who shared the nationalist outlook of Chopin, his compatriot and contemporary, but whose music has never caught on abroad to anything like the same extent.

Into the Table Mountains

Though they seldom rise above 900m and are almost as flat as their name suggests, the **Góry Stołowe** (Table Mountains) are the most enticing range in the Kłodzko Region. The nearest base is **KARŁÓW**, 11km east of Kudowa via the so-called "road of a hundred bends." However, there's only a campground here (plus a restaurant and a couple of bars), leaving Kudowa itself as the main alternative if you haven't a tent.

From Kudowa, the **green trail** makes a good basis for a day's walk. It leads north to the outlying hamlet of CZERMNA, where the **cemetery chapel** strikes a discordant note in this area of healthy living—its walls, ceiling, and altar are gruesomely covered with the skulls and bones of the dead of the Thirty Years' War, the Silesian Wars, and the Seven Years' War. The trail then goes northeast to the first of several fantastic rock formations in the range, the **Błędne Skały** (Erratic Boulders), then continues via PASTERKA to the **Szczeliniec Wielki** above Karłów, the highest point in the range at 919m. Here the rocks have been weathered into a series of irregular shapes nicknamed "the camel," "the elephant," "the hen," and so on.

Farther south, in the vicinity of ŁĘZNO, the route passes the **Sawanna Afrykańska**, a remnant of the upper layer of the mountains, formed fifty million years ago when the region was similar to the African savannahs of today. Trees bent into umbrella shapes by the wind add to the uncanny impression. The green trail continues south to LEWIN, but before that you can pick up the red trail which completes a circle back to Kudowa.

As an alternative, take the more direct **red trail** from the Błędny Skałny to Karłów. This then continues eastward to the largest and most scattered group of rocks in the area, the **Skalne Grzyby** (Rocky Mushrooms), which were formed by uneven erosion. Proceeding southward from here, you can switch to either the yellow route to Duszniki, or the blue route to Polanica; the red route itself descends in an hour or so to Wambierzyce (see below).

Wambierzyce

If hardly worthy of the title "the Silesian Jerusalem," **WAMBIERZYCE** (ALBENDORF) is nevertheless a highly distinctive place, which has drawn pilgrims since the twelfth century, when a blind man was cured by praying at a statue of the Madonna and Child placed here on a linden tree.

The Baroque **Basilica**, perched above a broad flight of steps, is the fourth on the site, and retains the outer walls of its predecessor, which collapsed soon after it was built. Its monumental exterior gives no hint of the intricate layout inside, where a broad **processional way** passes a variety of chapels, grottoes, and other nooks and crannies containing representations of scenes from the lives of Christ and the Virgin. The nave of the church is an octagon hung with six large altar-pieces by Michael Willmann, while the oval presbytery has a cupola illustrating the fifteen mysteries of the Rosary. A magnificent silver **tabernacle** from Venice bears the miraculous image, with a profusion of votive offerings to the side.

Scattered all around the village are nearly 100 **shrines** containing sculptures representing the minutiae of the Passion story. They are oddly grouped out of sequence, except towards the end, which culminates in the **Calvary** on the hill facing the basilica. Halfway up is the **Szopka** (April–Sept Tues–Sun 10am–5pm), a large mechanical contraption that presents Biblical and everyday local scenes, laid out like miniature theater sets.

Wambierzyce has only one very basic **restaurant**, *Turystyczny*, on the square below the Basilica; the local grocery store opposite is a good enough source for putting together a picnic. The restaurant may also have rooms for rent; otherwise the nearest **hotel** is *Graniczny* on the Rynek in RADKÓW, the next village to the northwest (☎26).

Bystrzyca Kłodzka

Midway down the valley south of Kłodzko, some 15km away, is **BYSTRZYCA KŁODZKA** (HABELSCHWERDT), its peeling medieval core reminiscent of a decayed Mediterranean town. This impression is particularly strong if, from the train station (for once conveniently sited), you circle the town to the left and cross the river. Bearing left, you'll shortly get a magnificent full-frontal view of the town's tier-like layout, which on a sunny day looks more Spanish than Polish.

Substantial sections of the **walls** survive, including the Kłodzko and Water gates and the Knights' Tower. The tower later became a belfry for the Protestant church, which dominates the smaller of the two central squares, the Mały Rynek. Now deconsecrated, it houses the **Museum of Fire-Making** (Tues–Sun 10am–4pm), okay if matchbox labels give you a buzz. In the middle of the main square, pl. Wolności, is the **Town Hall**, which has a nineteenth-century body tacked onto a Renaissance tower. Farther uphill, the parish church of **St Michael the Archangel** is a medley of different styles, featuring two well-crafted late Renaissance portals and an unusual double-naved interior.

Bystrzyca is not particularly well placed for **walks**, though the yellow route to Polanica and Duszniki is one of the best long hikes in the region; taking up the better part of a day, it passes through lonely high moorland.

The only **hotel** in Bystrzyca is the *Piast* at ul. Okrzei 26 (☎11-03-22). There are a couple of **restaurants** on pl. Wolności, *Regionalna* and *Rycerska*.

The Masyw Śnieznika

At the southeastern corner of the Kłodzko Region is the bracingly wild **Masyw Śnieznika**, the best of whose scenery can be seen in a good day's walk. The main jumping-off point is the straggling community of **MIĘDZYGÓRZE** (WÖLFESGRUND), 13km southeast of Bystrzyca; there's no train station, but it's served quite well by buses, which terminate in the village center, but also stop at the **hotel**, *Nad Wodospadem* (☎20), on the western outskirts. If you get down there, you can descend to see the Wilczka River's beautiful 27-meter **waterfall**; a bridge directly above lets you peer down at the roaring mass, while platforms at various levels on both sides of the river give a variety of downstream views.

The **red trail** leads all the way through Międzygórze, then rises steeply through lovely wooded countryside. After a couple of hours you come to the *Na Śnieżniku* **refuge**; though set in total isolation at over 1200m, this is actually a fully functioning post office which has dormitory accommodation and also serves cheap, homey meals. It's then a much gentler ascent to the plateau-like summit of **Śnieżnik** (1425m), the highest point in the Kłodzko Region, set right on the Czechoslovak border.

You can return to Międzygórze by a variety of routes, but it's better to descend northward by the yellow trail in the direction of KLETNO, which will bring you in about an hour to the **Bear's Cave** (Jaskinia Niedzwiedzia). Discovered in 1966 during quarrying, the cave takes its name from the bear fossils that predominate among the 24 species of prehistoric animal bones discovered there. As yet, no trace of human habitation has been found, but only a small part of the cave has so far been excavated. The extraordinary **stalactites and stalagmites** in the section of the cave opened to the public have been given nicknames like "the palace," "the corridor," "the Madonna and Child" and "the bat." Visits are by guided tour only; since opening hours are very variable and admission tightly controlled, it's best to check the current position with a local tourist office before setting out, or at least to make sure you arrive by the early afternoon.

The nearest bus stop to the Bear's Cave is some 3km farther north; even cars have to be left over 1km away. The yellow walking trail continues to the glass-making town of STRONIE ŚLĄSKIE, terminal of a train line from Kłodzko. Beyond, 5km to the north, is Lądek-Zdrój.

Lądek-Zdrój

LĄDEK-ZDRÓJ (BAD LANDECK) is an eastern competitor to the three valley resorts west of Kłodzko, of which it most resembles Duszniki, having a historic center as a counterbalance to the spa quarter. According to tradition, the waters here were known for their healing properties as early as the thirteenth century, when the bathing installations were allegedly destroyed by the Tartars. They have certainly been exploited since the beginning of the sixteenth century, and have attracted visitors as august as Goethe and Turgenev.

Centerpiece of the pompous Neoclassical **spa buildings**—the most grandiose in the Kłodzko Region—is the main sanatarium, a handsome domed building with extravagantly sculpted porticoes. In the older part of town, a sixteenth-century **bridge** over the Biała Lądecka River, a tributary of the Nysa Kłodzka, can still be seen. The **Rynek** is largely Baroque, with a number of fine gabled houses, above which soars the octagonal tower of the Town Hall.

The Masyw Śnieżnika is close enough to Lądek to be a goal for adventurous **walks**. However, the curiously named **Góry Złote** (Golden Mountains) immediately to the east of the town make a more obvious excursion. Following the blue trail southeast, you ascend within an hour to the ruined medieval castle on **Karpień** (776m) via a series of the fantastically weathered rocks typical of the region. You can see another group of these by transferring to the green trail north to LUTYNIA, before circling back to Lądek.

PTTK have an office at ul. Kościuszki 36 (☎255), between the old town and the spa quarter. The only two **restaurants**, *Pod Filarami* and *Ratuszowa*, are both on the Rynek; the first is particularly good. **Pensions** offering full or half board include *Złoty Lan*, ul. Żwirki Wigury 14 (☎243), *Maskiewicz*, ul. Wolności 10

(☎767), and *Watra*, ul. Brzozowa 14 (☎609). There's a **youth hostel** in the outlying hamlet of STÓJKÓW (☎540) to the south.

North of the Kłodzko Region

If you're traveling between Kłodzko and Wrocław by either road or rail, there are a couple of places on the way well worth stopping at for an hour or two.

The market town of **ZĄBKOWICE ŚLĄSKIE** (FRANKENSTEIN), 20km north, has been dubbed "the Silesian Pisa" on account of its fourteenth-century **leaning tower**, just off the Rynek. By the 1400s the ground on which it was built had shifted so much that a story was added perpendicular to the ground to try to straighten it. The opposite happened, and the thing now leans about five feet out of true. From the tower's appearance, you would think that it was a defensive structure, but it's actually the detached belfry of the church of **St Anne**, which stands in a peaceful garden behind.

A few blocks south is the shell of the **Castle**. Built at the end of the thirteenth century by Bolko I of Świdnica, it was transformed around 1530 into a palace for the Bohemian royal family by Benedict Rieth, who had previously designed the dazzling interiors of Prague's royal palace. Sadly, Ząbkowice's castle was burned out in the Thirty Years' War and, although the remains are substantial, there's little to hint at their former splendour.

Twelve kilometers northeast is **HENRYKÓW** (HEINRICHAU), which can be reached from Kłodzko by either bus or rail; trains are more frequent, but the station is more than 2km from the village. In 1220, the first **Cistercian abbey** in Silesia was founded here by Duke Henryk the Bearded, who immodestly named it after himself. Half a century later, the abbot, a man named Piotr, compiled a chronicle in which appears the earliest written sentence in the Polish language—a fact which has bestowed on Henryków a special place in the national consciousness.

In the late seventeenth and early eighteenth centuries, the monastery was greatly expanded in the monumental Baroque style then in vogue. These buildings still dominate the village, which, since the monastery's suppression, has been left with the problem of how to make full use of them. The architecture of the **church**, whose plain Gothic style reflects the Cistercians' ascetic principles, has survived largely intact, though its interior is swamped with Baroque furnishings, including much fine woodwork and several altarpieces by the ubiquitous Michael Willmann. The church is normally kept locked, so you may have to search out a priest to show you around.

Paczków to Nysa

Leaving the Kłodzko Region to the east, you immediately cross into the almost unrelievedly flat plateau of Upper Silesia, which stretches down to the Beskid mountains. The route runs through a string of small fortified towns associated for most of their history with the bishops of Breslau/Wrocław, who ruled an independent principality here from 1195 until its dissolution by Prussia in 1810. For covering this stretch, buses have the edge on trains for both convenience and frequency of service.

Paczków

In contrast to its neighbors, the quiet little market town of **PACZKÓW** (PATSCHKAU), 30km east of Kłodzko, has preserved its medieval fortifications almost intact—hence its designation as "the Polish Carcassonne." In reality, Paczków is hardly in that league, but has the advantage of being untouched by the hands of romantically inclined nineteenth-century restorers. In few other places does it require so little imagination to visualize how it must have looked in the Middle Ages.

Nowadays, the mid-fourteenth-century **ramparts** form a shady promenade in the center of the town; their visual impact is diminished by the enveloping later buildings, though it's a wonder that the town managed to grow so much without their demolition. As it is, nineteen of the twenty-four towers survive, as do 1200 meters of the original 1350 meters of wall, pierced by three gateways: the square Wrocław Gate of 1462 and the cylindrical Ząbkowice and Kłodzko gates from around 1550.

The area within the walls, set on a gentle slope, consists of just a handful of streets, but is focused on a **Rynek** as large as that of a big city. In the familiar off-center position is the **Town Hall**, so comprehensively rebuilt during the nineteenth century that only the belfry of its Renaissance predecessor is left; ask inside for permission to ascend for the best view of the town.

Rearing up behind the Rynek is the awesome parish church of **St John**, a strongly fortified part of the town's defenses. Begun soon after the completion of the walls, it was under construction for a century, with the crenellated attic not added until the Renaissance period. A section was lopped off the tower in the early eighteenth century, and a Baroque helmet put in its place. Inside, the box-like geometry of the design is particularly evident, with the chancel the same length as the main nave. The furnishings are almost all neo-Gothic, giving a fusty nineteenth-century feel to the interior.

Paczków's sole **hotel**, *Zacisze*, ul. Wojska Polskiego 31 (☎62-77), lies outside the ramparts but on a street leading directly off the Rynek; it is outrageously over-priced for its tacky condition, and doesn't serve meals. With that in mind, the **youth hostel**, which is even closer to the Rynek at ul. Kołłataja 9 (☎64-41), is a better bet. There's also a **campground** at ul. Jagiellońska 5 (☎65-09). Currently the only **restaurant** is *Kameralna* at ul. Wrocławska 11 which, although acceptable and very cheap, stops serving meals in the early evening. There are cafés on ul. Wojska Polskiego and the Rynek, the latter bearing the inevitable name of *Carcassonne*.

Otmuchów

OTMUCHÓW (OTTMACHAU), 14km east of Paczków, nestles between two artificial lakes formed by the damming of the Nysa Kłodzka River. The original capital of the prince-bishopric, it's nowadays a sleepy backwater which springs to life only with the summer influx of water sports enthusiasts.

Dominating the town is the **Castle**, originally twelfth-century Romanesque, which guarded an extensive fortification system that has vanished but for one ruined gateway. It was transformed into a palace in the sixteenth century, and in 1820 was sold to Wilhelm von Humboldt, founder of the University of Berlin and architect of Prussia's educational system. He lived here in retirement, the liberal views he had championed having fallen from official favor. Nowadays, it's a sanatarium; there's unrestricted access to the courtyard, but you'll have to ask for permission to climb the tower, which commands a fine view.

On the Rynek is the Renaissance **Town Hall**, adorned with a beautiful sundial. The square slopes upward to a well-kept floral garden and the **parish church**, a very Central European-looking Baroque construction with a rhythmical twin-towered facade. Its ample interior is richly decorated with stucco work by Italian craftsmen, and large painted altarpieces, including several by Michael Willmann.

The only accommodation possibilities are the **campgrounds** to the west of town, the nearer being at ŚCIBÓRZ (☎53-93), the other a few kilometers on at SARNOWICE (☎52-25). Each village has two **restaurants**. In Otmuchów itself there are the café-restaurant *Zamkowa* on the Rynek and the snack bar *Bazant* on ul. Świerczewskiego.

Nysa

The name of **NYSA** (NEISSE), 12km east of Otmuchów, has become synonymous with the trucks made there for export all over Eastern Europe. Yet industry is a relative newcomer to this town which, in spite of the devastation of 1945, still preserves memories of the days when it basked in the fanciful title of "the Silesian Rome," a reference to its numerous religious houses and reputation as a center of Catholic education. It came to the fore when the adoption of the Reformation in Breslau forced the bishops to reside outside the city; they then built up Nysa, the capital of their principality for the previous couple of centuries, as their power base.

The Town

Both the **bus** and **train stations** are at the eastern side of the town; from there, bear right along the edge of the park, then turn left into ul. Kolejowa which leads in a straight line towards the center. On the way, you pass the fourteenth-century **Wrocław Gate**, an unusually graceful piece of military architecture now left stranded by the demolition of the ramparts. It's a tantalizing reminder of Nysa's long role as a border fortress; first fortified in the twelfth century by Bolesław the Wrymouth in his struggles against his Bohemian-backed brother Zbigniew, it remained an important stronghold until World War II. The only other remnant of the fortifications is the **Ziębicka Gate** on ul. Krzywoustego farther down to the right, a severe brick tower lightened by the insertion of a marble carving of a lion.

Nysa's vast **Rynek** presents a very sorry appearance, having lost its town hall and all its old houses during the war. Only the jolly seventeenth-century **Weigh House**, which looks as if it belongs somewhere in the Low Countries, has been rebuilt. The sides of the square are now lined with concrete monstrosities.

Off the northeastern side of the Rynek is the huge church of **St James** (św. Jakuba), which long served as the cathedral of the exiled bishops. Constructed in just six years in the 1420s, it's a fine example of the hall-church style, with nave and aisles of equal height—a design much favored in Germany but rare in Poland. It's also unusual for this part of the world in having been very little altered, the only modifications being the reconstruction in Renaissance or Baroque style of three of the chapels. Entering through the graceful double portal, it's the spareness of the vast interior which makes the strongest impression. So crushing is the weight of the vault that many of the octagonal pillars, adorned with statues of the Apostles, have sagged under the strain. The chapels provide the only intimate note: fenced off by elegant grilles, they overflow with funerary plaques and monuments to the bishops and local notables. The squatness of the church's detached **belfry** is explained by the fact that it was abandoned after fifty years' work.

Southeast of St James' lies the well-preserved Baroque episcopal quarter. The **Bishops' Palace**, reached down ul. Jarosławka, is now decked out as a surprisingly good local **museum** (Tues, Wed & Fri 10am–3pm, Sat 11am–3pm, Sun 11am–4pm), with well-documented displays on the history of Nysa, including impressive fragments from demolished buildings.

From here turn right into ul. Grodzka, where the **Bishops' Residence**, which was built right up against the ramparts, stands forlorn and neglected. Farther up the street, the complex of **Jesuit buildings** has survived in better shape. The white-walled church is in the plain style favored by the order, though its austerity is softened by some recently discovered ceiling frescoes and a beautiful eighteenth-century silver tabernacle at the high altar. Adjoining it is the famous **Carolinum** college, whose luminaries included the Polish kings Michał Korybut Wiśniowiecki and Jan Sobieski.

South of the Rynek is the only other reminder of "the Silesian Rome" in the shape of the **Monastery of the Hospitallers of the Holy Sepulcher** (Klasztor Bozogrobców). This order moved to Nysa from the Holy Land at the end of the twelfth century, but the huge complex you see today dates from the early eighteenth century. It's now a seminary, and you'll probably have to ask at the reception on ul. św. Pawła to get into the resplendent Baroque church on the parallel ul. Bracka. This features a reproduction of the Holy Sepulcher in Jerusalem, and a cycle of highly theatrical frescoes by the brothers Christoph Thomas and Felix Anton Scheffler.

Practicalities

Nysa has only one **hotel**, the three-star *Piast* opposite the Ziębicka Gate at ul. Krzywoustego 14 (☎40-84). Otherwise, there's a **motel** on the outskirts of town at ul. Swierczewskiego 1a (only practical if you've got a car) and a **youth hostel** close to the station at ul. Warszawy 7 (☎37-31). Best **restaurants** are the one in the hotel, *Warszawianka* at no. 25 on the same street and *Pod Starą Wagą* on the Rynek; the last also has a café. **Orbis** is at ul. Wrocławska 14 (☎41-69).

Brzeg

Situated about 40km from both Wrocław and Opole, the old ducal seat of **BRZEG** (BRIEG) is an easily manageable and agreeable market town, with an impressive array of monuments that make it a good stopping-off point for a few hours. Originally a fishing village on the bank (*brzeg*) of the Odra, Brzeg was documented in the early thirteenth century as having a castle of a branch of the Piast dynasty. In 1311 it became a regional capital in the continuing subdivision of Silesia, and ousted Legnica as the main residence of the court. The Piasts remained there until 1675 when this family, a prominent dynasty throughout the recorded history of Poland, finally died out.

The Town

Brzeg's most historic area lies close to the river in tranquil isolation from the commercial center, at the opposite end of town from the train and bus stations. Seen from its spacious square, the **Palace** is a bit of a jumble: predominantly Renaissance, with the Gothic presbytery of St Hedwig's (the mausoleum of the Piasts), plus various misguided later additions. Badly damaged by Frederick the Great's troops in 1741, the palace was relegated for the next century and a half to the status of an arsenal. Only in the last decade has restoration returned parts of the structure to something like their former glory, which, in the case of the Renaissance sections, is something special. Built in the 1530s by a team of Italian masons, Brzeg became the prototype for a whole series of palaces in Poland, Bohemia, northern Germany, and Sweden.

The **gateway**, modeled on Dürer's woodcut of a triumphal arch in honor of Emperor Maximilian, is extravagantly rich. Above, in a shameless piece of self-glorification, are portrait figures of Duke George II and his wife, Barbara von Brandenburg. At the same level are pairs of knights whose coats of arms include those of Brzeg, Legnica, and the Jagiellonian monarchs of Poland—the last, given that Silesia had not been a part of Poland for the past three centuries, being an expression of unrequited loyalty. Two tiers of busts above the windows trace the duke's genealogy, beginning with the peasant Piast at the upper left-hand corner.

To some extent, the three-story **courtyard** resembles the Wawel palace in Kraków, above all in the lofty arcades. However, its carved decoration ultimately gives it a different character, with the heraldic motif continued on the more modest interior gate and antique-style medallions to the sides of the arcades. To the southwest corner of the courtyard rises the Lwów Tower, a survival of the medieval castle, along with part of its fortifications.

The halls of the second floor have been adapted to house the **Piast Museum** (Wed 10am–6pm, Thurs–Sun 10am–4pm). At the time of writing, exhibits from the National Museum in Wrocław were on display here, including an impressive array of devotional sculptures, and a magnificent group of canvases, particularly a hauntingly powerful series of *The Four Doctors of the Church* by Michael Willmann.

Across from the palace stands the **Piast College**, which was built some thirty years later. It has suffered even more from the vagaries of time, but once more a school is functioning behind the great portal. Directly opposite is the former Jesuit church of the **Holy Cross**, which dates back to the turn of the eighteenth century. Sober enough from the outside, its single interior space is encrusted with Rococo decorations.

Back towards downtown is the **Town Hall**, which belongs to the same architectural school as the palace, and again is an adaptation of an older structure, from which the tall belfry survives. It consists of two long parallel buildings, each terminating in a tower crowned by a bulbous Baroque steeple, joined together by the galleried facade. Farther on towards the stations is the market square, centered on the very German-looking fourteenth-century church of **St Nicholas** (św. Mikołaja). Its exterior was marred by a heightening of the towers during the last century—the builders lacked the sense to use bricks of matching color. However, the interior is pleasingly spacious and boasts a varied collection of memorial plaques of prominent families. If you come around the Mass times, you may get to see the Gothic wall paintings recently uncovered in the sacristy.

Practicalities

Brzeg has only one **hotel**, *Piast*, situated just a couple of minutes' walk from the station on the way to the town center at ul. Piastowska 14 (☎677). There's also a **youth hostel** at ul. Lechicka 4 (☎2404), but this is only open for a few weeks in midsummer. Classiest **restaurant** is the *Ratuszowa* in the town hall cellars, which opens at 1pm; several more basic snack bars can be found in the neighboring streets.

Opole and Around

If you're planning on spending a fair amount of time in Silesia, chances are you'll end up in **OPOLE** (OPPELN) sooner or later. Situated in the very heart of the province, midway down the train line between Wrocław and Katowice, and within easy reach of Nysa, the Kłodzko Region, and Częstochowa, the city makes a convenient touring base. Though ravaged by over twenty fires throughout its history, the center presents a well-balanced spread of old and new, ringed by a green belt and with the more unsightly industry banished to the outskirts.

One of Opole's main assets is its setting on the banks of the Odra. The river divides to form an island, the **Wyspa Pasieka**, which was inhabited in the ninth century by a Slavic tribe called the Opolanes. Bolesław the Brave established the island as a fortress, but Opole subsequently became divorced from its mother country, serving as the capital of a Piast principality from 1202 until this particular line died out in 1532.

The city and the highly productive agricultural land around were understandably coveted by the Polish state after World War I, but Opole voted to remain part of Germany in the plebiscite of 1921, subsequently becoming the capital of the German province of Upper Silesia. In contrast to most other places ceded to Poland after World War II, the Opole region retained a sizable **German minority**, and is the prime focus of German political troublemakers.

The City

The hub of Opole has long moved from the Wyspa Pasieka to the right bank of the Odra, where the central area is laid out on a grid-iron pattern. Nonetheless, the island in many ways makes the best place to begin an exploration, and can be reached in a few minutes from the main **train** and **bus** stations at the southern end of town via ul. Wojciecha Korfantego.

Of the four bridges crossing the arm of the river, look out for the second, one of several structures in Opole built around 1910 in the Secessionist style. Arched like a bridge in a Japanese garden, this steel construction was made so cheaply that it became known as the **Groschen Bridge** after the smallest coin then in circulation. It bears the curious coat of arms of the city, showing half an eagle and half a cross: the local Piasts allowed one side of the family's traditional blazon to be replaced by a symbol of the city's acquisition of a relic of the True Cross.

Of the medieval Piast **Castle**, almost nothing is left except a gaunt round tower, now partly hidden behind functional 1930s administrative buildings. The grounds have been converted into a park with a large artificial lake and an open-air amphitheater, the setting for a **Festival of Polish Song** held each June.

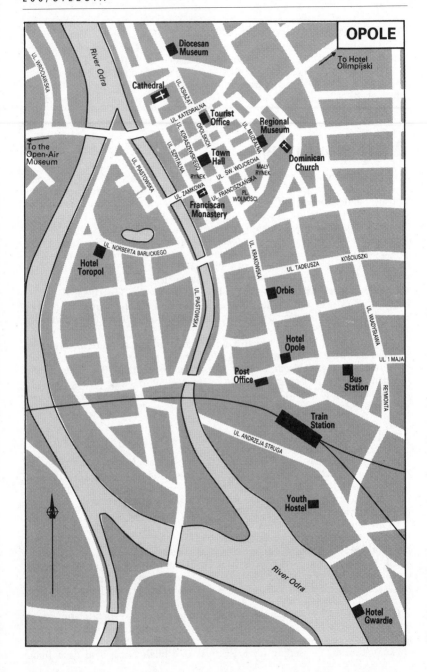

OPOLE

Diocesan Museum

Cathedral

UL WROCŁAWSKA

River Odra

To Hotel Olimpijski

UL KSIĄŻĄT
UL KATEDRALNA
OPOLSKICH

Tourist Office

UL KORASZEWSKIEGO

UL SZPITALNA

UL MUZEALNA

Regional Museum

Town Hall

Dominican Church

RYNEK

UL ŚW. WOJCIECHA

MAŁY RYNEK

UL PIASTOWSKA

UL ZAMKOWA

UL FRANCISZKAŃSKA

PL. WOLNOŚCI

Franciscan Monastery

UL NORBERTA BARLICKIEGO

To the Open-Air Museum

Hotel Toropol

UL KRAKOWSKA

UL TADEUSZA

KOŚCIUSZKI

Orbis

UL PIASTOWSKA

UL WŁADYSŁAWA

Hotel Opole

UL 1 MAJA

Post Office

Bus Station

REYMONTA

Train Station

UL ANDRZEJA STRUGA

Youth Hostel

River Odra

Hotel Gwardie

Continuing northward along ul. Piastowa, you get a good view of the old town on the opposite bank, and in particular of the former **wharf** directly opposite, with a picturesque jumble of buildings rising directly from the river.

Returning across the Odra by ul. Zamkowa, you soon arrive at the **Franciscan church**, a much-altered Gothic construction chiefly remarkable for the richly decorated Chapel of St Anne off the southern side of the nave. Endowed by the local Piasts to serve as their **mausoleum**, it has an exquisite stellar vault studded with keystones of the family eagle and painted with floral and heraldic motifs. The two magnificent double tombs were carved around 1380 by a member of the celebrated Parler family. Although he was still alive, an effigy of Duke Bolko III was made to accompany that of his recently deceased wife, with a similar monument created in belated memory of his two ancestral namesakes. The retable is from a century later, and shows Bolko I offering a model of this monastery to Saint Anne, while Ladislaus II presents her with a model of the great church of Jasna Góra in Częstochowa.

If you ring at any reasonable time at the door of the **Franciscan monastery** just around the corner on ul. Koraszewskiego, a monk will escort you through the complex, and will light up the chapel—a necessity for seeing it properly. You will also be taken down to the catacombs, which contain the unadorned coffins of other members of the dynasty, and a number of fourteenth-century frescoes, notably a faded but tragically powerful *Crucifixion*.

Immediately beyond the Franciscan monastery is the **Rynek**, whose cheerful mansions were badly damaged in World War II, but have been deftly restored. The **Town Hall** dates from the early Nazi years, and is a self-conscious pastiche of the Palazzo Vecchio in Florence, yet its unrelieved severity is suggestive more of a prison than of the civic headquarters.

Housed in the former Jesuit college on ul. św. Wojciecha just off the Rynek is the **District Museum** (Tues, Thurs & Fri 10am–4pm, Wed 10am–6pm, Sat & Sun 10am–3pm), whose main strength is the archaeology section, with exhibits from prehistoric to early medieval times. A steep stairway then ascends to a hill where Saint Adalbert (see "Gniezno," in Chapter Six) used to preach as Bishop of Prague, Opole being part of his diocese. The church of **Our Lady**, which now occupies the spot, was originally Gothic, though this is hardly apparent from the neo-Romanesque facade and Baroque interior decorations. Beyond stand the tower of the fourteenth-century fortress and remains of the sixteenth-century town wall.

From the Rynek, ul. Książąt Opolskich leads past the eye-catching Secessionist **Bank Rolników**, which was founded by the local Polish population in 1911—along with a newspaper—as a gesture of nationalist defiance. Farther down the street you come to the **Cathedral**, mixing fourteenth-century Gothic and nineteenth-century imitation. Raised to the status of a cathedral only a couple of decades ago, the church is chiefly famous for the allegedly miraculous, jewel-encrusted icon to the right of the main altar, known as the *Opole Madonna*.

The **Diocesan Museum** (Tues & Thurs 10am–noon & 2–5pm, first Sun in month 2–5pm) is located in a block of modern buildings at the beginning of ul. Buczka. Opened in 1987 largely as a result of voluntary effort, it's the object of considerable local pride as the first non-state museum in postwar Poland and one whose display techniques put the nationally owned collections to shame. Ask for the leaflet in English which describes the exhibits, all from churches in the Opole region. On the ground floor are several outstanding Gothic sculptures, including an *Enthroned Madonna* in the Parler style. Upstairs, pride of place is taken by the fourteenth-century reliquary made to house Opole's fragment of the True Cross; there's also a lovely *Virgin and Child* attributed to Fra Filippo Lippi. The small room next door features gifts to adorn the *Opole Madonna* from worthies ranging from King Jan Sobieski to the present pope. Imaginative exhibitions of contemporary religious art are also featured.

By the side of the main road to Wrocław, 8km west of the city center and reached by buses #5, #19, or #A, is an excellent **Open-Air Museum** (Muzeum Wsi Opolskiej; Tues–Sun 10am–5pm). Some sixty examples of the rural architecture of the region have been erected here, many grouped in simulation of their original environment. Particularly notable is the early seventeenth-century wooden church from Gręboszów, a typical example of what is still the main place of worship in many Silesian villages. Another highlight is an eighteenth-century water mill in full working order, which can be demonstrated on request.

Opole Practicalities

The **tourist office** on ul. Książąt Opolskich (Mon–Fri 9am–5/6pm, Sat 10am–3pm) has maps and booklets on Opole in Polish and German. **Orbis** is at ul. Krakowska 31 (☎363-36), while **Almatur** is at pl. Armii Czerwonej 1 (☎377-36).

The best accommodation bets are the **sports hotels**—*Toropol*, ul. Norberta Barlickiego 13 (☎366-91) on the Wyspa Pasieka, and *Gwardie*, ten minutes' walk south of the station at ul. Kowalska 4 (☎364-20). Cheapest of the other **hotels** is *Zajadz Kastelański*, well to the west of downtown at ul. Koszyka 29 (☎743-028), but close to over a dozen bus routes, including #2, #4, #5, #7, #8, and #9. The leading hotel is *Opole*, just across from the station at ul. Krakowska (☎386-51), a three-star place catering mainly to affluent German tourists, with prices to match. Similarly luxurious is the motel *Olimpijska*, not far from the northern suburban station of Opole-Wschodnie at ul. Oleska 86 (☎263-51); from the center take bus #3, #11, #C, #D, or #N. The **youth hostel** is to the rear of the main train station at ul. Struga 16 (July & Aug; ☎333-52). Another summer possibility is the **student hotel**, *Zygzak*, north of the motel at ul. ZSP 10 (☎262-57). Opole has no camping facilities.

Prices in the *Hotel Opole*'s **restaurant**, the *Hotelowa*, are bargain-basement in comparison with the accommodation, but the quality isn't outstanding either. Alternative choices for a full meal are *Europa*, pl. Wolności 1, and *Biełgorod*, ul. Kościuszki 3. More adventurous menus are available at *Karczma Słupska*, ul. Książąt Opolskich 6, specializing in huge pork knuckles and the Hungarian *czardasz*, east of downtown at ul. Ozimska 63, which has dancing in the evenings.

If you're after something less fancy, there are the **milk bars** *Krówka*, ul. Krakowska 11, and *Kubus*, ul. 1 Maja 1. There's also a snack bar for fish dishes: *Rybny*, ul. Władysława Reymonta 9. Among the many **cafés** are two on the Rynek, *Pod Arkadami* and *Melba*, and a couple more on ul. Krakowska, *Ptyś* and *Teatralna*.

Góra Świętej Anny

Forty kilometers southeast of Opole, conspicuous on its 410-meter hill, is the village of **GÓRA ŚWIĘTEJ ANNY** (SANKT ANNABERG). Associated with the cult of Saint Anne, mother of the Virgin Mary, it's one of the most popular places of **pilgrimage** in Poland, and is the scene of colorful processions on June 26 each year. Outside major church festivals, however, it's a moribund little place, the antithesis of the relentlessly busy Jasna Góra. For that, it can thank its relatively isolated situation; getting here by public transit is problematic, and is best done by taking a train from Opole to ZDZIESZOWICE, then covering the remaining 6km on foot or by bus. It's worth bringing a picnic, as the village has only a café and some tacky snack bars which aren't always open.

Although the cult of Saint Anne is long established in Silesia, Góra Świętej Anny's status as a major pilgrimage shrine dates back only to the mid-seventeenth century, when a **Franciscan monastery** was built to replace a modest Gothic votive chapel. As is the case with Jasna Góra, its popularity is intimately associated with Polish nationalism, fanned by the fact that the monks have been expelled three times (as a result of the policies of Napoleon, Bismarck, and Hitler). For five days in May 1921, the village was the scene of bitter fighting following the Upper Silesia plebiscite, which left it in German hands. Ill-feeling has persisted: it was only in 1989 that the outlawing of Masses in German, introduced when the monks returned in 1945 in retaliation for previous bans on Polish services, was rescinded.

The **church**, decorated in a restrained Baroque style, houses the source of the pilgrimage, a tiny miraculous statue of *St Anne with the Virgin and Child*, high above the main altar. An unassuming piece of folksy Gothic carving, it's usually decked out in gorgeous clothes. Below the monastery buildings is the mid-eighteenth century **Calvary**, an elaborate processional way with 33 chapels and shrines telling the story of the Passion. A large and less tasteful **Lourdes grotto** was added as the centerpiece in 1912.

The Katowice Conurbation

Poland's main industrial area consists of an almost continuously built-up conurbation of about a dozen towns, beginning around 65km southeast of Opole. Two million inhabitants make this the most densely populated part of the country, with 350,000 in the largest city, **KATOWICE** (KATTOWITZ).

Since the beginning of the *glasnost* era, the region has attracted worldwide attention because of the horrendous **pollution** of its outdated factories. It's officially classified as an environmental disaster area by the Polish Academy of Sciences and a large percentage of its inhabitants are constantly subjected to severe health hazards, as the large number of disease-ridden children testifies. Similarly, the effect on buildings goes beyond turning local stonework a delicate shade of spearmint green; the dispersion of the pollution is responsible for the severe damage caused to Kraków, some 70km to the east. And when Poland faces a tricky international soccer match, the odds are that it'll be played in Katowice—if the surroundings don't incapacitate the opposition with depression, the oxygen-free atmosphere should take a few yards off their pace.

The region's rich mineral seams have been extensively mined since the Middle Ages, but it wasn't until the nineteenth-century **industrial revolution** that the area became urbanized. In 1800, Katowice had just 500 inhabitants. Fifty years later, its population was a still modest 4000 before Upper Silesia mushroomed into the powerhouse of the Prussian state, in tandem with the broadly similar Ruhr at the opposite end of the country.

With a population composed almost equally of Germans and Poles, the fate of the area became a hot political issue after World War I. In each of the next three years, there were uprisings by Poles demanding to be included in the new Polish state, which would otherwise have been a poor agricultural country with no industrial base. As a result, the League of Nations held a **plebiscite** throughout Upper Silesia in 1921 to determine the fate of the area. By a small majority this was won by the Germans, but the League decided the distribution of votes justified splitting up the province, with the bulk of the conurbation going to Poland.

Katowice

Katowice is not a place you'll want to go out of your way to see; if you do find yourself here for any reason, there are a couple of spots where you could kill some time. At the end of the long ul. Wojciecha Korfanty, the **Silesian Museum** (Muzeum Śląskie; Tues–Fri 10am–5pm, Sat & Sun 11am–4pm) features changing exhibitions plus a variety of contemporary paintings downstairs, while the upstairs gallery has a selection of Polish art from 1800 to World War II. Major names such as Piotr Michałowski, Jan Matejko, and Stanisław Wyspiański are here, but the most intriguing work is a highly accomplished *Self Portrait* by Stanisław Ignacy Witkiewicz, better known for his brilliantly original novels and plays.

Continuing down the street to the end, you come to a traffic circle with a sports hall reminiscent of a flying saucer. On the right is the **Monument to the Silesian Uprisings**: three tall shapes in the form of clipped wings, symbolizing each of the attempts to gain freedom from German rule. In the nearby **Kościuszko Park** is another commemorative monument, this time to the victims of World War II and the Holocaust. It's a reminder of the parachute tower formerly occupying the site, where people learned how to jump; the Nazis continued to put it to use, without the parachutes.

Any tram going from the roundabout in the direction of Chorzów will bring you to Katowice's main recreation area, the **Wojewódzki Park**, which features a big wheel similar to the famous Prater in Vienna. Behind the huge soccer stadium (four stops farther on) is the **Górnośląski Park** (May–Sept daily 10am–dusk). If you don't have a chance to go into the mountains, the wooden buildings brought here from nearby rural communities will give you a fair idea of what you're missing.

Katowice Practicalities

The cheapest **hotels** are *Centralny*, beside the train station at ul. Dworcowa 9 (☎53-90-41), *Polonia* on ul. Kochanowskiego (☎51-40-51), and *Śląski*, ul. Mariacka 15 (☎53-70-11). Alternatively, there are two four-star Orbis hotels, with all the normal luxuries: *Silesia*, ul. Piotra Skargi 2 (☎59-62-11), and *Warszawa*, ul. Rozdzieńskiego 16 (☎59-60-11). There's also a **youth hostel** close to the station at ul. Graniczna 27a (☎51-94-57). The best **restaurants** are in the Orbis hotels: unlike the rooms, they're priced on a purely Polish scale. Other good choices in the city center are *Corner*, ul. 27 Go-Styczni, and *Best*, in the pedestrian precinct opposite the station. **Orbis** is at ul. Wojciecha Korfanty 2 (☎58-75-32), **Almatur** at ul. 3 Maja 7 (☎59-88-58).

Regular **concerts** are given by the Silesian Philharmonic, ul. Gen. Zawadzkiego 2 (☎52-62-61), and the Symphony Orchestra of Polish Radio and Television, pl. Dzierzyńskiego 2 (☎57-13-84). The *Teatr Stanisława Wyspiański* on the Rynek (☎59-89-76) presents high-quality **drama**, though its fame is eclipsed by the *Teatr Zagłębia* in the adjacent town of SOSNOWIEC.

Tarnowskie Góry

From a tourist point of view, the only worthwhile town in the area is **TARNOWSKIE GÓRY** (TARNOWITZ), at the far northern end of the conurbation and reached from Katowice in about an hour by train. It's a place with a far more venerable history: silver and lead deposits were discovered in the thirteenth century, and it was given an urban charter and mining rights in the sixteenth by the dukes of Opole. Some idea of its underground wealth is given in a document dated 1632, listing 20,000 places where minerals could be exploited.

There are two **historic industrial sites** in Tarnowskie Góry, which make a fascinating supplement to the famous salt mines of Wieliczka (see Chapter Four). Probably the best approach is to telephone the Friends of Tarnowskie Góry Association for a **guided tour** (daily 7:30am–3:30pm; ☎85-49-96), or to ask a tourist office to do it for you; they have guides who speak German plus a little English and French. Otherwise, you can just turn up at the sites and wait to tag on to the next organized group passing through; these are frequent in summer and on weekends. Warm clothing and shoes with a good tread are essential.

The first of the sites is the **Sylvester Mine and Museum** (9am–2pm; closed Tues). From Tarnowskie Góry station, take any bus going to BYTOM—if an express service, get off at the first stop; if a normal service, at the third. Alternatively, it can be reached directly from Katowice by taking express bus #A as far as Osada Janas. Dating back to medieval times, the mine was formerly worked for silver, lead, and copper. In the small museum you can see the old equipment, plus models of how the mine was worked and the water levels controlled.

A large wall map explains the connection between the levels of the mine and the **Black Trout Shaft** (Sztolnia Czarnego Pstrąg; daily 8:30am–dusk), 3km away. If you've signed on to a tour, the guide will accompany you from the Sylvester mine. By public transit the easiest approach is to return to the station, then take bus #19 as far as the hospital; the way is then signposted through the park. Here you make a spooky journey by boat along one of the former drainage channels through rock-hewn "gates." Each has a different name, with a legend attached: at one point, for instance, any woman wanting to find a husband within the year is invited to rap on the wall. At the end of the trip, wait until the water becomes still—the reflection from the ceiling creates the uncanny illusion that the water has disappeared.

Each September, Tarnowskie Góry hosts a costume **festival** in honor of the visit of King Jan Sobieski, who stopped off in 1683 on his way to relieve Vienna from the Turks.

South of Katowice

South of the Katowice conurbation there's a more agreeable and rural landscape, featuring several old ducal towns plus the westernmost part of the Beskids. The places below are served by plenty of trains and buses from the city, but beware that the latter sometimes stop running relatively early.

Pszczyna

The small town of **PSZCZYNA** (PLESS), reached from Katowice in about forty minutes by bus #31, is best known for its particularly unpronounceable name, which features in a favorite Polish tongue-twister. On a more serious note, it holds an honored place in Poland's history for having led the first Upper Silesian Uprising of 1919, but its main claim on your attention is likely to be the **Palace** (tours May–Oct Wed 9am–4pm, Thurs & Fri 9am–2pm, Sat & Sun 10am–2pm; Nov–April Wed 10am–4pm, Thurs–Sun 10am–2pm). The building's checkered history mirrors the area's turbulent past: a Piast hunting lodge from the twelfth century, it was expanded and rebuilt in the Gothic and Renaissance styles before gaining its largely Baroque appearance after a fire (other parts were added in the nineteenth century). It contains many period furnishings, some of them brought from other Polish stately homes. On the first and last Sunday of the month, chamber **concerts** are held in the beautiful Baroque ballroom; tickets are available at the booking office on the day of performance. The English-style park (free access) has a lake with water lilies and a wooden bridge straight out of a Monet painting.

In the town itself, the handsome late eighteenth-century **Rynek** is lined with fine mansions. At no. 18, look out for the bison sign which gives the *Pod Zubrem* restaurant its name. Other places to **eat** and **drink** can be found on the nearby ul. Piastowska. **PTTK** have an office at no. 3 on the Rynek (☎35-30); the same organization runs a **tourist hostel** at ul. Brama Wybrańców 2 (☎32-33).

Cieszyn

If you missed out on Berlin when it still had the Wall, then **CIESZYN** (TESCHEN), 80km southwest of Katowice, will give you a smaller-scale idea of the realities of life in a place arbitrarily divided by a line on a map. Formerly part of the Habsburg Empire, it was claimed after World War I by Czechoslovakia and Poland, both of whom had large numbers of nationals living there. In the end, the 1920 Conference of Ambassadors decided to use the Olza River as the frontier, so the right-bank part of town became Polish and the opposite side Czech. However, no attempt was made to rationalize the nationality problem, with chaotic results. Ethnic Poles living on the Czech side can cross over to work each day using special passes, whereas Poles may only cross in the other direction if armed with an official invitation and a visa, except on All Saints' Day, when the border is thrown open. This absurdity seems set to continue, in order to thwart traders out to exploit the price disparities between the two countries. So take great care if crossing—your Polish visa will be canceled and you won't get back in unless you have a re-entry permit.

The central **Rynek**, with the eighteenth-century Town Hall, is marred by heavy traffic, though that should soon be siphoned off by the new crossing point being built west of town, at the end of what will be the largest bridge in Poland. At the southwest corner of the square is the Gothic church of **St Mary Magdalene**, containing the mausoleum of the Piast dukes who established a principality here in 1290.

The main street, ul. Głebocki, leads from the Rynek down to the river. If you take ul. Sejmowa to the left and then the first turning right, you'll find yourself on ul. Trzech Braci (Street of the Three Brothers), where stands the **well** associated with the legend of the town's foundation. In the year 810 the three sons of King Leszko III met up at this spring after a long spell of wandering around the country, and were so delighted to see each other again that they founded a town named "I'm happy" (*cieszyćsię*).

Above the town rises a hill crowned by a Gothic **clock tower** (daily 9:30am–4pm, closed in winter in bad weather), the only survival from the Piast palace. From the top, there's a superb view over both sides of the town. Also on the hill are a nineteenth-century rebuild of a Romanesque rotunda and a "ruined" Romantic folly among the trees.

Orbis has a four-star **motel** at ul. Armii Ludowej 93 (☎204-51). Other accommodation possibilities are the **youth hostel** at ul. Wojsk Ochrony Pogranicza 3 and the **campground** *Olza*, ul. Jana Łysa 12. There's a PTTK **tourist office** at ul. Mennicza 48. If you're traveling in the direction of Katowice, note that the buses are much faster than the trains, but that the last service leaves around 5pm.

The Silesian Beskids

East of Cieszyn lies the Silesian section of the **Beskids**. These are best known as being the source of the Wisła, which rises on the slopes of one of the highest peaks, Barania Góra (1220m), and winds a serpentine 1090-kilometre course through Oświęcim, Kraków, Warsaw, and Toruń before emptying into the Baltic just east of Gdańsk.

Although there are the usual hiking opportunities in summer, these hills don't really compare with the more dramatic scenery of the eastern Beskids or the Sudetens farther north. However, as the area experiences prolonged and heavy snowfalls each winter, it has developed a number of **winter sports** resorts. The best of the bunch is **SZCZYRK**, set in a valley about 30km from Cieszyn; it ranks second to Zakopane as the most popular ski center in the country, and has an international-class downhill route. There are dozens of places to stay—just turn up and look for signs saying *Noclegi* or *Pokoje*. Many of these houses will provide dinner for a moderate amount, or allow you to do your own catering; otherwise there are plenty of snack bars around. The town's party atmosphere compensates for the frustrations of waiting in long lines for the ski-lifts.

ZYWIEC (SAYBUSCH), in a broad valley 17km southeast of Szczyrk, was founded in the fifteenth century by the dukes of Oświęcim. Their Renaissance **castle** was taken over by the Habsburgs, who extensively rebuilt it in the last century, retaining the original courtyard. The town's brewery annually produces 30 million liters of what's generally agreed to be the **best beer in Poland**. Although this is easily obtainable locally, you may have trouble finding it elsewhere in Poland, as much of it is made for export. If you need to stay, there's a **youth hostel** at ul. Waryńskiego 4 (☎26-39). Every August, there's a **festival** of local folklore, while the Christmas celebrations are among the most characterful in Poland.

travel details

Trains

Wrocław to Białystok (2 daily; 10hr 30min–13hr; couchettes); Bydgoszcz (7 daily; 4–5hr); Częstochowa (6 daily; 3–4hr); Gdańsk (6 daily; 6hr–7hr 30 min; couchettes); Jelenia Góra (19 daily; 2hr 30min–3hr); Kalisz (13 daily; 2hr–2hr 30min); Katowice (21 daily; 3–4hr); Kielce (3 daily; 5hr–6hr 30min); Kłodzko (7 daily; 2hr 30min); Kołobrzeg (3 daily; 8–10hr); Kraków (17 daily; 4–6hr); Legnica (22 daily; 1hr); Leszno (27 daily; 1hr–1hr 30min); Lublin (3 daily; 8hr 30min–9hr 30min; couchettes); Łódź (14 daily; 4–6hr); Olsztyn (2 daily; 7hr 30min–10hr; couchettes); Opole (42 daily; 1hr–1hr 30min); Poznań (26 daily; 2hr–3hr 30min); Przemyśl (5 daily; 8hr 30min; couchettes); Rzeszów (6 daily; 7hr; couchettes);

Słupsk (2 daily; 9–10hr); Szczecin (11 daily; 6hr–7hr 30min; couchettes); Świnoujście (3 daily; 7–8hr); Wałbrzych (20 daily; 1hr 30min); Warsaw (16 daily; 6–7hr; couchettes); Zakopane (1 daily; 8hr 30min; couchettes); Zielona Góra (10 daily; 2–3hr). Also **international connections** to Görlitz, Dresden, and Prague.

Jelenia Góra to Bydgoszcz (1 daily; 8hr; couchettes); Częstochowa (2 daily; 6hr); Gdańsk (1 daily; 10hr; couchettes); Kalisz (4 daily; 5hr–6hr 30min); Katowice (6hr 30min–8hr); Kielce (1 daily; 8hr; couchettes); Kłodzko (4 daily; 2hr); Kraków (2 daily; 9–10hr; couchettes); Leszno (3 daily; 4–5hr); Lublin (1 daily; 11hr 30min; couchettes); Łódź (4 daily; 6hr 30min–9hr); Opole (4 daily; 4hr–4hr 30min); Poznań (4 daily; 5hr–6hr 30min); Szczecin (1 daily; 9hr; couchettes); Wałbrzych (23 daily; 1hr); Warsaw (4 daily; 8hr 30min–9hr 30min); Wrocław (18 daily; 2hr 30min); Zielona Góra (2 daily; 4hr 30min–5hr 30min).

Katowice to Białystok (2 daily; 6–8hr; couchettes); Bydgoszcz (6 daily; 5–7hr; couchettes); Częstochowa (34 daily; 1hr 30min–2hr); Gdańsk (8 daily; 6hr 30min–9hr; couchettes);

Jelenia Góra (3 daily; 7hr); Kielce (11 daily; 2hr 30min–3hr 30min); Kołobrzeg (2 daily; 10hr 30min–1hr 30min; couchettes); Kraków (40 daily; 1hr 30min–2hr); Legnica (7 daily; 4–7hr); Leszno (7 daily; 4hr 30min–5hr); Lublin (5 daily; 6–7hr); Łódź (8 daily; 3hr 30min–5hr); Olsztyn (2 daily; 8hr 30min–11hr); Opole (23 daily; 2hr); Poznań (15 daily; 5–7hr); Przemyśl (7 daily; 5hr 30min); Rzeszów (8 daily; 4–5hr); Słupsk (2 daily; 10–13hr; couchettes); Szczecin (7 daily; 9–10hr); Świnoujście (3 daily; 10hr–1hr 30min); Wałbrzych (3 daily; 6hr); Warsaw (17 daily; 3hr 30min–5hr); Wrocław (23 daily; 3–4hr); Zakopane (3 daily; 5–7hr; couchettes); Zamość (2 daily; 8–10hr); Zielona Góra (4 daily; 5–6hr).

Buses

Wrocław to Kłodzko, Legnica, Oleśnica, Sobótka, Świdnica, Trzebnica.

Jelenia Góra to Bolków, Kamienna Góra, Karpacz, Kłodzko, Legnica, Szklarska Poręba.

Kłodzko to Kudowa-Zdrój, Lądek-Zdrój, Międzygórze, Paczków–Otmuchów–Nysa–Opole.

Katowice to Cieszyn, Pszczyna.

CHAPTER SIX

WIELKOPOLSKA AND POMERANIA

Wielkopolska and **Pomerania**, the two northwest regions of the country, constitute a large swath of modern Poland. Despite their proximity, however, the feel and history of each is highly distinct. Wielkopolska formed the core of the original Polish nation and has remained identifiably Polish through subsequent centuries; Pomerania, by contrast, bears the imprint of the Prussians, who ruled this area from the early eighteenth century through to 1945—the province only became Polish after 1945, and parts of "Lower Pomerania," to the west of Świnoujście, remain German territory.

In **Wielkopolska** the chief interest is supplied by the regional capital **Poznań**, an attractive city famed within Poland for the 1956 riots which were the first major revolt against communism. **Gniezno**, the ancient capital of the first Piast monarchs and still the seat of the Primate of Poland, is a big church center, full of seminaries and trainee priests. Out in the countryside, the outstanding attractions are the **Wielkopolska National Park**, and the Iron-Age village of **Biskupin**, Poland's most ancient preserved settlement.

Pomerania is dominated by the Baltic, with ports such as **Szczecin** playing a crucial role in the country's economy, in tandem with a network of seaside resorts that pulls in large numbers of Polish and foreign tourists. The Baltic may be not quite the Mediterranean, but temperatures climb high enough for summer swimming and the **beaches** sweep far enough for escapes from the crowds. Among the towns, **Kamień Pomorski** is the architectural high point, an old lagoon settlement with a wonderful cathedral, while the region has wildlife appeal, too, with a bison reserve in the forested **Woliński National Park**. Inland, the Pomeranian **lakeland** is less known than its counterpart in Mazury, but offers enjoyable, low-key pursuits for canoeists and hikers.

WIELKOPOLSKA

Much of the landscape of **Wielkopolska** is dull, but its human story is an altogether different matter, as its name—"Great Poland"—implies. This area has been inhabited continuously since prehistoric times, and it was here that the Polish nation first took shape. The name of the province and of Poland itself derive from a Slav tribe called the **Polonians**, whose leaders—the **Piast** family—were to rule the country for five centuries. Their embryonic state emerged under Mieszko I in the mid-tenth century, but the significant breakthrough was achieved under his son, Bolesław the Brave, who gained control over an area

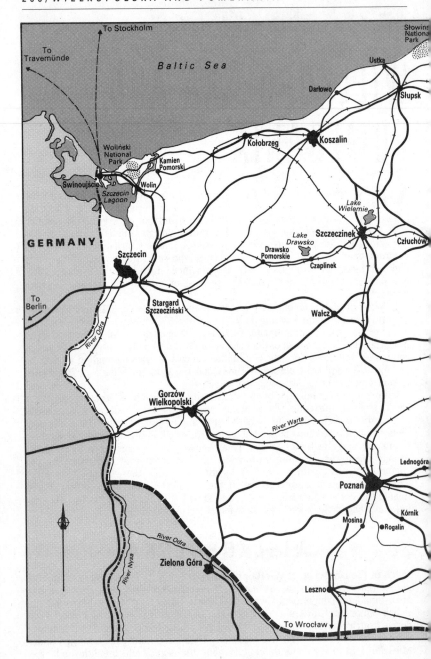

similar to that of present-day Poland, and made it independent from the German-dominated Holy Roman Empire. Though relegated to the status of a border province by the mid-eleventh century, Wielkopolska remained one of the indisputably Polish parts of Poland, fighting the Germanization which swamped the nation's other western territories.

The major survival from the early Piast period is at **Lake Lednica**, which is part of the established tourist trail known as the Piast Route; strangely enough, the region's prehistoric past is represented far more vividly, in the form of the Iron-Age village of **Biskupin**.

Gniezno was the first city to achieve dominance, but soon went into decline, accepting the consolation role of Poland's ecclesiastical capital. It was quickly supplanted as the regional center by nearby **Poznań**, which has retained its position as one of Poland's leading commercial cities. Even older than either of these is **Kalisz**, which dates back at least as far as Roman times. Another town in the province which has played an important part in Polish culture, albeit at a later date, is **Leszno**, once a major Protestant center. Yet this is predominantly a rural province, and perhaps its most typical attraction is the **Wielkopolska National Park**, epitomizing the region's glaciated landscape.

On the eastern border of Wielkopolska lies the ancient province of Kujawy; now scarcely distinguishable from Wielkopolska, it has one fairly interesting town, the historic capital of **Włocławek**.

As in the rest of Poland, there are plentiful trains and buses, with the former usually having the edge in terms of speed and convenience. A particularly diverting way of getting around is provided by a number of narrow-gauge rail lines, the most useful of which are described in the text.

Poznań

Thanks to its position on the Paris–Berlin–Moscow rail line, and as the one place where all international trains stop between the German border and Warsaw, **POZNAŃ** is many visitors' first taste of Poland. In many ways it's the ideal introduction, as no other city is more closely identified with Polish nationhood. *"Posnania elegans Poloniae civitas"* (Poznań, a beautiful city in Poland), the inscription on the oldest surviving depiction of the town, has been adopted as a local catchphrase to highlight its unswerving loyalty to the national cause over the centuries. Nowadays it's a city of great diversity, encompassing a tranquil cathedral quarter, an animated center focused on one of Europe's most imposing squares, and a dynamic business district whose trade fair is the most important in the country.

Poznań's History

In the ninth century the Polonians founded a castle on a strategically significant island in the Warta River, and in 968 Mieszko I made this one of the two main centers of his duchy, and the seat of its first bishop. The settlement that developed here was given the name **Ostrów Tumski** (Cathedral Island), which it still retains.

Although initially overshadowed by Gniezno, Poznań did not follow the latter's decline with the transference of the court to Kraków in the mid-thirteenth century. Instead, it became the undisputed capital of Wielkopolska, and the main bastion of Poland's western border. The economic life of the city then shifted to the west bank of the river, which was laid out in a chessboard pattern around a market square—an arrangement preserved today. Poznań's prosperity soared as it profited from the union of Poland and Lithuania, and the decline of both the Teutonic Order and the Hanseatic League, becoming a key junction of European trade routes as well as a leading center of learning.

Along with the rest of the country, decline inevitably set in with the Swedish wars of the seventeenth and eighteenth centuries. Revival of sorts came during the Partition period, when Poznań became the thoroughly Prussian city of Posen; sharing in the wealth of the Industrial Revolution, it also consolidated its reputation as a rallying point for **Polish nationalism**, resisting Bismarck's Germanization policy and playing an active role in the independence movements. An uprising in December 1918 finally forced out the German occupiers, ensuring that Poznań would become part of the resurrected Polish state. A university was founded in the following year, with the annual trade fair established two years after that.

Poznań's rapid expansion during the interwar period has been followed by accelerated growth, doubling in population to its present level of almost 600,000, and spreading onto the right bank of the Warta. The city's association with the struggle against foreign hegemony—this time Russian—was again demonstrated by the food riots of 1956, which were crushed at a cost of 74 lives. These riots are popularly regarded as the first staging post toward the formation of Solidarity, 24 years later.

> The Poznań telephone code is ☎061.

Arrival, Information, and Accommodation

The main **train station**, Poznań Główny, is southwest of the historic district; the front entrance, not immediately apparent, is situated between platforms 1 and 4. Trams #5 and #21 go from here to the city center. The **bus station** is five minutes' walk to the east along ul. Towarowa. Buses #59, #77, and #108 serve the **airport** in the western suburb of Ławica.

The main **tourist office** is located at Stary Rynek 77 (Mon–Sat 8am–4pm; ☎52-61-56); an alternative source of information is the PTTK bureau at no. 90 on the same square (☎52-18-39). International rail tickets can be purchased from the **Orbis** office at pl. Wolności 3 (☎52-40-11). Other conveniently located branches are at ul. Czerwonej Armii 33 and al. Karola Marcinkowskiego 21—worth knowing about if you want to buy domestic tickets, since the lines at the station are very often horrendous. The **Almatur** office is at al. Aleksandra Fredry 7 (☎52-36-45).

Finding a Place to Stay
Because of the trade fair, Poznań has plenty of accommodation, but hotel prices consequently tend to be western rather than Polish. Staying here on a tight budget shouldn't present any real problems, however, as the city has a better-than-average supply of hostels.

CHEAPER HOTELS

Grouped closely together near the very heart of the city are three **three-star hotels**: *Poznański*, al. Karola Marcinkowskiego 22 (☎52-81-21); *Wielkopolska*, ul. Czerwonej Armii 67 (☎52-76-31); and *Lech*, ul. Czerwonej Armii 75 (☎66-60-512). They charge identical rates, which are rather high by Polish standards. For a better bargain, you'll have to try your luck at one of the **sports hotels**. *POSiR*, just to the south of the center at ul. Marcina Chwiałkowskiego 34 (☎33-05-11), is the most convenient of these. Others to try are *Olimpia*, ul. Warmińska 1 (☎458-21), northwest of downtown and reached by tram #9 or #11; and *Naramowice*, ul. Naramowicka 150 (☎20-06-612), in the northern suburb of the same name, reached by bus #67 or #105.

LUXURY HOTELS

There are five **Orbis hotels**, all four-star. Unfortunately, by far the most enticing of these, the historic *Bazar* at al. Karola Marcinkowskiego 10 (☎512-51), is not scheduled to reopen until 1993. In the meantime, the flagship of the modern concrete alternatives is *Poznań* on pl. Gen. Henryka Dąbrowskiego (☎33-20-81), diagonally opposite the bus station; even if you're not staying there it's a useful place to know about, since its services include a travel bureau and a car rental office, and English is spoken. *Merkury*, ul. Franklina Roosevelta 20 (☎40-801), is convenient for its proximity to the train station. *Polonez*, to the north of the center at al. Niepodległości 54/68 (☎69-91-41), is quieter and not as expensive. *Novotel*, ul. Warszawska 64/66 (☎77-00-41), is on the eastern approach road, but still on various tram routes, including #6, which goes to the station.

PRIVATE ROOMS

For a room in a **private house**, you could try the *Biuro Zakwaterowania*, opposite the side entrance to the station at ul. Głogowska 16 (Mon–Fri 9am–7pm, Sat 9am–3pm; ☎603-13), but they're mainly interested in long stays and may have nothing for short-term rental. The inflated prices at the Orbis office in the *Hotel Poznań* may mean you'd be better off in a budget hotel. At the latter there's a hefty surcharge for stays of one or two nights.

HOSTELS

Poznań has no fewer than five official **youth hostels**, the handiest of which is at ul. Berwinskiego 2/3 (☎66-36-80), just to the southwest of the station. Almost equally convenient is the one on the top floor at al. Niepodległości 32/40 (☎567-06). Well to the west of the center, but close to tram routes #1, #3, #6, #13, #15, and #17, is the hostel at ul. Trybunalska 17 (☎67-33-40). Near the southern suburban Dębiec station is another hostel at ul. Jesionowa 14 (☎32-14-12). The largest of the group has no phone and inconveniently situated 10km southeast of the city at ul. Głuszyna 127—take a suburban train to Starołęka, then bus #58.

In total contrast, the final possibility for dormitory accommodation, the **tourist hostel** *Dom Turysty*, has an ideal location at Stary Rynek 91 (☎52-88-93).

CAMPGROUNDS

Both **campgrounds** are far from the center of things, entailing a bus ride of some 9km. *Strzeszynek*, ul. Koszalińska 15 (☎472-24), has a lakeside setting to the northwest and is reached by bus #95, while *Lawica*, ul. Wichrowa 100 (☎432-25), is at the extreme west of the city, and is served circuitously by bus #122. As an alternative to pitching a tent, chalet accommodation is available at each site.

The City

In spite of its size, most of Poznań's attractions are grouped in clusters which are no great distance from one another. Walking is the only way of getting to grips with the city, considerable parts of which are free from traffic. The trams, though forced to circumnavigate the most historic areas, do pass through the busy shopping streets to the west, and are also of use if you want to escape to the green belt.

The Stary Rynek

For seven centuries the grandiose **Stary Rynek** has been the hub of life in Poznań, even if nowadays it has lost its position as the center of political and economic power. Archetypally Polish, with the important public buildings sited in the middle, it was badly damaged in the last war, subsequently gaining the sometimes overenthusiastic attentions of the restorers. Their work has now been mellowed—successfully, in a bizarre sort of way—by the effects of pollution.

The **Town Hall** is in every way predominant. Originally a two-story Gothic brick structure, it was radically rebuilt in the 1550s by Giovanni Battista Quadro of Lugano, whose turreted facade gives it a quasi-military feel. Every day at noon, the effigies of two rams emerge onto the platform of the **clock** and butt their heads twelve times. This is in honor of the best-known local legend, which narrates that the two animals locked horns on the steps of the town hall, and thereby drew attention to a fire which had just begun there, so saving the city from yet another conflagration. In thanks, the rams were immortalized in the local coat of arms, as well as by this timepiece. Other sides of the building are inscribed with the words of Polish Renaissance sages, to which the restorers were forced to add extracts from the Communist constitution.

The interior is now the **Museum of the History of Poznań** (Tues & Thurs 9am–3pm, Wed & Fri noon–6pm, Sun 10am–3pm); though this is less didactic than it sounds, the main reason for entering is to see the building itself. Surviving from the Gothic period are the vaulted **cellars**, transformed into the prison in the sixteenth century; they now contain the earliest objects in the display, notably items excavated on Ostrów Tumski and the medieval pillory. However, the showstopper is the Renaissance **Great Hall** on the first floor, formerly the scene of council meetings. Its coffered vault bears polychrome bas-reliefs which embody the exemplary civic duties and virtues through scenes from the lives of Samson, King David, Venus, and Hercules. The southern section shows astrological figures, while the marble busts of Roman emperors around the walls are reminders of the weighty tradition of municipal leadership.

Outside the town hall stands a fine but horribly blackened Rococo **fountain**, alongside a copy of the **pillory**, in its traditional location. Farther to the south stand the colorful **Houses of the Keepers**, once home of the market traders, many of whom sold their wares in their arcaded passageway. The present structures, though very heavily restored, date from the sixteenth century and are thus the oldest in the square.

At the back is the **Weigh House** (Waga Miejska), the second most important public building in this great trading center; what you see today is a reproduction of the original, again the work of Quadro. Around the corner from here is the sternly Neoclassical **Guardhouse** (Odwach), built for "defense and decoration" of the city in the 1780s—just before the whole Polish state crumbled. In recent years,

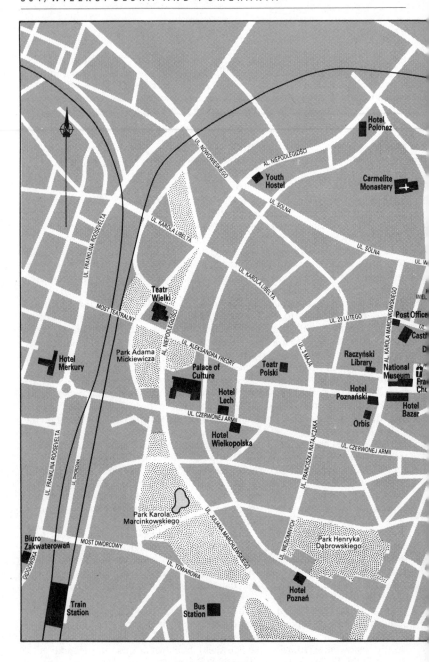

Hotel
Polonez

UL. NOWOWIEJSKIEGO

AL. NIEPODLEGIŁDŚCI

Youth
Hostel

Carmelite
Monastery

UL. SOLNA

UL. KAROLA LIBELTA

UL. SOLNA

UL. W

UL. KAROLA LIBELTA

WIEL

UL. FRANKLINA ROOSEVELTA

Teatr
Wielki

AL. KAROLA MARCINKOWSKIEGO

Post Office

UL. 23 LUTEGO

UL.

Castl

MOST TEATRALNY

AL. NIEPODLEGŁOŚCI

UL. ALEKSANDRA FREDRY

D

Park Adama
Mickiewicza

Teatr
Polski

Raczyński
Library

National
Museum

Fra
Chu

Hotel
Merkury

Palace of
Culture

Hotel
Poznański

Hotel
Bazar

Hotel
Lech

Orbis

UL. CZERWONEJ ARMII

UL. FRANCISZKA RATAJCZAKA

UL. 3 MAJA

Hotel
Wielkopolska

UL. CZERWONEJ ARMII

UL. FRANKLINA ROOSEVELTA

UL. DWORCOWA

Park Karola
Marcinkowskiego

UL. JULIANA MARCHLEWSKIEGO

UL. NIEZŁOMNYCH

Park Henryka
Dąbrowskiego

Biuro
Zakwaterowań

MOST DWORCOWY

UL. TOWAROWA

UL. GŁOGOWSKA

Hotel
Poznań

Train
Station

Bus
Station

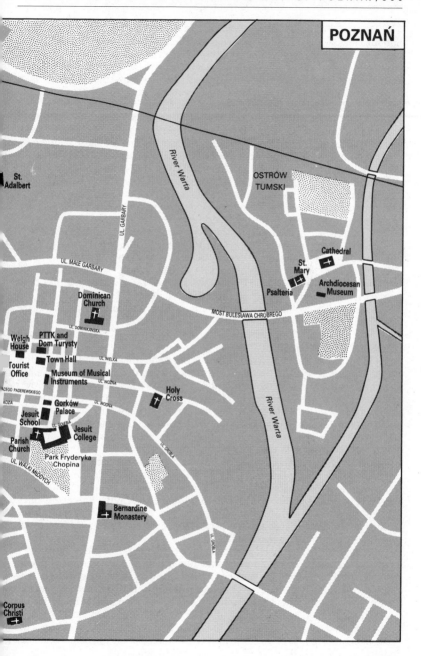

POZNAŃ

River Warta

OSTRÓW TUMSKI

St. Adalbert

UL. GARBARY

UL. MALE GARBARY

Cathedral

St. Mary

Psalteria

Archdiocesan Museum

Dominican Church

UL. DOMINIKAŃSKA

MOST BOLESŁAWA CHROBREGO

Weigh House

PTTK and Dom Turysty

Town Hall

UL. WIELKA

Tourist Office

Museum of Musical Instruments

UL. WOŹNA

NACEGO PADEREWSKIEGO

Holy Cross

KOZIA

Gorków Palace

UL. WODNA

Jesuit School

UL. ŚWIĘTOSŁAWSKA

UL. GROBLA

Jesuit College

Parish Church

UL. WALKI MŁODYCH

Park Fryderyka Chopina

River Warta

Bernardine Monastery

UL. GROBLA

Corpus Christi

a museum of the history of the working-class movement has been housed here, but this looks like it will end up a casualty of the backlash against the communist years. Between here and the Houses of the Keepers are two ugly structures which add the only discordant notes to the square—communist legacies which should be disowned even more urgently. One of them is now the **Wielkopolska Museum of Arms** (Tues–Sat 9am–6pm, Sun 10am–3pm), a moderately interesting display of weaponry in the province from the Middle Ages onward.

Many a medieval and Renaissance interior lurks behind the Baroque facades of the **gabled houses** lining the outer sides of the Stary Rynek, most of them shops, restaurants, cafés, or public offices. Particularly fine are those on the eastern side, where no. 45 is the **Museum of Musical Instruments** (Tues–Thurs & Sat 9am–6pm, Fri noon–6pm, Sun 10am–3pm), the only collection of its kind in Poland. Its exhibits range from folk instruments from all over the world, through Chopin memorabilia to a vast array of violins. The last is a reminder that every five years the city hosts the Wieniawski International Violin Competition, one of the most prestigious events for young virtuosi.

The western side of the square is almost equally imposing, above all because of the massive green and white **Działyński Palace** at no. 78, which was one of the headquarters of the nineteenth-century struggles to keep Polish culture alive. The houses at the extreme ends of this side were the homes of prominent Poznań personalities. Giovanni Battista Quadro lived in no. 84, whose facade has been painted with scenes narrating his life. Number 71 belonged to Jan Chróściejewski, twice the mayor of the city around 1600 and the author of the first book on children's diseases.

West of the Stary Rynek

Just to the west of the Stary Rynek stands a hill with remnants of the inner circle of the medieval walls. This particular section guarded the **Castle** (Zamek Przemysława), which was the seat of the rulers of Wielkopolska. Modified over the centuries, it was almost completely destroyed in 1945 but has been partly restored to house the **Museum of Decorative Arts** (Tues–Sun 9am–3pm). This features an enjoyable enough collection from medieval times to the present day, while the Gothic cellars are used for changing displays of posters, an art form taken very seriously in Poland.

Below the hill is the Baroque **Franciscan Church**, its transepts formed by sumptuous chapels dedicated to the Virgin and Saint Francis. Its decoration, including the ornate stalls and high altar, was executed by the Franciscan brothers (in both senses of the word) Adam and Antonin Swach, the former a painter, the latter a sculptor and stuccoist. On the interior of the west wall you can see examples of a uniquely Polish art: portraits of nobles painted on sheet metal, which were placed on the deceased's coffin.

From here it's only a short walk around the corner to the vast elongated space of **plac Wolności**, which formerly bore the name of Napoleon, then Kaiser Wilhelm, only gaining its present designation—Victory Square—after the Wielkopolska uprising in 1918. The **Bazar Hotel**, a favorite meeting place of Polish patriots throughout the Partition period, was where Paderewski lodged when he led the rebellion against the German garrison. Diagonally opposite stands another seminal center of the fight to preserve Polish culture, the **Raczyński Library**. Architecturally, it's one of the most distinguished buildings in the city, erected in the 1820s in the grand style of the Louvre.

THE NATIONAL MUSEUM

Directly facing the Raczyński Library is the ponderous **National Museum** (Tues–Sat 9am–6pm, Sun & hols 10am–3pm), on the first floor of which is one of the few important displays of old master paintings in Poland. The **Italian** section begins with panels from Gothic altarpieces by artists such as Bernardo Daddi and Lorenzo Monaco, and continues with Renaissance pieces such as Bellini's tender *Madonna and Child with Donor*, Bassano's *Venus in Vulcan's Forge*, Bronzino's *Cosimo de' Medici* and the fascinating *Game of Chess* by Sofonisba Anguisciola, one of the few celebrated woman painters of the period.

Dominating the gallery's small but choice **Spanish** section is the prize exhibit, Zurbarán's *Madonna of the Rosary*. This Counter-Reformation masterpiece was part of a cycle for the Carthusian monastery at Jerez, and features actual portraits of these silent monks. By the same artist is *Christ at the Column*, a sharply edged work from the very end of his career, and there are also a couple of notable works by his contemporary Ribera. In the extensive display of the **Low Countries**, highlights are a *Madonna and Child* attributed to Massys and the regal *Adoration of the Magi* by Joos van Cleve.

The **Polish** canvases are an anticlimax, but look out for the room dedicated to the versatile Jacek Malczewski, the historical scenes by Jan Matejko, the landscapes of Wojciech Gerson, and the subdued portraits of Olga Boznańska. Also hung in this section is Bellotto's huge *Election of Stanisław August*, a fascinating documentary record of the way a Polish king was chosen.

BEYOND PLAC WOLNOŚCI

Moving into the business thoroughfares which branch out west from plac Wolności, you shortly come to the **Theatr Polski** on ul. 27 Grudnia. Erected in the 1870s by voluntary contributions, this was yet another major cultural institution during the Partition period. The uphill nature of this struggle is reflected in the inscription on the facade: "The nation by itself."

An insight into the curious dichotomy of life in that time is provided by the large buildings in the streets beyond, which reflect the self-confidence of the German occupiers in the first decade of this century. Ironically, many of these cultural establishments and administration offices were taken over just a few years after they were built by an institution with very different values, the new University of Poznań. The most imposing of the group, the huge neo-Romanesque **Kaiserhaus** on ul. Czerwonej Armii, had an even more dramatic change of role. Built in imitation of the style favored by the Hohenstaufen emperors of early medieval Germany, it was intended to accommodate the kaiser whenever he happened to be in town. Instead, it has become a Palace of Culture with a distinctively populist stamp. In the park beyond are two huge crosses bound together, forming a **monument** to the victims of the Poznań food riots and also celebrating the birth of Solidarity. It was put up on the 25th anniversary of the former event in 1981—during martial law.

South and East of the Stary Rynek

Returning to the Stary Rynek and continuing along ul. Wodna soon brings you to the **Górków Palace**, which still preserves its intricate Renaissance portico and sober inner courtyard. The mansion now houses the **Archaeology Museum** (Tues–Fri 10am–4pm, Sat 10am–6pm, Sun 10am–3pm), where the displays are short on aesthetic appeal but commendably thorough. They trace the history of the region from the time of the nomadic hunters who lived here between 15,000 and 8000 BC, all the way to the early feudal society of the seventh century AD.

Down ul. Świętosławska is a complex of former Jesuit buildings, the finest examples of Baroque architecture in the city. The end of this street is closed by the facade of what's now generally known as the **Parish Church** (Kościół Frany), completed just forty years before the expulsion of the Jesuits in 1773. Its interior is all colored columns, gilded capitals, monumental sculptures, large altarpieces, and rich stuccowork, in the full-blown Roman manner. Over the high altar is a painting illustrating a legendary episode from the life of Saint Stanisław. Then a bishop, he was accused by King Bolesław the Generous of not having paid for a village he had incorporated into his territories. In order to prove his innocence, the saint resurrected the deceased former owner of the land to testify on his behalf.

Across the road is the **Jesuit School**, now one of Poland's main ballet academies; try to see its miniature patio, an architectural gem. To the east of the church is the front section of the **Jesuit College**, currently the seat of the city council. The Jesuits have returned to Poznań, though they were unable to reclaim the buildings they created. Instead, they now occupy the oldest left-bank building, the **Dominican church** to the northeast of the Stary Rynek. Despite a Baroque recasing, this still preserves original Romanesque and Gothic features, as well as a stellar-vaulted Rosary Chapel.

The late Baroque church of the **Holy Cross** (Kościół Wszystkich Świętych), almost due east of the Stary Rynek, is the epitome of a Lutheran church, with its democratic central plan layout and overall plainness. Although it survives as an almost complete period piece, the exodus of virtually all the Protestants during this century means that it's now used for Catholic worship, as is evidenced by the jarring high altar.

At no. 25 on the adjacent ul. Grobla is the lodge of the freemasons, now the **Ethnographical Museum** (Wed, Thurs, Sat & Sun 10am–3pm, Tues & Fri noon–6pm). Farther south is the very different Baroque church of the **Bernardine monastery**, which has been gleamingly restored by the monks who repossessed it following its wartime use as a workshop for the opera house. At the southern extremity of the old town is **Corpus Christi** (Kościół Bozego Ciała), a soaring, fifteenth-century Gothic church that once belonged to a Carmelite monastery.

North of the Stary Rynek

The northern quarters are best approached from plac Wielkopolski, a large square now used for daily markets. From here ul. Działowa passes two churches facing each other on the brow of the hill. To the right is the Gothic **St Adalbert** (św. Wojciecha), chiefly remarkable for its stumpy little seventeenth-century belfry, the only piece of wooden architecture left in the city. Opposite, the handsome Baroque facade of the **Carmelite monastery** makes a highly effective contrast. Farther uphill are the most exclusive cemetery in Poznań, reserved for people deemed to have made a valuable contribution to the life of Wielkopolska, and a monument to the defenders of the city in 1939.

Beyond, al. Niepodległości ascends to the vast former **Citadel**. This Prussian fortress was leveled after the war to make a public park, albeit one whose main appeal is to necrophiles. There's a cemetery for the 6000 Russians and Poles who lost their lives in the month-long siege which led to its capture, while to the east are the graves of British and Commonwealth soldiers.

Ostrów Tumski and the Right Bank

From the left bank the Bolesława Chrobrego bridge crosses to the holy island of **Ostrów Tumski**, a world away in spirit, if not in distance, from the hustle of the city. (Trams #4, #8, #16, and #17 go over the bridge.). Only a small portion of the island is built upon, and a few priests and monks comprise its entire population. Lack of parishioners means that there's not the usual need for evening Masses, and after 5pm the island is a ghost town.

The first building you see is the late Gothic **Psalteria**, characterized by its elaborate stepped gable. It was erected in the early sixteenth century as a residence for the cathedral choir. Immediately behind is an earlier brick structure, **St Mary's** (Kościół Mariacki); this lofty and unusually graceful chapel was given controversial but effective stained glass and murals after the war. Across the street is the **Archdiocesan Museum** (Tues–Sat 10am–3pm, Sun 1–3pm), with a homey spread of paintings, sculptures, textiles, and treasury items from the Middle Ages to the present day.

THE CATHEDRAL

The streets of the island are lined by handsome eighteenth-century houses, all very much in the shadow of the **Cathedral**. Over the centuries, the brickwork of the church was progressively hidden under Baroque and Neoclassical remodellings. When much of this was stripped away by wartime devastation, it was decided to restore as much of the Gothic original as possible. However, the lack of documentary evidence for the eastern chapels meant that their successors had to be retained. The Baroque spires on the two facade towers and the three lanterns around the ambulatory, which give a vaguely eastern touch, were also reconstructed.

Inside, the **crypt**, entered from below the northern tower, has been extensively excavated, uncovering remains of the pre-Romanesque and Romanesque cathedrals which stood on the site, as well as parts of the sarcophagi of the first two Polish kings, Mieszko I and Bolesław the Brave. Their current resting place is the **Golden Chapel** on the axis of the ambulatory. Miraculously unscathed during the war, this luscious creation, representing the diverse if dubious tastes of the 1830s, is the antithesis of the plain architecture all around it. Its decoration is a curious cooperation between mosaic artists from Venice (who created the patterned floor and the copy of Titian's *Assumption*) and a painter and a sculptor from the very different Neoclassical traditions of Berlin.

Of the many other **funerary monuments** which form one of the key features of the cathedral, the finest is that of Bishop Benedykt Izdbieński, just to the left of the Golden Chapel. This was carved by Jan Michałowicz, the one native Polish artist of the Renaissance period who was the equal of the many Italians who settled here. The other outstanding tomb is that of the Górka family, in the Holy Sacrament chapel at the northern end of the nave, sculpted just a few years later by one of these itinerant craftsmen, Hieronimo Canavesi. Other **works of art** to look out for are the late Gothic, carved-and-painted high altar from Silesia, the choir stalls from the same period, and fragments of sixteenth-century frescoes, notably a cycle of the Apostles.

ŚRÓDKA

Crossing Most Mieska I brings you to the right-bank suburb of **Śródka**, the second oldest part of the city, whose name derives from the word for Wednesday—market day here in medieval times. Though there's nothing special to see, something of the atmosphere of an ancient market quarter survives. Just beyond is another distinct settlement, known as **Komandoria** after the commanders of the Knights of Saint John of Jerusalem, who founded it towards the end of the twelfth century. The late Romanesque church of this community, **St John's**, survives with Gothic and Baroque additions, and now stands in splendid isolation beside one of the busiest traffic intersections in the city.

Eating, Drinking, and Entertainment

In choosing somewhere to eat and drink, the **Orbis hotels** (see above) should always be kept in mind. Each has a restaurant and café with prices that are a bit higher than elsewhere in town but still extremely cheap; they're also likely to serve much of what appears on the menu, and are among the few options if you want to eat late. The situation may well improve, but at the moment the city's other eateries tend to close at 7 or 8pm, with service often ending long before. Another snag is that they're heavily concentrated around the Stary Rynek, other quarters having nowhere to eat at all. Poznań is a major brewing center, and its beers—*Ratusz* and (especially) *Lech*—are not the inferior products their price tags would suggest.

Restaurants

U Dylla, Stary Rynek 37. One of two restaurants on the main square; good and reasonably priced food but your bill will be inflated by the fact that only western drinks are available.

Pod Koziołkami, Stary Rynek 64. Even cheaper, and serves Polish drinks at about a quarter of the cost of the competition.

Pod Korona, ul. Zamkowa 7. Just off the Stary Rynek, with menu of old Polish dishes.

Przyneta, ul. Czerwonej Armii 34. Specialty fish restaurant.

Smakosz, ul. 27 Grudnia 7. Open a bit later than most other restaurants, but can get crowded.

W-Z, ul. Aleksandra Fredry 12. Has even longer opening hours because of its nightly dances, for which there's a surcharge.

Krekucha, ul. Karola Libelta 37. On the fringes of the central area, worth the trek for its game dishes.

Bałtycka, ul. Franklina Roosevelta 20. Best of the restaurants near the station.

Adria, ul. Głogowska 14. Just across from the station, with its own nightclub.

Piracka, Park Sołacki. The only suburban restaurant justifying an excursion; situated to the northwest of the city and reached by trams #9, #11, or #24.

Snack Bars

Piccolo, Stary Rynek 74. A spaghetti house which is probably the cheapest and most popular snack bar in town.

Pod Rondlem, Stary Rynek 62. Quick-service joint with a reasonable choice of dishes.

As, pl. Wolności 18. Offers snack-type meals plus a beer garden.

Mewa, pl. Wolności 1. Good and very cheap milk bar.

Wyborowy, ul. Czerwonej Armii 41. Milk bar in the heart of the shopping area.

Cafés

Winiarnia Ratuszowa, Stary Rynek 55. A conventional enough café at ground-floor level, with a wonderfully atmospheric wine bar in the medieval cellars.

Eliksiv, Stary Rynek 61. Has an array of irresistible gooey puddings.

U Rajców, Stary Rynek 93. Tea house, with a sideline in mead.

Sukiennicza, Stary Rynek 98. Superb coffee, cakes, and ice cream in an unhurried setting, complete with resident pianist, reminiscent of Central Europe's pre-communist days.

Nightlife and Culture

Nightspots in Poznań are few and far between, unless you count the cabaret scene in the Orbis hotels and the restaurants around the station. Best chance of some action is to ask around the university buildings about **student clubs**: the largest, *Odnowa*, is at ul. Czerwonej Armii 80/82. The lively *Bratniak* peace and environmentalist group meets in Building B on ul. Dozynkowa to the north of the center, reached by tram #4, #16, or #22.

There's a far better choice if you want highbrow **culture** in the evening. The *Teatr Polski*, ul. 27 Grudnia 8 (☎52-56-27), presents classic plays, while the *Teatr Nowy*, ul. Jarosława Dąbrowskiego 5 (☎48-12-41), specializes in modern fare. **Opera** is performed at the *Teatr Wielki*, ul. Aleksandra Fredry 9 (☎52-82-91), and the *Polski Teatr Tańca*, ul. Kozia 4 (☎52-42-41), offers varied **dance** programs. Classical concerts are held at the *Filharmonia Poznańska*, ul. Czerwonej Armii 81. Musicals are put on at the *Teatr Muzyczny*, ul. Niezłomnych 1a (☎52-17-86), while puppet shows are among the attractions at the *Teatr Lalki i Aktora* in the *Pałac Kultury* at the corner of ul. Czerwonej Armii and al. Niepodległości (☎52-88-16).

Listings

Airlines *LOT*, ul. Czerwonej Armii 69 (☎549-85); *Pan Am*, in *Hotel Polonez*, al. Niepodległości 54/68 (☎699-141).

Bookshops Can be found on Stary Rynek, ul. Ignacego Paderewskiego, pl. Wolności, and at the corner of ul. 27 Grudnia and ul. Alfreda Lampego.

British Council Ul. Franciszka Ratajczaka at the corner with ul. 27 Grudnia.

Car rental Office in *Hotel Poznań*, pl. Gen. Henryka Dąbrowskiego (☎33-02-21).

Consulate *USA*, ul. Fryderyka Chopina 4 (☎52-95-86). There is no Canadian consulate.

Exchange facilities Best rates are from the banks: ul. Czerwonej Armii 81, al. Karola Marcinkowskiego 12, and ul. Karola Libelta 16/20.

Festivals Main folklore event is the *Jarmarkt Świętojański* (St John's Market) held during the International Trade Fair in the second week of June. There's a festival of boys' choirs every February, and the Wieniawski International Violin Competition will be next be staged in November 1991.

Gas station 24-hr station on ul. Warszawska, with a lead-free pump.

Post offices Head office is at the junction of al. Karola Marcinkowskiego and ul. 23 Lutego. A limited 24-hr service is available at the main train station.

What's happening A free monthly program in Polish and an English abridgement, both known as *iks*, are available from tourist information points.

Around Poznań

It's simple to escape from the big-city feel of Poznań, as its outskirts soon give way to peaceful agricultural villages set in a lake-strewn landscape. Within a 25-kilometer radius of the city is some of the finest scenery in Wielkopolska, along with two of Poland's most famous castles, each of which makes a relaxing day or half-day excursion.

Kórnik

KÓRNIK, site of one of the great castles of Wielkopolska, lies 22km southeast of Poznań on the eastern bank of lakes Skrzynki and Kónickie, the first two in a long chain of six. There are regular services from the city's main bus station and from the terminal at Rondo Rataje; don't go by train, as the station is 4km from the village.

Somewhat run down, Kórnik has an appealing rural feel to it, consisting essentially of one very long street, ul. Poznańska (where you'll find the best of the three restaurants, *Turystyczna*). This street culminates in a market square, dominated by the red-brick **parish church**, originally Gothic but heavily rebuilt during the last century. It contains tombs of the Górka family, the first owners of the town, though these are poor relations of their monument in Poznań Cathedral.

The Górkas built their **Castle** at the extreme southern edge of the village in the fifteenth century. A fragment of the original survives, as does the medieval layout with its moat, but the castle was rebuilt in neo-Gothic style last century by the German architect Karl Friedrich Schinkel, best known for his Neoclassical public buildings in Berlin. However, his designs were considerably modified, and credit for the final shape of the castle is due to the owner, Tytus Działyński, whose aim was as much to show off his collection of arms and armor, books, and *objets d'art* as to provide a luxurious home for himself.

In contrast to the plain grandeur of the exterior, with its mock defensive towers and battlements, the **interior** (April 15–Oct 15 Tues–Fri & Sun 9am–3pm, Sat 9am–2pm; rest of year closes 1hr earlier) is for the most part very intimate, and entry creates the impression of trespassing into a private residence of a century or more ago. The one really theatrical gesture is the spacious **Moorish Hall** on the first floor, which mimics the most spectacular of Arab palaces, the Alhambra in Granada. Ask to borrow the leaflet in English which gives descriptions of all the exhibits.

In order to see all sides of the castle's exterior, you have to visit the **Arboretum** (May–Oct daily 9am–6pm). Originally in the formal French style, this was transformed in the seemingly arbitrary manner of a *jardin anglais*. There are over 2000 species of trees and shrubs, many of them brought here from all corners of the world. The lakeside offers an even more pleasant stroll, particularly the western bank with its fine distant views.

Rogalin

With your own transport, it's easy to combine a visit to Kórnik with the castle in the hamlet of **ROGALIN**, 11km to the west on the road to Mosina (see overleaf). Unfortunately, only three daily buses pass this way in each direction, and the timetables don't work out for seeing both monuments on the same day, unless you're prepared to walk or take a chance on hitching.

The **Palace** (Wed–Sun 10am–4pm, last admission 3pm; May–Sept open until 6pm on Sat) was the seat of another eminent Poznań family, the Raczyńskis. In contrast to Kórnik, it's a grand country residence built in a style which shows the Baroque melting into Neoclassicism, and it forms the axis of a careful layout of buildings and gardens. At the time of writing, the palace was in the middle of a long-term restoration, and the central block is likely to be closed until at least 1992. In the meantime, you can visit the recently restored small rooms in the two wings, and the **art gallery** off the northern side; most of its paintings are second-rate, but there's a marvelous exception, Monet's *Landscape at Pourville*.

Fronting the palace courtyard is a long forecourt, to the sides of which are the stables and **coach house**, the latter crammed with old carriages once used by owners of this estate, along with the last horse-drawn cab to operate in Poznań. Passing outside the gates, a five-minute walk brings you to the **Mausoleum** of the Raczyński family. Set peacefully at the side of the road, this is a slightly reduced copy of one of the best-preserved monuments of classical antiquity, the Maison Carrée in Nîmes, built in a startlingly pink sandstone.

At the back of the main palace is an enclosed formal garden, now desperately in need of a gardener or two. More enticing is the English-style park beyond, laid out on the site of a primeval forest. This is chiefly remarkable for its **oak trees**, three of the most ancient of which have been fenced off for protection. Among the most celebrated natural wonders of Poland, they are at least 1000 years old—and thus of a similar vintage to the Polish nation itself. They are popularly known as Lech, Czech, and Rus, after the three mythical brothers who founded the Polish, Czech, and Russian nations; with all due modesty, the largest is designated as Rus.

If you intend to be here around lunchtime, it's best to bring your own picnic, though there's a **restaurant**, *Pod Dębami*, about 1km away from the palace, and another, *Na Skarpie*, in ROGALINEK, 3km to the west.

The Wielkopolska National Park

The only area of protected landscape in the province, the **Wielkopolska National Park** occupies an area of some 100 square kilometers to the south of Poznań. Formed in geologically recent times, it's a glacial and post-glacial landscape of low moraines, gentle ridges and lakes, several of them very substantial. Half the park is taken up by forest, predominantly pine and birch planted as replacements for the original hardwoods.

Although the scenery in the park is hardly dramatic, it is unspoiled by any kind of development and warrants a day's exploration. By public transit the main point of access from Poznań is **MOSINA**, a small, straggling rural community on the Poznań–Wrocław rail line, served by all except the express trains. The sole **hotel** in the immediate vicinity of the park, *Moreno* (☎546), also has the village's only restaurant, on the main road to **STĘSZEW**. The latter, 13km to the west on a regular bus route, and on the rail line between Poznań and Wolsztyn, is the other possible base if you want to stay in the area, as it has a **campground** (☎06), set on the banks of Lake Lipno just to the northeast. On the Rynek there's a restaurant, *Broniszanka*, along with the **Regional Museum** (Tues–Sun 9am–1pm).

For a day trip, however, the most convenient point of entry is OSOWA GÓRA, a station apparently serving nowhere, just to the west of Mosina at the end of a separate line from Poznań; there are half a dozen daily services in each direction, passing along the shore of one of the finest of the lakes, Budzyńskie.

Alternative approaches are the twin villages of **PUSZCZYKÓWKO** and **PUSZCZYKOWO**, on the left bank of the snaking Warta River immediately north of Mosina. Each has one restaurant, and the latter also has a couple of snack bars. Situated on the opposite side of the rail line from Puszczykowo proper is a **museum** (Tues–Sat 10am–3pm, Sun 10am–4pm) with displays on the evolution of the region's landscape.

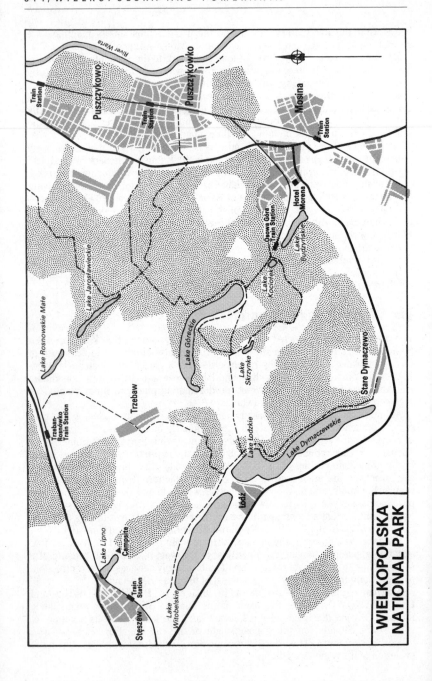

WIELKOPOLSKA
NATIONAL PARK

Walks in the Park

When exploring the park, it's best to stick to the three official **hiking paths**, which are generally well marked and unstrenuous. Each takes several hours to cover its entire length, though it's easy enough to switch from one to the other—the best idea if you're short on time.

Walking **from Osowa Góra** gets you into the best of the terrain quickly. From the parking lot above the station (which offers one of the park's few panoramic views), the **blue trail** leads around the small heart-shaped Lake Kociołek, which is beautifully shaded by trees, then continues through the forest to the southern end of Lake Góreckie. It then climbs through thick woods before passing through open countryside to Lake Łódźkie, on the far side of which—off the trail but on the main road—is the hamlet of ŁÓDŹ, clustered around a seventeenth-century wooden church. The route then leads along the northern shore of Lake Witobelskie to Steszew.

The **red trail** from Osowa Góra passes Lake Kociołek, then travels circuitously uphill, skirting the small Lake Skrzynka just before crossing the blue trail. It arrives at the bend in the sausage-shaped Lake Góreckie, from where there's a view across to an islet with a ruined castle: a former fortress of the Działyński family, and a meeting point for the Polish insurgents of 1863. The path then leads about halfway around the perimeter of the lake as far as JEZIORY, where there's another parking lot plus a restaurant and café. Two separate red paths proceed to Puszczykówko, while a third follows the long northerly route to Puszczykowo via Lake Jarosławieckie.

The **black trail** begins at the station of **Trzebaw-Rosnówko**, then traverses the fields to the hamlet of TRZEBAW, before continuing through the woods to Lake Łódźkie. It then follows the eastern bank of this lake and its much longer continuation, Lake Dymaczewskie—which together make up the largest stretch of water in the park—before ending at STARE DYMACZEWO, from where you can take a bus to Mosina or Steszew.

Leszno and Around

The last notable stop in Wielkopolska before Silesia is **LESZNO**, which lies some 90km south of Poznań. Nowadays a bustling market town, it hardly hints at the glittering role it has played in Poland's history. Its entire early story is bound up with one of the country's most remarkable dynasties, the Leszczyński family, who founded Leszno in the late fourteenth century. The last of the male line, **Stanisław Leszczyński**, deposed the hated Augustus the Strong of Saxony to become King of Poland in 1704, only to be overthrown by the same rival six years later. He briefly regained the throne in 1733, but met with far more success in exile in France, marrying his daughter to Louis XV, and himself becoming Duke of Lorraine and gaining a reputation as a patron of the arts.

The Town

The **train station** is to the west of the town center; from the entrance hall continue straight ahead until you come to an underpass on the left; this brings you out on to the beginning of the main street, ul. Słowiańska. Just up to the left from here is the **bus station**.

THE BOHEMIAN BRETHREN

Along with many other Polish grandees, the Leszczyńskis enthusiastically adopted the Reformation, though Stanisław, like Augustus the Strong, was forced to convert to Catholicism in order to launch his bid for the crown. In the first half of the seventeenth century Leszno became a refuge for the Bohemian Brethren, Czech Protestants who were forced to flee their homeland by the religious intolerance of the Thirty Years' War. The academy these exiles founded in Leszno developed into one of Europe's great centers of learning, thanks to the leadership of Jan Amos Komeński, known as **Comenius**. Creator of the first illustrated textbook, he was called to put his educational theories into practice in England, Sweden, Hungary, and Holland, and even received invitations from the Protestant-loathing Cardinal Richelieu in France and from Harvard University, which wanted him as its president. Though Comenius and his colleagues were eventually forced to leave Leszno by the Swedish Wars of the 1650s, the town remained a major educational center until the last century. The Brethren were later transformed into the Moravian Church, a body which continues to have an influence out of all proportion to its size, particularly in the USA.

Heading straight ahead brings you to the pedestrianized **Rynek**, one of Poland's most handsome squares. It's predominantly Baroque, having been rebuilt after the Swedish Wars, which left Leszno in ruins. The colorist approach favored by the architects—prominent among whom was the Italian Pompeo Ferrari—is shown to best effect in the red, yellow, and white **Town Hall**, which occupies the usual central position, its tall belfry serving as the main local landmark.

Just south of the Rynek, the exterior of the large church of **St Nicholas** (św. Mikołaja) strikes a more somber note. Its interior, on the other hand, has some extravagant Rococo furnishings, the most eye-catching being the huge monuments to the Leszczyńskis. A fascinating contrast with this richness is provided by the clean, sober lines of the **Holy Cross** (św. Kryza), a couple of minutes' walk to the southwest on pl. Metziga. On the same square is the **Museum** (Tues & Thurs 2–7pm, Wed & Fri 9am–2pm, Sat & Sun 10am–2pm), a miscellaneous local collection, featuring a room devoted to Comenius.

A few streets east of here, off ul. Bolesława Chrobrego, is the church of **St John**, aesthetically unremarkable but semi-interesting as the place where the Bohemian Brethren held their services.

There are two good and cheap **hotels** on ul. Słowiańska: *Leszno* at no. 11 (☎20-22-17) and *Centralny* at no. 30 (☎20-22-10). The latter has a café only, whereas the former boasts one of the better **restaurants** in town. A wide variety of other places to eat and drink can be found down the same street and on the Rynek. The **Orbis** office is at ul. Słowiańska 29 (☎20-25-65).

If you want an overnight stay with some panache, you could head for the palace designed by Pompeo Ferrari for the Sułkowski family—who bought Leszno from the Leszczyńskis—at RYDZYNA, 9km to the southeast and reached by regular buses; it has been coverted into a **hotel** and restaurant.

Rail Trips Around Leszno

There are two outstanding **narrow-gauge** lines within easy reach of Leszno, both accessible from the main line to Wrocław. For the first of these, get off at STARE

BOJANOWO, 18km away, then just cross the platform to take one of the four daily return trains to WIELICHOWA, 15km northwest. Modern, immaculately maintained little diesels serve the small communities strung out along the route, many of which have changed little in centuries, while a few others have been transformed by recent political and economic reforms—as the new German cars parked beside some of the farms testify. An even more fascinating narrow-gauge line can be seen by continuing down the main line from Stary Bojanowo to ZMIGROD, just over the border in Silesia (see Chapter Five).

Wolsztyn

If you have a nostalgia for the days of **steam**, head 50km northwest from Leszno to the little lakeside town of **WOLSZTYN**, where steam engines can be seen shunting throughout the day. You may even make the journey by steam, but double-decker commuter diesels are more common.

The town center has a few fine buildings, notably a Neoclassical palace and a Baroque church with an impressive frescoed vault. On the main street, ul. Piątego Stycznia, is the **Marcin Rozek Museum** (Tues–Fri 9am–4pm, Sat & Sun 10am–2pm), occupying the home of this artist, one of the best Poland ever produced, who was murdered in Auschwitz. It's his sculptures which stand out, notably the large reliefs on the rear of the house and the classically inspired portrait busts in the garden—mostly replicas of works destroyed by the Nazis.

Taking the back exit from here brings you to the shore of Lake Wolsztyn. If you follow its perimeter back towards the railroad, then continue away from the town, you shortly come to an **open-air museum** of traditional farm buildings; it's always accessible through an unlocked gate.

Kalisz and Around

At the extreme southeastern corner of Wielkopolska, 130km from Poznań, lies the heavily industrialized town of **KALISZ**. Almost universally held to be Poland's oldest city, it was referred to as Calissia by Pliny in the first century, and was described in the second century as a trading settlement on the "amber route" between the Baltic and Adriatic. Though apparently inhabited without interruption ever since, it failed to develop into a major city. Despite its history, Kalisz is not worth a special journey, but it makes a convenient stopover if you're passing this way, and is the obvious place from which to approach the palace at **Gołuchów**.

Kalisz Town

Both the **train** and **bus** stations are situated at the southwestern end of the city. To reach the center, take bus #19, #101, or #102; no buses run within the old quarter, which lies between the rivers Prosna and Bernardynka. The only reason for enduring the long, straight walk down ul. Górnośląska and ul. Śródmiejska is to take a close look at the two space-age churches which shoot up from parallel boulevards—potent symbols of the key role of Catholicism in modern Poland. If you do decide to walk, you can turn down ul. Tadeusza Kościuszki (on the left as you approach the old town) to see the **Kalisz Museum** at no. 12 (Tues, Thurs, Sat & Sun 10am–2:30pm, Wed & Fri noon–5:30pm), which contains material from the many archaeological excavations carried out in the area.

Ulica Śródmiejska terminates at the unprepossessing Rynek, with its large Baroque town hall. Down ul. Kanonicka at the northwestern end of the square is the brick Gothic church of **St Nicholas** (św. Mikołaja), which has been subject to a fair amount of neo-Gothic tinkering, though for once this is not entirely to its disadvantage. Inside, the prize item is the altarpiece of *The Descent from the Cross*, brought here from Rubens' workshop in Antwerp. Off the southeastern corner of the Rynek is a smaller square in front of the **Franciscan Church**, an older and simpler example of Gothic brickwork, but with ample Baroque interior decorations, including a pulpit in the shape of a boat.

From here, it's just a short walk to ul. Kolegialna, which defines the eastern perimeter of the old town. This is dominated by the long facade of the **Jesuit college**, a severe Neoclassical composition incorporating a Renaissance portal. The one part of it you can enter is the church, which is in the plain Baroque style of the Jesuits' most important church, the Gesù in Rome. Immediately beyond the college, standing beside the surviving fragment of the city's ramparts, is the single-towered **Collegiate Church**, a more adventurous example of Baroque which includes parts of its Gothic predecessor. The interior bristles with works of art, the most notable of which is a Silesian polyptych from around 1500—but unfortunately only the vestibule is normally kept open.

Kalisz Practicalities

Kalisz is reckoned prestigious enough to warrant its own luxury Orbis **hotel**, *Prosna*, ul. Górnośląska 53/55 (☎33-921), about a third of the way down the road from the bus station to the town. A better bet, though, is the *Europa*, al. Wolności 5 (☎720-31)—it's a classy place with a much better location by the river, but won't break the bank. Less convenient is the PTTK sports and tourist hotel, *Dom Wycieczkowy* (☎746-50), by the stadium to the east of the old town, the end of bus route #101. There's also a **youth hostel** in a small park east of the *Europa*, with the reception nearby at ul. Częstochowska 17 (☎726-36).

For **eating** and **drinking**, the hotels are probably the best choice. Pick of the other options are *Adria*, on ul. Piekarska due east of the Rynek, and *U Barbary i Bogumiła*, just up ul. Górnośląska from the bus station; there are more basic alternatives in and around the Rynek.

Orbis have an office at Śródmiejska 1 (☎738-16); the Rynek's information office has been closed down.

Gołuchów

Twenty kilometers away on the main road to Poznań, and reached by frequent interurban buses or by local bus #A, lies the village of **GOŁUCHÓW**, a nondescript place were it not for its **Palace**, the one outstanding monument in the Kalisz area.

It began as a small defensive castle, built for Rafał Leszczyński of the famous Leszno family in 1560. Early in the following century, his son Wacław completely transformed it into a palatial residence worthy of a man who had risen to be Royal Chancellor. Like the Polish state itself, it gradually fell into ruin. In 1853 it was bought by Tytus Działyński, the owner of Kórnik, as a present for his son Jan, who married Izabella, daughter of the formidable Adam Czartoryski. While her husband languished in exile for his part in the 1863 uprising, Izabella devoted herself to recreating the glory of the castle, eventually opening it as one of

Poland's first museums. Rather than revert to the Italianate form of the original, she opted for a distinctively French touch—with its steeply pitched roofs, prominent chimneys, towers and graceful arcaded courtyard, the palace looks as if it has been transported from the Loire Valley.

The small **apartments** (tours Tues–Sun 10am–3pm; leaflet in English available) are crammed with paintings and *objets d'art*. Highlight of the display are some magnificent antique vases—just part of an assembly whose other items are now kept in the National Museum in Warsaw. After the guided tour, you can wander off to the two rooms under the stairway, in which changing exhibitions from the castle's collection of engravings are held. If you ask the English-speaking curator, you might get to see rooms not included on the tour, such as the tiny library and the upstairs guest rooms.

Gołuchów's **park** is cultivated for serious scientific purposes, and contains a **Museum of Forestry** (Tues–Sun 10am–3pm); you'll also come across Izabella's neo-Gothic funerary chapel. For refreshments, there's a café in the park and a restaurant in the village.

If you want to stay, the sole possibility is the **campground**, which is well sign-posted from the main road.

Gniezno and Around

Despite the competing claims of Poznań, Kruszwica, and Lednica, **GNIEZNO** is normally credited as the first capital of Poland, a title based on the dense web of myth and chronicled fact which constitute the story of the nation's earliest years. Still Poland's ecclesiastical capital, with an unhurried atmosphere in keeping with the dominance of churchly affairs, the town is situated 50km east of Poznań and reached in an hour by express train, or in at least two hours by bus.

Gniezno lies on the **Piast Route** (Szlak Piastowski), a tourist trail between Poznań and Inowrocław which, as the name implies, offers constant reminders of the Piast dynasty. The first major sight east of Poznań is **Lake Lednica**, which is most easily reached from Gniezno and has therefore been included in this section.

Gniezno's History

Lech, the legendary founder of Poland, supposedly came across the nest (*gniazdo*) of a white eagle here; he founded a town on the spot, and made the bird the emblem of his people, a role it still maintains. Less fancifully, it's known for sure that Mieszko I had established a court here in the late tenth century, and that in the year 1000 it was the scene of one of the landmarks in the country's history.

The catalyst for this, ironically enough, was a Czech, **Saint Adalbert** (Wojciech), the first Bishop of Prague. Unable to cope with the political demands of his office, he retired to a monastery, but later bowed to pressure from Rome to take up missionary work. In 997 he set out from Gniezno to evangelize the Prussians, a fierce Baltic tribe who lived on Poland's eastern borders—and who quickly dispatched him to a martyr's death. In order to recover the body, Mieszko I's son, **Bolesław the Brave**, was forced to pay Adalbert's weight in gold, an astute investment as it turned out. At the pope's instigation, Emperor Otto III made a pilgrimage to Gniezno, bringing relics with him which would add to the site's holiness. Received in great splendor, he crowned Bolesław with his own crown, confirming Poland as a fully-fledged kingdom, and one which was independent of the German-dominated Holy Roman Empire. Furthermore, Gniezno was made the seat of Poland's first archbishopric; Adalbert's brother was the first to be appointed to the post.

Gniezno was soon replaced as capital by the more secure town of Kraków, and although it made a partial recovery in the Middle Ages, it never grew very big. Nevertheless, it has always been important as the official **seat of the Primate of Poland**. Throughout the period of elected kings, the holder of this office functioned as head of state during each interregnum, and it is still one of the most prestigious positions in the land. However, the archbishop now normally resides in Warsaw, spending no more than one week per month in Gniezno; consideration is now being given to stripping Gniezno of its role as ecclesiastical capital in return for a full-time bishop.

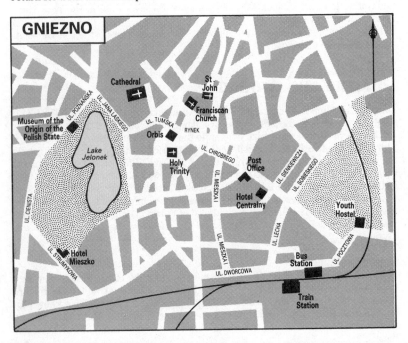

The City

The compactness of Gniezno is immediately evident: arriving at either the **train** or **bus station**, side by side to the south of the center, it's only a couple of minutes' walk straight down ul. Lecha to the main thoroughfare, ul. Bolesława Chrobrego. The shabby streets off it, particularly to the left, twist and turn in a medievally haphazard manner, though few buildings date back further than the last century. Even the **Rynek**, normally the showpiece of a Polish city, is distinctly run down.

There are, however, three Gothic churches worth a quick look. Just off the southern side of the Rynek is the **Holy Trinity** (św. Trójcy), partly rebuilt in the Baroque style following a fire, beside which stand the only surviving remains of the city walls. Off the opposite side of the Rynek towers the Franciscan church, while farther to the north is **St John's**. The latter, a foundation of the Knights Templar, preserves fourteenth-century frescoes in its chancel, and has carved bosses and corbels depicting virtues and vices.

The Cathedral

Downhill from the Rynek lies Gniezno's episcopal quarter, presenting an altogether smarter appearance than the commercial center. A flourishing seminary is the main focus of activity, but the most important monument is the **Cathedral**, beside which stands a statue of Bolesław the Brave. Strongly reminiscent of Poznań Cathedral, the basic brick structure was built in the fourteenth century in the severest Gothic style, but was enlivened in the Baroque period by a ring of stone chapels and by the addition of steeples to the twin facade towers. Not surprisingly, memorials to Saint Adalbert dominate the interior. At the entrance to the sanctuary, in the shadow of a fifteenth-century limewood crucifix, is his red marble **tomb**, carved around 1480 by Hans Brandt of Gdańsk. Another craftsman from the same city, Peter van Rennen, made the silver **shrine** above the high altar, to which one's eye is drawn down the whole length of the building. Surrounded by figures representing the different social classes, this features—like the tomb—an imaginary portrait of the saint, along with depictions of the chief events of his life.

An inevitable influence on van Rennen was the magnificent pair of **bronze doors** at the beginning of the southern aisle. Cast around 1170, these are among the finest surviving examples of Romanesque decorative art, and are unique in Poland. Adalbert's life from the cradle to beyond the grave is illustrated in eighteen scenes, going up the right-hand door and then down the left, all set within a rich decorative border. Quite apart from their artistic quality, the doors are remarkable as a documentary record: even the faces of the villainous Prussians are based on accurate observation. If you pass through the doorway, you can see the beautiful **portal** on the other side. Though its tympanum of *Christ in Majesty* is orthodox enough, the carvings of animals and the prominent mask heads give it a highly idiosyncratic flavor.

On the west wall are two outstanding **monuments**. The marble slab of Zbigniew Oleśnicki is a masterpiece by Veit Stoss, and one of his few works to be found outside Nuremberg and Kraków. It contrasts with the nervy line of the brass memorial to Jakub ze Sienna alongside, made earlier in the fifteenth century by Flemish artisans. Other monuments to prominent local clerics and laymen can be found throughout the cathedral. One which can hardly fail to catch your attention is that to **Primate Stefan Wyszyński**, in the north side of the ambulatory. Cardinal Wyszyński was instrumental in making the Church a focus of opposition to the Russian-imposed regime—being imprisoned for three years in the 1950s for criticizing the government—and played a key role in the events leading up to the birth of Solidarity. In making the Polish Church a conspicuous presence on the European scene, he also paved the way for his protegé, Karol Wojtyła, to become the first Polish pope.

Directly opposite the bronze doors is another porch only accessible from the interior. Off it, the **museum** contains one of Poland's most important treasuries, with the star item being a chalice said to have belonged to Saint Adalbert. You'll probably need a bit of guile to get to see the manuscripts kept in the adjacent **archive**. The most beautiful of these is the eleventh-century *Golden Codex*, made for Gniezno at Reichenau in southwestern Germany, the most inventive center of European book illumination at the time. A far simpler gospel book from a couple of centuries earlier has annotations by Irish missionaries, which has prompted the suggestion that it was the Irish who converted the Polish tribes.

Lake Jelonek

Just west of the cathedral is Lake Jelonek, a peaceful spot with a wonderful view of the town. Overlooking its far bank, but best approached via the main road, is a large modern building containing a college and the **Museum of the Origins of the Polish State** (Tues–Sun 10am–5pm). This contains archaeological finds from various Wielkopolska sites, along with changing art exhibitions. There's also a video show on the early history of Poland, with screenings in English on request.

Gniezno Practicalities

There's little evidence that Gniezno is expecting foreign tourists. Both **Orbis** and **PTTK** have offices on the Rynek, but neither has any tourist information. Cashing a traveler's check also presents problems: Orbis refuses to do it, which leaves only the bank at ul. Sienkiewicza 17, where you'll probably have to wait for well over an hour.

There are just three possibilities for **accommodation**, which is a pity as Gniezno makes a good touring base. Until recently the only **hotel** was the decrepit *Centralny*, ul. Bolesława Chrobrego 32 (☎37-14). However, there's now the alternative of the *Mieszko*, beside the sports stadium above Lake Jelonek (☎46-25); this is on the model of an expense-account motel, but with prices about a quarter of what they would be in the west. Its bistro is one of the livelier night-spots in a town which is generally quiet of an evening. The **youth hostel** is conveniently close to the stations at ul. Pocztowa 11 (☎46-09).

Best **restaurant** downtown is *Gwarna* at the corner of ul. Mieszka I and ul. Bolesława Chrobrego; others to try are *Teatralno* on the latter street, and *Robotnicza* at the corner of ul. Mieszka I and ul. Dąbrówki. There are several **cafés** on and around the Rynek.

Lake Lednica

One of the key places in the early life of Poland is the long, narrow **Lake Lednica**, 18km west of Gniezno and easily reached by bus. The place to get off is across from the entrance to the **Wielkopolska Ethnographic Park** (April 15–Oct 31 Tues–Sun 9am–5pm), by the turn off to DZIEKANOWICE. Laid out in an exhilarating location by the side of the lake, this open-air museum consists of about fifty traditional rural buildings from the last 250 years or so, mostly origi-nals—including three working windmills, a Baroque cemetery chapel with all its furnishings, and several farmsteads.

From here, continue on to the village, bear left along the main street, then right at the grocery store; it's then a walk of twenty minutes or so to the disparate tourist complex known as the **Museum of the First Piasts at Lednica** (same hours). Entered through an impressive wooden gateway, whose upper story turns out to be a snack bar, this features a few more rural buildings, a craft shop in yet another windmill, a small collection of archaeological finds, and over-life-sized statues of Polish warriors of a millennium ago. More importantly, it's the departure point for **Ostrów Lednicki**, the largest of the three islands in Lake Lednica, which is reached in a couple of minutes by the chained ferry.

This unlikely site, uninhabited for the last six centuries, was once a royal seat equal to Poznań and Gniezno in importance: Bolesław the Brave was born here, and it may also have been where his coronation by Emperor Otto III took place, rather than in Gniezno. It began life in the ninth century as a fortified town covering about a third of the island and linked to the mainland by a causeway. In the following century a massive **palace** was constructed, along with a church—the excavated remains only hint at its former grandeur, but the presence of stairways prove it must have been at least two storys high. The buildings were destroyed in 1038 by the Czech prince Brzetysław, but the church was rebuilt soon afterwards, only to gradually fall into disuse, along with the town itself. For centuries the island served as a cemetery, to be recently coaxed out of its sleep by tourism.

Biskupin

The Iron-Age village of **BISKUPIN**, 30km north of Gniezno, is one of the most evocative and exciting archaeological sites in Europe. Though the area has long been a fruitful source for excavations, its full significance only became apparent in 1933, when the local schoolmaster noticed some hand-worked stakes standing in the reeds at the edge of Lake Biskupin. He also learned from a landowner that other artifacts had been found during peat-cutting. Experts from Poznań soon pronounced that the site had been a **fortified village** of the Lusatian culture, founded around 550 BC and destroyed in tribal warfare some 150 years later. The subsequent uncovering of the settlement has thrown fresh light on the tribal life of the period, enabling the solution of many previously unresolved questions.

The only way of reaching Biskupin by public transit is by taking a bus to **GĄSAWA**, 2km south of Biskupin, then switching to the **narrow-gauge steam train** which stops right in front of the site up to five times daily. Unlike most of the many other historic lines in Poland, it exists solely for tourist purposes and runs only when the site is open. Nonetheless, the open-windowed red and yellow carriages are sufficiently unkempt to seem authentic and add a distinctive note to the otherwise monotonously green landscape. (For more on the railroad, see below.)

The Site

In contrast to the overcautious approach which makes so many famous archaeological sites disappointing to non-specialists, it was decided to reconstruct the original appearance of a section of the village. The price to be paid for this approach is evident at the entrance to the **Archaeological Park** (daily mid-April to end Sept 8am–7pm; Oct 8am–6pm subject to weather), where ramshackle snack bars, tacky souvenir shops, and amusement booths are overrun by endless busloads of schoolkids in early summer. There's also a small tourist office which sells an excellent booklet to the site in English.

From the entrance, it's best to go straight ahead past a re-erected old farmhouse to the **Museum**, which contains all manner of objects dug up here—tools, household utensils, weapons, jewelry, ornaments, and objects for worship. Piecing together the evidence, archaeologists have been able to draw a picture of a society in which hunting had been largely superseded by arable farming and livestock breeding. Their trade patterns were surprisingly extensive: their iron seems to have come from Transylvania, and there's a fascinating group of exhibits imported from even farther afield, the most exotic being some Egyptian beads. Most remarkable of all was the tribe's prowess in building, as can be seen in the model reconstruction of the entire village. Beyond the museum buildings is an enclosure for tarpans, miniature dray horses which have evolved very little since the time of the settlement.

Returning to the farmhouse, it's only a couple of minutes' walk down the path to the right to the **excavations**. The foreground consists of the uncovered foundations of various buildings, some from as late as the thirteenth century; of more interest are re-creations of the Iron-Age buildings—although only a section of each has been built, and not exactly on their former site, it requires little imagination to picture what the whole must have looked like. For the best view of the settlement, take a **cruise** on the old steamer which chugs around the lake all day: departure times are posted on the jetty, and the cost is nominal.

The **palisade** was particularly ingenious: it originally consisted of 35,000 stakes grouped in rows up to nine deep and driven into the bed of the lake at an angle of 45°. It acted both as a breakwater and as the first line of the fortifications. Immediately behind was a circular **wall** of oak logs guarded by a tall watchtower, this latter the most conjectural part of the whole restoration project. Inside the defenses were a circular road plus eleven symmetrical streets, again made of logs and filled in with earth, sand, and clay; the **houses** were grouped in terraces ranged from east to west to catch the sun. An entire extended family would live in each house, so the population of the settlement probably numbered over 1000. As you can see from the example open for inspection, each house had two chambers. Pigs and cattle—the most important privately owned objects—were kept in the lobby, while the main room, where the family slept in a single bed, was also equipped with a loft for the storage of food and fuel.

The Biskupin Railroad

Next stop after Biskupin on the narrow-gauge railroad is **WENECJA**, which is itself well worth a visit. This hamlet's name is the Polish word for Venice, fancifully justified by the fact that it is almost surrounded by water, lying as it does between two lakes. Nearby communities are equally improbably styled "Rome," "Paris" and "Scotland." To the right of the station are the remains of the fourteenth-century **castle** of Mikołaj Nałęcz, a notorious figure known by the nickname of "the Bloody Devil of Wenecja." Only the lower parts of the walls survive, admittedly in good shape, but to see inside you have to take a leaf out of the book of a medieval attacker and scale them. On the opposite side of the tracks is the open-air **Museum of Narrow-Gauge Railroads** (daily 9am–5pm), which has a collection of engines and rolling stock from all over Europe.

The terminal of the twelve-kilometer route is **ZNIN**, a small town again set between two lakes, part of a long north–south chain. In the center of its Rynek stands the remarkable and forlorn tower of the demolished fifteenth-century

Town Hall, whose interior has been fitted out as the local museum (Tues–Fri 9am–4pm, Sat 9am–3pm, Sun 10am–3pm). There are several restaurants, cafés and bars here, and a couple of **accommodation** options if you fancy a night in a quiet location—*Hotel Brda*, ul. 700 Lecia 1 (☎207), and a campground (☎76) by Lake Mały Znin to the south.

It's easy to move on from Znin: in addition to main line and narrow-gauge trains, it's also well served by buses on the main road between Gniezno and Bydgoszcz.

Trzmesno to Inowrocław

Sixteen kilometers east of Gniezno, the Piast Route winds through **TRZMESNO**, a straggling little lakeside community that was founded, according to tradition, by Saint Adalbert. It can be reached either by bus or Baltic-bound train—the latter involving a fairly long walk through the fields to the town.

The ancient church which Adalbert is said to have established was succeeded by a Romanesque structure, parts of which are incorporated in the Baroque **Basilica** which dominates the town. From the outside it appears austere, but the interior is lavishly decorated from the tiled sidewalk to the frescoed dome. In the main square is a monument to the local hero, the shoemaker Jan Kiliński, who played a leading role in the 1794 insurrection (see "Warsaw"). Next to the church is the *Hotel Czeremcha* (☎234), which also has the town's only restaurant.

Mogilno

A farther 16km northeast is **MOGILNO**, again set on the bank of a lake. Here the railroad splits, with a branch slowly and circuitously following the Piast Route, offering an alternative to the more regular buses. Mogilno itself isn't a place you'll want to hang around for long, but it does have a couple of worthwhile churches, the Gothic St James in the town center and the eclectic St John the Evangelist by the side of the lake. The latter preserves its Romanesque crypt and apse, complete with carved frieze, though the building was heavily transformed in both the Gothic and Baroque epochs.

Strzelno

The Piast Route's most important artistic treasures are found 17km east of Mogilno in the archetypally Polish rural town of **STRZELNO**. Both the bus and train stations are set at the western fringe of town; from there, walk straight ahead, turning left at the *Hotel Dom Wycieczkowy* (☎36)—at the end of this street is the rather run-down main square. Continuing down to the right brings you to the far end of town. Enclosed in a precinct—a haven of peace when the tour groups aren't there—are two outstanding Romanesque buildings.

The monastery of the **Holy Trinity** is a typically Polish accretion: brick Gothic gables reminiscent of the Baltic ports and a monumental Baroque facade sprout from a dignified late twelfth-century Romanesque shell. After the war, some of the interior encrustations were removed, to reveal, in well-nigh perfect condition, four original nave **pillars**. Two of these, adorned with figurative carvings set in a foliage surround, are crafted with a delicacy found in few other European sculptures of the period; a third is reminiscent of Arab art in its geometrical shapes. Another column of almost equal quality forms the sole support of the beautiful vault of the Chapel of St Barbara, to the right of the chancel.

Beside the monastery church stands the slightly older little red sandstone rotunda of **St Procopius**. In contrast to its neighbor, this has preserved the purity of its original form, its round tower perfectly offset against the protruding apses. It's normally kept locked, but you should be able to get in if you ask in Holy Trinity or the buildings alongside.

Incidentally, the churches are not the earliest evidence of worship on this site: the large stone block in front of them is thought to have been used for pagan rites.

Kruszwica

As the Piast Route moves on to sleepy **KRUSZWICA**, 16km northeast of Strzelno by road but much farther by rail, it enters the tiny province of Kujawy. Standing at the head of the pencil-slim **Lake Gopło**, the largest of all western Poland's lakes, Kruszwica is enshrined in Polish folklore as the cradle of the Piast dynasty.

The legend goes that the descendants of Lech were ousted as the nation's rulers by the evil Popiel family. To ensure there was no competition for his succession, the last King Popiel killed off all his male kin except his own children, then established himself at a castle in Kruszwica, where he subjected his people to a reign of terror. One day, Saints John and Paul came in the guise of poor travelers, but the king refused them hospitality and they were forced to lodge with a peasant named Piast. They baptized him and his family, and predicted that he would be first in a long line of monarchs, whereupon they vanished into thin air. Shortly afterward, the Poles rose up against their evil ruler. He took refuge in his castle tower, where he was eventually devoured by rats and mice. The people then unanimously chose the worthy Piast as his successor.

The brick octagon overlooking the lake is known as the **Mouse Tower** (Mysia Wieza) and is allegedly where the rodent feast took place; in fact, ironically enough, it was part of a castle built by the last of the Piast kings, Kazimierz the Great. The only other historic monument is the early twelfth-century **Collegiate church**, a grim granite basilica which has been stripped of most of its later additions, except for the Gothic tower. Supposedly occupying the miraculous site of Piast's cottage, it served as a cathedral for the first half-century of its life, but was then supplanted by Włocławek.

Inowrocław

The end of the Piast Route comes 15km north of Kruszwica at **INOWROCŁAW**, where the main monument is the Romanesque **Church of the Assumption**, a building devalued by remodelling early this century. Also of note is **St Nicholas**, a Gothic church with Renaissance and Baroque additions. Around the time this was being built in the fifteenth century, salt springs were discovered in the area, but it was not until the 1870s that Inowrocław became a popular **spa**, with thermal establishments going up to the west of the old town. Though the baths are still in use, the modern town has harnessed the waters for a chemical industry which has led to heavy pollution and a ring of concrete suburbs.

Given the current appearance of Inowrocław, it's not likely to rate as an overnight stop. If you do want to use it as a touring base, then there are two fairly basic **hotels**, *Centralny* (☎35-17) and *Polonia* (☎28-18), both on ul. Królowej Jadwigi between the bus and train stations. In the same area are the best of the places to eat and drink.

The town offers a wide choice of connections onward to Toruń and Bydgoszcz, or else back to Gniezno either directly or via Znin.

Włocławek

Other than Kruszwica, the only place of any real interest in Kujawy is the province's historic capital, **WŁOCŁAWEK**, 60km southeast of Inowrocław. It's best reached by bus: to get there by train involves a long detour via Toruń. Nowadays it's a grim industrial town, with a huge paper mill fed by the neighboring forests, but is best known as the source of one of Poland's favorite tourist souvenirs—glazed pottery, hand-painted with brown floral motifs. Włocławek's early development owed much to its strategic position on the Wisła River; it has been the seat of a bishop since the mid-twelfth century and for long operated a rigid anti-Semitic policy, with Jews prohibited from settling until the eighteenth century.

The old town is centered on a small Rynek with houses from the seventeenth to the nineteenth centuries. Also on the square is the parish church of **St John**, originally Gothic but heavily remodeled in the Baroque period. A short distance to the east lies the **Cathedral**, which has preserved its Gothic form far more fully. It was begun in 1340, a few years after a fire which completely destroyed its predecessor along with much of the rest of the town. Subsequently it was embellished with a number of chapels, of which the finest is that dedicated to St Joseph, containing the **tombs** of Bishop Piotr Moszyński, beautifully carved in Hungarian marble by Veit Stoss, and of Monseigneur Karnowski, by an anonymous sculptor from Nuremberg. Also worth a look is the late Renaissance chapel of the Tarnowski family, richly adorned with statues and busts.

Orbis has an office at pl. Wolności 8/9 (☎245-22). There are a couple of places to stay: the **hotel** *Victoria*, ul. Przechodnia 1 (☎31-18), and the **youth hostel**, ul. Chmielna 24 (☎273-63).

POMERANIA (POMORZE)

Pomerania's long, sandy coastline is its major attraction, and a couple of days holed up on the Baltic here is one of the most pleasant ways of unwinding that the country can offer. Less known but equally appealing, though, is the inland forested lake district, with its market towns, Prussian peasant houses, and marvelous Gothic brick churches.

Bydgoszcz, a major industrial center, is a place to avoid, save for its transportation links north to the **lakes**. For these, the best base is **Czaplinek**, on the shores of **Lake Drawsko**, as attractive a stretch of water as any in Mazury. On the coast there are plenty of resorts to choose from: **Łeba** combines beaches with the **Słowiński National Park**; the old port of **Darłowo** preserves a distinctively Pomeranian character; while to the west, many of the finest beaches are to be found in the **Kołobrzeg** and **Świnoujście** areas—the latter easily reached from the port of **Szczecin**, hard up against the German frontier. Finally, for architecture, **Kamień Pomorski cathedral** is not to be missed, nor, for organ and chamber music enthusiasts, is its **summer festival**.

Public **transportation** within Pomerania is good: there's a reasonable train service that runs parallel to the coast on the Gdańsk–Szczecin line, with local connections up to the coastal resorts and buses for excursions into the countryside.

A Brief History of Pomerania

In prehistoric times the southern Baltic coast was inhabited by the Celts, who were later displaced by a succession of Germanic tribes. By the end of the fifth century they too had been ousted by Slav people known as the **Pomorzanie**, relics of whose settlements are preserved on Wolin Island, in the west of the region. The lands of the Pomorzanie were in turn conquered by the Piast **King Mieszko I**, who took Szczecin in 979—a campaign which is cited by the Poles in support of their claim to ownership of this often disputed territory. Thereafter the picture gets more complicated. Throughout the medieval era Pomerania evolved as an essentially independent dukedom ruled by a local Slav dynasty commonly called the **Pomeranian princes**, who nonetheless owed loyalty to the Polish monarch. Eastern Pomerania was conquered by the Teutonic Knights in 1308, and was later known as Royal Prussia; this part of the region returned to the Polish sphere of influence under the terms of the 1466 Treaty of Toruń (see "Malbork," in Chapter Two).

The ethnic mix of the region played a dominant part in governing its allegiances. While a Slav majority retained its hold on the countryside, heavy German colonization of the towns inexorably tilted the balance of power to the territorially ambitious Brandenburg margravate. In line with the westward drift, the Pomeranian princes finally transferred formal allegiance to the Holy Roman Empire in 1521, and the inroads of the Reformation further weakened the region's ties with Catholic Poland, which anyway was more interested in its eastern borderlands than its western terrains.

Control of the region was fiercely disputed during the Thirty Years' War, the Swedes soon occupying much of the coastal region and keeping a foothold in western Pomerania throughout the later hostilities. The Treaty of Westphalia (1648) divided western Pomerania between Brandenburg and Sweden, the eastern section remaining under Polish control. With the departure of the Swedes in the 1720s, Prussia (as Brandenburg had now become) was able to incorporate all of western Pomerania into its territories, with the rest of Pomerania being absorbed during the Partitions. Prussian control was undisturbed until after the Versailles Treaty, when a strip of the eastern fringe became the so-called "Polish Corridor"; the western part—the region covered in this chapter—became Polish only in 1945. Mass emigration of Pomerania's German population followed the fall of the Third Reich, their place being taken by Polish settlers, mainly from the relinquished eastern territories.

Bydgoszcz

The provincial capital of **BYDGOSZCZ** is a sprawling industrial center, developed around a fortified medieval settlement, strategically located on the borders of Wielkopolska and Pomerania. Unlike much of the region to the north, it has been Polish since 1920, when the territory was ceded by Prussia. During the last war, however, the town suffered particularly badly at the hands of the Nazis: mass executions followed its fall to German troops, and by the end of the war over 50,000 people—a quarter of the population—had been murdered on the town square, with many of the rest deported to labor and concentration camps. Wartime destruction has left precious few buildings standing, the few remaining monuments being centerd on the right bank of the Brda River.

From the **train station** in the north of town it's a short tram ride down ul. Dworcowa to the bridge over to the old town. As usual the area hinges on the **Rynek**, where the main feature is a large memorial to the Nazis' victims. A little back from the square, overlooking the river, is the late fifteenth-century **Cathedral**, its western front topped by a fine Gothic gable. Interior ornamentation is the usual Baroque, a notable exception being the late Gothic *Virgin with a Rose* on the high altar.

If you have more time to fill, wander down to the **waterside**, where a number of stocky timbered **granaries** are dotted along the banks, one of them housing a local museum (Tues–Sat 10am–4pm). A red brick building beyond sells tickets for summer **boat excursions** along the Brda, a tributary of the Wisła.

Practicalities

The city **tourist office** is at ul. Zygmunta Augusta 10, across the road from the train station. **Hotels**, in ascending order of price, include the *Centralny*, ul. Dworcowa 85 (☎228-876), the *Budowlani*, ul. Forordońska 112 (☎426-082), the *Brda*, ul. Dworcowa 94 (☎224-061), the *Ratuszowy*, ul. Długa 37 (☎228-861), and the smart Orbis-run *Pod Orłem*, al. 1 Maja 14 (☎221-861). Cheapest of all is the **youth hostel** at ul. Sowińskiego 5 (☎227-570).

For an evening's entertainment, the *Bydgoszcz Philharmonia* at ul. Libełta 1b, north of the old town, is a well-known **concert venue** featuring top-notch piano recitals.

The Pomeranian Lakeland

The **Pomeranian Lakeland** lies over to the northwest of Bydgoszcz, centered on the resort town of **Szczecinek**. A marshy, green area, with quiet, tree-lined roads and small market towns, it is dotted with over 1000 lakes which are connected by a trellis of east–west and north–south waterways, making it possible to travel all over the area by boat. There is very little tourist infrastructure as yet, though many Poles have holiday *dachas* on the lakesides. Perhaps the most attractive area to make for is around **Lake Drawsko**, with its relaxed little town of **Czaplinek**.

Although some train lines weave their way across the district, **buses** are the best way of getting into the heart of the lakeland—either from Bydgoszcz, Szczecin, or Gdańsk, or from the coastal resorts. If you want to walk, or have a **car**, you can get well off the beaten track to lakes that haven't made it into this section—or into any of the Polish tourist literature, in which Pomerania remains oddly played down. In the remoter reaches, the tradition of Polish hospitality compensates for the lack of formal **accommodation**: turn up at a bar and ask, and someone can usually arrange a room for the night.

Chojnice and Around

Some 50km north of Bydgoszcz, near Lake Charzykowskie, lies **CHOJNICE**, a quiet, unpretentious place with a dusty, open square: the setting for its main bit of animation, a weekly market, when the streets are filled with horse-drawn carts. Architecturally, the town has a few reminders of its past as the last Polish stronghold of the Teutonic Knights. The most impressive of these buildings is the

Gothic **parish church**, a sturdy brick construction whose high tower dominates the town center. Sections of the town **walls** have also survived the battering of the centuries, most notably the five-storey **Czuchołow Gate** (Brama Czuchołowoska), off the western edge of the Rynek.

Few foreign visitors will want to stay in Chojnice. Should you need to do so, the Orbis ofice at pl. Bojownikow 3 can provide information on private rooms and **hotels**. At present there are just two rather basic places—the *Olimp*, ul. Kościerska 9 (☎36-29), and the *Turystyczny*, ul. Myśliboja 5 (☎24-72)—and a summer **youth hostel** at ul. 31 Stycznia 21/23 (☎50-39).

Lake Charzykowskie and the Tucholski Forest

A few kilometers north of Chojnice, a series of lakes and waterways extends for an unbroken sixty kilometers towards the edges of Kashubia (see Chapter Two). The place to start out at is **Lake Charzykowskie**, approached from the village of CHARZYKOW, a five-kilometer bus ride to the north of town.

East of Chojnice stretches the huge **Tucholski Forest** (Bory Tucholski), a dense expanse of woodland punctuated by lakes and crisscrossed by streams and rivers, the largest being the Brda, flowing north from Bydgoszcz. In the heart of the forest are a string of peasant villages and, on the banks of the Brda, a scattering of holiday centers.

Odry Stone Circle

Just outside the village of **ODRY**, 20km northeast of Chojnice (served by sporadic buses), a wooded nature reserve hides a well-preserved megalithic site. A sequence of irregular **stone circles** and overgrown burial mounds, it covers an area about half the size of a soccer field. It has been dated to the first or second century AD, though little is known of its origins.

To find the clearing in which it stands isn't easy, adding to the enjoyment of the site when you finally arrive; before setting out from the village ask directions for the *Kręgi Kamieniece*. Most of the year, you're likely to be on your own, though at the midsummer solstice the circle attracts the Gdańsk contingent of hippies, alternatives, and New Agers.

Szczecinek and Lake Drawsko

One of the most popular lakeland bases is **SZCZECINEK**, due west of Chojnice. A modern and rather over-functional holiday center, it stands a kilometer back from the enticing **Lake Wielimie**. As you'd expect, there's plenty of water-sports facilities, with an increasing number of rental places for the general demand.

Accommodation in town is provided by the **hotels** *Zamek*, ul. Mickiewicza 2 (☎420-74), *Pomorski*, ul. Bohaterów Warszawy (☎409-51), and *Fala*, ul. Kilińskiego 7 (☎401-11), or the all-year **youth hostel** at pl. Wazów 1 (☎4336).

Czaplinek and Lake Drawsko

The best-known lake area is the Drawskie region, 40km west of Szczecinek. **Lake Drawsko**, the center of the district, is one of the largest Pomeranian lakes, a tranquil expanse of deep, clear water some ten kilometers in length. In summer you'll find groups of Polish canoeists powering their way through the area; if you feel like joining them, there are rent facilities in town. Walking is wonderful, too, with paths rambling off through the lakeside woods for miles in all directions.

On the banks of Drawsko is **CZAPLINEK**, an early Slav stronghold eventually incorporated into the Brandenburg domains. The town has a drowsy charm about it, with eighteenth-century wooden houses adding character to the modern center, and tourism doesn't seem to have much affected the easy-going life of the place. Despite the popularity of the lake, **accommodation** is limited to two basic *Dom Wycieczkowe*, the *Pomorski*, ul. Jagiellońska 11 (☎853-63), and the *Czapla*, ul. Piaskowa 1 (☎452-55), and a lakeside **campground**.

Łeba and Around

Northwest of Gdańsk the hills of Kashubia merge into the lush wooded coastline of eastern Pomerania. The easternmost resort is **ŁEBA**, an attractive old fishing village at the mouth of the river of the same name; it's 90km from Gdańsk with reasonable train and bus connections via Lębork—which is also the route taken by trains from Słupsk, Koszalin (see p.334) and points west. Buses from Gdańsk take the main roads; if you're coming by car, a more appealing approach is on the backroads, taking you through the tiny hamlets and along the delightful tree-lined avenues that characterise this part of the country. To avoid getting lost you'll really need the *Pobrzeze Baltyku mapa turystyczna*, which marks all the minor roads.

The **village** itself is set some way back from the sea; dunes and beaches cover the original site of the village, which was forced to move inland in the late sixteenth century because of shifting sands and erosion. Both bus and train drop you just off ul. Kościuszki, the street running down the middle of the village. Lined with attractively gabled fishermen's houses, the street bustles in summer with tourist traffic heading for the long sandy **beaches** just to the north, which are widely regarded as among the cleanest on the Baltic coast. Poles aren't the only people who have enjoyed the bracing location: wandering through the park that provides the main approach to the beaches, you'll pass the summer house used by Nazi propaganda chief Josef Goebbels. Closer to the sea, the ruins of a Gothic church loom from the sand dunes, a lone reminder of the village's former location.

Even in season, **accommodation** shouldn't be too much of a problem here: there's a PTTK **hostel** at ul. 1 Maja 6 (☎613-24), plus a whole host of private and vacation homes available. The *Przymorze* tourist information office at ul. Dworcowy 1, by the station, can help out with these. One attractive option is the workers' vacation home in neighboring Rąbka (see overleaf), though it's best to check with the *Przymorze* office before heading out there. There's an attractive **campground** nearby too. Best of the numerous tourist **restaurants** is the *Karczma Słowińska* on ul. Kościuszki: decent menu plus excellent local *Hewelius* beer.

The Słowiński National Park

West of Łeba are the lakes and sand dunes of the **Słowiński National Park**, one of the country's strangest but most memorable natural attractions, special enough to be included in UNESCO's list of world Biosphere Reserves. The park gets its name from the **Slovincians**, a small ethnic group of Slav origin who, like their neighbors the Kashubians, have retained a distinctive identity despite centuries of Germanization.

This area is an ornithologist's paradise, with over 250 **bird** species either permanently inhabiting the park or using it as a migratory habitat. The lakes, stretching some 30km along the coast, are shallow lagoons separated from the sea by a long expanse of sand dunes—which during World War II provided an ideal training ground for units of the Afrika Korps. In the latter stages of the war the park was turned into one of several launch sites for the fearsome V1 and V2 rockets that bombarded London.

Access to the park is from **RĄBKA**, a small holiday village on the shores of **Jezioro Łebsko**, the largest and best-known of the lagoons, a bus ride or twenty-minute walk west of Łeba. The shores are covered with thick reeds, making access to the water difficult but providing ideal cover for the birds: sanctuaries at several points protect the main breeding sites. Though it is possible to skirt some of the southern edge, most visitors continue along the **northern** side, on a road into the dune territory that is the park's distinguishing feature. From July to August tourist buses from Łeba and Rąbka run west to the edge of the sands; at any other time of year you'll have to walk the whole way. Most people are content to venture a kilometer or so beyond where the bus finishes, returning either with the bus or by a parallel path running along the coast, but if you're feeling up to a sterner challenge you could walk on to the village of Smołdzino (see below)—12km from where the bus stops. You could then return to Łeba by a roundabout bus route in the evening, or even stay overnight.

Even a brief hike will give you the flavor of the terrain, though. A short distance out of the lakeside woods, huge dunes are piled up to thirty meters high; dried by the sun and propelled by the wind, they migrate over ten meters per year on average, leaving behind the broken tree stumps you see along the path. Out in the middle of the dune area there's a desert-like feeling of desolation with the sands rippling in the wind, giving an unsettling sense of fluidity as the dunes change their form around you.

FAUNA IN THE PARK

Birds in the park are classified into three main groups: nesting, migratory, and wintering species. Nesters include such rare species as the white-tailed eagle, black stork, crane, ruff, and eagle-owl. During the late autumn migration period you'll see large flocks of wild **geese** winging over the lakes, and in winter you'll find ducks and other fowl from the far north of Europe sheltering here on the warmer southern shores of the Baltic—velvet scoters, mergansers, auks, and whooper swans included. Mammals are numerous too, the shores of the lakes harboring deer and boar, with elks, racoons, and badgers in the surrounding woods.

Smołdzino

SMOŁDZINO is the site of the park's **natural history museum** (Tues–Sat 9am–5pm), which contains an extensive display of the park's flora and fauna; the park offices here can provide you with detailed information about the area, including advice on bird-watching around the lake. Just to the west of the village is **Rowokół** hill, whose observation tower at the top affords a panoramic view over the entire park area. There's a summer youth hostel and a farm hostel in the village as well.

Kluki

Five kilometers east of Smołdzino, on the western edge of Lake Łebsko and at the end of a minor road, is the little village of **KLUKI**, which is served by occasional buses from Smołdzino and more frequent ones from Słupsk. Entirely surrounded by woods, Kluki has an enjoyable *skansen* of Slovincian wooden architecture (May–Sept Tues–Sun 9am–4pm; Oct–April 9am–2pm), providing a flavor of the traditional way of life of these tough seafaring and fishing people.

Słupsk and the Central Coast

Continuing west, the next place of any significance is **SŁUPSK**, 20km beyond the nondescript town of LEBORK on the main road and rail line. An early Slav settlement, ruled by Pomeranian princes and Brandenburg margraves for much of its history, Słupsk was completely wrecked in 1945. Faceless postwar developments now dominate the town, which is probably best known in Poland for its annual **piano festival**, held in September. Of late it's been in the news as the center of industrial unrest against the Solidarity government, with Słupsk rail workers helping to paralyze the rail network of the northwest in protest at the austerity policies. It's not a place to detain you, but it can be useful as a base for exploring the Słowiński National Park, to which the **Orbis** office at ul. Wojska Polskiego 1 (☎236-14) organizes summer excursions.

What little there is worth seeing in the town center can be covered in an hour or two. On the banks of the river, the Renaissance castle houses a **regional museum** (Tues–Sun 10am–4pm); alongside displays of local ethnography, there's a large collection of modern Polish art, most notably a series of canvases by Stanisław Ignacy Witkiewicz. The old castle **mill** is one of the earliest specimens of its kind in the country, while the reconstructed Gothic **Dominican church** contains a fine Renaissance altarpiece and the tombs of the last Pomeranian princes.

This scattering of historic sites aside, the town's main attractions are two highly reputable **restaurants**, the *Karczma Słupska* at ul. Wojska Polskiego 11 and the *Pod Kluką* at ul. Kaszubska 22—both downtown, both offering a spread of traditional Polish cuisine with a sprinkling of regional specialties.

Accommodation is provided by the passable *Przymorze* **motel**, ul. Szczecińska 41 (☎308-52), the *Piast* **hotel**, ul. Jednosci Narodowej 2 (☎252-86), and the *Zamkowy* hotel, ul. Dominikańska 9 (☎252-94). **Private rooms** are arranged by the *Biuro Zakwaterowania*, ul. Dominikańska 9 (Mon–Sat 7:30am–3:30pm).

Ustka

USTKA, 20km northwest of Słupsk by bus or local train, is a one-time member of the Hanseatic League that's been a popular holiday resort for well over a century. A decent set of beaches is the only real attraction here; the town itself has little character, the old fishing village having long been replaced by a nondescript modern harbor.

Darłowo and Darłówko

A more attractive proposition than Ustka is **DARŁOWO**, 40km farther west and a couple of kilometers inland on the Wieprza River, though here the drawback is the difficulty of access by public transit—trains from Słupsk involve a change at Sławno, and buses take nearly two hours.

The beaches north of the town, around the resort of DARŁÓWKO, are as popular as any, but what makes Darłowo special are the buildings of the old Hanseatic fishing center. The **Rynek**, still a marketplace, is dominated by a gracefully reconstructed Baroque town hall, complete with its Renaissance doorway. On one side of the Rynek sits the Gothic **St Mary's** church, an attractive brick building with a relatively restrained Baroque interior overlay; among a clutch of royal tombs is that of the notorious Scandinavian ruler King Erik VII (1397–1459), a relative of King Kazimierz the Great, who was deposed in 1439 and lived out the last years of his life in exile here. Farther out from the center you'll find parts of the fifteenth-century **walls**, including the town gate, just beyond which is **St Gertrude's**, another impressive Gothic structure with an unusual twelve-sided ambulatory. On the other side of town, the well-preserved fourteenth-century castle of the Pomeranian princes now houses an extensive **regional museum** (Tues–Sun 8am–4pm), focusing on the town's maritime past.

The **information office** by the town gate might be able to arrange **private rooms**, but they're more likely to direct you to the PTTK *Dom Wycieczkowy* (☎27-56) in Darłówko. This basic hotel-restaurant is well located in a quiet spot by the river, the peace broken by holiday-time discos at the bar across the sound. Privatization of workers' **holiday homes** means there may well be some extra accommodation options near the beach by this summer. There's also a camping place (☎28-72) near the sea.

West from Darłowo

If you've a car and time on your hands, it's worth taking the backroads west from Darłowo, which pass through an attractive open landscape of fields, woods, and quiet old Pomeranian villages. The sturdy German farm buildings are still standing, as in several cases are the Gothic brick churches, often in better condition than those in the major towns. A characteristically beautiful example is at **IWIECINO**, a tiny village stuck in the middle of nowhere halfway between Darłowo and Koszalin. The fourteenth-century structure has a beautifully decorated wooden ceiling, painted sixteenth-century pews, a delicate Renaissance altarpiece and a splendid late Baroque organ.

Koszalin

KOSZALIN, the provincial capital 25km west of Darłowo, is an anonymous place. Like so many towns in this region, the old town was badly damaged during 1945, and postwar reconstruction of the newly vacated German city was more about residential blocks and intensive industrial development than aesthetic statements. Most Polish vacationers head straight through en route for the beaches and resorts north of the city, like MIELNO and UNIEŚCIE. Neither is especially compelling.

Kołobrzeg

Beyond Darłowo the next coastal town of any size is **KOŁOBRZEG**, a largish town clumped around the mouth of the Parseta River, a forty-kilometer bus or train ride west of Koszalin. With one and a half million visitors annually, it's one of the country's busiest seaside resorts, with a decent collection of vacation-oriented amenities integrated into its otherwise drab landscape.

The paucity of ancient buildings belies the town's history. One of the oldest Pomeranian settlements, it grew on the economic foundations of the **salt works** that were established here in the seventh century. By the mid-800s a decent-sized fortified town had developed, and in 1000 Bolesław the Brave founded one of the early Piast bishoprics in what was becoming a significant port. A steady influx of German merchants and sailors eventually led to its incorporation into the Hanseatic League in the mid-thirteenth century. Badly hit by the Thirty Years' War, in 1655 it passed into the control of the Brandenburg Margraves, who established a fortress here. A change of emphasis came two centuries later when a new spa resort began to develop, attracting crowds from all over the Baltic region. The Germans defended the town to the last in 1945, leaving the place a ruin by the time the Polish and Russian armies arrived in March. A band of the liberators gathered on the beach to swear an oath that this ancient Piast town would thenceforth be Polish for ever, sealing the vow in suitably dramatic style by hurling a wedding ring into the sea—"Poland's Reunion with the Sea" as the event came to be known.

The Town and the Beach

Architecturally, the only remotely interesting bit of Kołobrzeg is the old town area, fifteen minutes' walk south of the train and bus stations in the center of town. The hall-shaped **Collegiate Church of St Mary**, a large red brick Gothic structure, was badly damaged in 1945 but nevertheless retains significant elements of the original decoration, some Gothic triptychs, and a bronze fourteenth-century font included. In the surrounding streets you'll find a number of Gothic burghers' houses, many of them well reconstructed, but apart from that there's really nothing else to look at.

It's the sand that the visitors come for, and throughout the summer you'll find throngs of Polish vacationers soaking up the sun on the main strand a short walk north of the station. Like many of the Pomeranian resorts the beach has a slightly downbeat, old-fashioned feel, with wicker chairs, weather-beaten hot-dog stands, and tawdry snack bars. And it's long enough for a decent stroll, with a pier and a seafront parade edging an attractive park. Beyond the pier at the western end there's a tall brick lighthouse and a stone monument marking the spot where Kołobrzeg married the ocean.

Practicalities

The main **information** office is at ul. Dworcowa 4, in the center of town. **Accommodation** is available at the *Monika pensjonat*, ul. 22 Lipca 18a (☎32-32), the Orbis-run *Solny*, ul. Fredry 4 (☎24-00), and the similarly upscale *Skanpol*, ul. Dworcowa 10 (☎34-11). **Private rooms** are arranged by the *Biuro Zakwaterowań* at ul. Lenina 2 (Mon–Sat 7am–3pm), and there's a summer **youth hostel** at ul. Łopuskiego 13 (☎21-31). The town **campground**, the *Bałtywia*, is at ul. IV Dywizji WP 1 (☎45-69). Best **restaurants** in town are the *Fregata*, ul. Dworcowa 12, and those in the *Solny* and *Skanpol* hotels.

Kamień Pomorski

Some sixty kilometers west of Kołobrzeg lies the quiet little lakeside town of **KAMIEŃ POMORSKI**, an atmospheric Pomeranian center which demands a visit for its fine cathedral. For public transit from Kołobrzeg you'll have to rely on buses to take you cross-country; there are no train connections along this bit of the coast, only northward from Szczecin. Traveling on the main routes it's easy to miss this town, since it's not on the major coastal road to Świnoujście, and getting there by any means of transportation involves a detour.

The town's history starts in the ninth century, when a port was established here on the Dziwna River, a short stretch of water connecting the huge Szczecin lagoon (Zalew Szczeciński) with the smaller Kamień lagoon (Zalew Kamieński). By the late twelfth century Kamień was significant enough to be appointed the seat of the bishopric of West Pomerania, a position it retained for nearly 400 years. The Swedes seized the town during the Thirty Years' War, but by the late seventeenth century it had been appropriated by the Brandenburg rulers, not coming under Polish control until after World War II. Despite extensive wartime damage, Kamień Pomorski seems to have come out better than most towns in the area: concrete blocks fill in the huge gaps between the occasional burghers' mansions, yet there's enough of the older architecture to retain a sense of times past.

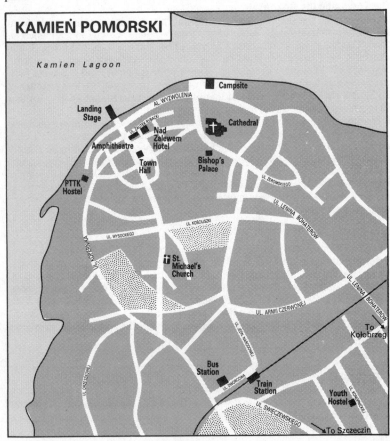

KAMIEŃ POMORSKI

The Town

All Kamień's sights are located some way north of the bus and rail stations, on and around the **Rynek**, where proximity to the lagoon lends a maritime feel. The fifteenth-century **Town Hall**, plumped right in the middle, is a careful reconstruction, its solid symmetrical brick archways rising to the familiar stepped gables at each end. Parts of the walls ringing the old town have survived, most notably the **Brama Wolińska** to the west of the square, an imposing Gothic gateway, surrounded by apartment blocks.

East of the square stands the magnificent **Cathedral**, one of the finest Romanesque structures in the country, made yet more startling by its backwater location. Construction of the brick and stone basilica began in the 1170s, following the creation of the Kamień bishopric, with many subsequent additions over the following centuries. Entrance to the building is through the fine Romanesque portal of the southern transept, adorned with weathered mid-thirteenth-century statues of the saints. Inside the cathedral you're enveloped by majestic Gothic vaulted arches; the presbytery is older, and is covered with flowing early thirteenth-century decoration. Other sections of the earliest polychromy are tucked away in corners around the transept, including a stern *Christ Pantocrator* and a fine *Crucifixion* that was uncovered in the 1940s. The focus of attention, though, is the superb fifteenth-century triptych gracing the altar, the most outstanding of many such Gothic pieces in the building—the rest are in the **sacristy museum**. A central *Coronation of Mary* is surrounded by scenes from the lives of the saints, most notably John Chrysostom, to whom the building is dedicated. To the right of the altar is another finely sculpted Romanesque portal, leading to the sacristy.

The cathedral's most famous feature, however, is its massive Baroque organ, at the back of the building, its forest of silver pipes and exuberant detail crowned by a procession of dreamy gilded saints. Approaching from the nave, a portrait of the instrument's creator, a local bishop by the name of Bogusław de Croy i Archot, stares down on the congregation from a cherub-encircled frame. From June to August the cathedral hosts an international organ and chamber music festival, with concerts every Friday: details from tourist offices throughout the region.

To complete the ensemble, across plac Katedralny is the **bishop's palace**, a stately late Gothic structure with a finely carved attic.

Practicalities

In summer the tourist **information point** on plac Katedralny dispenses maps and information; otherwise try the Orbis office on the Rynek. Best **accommodation** option is the *Nad Zalewem*, Zaułek Rybacki 1 (☎208-17), just off the Rynek with a view of the lagoon. Otherwise there's the less salubrious *Dom Pracy Twórczej* at ul. H. Sawickiej 1 (☎207-49), the PTTK *Dom Wycieczkowy* at ul. Słowackiego (☎202-41), a summer **youth hostel** at ul. Konopnickiej 19 (☎207-84), and a **campground** by the lagoon on al. Wyzwolenia (☎212-80). The only half-decent **restaurants** are the *Steńka*, ul. Rejtana 25, and the *Pod Muzami* on the Rynek.

Wolin and Westward

South of Kamień Pomorski, the main Szczecin–Świnoujście road crosses the water west to **WOLIN**, a small town on the site of one of the oldest Slav settlements in the country. According to early chronicles, a pagan tribe known as the Wolinians established themselves here in the eighth century, developing one of the most important early Baltic ports. A temple to Trzygłów and to Światowid, a triple-headed Slav deity, existed here until the early twelfth century, and was presumably destroyed by the Christian Poles when they captured the stronghold.

Echoes of the town's pagan past are present in the totem-like reconstructed wooden figures dotted around close to the water, all depicting Slav gods. The desolate ruins of a medieval church just up from the main square only add to the haunted atmosphere of the place. Recent excavations have uncovered plentiful evidence of the Wolinian settlement; you can see their discoveries in the local **museum** (Tues–Sun 10am–4pm) on the main road through town.

For an overnight stay there's one rudimentary **hotel**, the *Wineta* on the main road (✆618-84), a summer **youth hostel** at ul. Mickiewicza, and a camping space right by the water's edge, popular with fishermen and sailors.

The Woliński National Park

West from Wolin, the main road soon begins an exhilarating climb through the wooded slopes of the **Woliński National Park**, a large and beautiful expanse of oak and beech forests, terminating at the pine-covered sand dunes. Right in the heart of the forest there's a small **bison reserve**, and another one for wild swans in the glacial lake region on the remote eastern edge of the park. For anyone with a day to spare, a walk in these delightful surroundings would definitely be worth-while; regular bus services between Wolin and Świnoujście stop halfway through the forest, allowing you the chance to hike off on one of the marked paths. If you're going to do this you'll need the detailed local map—*Zalew Szczeciński: mapa zeglarskoturystyczna* (1:75 000).

Świnoujście

The road eventually descends to the port of ŚWINOUJŚCIE, located on one of the more attractive sections of the Baltic coast, right on the German border. Getting to the main part of town involves a short (free) ferry trip across the Świna River, at a point just before it opens out onto the Baltic; the rail station and main port are stranded on the near side of the river.

Świnoujście is another sprawling beach and spa resort, as popular with Swedes and Germans as with the Poles themselves—the border crossing and interna-tional ferry connections with Sweden ensure a regular procession of foreign vehi-cles throughout the summer. So the town's well used to tourists, and you'll find plenty of *pensjonats*, hotels, and other **accommodation**: hotels include the *Albatros*, ul. Kasprowicza 2 (✆23-36), which also has a decent restaurant, the *Bałtyk*, ul. Armii Czerwonej 5 (✆23-91), and the *Atol pensjonat* at ul. Orkana 3 (✆30-10). There's also a summer **youth hostel** at ul. Gdyńska 26 (✆59-61) and a **campground** at ul. Słowackiego 5. For **private rooms** ask at the *Biuro Zakwaterowań* by the waterfront at ul. Armii Czerwonej 14a.

The main **Orbis office**, ul. Armii Czerwonej 2 (Mon–Sat 8am–4pm; ✆22-84), has plenty of maps and information. They also organize excursions into the Woliński National Park—most of which start from Międzyzdroje (a 30-min bus ride east)—and provide timetables for the regular Szczecin–Świnoujście hydrofoil service. In summer **ferries** operate along the coast to Kołobrzeg, Darłówko, Ustka, and other ports: details and reservations from the Warsów marine terminal (✆30-06) or the Orbis office. For **ferry services** to Scandinavia you'll need to contact Orbis or the *Polferries* office in Szczecin, at ul. Wyszyńskiego 28 (Mon–Sat 11am–4:30pm).

Szczecin

The largest city in northwestern Poland, with 400,000 inhabitants, **SZCZECIN** sprawls around the banks of the Odra in a tangle of bridges, cranes and dock machinery: a sort of Polish Newport News. *Szczecin zawsze Polski*—"Szczecin, for ever Polish"—proclaims the billboard on the main road approach, betraying a certain nervousness about the ownership of this long-time German city.

The Slav stronghold established here in the eighth century was taken by the first Piast monarch, Mieszko I, in 967—a point much emphasized in Polish histories. From the early twelfth century Szczecin became the residence of a local branch of Piast princes, rulers of Western Pomerania, but German colonists were already present in force by the time the city joined the Hanseatic League in the mid-thirteenth century. The next key event was the port's capture by the Swedes in 1630, after which it was held by them for nearly a century. Sold to the Prussians in 1720, it remained under Prussian rule until 1945, when it became an outpost on the newly established western frontier. With the border just west of the city limits and Berlin—for which Stettin/Szczecin used to be the port—only an hour's car journey south on the expressway, the German presence is still palpable.

Wartime pummelling destroyed most of the old center, which never received quite the same restorative attention as some less controversially Polish cities. Despite the city's size, there isn't that much to take in—a full day is enough to cover all the main sights.

Arrival, Information, and Accommodation

The central **train station** and the nearby **bus terminal** are located near the water's edge, from where it's a fifteen-minute walk or a quick tram ride up the hill to the town center. For details of the comprehensive **bus and tram** routes you'll need to track down a copy of the rare *Szczecin: plan miasta*.

Szczecin **airport**—chiefly for internal flights but with some international services—is in fact at GOLENIOW (☎27-08), 45km north of the city, with bus services to and from the *LOT* office at al. Wyzwolenia 17 (☎399-26).

For city **information**, the *Pomerania* tourist office at al. Jednosci Narodowej 50 (☎428-32) has all the maps and brochures you might want; they're supposed to be able to help with accommodation, but experience indicates they're not much help in this department. Almatur, ul. Wawrzyniaka 7 (☎233-678), will be able to tell you where the international student hotels are operating—locations are changeable. Orbis, at pl. Zwycięstwa 1 (☎358-08), deals with train tickets.

Finding a Place to Stay

There's a fair spread of **accommodation** in town, ranging from Orbis-run luxury places to very basic hostels, and even in high summer you shouldn't have too much trouble finding a bed for the night.

CHEAP HOTELS

Dom Turysty PTTK, pl. Batorego 2 (☎458-33). Close to the station; noisy and crowded.
Domu Sportu Wojew, ul. Unisławy. (☎222-856). Out of town sports hotel.
Pogoń, ul. Twardowskiego 12 (☎782-78). Basic overnighter, run by a sports club.

MODERATE HOTELS

Gryf, al. Wojska Polskiego 49 (☎340-35). West of downtown; nicest of the mid-range bunch, with colorfully furnished rooms, but not always with private bathrooms.

Piast, pl. Zywcięstwa 3 (☎30-71). Unspectacular rooms in busy central location.

Pomorski, Brama Portowa 4 (☎360-51). Cheaper alternative in same part of town.

EXPENSIVE HOTELS

Arkona, ul. Panieńska 10 (☎360-61). Concrete block right in the middle of town,

Neptun, ul. Matejki 18 (☎240-111). Luxury joint by the water.

Reda, ul. Cukrowa 2 (☎822-461). Another plush option, farther out from the center.

HOSTELS AND CAMPGROUNDS

Ul. Unisławy 26 (☎232-566). Main hostel, on top floor of a school building; open all year. Take tram #2 or #3 to plac Kilińskiego, north of downtown.

Ul. Grodzka 22 (☎894-24). In the center; open July & Aug only.

Ul. Reymonta 23 (☎730-32). Also summer only.

PTTK Camping, ul. Przestrzenna 24 (☎613-264). In Dąbie, 3km east of town—take the local train to Szczecin-Dąbie station. Open May–Sept; tent space and bungalows available.

The City

All of the city's historic sites are located in and around the medieval Old Town, laid out between the river and al. Niepodległości, over the crest of the hill. Beyond Niepodległości stretches the New Town, with its Parisian boulevards radiating out from plac Grunwaldzki.

Climbing the hill from the train station up ul. Dworcowa brings you to plac Zwycięstwa, the largest and busiest central square. On the edge of the square, engulfed by traffic, is the **Harbor Gate** (Brama Portowa), a stately Baroque archway built by the Prussians in 1725 to mark the purchase of the city; a good scrub would do wonders. Back downhill along ul. Wielka brings you to **St James's Cathedral** (św. Jakuba), a massive Gothic brick structure almost totally rebuilt after 1945. Like St Mary's in Gdańsk, the triple-naved interior is a colder place than it used to be, as is emphasized by the delicate vaulting in the only surviving original chapel—one out of a total of thirty. The tower, once 120 meters high, is only half that now: its five-and-a-half-ton bell sits outside by the restored Gothic rectory.

The Castle

North from St James's along ul. Grodzka takes you to the **Castle** of the Pomeranian princes, commanding the river from its hillside perch. A Slav fortified settlement on this spot was replaced in the mid-fourteenth century by a stone structure, the oldest section of the current building. The whole thing was given a Renaissance enlargement in the late sixteenth century, and again remodeled in the 1720s. Princes and dukes aside, the building has been used as a brewery, offices, barracks, and anti-aircraft emplacement—the last function being the direct cause of its flattening in an air raid in 1944. Reconstruction continued into the 1980s; since then it's been turned into a museum and cultural center. Much of the building is closed to the public, the **museum** (Tues–Sun 10am–4pm) occupying scattered parts of the castle.

The fourteenth-century chapel on the ground floor of the north wing has been turned into a concert hall, while the upper floor has several spartan exhibition

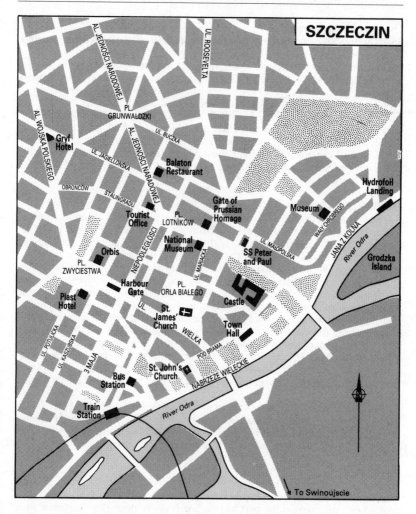

rooms, the principal source of interest being a smattering of contemporary Polish art. The main exhibition rooms are in the three-story west wing, and contain a forgettable display of paintings and *objets d'art*. In the east wing, much of the wall and ceiling decoration has been carefully reworked; most of this section is now taken up by a theater and other cultural facilities. Renaissance tin sarcophagi and the decorated burial vaults of the Pomeranian princes still occupy the cellars, one of the few parts to come through the war intact.

After a visit to the castle café—a popular rendezvous point, lined with pictures of prewar Szczecin—it's worth climbing the **bell tower** for the view over the city, port, and surroundings. If you're here in summer, you might get to hear an open-air concert in the castle square.

The Rynek and Beyond

South of the castle stands the old **Town Hall**, an attractive gabled brick structure looking lost in the concrete surrounding the Rynek. It's an artful reconstruction of the fourteenth-century original, which was given a Baroque face-lift by the Swedes in the 1670s. These days the building serves as a small **museum of local history** (Tues–Sat 10am–4pm). West of the town hall stands the Maiden's Tower, one of very few remaining parts of the town's fifteenth-century fortifications.

Back up the hill along the broad ul. Wyszaka you pass the beguiling four-teenth-century **Saints Peter and Paul**, a Gothic church built on the site of one established by Polish missionaries in the early twelfth century. In a rich ensemble of original ornamental detail the most striking elements are the seventeenth-century memorial tablets, the German inscriptions reminding you of the city's Teutonic heritage.

The National Museum

A little farther north on plac Zolnierza Polskiego stands another Germanic monument, the Baroque **Gate of Prussian Homage**, its sculpted arches echoing the Harbor Gate. Across the square on the corner of ul. Staromlyńska rises an elegant Baroque palace, formerly the Pomeranian parliament and now home of a section of the **National Museum** (Tues & Wed 10am–5pm, Thurs–Sun 10am–4pm). The main building is devoted to Pomeranian art and sculpture from the thirteenth to sixteenth centuries, highlighting an impressive array of medieval Pomeranian sculpture and expressive Gothic triptychs. Later sections emphasise Polish painters, with a perhaps tokenistic German work thrown in occasionally.

Works from the nineteenth century and onward are on display across the road. The ground floor features several important Polish artists, most notably Waliczewski, Merkel, and the broodingly introspective Jacek Malczewski. Upstairs there's plenty of 1970s Polish sci-fi art by popular artists like Ryszard Szymański, alongside an evocative collection of paintings by local artists on sea-based themes.

Back towards the river and north along Wały Chrobrego—a showpiece boulevard lined with towering prewar German buildings—there's another section of the National Museum (same hours), this one devoted to maritime history, notably the seafaring culture of the early Pomeranian Slavs.

The Harbor

Szczecin is one of the largest ports on the Baltic, with a highly developed shipping industry, and you'll appreciate the essence of the city more fully if you take a **boat trip** around the port and harbor. Two- to three-hour excursions set out from the **Dworzec Morski** terminal, north from Wały Chrobrego, from where there are also regular boat and hydrofoil departures across the vast Szczecin lagoon to Świnoujście. The border with Germany cuts across the middle of the lagoon, but the demise of the GDR means this isn't the source of tension it used to be for local sailing enthusiasts.

Eating, Drinking, and Entertainment

Though the city is no great gastronomic center, it does have a fair number of restaurants, and there will doubtless be additions as the new penchant for private ventures begins to take effect. As usual, places close early—even on weekends expecting anything after 9pm is chancing your luck, except in the Orbis hotels *Arkona, Nepun,* and *Reda* (addresses p.340), where you should be all right for a meal till 10:30pm. If you discount the ghastly hotel nightspots, bars are in shorter supply, but the students in town provide some action during semester.

Restaurants

Balaton, pl. Lotników 3. Respectable offerings of Hungarian nosh and wine.
Chief, ul. Świerczewskiego 18. Just off pl. Grunwaldzki. Good selection of fish dishes.
Gryf, al. Wojska Polskiego 49. Reasonable hotel restaurant.
Jasołka, ul. Królowej Jadwigi. Established private venture; closes early.
Ryska, al. Piastów 16. Russian and Lithuanian specialties.
Tulska, ul. Jagiellońska 7. Traditional Polish fare.

Bars

U Wyszaka, pl. Rzepichy. Trendy upscale hang-out in the old town hall cellars.
Bajka, ul. Niepodległości 30. Boozy local nightspot.
Ali-Baba, al. Jednosci Narodowej 43. Archetypal "drink bar."
Zamkowa, ul. Rycerska. *Kawiarnia* inside the castle.

Nightlife

There are a number of student clubs, the top outlets being the *Pod Wiezą* at ul. Rybacka 1, and the place at Wawrzyniaka 7a; details of where the current action is can be obtained from the Almatur office.

The *National Filharmonia,* pl. Dzierzińskiego 1, has a regular program of **classical music** concerts. The local press and main tourist office will have details of other events.

Stargard Szczeciński

A thirty-kilometer bus or train ride east of Szczecin takes you to **STARGARD SZCZECIŃSKI,** a largish industrial center straddling a tributary of the Odra. An old Pomeranian settlement on the trade routes to the coast, the town was almost completely destroyed in 1945, but the medieval center was carefully reconstructed after the war and gives ample evidence of a prosperous past.

The Old Town

From the station it's a short bus ride to the old town, encircled by stone **walls,** most of which somehow survived the war intact, Gothic gates and bastions included. In among the newer buildings on the **Rynek** are a number of impressive reconstructed burghers' houses, and at the center of it all the mid-sixteenth-century **Town Hall,** topped by a lavish Renaissance gable capped with terra-cotta tracery.

Even better is the Gothic parish church of **St Mary,** a hall-like late thirteenth-century structure subsequently enlarged with an ambulatory and octagonal chapel devoted to the Virgin. The exterior is studded with ceramics, while the interior has a wonderful vaulted ceiling supported by high brick arches. An offbeat sense of humor is revealed in the long-mouthed figures in the Virgin chapel, counterpointing the poker-faced saints and other worthies on the chapel's ceiling bosses.

Practicalities

For **tourist information**, check out the Orbis office at Rynek Staromeijski 5 on the main square. There's just one hotel in town, the *Morena* at ul. Czarnieckiego 15 (☎77-64-63), though additional accommodation is provided by a PTTK **hostel** at ul. Kuśnierzy (☎731-91), and an all-year **youth hostel** at ul. 1-go Maja 9 (☎77-67-77).

For a bite to eat, the **café-restaurant** across the road from the church will do the honors.

travel details

Trains

Poznań to Białystok (1 daily; 10hr 30min; couchettes); Bydgoszcz (12 daily; 2hr–2hr 30 min); Częstochowa (8 daily; 4–6hr); Gdańsk (7 daily; 4hr); Gniezno (hourly; 1hr); Inowrocław (12 daily; 2hr); Jelenia Góra (5 daily; 5–6hr); Kalisz (5 daily; 2hr 30min–3hr 30min); Katowice (15 daily; 5–6hr); Kołobrzeg (5 daily; 5hr); Kraków (8 daily; 7hr); Leszno (34 daily, 1hr–1hr 30min); Łódź (7 daily; 4–5hr); Olsztyn (4 daily; 4hr 30min–6hr); Opole (9 daily; 3hr 30min–4hr 30 min); Przemyśl (3 daily; 11–13hr; couchettes); Rzeszów (3 daily; 10–11hr; couchettes); Słupsk (4 daily; 5–7hr); Szczecin (18 daily; 3–4hr); Świnoujście (7 daily; 4–5hr); Toruń (8 daily; 2hr 30min–3hr); Wałbrzych (4 daily; 4–5hr); Warsaw (20 daily; 4–5hr); Wrocław (26 daily; 2hr–3hr 30 min); Zakopane (2 daily; 11–13hr; couchettes); Zielona Góra (6 daily; 2hr 30min–3hr). Also **international connections** to Berlin, Leningrad, Moscow, and Riga.

Kalisz to Białystok (1 daily; 8hr); Jelenia Góra (4 daily; 5–6hr 30min); Legnica (5 daily; 4hr 30min–5hr 30 min); Leszno (3 daily; 2hr 30 min); Lublin (3 daily; 7hr); Łódź (25 daily; 1hr 30min–2hr); Poznań (6 daily; 2hr 30min–3hr 30 min); Szczecin (2 daily; 6hr); Wałbrzych (4 daily 4–5hr); Warsaw (11 daily; 3hr–4hr 30 min); Wrocław (14 daily; 2hr–3hr 30 min); Zielona Góra (3 daily; 4–5hr).

Leszno to Białystock (1 daily; 12hr); Bydgoszcz (5 daily; 3hr 30min–4hr 30 min); Gdańsk (6 daily; 5hr 30min–6hr 30 min); Jelenia Góra (4 daily; 4hr–4hr 30min); Kalisz (3 daily; 3hr 30min); Katowice (6 daily; 4hr 30min–5hr 30min); Kraków (4 daily; 6hr 30min); Łódź (3 daily; 4hr); Olsztyn (2 daily 6-8hr; couchettes); Opole (9 daily; 2hr 30min–3hr 30 min); Poznań (36 daily; 1hr–1hr 30min); Przemyśl (1 daily; 10hr 30min; couchettes); Rzeszów (1 daily; 9hr; couchettes); Słupsk (2 daily; 7hr 30min–8hr 30min; couchettes); Szczecin (7 daily; 5–6hr); Świnoujście (1 daily; 6hr); Toruń (2 daily; 3–4hr); Wałbrzych (4 daily; 3–4hr); Warsaw (2 daily; 6hr); Wrocław (26 daily; 1hr 30min–2hr); Zakopane (1 daily; 10hr; couchettes); Zielona Góra (2 daily; 2hr).

Bydgoszcz to Częstochowa (5 daily; 5–6hr); Gdańsk (hourly; 2hr); Kołobrzeg (8 daily; 5hr); Kraków (3 daily; 7–8hr); Łódź Kaliska (11 daily; 3–4hr); Poznań (11 daily; 2–4hr); Szczecin (2–3 daily; 4–6hr); Toruń (hourly; 40min); Warsaw (6 daily; 4–5hr).

Słupsk to Gdańsk (12 daily; 2–4hr); Kołobrzeg (4 daily; 2–2hr 30min); Koszalin (hourly; 1hr); Szczecin (9 daily; 3–4hr); local trains to Ustka (via Sławno) and Darłowo.

Kołobrzeg to Bydgoszcz (6 daily; 5hr); Gdańsk (4 daily; 4–5hr); Koszalin (9 daily; 1hr); Szczecin (4 daily; 4–5hr); Warsaw (8 daily; 8–10hr).

Kamień Pomorski to Szczecin (1 daily; 2hr 30min).

Świnoujście (all via Szczecin) to Kraków (2 daily; 12–13hr; sleeper); Poznań (7 daily; 4–5hr); Szczecin (18 daily; 2hr–2hr 30min); Warsaw (3 daily; 8–10hr; sleeper).

Szczecin to Bydgoszcz (3 daily; 4–5hr); Gdańsk (7 daily; 5–6hr); Kołobrzeg (6 daily; 3–4hr); Kraków (6 daily; 10–11hr); Łódź (4 daily; 6–7hr); Poznań (20 daily; 3–4hr); Słupsk (9 daily; 3–4hr); Świnoujście (20 daily; 2hr–2hr 30min); Warsaw (7 daily; 5–8hr; sleeper).

Szczecinek to Czaplinek (8 daily; 1hr); Kołobrzeg (4 daily; 2hr–2hr 30min).

Buses

Poznań to Kórnik/Rogalin/Mosina, Gniezno, and Kalisz.

Gniezno to Gąsawa (for Biskupin), Mogilno, Znin/Bydgoszcz.

Leszno to Gołuchów/Kalisz.

Bydgoszcz to Toruń, Chojnice, and Szczecinek.

Szczecinek to Czaplinek, Słupsk, and Szczecin.

Łeba to Słupsk and Gdańsk.

Słupsk to Darłowo, Ustka, and Koszalin.

Kołobrzeg to the coast (Sarbinowo, Mielno), Kamień Pomorski, and Świnoujście.

Kamień Pomorski to Świnoujście, Wolin, Szczecin, and Kołobrzeg.

Świnoujście to Wolin, Międzyzdroje, and Szczecin Kołobrzeg via Trzebiatów.

Szczecin to Stargard Szczeciński, Wolin, and Świnoujście.

PART THREE

THE
CONTEXTS

THE HISTORICAL FRAMEWORK

No other European country has had so checkered a history as Poland. At its mightiest, it has been a huge common-wealth stretching deep into what is now the Soviet Union; at its nadir, it has been a nation that existed only as an ideal, its neighbors having on two occasions conspired to wipe it off the map. Yet, despite all this, a distinctive Polish culture has survived and developed with-out interruption for more than a millennium.

THE BEGINNINGS

The great plain that is present-day Poland, stretching from the Odra (or Oder) River in the west all the way to the Russian steppes, has been inhabited since the Stone Age. For thou-sands of years it was home to numerous tribes—some nomadic, others settlers—whose traces have made Poland a particularly fruitful land for archaeologists. Lying beyond the frontiers of the Roman Empire, it did not sustain anything more socially advanced than a tribal culture until a relatively late date.

The exact period when this plain was first settled by **Slav** tribes is uncertain, but it may have been as late as the eighth century. Although diffuse, the various Slavs groups

shared a common culture—certainly to a far greater extent than is true of the Germanic tribes to the west—and the Polish language can be said to have existed before the Polish state.

It was the **Polonians** (the "people of the open fields"), based on the banks of the Warta River between Poznań and Gniezno, who were ultimately responsible for the forging of a recognizable nation, which thereafter bore their name. From the early ninth century, they were ruled by the **Piast dynasty**, whose early history is shrouded in legend, but emerges into something more substantial with the begin-nings of recorded history in the second half of the tenth century.

In 965, the Piast **Mieszko I** married the sister of the Duke of Bohemia, and underwent public baptism, thus placing himself under the protection of the papacy. Mieszko's motives appear to have been political: Otto the Great, the Holy Roman Emperor, had extended Germany's border to the Odra and would have had little difficulty in justifying a push east-ward against a pagan state. By 990, Mieszko had succeeded in uniting his tribal area, hence-forth known as Wielkopolska (Great Poland), with that of the Vistulanian tribe, which took the name of Małopolska (Little Poland). Silesia, settled by yet another Slav tribe, became the third component of this embryonic Polish state.

Mieszko's policies were carried to their logi-cal conclusion by his warrior son **Bolesław the Brave**. In 1000 the Emperor Otto III was dispatched by the pope to pay tribute to the relics of the Czech saint Adalbert, which Bolesław had acquired. During his stay, he crowned Bolesław with his own crown, thus renouncing German designs on Polish territory. Subsequently, Bolesław established control over Pomerania, Kujawy, and Mazovia; he also gained and lost Bohemia, and began Poland's own easterly drive, pushing as far as Kiev. The name "Poland" now came into general use, and its status as a fully fledged kingdom was underlined by Bolesław's decision to undergo a second coronation in 1022.

PIAST POLAND

By the middle of the eleventh century, Małopolska had become the center of the nation's affairs and Kraków had replaced Gniezno as capital, owing to Wielkopolska's vulnerability to the expansionist Czechs and Germans. Political authority was in any case overshadowed by the **power of the Church**: when Bishop Stanisław of Kraków was murdered in 1079 on the orders of Bolesław the Generous, the clergy not only gained a national saint whose cult quickly spread, but also succeeded in dethroning the king.

In the early twelfth century, centralized monarchical power made a comeback under **Bolesław the Wrymouth**, who regained Pomerania—which had become an independent duchy—and repulsed German designs on Silesia. However, he undid his lifetime's work by his decision to divide his kingdom among his sons: for the rest of the century and beyond, Poland lacked central authority and was riven by feuds as successive members of the Piast dynasty jostled for control over the key provinces. Pomerania fell to Denmark, while Silesia began a long process of fragmentation, becoming increasingly Germanic.

In 1225 Duke Konrad of Mazovia, under threat from the heathen Prussians, Jacwingians, and Lithuanians on his eastern border, invited the **Teutonic Knights**, a quasi-monastic German military order, to help him secure his frontiers. The Knights duly based themselves in Chełmno, and by 1283 they had effectively eradicated the Prussians. Emerging as the principal military power in mainland Europe, the Knights built up a theocratic state defended by some of the most awesome castles ever built, ruthlessly turning on their former hosts in the process. They captured the great port of Gdańsk in 1308, renaming it Danzig and developing it into one of Europe's richest mercantile cities. At the same time, German peasants were encouraged to settle on the fertile agricultural land all along the Baltic. Poland was left cut off from the sea, with its trading routes severely weakened as a result.

If the Teutonic Knights brought nothing but disaster to the Polish nation, the effects of the **Tartar invasions** of 1241–42 were more mixed. Although the Poles were decisively defeated at the Battle of Legnica, the Tartars' crushing of the Kiev-based Russian empire paved the way for Polish expansion eastward into White and Red Ruthenia (the forerunners of Byelorussia and Ukraine), whose principalities were often linked to Poland by dynastic marriages. On the down side, the defeat

spelled the beginning of the end for Silesia as part of Poland. It gradually split into eighteen tiny duchies under the control of Bohemia, then the most powerful part of the Holy Roman Empire.

KAZIMIERZ THE GREAT

It was only under the last Piast king, **Kazimierz the Great** (1333–70), that central political authority was firmly re-established in Poland. Kraków took on some aspects of its present appearance during his reign, being embellished with a series of magnificent buildings to substantiate its claim to be a great European capital. It was also made the seat of a university, the first in the country and before long one of the most prestigious in the continent. Kazimierz's achievements in **domestic policy** went far beyond the symbolic: he codified Poland's laws, created a unified administrative structure with a governor responsible for each province, and introduced a new silver currency.

With regard to **Poland's frontiers**, Kazimierz was a supreme pragmatist. He secured his borders with a line of stone castles, and formally recognized Bohemia's control over Silesia in return for a renunciation of its claim to the Polish crown. More reluctantly, he accepted the existence of the independent state of the Teutonic Knights, even though that meant Poland was now landlocked. To compensate, he extended his territories eastward into Red Ruthenia and Podolia, which meant that, although the Catholic Church retained its prominent role, the country now had sizable Eastern Orthodox and Armenian minorities.

Even more significant was Kazimierz's encouragement of **Jews**, who had been the victims of pogroms all over Europe, often being held responsible for the Black Death. A law of 1346 specifically protected them against persecution in Poland, and was a major factor in Poland's centuries-long position as the home for the largest community of world Jewry.

THE JAGIELLONIANS

On Kazimierz's death, the crown passed to his nephew Louis of Anjou, King of Hungary, but this royal union was short-lived, as the Poles chose Louis' younger daughter **Jadwiga** to succeed him in 1384, whereas her sister ascended the Hungarian throne. This event was important for two reasons. Firstly, it was an assertion of power on the part of the aristocracy and the beginnings of the move towards an elected monarchy. Secondly, it led soon afterwards to the most important and enduring alliance in Polish history—with **Lithuania**, whose Grand Duke, **Jagiełło**, married Jadwiga in 1386. Europe's last pagan nation, Lithuania had resisted the Teutonic Knights and developed into an expansionist state which now stretched from its Baltic homeland all the way to the Crimea.

After Jadwiga's death in 1399, Jagiełło ruled the two nations alone for the next 45 years, founding the Jagiellonian dynasty—which was to remain in power until 1572—with the offspring of his subsequent marriage. One of the first benefits of the union between the two countries was a military strength capable of taking the offensive against the Teutonic Knights, and at the **Battle of Grunwald** in 1410, the Order was defeated, beginning its long and slow decline. A more decisive breakthrough came as a result of the **Thirteen Years' War** of 1454–66. By the Treaty of Toruń, the Knights' territory was partitioned: Danzig became an independent city-state, run by a merchant class of predominantly German, Dutch, and Flemish origin, but accepting the Polish king as its nominal overlord; the remainder of the Knights' heartlands around the Wisła (Vistula) became subject to Poland under the name of Royal Prussia; and the Order was left only with the eastern territory thereafter known as Ducal Prussia or East Prussia, where it established its new headquarters in the city of Königsberg.

Towards the end of the fifteenth century, Poland and Lithuania began to face new dangers from the east. First to threaten were the Crimean Tartars, whose menace prompted the creation of the first Polish standing army. A far more serious threat—one which endured for several hundred years—came from the **Muscovite czars**, the self-styled protectors of the Orthodox faith who aimed to "liberate" the Ruthenian principalities and rebuild the Russian empire which had been destroyed by the Mongol Tartars. The Jagiellonians countered by building up their power in the west. The Bohemian crown was acquired by clever politicking in 1479 after the religious struggles of the Hussite Wars; that of Hungary followed

in 1491. However, neither of these unions managed to last.

THE RENAISSANCE AND REFORMATION

The spread of **Renaissance** ideas in Poland—greatly facilitated by the country's religious connections with Italy—was most visibly manifested in the large number of Italianate buildings constructed throughout the country, but science and learning also prospered under native Polish practitioners such as Nicolaus Copernicus.

This period saw a collective muscle-flexing exercise by the Polish nobility (*szlachta*). In 1493, the parliament or **Sejm** was established, gaining the sole right to enact legislation in 1505 and gradually making itself an important check on monarchical power.

The **Reformation** had a far greater impact on Poland than is often admitted by Catholic patriots. Its most telling manifestation came in 1525, with the final collapse of the Teutonic Order when the Grand Master, Albrecht von Hohenzollern, decided to accept the new Lutheran doctrines. Their state was converted into a secular duchy under the Polish crown but with full internal autonomy—an arrangement that was to be disastrous for Poland in the long term, but which removed any lingering military strength from the Order. Lutheranism also took a strong hold in Danzig and the German-dominated cities of Royal Prussia, while the more radical Calvinism won many converts among the Lithuanian nobility. Poland also became home for a number of refugee sects; along with the acceptance already extended to the Jewish and Orthodox faiths, this added up to a degree of religious tolerance unparalleled elsewhere in Europe.

THE REPUBLIC OF NOBLES

Lacking an heir, the last of the Jagiellonians, **Zygmunt August**, spent his final years trying to forge an alliance strong enough to withstand the ever-growing might of Moscow. The result of his negotiations was the 1569 **Union of Lublin**, whereby Poland, Royal Prussia, Livonia (subsequently Latvia) and Lithuania were formally merged into a commonwealth. In the same year the Sejm moved to Warsaw, a more central location for the capital of this new agglomeration; its capital status became official in 1596.

On the death of Zygmunt August in 1572, the Royal Chancellor, Jan Zamoyski, presided over negotiations which led to the creation of the so-called **Republic of Nobles**: thenceforth kings were to be elected by an assembly of the entire nobility, from the great magnates down to holders of tiny impoverished estates. On the one hand this was a major democratic advance, in that it enfranchised about ten percent of the population, by far the largest proportion of voters in any European country; on the other hand it marked a strengthening of a **feudalistic social system**. Capitalism, then developing in other European countries, evolved only in those cities with a strong German or Jewish burgher class(predominantly in Royal Prussia), which remained isolated from the main power structures of Polish society.

In 1573, the Frenchman Henri Valois was chosen as the first elected monarch, and, as was the case with all his successors, was forced to sign a document which reduced him to a managerial servant of the nobility. The nobles also insisted on their **Right of Resistance**—a license to overthrow a king who had fallen from favor. The Sejm had to be convened at two-yearly intervals, while all royal taxes, declarations of war and foreign treaties were subject to ratification by the nobles.

Although candidates for the monarchy had to subscribe to Catholicism, the religious freedom which already existed was underpinned by the **Compact of Warsaw** of 1573, guaranteeing the constitutional equality of all religions. However, the Counter-Reformation left only a few Protestant strongholds in Poland: a large section of the aristocracy was re-converted, while others who had recently switched from Orthodoxy to Calvinism were persuaded to change allegiance once more. The Orthodox Church was further weakened by the schism of 1596, leading to the creation of the Uniate Church, which recognized the authority of Rome. Thus Poland gradually became a fervently Catholic nation once more.

The Republic of Nobles achieved some spectacular successes early on, particularly under the second elected king, the Transylvanian prince **Stefan Bathory**. Having carried out a thorough reform of the army, he waged a brilliant campaign against the Russians in 1579–82, neutralizing this particular threat to Poland's eastern borders for some time to come.

THE WAZA DYNASTY AND ITS AFTERMATH

The foreign policy of the next three elected monarchs, all members of the Swedish **Waza** dynasty, was less fortunate. Zygmunt August Waza, the first of the trio, was a Catholic bigot, and soon came into conflict with the almost exclusively Protestant population of his native land, and was deposed in Sweden in 1604. Though his ham-handedness meant that Poland now had a new (and increasingly powerful) enemy, he continued as the Polish king for the next 28 years, having fought off a three-year-long internal rebellion.

In 1618, Poland's situation became even more precarious, as John Sigismund von Hohenzollern inherited Ducal Prussia as well as the Electorate of Brandenburg. A couple of decades later, the Hohenzollerns inherited much of Pomerania as well, with another section being acquired by Sweden. Poland managed to remain neutral in the calamitous series of religious and dynastic conflicts known as the **Thirty Years' War**, from which Sweden emerged as Europe's leading military power.

The reign of the third of the Wazas, **Jan Kazimierz**, saw Poland's fortunes plummet. In 1648, the year of his election, the Cossacks revolted in the Ukraine, eventually allying themselves with the Russian army, which conquered eastern Poland as far as Lwów. This diversion inspired the Swedes to launch an invasion of their own, known in Polish history as the "Swedish Deluge," and they soon took control of the remainder of the country. A heroic counterattack was mounted, ending in stalemate in 1660 with the Treaty of Oliwa, in which Poland recovered its former territories except for Livonia. Three years earlier, the Hohenzollerns had wrested Ducal Prussia from the last vestiges of Polish control, merging it with their other territories to form the state of Brandenburg-Prussia (later shortened to Prussia).

As well as the territorial losses suffered, these wars had seen Poland's population reduced to four million, less than half its previous total. Another crucial development of this period had been the first use in 1652 of the **liberum veto**, whereby a single vote in the Sejm against a measure was enough to cancel it. In principle, the nobility governed the republic as a sort of collective conscience in a wholly disinterested manner—and thus would be expected to act with unanimity. The first time someone objected to a measure, there was some debate as to whether his veto was sufficient to override the will of the majority: once it had been ruled that indeed it was, the practice soon became widespread in the protection of petty interests, and Poland found itself on the slippery slope down toward ungovernability. This process was hastened when it was discovered that one dissenter was constitutionally empowered to object not only to any particular measure, but to dissolve the Sejm itself—and in the process repeal all the legislation it had passed. Meanwhile, the minor aristocracy gradually found themselves squeezed out of power, as a group of a hundred or so great **magnates** gradually established a stranglehold.

JAN SOBIESKI

Before repeated use of the *liberum veto* led to the final collapse of political authority, Poland had what was arguably its greatest moment of glory in international power politics—a consequence of the **Ottoman Turks'** overrunning of the Balkans. They were eventually beaten back by the Poles, under the command of **Jan Sobieski**, at the Battle of Chocim in 1673—as a reward for which Sobieski was elected king the following year. In 1683 he was responsible for the successful **defense of Vienna**, which marked the final repulse of the Turks from Western Europe.

However, Poland was to pay a heavy price for the heroism of Sobieski, who had concentrated on the Turkish campaign to the exclusion of all other issues at home and abroad. His relief of Vienna exhausted Poland's military capacity while enabling Austria to recover as an imperial power; it also greatly helped the rise of the predatory state of Prussia, which he had intended to keep firmly in check. His neglect of domestic policy led to the *liberum veto* being used with impunity, while Poland and Lithuania grew apart as the nobility of the latter engaged in a civil war.

THE DECLINE OF POLAND

Known as "Augustus the Strong" owing to his fathering of over 300 children, Sobieski's successor, **Augustus Wettin**, was in fact a weak ruler, unable to shake off his debts to the Russians who had secured his election. In 1701

Friedrich III of Brandenburg-Prussia openly defied him by declaring Ducal Prussia's right to be regarded as a kingdom, having himself crowned in Königsberg. From then on, the Hohenzollerns plotted to link their territories by ousting Poland from the Baltic; in this they were aided by the acquisition of most of the rest of Pomerania in 1720. Augustus's lack of talent for power politics was even more evident in his dealings with Sweden, against whom he launched a war for control of Livonia. The conflict showed the calamitous decline of Poland's military standing, and the victorious Swedes deposed Augustus in 1704, securing the election of their own favored candidate, **Stanisław Leszczyński**, in his place.

Augustus was reinstated in 1710, courtesy of the Russians, who effectively reduced Poland to the role of a **client state** in the process. The "Silent Sejm" of 1717, which guaranteed the existing constitution, marked the end of effective parliamentary life. The Russians never hesitated to impose their authority, cynically upholding the Republic of Nobles as a means of ensuring that the liberal ideals of the Age of Reason could never take root in Poland, and that the country remained a buffer against the great powers of Western Europe. When Leszczyński won the election to succeed Augustus the Strong in 1733, they intervened almost immediately to have him replaced by the deceased king's son, who proved to be an even more inept custodian of Polish interests than his father. Leszczyński was forced into exile, spending the last thirty years of his life as the Duke of Lorraine.

When the younger Augustus Wettin died in 1763, the Russians again intervened to ensure the election of **Stanisław-August Poniatowski**, the former lover of their empress, Catherine the Great. However, Poniatowski proved an unwilling stooge, even espousing the cause of reform. Russian support of the Orthodox minority in Poland led to a growth of Catholic-inspired nationalism, and by obstructing the most moderately liberal measures, Russian policy led to an outbreak of revolts. By sending armies to crush these, they endangered the delicate balance of power in Eastern Europe.

In 1740 Frederick the Great launched the **Silesian Wars**, which ended in 1763 with Prussia in control of all but a small part of the province. As a result, Prussia gained control over such parts of Poland's foreign trade as were not subject to Russia. The long-cherished ambition to acquire Royal Prussia and thus achieve uninterrupted control over the Baltic's southern coast was Frederick's next objective.

THE PARTITIONS

Russia's Polish policy was finally rendered impotent by the revolt of the **Confederacy of Bar** in 1768–72. A heavy-handed crackdown on these reformers would certainly have led to war with Prussia, probably in alliance with Austria; doing nothing would have allowed the Poles to reassert their national independence. As a compromise, the Russians decided to support a Prussian plan for the **Partition of Poland**. By a treaty of 1772, Poland lost almost thirty percent of her territory. White Ruthenia's eastern sectors were ceded to Russia, while Austria received Red Ruthenia plus Małopolska south of the Wisła—a province subsequently rechristened Galicia. The Prussians gained the smallest share of the carve-up in the form of most of Royal Prussia, but this was strategically and economically the most significant.

Stung by this, the Poles embarked on a radical program of reform, including the partial emancipation of serfs and the encouragement of immigration from the three empires which had undertaken the Partition. In 1791, Poland was given the first **codified constitution** in Europe since Classical antiquity and the second in the modern world, after the United States. It introduced the concept of a people's sovereignty, this time including the bourgeoisie, and adopted a separation of powers between executive, legislature, and judiciary, with government by a cabinet responsible to the Sejm.

This was all too much for the Russians, who, buying off the Prussians with the promise of Danzig, invaded Poland. Despite a tenacious resistance under **Tadeusz Kościuszko**, erstwhile hero of the American War of Independence, the Poles were defeated the following year. By the **Second Partition** of 1793, the constitution was annulled; the Russians annexed the remaining parts of White and Red Ruthenia, with the Prussians gaining Wielkopolska, parts of Mazuria, and Toruń in addition to the star prize of Danzig. This time the Austrians held back and missed out on the spoils.

In 1794, Kościuszko launched a national **insurrection**, achieving a stunning victory over the Russians at the Battle of Racławice with a militia largely composed of peasants armed with scythes. However, the rebellion was put down, Poniatowski forced to abdicate, and Poland wiped off the map by the **Third Partition** of 1795. This gave all lands east of the Bug and Niemen rivers to Russia, the remainder of Małopolska to Austria, and Prussia the rest of the country, including Warsaw. By an additional treaty of 1797, the Partitioning powers agreed to abolish the very name of Poland.

NAPOLEON AND THE CONGRESS OF VIENNA

Revolutionary France was naturally the country that Polish patriots looked to in their struggle to regain national independence, and Paris became the headquarters for a series of exiles and conspiratorial groups. Hopes eventually crystalized around **Napoleon Bonaparte**, who assumed power in 1799, but when three Polish legions were raised as part of the French army, Kościuszko declined to command them, regarding Napoleon as a megalomaniac who would use the Poles for his own ends.

Initially, these fears seemed unfounded: French victories over Prussia led to the creation of the **Duchy of Warsaw** in 1807 out of Polish territory annexed by the Prussians. Although no more than a buffer state, this seemed an important first step in the re-creation of Poland, and encouraged the hitherto uncommitted **Józef Poniatowski**, nephew of the last king and one of the most brilliant military commanders of the day, to throw in his lot with the French dictator. As a result of his successes in Napoleon's Austrian campaign of 1809, part of Galicia was ceded to the Duchy of Warsaw.

Poniatowski again played a key role in the events of 1812, which Napoleon dubbed his "Polish War," and which restored the historic border of Poland-Lithuania with Russia. The failure of the advance on Moscow, leading to a humiliating retreat, was thus as disastrous for Poland as for France. Cornered by the Prussians and Russians near Leipzig, Poniatowski refused to surrender, preferring to lead his troops to a heroic, suicidal defeat. The choice faced by Poniatowski encapsulated the nation's hopeless plight, and his act of self-sacrifice was to serve as a potent symbol to Polish patriots for the rest of the century.

The **Congress of Vienna** of 1814–15, set up to organize post-Napoleonic Europe, decided against the re-establishment of an independent Poland, mainly because this was opposed by the Russians. Instead, the main part of the Duchy of Warsaw was renamed the **Congress Kingdom** and placed under the dominion of the Russian czar. The Poznań area was detached to form the **Grand Duchy of Posen**, in reality no more than a dependency of Prussia. Austria was allowed to keep most of Galicia, which was governed from Lwów (renamed Lemberg). After much deliberation, it was decided to make Kraków a city-state and "symbolic capital" of the vanished nation.

THE ARMED STRUGGLE AGAINST THE PARTITIONERS

The most liberal part of the Russian Empire, the Congress Kingdom enjoyed a period of relative prosperity under the governorship of **Adam Czartoryski**, preserving its own parliament, administration, educational system, and army. However, this cosy arrangement was disrupted by the arch-autocrat Nicholas I, who became czar in 1825 and quickly imposed his policies on Poland. An attempted **insurrection** in **November 1830**, centered on a botched assassination of the czar's brother, provoked a Russian invasion. Initially, the Polish army fared well, but was handicapped by political divisions (notably over whether the serfs should be emancipated) and lack of foreign support, despite the supposed guarantees provided by the Vienna settlement. By the end of the following year, the Poles had been defeated; their constitution was suspended and a reign of repression began. These events led many to abandon all nationalist hopes: the first great wave of Polish **emigration**, principally to America, began soon after.

An attempted insurrection against the Austrians in 1846 also backfired, leading to the end of Kraków's independence with its re-incorporation into Galicia. This setback was a factor in Poland's failure to play an active role in the European-wide revolutions of 1848–49, though by this time the country's plight had attracted the sympathy of the emergent socialist movements. Karl Marx and Friedrich Engels went so far as to declare that Polish liberation should be single most important immediate objective of the workers' movement. The last major **uprising**, against the Russians in 1863–64, attracted the support of Lithuanians and Galicians, but was hopelessly limited by Poland's lack of a regular army. Its failure led to the abolition of the Congress Kingdom and its formal incorporation into Russia as the province of "Vistulaland." However, it was immediately followed by the **emancipation of the serfs**, granted on more favorable terms than in any other part of the Czarist empire—in order to cause maximum ill-feeling between the Polish nobility and peasantry.

CULTURAL AND POLITICAL RESISTANCE

Following the crushing of the 1863–64 rebellion, the Russian sector of Poland entered a period of quiet stability, with the abolition of internal tariffs opening up the vast Russian market to Polish goods. For the next half-century, Polish patriots, wherever they lived, were concerned less with trying to win independence than with keeping a distinctive **culture** alive. In this they were handicapped by the fact that this was an era of great empires, each with many subjugated minorities whose interests often conflicted: Poles found themselves variously up against the aspirations of Lithuanians, Ukrainians, and Czechs. They had the greatest success in Galicia, because they were the second largest ethnic group in the Habsburg Empire, and because the Habsburgs had a more lax attitude towards the diversity of their subjects. The province was given powers of self-government and, although economically backward and ruled by a reactionary upper class, flourished once more as a center of learning and the arts.

Altogether different was the situation in Prussia, the most efficiently repressive of the three partitioning powers. It had closely followed the British lead in forging a modern industrial society, and Poles made up a large percentage of the workforce in some of its technologically most advanced areas, notably the rich minefields of Upper Silesia. The Prussians, having ousted the Austrians from their centuries-long domination of German affairs, proceeded to exclude their rivals altogether from the **united Germany** they created by 1871, which they attempted to mold in their own Protestant and militaristic tradition.

For the Poles living under the Prussian yoke, the price to be paid for their relative prosperity was a severe clampdown on their culture, seen at its most extreme in the **Kulturkampf**, whose main aim was to crush the power of the Catholic church, with a secondary intention of establishing the unchallenged supremacy of the German language in the new nation's educational system. It misfired badly in Poland, giving the clergy the opportunity to whip up support for their own fervently nationalistic brand of Catholicism.

Meanwhile, an upswing in political life came with the establishment, in response to internal pressure, of representative assemblies in Berlin, Vienna, and St Petersburg. Toward the end of the century, this led to the formation of various new Polish **political parties and movements**, the most important of which were: the Polish Socialist Party (PPS), active mainly in the cities of Russian Poland; the Nationalist League, whose power base was in the peripheral provinces; the Peasant Movement of Galicia; and the Christian Democrats, a dominant force among the Silesian Catholics.

THE RESURRECTION OF POLAND

World War I smashed the might of the Russian, German, and Austrian empires and allowed Poland to rise from the dead. Desperate to rally Poles to their cause, both alliances in the conflict made increasingly tempting offers: as early as August 1914 the Russians proposed a Poland with full rights of self-government, including language, religion, and government, albeit one still ultimately subject to the czar.

When the German and Austrian armies overran Russian-occupied Poland in 1916, they felt obliged to trump this offer, promising to set up a **Polish kingdom** once the war was over. The foundations of this were laid immediately, with the institution of an interim administration—known as the Regency Council—and the official restoration of the Polish language. Even though carried out for cynical reasons, these initial steps were of crucial importance to the re-launch of a fully independent Poland, a notion which had soon gained the support of the US President Woodrow Wilson and of the new Bolshevik government in Moscow.

Meanwhile two bitter rivals had emerged as the leading contenders for leadership of the Polish nation. **Józef Piłsudski**, an impoverished noble from Lithuania and founding member of the PPS, had long championed a military solution to Poland's problems. During the war, his legions fought on behalf of the Germans, assuming that the defeat of the Russians would allow him to create the new Polish state on his own terms. In this, he favored a return to the great tradition of ethnic and religious diversity of centuries past. **Roman Dmowski**, leader of the Nationalist League, represented the ambitions of the new middle class and had a vision of a purely Polish and staunchly Catholic future, in which the Jews would, as far as possible, be excluded. He opted to work for independence by purely political means, in the hope that victory over Germany would lead the western allies to set up a Polish state under his leadership.

In the event, Piłsudski came out on top: the Germans, having held him in internment for well over a year, released him the day before the **armistice of November 11, 1918**, allowing him to take command of the Regency Council. He was sworn in as head of state three days later. Dmowski had to accept the consolation prize of head delegate to the Paris Peace Conference, though his associate, the concert pianist Ignacy Jan Paderewski, became the country's first prime minister.

POLAND REDEFINED

The new Poland lacked a defined territory. Initially, it consisted of the German and Austrian zones of occupation, centered on Warsaw and Lublin, plus Western Galicia. Wielkopolska was added a month later following a revolt against the German garrison in Poznań, but the precise frontiers were only established during the following three years on an *ad hoc* basis. Yet, though the Paris Conference played only a minor role in all this, it did take the key decision to give the country access to the sea by means of the **Polish Corridor**, a strip of land cut through the old Royal Prussia, which meant that East Prussia was left cut off from the rest of Germany. Despite intense lobbying, it was decided to exclude Danzig from the corridor, on the grounds that its population was overwhelmingly German; instead, it reverted to its former tradition as a city-state—an unsatisfactory compromise which was later to have tragic consequences.

The **Polish-Soviet War** of 1919–20 was the most significant of the conflicts that crucially determined the country's borders. Realizing that the Bolsheviks would want to spread their revolution to Poland and then to the industrialized west, Piłsudski aimed to create a grouping of independent nation-states stretching from Finland to Georgia to halt this new expansionist Russian Empire. Taking advantage of the civil war between the Soviet "Reds" and the counterrevolutionary "Whites," his army marched deep into Byelorussia and the Ukraine. He was subsequently beaten back to Warsaw, but skillfully regrouped his forces to pull off a crushing victory and pursue the Russians eastward, regaining a sizable chunk of the old Polish-Lithuanian Commonwealth's eastern territories in the process, an acquisition confirmed by the Treaty of Riga of 1921.

At the very end of the war, Piłsudski seized his home city of Wilno (Vilnius), which had a predominantly Polish population, but was wanted by the Lithuanians—who had opted for independence rather than a revival of the union. The grudge borne by Lithuania over this proved costly to them, as they became dependent on, and were later annexed by, the Soviet Union. Other border issues were settled by **plebiscites** organized by the League of Nations, the new international body set up to resolve such matters. In the most significant of these Germany and Poland competed for Upper Silesia. The Germans won, but the margin was so narrow that the League felt that the distribution of votes justified the partition of the province. Poland gained most of the Katowice conurbation, thus ensuring that the country acquired a solid industrial base.

THE INTER-WAR YEARS

Although the Polish state managed to develop coherent political, economic, and educational institutions, plus a transport and communications network, all were essentially fragile creations, as became obvious when Piłsudski refused to stand in the **1922 presidential elections** on the grounds that the office was insufficiently powerful. Worse, the victor, Gabriel Narutowicz, was hounded by the

Nationalists for having won as a result of votes cast by "non-Poles," and was assassinated soon afterward. For the next few years, Poland was governed by a series of weak governments presiding over hyper-inflation, feeble attempts at agrarian reform, and a contemptuous army officer class.

In May 1926, Piłsudski staged a military coup, ushering in the so-called **Sanacja** regime, named after a slogan proposing a return to political "health." Piłsudski functioned as the state's commander-in-chief until his death in 1935, though he held no formal office after an initial two-year stint as prime minister. Parliamentary life continued, but opposition was emasculated by the creation of the so-called Non-Party Bloc for Co-operation with the Government, and disaffected groups were brought to heel by force if necessary.

Having a country led by Stalin on one frontier was bad enough; when Hitler seized power in Germany in 1933, Poland was a sitting duck for two ruthless dictators, despite managing to sign ten-year non-aggression pacts with each. Hitler had always been open about his ambition of wiping Poland off the map again, regarding the Slavs as a race who were fit for no higher role than to be slaves of the Aryans. His foreign policy objectives were quickly put into effect by his annexation of Austria in 1937 and of parts of Czechoslovakia—with British and French connivance—in 1938. Turning his attentions towards Poland, his foreign minister Joachim von Ribbentrop and his Soviet counterpart Vyacheslav Molotov concluded the notorious **Nazi-Soviet Pact** in August 1939, which allowed either side to pursue any aggressive designs without the interference of the other. It also included a secret clause which agreed on a full partition of Poland along the lines of the Narew, Wisła, and San rivers.

WORLD WAR II

On September 1, 1939, Hitler **invaded Poland**, beginning by annexing the free city of Danzig, thereby precipitating World War II. The Poles fought with great courage, inflicting heavy casualties, but were numerically and technologically in a hopeless position. On September 17 the Soviets invaded the eastern part of the country, claiming the shareout agreed by the Nazi-Soviet Pact. The Allies, who had guaranteed to come to Poland's defense, initially failed to do so, and by the end of the first week in October the country had capitulated. A government-in-exile was established in London under **Władysław Sikorski**.

Millions of civilians—including virtually every Jew in Poland—were to be slaughtered in the Nazi **concentration camps** that were soon being set up on the occupied territory. And as this was going on, prisoners of the Soviets were being transported eastward to the **Gulag**, while wholesale murders of the potentially troublesome elements in Polish society were being carried out, such as the massacre of Katyn, where 4500 officers were shot.

With the Nazi disavowal of the 1939 pact and the invasion of the Soviet Union in June 1941, the Polish resistance, led by the **Home Army** (AK), no longer had to fight on two fronts, as it prompted Stalin to make an alliance with Sikorski. The Soviet victory at Stalingrad in 1943 marked the beginning of the end for the Nazis, but it enabled Stalin to renege on his agreement with the government-in-exile. At the **Tehran Conference** in November, he came to an arrangement with Britain and America with regard to future spheres of influence in Europe, making it almost inevitable that postwar Poland would be forced into the Soviet camp. He also insisted that the Soviet Union would retain the territories it had annexed in 1939. Allied support for this was obtained by reference to the current border's virtual coincidence with the so-called "Curzon Line," which had been drawn up by a former British Foreign Secretary in 1920 in an unsuccessful attempt at mediation in the Polish-Soviet War.

During the **liberation of Poland** in 1944, the Soviets installed a hand-picked Polish regime as the official government: any possibility of reasserting genuine Polish control depended on the outcome of the **uprising in Warsaw** against the Nazi occupiers. On July 31, with the Soviets poised on the outskirts of the city, the Home Army was forced to act. The Red Army lay in wait during the ensuing bloodbath. When the insurgents were finally defeated at the beginning of October, Hitler ordered that the city be razed before leaving the ruins to the Red Army. In early 1945, as the Soviets pushed onward through Poland, the Nazis set up last-ditch strongholds in Silesia,

but these were overrun by the time of the final armistice in April.

No country suffered so much from World War II as Poland. In all, around 25 percent of the population died, and the whole country lay devastated. Moreover, although the Allies had originally gone to war on its behalf, it found itself **reduced in size** and **shifted westward** across the map of Europe by some 200 kilometers, with its western frontier fixed at the lines of the Odra and Nysa rivers. Stalin had in effect achieved his twin aims of moving his frontiers and his sphere of influence well to the west.

The losses in the east—including Lwów and Wilno, both great centers of Polish culture—were painful, and involved the transfer of millions of people across the country in the following two years. There were compensations, however: Pomerania and the industrially valuable Silesia were restored after a gap of some seven centuries, and the much-coveted city of Danzig, which had been detached since its seizure by the Teutonic Knights, was also returned—and as Gdańsk was later to play a major role in the formation of postwar Poland.

THE RISE OF POLISH COMMUNISM

The Polish communists took power, not through popular revolution—as their Soviet counterparts had—nor even with significant public support—as the Czech communists had—but through the military and political dictate of an occupying force. Control was seized by the **ZPP** (Union of Polish Patriots), an organization formed by Stalin in 1943 from Polish exiles and Russian cadres with polonized names. As the Red Army drove the Germans westward, the ZPP established a Committee for National Liberation in Lublin, under the leadership of Bolesław Bierut. This was to form the core of the Polish government over the next few years.

Political opposition was fragmented and ineffectual. From the government in exile, which was effectively abandoned by the Allies at Yalta and Potsdam, only a single prominent figure returned to Poland after 1945—Stanisław Mikolajczyk, leader of the prewar Peasants' Party. He was to leave again in 1947, narrowly avoiding imprisonment.

The Polish communists and socialists who had remained in Poland during the war now regrouped. The communists, though suspicious

of Moscow, joined the ZPP to form the Polish Workers' Party under general-secretary **Władisław Gomułka**, as the socialists attempted to establish a separate party. Meanwhile the Soviets ran the country as an outlying province, stripping factories of plant and materials, intimidating political opponents, and orchestrating the brutal suppression of a nationalist uprising in the Western Ukraine by the Polish army, in what is referred to as the **Civil War** (1945–47).

The economic and political framework of Poland was sealed by the elections of 1947. The communists and socialists, allied as the **Democratic Bloc**, won a decisive victory over their remaining opponents, through an extended campaign of political harassment and manipulation. After the forcible merger of the socialists and communists in 1948 as the **PZPR** (Polish United Workers' Party), it only remained for the external pressures of the emerging Cold War to lock Poland completely into the Soviet sphere of influence and the Soviet model of economic and political development.

THE TRANSFORMATION OF POLAND

Polish history from 1947 to 1955 must be understood against the backdrop of an emergent Cold War. After the Berlin Blockade (1948), the formation of NATO (1949) and the rearmament of the German Federal Republic, the Soviet Union regarded a stable, communist Poland as an essential component of its defense. The realpolitik of Soviet foreign policy was not lost on the Polish communists, who, though subordinate in many areas, retained a degree of independence from Moscow. Thus, while foreign policy was determined by Moscow, and Poland joined the Warsaw Pact on its formation in 1955, some leeway remained in domestic policy. For example, First Secretary Gomułka, although deposed and arrested in 1951, was not executed, unlike other disgraced leaders in Eastern Europe. Nor were the purges of the party and the suppression of civil opposition as savage as elsewhere.

Nonetheless, the new constitution of 1952 enshrined the leading role of the PZPR in every aspect of Polish society, designating the country as the **Polish People's Republic**. Further, while the trappings of elections and a two-house parliament were retained, the other parties—the Democratic Party (SD) and the reconstituted Peasants' Party (ZSL)—were under the effective political control of the PZPR. Real power lay with the Politburo, Central Committee, and the newly formed economic and administrative bureaucracies. Only the Catholic Church, although harassed and extensively monitored by the authorities, retained a degree of independent political and cultural organization—a defiance characterized by **Cardinal Wyszinski**, arrested in 1953 for "anti-state" activities and imprisoned for three years.

Nationalization continued throughout this period, accelerated through the first **Three Year Plan** (1947–50) and the first **Six Year Plan** (1950–1956). Although the former retained some emphasis on the role of private ownership, the thrust of both was toward the collectivization of agriculture and the creation of a heavy industrial base. Collectivization proved impossible in the absence of the sort of force used by Stalin against the Kulaks; the program slowed in the mid-Fifties and was tacitly abandoned thereafter. Industrially the plans proved more successful: major iron and steel industries were established, mining extensively exploited in Silesia, and an entire ship-building industry developed along the Baltic coast—most notably in Gdańsk. There were, inevitably, costs: standards of living remained almost static, food was scarce, work was long, hard, and often dangerous, and unrestrained industrialization resulted in terrible pollution and despoliation of the land. Perhaps the most significant achievement of the period was the creation of an **urban industrial working class** for the first time in Polish history. Paradoxically, these very people proved to be the backbone of almost every political struggle against the Party in the following decades.

1956—THE POLISH OCTOBER

In Poland, as in Hungary, **1956** saw the first major political crisis of the communist era. Faction and dissension were already rife, with intellectuals calling for fundamental changes, splits within the Party leadership, and increasing popular disenchantment with the excesses of Stalinism. In February 1956 **Khrushchev** made his famous "secret" speech to the Twentieth Congress of the Soviet Communist Party, denouncing Stalin and his crimes. For

Bolesław Bierut, President and First Secretary of the PZPR, as for other Eastern European leaders, the speech was a bombshell, unmasking the lie of the absolute correctness of Stalin's every act. Reform-minded members of the Party in Poland were the first to make copies available in the west, but for Bierut and the hardline leadership it was the end: Bierut died directly after the congress, many suspecting that he had committed suicide.

Then in June workers in Poznań took to the streets over working conditions and wages. The protest rapidly developed into a major confrontation with the authorities, and in the ensuing street battles with the army and security police up to eighty people were killed and many hundreds of others wounded. Initial government insistence that "imperialist agents" had instigated the troubles gave way to an admission that some of the workers' grievances were justified and that the Party would try to remedy them.

The Poznań riots further divided an alarmed and weakened party. Hardliners pushed for defense minister General Rokossowski to take over the leadership, but it was Gomułka, with his earnest promises of reform, who carried the day. In October the Party plenum re-elected Gomułka as the new leader, without consulting Moscow. An enraged Khrushchev flew to Warsaw to demand an explanation of this unprecedented flouting of Moscow. East German, Czech, and Soviet troops were mobilized along Poland's borders, in response to which Polish security forces prepared to defend the capital. Poland held its breath as Gomułka and Khrushchev engaged in heated debate over the crisis. In the end, Gomułka assured Khrushchev that Poland would remain a loyal ally and maintain the essentials of communist rule. Khrushchev returned to Moscow, Soviet troops withdrew, and four days later Gomułka addressed a huge crowd in Warsaw as a national hero. The Soviet invasion of Hungary to crush the national uprising there in early November 1956 provided a clear reminder to Poles of how close they had come to disaster.

The **Polish October**, as it came to be known, raised high hopes of a new order, and initially those hopes seemed justified. Censorship was relaxed, Cardinal Wyszinski was released and state harassment of the church and control over the economy eased.

But the impetus for reform quickly faded, and the 1960s saw a progressive return to centralized planning, a stagnant economy, and steadily increasing levels of political control.

1970–79: FROM GOMUŁKA TO GIEREK

The final days of the Gomułka years were marked by a contrast between triumph in foreign policy and the harsh imposition of economic constraint. Pursuing his policy of Östpolitik, Willy Brandt—SDP Chancellor of the German Federal Republic—visited Poland in December 1970, and laid to rest some of the perennial concerns of postwar Polish foreign policy. In signing the Warsaw Treaty, West Germany recognized Poland's current borders and opened full diplomatic relations. And in an emphatic symbolic gesture, Brandt knelt in penance at the monument to those killed in the Warsaw Uprising.

A few days later, on December 12, huge food price rises were announced, provoking a simmering discontent that was to break out in strikes and demonstrations along the Baltic coast, centering on Gdańsk. When troops fired on demonstrators, killing many, the protests spread like wildfire, to the point of open insurrection. A traumatized central committee met five days before Christmas, hurriedly bundling the moribund Gomułka into retirement and replacing him as First Secretary with **Edward Gierek**, a member of the Party's reformist faction in the 1960s. Price rises were frozen and wage increases promised, but despite a Christmas calm, strikes broke out throughout January 1971, with demands for free trade unions and a free press accompanying the more usual economic demands. Peace was only restored when Gierek and the Minister of Defense, General **Wojciech Jaruzelksi**, went to the Gdańsk shipyards by taxi, to argue their case and admit their errors to the strikers.

The Gierek period marked out an alternative route to social stability. Given access to western financial markets by Brandt's reconciliation, the Gierek government borrowed heavily throughout the early Seventies. Food became cheaper and more plentiful as internal subsidies were matched by purchases from the west and the Soviet Union. Standards of living rose and a wider range of consumer goods became more freely available. However, the international economic recession and oil crises of the mid-Seventies destroyed the Polish boom at a stroke. Debts became impossible to service, new loans harder to obtain, and it became apparent that earlier borrowing had been squandered in unsustainable rises in consumption or wasted in large-scale projects of limited economic value.

By 1976, the wheel had turned full circle with remarkable rapidity. The government announced food price rises of almost treble the magnitude of those proposed in the early Seventies. This time the ensuing strikes were firmly repressed and many activists imprisoned, and it is from this point that one can chart the emergence of the complex **alliance between Polish workers, intellectuals, and the Catholic Church**. In response to the imprisonment of strikers, the KOR (Committee for the Defense of Workers) was formed. Consisting of dissident intellectuals, it was to provide not only valuable publicity and support for the opposition through western contacts, but also new channels of political communication through underground *samizdat* publications, plus a degree of strategic sophistication that the spontaneous uprisings had so far lacked.

But perhaps even more decisive was the election of **Karol Wojtyła**, Archbishop of Kraków, as **Pope John Paul II** in 1978. A fierce opponent of the communist regime, he visited Poland in 1979 and was met by the greatest public gatherings that Poland had ever seen. For the Polish people he became a symbol of Polish cultural identity and international influence, and his visit provided a public demonstration of their potential power.

1980–89: SOLIDARITY

Gierek's announcment of 100 percent price rises on foodstuffs in July 1980 led inevitably to more strikes, focused on the **Gdańsk shipyards**. Attempts by the authorities to have a crane operator, Anna Walentynowicz, dismissed for political agitation intensified the unrest. Led by a shipyard electrician, **Lech Wałęsa**, the strikers occupied the yards and were joined by a hastily convened group of opposition intellectuals and activists, including future prime minister Tadeuz Mazowiecki. Together they formulated a series of demands—the so-called **Twenty-one Points**—that were to serve not only as the

principal political concerns of the Polish opposition, but to provide an intellectual template for every other oppositional movement in Eastern Europe.

Demands for popular consultation over the economic crisis, the freeing of political prisoners, freedom of the press, the right to strike, free trade unions, and televised Catholic Mass were drawn up along with demands for higher wages and an end to party privileges. Yet the lessons of Hungary in 1956 and Czechoslovakia in 1968 had been learned, and the opposition was careful to reiterate that they "intended neither to threaten the foundations of the Socialist Republic in our country, nor its position in international relations."

The Party caved in, after protracted negotiations, signing the historic **Gdańsk Agreements** in August 1980, after which free trade unions, covering over 75 percent of Poland's 12.5 million workforce, were formed across the country, under the name *Solidarność*—**Solidarity**. Gierek and his supporters were swept from office by the Party in September 1980, but the limits of Solidarity's power were signaled by an unscheduled Warsaw Pact meeting later in the year. Other Easter European communist leaders perceptively argued that Solidarity's success would threaten not only their Polish counterparts' political futures, but their own as well. Accordingly, Soviet and Warsaw Pact units were mobilized along Poland's borders. The Poles closed ranks: the Party reaffirmed its Leninist purity, while Solidarity and the Church publicly emphasized their moderation.

Throughout 1981 deadlock ensued, while the economic crisis gathered pace. Solidarity, lacking any positive control over the economy, was only capable of bringing it to a halt, and repeatedly showed itself able to do so. General Jaruzelski took control of the Party in July 1981 and, in the face of threats of a general strike, continued to negotiate with Solidarity leaders, but refused to relinquish any power. A wave of strikes in late October 1981 were met by the imposition of **martial law** on December 12, 1981: occupations and strikes were broken up by troops, Solidarity was banned, civil liberties suspended, and union leaders arrested. However, these measures solved nothing fundamental, and after a second visit by Pope John Paul II in 1983 martial law was lifted.

The period 1984 to 1988 was marked by a final attempt by the Jaruzelski government to dig Poland out of its economic crisis. The country's debt had risen to an astronomical $39 billion, wages had slumped, and production was hampered by endemic labor unrest. In 1987 Jaruzelski submitted the government's program of price rises and promised democratization to a referendum. The government lost, the real message of the vote being a rejection not merely of the program but of the notion that the Party could lead Poland out of its crisis. As the Party's route lay blocked by popular disenchantment, the opposition's opened up after major strikes in May 1988.

Jaruzelski finally acknowledged defeat after a devastating second wave of strikes in August of that year and called for a "courageous turnaround" by the Party, accepting the need for talks with Solidarity and the prospect of real power-sharing—an option of political capitulation probably only made possible by the accession of Gorbachev to the Kremlin.

1989–90: THE NEW POLAND

The **Round Table talks** ran from February to April 1989, the key demands being the absolute acceptance of the legal status of Solidarity, the establishment of an independent press, and the promise of what were termed semi-free elections. Legalization of Solidarity was duly agreed, opposition newspapers were to be allowed to publish freely, and all 100 seats of a reconstituted upper chamber, the Senate, were to be freely contested. In the lower house of parliament, the Sejm, 65 percent of seats were to be reserved for the PZPR and its allied parties, with the rest openly contested.

The communists suffered a humiliating and decisive defeat in the consequent **elections** of **July 1989**, whereas Solidarity won almost every seat it contested. Thus while the numerical balance of the lower chamber remained with the PZPR, the unthinkable became possible—a Solidarity-led government. In the end, the parties allied to the PZPR broke with their communist overlords and voted to establish the journalist **Tadeuz Mazowiecki** as prime minister in August 1989, installing the first non-communist government in Eastern Europe since the war. Subsequently the PZPR rapidly

disintegrated, voting to dissolve itself in January 1990 and then splitting into two notionally social democratic currents.

The tasks facing Poland's new government were formidable: economic dislocation, political volatility, and a rapidly changing foreign scene in the rest of Eastern Europe. For the most part, the government retained a high degree of support in the face of an **austerity program** far stiffer than anything proposed under the communist regime.

Lech Wałęsa, long out of the main political arena, forced the pace in the **presidential election of 1990**, calling for the removal of Jaruzelski, a faster pace of reform, and a concerted effort to remove the accumulated privileges of the senior Party men. Against him stood Prime Minister Mazowiecki and the previously unknown Jan Tymiński, a Canadian-Polish businessman employing free-market rhetoric and western-style campaigning techniques. Although clearly in the lead in the first round of voting in December 1990, Wałęsa was required to face a second round against Tymiński. Mazowiecki, having finished a disappointing third, then resigned as prime minister, taking the whole government with him. Wałęsa won the second round comfortably and pieced a new government together in early 1991, under Prime Minister Bielicki, a leading intellectual force within Solidarity.

The Polish people once again face terrible difficulties. Inflation has been brought under control, but living standards are falling still further and unemployment is soaring. The specter of anti-Semitism, a recurrent feature of Polish history, threatens to return from the margins, and the environmental disasters of the last forty years remain unresolved and expensive. Perhaps most problematic of all, the country is having to learn the complex operation of a politically plural society, and there is much to suggest that the Solidarity coalition will gradually fragment to produce political parties of more recognizably western orientations. There can be little doubt as to the fortitude and integrity of the Polish people in the forty years or so since the end of World War II. There is equally little doubt that they will need to draw on those resources as much again in the years to come.

MONUMENTAL CHRONOLOGY

1500 BC	Iron-Age tribes of Lusatian culture.	Fortified settlement of **Biskupin**.
10C	Creation of Polish state.	Ruins of palace at **Ostrów Lednicki**, St Mary on the Wawel, **Kraków**.
11–12C	Poland under the early Piasts.	**Romanesque** architecture—cathedrals of **Gniezno** (bronze doors only survive) and **Kraków** (crypt); Collegiate church, **Kruszwica**; Premonstratensian monastery, **Strzelno**.
Early 13C	Monasticism spreads to Poland; Teutonic Knights invited into the country.	**Transitional** style introduced by Cistercians—monasteries at **Trzebnica** and **Henryków**. Fully-fledged **Gothic** first appears in Dominican and Franciscan churches in **Kraków**. First Teutonic buildings: castle of **Kwidzyn**, beginning of construction of fortress at **Malbork**.
14C	Teutonic Knights establish a Baltic state; reign of Kazimierz the Great (1333–70); Bohemian control of Silesia recognized.	Great century of Gothic building, particularly of brick, in the Teutonic territories. Middle Castle, **Malbork**; castle at **Lidzbark Warmiński**; town hall and churches of St Mary and St John, **Toruń**; town hall, Great Mill, St Mary, **Gdańsk**; cathedral, **Frombork**. **Kraków** adorned with Gothic buildings—Sukiennice (Cloth Hall), churches of Corpus Christi and St Catherine, suburb of Kazimierz. Laying out of new town of **Kazimierz Dolny**; stone castles of the **Eagles' Nest Trail**; cathedrals of **Gniezno** and **Poznań** rebuilt. Series of brick churches in **Wrocław** (Breslau)—cathedral, Holy Cross, St Mary of the Sands; fortifications of **Paczków**.
Late 14C, 15C	Poland under the Jagiellonians; Silesia officially part of Bohemia.	**Late Gothic** buildings—university and town gates, **Kraków**; town hall and more brick churches, **Wrocław**; St James, **Nysa**.
16C	Last of Jagiellonian dynasty; creation of Republic of Nobles (1572).	Italian architects bring **Renaissance** to Poland, introduced at Wawel Castle, **Kraków**. In same city, Zygmuntowska Chapel in Wawel Cathedral, reconstruction of Sukiennice, Old Synagogue. Palaces at **Brzeg** and at **Krasiczyn**; rebuild of town hall at **Poznań**. **Late Renaissance** and **Mannerist** styles practised from 1570s until around 1610. Layout of planned town of **Zamość**, including town hall, collegiate church, and synagogue, by Bartolomeo Morandi. Beginning of construction of Royal Palace, **Warsaw**. Armory and Golden House, **Gdańsk**; other town mansions in **Kraków**, **Kazimerz Dolny**, **Sandomierz**, and **Wrocław**.

1587– 1668	The Waza dynasty.	Early **Baroque** style of the Jesuits introduced with Saints Peter and Paul, **Kraków**. Rebuilding of monastery of Jasna Góra, **Częstochowa**, and palace of **Łańcut**. Waza Chapel in Wawel Cathedral, **Kraków**, marks Polish debut of full-blooded Baroque.
Late 17C	Turkish Wars; Poland at height of its international prestige.	Extensive building in **Warsaw**, including palace of Wilanów, the more restrained Krasiński and Radziwiłł palaces, and Church of Holy Sacrament. All except the first designed by Tylman of Gameren, architect also of St Anne, **Kraków**, and the palace of **Nieborów**.
Late 17C, early 18C	Poland under the Saxon kings; Silesia part of Habsburg Empire	Italianate Baroque in parish church, **Poznań**; town hall and churches, **Leszno**. Additions to Royal Palace, **Warsaw**. Buildings by Baroque architects from Vienna and Prague in Silesia: Ossoliński Library, Elector's Chapel in cathedral, Church of Holy Name and university, **Wrocław**; St Joseph and Monastery Church, **Krzeszów**; monastery of **Legnickie Pole**.
1764– 1795	Reign of Stanisław-August Poniatowski; Silesia under Prussian rule.	**Neoclassicism** appears in additions to Royal Palace and in Łazienki Palace, **Warsaw**. Period of great country houses, including **Arcadia** and **Rogalin**. More severe version of Neoclassical style is adopted in Silesia—university library and royal palace, **Wrocław**; fortress at **Kłodzko**.
1795– 1914	Poland under Partition.	Late Neoclassical buildings include Raczyński Library, **Poznań**, and theater, **Wrocław**. Neo-Gothic of Berlin architect Karl Friedrich Schinkel in palace of **Kórnik** and castle of **Legnica**; castle in **Lublin** is in similar vein. Grandiose, derivative styles characteristic of the nineteenth century best illustrated in Polish Bank and Grand Theater in **Warsaw** and in factories and houses of **Łódź**. In early twentieth century, notable public works in **Wrocław**—Grunwaldzki Bridge and Max Berg's Hala Ludowa. Also **Jugendstil** and **Secessionist** styles in then German cities such as Zielona Góra and Opole.
1918– present	Resurrection of Polish state; World War II; Poland under communism; democracy restored.	**Nazi** architecture in German lands, notably Wolf's Lair, **Gierłoz**. Postwar concentration on factories and housing estates, with occasional showpieces, such as Palace of Culture, **Warsaw**. After an initial ban, spectacular modern churches built; two of the finest are in Kraków suburb of **Nowa Huta**.

BOOKS

A vast amount of writing both from and about Poland is available in English, and the quantity looks set to increase at an accelerated pace with the advent of the post-communist regime. Most of the books listed below are in print either in the US or Poland, and those that aren't should be easy enough to track down in second-hand bookshops.

HISTORY

Adam Zamoyski *The Polish Way* (Watts $27.50). The most accessible history of Poland, going right up to the 1989 elections. Zamoyski is an American emigré Pole, and his sympathies—as you would expect in a member of one of Poland's foremost aristocratic families—are those of a thoroughly blue-blooded nationalist.

Norman Davies *The Heart of Europe: A Short History of Poland* (OUP $10.95). An excellent treatment of modern Polish history, beginning with the events of 1945 but looking backwards over the past millennium to illustrate the author's ideas. Scrupulously gives all points of view in disentangling the web of Polish history.

Norman Davies *God's Playground* (2 vols; Columbia Univ. Press $40 set). A masterpiece of erudition, entertainingly written and pretty much definitive for the pre-Solidarity period.

Norman Davies *White Eagle, Red Star: The Polish Soviet War, 1919–20* (Hippocrene Books $14.95). Fascinating account of a little-known but critical episode of European history, when Lenin looked set to export the Soviet Revolution into Europe.

Oskar Halecki *History of Poland* (Routledge, UK only). An alternative to Davies if you want a manageable chronological account of Polish history, but its nationalistic bias puts it at a severe disadvantage.

Neal Ascherson *The Struggles for Poland* (Random $19.95). Ascherson's book was designed to accompany the British Channel 4 TV series and its focus is squarely on the twentieth century, with just a thirty-page chapter on the previous thousand years. For most general readers, though, this is the best possible introduction to modern Polish history and politics.

Józef Piłsudski *Memoirs of a Polish Revolutionary and Soldier* (AMS Press $27.50). Lively stuff from Lech Wałęsa's hero, who—after a dashing wartime career—was Poland's leader from 1926 to 1934.

Wacław Jedrzejewicz *Piłsudski—a Life for Poland* (Hippocrene Books $11.95). Comprehensive biography of the enigmatic military strongman.

Patrick Brogan *Eastern Europe: The Fifty Years War, 1939–89* (Bloomsbury, UK only). Useful summaries of the eight European communist nations (plus the Baltic Republics) from conception to collapse.

Chimen Abramsky, Maciej Jachimczyk and Antony Polonsky (ed.) *The Jews in Poland* (Basil Blackwell $16.95). Historical survey of what was for centuries the largest community of world Jewry.

WORLD WAR II AND THE HOLOCAUST

Józef Garlinski *Poland in the Second World War* (Hippocrene Books $14.95). General history by a UK-based emigré, from a partisan standpoint.

Jan Ciechanowski *The Warsaw Uprising of 1944* (CUP $49.50). Compelling, day-by-day account—the best of many on this subject.

Gustaw Herling *A World Apart* (Arbor House, o/p). An account of deportation to a Soviet labor camp, based on the author's own experiences.

Jan Nowak *Courier for Warsaw* (Books Demand UMI $124.60). Racily written memoir of the Polish underground resistance.

Martin Gilbert *The Holocaust* (H. Holt & Co. $14.95). The standard work, providing a trustworthy overview on the slaughter of European Jewry—and the crucial role of Poland, where most Nazi concentration camps were sited.

The Warsaw Ghetto (Interpress, Warsaw). Official state publication, issued in several languages, that documents the destruction of the capital's Jewish population.

Dan Kurzman *The Bravest Battle* (Putnam, o/p). Detailed account of the 1943 Warsaw Ghetto Uprising, conveying the incredible courage of the Jewish combatants.

Alan Adelson and Robert Lapides *The Łódź Ghetto—Inside a Community under Siege* (Viking Penguin $16.95). Scrupulously detailed narrative of the 200,000-strong ghetto, with numerous personal memoirs and photographs.

Primo Levi *If this is a Man & The Truce* (o/p); *Moments of Reprieve* (Viking Penguin $6.95); *The Drowned and the Saved* (Random $8.95); *The Periodic Table* (Schocken $8.95); *If Not Now, When?* (Viking Penguin $8.95). An Italian Jew, Levi survived Auschwitz because the Nazis made use of his training as a pharmacist in the death-camp factories. Most of his books, which became ever bleaker towards the end of his life, concentrate on his experiences during and soon after his incarceration in Auschwitz, analysing the psychology of survivor and torturer with extraordinary clarity. *If Not Now, When?* is the story of a group of Jewish partisans in occupied Russia and Poland; giving plenty of insights into Eastern European anti-Semitism, it's a good corrective to the mythology of Jews as passive victims.

Janina Bauman *Winter in the Morning* (Free Press $24.95); *A Dream of Belonging* (Trafalgar Square $12.95). Bauman and her family survived the Warsaw ghetto, eventually leaving the country following the anti-Semitic backlash of 1968. *Winter* is a delicate and moving account of life and death in the ghetto. Less dramatic but equally interesting, *Belonging*, the second volume of her autobiography, tells of life in the Communist Party and disillusionment in the early postwar years.

Betty Jean Lifton *Janusz Korczak: The King of the Children* (Farrar, Straus & Giroux $22.50). Biography of the Jewish doctor who died in Treblinka with the orphans for whom he cared. He was the eponymous subject of Andrzej Wajda's latest film.

Art Spiegelman *Maus* (Pantheon $9.95). Spiegelman, editor of the cartoon magazine *Raw*, is the son of Auschwitz survivors. *Maus* is a brilliant comic-strip exploration of the ghetto and concentration camp experiences of his father, recounted in flashbacks. The story runs through to Art's father's imprisonment at Auschwitz; subsequent chapters of the sequel—covering Auschwitz itself—have been printed in recent editions of *Raw*.

Rudolf Höss *Kommandant at Auschwitz* (o/p). Perhaps the most chilling record of the barbarity: a remorseless autobiography of the Auschwitz camp commandant, written in the days between his death sentence and execution at Nuremberg.

Tadeusz Borowski *This Way for the Gas, Ladies and Gentlemen* (Viking Penguin $7.95). These short stories based on his Auschwitz experiences marked Borowski out as the great literary hope of communist Poland, but he committed suicide soon after their publication, at the age of 29.

Ida Fink *A Scrap of Time* (Schocken $6.95). Haunting vignettes of Jews striving to escape the concentration camps—and of the unsung Polish Gentiles who sheltered them.

POLITICS AND SOCIETY

Timothy Garton Ash *The Polish Revolution: Solidarity 1980–82* (Random $10.95); *The Uses of Adversity* (Random $12.95); *The Magic Lantern The Revolution of 89* (Random $17.95). Garton Ash has been the most consistent and involved western reporter on Poland in the Solidarity era, displaying an intuitive grasp of the Polish mentality. His *Polish Revolution* is a vivid record of events from the birth of Solidarity—a story extended in the climactic events of 1989, documented as an eyewitness in Warsaw, Budapest, Berlin, and Prague.

Jan Josef Lipski *A History of KOR—The Committee for Workers' Self-Defence* (University of California Press $47.50). Detailed history of key 1970s opposition movement that is regarded as one of Solidarity's main inspirations. A resistance veteran and leading light in KOR, Lipski shows how it developed ideas and strategies of non-violence and an "independent civil society" as a response to totalitarianism. A demanding but worthwhile read.

Grazyna Sikorska *Jerzy Popiełuszko, a Martyr for Truth* (Eerdmans Pub. Co., o/p). Hagiographic biography of the murdered Catholic priest and national hero.

Misha Glenny *The Rebirth of History: Eastern Europe in the Age of Democracy* (Penguin, UK only, £4.99). One chapter deals with Poland, homing in on the economic and political difficulties of post-communist reconstruction.

Grupa Publikacyjna Forum *Forum Polek: Polish Women's Forum* (available in UK only from POSK, 238–246 King St, London W6 0RF; £5.95). Highly worthwhile anthology—in English and Polish—of essays, memoirs, fiction, and poetry by London-based émigre (and second generation émigre) writers.

Stewart Steven *The Poles* (Macmillan, o/p). Excellent journalistic account of all aspects of society in early 1980s Poland.

ESSAYS AND MEMOIRS

Adam Michnik *Letters From Prison* (University of California Press $10.95). Collection of writings by prominent opposition intellectual and editor of the *Gazeta Wyborcza*, once Solidarity's house newspaper, now critical of (and disowned by) Wałęsa. The essay "A New Evolutionism" is a seminal piece of new political writing, and the more historical pieces are fascinating, too.

Adam Zagajewski *Solidarity, Solitude* (Ecco Press $19.95). One of Poland's finest contemporary poets responds in essay form to recent (published 1990) events.

Kazimierz Brandys *Warsaw Diary 1977–81* (Random, o/p). This account by a major Polish journalist and novelist brilliantly captures the atmosphere of the time, and especially the effect of John Paul II's first papal visit in 1979. During martial law, possession of this book carried an automatic ten-year jail sentence.

Teresa Toranska *Them: Stalin's Polish Puppets* (Harper Collins $22.45). Interviews with Polish communists and Party leaders from the Stalinist era carried out during the Solidarity era by investigative journalist Toranska. The result is a fascinating insight into how Stalin established Soviet control over Eastern Europe, and Poland in particular.

Lech Wałęsa *A Way of Hope: An Auobiography* (H. Holt & Co. $19.95). Ghostwritten, it would seem, by a Solidarity committee, in the years before Lech split the party and created his own role as "axe-wielding" president.

Hans Magnus Enzensberger *Europe, Europe* (Pantheon $13.95). A tour de force from the German anarchist, delving outside the mainstream to answer the question "What is Europe?." The section on Poland is a wonderfuly observant roam around the main cities in 1986.

Czesław Miłosz *The Captive Mind* (Random $6.95). Penetrating analysis of the reasons so many Polish artists and intellectuals sold out to communism after 1945, with four individual case-studies supplementing a confession of personal guilt.

Czesław Miłosz *Native Realm* (Univ. of California Press $9.95). An unorthodox autobiography of the years before Miłosz defected to the west; especially illuminating on the Polish–Lithuanian relationship.

Ryszard Kapusciński *The Soccer War* (Granta, UK only, £12.99). For many years Kapusciński was the only full-time Polish foreign correspondent, and he's best known for his trilogy on the dictators of Iran, Angola, and Ethiopia. His latest book, a collection of sketches of Third World politics, offers many wry insights into his native land.

CULTURE, ART AND ARCHITECTURE

Jan Kott (ed.) *Four Decades of Polish Essays* (Northwestern University Press $12.95). Culture-based anthology—on art, literature, drama, plus politics—that features most of the major intellectual names of postwar Poland.

The Polish Jewry: History and Culture (Interpress, Warsaw). Wide-ranging collection of essays and photographs on all aspects of culture—from customs and family life to theater, music, and painting. A beautiful production.

David Buxton *The Wooden Churches of Eastern Europe* (CUP $95). Wonderful illustrations of Poland's most compelling architectural style. Well worth hunting out in libraries: it will make you want to traipse around Silesia, the Bieszczady mountains, and Czech borderlands.

Les Icones de Pologne (Editions de Cerf/Arkadia, o/p). Good reproductions of most of the major icons from Poland's regional museums. Scour the *antiquariats* of the big cities for a copy.

POLISH FICTION

Joseph Conrad A Personal Record (with The Mirror of the Sea, OUP $7.95). An entertaining, ironic piece of "faction" about Conrad's family and his early life in the Russian part of Partition Poland, addressing the painful subjects of his loss of his own country and language. •

Tadeusz Konwicki A Minor Apocalypse (Random $7.95); A Dreambook for our Time (Viking Penguin $6.95); The Polish Complex (Viking Penguin $6.95). A convinced Party member in the Fifties, Konwicki eventually made the break with Stalinism: since then a series of highly respected novels, films, and screenplays have established him as one of Poland's foremost writers. Describing a single day's events, A Minor Apocalypse is narrated by a character who constantly vacillates over his promise to set fire to himself in front of the Party headquarters. Dreambook is a hard-hitting wartime tale, while The Polish Complex is a fascinating, often elusive exploration of contemporary life in Poland. Like Miłosz and many others who grew up in Wilno, now the capital of Lithuania, Konwicki betrays a yearning for a mystic homeland.

Czesław Miłosz The Seizure of Power (Farrar, Straus & Giroux $6.95); The Issa Valley (Farrar, Straus & Giroux $9.95). The Seizure of Power, the first book by this Nobel Prize-winning writer, is a wartime novel, while the semi-autobiographical Issa Valley is a wonderfully lyrical account of a boy growing up in the Lithuanian countryside.

Jerzy Andrzejewski Ashes and Diamonds (Viking Penguin $4.95). Spring 1945: resistance fighters, communist ideologues, and black marketeers battle it out in small-town Poland. A gripping account of the tensions and forces that shaped postwar Poland, and the basis for Andrzej Wajda's film of the same title.

Stanisław Ignacy Witkiewicz Insatiability (Salem House Pub. $11.95). Explicit depiction of artistic, intellectual, religious, and sexual decadence against the background of a Chinese invasion of Europe. The enormous vocabulary, complicated syntax and philosophical diversions don't make an easy read, but this is unquestionably one of the most distinctive works of twentieth-century literature.

Witold Gombrowicz Ferdydurke (Viking Penguin $7.95). Takes as its theme humanity's infantile and juvenile obsessions, and the tensions between urban life and the traditional ways of the countryside.

Isaac Bashevis Singer The Magician of Lublin (Fawcett $2.95); The Family Moskat (Farrar, Straus & Giroux $12.95); Collected Stories (Farrar, Straus & Giroux $12.95); The Slave (Avon $1.95); Satan in Goray (Fawcett $2.50); The King of the Fields (NAL Dutton $8.95). Singer, who emigrated from Poland to the USA in the 1930s, writes in Yiddish, so his reputation rests largely on the translations of his novels and short stories. Only a selection of his vast output is mentioned here. The Magician of Lublin and The Family Moskat, both novels set in the ghettoes of early twentieth-century Poland, are masterly evocations of life in vanished Jewish communities. The Slave is a gentle yet tragic love story set in the seventeenth century, while Satan in Goray is a blazing evocation of religious hysteria in the same period. His latest, The King of the Fields, re-creates the early life of the Polish state, and is his only novel without a Jewish emphasis.

Israel Joshua Singer The Brothers Ashkenazi (Carroll & Graf $9.95). In contrast to his younger brother, I. J. Singer was a non-believer, and was happiest writing in the grand manner, as in this epic of the rise and fall of a Jewish family in Łódź.

Shmuel Yosef Agnon The Bridal Canopy (Schocken, o/p). Agnon is a Nobel Prize-winner, and is regarded as the father-figure of modern Hebrew literature. The Bridal Canopy is a saga of Jewish life in Poland.

Jan Potocki Tales from the Saragossa Manuscript: Ten Days in the Life of Alphonse von Worden (Hippocrene Books $8.95). A self-contained section of a huge unfinished gothic novel written at the beginning of the nineteenth century by a Polish nobleman: a rich brew of picaresque adventures, dreams, hallucinations, eroticism, philosophical discourses, and exotic tales.

Henryk Sienkiewicz Quo Vadis? (Hippocrene Books $8.95); Charcoal Sketches and Other Tales (Dufour $16.95). Sienkiewicz's reputation outside Poland largely rests on Quo Vadis? (which won him the Nobel Prize), treating the early Christians in Nero's Rome as an allegory of Poland's plight under the Partitions. All the author's other blockbusters (including *Knights of the Cross* and the trilogy *With Fire and Sword*, *The Deluge*, and *Pan Michael*) are set in various periods of Poland's past; badly translated, they are all out of print now, but should be available from libraries. The recently published novellas, which focus on the classes of nineteenth-century Polish rural society, at last do justice to Sienkiewicz's prose and will hopefully be followed up by new versions of his more ambitious works.

Władysław Reymont *The Peasants*; *The Promised Land* (both o/p). Reymont won the Nobel Prize for *The Peasants*, a quartet of novels about village life (one for each season of the year), but its vast length has led to its neglect outside Poland. *The Promised Land*, which was filmed by Wajda, offers a comparably unromanticized view of industrial life in Łódź.

Bruno Schulz *Street of Crocodiles* (Viking Penguin $6.95); *Sanitorium under the Sign of the Hourglass* (Viking Penguin $6.95). These kaleidoscopic, dream-like fictions, vividly evoking life in the small town of Drohobycz in the Polish Ukraine, constitute the entire literary output of their author, who was murdered by the SS.

Marek Hłasko *The Eighth Day of the Week* (Greenwood $35); *Next Stop—Paradise* (o/p); *The Graveyard* (Greenwood $35); *Killing the Second Dog* (Cane Hill Press $8.95). Poland's "Angry Young Man," Hłasko articulated the general disaffection of those who grew up after World War II, his bleak themes mirrored in a spare, taut prose style.

Aleksander Wat *Lucifer Unemployed* (Northwestern University Press $8.95). Comic reversals of religion, politics, and culture by Poland's leading Futurist: an attempted revolution in England peters out into a soccer match; a Jew becomes pope; the Devil comes to terms with unemployment in the face of Europe-wide depravity. Slightly dated, but still hilarious.

Stanisław Lem *Return from the Stars*; *Tales of Pirx the Pilot*; *His Master's Voice* (Harcourt Brace Jovanovich $6.95–7.95 each). The only recent Polish writing to have achieved a worldwide mass-market readership, Lem's science fiction focuses on the human and social predicament in the light of technological change.

Janusz Anderman *Poland Under Black Light* (Readers International $6.95); *The Edge of the World* (Readers International $7.95). Stark, highly cinematic stories and sketches of life in Poland under martial law, with more than a dash of black humor in the second collection.

Henia Karmel-Wolfe *The Baders of Jacob Street* (Lippincott, o/p). Kraków-set tale of the impact of German occupation on a Jewish family.

Adam Gillon (ed.) *Introduction to Modern Polish Literature* (Hippocrene Books $12.95). An excellent anthology of short stories and extracts from novels, many of them (eg Reymont's *The Peasants*) out of print in English.

POLISH POETRY

Adam Mickiewicz *Pan Tadeusz* (Cherry Hill Books, o/p); *Konrad Wallenrod* & *Grazyna* (University Press of America $24.50). Poland's national epic, set among the gentry of Lithuania at the time of the Napoleonic invasion, is here given a highly effective verse translation. In contrast to the self-delusion about Polish independence shown by the characters in *Pan Tadeusz*, *Konrad Wallenrod* demonstrates how that end can be achieved by stealth and cunning; like *Grazyna*, its setting is Poland's struggle with the Teutonic Knights.

Karol Wojtyła *Easter Vigil and Other Poems* (Random House, o/p). Pope John Paul II followed a sideline career in poetry throughout his priesthood. This selection of his verses casts light on the complex private personality of a very public figure.

Adam Zagatewski *Tremor* (Farrar, Straus & Giroux $8.95). The early poems here belong to the "angry generation" of 1968; the later, more metaphysical work, sometimes focuses on the poet's native city of Lwów.

Zbigniew Herbert *Selected Poems* (Ecco Press $7.50); *Report from the Besieged City* (Ecco Press $8.50). Another fine contemporary poet, with a strong line in poignant observation; intensely political but never dogmatic.

Czesław Miłosz (ed.) *Polish Postwar Poetry* (University of California Press $8.95). Useful anthology selected and mostly translated by Miłosz, with an emphasis on poetry written after the thaw of 1956. The closer you get to the 1980s the grittier and more acerbic they come, as befits the politics of the era.

Adam Czerniawski (ed.) *The Burning Forest* (Dufour £$17.95). Selected by one of Poland's leading contemporary poets, this anthology covers Polish poetry from the laconic nineteenth-century verses of Cyprian Norwid, through examples of Herbert, Rozewicz, and the editor, up to young writers of the present day.

Susan Bassnett and Piotr Kuhiwczak (eds.) *Ariadne's Thread: Polish Women Poets* (Three Continents $14). Eight contemporary poets with distinctive voices and range, from reinterpretations of classical myth to the horrors of torture.

POLISH DRAMA

Juliusz Słowacki *Mary Stuart* (Greenwood $35). Słowacki ranks second only to Mickiewicz in Polish esteem, but his reputation hasn't traveled. Nonetheless, this is a fine example of Romantic drama, set against the backdrop of the murders of David Riszio and Mary's husband, Henry Darnley.

Stanisław Ignacy Witkiewicz *The Madman and the Nun, The Water Hen & The Crazy Locomotive* (Applause $8.95). Witkiewicz created a Theater of the Absurd twenty years before the term came into common use through the work of Ionesco and Beckett. This volume makes the ideal introduction to the versatile avant-garde painter, novelist, and playwright.

Witold Gombrowicz *The Marriage* (Northwestern University Press $9.95). A play exploring similar themes to those found in Gombrowicz's novels.

Sławomir Mrozek *Tango* (Grove Weidenfield $3.95); *Vatzlav* (Applause $5.95); *Striptease, Repeat Performance* & *The Prophets* (Applause $5.95). Mrozek is the sharpest and subtlest satirist Poland has produced, employing nonsensical situations to probe the most serious political issues.

Tadeusz Rozewicz *The Card Index and Other Plays* (Grove Press, o/p); *Marriage Blanc* & *The Hunger Artist Departs* (M Yoars $7.95). The best works by an unremittingly inventive experimentalist.

Tadeusz Kantor *Wielopole/Wielopole* (M Boyars $17.95). One of the most successful products of Poland's experimental theater scene, complete with a lavish record of its production plus the author/director's rehearsal notes.

Solomon Anski *The Dybbuk* (Regnery Gateway $6.95). Written by a prominent member of the Jewish socialist movement in Poland, this drama of divine justice is the masterpiece of Yiddish theater. Also included in the anthology is a work on a similar theme, *God of Vengeance* by Scholem Asch.

LITERATURE BY FOREIGN WRITERS

E. T. A. Hoffmann *Best Tales of Hoffmann* (Dover $7.95); *Tales of Hoffmann* (Viking Penguin $5.95) Hoffmann began writing his masterly stories of the macabre while a bored civil servant in Prussian Poland; included here are two with a specifically Polish setting.

Gerhart Hauptmann *The Weavers* (in *Three Plays: The Weavers, Mannele, The Beaver Coat* Ungar $7.95). Taking as its background a futile mid-nineteenth-century uprising by the Silesian weavers against the mill owners, this intense drama gained its reputation as the first "socialist" play by having a collective rather than a single hero.

Isaac Babel *Red Cavalry* (in *Collected Stories*, NAL-Dutton $9.95). A collection of interrelated short stories about the 1919–20 invasion of Poland, narrated by the bizarrely contradictory figure of a Jewish Cossack communist, who naturally finds he's torn by conflicting emotions.

John Hersey *The Wall* (Random House $9.95). Tale of Jewish resistance to the Nazi occupation.

Günter Grass *The Tin Drum* (Random $9.95); *Dog Years* (Harcourt Brace Jovanovich $12.95); *Cat and Mouse* (Ameron Ltd. $12.95). These three novels, known as the "Danzig Trilogy," are one of the highpoints of modern German literature. Set in Danzig/Gdańsk, where the author grew up, they hold up a mirror to the changing German character this century.

Leon Uris *Mila 18* (Bantam $5.95). Stirring tale of the Warsaw Ghetto Uprising—Mila 18 was the address of the Jewish resistance militia's HQ.

James Michener *Poland* (Fawcett $6.95). Another of Michener's blockbusting sagas, larded with highly symbolic peasants and aristocrats. Characterization is wooden and schematic, but a lot of research went into its writing, and it's no bad introduction to the intricacies of Polish history.

Thomas Keneally *Schindler's List* (Viking Penguin $8.95). Based on the life of Oskar Schindler, a German industrialist who used his business operations to shelter thousands of Jews, this powerful and moving novel won the 1982 Booker Prize.

Piers Paul Read *Polonaise* (Avon $1.95). Aristocratic family saga, its prewar sections set in Poland.

Brian Moore *The Color of Blood* (Nal-Dutton $7.95). Superb thriller of ecclesiastical and state maneuverings, set in unnamed Poland in the early 1980s.

John Simpson *A Fine and Private Place* (St Martin $13.95). A Kraków location and various oddments of history and politics add spice to this espionage thriller, written by one of the BBC's former Eastern European correspondents.

FILM

Andrzej Wajda *Double Vision: My Life in Film* (H. Holt & Co. $19.95). Autobiography of Poland's most famous director; somewhat more rewarding than some of his recent celluloid creations.

LANGUAGE

Polish is one of the more difficult European languages for English-speakers to learn. Even so, it is well worth acquiring the basics: not only is Polish beautiful and melodious, but a few words will go a long way. This is especially true away from the major cities where you won't find a lot of English spoken. (Knowledge of German, however, is quite widespread.)

The following features provide an indication of the problems of Polish grammar. There are three genders (masculine, feminine and neuter) and no word for "the." Prepositions (words like "to," "with," "in" etc) take different cases, and the case changes the form of the noun. Thus, "miasto" is the Polish for "town," but "to the town" is "do miasta" and "in the town" is "w mieście." You don't have to learn this sort of thing off by heart, but it can be useful to be able to recognize it.

Such grammatical complexity is a product of Polish history. During the periods when Poland didn't even exist as a nation, Polish was taught as virtually a foreign language, and the teachers were determined that nothing should be lost. Hence the "conservative" retention of so many archaic features.

Finally, a brief word on how to address people. The familiar form used among friends, relations and young people is "ty," like French "tu" or German "du." However, the polite form which you will usually require is "Pan" when addressing a man and "Pani" for a woman (literally "Sir" and "Madam"). ALWAYS use this form with people obviously older than yourself, and with officials.

PRONUNCIATION

While Polish may look daunting at first, with its apparently unrelieved rows of consonants, the good news is that it's a phonetic language—ie it's pronounced exactly as spelled. So once you've learnt the rules and have a little experience you'll always know how to pronounce a word correctly.

Stress:
Usually on the penultimate syllable, eg Warszawa, przyjaciel, matka

Vowels:
a: as "u" in "run."
e: "e" in "neck."
i: "i" in "Mick," never as in "I."
o: "o" in "lot," never as in "no" or "move."
u: "oo" in "look."
y: unknown in Standard English; cross between "e" and Polish "i."

Three **specifically Polish** vowels:
ą: nasalized—like "ong" in "long" or French "on."
ę: nasalized—like French "un" (eg Lech Wałęsa).
ó: same sound as Polish "u."

Vowel combinations:
ie: pronounced y-e, eg "nie wiem" (I don't know): ny-e vy-em (not nee-veem).
eu: each letter pronounced separately as above, eg "E-u-ropa" (Europe).
ia: rather like "yah," eg "historia" (history): histor-i-yah.

Consonants

Those which look the same as English but are different:
w: as "v" in "vine," eg "wino" pronounced "vino" (wine).
r: trilled (as in Scottish pronunciation of English r).
h: like the "ch" in Scottish "loch."
Some consonants are pronounced differently at **the end of a word** or syllable: b sounds like p, d like t, g like k; w sounds like f.

Specifically Polish consonants:
ć = ci: "ch" as in "church."
ł: "dark l" sounding rather like a "w".
ń = ni: "soft n," sounding like "n-ye," eg "koń" (horse): kon-ye.

ś = si: "sh" as in "ship."

ź = zi: like the "j" of French "journal."

ż = rz: as in French "g" in "gendarme." (Note that the dot over the z is sometimes replaced by a bar through the letter's diagonal.)

Consonantal Pairs

cz: "ch" (slightly harder than "ć" and "ci").

sz: "sh" (ditto "ś," "si").

dz: "d" as in "day" rapidly followed by "z" as in "zoo," eg "dzwon" (bell): d-zvon. At the end of a word is pronounced like "ts" as in "cats."

dż: "d-sh," eg "dżungla" (jungle): d-shun-gla.

dź: sharper than the above; at the end of a word is pronounced like "ć" (ch).

szcz: this fearsome-looking cluster is easy to pronounce—"sh-ch" as in "pushchair," eg "szczur" (rat): sh-choor.

BASIC WORDS

Tak	Yes	*Teraz*	Now	*Więcej*	More
Nie	No/not	*Później*	Later	*Mniej*	Less
Proszę	Please/you're welcome	*Otwarty*	Open	*Mało*	A little
		Zamknięty	Closed/shut	*Duzo*	A lot
Proszę bardzo	More emphatic than "proszę"	*Wcześniej*	Earlier	*Tani*	Cheap
		Dosyć	Enough	*Drogi*	Expensive
Dziekuję; dziekuję bardzo	Thank you	*Tam*	Over there	*Dobry*	Good
		Ten/ta/to	This one (masc/ fem/neuter)	*Zły/niedobry*	Bad
Gdzie	Where			*Gorący*	Hot
Kiedy	When	*Tamten/ tamta/tamto*	That one	*Zimny*	Cold
Dlaczego	Why			*Z*	With
Ile	How much	*Wielki*	Large	*Bez*	Without
Tu; tam	Here; there	*Mały*	Small	*W*	In
				Dla	For

BASIC PHRASES

Dzień dobry	Good day; hello	*Co to znaczy po Polsku?*	What's the Polish for that?
Dobry wieczór	Good evening		
Dobra noc	Good night	*Jestem tu na urlopie*	I'm here on holiday
Cześć!	"Hi!" or "'Bye" (like Italian "ciao")	*Jestem Amerykanką/ Amerykaniniem*	I'm American (male/ female)
Do widzenia	Goodbye	*Kanadyjczykiem/ Kanadyjką*	Canadian
Dobrze!	Fine!		
Przepraszam	Excuse me (apology)	*Mieszkam w . . .*	I live in . . .
Proszę Pana/Pani	(ditto) requesting information	*Dzisiaj*	Today
		Jutro	Tomorrow
Jak się masz?	How are you? (informal)	*Pojutzre*	Day after tomorrow
Jak się Pan/Pani ma?	(ditto: formal male/female)	*Wczoraj*	Yesterday
		Chwileczką	Moment! Wait a moment
Dobrze	Fine		
Czy Pan/Pani mówi po angielsku	Do you speak English?	*Rano*	In the morning
		Po południu	In the afternoon
Rozumiem	I understand	*Wieczorem*	In the evening
Nie rozumiem	I don't understand	*Gdzie jest . . .*	Where is
Nie wiem	I don't know	*Jak dojechać do . . . ?*	How do I get to . . . ?
Proszę mówić trochę powolniej	Please speak a bit more slowly	*Która (jest) godzina?*	What time is it?
		Jak daleko jest do . . . ?	How far is it to . . . ?
Nie mówię dobrze popolsku	I don't speak Polish very well	*Co to znaczy po polsku?*	What's it called in Polish?

ACCOMMODATION

Hotel	Hotel	*To drogo*	That's expensive.
Noclegi	Lodgings	*To za drogo*	That's too expensive.
Czy jest gdzieś tutaj hotel?	Is there a hotel nearby?	*Czy to obejmuje śniadanie?*	Does that include breakfast?
Czy Pan/Pani ma pokój?	Do you have a room?	*Czy nie ma tańszego?*	Do you have anything cheaper?
Pojedynczy pokój	Single room		
Podwójny pokój	Double room	*Czy mogę zobaczyć pokój?*	Can I see the room?
Będziemy jedną dobę	For one night (doba: 24 hours)	*Dobrze, wezmę*	Good, I'll take it.
Dwie nocy	Two nights	*Mam rezerwację*	I have a booking.
Trzy nocy	Three nights	*Czy możemy tu rozbić namioty?*	Can we camp here?
Tydzień	A week		
Dwa tygodnie	Two weeks	*Czy jest gdzieś tutaj camping?*	Is there a camp-ground nearby?
Pokój z łazienką	With a bath		
Z prysznicem	With a shower	*Namiot*	Tent
Z balkonem	With a balcony	*Schronisko*	Cabin
Z ciepłą wodą	Hot water	*Schronisko młodzieżowe*	Youth hostel
Z bieżącą wodą	Running water	*Proszę o jadłospis*	The menu, please
Lle kosztuje?	How much is it ?	*Proszę o rachunek*	The bill, please

TRAVELLING

Auto	Car	*w jedną stronę*	Single
Samolot	Aircraft	*Proszę o miejscówką*	I'd like a seat reservation.
Rower	Bicycle	*Kiedy odjeżdża pociąg do Warszawy?*	When does the Warsaw train leave?
Autobus	Bus		
Prom	Ferry	*Czy muszę się przesiadać?*	Do I have to change?
Pociąg	Train		
Dworzec, samochód, stacja	Train station	*Z jakim peronu odejdzie pociąg?*	Which platform does the train leave from?
Autobusowy	Bus station	*Ile kilometrów jest?*	How many kilometers is it?
Taksówka	Taxi	*Ile czasu trwą podróż?*	How long does the journey last?
Autostop	Hitchhiking		
Piechotą	On foot	*Jakim autobusem do . . ?*	Which bus is it to . . . ?
Prosze bilet do . . .	A ticket to . . . , please	*Gdzie jest droga do . . . ?*	Where is the road to . . . ?
Bilet powrotny	Return	*Następny przestanek, proszę*	Next stop, please.

SOME SIGNS

Wejście; wyjście	Entrance; exit/way out	*Peron*	Platform
Wstęp wzbroniony	No entrance	*Kasa*	Cash desk
Toaleta	Toilet	*Stop*	Stop
Dla panów; męski	Men	*Granica międzynarodowa*	Polish state frontier
Dla pan; damski	Women	*Rzeczpospolita Polska*	Republic of Poland
Zajęty	Occupied	*Uwaga; baczność*	Beware, caution
Wolny	Free, vacant	*Uwaga; niebezpieczeństwo*	Danger
Przyjazd; odjazd	Arrival; departure (train, bus)	*Policja (formerly: milicja)*	Police
Przylot; odlot	(ditto for aircraft)	*Informacja*	Information
Remont	Closed for renovation/ stocktaking	*Nie palić; palenie wzbronione*	No smoking
Ciągnąć; pchać	Pull; push	*Nie dotykać*	Do not touch
Nieczynny	Out of order; closed (ticket counters, etc)		

DRIVING

Samochód, auto	Car	*Benzyna*	Gas
Na lewo	Left	*Stacja benzynowa*	Gas station
Na prawo	Right	*Olej*	Oil
Prosto	Straight ahead	*Woda*	Water
Parking	Parking	*Naprawić*	To repair
Objazd	Detour	*Wypadek*	Accident
Koniec	End (showing when a previous sign ceases to be valid)	*Awaria*	Breakdown
		Ograniczenie	Speed limit
Zakaz wyprzedzania	No passing	*prędkości*	

DAYS, MONTHS AND DATES

Poniedziałek	Monday	*Kwiecień*	April	*Poniedziałek, pierwsy*	Monday, 1st
Wtorek	Tuesday	*Maj*	May	*Kwiecień*	April
Środa	Wednesday	*Czerwiec*	June	*. . . drugi Kwiecień*	. . . 2nd April
Czwartek	Thursday	*Lipiec*	July	*. . . trzeci Kwiecień*	. . . 3rd April
Piątek	Friday	*Sierpień*	August	*Wiosna*	spring
Sobota	Saturday	*Wrzesien*	September	*Lato*	summer
Niedziela	Sunday	*Październik*	October	*Jesień*	autumn
Styczeń	January	*Listopad*	November	*Zima*	winter
Luty	February	*Grudzień*	December	*Wakacje*	holidays
Marzec	March			*Święto*	bank holiday

NUMBERS

Jeden	1	*Jedenaście*	11	*Trzydzieści*	30
Dwa	2	*Dwanaście*	12	*Czterdzieści*	40
Trzy	3	*Trzynaście*	13	*Pięćdziesiąt*	50
Cztery	4	*Czternaście*	14	*Sześćdziesiąt*	60
Pięć	5	*Piętaście*	15	*Siedemdziesiąt*	70
Sześć	6	*Szesnaście*	16	*Osiemdziesiąt*	80
Siedem	7	*Siedemnaście*	17	*Dziewięćdziesiąt*	90
Osiem	8	*Osiemnaście*	18	*Sto*	100
Dziewięć	9	*Dziewietnaście*	19	*Dwieście*	200
Dziesięć	10	*Dwadzieścia*	20	*Trzysta*	300

Czterysta	400
Pięłset	500
Sześćset	600
Siedemset	700
Osiemset	800
Dziewięćset	900
Tysiąc	1 000
Milion	1 000 000

Dwadzieścia pięć	25
Sześćset dziewięćdziesiąt cztery	694
Trzy tysiące dwieściesiedemdziesiąt osiem	3278

GLOSSARIES

GENERAL TERMS

ALEJA Avenue (abbreviation al.).

BESKIDY Range of hills, eg Beskid Niski.

BIURO ZAKWATEROWANIA
Accommodation office.

BRAMA Gate.

CERKIEW (pl. CERKWI) Orthodox church, or a church belonging to the Uniates, a church loyal to Rome but following Orthodox rites.

CMENTARZ Cemetery.

DOLINA Valley.

DOM House.

DOM KULTURY Community arts and social center, literally a "Cultural House."

DOM WYCZIECZKOWE Cheap, basic type of hotel.

DROGA Road.

DWORZEC Station.

GŁÓWNY Main—as in Rynek Główny, main square.

GÓRA (pl.GÓRY) Mountain.

GRANICA Border.

JEZIORO Lake.

KAPLICE Chapel.

KAWIARNIA Café.

KATEDRA Cathedral.

KLASZTOR Monastery.

KOŚCIÓŁ Church.

KSIĄDZ Priest.

KSIĄŻĘ Prince, duke.

KRAJ Country.

LAS Wood, forest.

MASYW Massif.

MIASTO Town. (Stare Miasto—old town; Nowe Miasta—new town.)

MOST bridge.

NARÓD Nation, people.

NYSA Neisse River.

ODRA Oder River.

OGRÓD Gardens.

PAŁAC Palace.

PIWNICE Pub.

PLAC Square.

PLAZA Beach.

POKÓJ Room.

POLE Field.

PROM Ferry.

PRZEDMIEŚCIE Suburb.

PRZYSTANEK Bus stop.

PUSZCZA Ancient forest.

RATUSZ Town Hall.

RESTAURACJE Restaurant.

RUCH Kiosk.

RYNEK Marketplace, commonly the main square in a town.

RZEKA River.

SEJM Parliament.

SKAŁNA Rock, cliff.

SKANSEN Open-air museum with reconstructed folk architecture and art.

STOCZNIA Shipyards.

ŚWIĘTO Saint (abbreviation św.).

STAROWIERCY (Old Believers) Traditionalist Russian Orthodox sect, small communities of which survive in east Poland.

STARY Old.

ULICA Street (abbeviation ul.).

WOJEWÓDZTWO Administrative district.

WIEŚ (pl. WSI) Village.

WIEŻA Tower.

WINIARNIA Wine cellar.

WISŁA River Vistula.

WODOSPAD Waterfall.

WZGÓRZE Hill.

ZAMEK Castle.

ZDRÓJ Spa.

ZIEMIA Region.

ART/ARCHITECTURAL TERMS

AISLE Part of church to the side of the nave.

AMBULATORY Passage round the back of the altar, in continuation of the aisles.

APSE Vaulted termination of the altar end of a church.

BAROQUE Exuberant architectural style of the seventeenth and early eighteenth centuries, characterized by ornate decoration, complex spatial arrangement and grand vistas. The term is also applied to the sumptuous style of painting of the same period.

BASILICA Church in which nave is higher than the aisles.

BLACK MADONNA National icon, an image of the Virgin and Child housed in the Jasna Góra monastery in Częstochowa.

CAPITAL Top of a column, usually sculpted.

CHANCEL Section of the church where the altar is situated, usually the east end.

CHOIR Part of church in which service is sung, usually beside the altar.

CRYPT Underground part of a church.

FRESCO Mural painting applied to wet plaster, so that colors immediately soak into the wall.

GOTHIC Architectural style with an emphasis on verticality, characterized by pointed arch and ribbed vault: introduced to Poland in the thirteenth century, surviving in an increasingly decorative form until well into the sixteenth century. The term is also used of paintings and sculpture of the period.

HALL CHURCH Church design in which all vaults are of approximately equal height.

JUGENDSTIL German version (encountered in Western Poland) of Art Nouveau, a sinuous, highly decorative style of architecture and design from the period 1900–15.

MANNERISM Deliberately over-sophisticated style of late Renaissance art and architecture.

MŁODA POLSKA (Young Poland) Turn-of-the-century cultural movement centerd on Kraków.

NAVE Main body of the church, generally forming the western part.

NEOCLASSICAL Late eighteenth- and early nineteenth-century style of art and architecture returning to classical models as a reaction against Baroque and Rococo excesses.

RENAISSANCE Italian-originated movement in art and architecture, inspired by the rediscovery of classical ideals.

ROCOCO Highly florid, light and graceful style of architecture, painting and interior design, forming the last phase of Baroque.

ROMANESQUE Solid architectural style of the late tenth to mid-thirteenth century, characterized by round-headed arches and geometrical precision. The term is also used for paintings of the same period.

ROMANTICISM Late eighteenth- and nineteenth-century artistic movement, rooted in adulation of natural world and rediscovery of

the country's rich historic heritage, strongly linked in Poland to the cause of national independence.

SECESSIONIST Style of early twentieth-century art and architecture, based in Germany and Austria, which reacted against academic establishments.

STUCCO Plaster used for decorative effects.

TRANSEPT Arms of a cross-shaped church, placed at ninety degrees to nave and chancel.

TRANSITIONAL Architectural style between Romanesque and Gothic.

TRIPTYCH Carved or painted altarpiece on three panels.

TROMPE L'OEIL Painting designed to fool the onlooker into believing that it's actually three-dimensional.

HISTORICAL AND POLITICAL GLOSSARY

AUSTRO-HUNGARIAN EMPIRE Vast Habsburg-ruled domain incorporating most of Central Europe, enlarged to include Polish province of Galicia during the Partition period.

BALCEROWICZ, LESZEK Finance minister since the 1989 elections; responsible for introducing the current program of radical, free market economic reform.

BARTOSZCZE, ROMAN Leader of the Peasant Party, which plays a major part in the government coalition.

BIELICKI, JAN Solidarity advisor and young technocrat, based in Gdańsk; became prime minister at the end of December 1990.

CENTRE AGREEMENT Political grouping formed by Lech Wałęsa in 1990, critical of the supposedly slow pace of government reforms.

CITIZENS MOVEMENT-DEMOCRATIC ACTION (ROAD) Coalition of intellectuals and former Solidarity activists formed to oppose Wałęsa's Center Agreement. Key figures included the then prime minister Mazowiecki, Adam Michnik, Zbigniew Bujak, and Bronisław Geremek.

COMMONWEALTH Union of Poland, Lithuania, Royal Prussia, and Livonia (Latvia); formed by Lublin Union (1569), it lasted until the Third Partition of 1795.

CONGRESS KINGDOM OF POLAND Russian ruled province of Poland established in 1815, following the Congress of Vienna.

DUCAL PRUSSIA (East Prussia) The eastern half of the territory of the Teutonic Knights, converted into a secular duchy in 1525 and divided in 1945 between Poland and the Soviet Union.

GALICIA Southern province of Poland including Kraków incorporated into Austro-Hungarian Empire during the Partition period, granted autonomy in latter half of nineteenth century.

GEREMEK, BRONISŁAW Medieval historian at Warsaw University who acted as advisor to Wałęsa and the Solidarity movement. Elected leader of the Solidarity group in parliament after the June 1989 elections but resigned in November 1990.

GIEREK, EDWARD Leader of the Communist Party in the 1970s, until replaced by Stanisław Kania following the strikes of summer 1980.

HABSBURG The most powerful family in medieval Germany, operating from a power base in Austria.

HANSEATIC LEAGUE Medieval trading alliance of Baltic and Rhineland cities, numbering about 100 at its fifteenth-century peak. Slowly died out in seventeenth century with competition from the Baltic nation-states, and rise of Brandenburg-Prussia.

HOLY ROMAN EMPIRE Name of the loose confederation of German states (many now part of Poland) which lasted from 800 until 1806.

JAGIELLONIAN Dynasty of Lithuanian origin which ruled Poland-Lithuania from 1386 to 1572.

JARUZELSKI, WOJCIECH General of the armed forces, called in by the Party in 1981 to institute martial law and suppress Solidarity. His subsequent flexibility and negotiating skill helped to usher in democracy and he became president after the June 1989 elections, until the election of Wałęsa in December 1990.

KULTURKAMPF Campaign launched by German Chancellor Bismarck in the 1870s, aimed at suppressing Catholic culture (including the Polish language) inside German territories.

KUROŃ, JACEK Veteran opposition activist and key figure in Solidarity movement; served as minister of labor in the Mazowiecki government.

MARTIAL LAW Military crackdown instigated by General Jaruzelski in December 1981 and remaining in effect until summer 1983.

MAZOWIECKI, TADEUSZ Catholic lawyer and journalist and longtime advisor to Solidarity. Became prime minister after the June 1989 elections and ran unsuccessfully for president against Wałęsa in December 1990.

MICHNIK, ADAM Warsaw academic and leading Solidarity theoretician and activist. Currently member of parliament and chief editor of the independent daily *Gazeta Wyborcza*, now intractably opposed to his old friend and ally Wałęsa, whom he sees as an anti-democratic force.

NAZI–SOVIET PACT (or MOLOTOV–RIBBENTROP PACT) 1939 agreement between Nazi Germany and the Soviet Union, which contained a secret clause to eliminate Poland from the map.

ODER-NEISSE LINE Western limit of Polish territory set by Yalta Agreement, 1945.

PARTITION PERIOD Era from 1773 to 1918, during which Poland was on three occasions divided into Prussian, Russian and Austrian territories.

PIASTS Royal dynasty which forged the Polish state in the tenth century and ruled it until 1370; branches of the family continued to hold principalities, notably in Silesia, until 1675.

POLISH UNITED WORKERS PARTY (PZPR) Former communist party which disbanded itself in January 1990, the majority forming a new Social Democratic Party.

POLONIANS Slav tribe which formed the embryonic Polish nation.

PRUSSIA Originally a Slavic Eastern Baltic territory, now divided between Poland and the Soviet Union. It was acquired in 1525 by the Hohenzollerns, who later merged it with their own German possessions to form Brandenburg-Prussia (later shortened to Prussia).

ROUND TABLE AGREEMENT Groundbreaking bi-partisan agreement between Jaruzelski's communist government and the Solidarity opposition in spring 1989, leading to the elections in June of that year.

ROYAL PRUSSIA (West Prussia) Territory centered on the Wisła delta, originally the easternmost sector of Pomerania, renamed after its capture from the Teutonic Knights in 1466.

RUTHENIA A loose grouping of principalities, part of which formed Poland's former Eastern Territories.

SOLIDARITY (Solidarność) The Eastern Bloc's first independent trade union, led by Lech Wałęsa, suppressed under martial law and relegalized in 1989, before forming the core of the new democratic government. Now irrevocably split into pro- and anti-Wałęsa factions.

TARTARS Mongol tribe who invaded Poland in the thirteenth century, some settling subsequently.

TEUTONIC KNIGHTS Quasi-monastic German military order who conquered parts of the eastern Baltic, establishing their own independent state 1225–1525.

WAŁĘSA, LECH Shipyard electrician who led strikes in the Gdańsk shipyards in 1980, leading to the establishment of the independent trade union, Solidarity, of which he became chairman. In this role, he opposed the communist government throughout the 1980s, and led negotiations in the Round Table Agreement of 1989. Following the June 1989 elections, he parted company with many of his former Solidarity allies, forcing a presidential contest, which he won in December 1990. Awarded the Nobel Peace Prize in 1983.

WAZA (Vasa) Swedish royal dynasty which ruled Poland 1587–1668.

WORKERS DEFENSE COMMITTEE (KOR) Opposition group formed in the mid-1970s, regarded by many as a precursor to Solidarity.

YALTA AGREEMENT 1945 agreement between the victorious powers which established Poland's (and Europe's) postwar borders.

ACRONYMS AND ORGANIZATIONS

ALMATUR Official student organization and travel office.

IT (Informator Turystyczny) Tourist information office.

ORBIS State travel agency; abroad, Orbis offices are called POLORBIS.

PO (Policja Obywatelska) Police.

PKO (Polska Kasa Oszczędności) State savings bank.

PKP (Polskie Koleje Państwowe) State railroads.

PKS (Polska Komunikacja Samochodowa) State bus company.

PTTK (Polskie Towarzystwo Turystyczno-Krajownawcze) Tourist agency—literally "Polish Nature Lovers' Association".

PZMot (Polski Związek Motorowy) National automobile club.

PZPR (Polska Zjednoczona Partia Robotnicza) Polish Communist Party—now defunct.

WOP (Wójskowe Ochrony Pogranicza) Border police.

INDEX